NETHERLANDISH ART
IN THE RIJKSMUSEUM
1600–1700

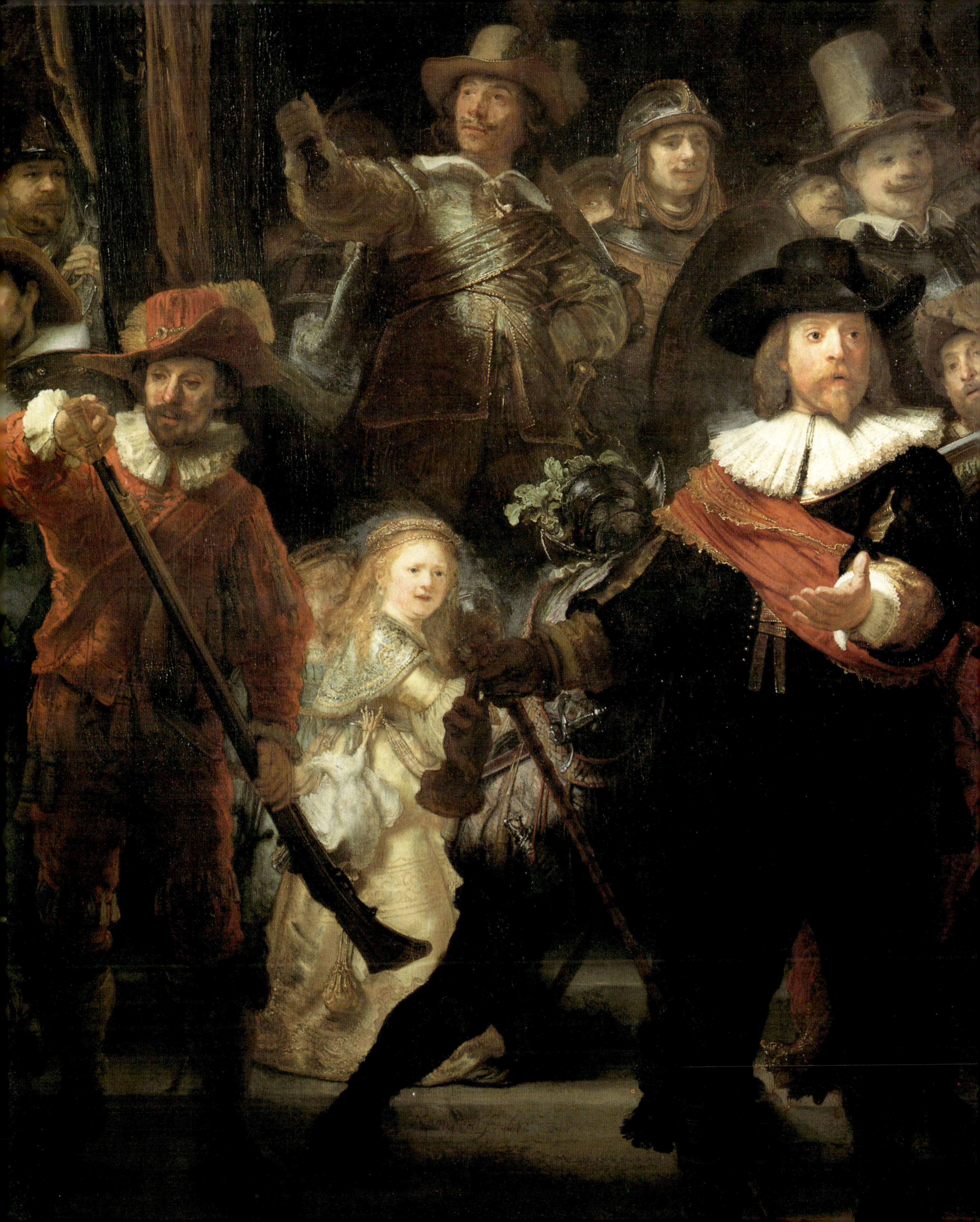

Netherlandish art
IN THE RIJKSMUSEUM
1600–1700

Jan Piet Filedt Kok
Reinier Baarsen
Bart Cornelis
Wouter Kloek
Frits Scholten

WITH CONTRIBUTIONS BY
Jan Daan van Dam
Ebeltje Hartkamp-Jonxis
Guido Jansen
Arjan de Koomen
Jan Rudolph de Lorm
Ger Luijten
Bianca du Mortier
Wouter Ritsema van Eck
Marijn Schapelhouman
Peter Sigmond
Arie Wallert

WAANDERS PUBLISHERS
RIJKSMUSEUM, AMSTERDAM

NETHERLANDISH ART IN THE RIJKSMUSEUM

volume 1: Netherlandish art in the Rijksmuseum 1400-1600, 2000
volume 2: Netherlandish art in the Rijksmuseum 1600-1700, 2001
to be published between 2003 and 2005:
volume 3: Netherlandish art in the Rijksmuseum 1700-1800
volume 4: Netherlandish art in the Rijksmuseum 1800-1900

Editors: Jan Piet Filedt Kok, Reinier Baarsen, Bart Cornelis,
Wouter Kloek, Frits Scholten, with many thanks to
Fennelies Kiers and Otto de Rijk

Final editing: Jan Piet Filedt Kok and Annemiek Overbeek,
with the assistance of Mark Poysden
Translation: Michael Hoyle
Design: René Staelenberg
Photographs: Photographic Department of the Rijksmuseum
(Peter Mookhoek and assistants), unless otherwise specified
Printing: Waanders Printers, Zwolle

ISBN 90 400 9552 3
Nugi 921/911

For more information on the activities of Waanders Publishers
and the Rijksmuseum, please visit www.waanders.nl and
www.rijksmuseum.nl

Cover (front):
Frans Hals and Pieter Codde, *The meagre company* (detail), 1637 [43]
Cover (back):
Johannes Lutma, *Two salts*, 1639 [33]
Frontispiece:
Rembrandt van Rijn, *The night watch* (detail), 1642 [44]

The numbers in square brackets refer to one of the works of art
discussed in this book.
[44], for instance, refers to 44, Rembrandt van Rijn, pp. 129-131

Contents

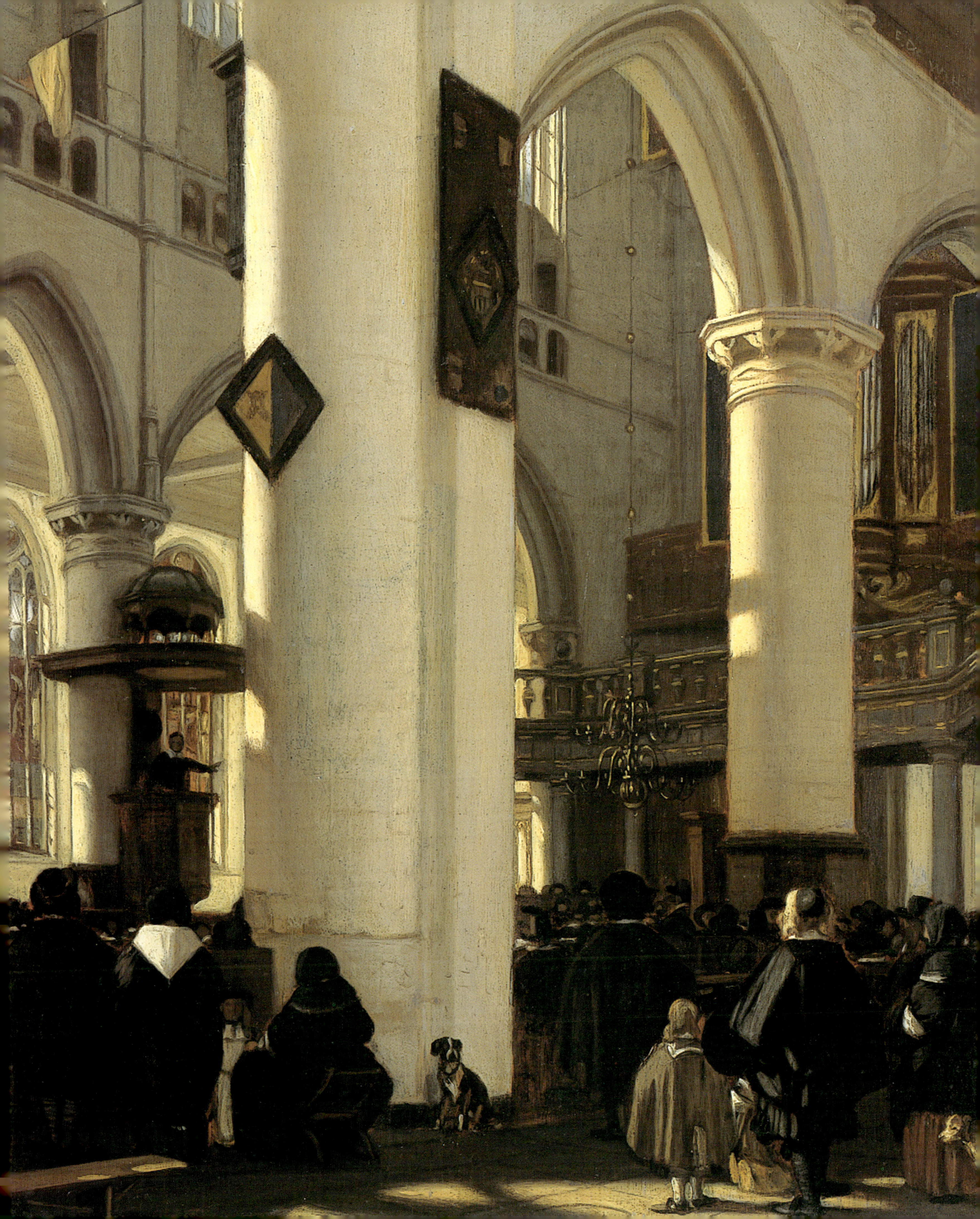

The art of specialists

The strength of 17th-century Dutch painting lies not only in the fact that the Golden Age brought forth great geniuses like Rembrandt, Frans Hals and Johannes Vermeer. The strength lies also, and importantly, in the abundance of paintings of an extraordinarily high standard by artists unranked among the great masters but who nonetheless did outstanding work. Streets in Dutch towns are proudly named after artists of greater and lesser fame: Amsterdam boasts not only a Johannes Vermeerstraat and a Rembrandtplein, but also an Adriaen van Ostadestraat, a Hobbemakade, a Moreelsestraat, to name but a few. Many Dutch towns thus have their own heroes, and there is no denying that people in Leiden are justly proud of their Jan van Goyen and Gerard Dou, in Utrecht of Joachim Wtewael and Hendrick ter Brugghen, in Zwolle of Gerard ter Borch. There were so many good painters from important towns like Amsterdam, Haarlem, Leiden, Utrecht and Dordrecht—and from smaller places too—that visitors from abroad could only marvel. Visiting Holland in 1667/68, the Italian Cosimo III de'Medici viewed work by Willem van de Velde the Elder, Rembrandt, Otto Marseus van Schrieck, Maria van Oosterwijck, Willem van Aelst, all artists whose work is still well known and admired today.

It is estimated that several million pictures were painted in the 17th century in a country with a population of some five million.

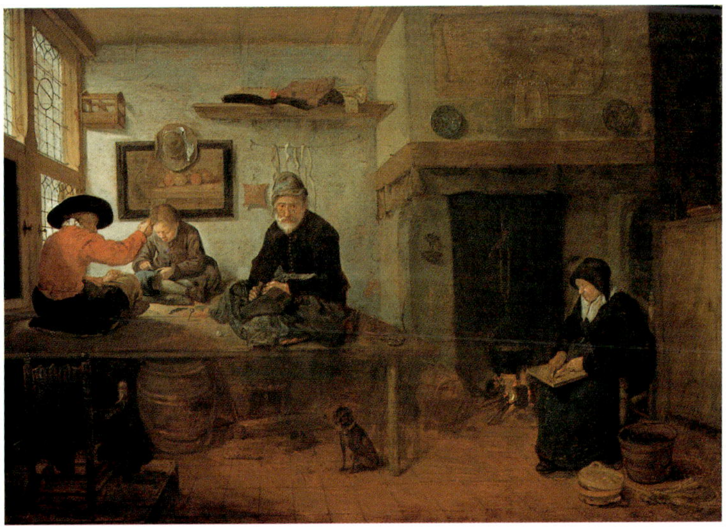

fig. 1 Quirijn van Brekelenkam, *The tailor's shop*; oil on panel, 60 x 85 cm. Worcester, Worcester Art Museum

Paintings were popular in all walks of life; according to French and English travellers they were to be found in every home, be it that of a nobleman or a peasant. In an amusing work by the painter Quirijn van Brekelenkam (*fig. 1*) there is a still life on the wall of a tailor's shop; we also see that the tailor has irreverently hung his hat on the same nail as the picture. Be that as it may, paintings of varying quality were produced on a vast scale and of varying quality in the 17th-century Netherlands, ranging from undisputed masterpieces, to highly or moderately professional works, down to endearing or inane experiments. What is so striking about the surviving corpus of 17th-century Dutch painting is that in addition to the masterpieces by artists of true genius, the works produced of the large group of artists ranking just below them are of a relatively high quality. Strolling through the rooms in the Rijksmuseum, which houses the most representative survey of paintings from this period, one is astonished to see how many good to outstanding painters there are. Their numbers show that 17th-century culture in Holland evidently offered plenty of scope for the development of individual talent. Countless artists were able to put their ability to the test, and many of them reached great heights.

Searching for an explanation for this singular phenomenon, one soon realises that specialisation offered a surprising range of possibilities to individual talents. Some excelled in landscapes, others were first-rate portraitists, others had less of an aptitude for flowers but painted fruit quite beautifully. Hendrick Avercamp [*6*] could convey the atmosphere of a wintry day, with snow and ice, in calm, slightly hazy weather—the perfect conditions for pastimes on the frozen water. Indeed, he painted virtually nothing but scenes on the ice throughout his life. Adriaen Coorte [105] was an expert painter of small quantities of fruit, vegetables or shells on a table, lit by a ghostly light. Small things were his forte, and his attempts at more ambitious compositions were failures. Some architectural painters were so specialised that they took the interior of just a single church as their subject. A contemporary stated that Anthonie Delorme made a speciality of painting the Church of St Lawrence in Rotterdam. His teacher, Jan van Vucht, took his specialisation to such extremes that he calculated the price of his pictures on the basis of the number of columns they contained. A greater talent in this area, Emanuel de Witte, likewise concentrated on church interiors, but seems to have been more interested in the artistic effect. He was not concerned whether the interior was recognisable (*figs. 2, 3*), and also abandoned a focused perspective, instead creating

◂ Detail of fig. 3

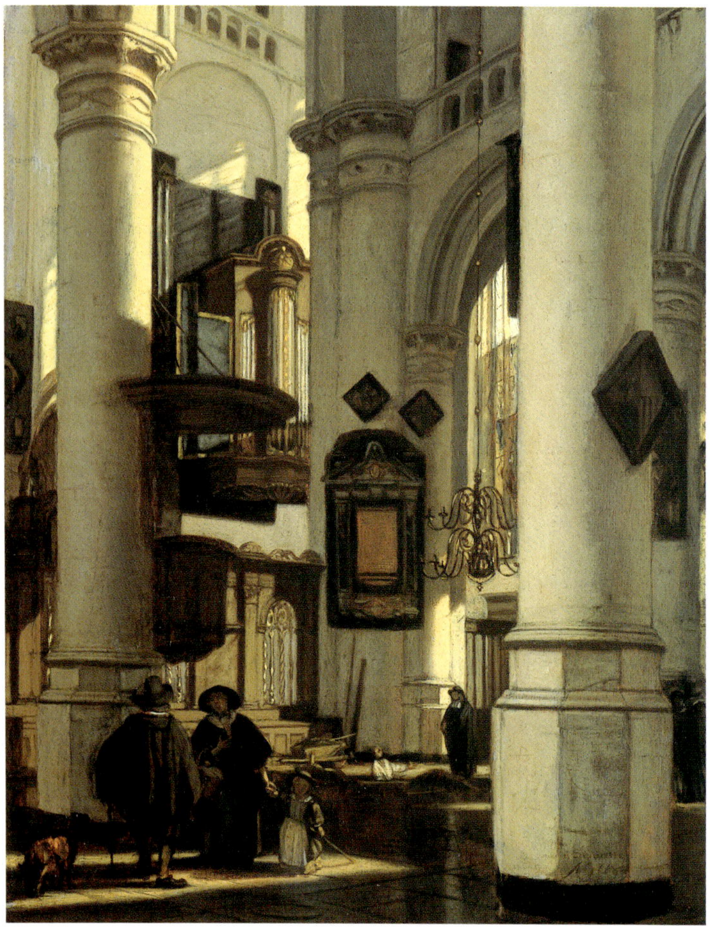

fig. 2 Emanuel de Witte, *Interior of a Protestant Gothic church with motifs from the Oude and the Nieuwe Kerk in Amsterdam*, 1669; oil on panel, 44.5 × 33.5 cm. Amsterdam, Rijksmuseum

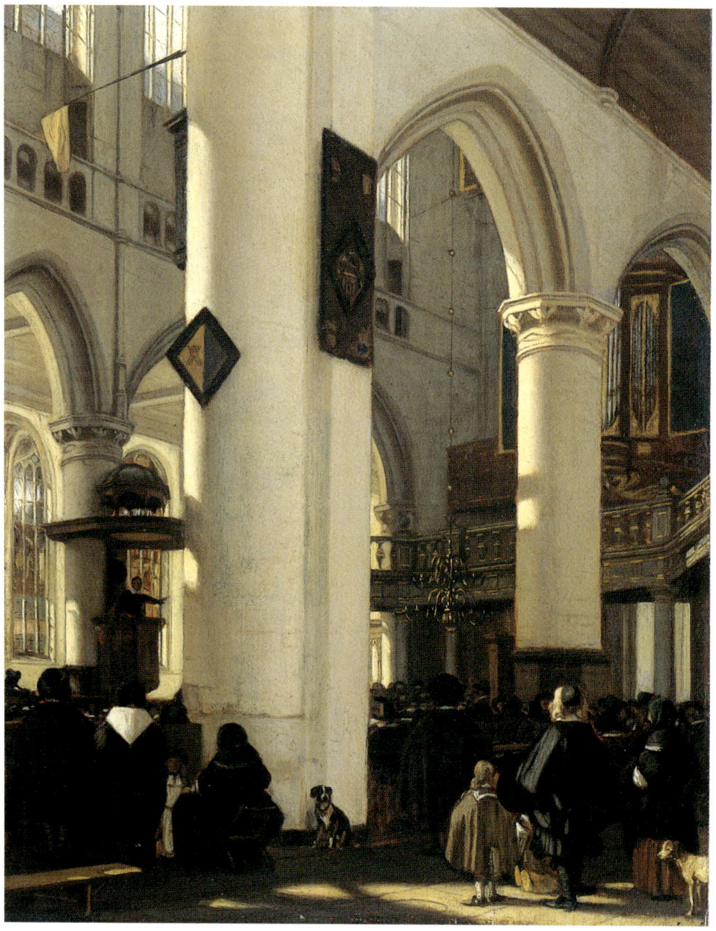

fig. 3 Emanuel de Witte, *Interior of a Protestant Gothic church with motifs from the Oude Kerk in Amsterdam*, 1669; oil on panel, 44.5 × 33.5 cm. Amsterdam, Rijksmuseum

an impression of depth with the effects of light and shade. Once in a while he would try his hand at other subjects, and although the results are not at all bad, he confined himself chiefly to churches. There is no need to cite further examples. Most artists in the northern Netherlands chose a speciality.

There are, of course, exceptions, and Rembrandt, needless to say, is a special case. In addition to history paintings—scenes with biblical, mythological or allegorical subjects—portraits and faces, he painted landscapes and the odd still life. His free spirit is expressed most vigorously in his candid etchings of landscapes or scenes from daily life. He is not the only exception, though. A little-known painter like Adriaen van Nieulandt made history paintings, kitchen still lifes, landscapes, a few portraits and the occasional flower piece. Van Nieulandt's 'generalism' is all the more remarkable in that he worked in Amsterdam, the city with the greatest concentration of painters. In that respect he was the polar opposite of Ludolf de Jongh, a master who supplied Rotterdam, still quite a small city at the time, with paintings covering a startling range of subjects: portraits, genre pieces, hunting scenes and interiors. De Jongh was a prosperous man who played a prominent part in the life of the city, among other things as a major in the civic guard. As such he was one of a small group of artists who met the varied demands of a local market while at the same time shouldering a share of civic responsibilities.

Numerous painters concentrated on more than one subject. Sometimes the combination is quite natural, as in the case of Gerard ter Borch, who coupled genre scenes—scenes from everyday life—with portraits. Rendering the texture of clothing required similar expertise, and there is a close correspondence between his genre scenes and his portraits in the way he placed his figures in the picture space (he paid scant attention to the background in most of his work). From time to time he also included members of his own family in his genre scenes, giving them clearly individualised features. A case in point is the *Seated girl in peasant costume* (*fig. 4*), for which his sister Gesina was the model. Scenes from everyday life offered him greater freedom, and he quite enjoyed that artistic latitude. The portraits will have ensured him of a regular income. For other painters the different specialities were not so compatible. That Abraham van Beijeren combined sumptuous still lifes with fish still lifes is understandable, but the river landscapes he also painted are somewhat surprising.

By and large, most Dutch painters opted for a limited field of operation, some limiting themselves more than others. The majority realised that specialisation offered an opportunity to excel within those limits, to attain a high standard in a particular field—perhaps the very highest. Competition must have been fierce, so it was to most painters' advantage to have fewer strings to their bow, to restrict themselves to the strength of their speciality and show what they were really good at. In any case, they imitated one another. Many a pupil first learned to work in the manner of his teacher and then tried to outdo him by developing a style of his own. Such artists adhered to the concept of *aemulatio*, the principle formulated by classical authors that the pupil should imitate his master, endeavour to equal him and then to surpass him. Gerard Dou, for instance, modelled his early work on that of his teacher, Rembrandt, and the young Frans van Mieris was in turn heavily indebted to Dou's mature work. The young Jan van Goyen imitated his master Esaias van de Velde, later developing a highly personal style. Pieter Claesz's early still lifes are very similar to those of his fellow townsman Floris van Dijck—a teacher-pupil relationship is far from certain—and in turn Willem Heda developed the devices invented by Claesz around 1630, eventually arriving at a much more tonal style of his own. Relationships like these are a good example of how 17th-century artists looked over each other's shoulders and clambered onto those shoulders in order to reach greater heights.

fig. 4 Gerard ter Borch, *Seated girl in peasant costume*; oil on panel, 28 x 23 cm. Amsterdam, Rijksmuseum

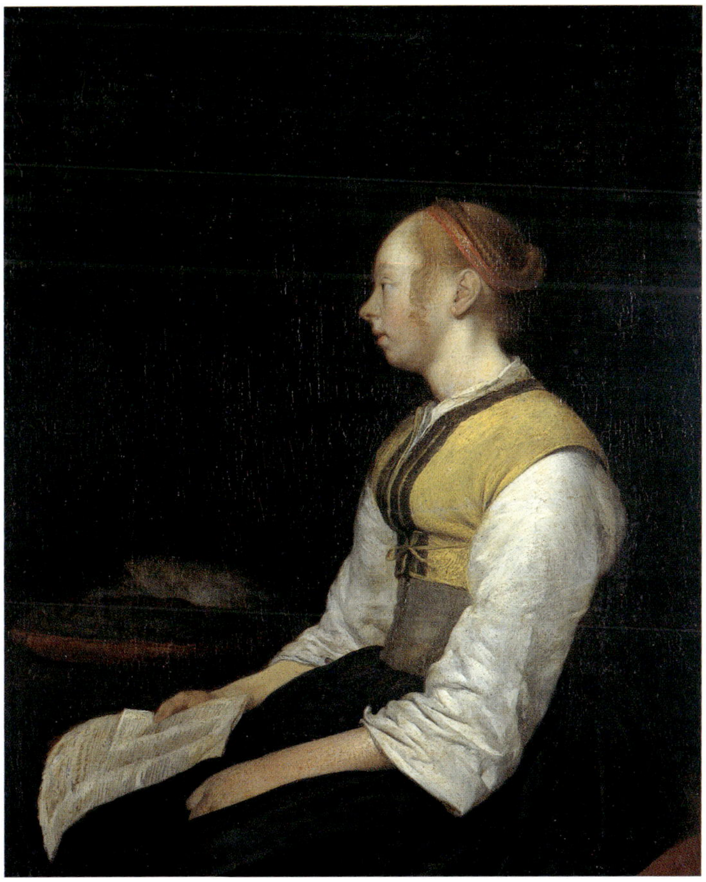

THE ASTONISHING HEYDAY OF 17TH-CENTURY PAINTING

The enormous success of painting in the Protestant Netherlands is nothing short of amazing. Most Protestants—and Protestantism dominated religious life in the northern Netherlands—set great store by strict adherence to the Ten Commandments as laid down in the Bible. The second of these commandments explicitly forbids the making of images of anything that is in heaven above, i.e. God the Father, or on the earth below or even under the earth, so it is quite remarkable that paintings were produced on such a vast scale in, of all places, the Protestant Netherlands.

For a proper understanding of this, some knowledge of religious developments during this period is required. Until well into the 16th century, art's main function was religious: most paintings were made for churches, as altarpieces or for other devotional purposes. They might depict an episode from the Bible or the life of a saint, help the faithful to think of Mary's love of the Infant Jesus, or remind them of Christ's sufferings. From about the middle of the century, worshippers became increasingly dissatisfied with the Catholicism shaped by the Church of Rome. Martin Luther's followers sought a purer form of worship, and their movement attracted a growing number of adherents. The differences between the various persuasions subsequently led to serious dissension and eventually to the formation of a number of factions. The Protestants opted for a form of religion based first and foremost on the Bible. Many churchgoers no longer appreciated the visual assistance of paintings. Art had not been exclusively at the service of religion up to then, but for the main part it had. Things reached a dramatic climax in 1566, when iconoclastic fury raged through the Netherlands. Not only were vast numbers of important works of art destroyed, the development of painting itself took an astonishing turn. While painters in the southern Netherlands were set to work repairing the damage caused by the Iconoclasm, the Protestants in the north wanted the interiors of their churches to be as bare as possible. Not only was much of the art that remained removed in a sort of 'stealthy Iconoclasm', but no new church commissions were awarded.

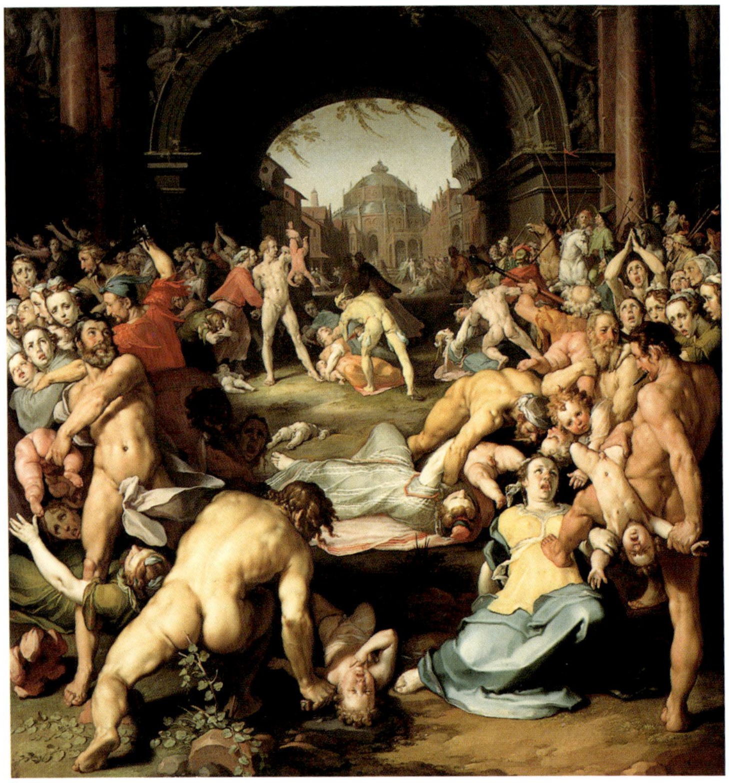

fig. 5 Cornelis Cornelisz van Haarlem, *Massacre of the Innocents*, 1592; oil on canvas, 270 x 255 cm. Haarlem, Frans Halsmuseum

However, the need for art—and we do not know whether the artists themselves or their patrons were the crucial factor here—was evidently so strong that new openings for painting were energetically sought. As a result, in the last decades of the 16th century, paintings of impressive size and with unusual biblical or mythological subjects were ordered by secular patrons. An example is Cornelis Cornelisz's *Massacre of the Innocents* (*fig. 5*) of 1592, commissioned by the City of Haarlem for Prince Maurits's apartments in the Prinsenhof. It seems as if the first generation of artists after Protestantisation wanted to prove with such spectacular scenes that there was indeed a future for art without the church's patronage. A little later, around 1600, the surprising development of the specialisations followed in an amazing interaction between painters and their patrons: burghers bought the pictures that artists wanted to paint.

Post-Protestantisation seems to have been a period of mutual understanding, never formulated but almost certainly practised, that allowed for the sanctioning of art without a religious function of any significance. Its radical prohibition was evidently felt to be going too far by the lively society of the early 17th century. Although paintings of biblical subjects were still produced, they almost never invite active devotion. The painting or sculpture was no longer an earthly reflection of a venerated saint or a convincing representation of Christ's self-sacrifice. The Bible's message was communicated verbally in church, and art no longer played any part in this. In other words, while plenty of art was made, works which incited devoutness or enabled the beholder to link the image with religious intentions no longer had any place within the Protestant mindset of the leading groups in the Republic. Artists, in turn, sought out new opportunities and exploited them to the full.

The need to explore new avenues, and the huge enthusiasm they generated, manifested itself mainly around 1600. Karel van Mander, whose *Schilder-boeck* containing biographies of painters was published in 1604, writes that hard times compelled Michiel van Mierevelt to specialise in portraiture. Van Mander stresses that as a young man Van Mierevelt was inventive and had produced competent figure pieces of which his critical biographer approved. 'Had he directed himself solely to the design and painting of histories, had he made this his speciality, he would have made very excellent works [...]. But in our Netherlands there is this deficiency or unfortunate situation, especially in these present times, that there is little work to be had that requires composition so as to give the youngsters and painters the opportunity to become excellent at histories, figures and nudes through practice. For it is most portraits that they get the opportunity to paint; so that most of them, because of the allure of profit, or for their own survival, usually take this side-road of art (to wit, portrait painting) and set off without having the time or inclination to seek out or follow the road of history and figures that leads to the highest perfection. So it is that many a clever, subtle talent must remain, as it were, barren and without fire, to the misery of art.' This passage is so well known because Van Mander explicitly states that painting histories, events from the Bible, mythology or ancient history, is the painter's highest goal. What is of prime importance here, though, is that he associates the fact that Van Mierevelt saw no chance of devoting himself to that high calling with the circumstances of the day which, as we know, were not conducive to art.

Around the same time, shortly before 1600, Hendrick Vroom was enjoying his first successes as a marine specialist: he painted naval battles, ships in distress, harbour scenes and portraits of ships. As a young man he had gone on a number of long and dangerous voyages, earning his keep by painting 'small devotional pieces'. Van Mander relates that after suffering a shipwreck he painted 'his own adventure and shipwreck', which he sold 'in Lisbon to a great lord for much money so that he was very grateful to Vroom and wanted yet more sea pieces and ships from him'. Although it is surprising, to say the least, to find an artist painting his own travel adventures (none of Vroom's early work has survived, nor are there any other examples known of painters recording their own escapades), the story is a good illustration of the interaction between art-lover and artist that gave birth to his specialisation. Vroom concentrated entirely on marine painting after his return to Haarlem, partly on the advice of his Haarlem colleagues (one of whom was Van Mander, the teller of the tale), who probably did not want to see yet another competitor joining the already crowded market for paintings with figures. As it happens, Vroom had a following wind, and was soon commanding high prices for his work. One of his earliest surviving paintings, executed in 1599, shows the triumphal homecoming to Amsterdam of four heavily laden ships under the command of Captain Jan van Neck. It was the second time that Dutch ships had returned from the East Indies archipelago, and the first time that trade with the Far East had generated large profits (*fig. 6*). Vroom had evidently discovered a clientele of wealthy shipowners and prosperous town corporations willing to pay large sums of money for meticulously detailed representations of the successful vessels and proud cities. The course which Vroom had adopted out of necessity turned out to be most expedient.

THE DIVISION OF LABOUR AS A HARBINGER OF SPECIALISATION

The surprising development of specialities around 1600 stemmed partly from the division of labour practised in the big Antwerp workshops earlier in the 16th century. The leading Antwerp painters were accustomed to leaving the execution of considerable parts of their pictures to other artists. They acted like true entrepreneurs. As heads of workshops they decreed the choice of subjects and the style of execution; they also supplied the design and maintained contacts with customers. Parts of a painting were often entrusted almost entirely to an assistant. He might be responsible for all the landscape backgrounds, or for all the draperies in a painting with large figures, adding the details and the folds. In the case of Jan Sanders van Hemessen, an artist-entrepreneur who usually painted the figures in his compositions himself, the backgrounds were left to several different artists. Modern art history has established a distinction between these artists and given them invented names. Independent paintings by some of them, such as the Brunswick Monogrammist and the Master of Paul and Barnabas, have been identified. They are generally landscapes or architectural paintings in which the assistant exploited his own particular speciality (*fig. 7*). Due to the insertion of small biblical scenes, such works do not qualify as independent landscapes or architectural paintings, but they must certainly be regarded as an important contribution to the development of the independent genres. Furthermore, these paintings dominated by a richly detailed landscape or the ingenious perspective of the architecture, were not made for the church but for a private market. The same applies to those assistants who were charged with the painting of draperies

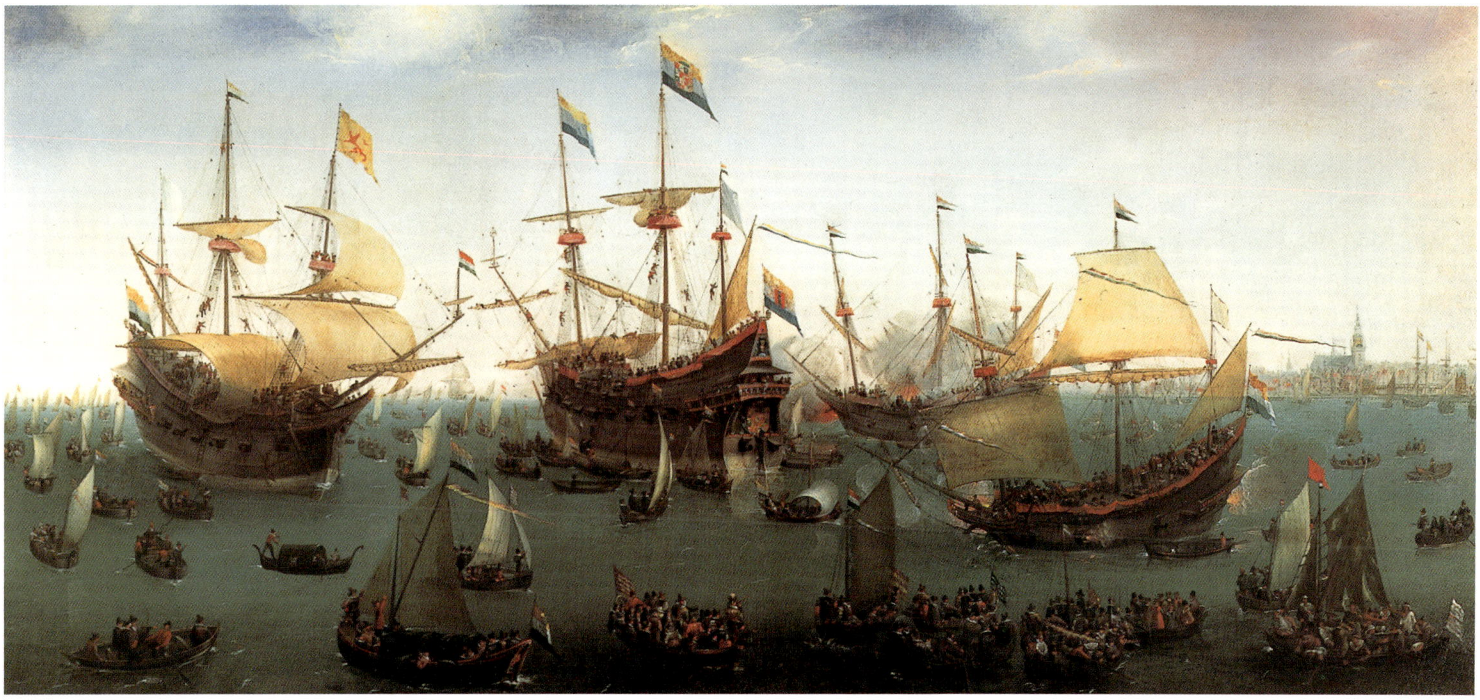

fig. 6 Hendrick Cornelisz Vroom, *The return to Amsterdam of the second expedition to the East Indies, 19 July 1599*, 1599; oil on canvas, 110 x 220 cm. Amsterdam, Amsterdams Historisch Museum (on loan from the Rijksmuseum, Amsterdam)

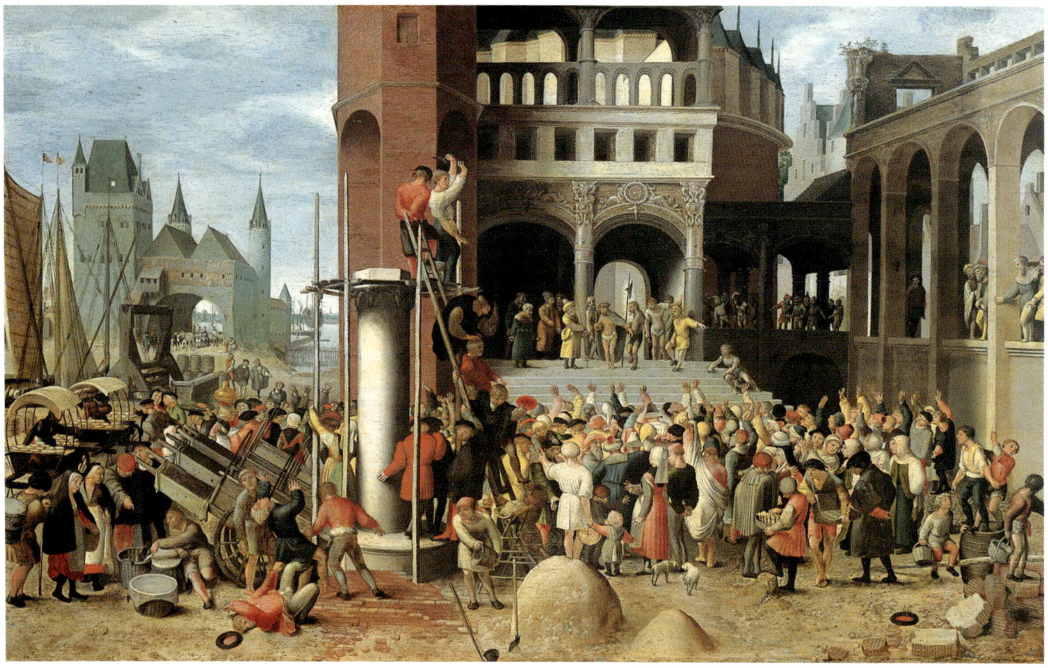

fig. 7 Brunswick Monogrammist, *Ecce homo*; oil on panel, 55 x 89.5 cm. Amsterdam, Rijksmuseum

and suchlike and who concentrated increasingly on texture. Art-lovers were fascinated by the magic of objects in paintings which were almost palpable. In the numerous pictures of St Jerome in his study for instance (*fig. 8*)—many of them painted in the 16th century—there is always a beautifully painted skull, a candle, a book, an hourglass or a clock on the wall. The still life as a speciality seems to have developed from such works of its own accord.

When the northern and southern Netherlands were separated towards the end of the 16th century, the southern provinces remaining Catholic and the northern espousing Protestantism, art too was significantly divided. In the south, the workshop tradition was preserved to a considerable extent. Here, great masters shaped the face of art: Peter Paul Rubens, Anthony van Dyck, David Teniers and Jacob Jordaens. In their workshops were to be found specialist masters who often collaborated in large productions and sometimes built up their own production lines. In the north, painters opted for greater freedom. Many of them, incidentally, had come from the southern provinces in search of freedom of worship—and, by the same token, the freedom to be masters of their own fate. The northern scene was dominated by a large number of independent painters who valued the chance to exploit their own talent. Of less significance is the large complement of Catholic artists in the north, for in general they too endeavoured to express their individual qualities.

fig. 8 Studio of Marinus van Roemerswaele, *St Jerome*; oil on panel, 80.5 x 109 cm. Amsterdam, Rijksmuseum

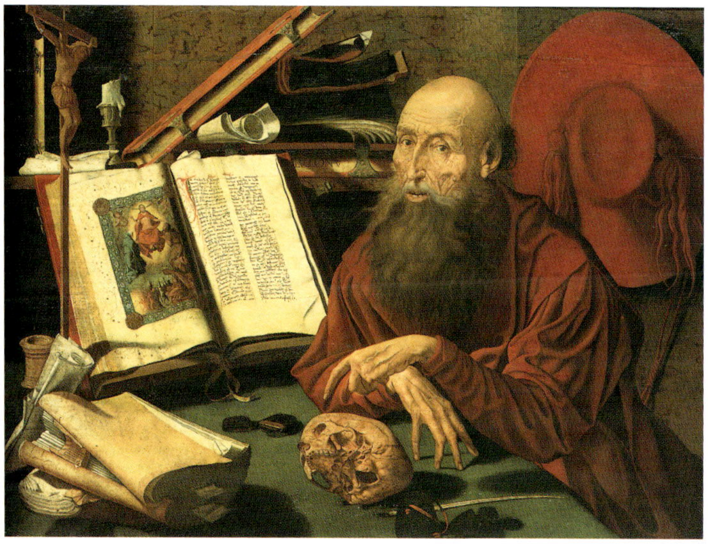

MANIFESTATIONS OF SPECIALISATION

In the 17th century there were many genuine specialists in the Netherlands: Jan van Goyen concentrated almost exclusively on landscapes, Pieter Saenredam confined himself to architectural paintings, Pieter Claesz to still lifes, Melchior d'Hondecoeter to birds. Again, an artist could exploit such a narrow field, constantly improving his own formula in his effort to reach the highest possible level. Sometimes this tactic backfired. In the work of some portraitists all the sitters look alike; in such cases the speciality was obviously cultivated for the sake of convenience. However, some painters appear to have pulled out all the stops in their chosen speciality. Such is the case with Frans Hals, who specialised in the portrait and set out to capture his sitters in a highly personal, loose manner [29]. His speciality emboldened him to perform all kinds of experiments. Pieter Codde, in turn, was not really up to tackling the large group portrait [43] that Hals had left unfinished, but he displays his consummate mastery in a smaller format and in silvery white and grey [25]. A cautious artist like Bartholomeus van der Helst exemplifies how a speciality could lead to great heights. Throughout his career Van der Helst concentrated almost entirely on portraits, seeking variation in the compositions. A number of group and double portraits demonstrate how well he could perform within the narrow limits he had set himself. Unlike Rembrandt in his *Night watch* [44], Van der Helst did not take the liberty of pushing important personages to the fore. In his large *Peace of Münster* [48] he accords almost equal treatment to all the figures, while at the same time managing to devise a composition that conveys a rich and varied impression.

In Leiden, from the second quarter of the 17th century on, the so-called 'Leiden *Feinmaler*' specialised in meticulously executed works. With their minutely detailed paintings, notably Gerard Dou [73] and Frans van Mieris [102] opted less for a category of subjects than for a technique of such smoothness that the brushstroke was invisible. The rendering of textures called for great skill on the artist's part, as Philips Angel, a lesser-known painter, declared in a eulogy on painting in 1642. According to Angel, a good artist should be able to depict the various kinds of metal in such a way that the beholder can perceive all the differences. The discerning beholder, he added, should also be able to discriminate between satin and silk from Tours. This manner of painting earned high praise at first, but a little later on in the century criticism was already being voiced. Writers on art deplored the lack of depth in the artists' choice of subject matter. Eventually all this sophistication palled on the connoisseurs, and there were periods in which appreciation for Dou and his fellows plummeted.

Many of the Italianate painters, so-called because of the Italian inspiration in their landscapes, concentrated less on actual Italian themes than on the bright Mediterranean light. There was evidently a demand in the 17th century for paintings of shepherds and cattle in an imaginary and hilly foreign land in which enthusiasts undoubtedly recognised Arcadia. Jan Both [55], Nicolaes Berchem (*fig. 9*) and Karel Dujardin were masters of the genre, as were Jan Asselijn and Adam Pynacker [56]. Non-Dutch landscapes, with mountains in the distance or lakes in a rocky terrain, were rendered with considerable proficiency. The addition of a few figures conveyed the impression that these were delightful places to be. Here we have masters of a non-existent world, but a world which exercised a strong attraction. Around 1650 Aelbert Cuyp, whose early work had been strongly influenced by Jan van Goyen, developed a Dutch variant of the Italian landscape in the evening sun [57]. It was with this device that he found his form. The subjects of his landscapes vary: they may be river landscapes near Nijmegen or harbour views near Dordrecht, but all his masterpieces are pervaded by the warm light of a low sun, his trademark, a light only seen in the Netherlands rarely, late on a warm summer evening.

That specialisation need not always be equated with a limited range of subjects or with their rendering in a particular style is

fig. 9 Nicolaes Berchem, *Ruins in Italy*, 1658; oil on panel, 51.5 x 41.5 cm. Utrecht, Centraal Museum (on loan from the Rijksmuseum, Amsterdam)

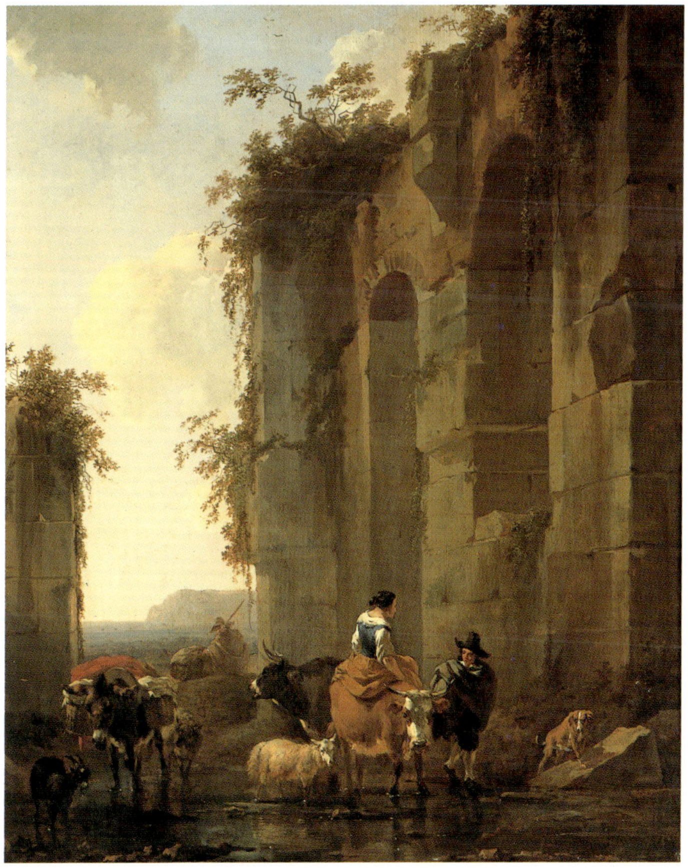

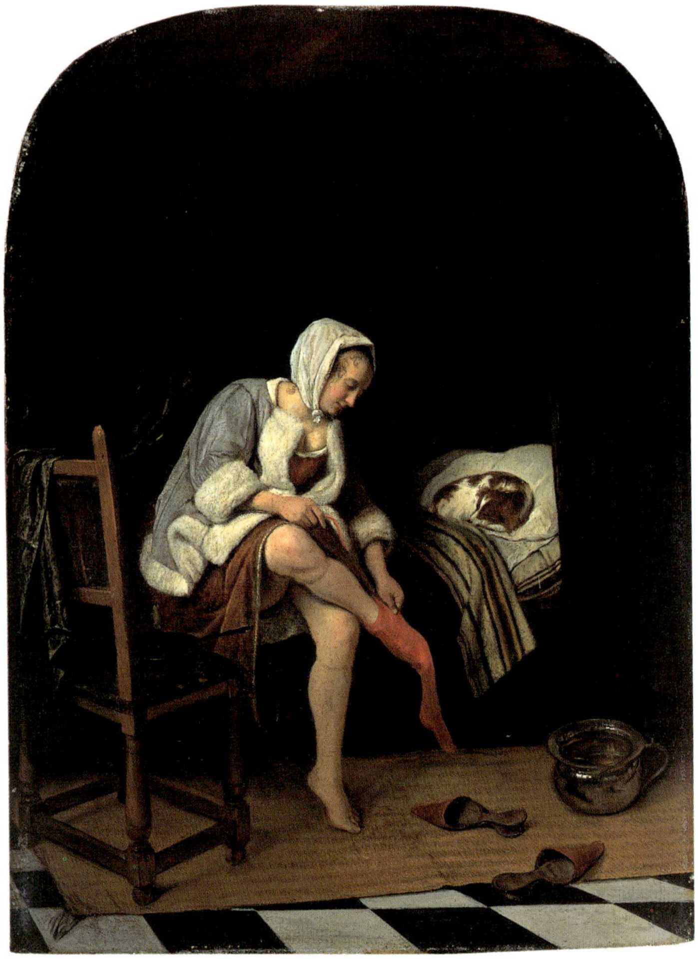

fig. 10 Jan Steen, *Woman at her toilet*; oil on panel, 37 x 27.5 cm. Amsterdam, Rijksmuseum

exemplified by the oeuvre of Quirijn van Brekelenkam (*fig. 1*), who is known for his depictions of various trades. To some extent this counteracts the advantages of repetition, for painting a woman selling fish in a market has little in common with painting a tailor in his workshop. Here, it is less a matter of a specific expertise than of embroidering on a specific theme, rendered with less sophistication but clearly with a particular clientele in mind. Brekelenkam, then, was obviously looking for a gap in the market.

Even less style-bound but nonetheless specialised in a way is the oeuvre of Jan Steen, the master of drollery, of the witty anecdote [74]. With routine expertise he plays one prank after another. Steen must have sensed people's need for comical paintings, for he produced a prodigious number of them, and in a host of different styles. Sometimes he painted small pictures in the manner of the Leiden *Feinmaler* (*fig. 10*); other works were conceived on a grander scale. He appropriated all kinds of styles with the greatest of ease. The humorous narrative element is never absent, not even in most of his biblical and mythological subjects.

Finally, a certain aspect of Rembrandt's artistic achievement may be deemed a speciality. The depiction of personal emotion is highly significant in his work. In his *Self-portrait as the apostle Paul* (*fig. 11*) he has endeavoured to convey the emotion of the writer who desires to hearten the recipients of his epistles but is himself imprisoned and knows he will die by the sword. Rembrandt has brilliantly captured the emotional strain in this painting. In other works he depicts the psychological tension between two or more protagonists. In his *Tobias* (*fig. 12*), the mood of the blind old man suddenly becomes one of suspicion and despair when he wonders how his wife, Anna, has managed to lay her hands on a kid. She in turn is baffled by his mistrust. To Rembrandt, capturing the emotional moment was a specific skill. His interest in this aspect had been kindled by his teacher Pieter Lastman, who in his best work beautifully succeeded in conveying the drama of a particular moment. Lastman's *Orestes and Pylades disputing at the altar* [11] focuses on the tension created by the necessity for a human sacrifice in Aulis and on the dispute between the two friends Orestes and Pylades, each of whom is prepared to sacrifice himself for the other. Rembrandt was later to employ an extra effect, intensifying the drama of his paintings

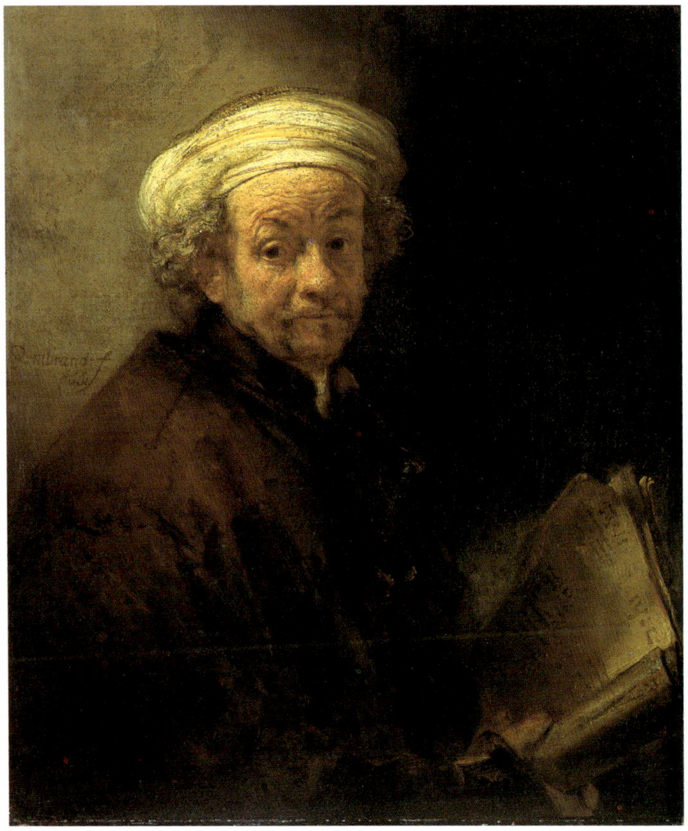

fig. 11 Rembrandt, *Self-portrait as the apostle Paul*, 1661; oil on canvas, 91 x 77 cm. Amsterdam, Rijksmuseum

with chiaroscuro, which became an important, specialist feature of his art.

All these examples show what clever use artists made of their freedom and how they turned the constraints of specialisation to their advantage in a constant exploration of their own artistic potential.

THE APPRECIATION OF SPECIALITIES

The success of landscapes, still lifes and scenes from daily life can be deduced only from their evident popularity, not from contemporary written sources. Writers of the time ranked figural paintings of important events in the highest category. This opinion merely reflected the theory and corresponded only partly with reality. Not surprisingly, really: prosperous burghers tended to be less interested in opulent or edifying scenes from the Bible or mythology. What they wanted were attractive paintings which would arouse general admiration or prompt a lively conversation about their qualities. Not even the theorists always managed to stick to their own rules. Karel van Mander repeatedly stressed that 'memorable histories', figure pieces with an interesting narrative content, constituted the most important task for the artist. He himself, however, painted a few peasant scenes which would have scored fairly low in the hierarchy of the arts; work that would have merely earned him a nice little extra on the side. Gerard de Lairesse was decidedly opposed in his writings to joint artistic efforts, to a division of labour by specialisation. However, he occasionally left the landscape backgrounds in his paintings to Johannes Glauber (*fig. 13*).

The painter Samuel van Hoogstraeten, who also wrote about art, dubbed still-life painters 'foot-soldiers in the army of art'. By this he meant that a specialist has his merits, like a soldier in the field, but that he lacks the complete overview that a general ought to have. A somewhat snide remark in view of the situation in the 17th-century Netherlands, where there was virtually no market for large figural paintings. Even so, we should take serious note of Van Hoogstraeten's observation, for many artists may well have hoped to be asked to paint more elevated subjects without ever having those hopes fulfilled. In practice, moreover, it appears that the theorists' pronouncements were modified by their own writings. An example: Van Hoogstraeten—as Van Mander had done before him—relates the story of Zeuxis, a Greek painter of antiquity who painted grapes exquisitely but was not so good at faces. The message here, in other words, is: painter, do what you are best at and don't try to do what you can't. Furthermore, Van Hoogstraeten ridiculed painters with only one forte which they used all the time, whether suitable or not. To illustrate his point he cites an artist whose speciality was cypresses. When asked to paint a shipwreck for somebody who had actually suffered such a calamity, the artist inquired whether the customer wanted a cypress in the picture. Perhaps an unduly sarcastic story, but it does underline the fact that a limited repertoire can entail imperfect mastery.

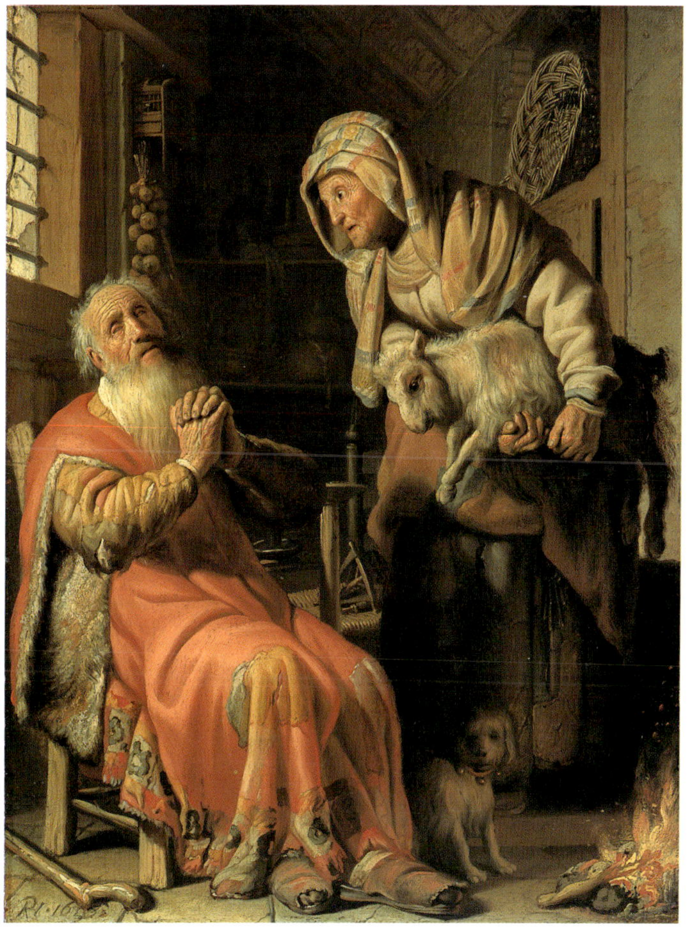

fig. 12 Rembrandt, *Tobias accusing Anna of stealing the kid*, 1626; oil on panel, 39.5 x 30 cm. Amsterdam, Rijksmuseum

Not all those who wrote about art had such negative views on specialisation. The third section of Van Mander's *Schilder-boeck* is a long poem offering advice to young artists. In it, Van Mander lists the many subjects in which the painters of antiquity specialised. Figural paintings of momentous events rank highest, but those unable to rise to such heights might try their hand, Van Mander suggests, at 'animals, kitchens, fruit, flowers, landscapes, architecture, prospects, rooms, grottoes, nights, fires, portraits from life, seas and ships'. Although Van Mander saw the development of some of these specialities in his own day—Hans Vredeman de Vries painted perspectives, Hendrick Vroom naval battles, Jacques de Gheyn flower pieces, Michiel van Mierevelt portraits—he did not live to see the heyday of specialisation. Reading between the lines, we often see that he could not condone the promotion of secondary matters to the status of main issue.

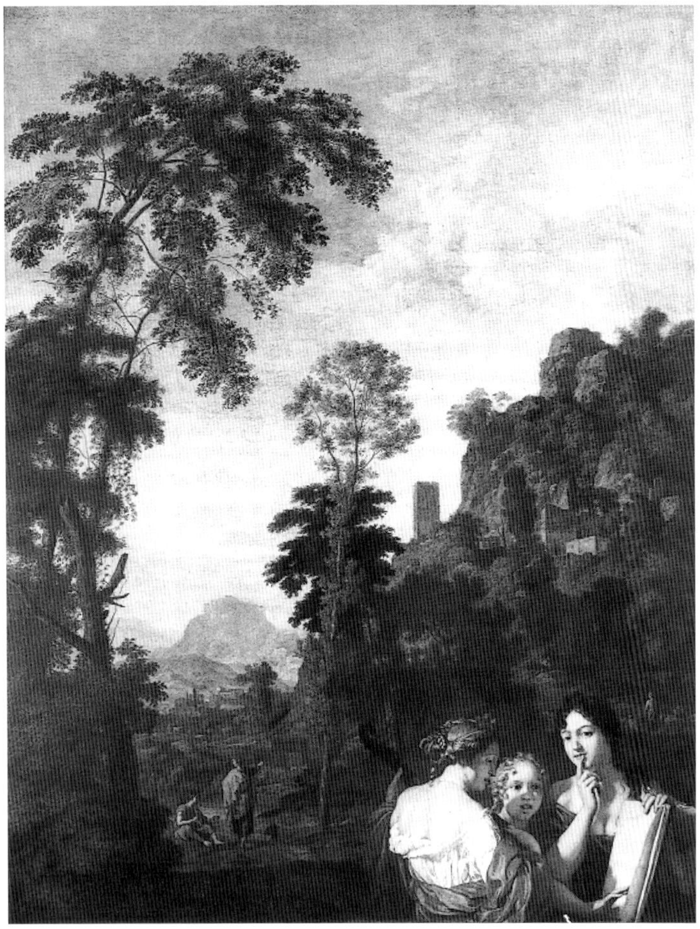

fig. 13 Gerard de Lairesse and Johannes Glauber, *Italian landscape with three women making music*; wall painting on canvas, 290 x 210 cm. Amsterdam, Rijksmuseum

Although De Gheyn sold a flower still life to Emperor Rudolf II in Prague, he preferred making figure pieces, and rightly so, according to Van Mander. In his biography of Bartholomeus Spranger, Van Mander states that painting landscapes is a minor occupation, and elsewhere he refers to specialist activity as 'trifling'. All in all, his attitude is ambivalent. On the subject of his successful fellow townsman Hendrick Vroom he observes, somewhat tartly, that he certainly did the painting profession no disservice, since anyone who wanted a painting by Vroom had to fork out a considerable sum of money. This latter aspect was important to Van Mander, for an artist's achievement was confirmed in part by the high prices he commanded.

Two authors whose writings were published halfway through the century had absolutely no reservations about specialisation. Philips Angel regarded the accurate representation of diverse materials as the highest good. He viewed his fellow townsman Gerard Dou—a representative of the Leiden *Feinmaler* who had made a speciality of meticulous detail, elevating it to the highest goal—as a master who had realised that aspiration. His Flemish colleague Cornelis de Bie regarded an artist's aptitude as a good motivation for making choices. He put it nicely: 'The one who excels in landscape will be unaccustomed to figures, conversely, the figure painter will be unversed in landscape, a second will excel in fruit, the other in flowers, a third in water, the other in fire, and so forth. Rarely will a painter be experienced in all these, but in particular forms of art the one will outdo the other.'

Willem Goeree of Middelburg brings us back to a theorist who deems history painting the principal aim and says that a good painter should be accomplished in every aspect of his profession. Goeree was particularly opposed to works in which more than one artist had collaborated, each displaying his prowess in what he did best. He called such joint efforts 'whoresons', works born of more than one father. His preference for a hierarchy with figural painting on the top rung of the ladder was whole-heartedly endorsed by later authors like Gerard de Lairesse and Arnold Houbraken, whose works were published in the 18th century but whose thinking must have been shaped in the closing decades of the previous one. The former suggested that still lifes were the products of the less gifted. As it happened, his opposition to specialisation eventually had an odd, ambivalent outcome. One of his chief patrons at the end of the 17th century was King-Stadholder Willem III, whose taste was for paintings of mythological subjects and of animals. The works he commissioned from De Lairesse for the bedroom in his Soestdijk hunting lodge showed Diana, in an allusion to the function of the house, and mythological love stories (*fig. 14*). He also enlisted the services of Melchior d'Hondecoeter [100], whose skill in rendering animals, a full-blooded speciality, came in useful for portraying the birds—domestic fowl or exotic specimens from a

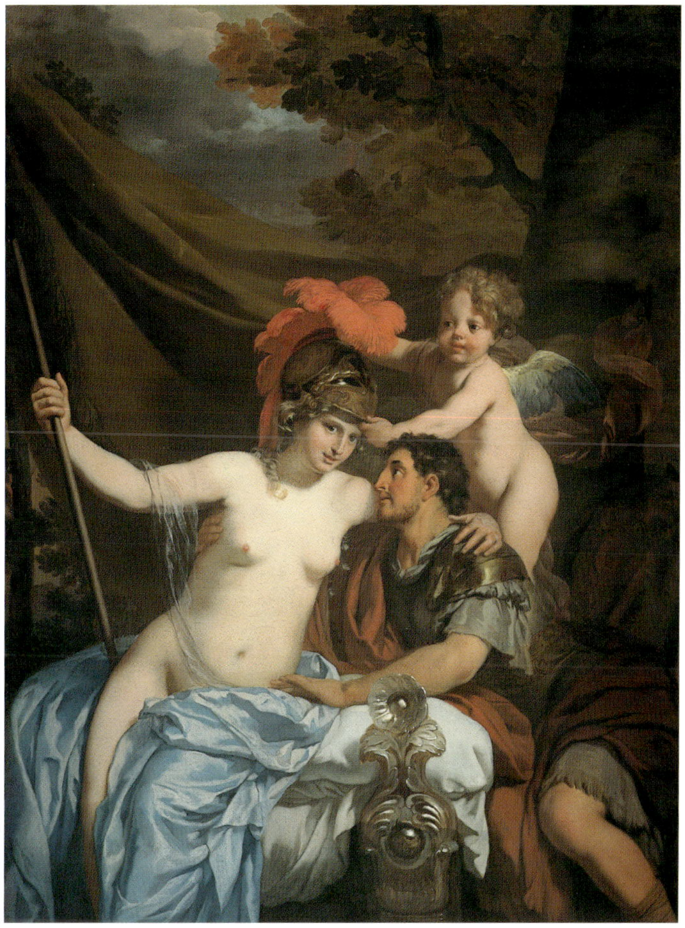

fig. 14 Gerard de Lairesse, *Odysseus and Calypso*; oil on canvas, 125 × 94 cm. Amsterdam, Rijksmuseum

menagerie or aviary—which were the pride of the country seats of the highest in the land. Although De Lairesse's ideas certainly found an echo in the closing decades of the 17th century, it was specialists like Jan Weenix, Rachel Ruysch and Jan van Huysum who continued to enjoy the greatest successes. What did happen is that some subjects, among them the peasant genre, virtually disappeared from painters' repertoires, so the condemnation of specialisation did ultimately lead to a restriction in choice.

STRENGTH AND WEAKNESS

In the end, specialisation survived as the forte of Dutch painting. Now and again we see a speciality develop from a not particularly convincing gimmick into an art form with outstanding results. Architectural painting has already been mentioned as one of the early specialities. One of its first practitioners was Hans Vredeman de Vries, whose particular talent was perspective, the art of suggesting depth in the flat plane. Rather like an itinerant showman, he travelled from one European court to the next, displaying his skill. He was less accomplished as a figure painter, and often left this element to others. As we have seen, such division of labour was not uncommon. Vredeman de Vries's son Pauwels worked in a similar manner, as witness his collaboration with David Vinckboons, for instance. Later in the century the architectural painter Bartholomeus van Bassen likewise resorted to collaborators, leaving the figures in his painting to such artists as Esaias van de Velde. In the Rijksmuseum's painting (*fig. 15*), Van de Velde painted the figures with verve, Van Bassen the architecture with great skill. In the final analysis, though, the work is little more than a demonstration of expertise, notably in the difficult rendering of the complex ceiling. With Pieter Saenredam, however, a true specialist appeared on the scene, a painter who cleverly placed perspective theory at the service of a singularly artistic final product. His architectural representations are no longer mere demonstrations of ingenious perspectives but carefully chosen portraits of buildings. The beauty of the building itself is paramount, and the love with which Saenredam acquitted himself of his task contributes enormously to the superior quality of the work [42]. Finally, Emanuel de Witte, doubtless motivated by his speciality, responded to the tricky use of perspective in the art of the first half of the 17th century by devising new, more painterly solutions (*figs. 2, 3*). Generally speaking, there was room for quite a number of specialists in architectural painting (more than are named here). However, the profession also passed through a development that gradually departed from the established pattern of perspective, leading to an artistic *tour de force*. In this field there is no denying that the stimulus of specialisation and competition produced a final result of high artistic quality.

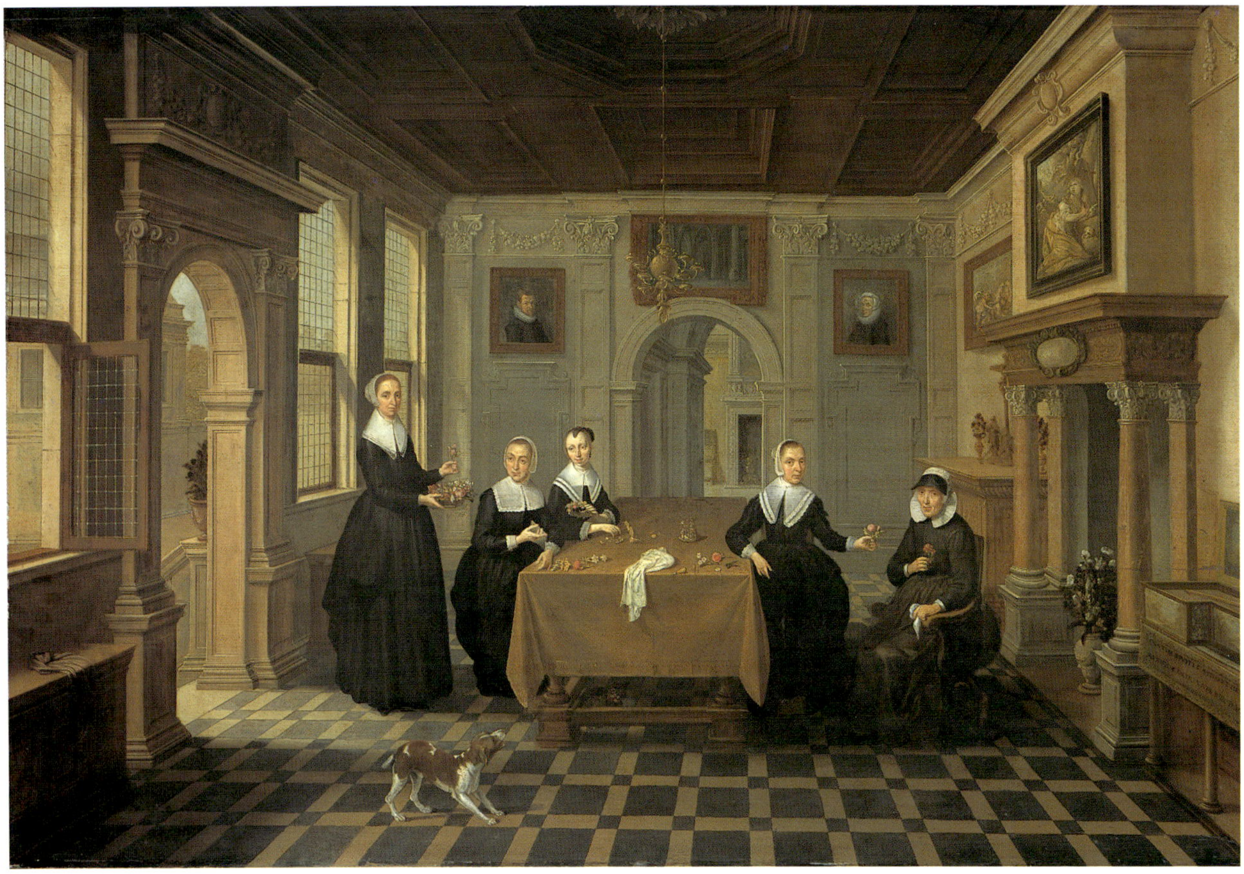

fig. 15 Bartholomeus van Bassen and Esaias van de Velde, *A company in an interior*; oil on panel, 72 x 100 cm. Amsterdam, Rijksmuseum

The same applies to marine painting. Here, too, we see a few specialists with a knowledge of marine architecture and rigging. The aforementioned Hendrick Vroom was the first practitioner of the genre. However, with Willem van de Velde the Elder [90] the speciality seems to have changed course, catering to the exclusive gratification of buffs familiar with historical details. His renderings of naval battles, done with pen and ink on a white ground, were highly successful. His amazing pen paintings, though strikingly accurate in detail, are artistically difficult to enjoy. Even so, Van de Velde was an accomplished draughtsman with an excellent command of perspective and a talent for ingenious arrangement which he displayed in his massed sea battles. This enabled him to rise to great heights within the narrow confines of his speciality. However, it was his son, Willem the Younger, who raised the marine to the highest level of all (*fig. 16*). His oeuvre embraces both the accurately detailed ship's portrait and the imposing naval review; serene, calm seas as well as dramatic tempests. He coupled this varied subject matter with a rich imagination and a keen interest in weather conditions. With masterly panoramas and subtle mood paintings, he added depth to marine art.

The danger of repetition is specialisation's weak point. Looking at only the very best still lifes—and, carefully selected, there are still plenty of them to be enjoyed—provides a one-sided view. The high quality of still-life painting is due not only to uniquely talented artists but to constant attempts to do the same sort of thing over and over again. If all 17th-century flower pieces were placed in a row—a sobering thought—the genre might become unpalatable in the long run. Lovers of the still life who wish to retain their enthusiasm ought to make careful choices from time to time. The same holds true for other specialities.

A similar danger threatens in the oeuvres of individual artists. A prolific landscapist like Jan van Goyen, with an estimated output of 1,400 paintings, strove to convey a convincing impression of the Dutch landscape without ever feeling impelled to document that landscape faithfully. This enables us to see Van Goyen's work as a phenomenal artistic explosion, as the work of an artist who never tires of the opportunity to bend reality to his will, to create landscape as he sees fit. One would, however, have to be a fervent admirer of Jan van Goyen to experience a broad selection from his oeuvre as a constantly surprising view of the Dutch landscape.

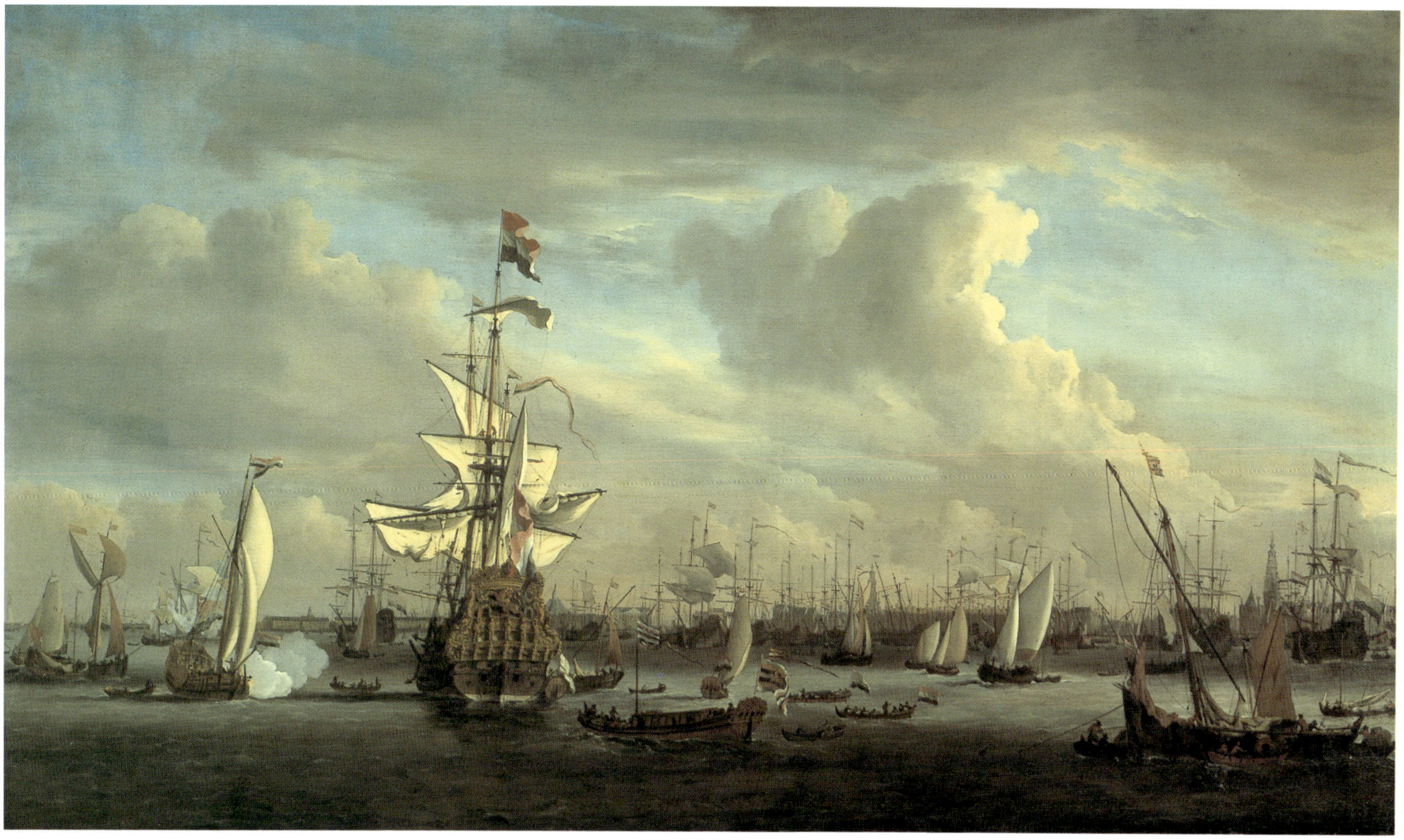

fig. 16 Willem van de Velde the Younger, *The IJ at Amsterdam with the Gouden Leeuw*, 1686; oil on canvas, 179.5 x 316 cm. Amsterdam, Amsterdams Historisch Museum

Another weakness is the tendency towards extreme expertise. This is best seen in the late flower still lifes of Rachel Ruysch and above all Jan van Huysum. In those of the latter, the emphasis on exceptional technical ability was so strong that it surely frustrated the free creative impulse of his colleagues in the genre. For decades, but without signal success, Van Huysum's emulators tried to equal his highly sophisticated still lifes. The products of his supreme virtuosity represent an unconquered peak in flower painting, but they also put an end to the glorious tradition of the Dutch still life.

The enormous strength of all these specialisations, finally, is the variation. The abundance of subjects that Dutch painters mastered never fails to amaze us. Portraits, landscapes by moonlight, marines, historic events, still lifes with flowers, books, views of churches, illustrations of trades, ice scenes—the repertoire was prodigious. That, too, is one of the great qualities of Dutch 17th-century painting.

FURTHER READING

In general: Haak 1984 and Slive 1995; on the production of paintings: Van der Woude 1997; on art in Delft: Montias 1982; on the immigration of Flemish artists: Briels 1987; for views about still lifes: exhib. cat. Amsterdam/Cleveland 1999-2000, pp. 51-57; contemporary writings on art: Angel 1642 (see also Hoyle & Miedema 1996); De Bie 1661; Goeree 1670; Van Hoogstraeten 1678; Houbraken 1718-21; De Lairesse 1740

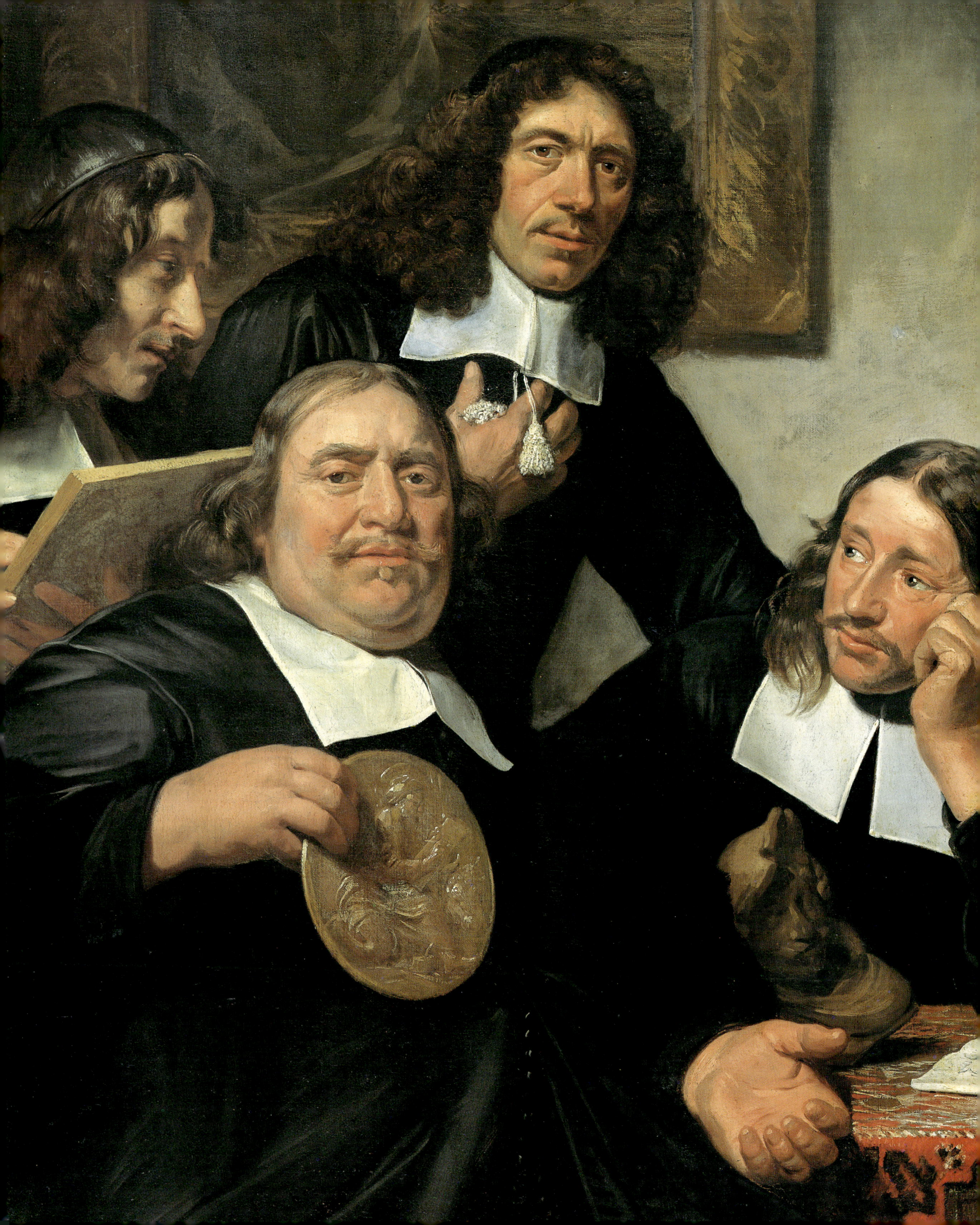

The world of the 17th-century artist

The abiding power of 17th-century Dutch paintings lies in their ability to offer glimpses of a real world. It is this that sets them apart from the art of earlier periods and other countries, bound as it was by convention. Dutch painting, by contrast, seems to open a fresh window on people going about their daily lives. We see their heads (some more evocative than others) and those of their children in portraits which tell us precisely how they wore their hair, which lace ruffs and collars were in vogue, and the shoes they felt matched their worsted suits and satin gowns. In genre painting we see them going about their daily business, from a quiet conversation between a mistress and maid by a linen cupboard or a woman absorbed in writing a letter, to the rowdy goings-on in taverns and brothels. Cityscapes record the facades of their houses and the newly-laid streets. Still lifes present us with their possessions and food. Even landscapes contain human cameos: skating by city walls, a coach halting by an inn in the coastal dunes, or a ferryboat laden with people and cattle.

One could go on describing these well-observed impressions, but one thing is perfectly clear: Dutch painters had a keen eye for the world around them. It is almost as if seems they had a visual gift for spotting what was of lasting artistic value in the passing world. Art historians constantly warn against taking this realistic art at face value, against regarding it as a mirror of everyday life. They stress that such paintings always present an air-brushed reality which was subject to intractable artistic conventions and no less coercive moral convictions. it should also be realised that many situations in real 17th-century life were never depicted at all. These qualifications may be important, but the fact remains that 17th-century Dutch art is unrivalled for the immediacy with which it portrays the outside world.

That world, in its turn, seems to have taken its artists to its heart. This can be inferred from the fortunate conjunction of quantity and quality. A surprisingly large proportion of the countless works of art produced in the 17th century (estimates put the output of paintings alone at more than 5 million) are of superb quality.[1] It was an age when talent was widespread, in both the personal and geographical senses. Gifted painters were not concentrated in just one centre; art flourished in many towns simultaneously: in Amsterdam, Haarlem, Utrecht, Leiden, Middelburg, Delft, The Hague and Dordrecht. Even smaller places like Alkmaar, Zwolle, Kampen, Deventer and Leeuwarden produced masters now held in high regard. It appears to have been a society which created a climate in which art could thrive across the full spectrum as never before nor since. A society with a fascination for art which stimulated artists to that remarkable collective achievement known as the Golden Age.

PAINTING AND THE OTHER ARTS

When speaking of 17th-century art one soon finds oneself, often inadvertently, talking of painting alone. Some may also think of drawings and prints. And perhaps there is a realisation that Delft faience is part of the legacy of that century, but the other arts barely intrude on the public perception of the Golden Age. On the one hand that is odd, because marble sculptures, tapestries, carved ivory, gold boxes, silver dishes, gilt-leather hangings, furniture upholstery and cabinets with delicate marquetry work often contributed more to the status and splendour of a house than paintings did. Generally, too, such objects were far more expensive and were produced in large numbers in these prosperous regions. The present focus on paintings is certainly one-sided, but it is not entirely ahistorical, for in the 17th century, too, it was painting that excited the greatest admiration and set the most tongues and pens in motion. It is telling, for example, that Karel van Mander (1604), Cornelis de Bie (1661), Joachim van Sandrart (1675) and Arnold Houbraken (1718-1721) wrote the biographies of painters but say nothing about the practitioners of other arts, whose lives were recorded by no one.[2] Nor do the theoretical treatises about painting, like those by Van Mander again (1604), Franciscus Junius (1641), Philips Angel (1642), Willem Goeree (1670), Samuel van Hoogstraeten (1678) and Gerard de Lairesse (1707) have their equivalents in the other artistic disciplines.[3]

That there was a new fascination with painting can also be deduced from incidental remarks that were recorded at the time. Constantijn Huygens, the erudite secretary to Stadholder Prince Frederik Hendrik, wrote that 'in the realm of painting (with which one is everywhere confronted these days) one cannot arrive at an opinion that is in any way well-founded if one has not practised the principles of that art oneself'.[4] This tells us not only that paintings were ubiquitous in 1631, but that people felt they had to speak of them discerningly, which made it advisable for even lay people to have taken up the brush themselves.

An interest in painting was not restricted to the sophisticated circles in which Huygens moved. David Beck, a schoolmaster and another amateur painter from The Hague, was equally enthusiastic.

◂ Detail of fig. 21

In his diary for 1624 he relates that during a journey on a passage-boat to Delft he fell in with a kindred spirit, a cabinetmaker called Master Anthonie, 'with whom I conversed endlessly about art'. He also says that each evening he was in the habit of reading 'for a good hour in Van Mander's *Schilder-boeck*'.[5]

The interest in painting was so widespread that it attracted the attention of several foreigners visiting the Republic. The Frenchman Samuel Sorbière, who was there in 1640, spoke of 'l'excessive curiosité pour les peintures' on the part of the Dutch.[6] The Englishman Peter Mundy was equally struck by the 'enclination and delight that these countries have to Paintings', which was so pervasive that even butchers, blacksmiths and cobblers had them hanging on the walls of their shops or workplaces.[7] One well-known reaction is found in the diary of John Evelyn, who was astonished in 1641 by the number of paintings on display at the annual market in Rotterdam. His explanation for this abundance was that people invested their money in them because of the shortage of land. He had been told that even a 'common Farmor' would invest between two and three thousand pounds in this way, and that he could sell his paintings on at great profit at the fairs.[8] It is doubtful whether Evelyn's economic explanation is a valid one, for it is no more than an observation made by someone passing through, but that does detract from his amazement about the way paintings were presented. Contemporary observations of this kind demonstrate that the Dutch Golden Age was indeed a triumph of painting.

The numbers confirm this. It has been estimated that there must have four times as many painters in the Republic in 1620 as in 1600—a quite remarkable expansion of a professional group, far outstripping the increase in the general population in the same period.[9] A more precise count of the painters in Haarlem, for example, reveals that at the beginning of the century, in 1605, there was one painter per 2,000-3,000 inhabitants. Ten years later the ratio was around one per 1,000-2,000, rising to one in 750-1,000 by 1625, and reaching one in 450-525 in 1635.[10] An almost fivefold increase, in other words. There was also a sharp rise in Utrecht in the early decades of the century which peaked in the 1640s before levelling off, and more serious after 1672, the 'year of disaster'.[11] Censuses of this kind have not been carried out for other groups. All the artistic sectors undoubtedly expanded greatly as a result of the general population increase and rising prosperity, but it is unlikely that they matched the kind of growth enjoyed by painters. The practitioners of the other arts may occasionally have had reason to envy the amount of attention given to painting. Gerard de Lairesse writes of a despondent sculptor who told him that he had 'changed stone into canvas and chisels into palette and brushes' because there was no living to be made from marble.[12]

GUILDS AND PROFESSIONAL EMANCIPATION

If painting could rise to such heights in quantity, quality and appreciation, one wonders whether it had found a new place in society. Not really, or at least not as regards training and professional organisation. Like most crafts, the arts were organised in guilds. A guild can be defined as 'a body of professional colleagues with powers sanctioned by the government to supervise admission to the profession and the manner in which it was practised'.[13] Guilds were organised at an urban level, which meant that their officials had to submit important decisions to the city council for its approval. Art, in other words, was ultimately a question of civic politics, which could vary from one town to the next.

The guild's main task was to decide who could practise a particular profession by only awarding the title of master to those who had received a thorough training and who had passed the masterpiece test. The guild also regulated the nature and duration of an apprentice's training, as well as protecting its members from outside competition, supporting them in times of illness, paying for their funerals, and providing financial assistance to widows threatened with poverty.

Most crafts were united in the Guild of St Luke: fine art painters and house painters (also known as broad-brush or coarse painters), tapestry weavers, engravers, stained-glass painters, and so on. In some towns sculptors were also included, but in others they were members of the stonemasons' guild. The position of precious metal workers could also vary. They often belonged to the Guild of St Luke, but in Amsterdam, for example, they had a guild of their own. The Delft faience makers were admitted to the Guild of St Luke in 1648, leaving the other potters behind in the St Michael's Guild. Cabinetmakers and others who worked with wood had their own Guild of St Joseph.

In many cases, then, there were several different professional groups within one and the same guild. In Haarlem, for instance, painters and goldsmiths found themselves in a corporation alongside not only engravers and sculptors, but pewterers, coppersmiths, tinsmiths, secondhand dealers and sellers of pottery and rags. Such a mixed bag of occupations, some of them very humble, would not appear to be the most stimulating surroundings for the practitioners of the higher forms of art. Matters were arranged differently in other countries. The painters of Florence had left the guild in 1563 to join forces with the sculptors and architects in forming an academy of art which was christened the Accademia del Disegno because of the importance of drawing to all three groups. Art academies were then founded elsewhere in Italy and Europe. The name alone, taken as it was from Plato's school of philosophy in Athens, signalled a totally different, more intellectual approach to the practice of art. It was only to be expected that in a period of such cultural flowering the artists of the Republic were attracted to the scholarly and prestigious image of the modern artist imported from Italy, and that they experienced the guilds largely as an unseemly straitjacket.

A struggle for emancipation was thus inevitable. However, it is extremely difficult to get an idea of just how satisfied or dissatisfied artists were with the guild system. It turns out that theory and practice were not entirely in step. The guilds were roundly condemned in writings about art. Van Mander, for instance, indignantly said that 'a guild is made of the noble art of painting, as is done with all manner of coarse handicrafts and crafts like weaving, stitching furs, carpentry, smithing and the like'.[14] In 1670, Willem Goeree also fulminated against a system which did not elevate art to the highest level but rewarded mediocrity: '[...] due to a lack of knowledge about the nature of the arts and the scant respect accorded them, unreasonable regulations have crept in from time to time which protect many a bungler under the pretence of a civic right or, rather, encourage them in their ignorant sloth'. Like Van Mander, Goeree regarded art as rather more than a craft. It is 'free by nature, and so full of lofty studies and sciences [...] that it encompasses all wisdom in a single bundle'.[15] Interestingly, Goeree cites the economic essay *Hollands Interest* written in 1660 by Pieter de la Court, in which the author extols the virtues of the free market and argues for the abolition of the guilds.

Such expressions of dissatisfaction have been associated with various attempts by painters to break free of the guild system and associate only with their immediate colleagues. Examples of this abound. The Utrecht painters and wood-carvers left the saddlemakers' guild in 1611, the painters then shook off the woodcarvers in 1639, and by 1644 there was no more talk of a guild but of a 'College of Painters'.[16] In 1616, the Middelburg art painters tried to distance themselves from the broad-brush painters, but the city authorities stepped in to prevent it. A 'Brotherhood or Confraternity of St Luke' was founded in Dordrecht in 1642, which Houbraken later explained was 'as if the noble art was dishonoured to be counted among the crafts'.[17] A similar fraternity was set up in Amsterdam in 1653, and served alongside the guild as a place where the members could socialise. A 'Confrèrie' was founded in The Hague in 1656 (grandly renamed 'Confrèrie Pictura' a few years later) after a disdainful secession from the guild of house-painters and glaziers, although sculptors, engravers, glass engravers and amateurs were allowed to join. In 1670, the Confrèrie commissioned a silver goblet which took on a ritual function during the installation of new members (*fig. 17*). In honour of the members' newly acquired status, the four branches of the Confrèrie are represented in cartouches on the base: 'Schilder Const' (Painting), 'Beelt Houwerie' (Sculpture), 'Glas Schrijverije' (Glass engraving)

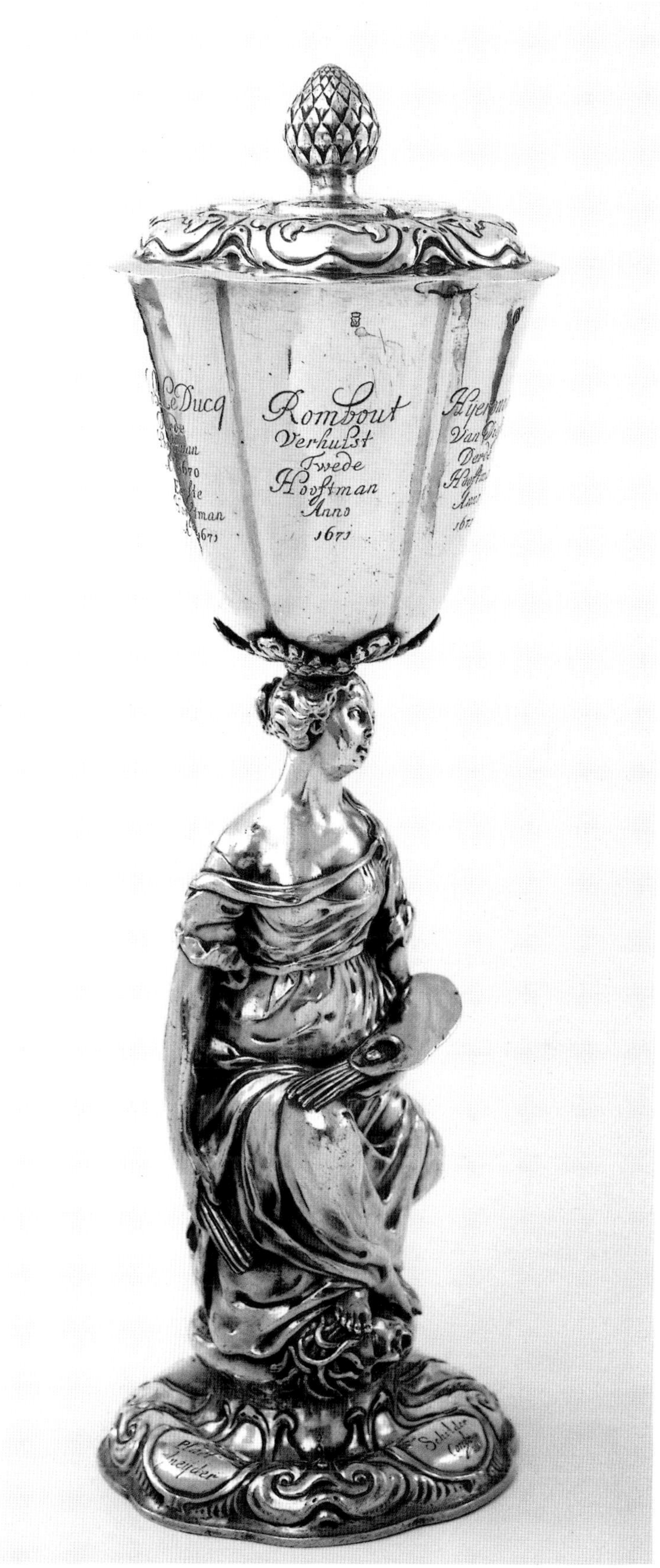

fig. 17 Jonas Gutsche, *Goblet of the Hague Confrèrie*, 1670; silver, h. 34 cm. Rotterdam, Museum Boijmans Van Beuningen

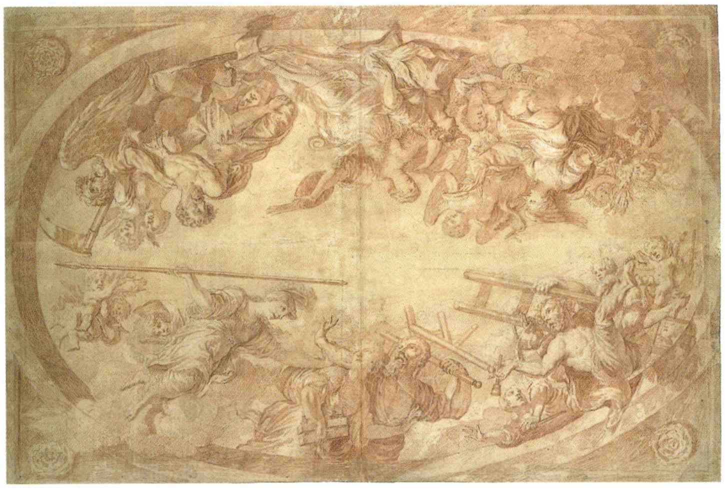

fig. 18 Mattheus Terwesten after Willem Doudijns, *Allegory of the secession of the Confrèrie Pictura from the Guild of St Luke, 1686*; red chalk, heightened with white chalk, over a sketch in black chalk, 62 x 84.3 cm. Amsterdam, Rijksmuseum, Rijksprentenkabinet

and 'Plaet Sneijder' (Engraving). The bowl, however, is not supported *en quatre* but by a single figure personifying painting. She is seated on a globe, trampling a head with writhing snakes for hair to proclaim that painting rules the world and conquers envy. The latter may well be a reference to the antagonism of the former guild which the departing painters had to overcome. Engraved on the bowl are the names of the board members in office at the time, among whom were the sculptor Rombout Verhulst and the history painter Willem Doudijns.

In 1686, the selfsame Doudijns mercilessly expressed the Hague painters' feeling of deliverance in a ceiling painting in Pictura's premises on the Korenmarkt (*fig. 18*).[18] The surviving drawing for this allegorical scene shows how, to echo Houbraken, 'Pallas and the love of art passionately banish the broad-brush painters with ladder and paint-pot, the bookbinders with screw and press, and the chair-makers with their tools from the artistic heavens'.[19]

One finds a similar hierarchical distinction between artists and craftsmen in the proposals which Salomon de Braij submitted for reforming the Haarlem Guild of St Luke in 1631. He suggested a division in which those who were 'engaged in art' were placed in an upper echelon headed by the painters, while manual workers such as goldsmiths, bookbinders and coppersmiths were relegated to a 'lower group'.[20] The city authorities rejected the proposals, but De Bray had no intention of abandoning his ideas. Four years later, when he designed 'coffin adornments' for deceased members of the Guild of St Luke, he suggested that the bier of a painter should be adorned 'in the most magnificent manner' with the coats of arms of all 16 crafts represented in the guild, that a sculptor's should have eight coats, a goldsmith's six (without that of the painters)

fig. 19 Anonymous artist after Salomon de Braij, *Example and sketches of coffin adornments, or ornaments in greater and lesser degrees, 1635*. Haarlem City Archives, Gildearchieven 194, fols. 26r and 27r

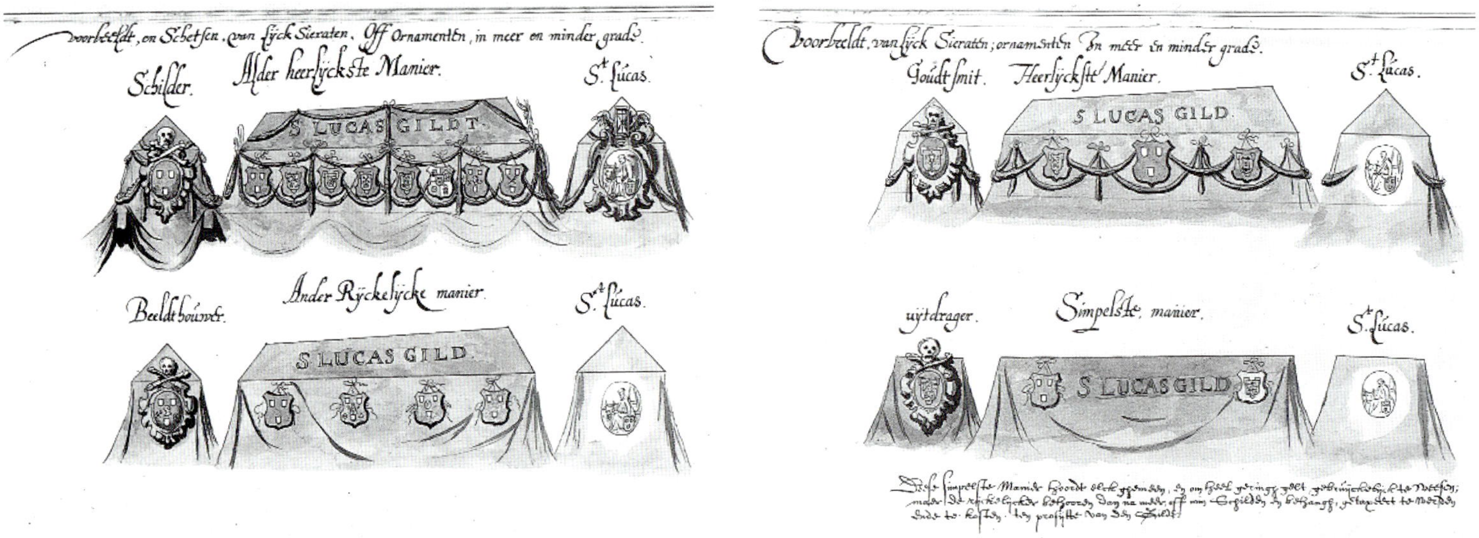

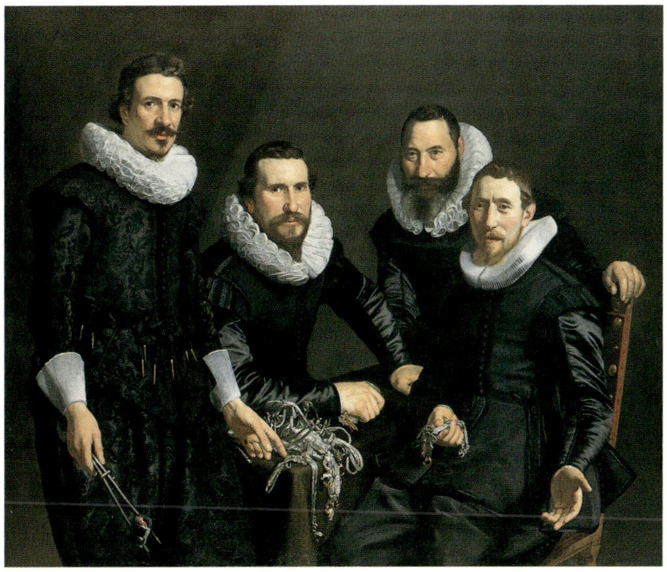

fig. 20 Thomas de Keyser, *The syndics of the Amsterdam goldsmiths guild*, 1627; oil on canvas, 127.2 x 152.4 cm. Toledo (Ohio), Toledo Museum of Art

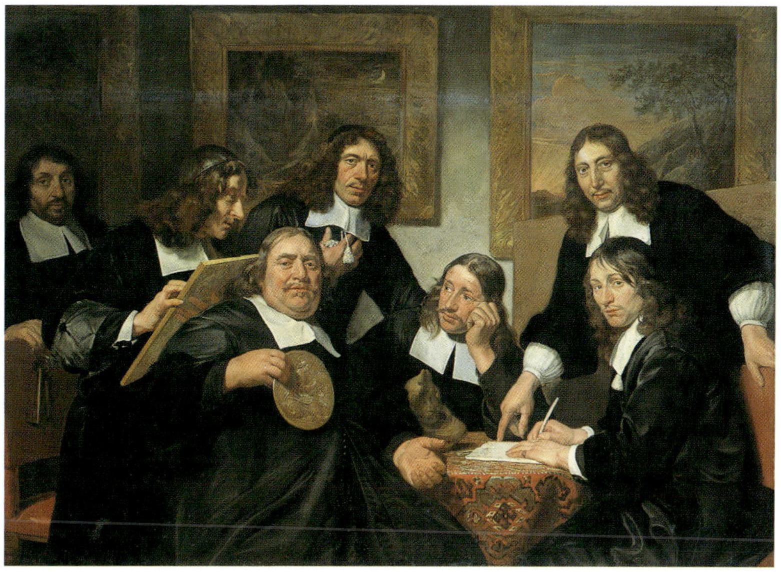

fig. 21 Jan de Braij and others, *The governors of the Guild of St Luke, Haarlem*, 1675; oil on canvas, 130 x 184 cm. Haarlem, Frans Halsmuseum (on loan from the Rijksmuseum, Amsterdam)

and a secondhand dealer's, 'in the simplest manner', no more than four (*fig. 19*).[21]

The biers in Haarlem and the ceiling in The Hague sent out an unequivocal message. They are expressions of a professional pride, of a professional self-importance even, at the expense of the more craft-oriented members of the guild or former guild. Other instances of attempts to break away from the Guild of St Luke, whether or not they were successful, cannot automatically be described as emancipatory. When the petitions were backed by reasons, the arguments are always protectionist and organisational, with not a word being said about the intellectual or free nature of art. As a fast-growing professional group, the painters had no wish to see their interests being diluted in the craft conglomerate which the Guild of St Luke so often was. That there was no general aversion to the guild system among painters is further demonstrated by the fact that in 1610 and again in 1642, the painters of Leiden took the initiative to form a Guild of St Luke because there had not been one for several decades and because they felt too exposed to competition from outside the town.

The guilds as such, in other words, were not held in contempt. On the contrary, the literary broadsides notwithstanding, they were generally accepted as a welcome form of protection. Having said that, one is struck by the fact that there are so few depictions of guild activities in 17th-century art. While the men of the civic guards, the superintendents of the ports, the governors of charitable institutions, the officers of the vintners' guild and the surgeons' guild frequently had themselves immortalised in group portraits, that custom, oddly enough, did not take root within the Guild of St Luke. There are only a few exceptions. The earliest does not actually involve St Luke's Guild but the officials of the Amsterdam goldsmiths' guild of 1627 (*fig. 20*). One nice touch is that the painter, Thomas de Keyser, included the attributes involved in one of the guild's most important tasks, namely to assay the content of precious metals. The man on the left, Loeff Vredericx, is holding as pair of tongs with the glowing coals used to test the purity of silver. Hanging from the cord knotted around his waist are the assaying rods used to determine the gold content. On the table lies a tangle of châtelaine girdles which women wore below their outer garments. Unfortunately, nothing is known about the circumstances surrounding this commission.[22]

That is also the case with the exceptional group portrait of the officials of Haarlem's Guild of St Luke painted in 1675 (*fig. 21*). The work goes under the name of Jan de Braij, the man second from left with a brush in his hand. The unusual, corporative aspect of the painting is that it is probably the work of no fewer than four hands. The painters Jan de Jong and Jan van Hotingh painted their own likenesses, while the brothers Jan and Dirck de Braij painted each other.[23] The other three sitters were not painters and were portrayed by Jan de Braij. One of them is the dean of the guild, the coppersmith Gerrit Mulraet, who is shown with the work which he had donated to the guild. It is not without irony that it was the son of Salomon de Braij who painted the coppersmith as the chief officer of the guild; Salomon himself would probably not have bothered getting his brush out.

That there are no other scenes glorifying the guild or immortalising its officials probably indicates that professional pride was experienced not so much within the collective ambience of the guild. Perhaps, then, one could characterise the relationship between artist and guild as one of indifference. And maybe that was not such a bad thing. It would have enabled new ideas about the practice of art, drawing instruction and the sale of artworks to evolve along fairly modern lines within the guilds without the latter holding the reins too tight. That indifference might even explain why the guilds actually managed to survive in the 17th century.[24]

THE ARTIST THROUGH HIS OWN EYES

The dearth of group portraits of the officials of St Luke's Guild is in marked contrast to the large number of self-portraits by 17th-century painters. Individual presentation evidently befitted the practice of art more than a collective one. In fact, no other cultural region produced so many self-portraits. Rembrandt leads the field with some 40, but other painters, like Jan Steen, Gerard Dou and Frans van Mieris were no shrinking violets either. Those large numbers indicate that the paintings were not made for the artist's home or family, but that there was a market for them among art-lovers, who regarded painters as a species of *uomini illustri*. Buyers of this kind had their dearest desires satisfied by a painting which united the artist's person and work.[25] Self-portraits (the word did not yet exist in the 17th century) should accordingly be regarded not as examples of psychological introspection but as the artist's contribution to the propagation of his own fame. It was at its most successful when the artist came up with an original variant of the genre, which is why self-portraits often contain so many 'ingenious accoutrements', unusual costumes and pleasing visual inventions.

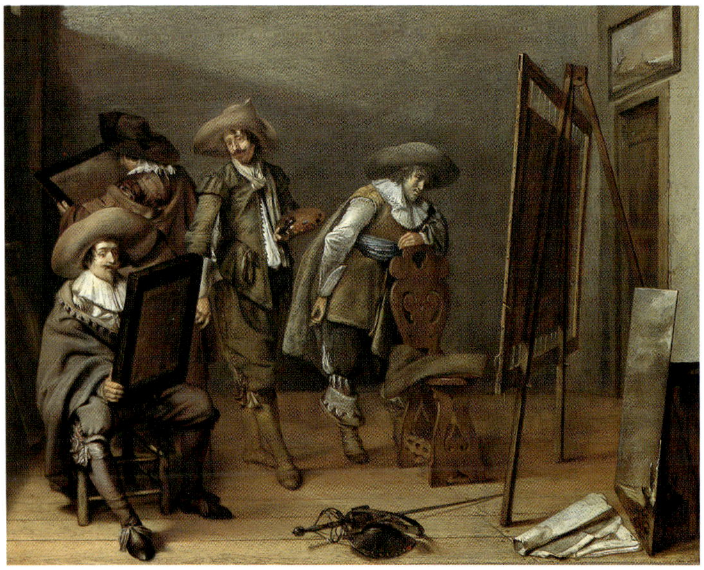

fig. 22 Pieter Codde, *Art-lovers in a painter's studio* , c. 1630; oil on panel, 38.3 x 49.3 cm. Stuttgart, Staatsgalerie

The related genre of people seen visiting an artist's studio is often crammed with artistic references. Moreover, it can provide interesting information about the social reality of the painter's workplace. Interestingly, this genre came into its own at a time when art dealing was on the rise. That prompts the question why these studios were thrown open to the public, as it were. The likely answer is that such paintings refer to the practice of true devotees and connoisseurs of painting visiting artists in their studios. The importance of those occasions emerges, among other places, in Constantijn Huygens's autobiography of 1631, which has been cited above. He stated that he enjoyed befriending artists, and wrote of his visits to them and the ensuing conversations about art, such as the time he called at the Leiden studio of the young Rembrandt and Lievens in 1629. The travel accounts of foreigners confirm that visiting a studio was a hallowed custom. When Cosimo III de'Medici toured the Republic in 1667/68 he called on no fewer than 15 artists, among them the elderly Rembrandt.[26] In 1625, the French painter Pierre Lebrun actually wrote a guide for studio visits in which he advised that 'in order to discourse about this noble profession one must have frequented the studio and disputed with the masters, and have seen how they handle their brush'.[27] He even supplied a list of remarks and comments which would enable the reader to cut a dash in the company of painters and art-lovers.

The object of such studio visits was not to buy a work from the artist but above all to discuss art with him and with like-minded devotees. This may be the subject of a painting by Pieter Codde of three elegantly-clad gentlemen who appear to be well-acquainted with this particular studio (*fig. 22*).[28] A painting by Frans van Mieris is even more interesting (*fig. 23*). A black-garbed visitor who has just entered, judging by the cape half-off his shoulders and the hat he is still holding in his hand, is not looking at the unfinished painting on the easel but at a piece of sculpture standing on a covered table. The connoisseur had evidently come not just to admire the painter's work but also to examine a variety of intriguing artefacts of art and science, which are accordingly arranged in a lavish display in most studio scenes.

It is fair to assume that art-lovers who shared this involvement in the artist and his world were the most likely group for which studio scenes were painted. That does not mean to say that those paintings were necessarily records of actual visits, but they do either depict or allude to discriminating taste. It is even possible that pictures of studios in which there are no visitors refer to this custom. For instance, one could interpret the way in which the painter looks at the viewer in a picture by Michiel van Musscher as a welcome to his imaginary workplace (*fig. 24*).

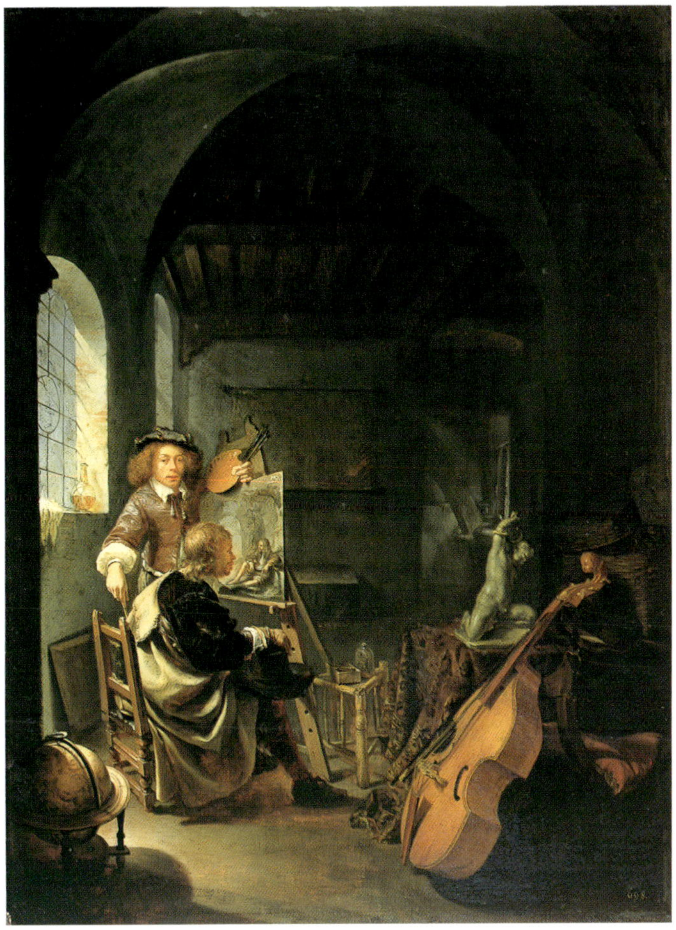

fig. 23 Frans van Mieris the Elder, *The painter's studio*, c. 1659; oil on panel, 59.5 x 47 cm. Dresden, Gemäldegalerie Alte Meister

THE ARTIST'S CALLING

The need to choose a profession came early in life in the 17th century. An apprenticeship usually began when a child was around ten years old, although it was not uncommon for aspiring artist to start later. Since the pupil was still a minor, the choice was generally made by the parents (or the guardian or local chamber of orphans). There were no schools or academies for a training in the arts, so a suitable teacher had to be found. A contract was drawn up between him and the parents stipulating the length of the apprenticeship, the tuition fees and the obligations on both sides. The teacher had to discharge his task to the best of his ability, and take good care of the child, even, as so often stated in such contracts, as if it 'were his own'.[29] Under the guild regulations, a teacher could not take on more than one or two new pupils a year, so that he had sufficient time to devote to them. The pupil had to obey his master. The level of tuition fees depended on various factors: whether the boy lodged with the master and whether his parents paid for his clothing, and also whether he was just an apprentice or was expected to assist in the workshop. Another consideration was whether the apprentice remained in the

fig. 24 Michiel van Musscher, *The painter's studio*, 1679; oil on panel, 57 x 46.5 cm. Rotterdam, Historisch Museum Het Schielandhuis

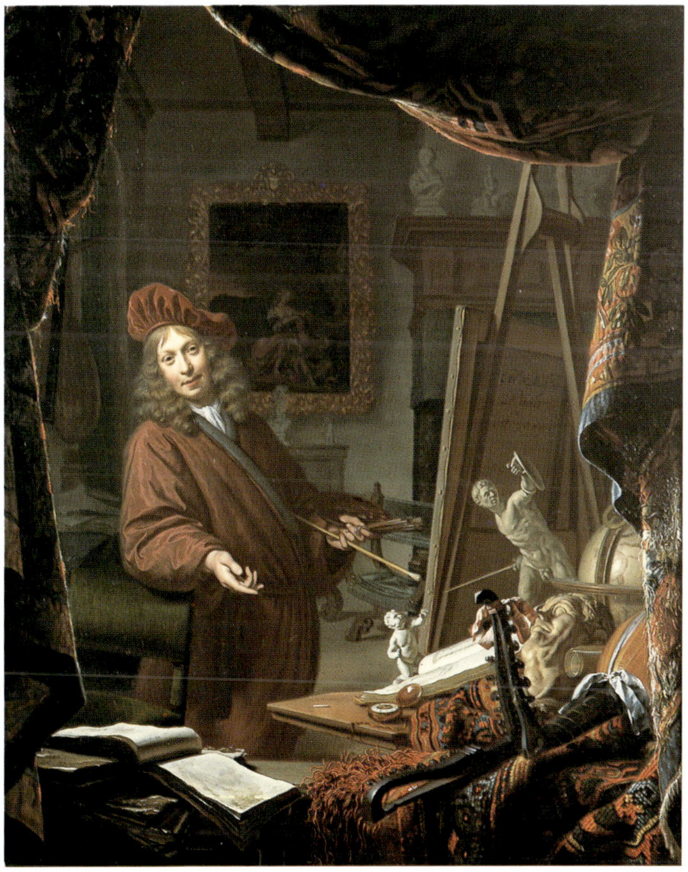

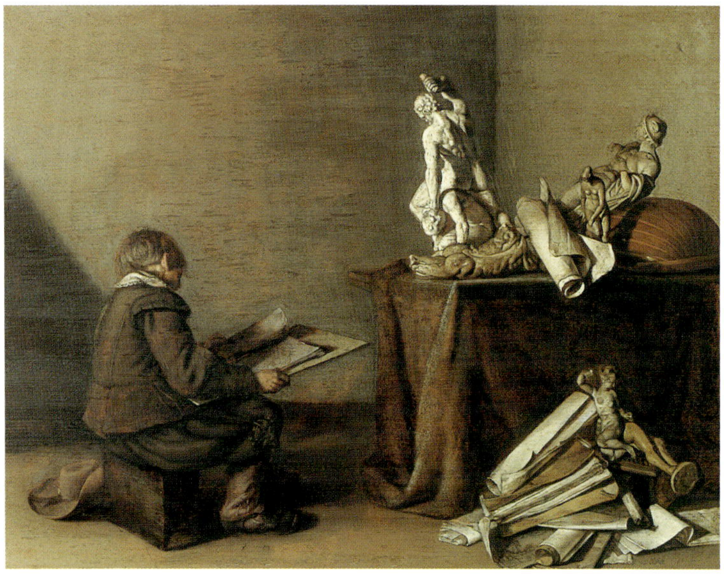

fig. 25 Pieter Codde (attributed to), *The young draughtsman*, c. 1630; oil on panel, 28 x 36.5 cm. Brussels, Koninklijke Musea voor Schone Kunsten

fig. 26 Jacob Ochterveld, *The drawing lesson*; oil on canvas, 72.5 x 59 cm. Bonn, Rheinisches Landesmuseum

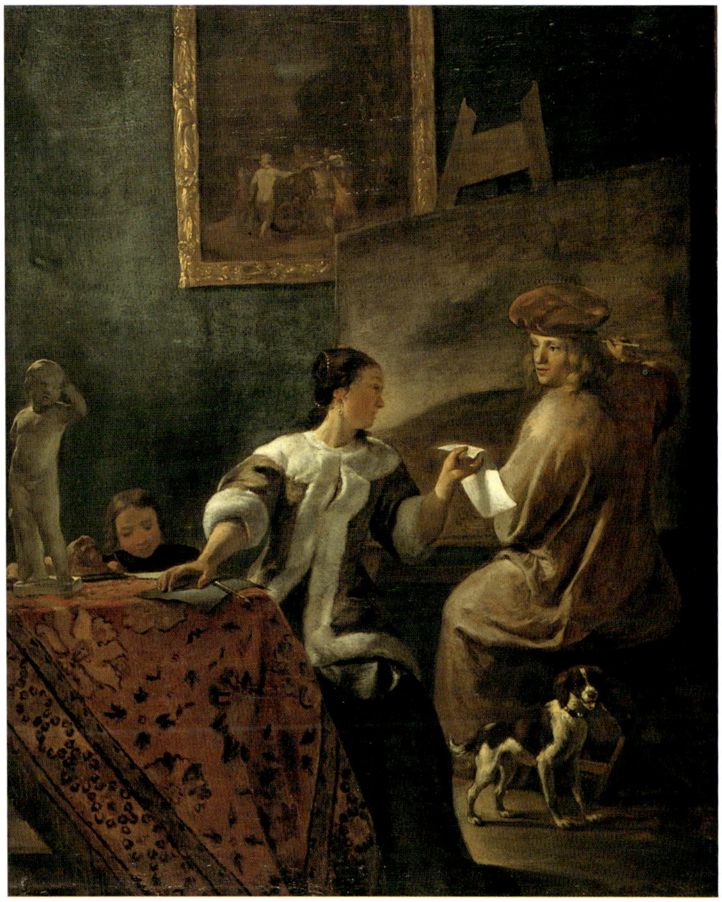

shop long enough to recoup the time invested in his tuition by contributing to the shop's output. The longer the contract the lower the fees.[30] The risks that the master ran if he lost his pupil before the profitable period began were covered by a penalty clause stipulating that a sizable sum was to be paid if an apprentice abandoned his studies early or died. Contracts ran for between one and seven years, the length being determined by whether it was to be a full apprenticeship resulting in the pupil becoming a master himself, and whether he had already studied with another artist. In any event, it took at least four years to reach the status of master.

The fees were higher for painting than for other crafts because the apprenticeship was longer. It is possible that they were inflated because the children of rich parents also applied for training in drawing, but it is not entirely clear whether the two groups intermingled. The parents of a painting apprentice certainly had to have some means. The poor simply could not afford the fees. It was first and foremost a profession for the middle classes,[31] one scorned by the children of the nobility, regents and rich merchants. All branches of the visual arts involved manual work, which placed them beneath the dignity of society's upper crust.

Remarkably little is known about the structure and content of the curriculum, apart from the fact that it differed from one teacher to the next.[32] We are best informed about a painter's apprenticeship, because snippets of information appear here and there in treatises and drawing books. They recommend that the beginner should first master the art of drawing. A possible explanation for the fact that so few of these pupils' drawings have survived is that they were not made on expensive paper but on erasable tablets.[33]

The apprentice would then have followed a course of study that started with grinding pigment and preparing the master's palette and ended with executing increasingly difficult passages in his paintings. Some apprentices remained with their masters on salary because they lacked either the money or the enterprise to head workshops of their own. If they did have that ambition they had to take a masterpiece test set by the guild. Having passed that, many young artists applied to another teacher to round off their training, or went to Italy instead to study the classical artists and the great Renaissance masters.

Some aspects of this apprenticeship were depicted frequently, others not at all. There are various paintings of children drawing, for instance, mostly from plaster models (*fig. 25*). It is possible that the painters of these works wanted to stress the importance of drawing in an artist's training. Another explanation is that these are children from prosperous homes taking drawing lessons, and the fact that some of them are girls would seem to bear this out. One such scene is Jacob Ochterveld's painting of a young woman showing her latest effort to a painter behind his easel (*fig. 26*).[34]

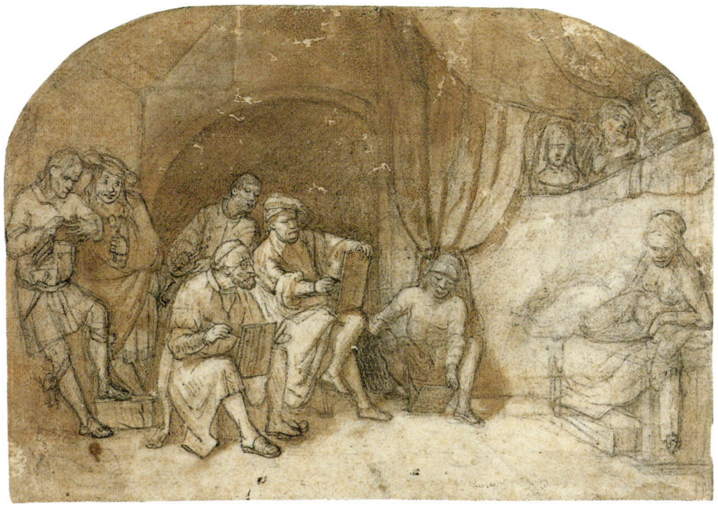

fig. 27 Studio of Rembrandt, *Drawing from the nude model in Rembrandt's studio*, 1650-1660; pen and brush in a brown wash over a chalk drawing, 18 x 26.6 cm. Darmstadt, Hessisches Landesmuseum

fig. 28 Crispijn de Passe, *A drawing school*, engraving in *Van 't licht der teken en schilderconst*, Amsterdam 1643

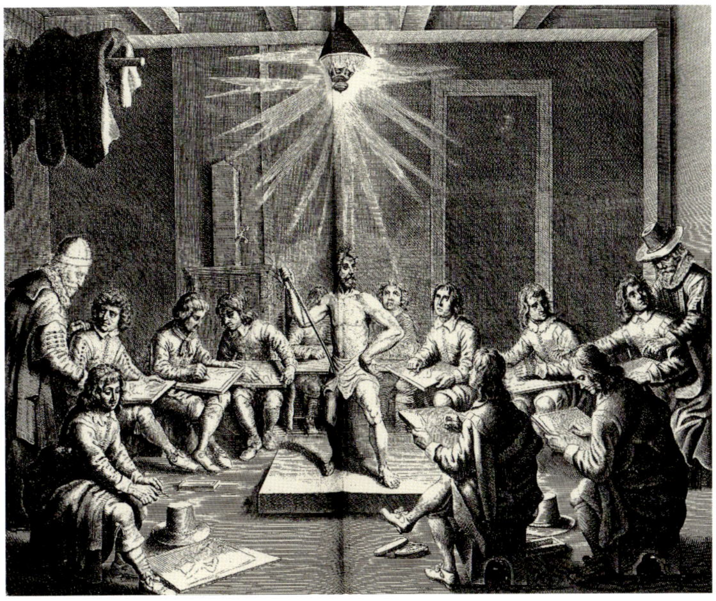

There are also several pictures of people drawing in groups. Working from the live model was an important part of Rembrandt's teaching method, for instance, and one of his pupils recorded the entire drawing class at work (*fig. 27*). In addition to the standard training there were various initiatives in several towns to set up drawing academies at which both amateurs and advanced artists could study. One of the visual records of this group activity is a print in Crispijn de Passe's drawing book *Van 't licht der teken en schilderconst*, published in 1643 (*fig. 28*). In the foreword he related that in Utrecht he had attended 'a famous drawing school that was taught by principal masters at that time'. It has been demonstrated beyond doubt that the print is a recollection of that specific academy, and that the two teachers are Abraham Bloemaert (left) and Paulus Moreelse (right).[35]

ART AND THE MARKET

Samuel van Hoogstraeten identified three reasons for devoting one's life to art: for the love of it, in search of honour, and for financial gain.[36] The latter suggests that there was a good living to be made from the arts. What, though, were the financial fortunes of artists? Many remained or died poor—a fate recorded in a number of prints.[37] An engraving after Andries Both, for example, takes a look at the shabby studio of a down-at-heels painter (*fig. 29*). Dressed in rags, unshaven, and with a bulbous drinker's nose, he makes excuses for himself in the accompanying French poem by claiming that his art is superb but the times are against him. His wife and children know better, saying that the family is in trouble because he cannot resist the bottle and the pipe. A print like this was designed to evoke laughter, not sympathy, but the ridicule would not have worked if the impoverished painter was not a real, recognisable type.

The successful artist was no less a social reality, however. No Dutch artist was ever as rich as Rubens in Flanders, with his urban palace, country estate and art collection, but if an artist had sound business sense there was good money to be made in prosperous Holland, and some artists did very well indeed. Gerard Dou, for instance, sold each of his paintings for several hundred guilders, and invested the proceeds wisely. Gerard van Honthorst, who worked for Stadholder Frederik Hendrik, could even permit himself the luxury of a private coach. Successful craftsmen working in the field of the decorative arts could amass even more wealth. Hendrick Marcelisz van Gogh and his wife Elisabeth owned the Delft faience factory De Porceleynen Schotel, and left a capital sum of no less than 125,533 Carolus guilders in 1661. Earlier in the century, in the same town, the Spiering tapestry-weaving family had become fabulously wealthy. The goldsmith Johannes Lutma was also accustomed to handling large sums, receiving 44,000 guilders in commissions from the city of Amsterdam alone.

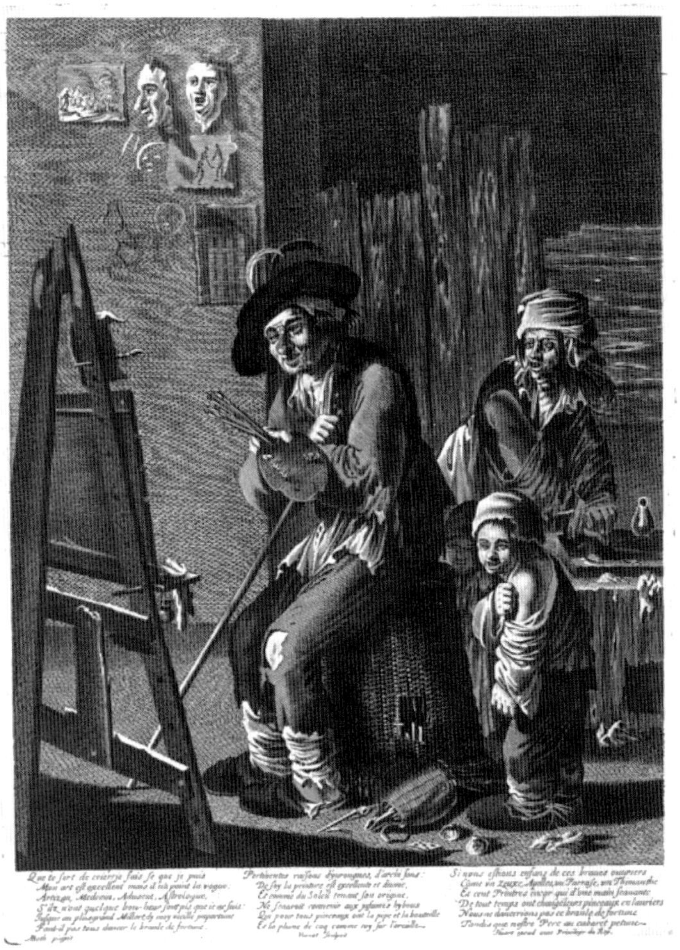

fig. 29 Nicolas Viennot after Andries Both, *The poor painter in his studio*, c. 1635; engraving, 33 x 24.7 cm. Amsterdam, Rijksmuseum, Rijksprentenkabinet

Hans le Maire, a maker of gilt-leather hangings, lived on the chic Keizersgracht, and the fact that the ebonist Herman Doomer and his wife had their portraits painted by Rembrandt testifies to their financial success. Speaking of Rembrandt, he too lived very well indeed in his early years in Amsterdam. In 1646, the value of his estate was put at more than 40,000 guilders. But the tide can always turn, and the same Rembrandt filed for bankruptcy in 1656, as did many others during the economic depression following the First Anglo-Dutch War (1652-1654).

So the financial prospects were anything but secure when an apprentice embarked on his career. The artistic professions were risky, just as they are today. Unlike a baker or cloth merchant, output was extremely sensitive to the short-term business cycle, and depended on what happened to catch the public's fancy. In short, when choosing to become an artist it was better if the love of art was stronger than the desire to make money. There were very good reasons why many artists had a second string to their bow in the form of a steady job.

Some branches of the decorative arts demanded such a high investment that councils lured them to a city by providing a workplace or interest-free loans. The tapestry works of the Spiering family was offered the St Agatha's Convent in Delft free of charge, and the authorities also protected it against competing establishments. Similarly, Amsterdam gave the gilt-leather maker Hans le Maire a house on St Anthony's Bastion in 1617. Glassblowers were also given sites or housing for free in Amsterdam, and the craftsmen were exempted from service in the civic guard. It is clear that cities subsidised or protected certain entrepreneurs in order to stimulate quality crafts, but that by no means ensured that the undertakings would be a success.

Much of the art that was produced had to find buyers on the open market, as it had in Antwerp back in the 16th century. The freedom of that market, though, extended only as far as the city walls, for the guilds obstructed a truly open economy. Moreover, all sorts of artistic products continued to be made on commission: portraits, tombs, medallions, graphic art commemorating a special occasion, faience with family coats of arms and inscriptions, and decorated interiors. The same applied to works of art that required heavy investment. No tapestry, for instance, was woven unless there was already a buyer.

Nevertheless, most works of art were sold on the open market, meaning that they were made for an unknown buyer. Often they were sold from shops, some of which were attached to the workplace, but which increasingly became independent businesses run by people who were not artists themselves. The art dealer thus became an important force in the market, for he was in a better position than the artist to specialise in finding purchasers. Good contacts with dealers were vital for artists. The fact that Saskia was a niece of the Amsterdam art dealer Hendrick van Uylenburgh may have made her particularly desirable to Rembrandt.

The existence of shops and dealers automatically increased the price of a work of art, which did not always make the dealer popular.[38] The benefits for the artist, though, were that he no longer needed to find his own way in the increasingly complex market, his sales were more constant, and workshops no longer had to be situated on expensive shopping streets. This new sales system with larger stocks of merchandise could of course only exist if there was sufficient confidence in an expanding market for luxury goods. In addition, it also required society as a whole to adopt a mercantile mentality, with buyer and producer being prepared to allow the commercial middleman to turn a profit. That mentality gained ground, as demonstrated by the fact that even goldsmiths and silversmiths, who had previously worked solely on commission because of the high cost of their materials, began producing for shops in the 17th century.[39] There is a small painting of one such establishment showing the saleswoman and a female customer (*fig. 30*).

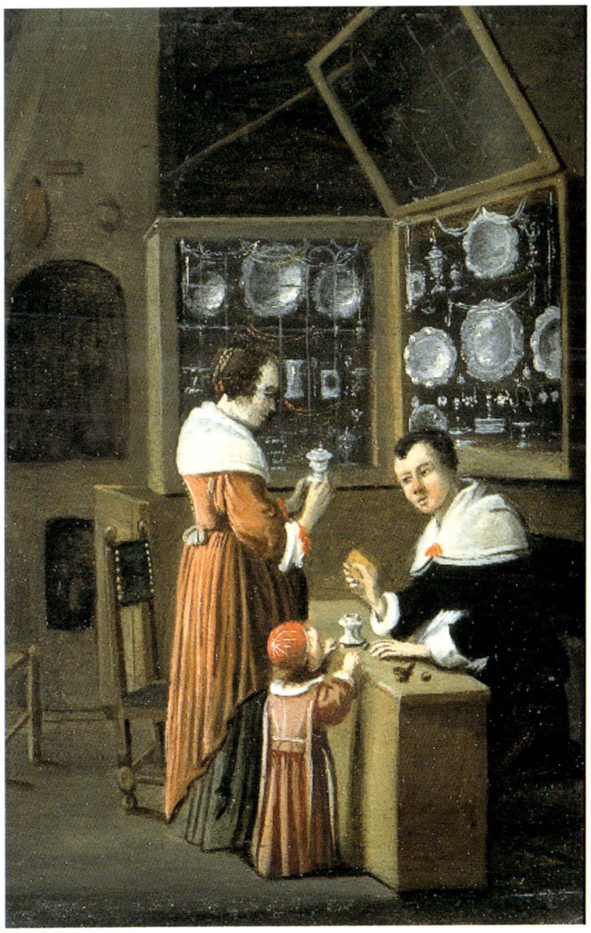

fig. 30 Anonymous artist, *Interior of a Dutch shop selling gold and silver*, c. 1660; oil on panel, 28 x 22 cm. Private collection

Trading through a middleman was not really in keeping with the tradition of the guilds, but they adapted to the development and introduced membership specifically for dealers. The battle against unregulated sales outside the purview of the guild continued unabated, however. Some guilds and confraternities also held sales in their own halls. The Amsterdam cabinetmakers in Kalverstraat, for example, had rooms where furniture could be displayed for sale under the supervision of a 'guild member's wife', who was replaced by another wife every eight days.[40]

Working for a free market sharpened competition and forced an artist to develop a keen nose for changing tastes. The prices of artworks must have fluctuated far more in a free market than in an economy based on commission. Purchasers now paid not for the sum total of materials and hours worked but for the desirability of the work, which must have had several consequences. Since the working hours invested could not automatically be passed on to the buyer it was essential to speed up the production process, which may explain the development of specialisation in painting (see pp. 7-19). It might even account for the appearance of tonal paintings in the 1630s, at the very time when the market was expanding most rapidly, which were inexpensive because less time was spent preparing the palette.[41]

One important and basic characteristic of the free market economy is that the stimulus for production comes not from the purchaser but from the producer. He somehow has to put that little extra into his work to persuade an unknown customer to buy it. Perhaps this is the secret behind that quintessentially Dutch detection of the visual attractions of the everyday world, for the painter constantly had to market new motifs which had an illusionistic enchantment.

Works were also sold at auctions in the 17th century, but the guilds disapproved because it could disrupt the regular market. This led to an interesting incident. In 1642, the officials of Haarlem's Guild of St Luke urged the city authorities to ban all public auctions of paintings. A group of painters, among them Pieter de Grebber, Salomon van Ruysdael and Frans Hals, objected to this petition because they had a totally different view of the workings of the marketplace. They said that sales of cheap paintings need not be a threat to established painters, for they attracted a public which would not otherwise be interested in buying art. Auctions thus created new art-lovers, which could only increase the demand for paintings. Moreover, auctions would enable young painters to capture a place in the market. The protesters suspected that it was mainly the 'shopkeepers, or sellers of art' who were behind the petition because they were afraid of having their high prices undercut.[42] The city authorities were not interested in the arguments of the 'liberal' painters. Auctions were prohibited, except for estate and bankruptcy sales. Other towns were less restrictive, so auctions of contemporary art did play a role in the 17th-century art market, as they already did for collectors of earlier art.

Another way of bringing art to the people was through lotteries, which again were opposed by the guilds because they supposedly undermined prices. Town councils repeatedly banned lotteries but were unable to stamp them out. Whether or not lotteries were beneficial to the entire profession is a macroeconomic question, but for the individual artist or dealer it was an ideal way of disposing of a large stock. Needless to say, the prizes had to appeal to a wide public. It is interesting that in addition to silver, which always held its value, there were also lotteries for furniture and paintings, so it was evidently considered that, in principle, even paintings were suitable for any interior.

Announcements for some lotteries took the form of magnificent prints, one such being the etching published to announce the important lottery held in 1689 to raise money to rebuild Durgerdam (*fig.* 31).[43] The prizes are displayed in an imaginary cabinet below the scene of the burning village. First prize was a gold chain and medallion worth 800 guilders plus a lump sum of 1,200 guilders. The other objects are silver dishes, candlesticks, oil cruets, mustard pots, salt-cellars, spoons and, hanging from the trumpet at the bottom, more châtelaine girdles of the kind already encountered above.

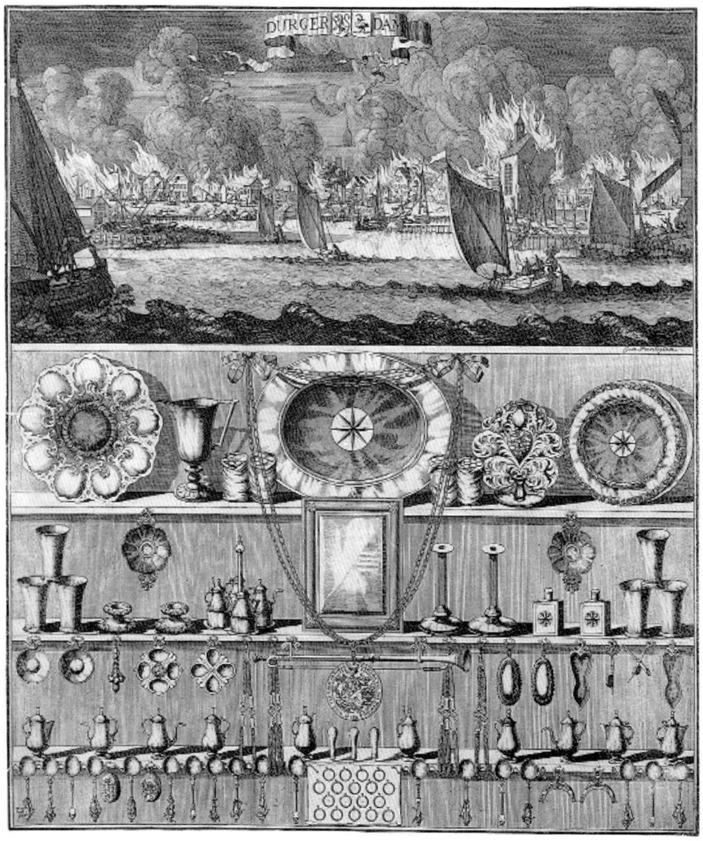

fig. 31 After Jan Luyken, *Print advertising the Durgerdam lottery*, 1688; etching, 58.2 x 51.5 cm. Amsterdam, Rijksmuseum, Rijksprentenkabinet

There were, naturally, fluctuations in the 17th-century market for works of art. The total amount that society paid for them went up and down. At first the trend was upwards, particularly during the prosperous days of the Twelve Years' Truce (1609-1621), when more and more Dutch people began buying art. Crises like the First Anglo-Dutch War and the disastrous year of 1672 have already been mentioned. The art market as a whole was very susceptible to depressions of this kind, but interestingly enough its top end was relatively immune. Expensive paintings and other luxury items were actually in great demand in those periods. What happened was that the market shrunk to a group of extremely rich buyers who wanted nothing but the best and for whom the purchase of a work of art represented just a tiny fraction of their wealth.

There were also shifts in taste. At the beginning of the century history paintings, both secular and religious, were all the rage, but by 1700 interest in them had dropped off sharply, from 45% to around 15% of the total stock. Landscapes, on the other hand, showed precisely the opposite trend.[44] In tapestry-making there was a similar switch from historical and allegorical subjects to decorative designs and landscapes.[45] The significance of figures of this kind, which are based on counts made in inventories, is that they also give an idea of a changing appreciation of art. At the beginning of the 17th century importance was attached to the content of the scene, whereas later it seems that decorative and artistic aspects were valued more highly.

INSTITUTIONAL COMMISSIONS

In addition to the free market there were a number of large organisations which patronised the arts. The church had always been the most important of them, but with the Calvinists' repudiation of images it dropped out of the picture almost entirely. Not completely, for eventually modest decorative programmes were permitted in Protestant churches—a development which did not meet with universal approval among the men of the cloth. Artists were employed on the manufacture, carving and painting of organs, the decoration of pulpits and churchwardens' stalls, metal or wooden screens, painted wall tablets, brass chandeliers and silver vessels for the celebration of the Lord's Supper. Tombs, some of them with sculpted portraits of the deceased and ornate decoration, were also installed in churches, but were always paid for by others.

fig. 32 Wall of the Oranjezaal with Jacob Jordaens's *Triumph of Frederik Hendrik*, 1647-1652. The Hague, Huis ten Bosch (Koninklijk Huisarchief)

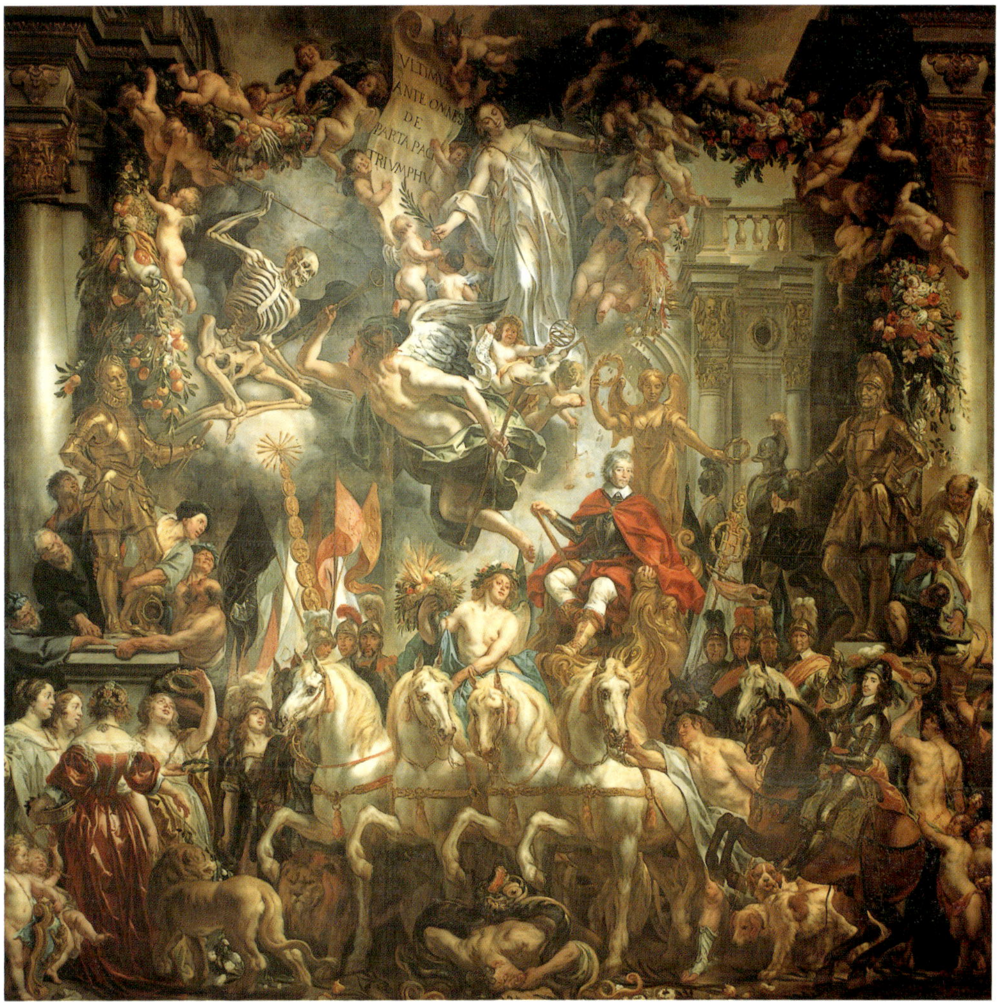

The Catholic Church, although officially banned, was also responsible for the creation of a considerable number of artworks. Especially when it became clear after the Synod of Dordrecht in 1618 that Catholicism would not triumph in the Republic, its supporters furnished clandestine churches with the profuse imagery so dear to the Old Church. Understandably, the commissions for those works, such as altarpieces, were mainly awarded to Catholic artists, of whom there were plenty in Utrecht and Haarlem.

Art historians had long been rather dismissive of the role of the stadholders in the patronage of art, but recent research has corrected that picture. Only Prince Maurits, who was stadholder until 1625, was a relatively inactive patron. He was interested in architecture and landscape gardening, indeed made designs of his own, as well as promoting the work of armourers and jewellers.

Maurits's successor Frederik Hendrik and his wife Amalia van Solms were more at ease with princely pomp. In this they owed a great debt to Constantijn Huygens, who administered their artistic affairs as part of his duties as the stadholder's secretary. They built three palaces: Honselaarsdijk, Huis ter Nieuburch and Huis ten Bosch. Two of them were demolished long ago, so their splendour can only be reconstructed with the aid of archival material, which reveals that the main rooms were hung with tapestry series and that others were decorated with paintings by Dutch and foreign artists—a collection which has now been totally dispersed through inheritance. As far as painting was concerned, the stadholder and his wife were heavily biased towards the Flemish masters Rubens and Van Dyck, but they also commissioned work from Dutch painters like Rembrandt, Honthorst and Poelenburch. After Frederik Hendrik's death in 1647, Amalia van Solms had the great hall of Huis ten Bosch decorated with paintings in memory of her husband. In doing so she created the greatest 17th-century monument to painting, although the amalgam of Flemish and Dutch masters did make for a rather hybrid result (*fig. 32*).

After the First Stadholderless Period (1650-1672) came Willem III, whose love of the arts was expressed in his Soestdijk hunting

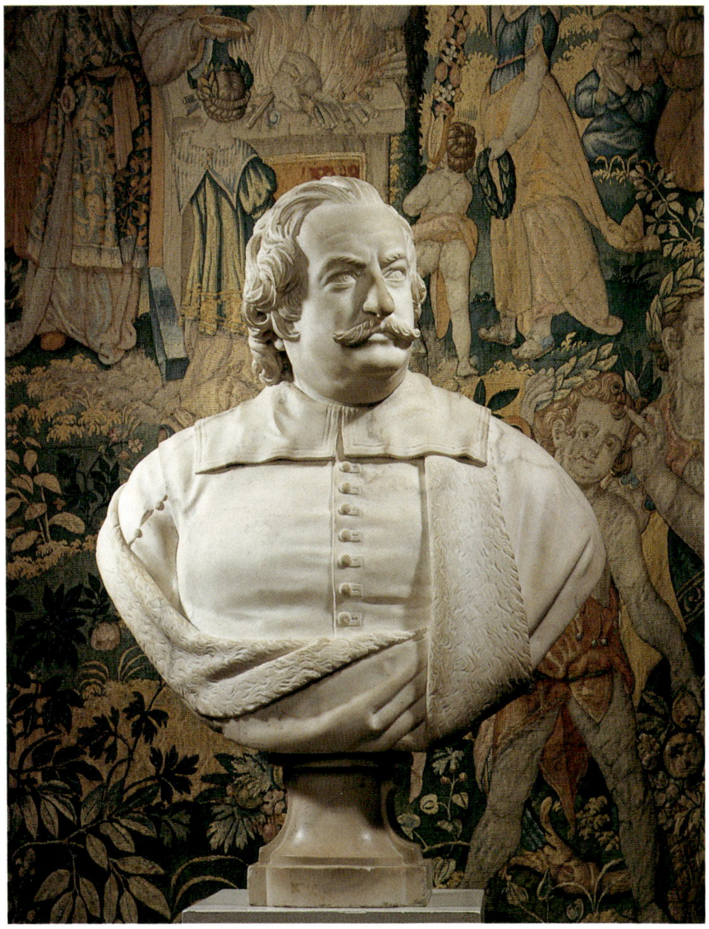

fig. 33 François Dieussart, *Portrait bust of Pieter Spiering*, c. 1645-1650; marble, h. 89 cm. Amsterdam, Rijksmuseum

lodge and at Het Loo summer palace, with its formal gardens. His importance to art history lies mainly in his encouragement of all forms of applied arts, in which he was guided chiefly by Daniel Marot, a French designer who, like many of his colleagues, emigrated to the Republic when Louis XIV revoked the Edict of Nantes in 1685 [107].

Then there were the agents who bought art for foreign courts. Amsterdam became the purchasing centre for all the exclusive products made in the Republic, mainly for the Protestant princes of northern Europe. In addition to paintings they were chiefly interested in tapestry series, and gilt-leather hangings. It is telling, for instance, that Pieter Spiering, a scion of the Delft tapestry-making family which supplied its products to many courts, became the art agent and even treasurer of Queen Christina of Sweden. Like the queen he served, he had himself immortalised in white marble (*fig. 33*).[46]

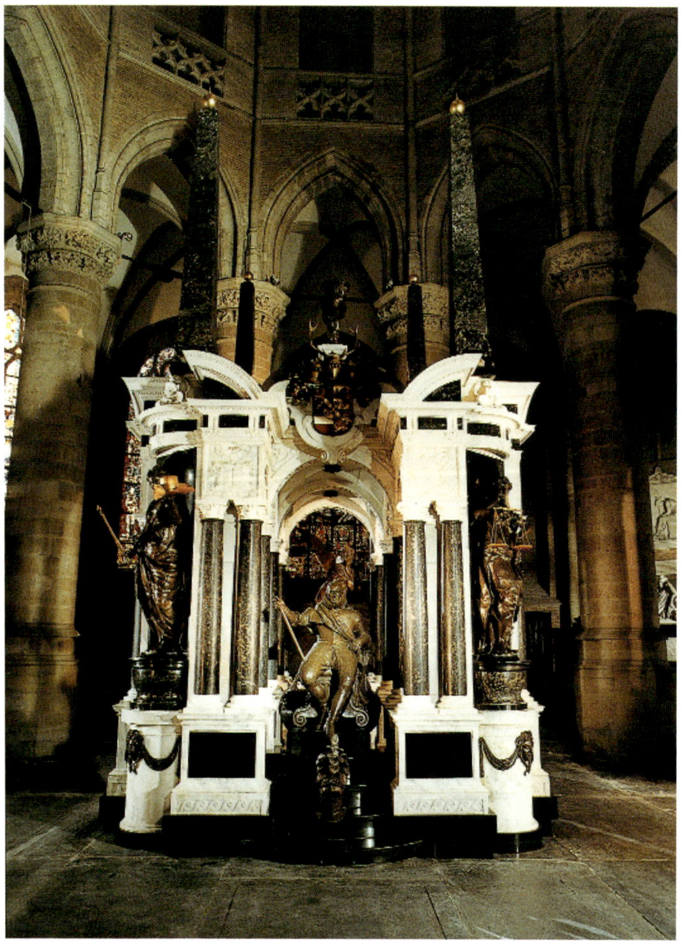

fig. 34 Hendrick de Keyser, *Tomb of William of Orange*, 1614-1621. Delft, Nieuwe Kerk

The States-General, the supreme authority in the Republic, also commissioned works of art. It was responsible for the tomb of William the Silent in the Nieuwe Kerk in Delft, which was ordered from Hendrick de Keyser during the Twelve Years' Truce. It was a late initiative to honour the father of the fatherland, 30 years after his death, and should accordingly be seen primarily as a monument to the young Republic, which had only recently won international recognition (*fig. 34*). Other politically inspired commissions were tapestry series for presentation on state visits, or mementoes commemorating feats of arms. One generous example of the latter is the gold goblet presented to Admiral Michiel Adriaansz de Ruyter to mark his rout of the English fleet at Chatham in the Second Anglo-Dutch War (1665-1667) [89].

Municipal authorities commissioned far more art than the States-General, with the decoration of public buildings, in particular, providing work for artists of every description. The grandest undertaking was the decoration of Amsterdam's new Town Hall between 1650 and 1660. The bulk of it was sculptural work, for which the city employed the services of Artus Quellinus of Antwerp for want of a Dutch master with sufficient experience of marble. Some of the sketches and terracotta models which Quellinus submitted to the burgomasters and used to instruct his sculpting assistants are preserved in the Rijksmuseum [51]. It is often not fully appreciated that the commission awarded to Quellinus was one of the largest in the whole of 17th-century Europe, on a par with projects initiated by the popes in Rome or Louis XIV at Versailles—no mean feat for a country with such a modest reputation in the field of sculpture.

Smaller bodies also ordered art on a large scale. Civic guards, guilds, charitable institutions, houses of correction, water drainage boards, admiralties and trading companies employed artists to lend added lustre to their activities and status. This list shows yet again the breadth of the appeal made to the arts in the 17th century.

MOBILITY

A land that was rich and had a reputation for tolerance must have been very attractive to people from less fortunate parts of Europe. Just as French Protestants fled to the Dutch Republic after the revocation of the Edict of Nantes in 1685, many German craftsmen came to try their luck in the expanding Dutch economy when their country was being ravaged by the Thirty Years' War. Crafts like ebony working and goldsmithing, in particular, profited from this German immigration.

The largest and most important influx was of Calvinists who left the southern Netherlands for the northern provinces around 1600. As has so often been pointed out, this wave of immigrants provided a crucial impulse for various arts in the Republic, particularly painting, printmaking and tapestry weaving. More than 100 weavers, most of them from Oudenaarde, ended up in Delft, Middelburg, Leiden, Amsterdam and Haarlem. Research has also been done on the goldsmiths, book printers and engravers who were part of that migration, but once again it is the painters who have received the most attention. One author counted 236 who moved from the southern Netherlands to the north as a result of war or their religious convictions.[47] Others consider that number exaggerated, and identify only a few genuine painters among those immigrants, arguing that they were far more strongly represented in the second generation, when the number of painters in the Republic began its explosive growth around 1610.[48] A more important factor than the number of painters was the lifestyle and taste which the immigrants brought with them. They took the possession of works of art for granted, and in general were more enamoured of finery than the sober Hollanders—a contrast which Gerbrand Bredero highlighted in his popular farce of 1617, *De Spaansche Brabander* (The Spanish Brabanter).

The Twelve Years' Truce (1609-1621), which brought about a provisional separation between the Spanish Netherlands and the Dutch Republic, would have persuaded many immigrants to abandon any hope of returning to their native country, so they decided to settle in the Republic permanently. The money they had earned they now spent on buying houses and decorating them. They were also the ideal group to buy the paintings from Antwerp which flooded the Dutch market once the borders were opened. According to one author, this development had a decisive impact

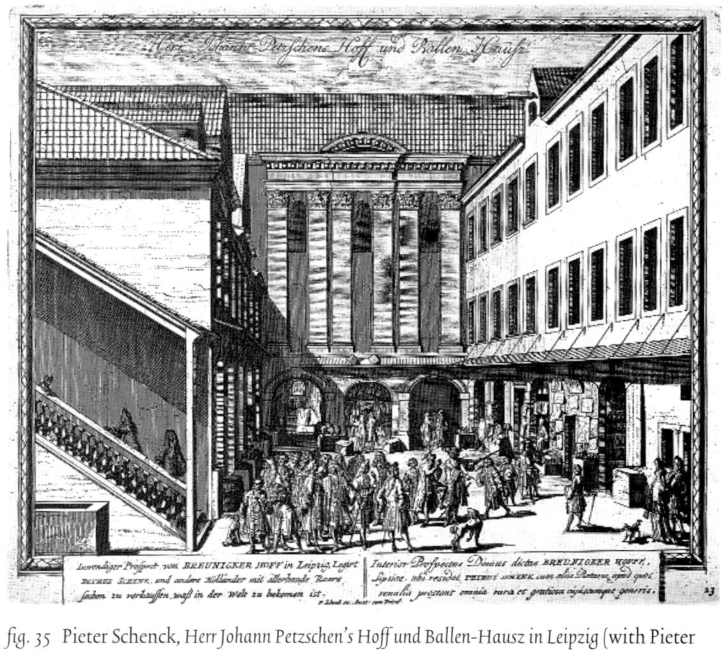

fig. 35 Pieter Schenck, *Herr Johann Petzschen's Hoff und Ballen-Hausz in Leipzig* (with Pieter Schenck's print shop on the right); etching, 21.4 x 26.5 cm. Amsterdam, Rijksmuseum, Rijksprentenkabinet

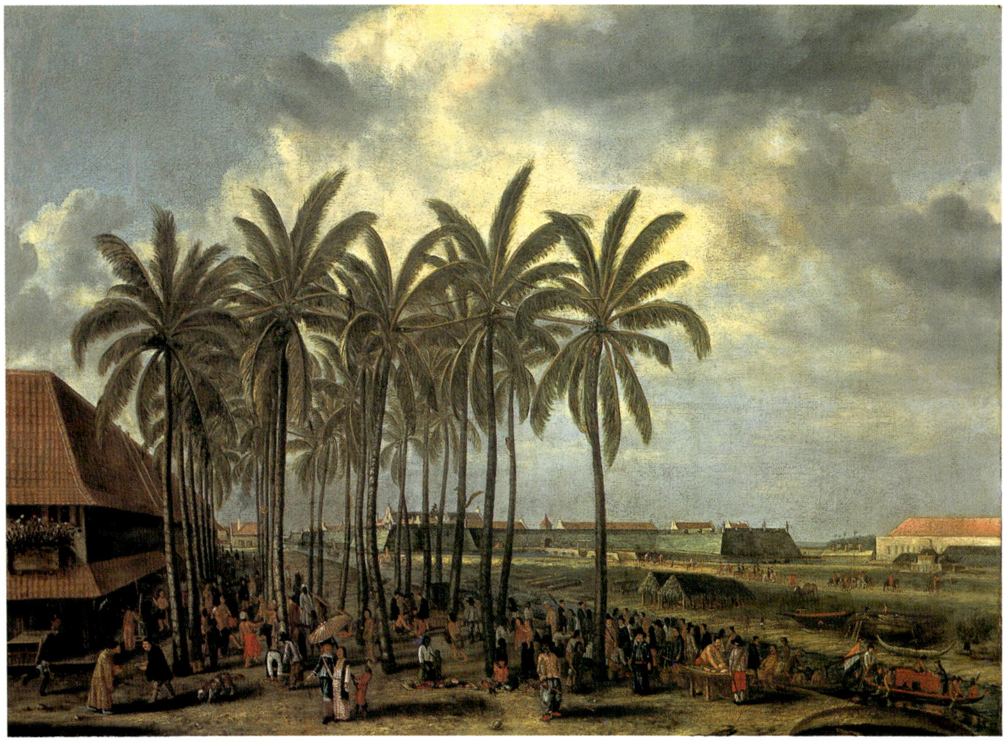

fig. 36 Andries Beeckman, *The castle of Batavia, seen from Kali Besar West*, c. 1656; oil on canvas, 108 x 151.5 cm. Amsterdam, Rijksmuseum

on Dutch painting.[49] The influx of foreign pictures naturally gave local painters a sharp shock. They called them 'Brabant dross', and warned that many copies were being passed off as originals. The guilds tried to persuade the city authorities to forbid such sales, evidently with little success, for they had to keep repeating their pleas. But instead of stealing the bread from the mouths of local painters, according to this theory, these imports generated a greater demand for paintings. It also forced Dutch artists to produce works which could rival the imports in quality and price.

Even more important than the influx of artists and works of art was the exports of both. The foreign market for luxury goods was huge. Delft faience was the finest quality of ceramics being produced anywhere in Europe, and as such it had the entire continent as its market. The Republic was also the largest production centre for gilt leather, which was exported not only throughout Europe but as far afield as Japan. Dutch and foreign merchants often played a key role in European exports, and even entered into long-term contracts in order to guarantee the supply of large quantities of objects. Occasionally the producers had to take to the road themselves to open up foreign markets. The managers of the large tapestry-making shops in Delft travelled from one princely court to another drumming up business. Missions of that kind, of course, could only be afforded by such a lucrative branch as tapestry-weaving, and even then it was risky. Karel van Mander III, who headed a tapestry workshop that tried to compete with the Spierings, ruined his business partly because of his expensive foreign journeys. The owners of large print-publishing houses also travelled to present their wares at fairs like those of Frankfurt and Leipzig. The Amsterdam publisher Schenck depicted the shop which his firm fitted out each year for the Leipzig fair in the right background of a print in a series of views of German cities (*fig. 35*).

What is also striking is the large number of Dutch artists who sought work abroad. Van Mander wrote as early as 1604 that artists 'from our nation are more disposed to travel than those of any other in the world'. Modern historical research has confirmed that they were indeed the most travelled in Europe.[50] The mobility of artists is of course not at all surprising for a society with a mercantile empire that spanned the globe. However, it is not true that artists (with the exception of cartographers) travelled in large numbers to distant continents in the wake of the ships of the Dutch East and West India companies. That happened only incidentally. Andries Beeckman painted views of 17th-century Batavia (modern Jakarta) which are not without merit (*fig. 36*), but unfortunately we have no visual record of the lost paintings of the East Indies and the 'Southland' (Australia) by Rembrandt's pupil Jan Victors. The only overseas adventure to make full use of artists was Johan Maurits of Nassau's governorship of north-west Brazil (1632-1644). He included the landscapist Frans Post [60] and the figure painter Albert Eckhout in his retinue, and he had the flora, fauna and cultural life of the Indians of the region recorded on thousands of painted and drawn sheets. There was a similar documentary interest in the East Indies later in the century.

Dutch artists occasionally pop up in the most unexpected places as a result of the country's trading contacts. One such surprise is that several shahs of Persia lured Dutch painters and goldsmiths to their courts in the 17th century, and that one of them took drawing lessons from Philips Angel, the artist who had delivered his learned address *De lof der schilder-konst* (Praise of painting) in Leiden in 1642, but who turned up in Persia after taking up a career as a merchant with the Dutch East India Company from 1645 to 1656. The Dutch presence was so pervasive that when the traveller and amateur painter Cornelis de Bruyn arrived in Persia in 1704 and was asked to paint the shah's portrait, he was presented with Dutch pigments to help him in his task.[51]

In general, though, the Dutch artist abroad was an incidental phenomenon. Dutch world trade influenced art production more through the cargoes than the artists that it carried. A familiar example of this is Delft faience, which really came into its own when the trade in Chinese porcelain ceased in 1647 and the Dutch developed a kind of imitation blue-and-white earthenware. The number of faience factories in Delft more than doubled between 1648 and 1661. Furniture-making, in turn, profited from the imports of new types of wood, like ebony, and exotic materials for marquetry work, such as whalebone, mother-of-pearl and tortoiseshell. Another material imported by sea was Italian marble. Trade with Livorno and Genoa flourished during the Twelve Years' Truce, and it was then that Hendrick de Keyser began using marble for works like the bust of Vincent Coster [4] and the tomb of William the Silent in Delft.[52] In the second half of the century, after the 1648 Treaty of Münster, Amsterdam actually became the European centre of the marble trade, which was used extensively in Artus Quellinus's decoration of the new Town Hall.

The worldwide trading operations of the Dutch had an impact on the history of 17th-century Dutch art, but artists generally followed very different routes from the merchantmen. The major centres of culture rarely coincided with the lucrative trading stations, and it was there, in Europe's wealthy cities and royal courts, that the skills of Dutch artists were most sought after.

In some cases, migration had drawbacks for the development of art in the Republic. Many sculptors moved abroad as a result of the triumph of Calvinism and the war with Spain, which was a serious blow to the country's sculpture tradition. Major commissions accordingly went to sculptors from the Spanish Netherlands. After 1672, the 'year of disaster', several of the best Dutch artists went abroad. In the Third Anglo-Dutch War (1672-1674) the Republic not only lost its hegemony of the seas to the English but also two of its most talented marine artists: Willem van de Velde, father and son. England had long been an enticing destination, because its art lagged way behind that of the Dutch while interest in it was rising sharply. In addition, Stadholder Willem III, after becoming king of England in 1689, also held court in London. The love of splendour of Louis XIV and several German princes also proved an irresistible lure for a considerable number of artists.

In general, though, migration had no adverse effect at all on the development of art. The expansion of the market and the associated international prestige led to enormous growth in the artistic professions. The dispersion of Dutch artists throughout Europe has not yet been charted. Only the *Ausbreitung* of 17th-century painting has produced an imposing survey, but that was published many years ago.[53] Such studies have yet to be written for other branches of the arts, but they will probably present a similar picture of an amazing mobility.

STUDYING IN ITALY

One aspect of mobility was the journey to Italy undertaken by countless Netherlandish artists from the beginning of the 16th century on. The idea was that they could only raise their profession to the very highest level if they had personally become acquainted with works of art from classical antiquity and those by the great masters of the Renaissance. The journey differed from other forms of artistic migration in that the economic motive was no goal in itself. It is true that the artists had to find work in Italy in order to pay their way, but the basic principle of the trip was to study the monuments of Italy. The reward was the greater professional prestige enjoyed by the artist on his return home.

In the 16th century almost every artist of any consequence made the artistic pilgrimage to Rome, and the tradition was still going strong at the beginning of the 17th century. Most of the early 17th-century history painters visited Rome, among them Van Mander and Goltzius [12], Wtewael, Moreelse, Lastman [11] and Jacob Pynas, as did the Utrecht artists who became the followers of Caravaggio, such as Ter Brugghen [13], Honthorst [14] and Van Baburen. Later in the century, though, artists no longer felt the same need to round off their studies in Italy.

One such departure from the trend is described in the encounter between Constantijn Huygens and Rembrandt and Jan Lievens.[54] Huygens visited their studio in 1629 and enthused over this 'noble pair of young men'. They did disappoint him in one respect, for they were so cocksure that they saw no point in going to Italy. 'This is plainly a touch of idiocy in intelligences which in other respect are quite exceptional', Huygens commented. In his view, it was only in Rome that they could perfect their art, and with their talent they could even outstrip the Italians. He looked forward to

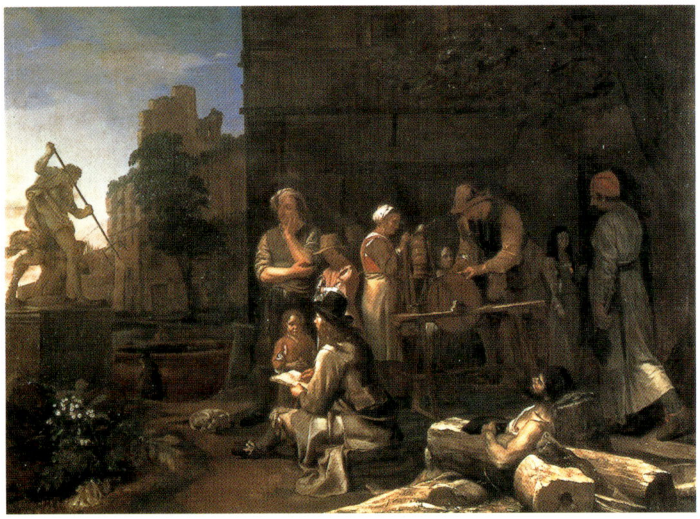

fig. 37 Michiel Sweerts, *Young artist drawing Bernini's Neptune and Triton*; oil on canvas, 85.5 x 120 cm. Rotterdam, Museum Boijmans Van Beuningen

the prospect of these two forcing the Italians to make the artistic pilgrimage to the north. They did not want to go, however, for 'they are now, they say, in the best years of their lives, and must above all benefit from them; they have no time to waste on long journeys'. They had another argument, which was that the best Italian paintings were now to be seen in royal collections north of the Alps. It is interesting that the two young artists preferred to remain at home not out of any lack of enterprise or dislike of Italian art, but precisely because of their high ambitions.

Nor was the study trip to Italy made by Rembrandt's pupils, such as Govert Flinck [32], Ferdinand Bol [79], Gerbrandt van den Eeckhout and Jan Victors (who did travel to the East Indies), despite the fact that some of them abandoned Rembrandt's style later in their careers in favour of a Classicism inspired by the antique. History painters who were not part of Rembrandt's immediate circle, such as Salomon and Jan de Braij [78], Jacob van Loo, Jacob Backer, Abraham van den Tempel, Johannes Vermeer [83, 84] and Caesar van Everdingen [76], also stayed at home. And that is even true of leading lights of Classicism like Gerard de Lairesse [99] and Adriaen van der Werff [104].

Seen in this light, Houbraken's pronouncement that 'it seems to me that that century [the 17th] had no regard for artists if they had not seen Rome for themselves', cannot be true. It seems more an expression of an ideal cherished by Karel van Mander and his generation. However, that does not mean that the tradition died out completely. Many young Dutch artists continued going to Italy until well into the 18th century, but for a different purpose. In addition to their pious study of classical and Renaissance works of art, they were captivated by the charms of the southern landscape, with its ruins and warm sunlight. Painters like Poelenburch [37], Breenbergh and other Italianate artists turned those landscapes into a distinct and highly-praised genre. Yet another group of Dutch painters known as the Bamboccianti developed a surprising fascination for the street life of Rome, painting beggars, herdsmen, washerwomen, hawkers, quacks, denizens of ale-houses, and cattle amidst ruins and shaded places. A painting by Michiel Sweerts (*fig. 37*) is a marvellous composite of all the different kinds of inspiration which Rome could offer. A young artist is drawing a modern sculpture by Bernini, while further off there are classical ruins and a glimpse of landscape, and on the right a busy scene with hawkers and beggars.

It is interesting that the journey to Italy, which was initially part of the training of the humanist breed of artist, became increasingly important in the course of the 17th century for the 'inferior' categories of landscape and genre scenes.

THE 'BENTVUEGHELS' IN ROME

Perhaps the Dutch painters developed such an eye for Roman street life because they themselves were forced by a lack of funds to live in rough neighbourhoods, notably around the Spanish Steps, and kept company with people of that kind. We know from police reports that the *fiamminghi* were well known for their misbehaviour in the taverns of Rome. Out of that culture of drink and amusement emerged a new form of social life when, in 1623, Poelenburch, Breenbergh, Pieter van Laer and other Dutch formed a sort of brotherhood, the members of which were known as

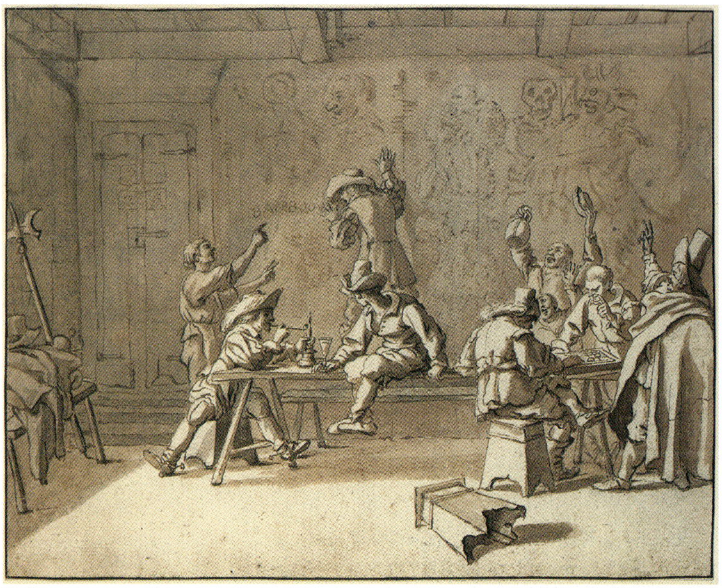

fig. 38 Pieter van Laer, *Bentvueghels in a Roman tavern*, c. 1625; pen in brown wash over a drawing in black chalk, 20.3 x 25.8 cm. Berlin, Kupferstichkabinett

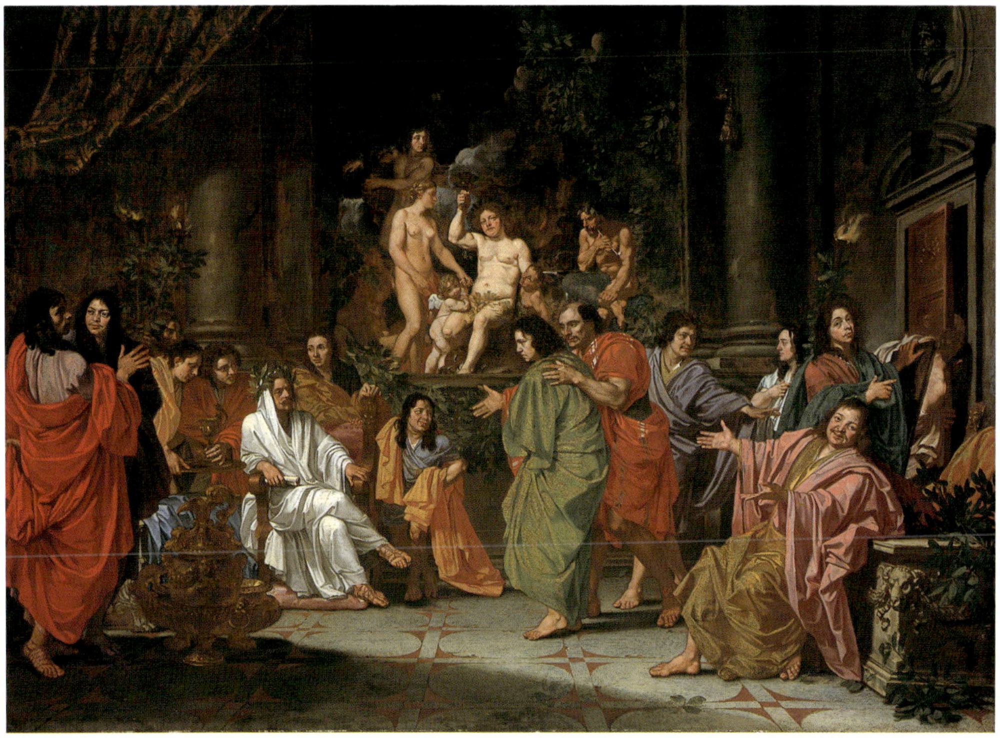

fig. 39 Dutch school, *Initiation of a Bentvueghel in Rome*, c. 1660; oil on canvas, 95.5 x 134 cm. Amsterdam, Rijksmuseum

Bentvueghels (literally: birds of the flock). Every newcomer from the north could join the club, but first had to undergo a farcical induction ritual.

A record of such an initiation later in the century was left by Cornelis de Bruyn, who was in Rome in 1675 (and later travelled to Persia).[55] He relates that he was led into a room filled with members in fancy dress. 'In the manifestation there is just one, called the hedge pope, who does all the talking. He sits in great state on an elevated seat and expounds to the greenhorn [as he who is to be initiated is called] with much argumentation certain laws and regulations regarding the study of painting and the indissoluble institutions of the Bent. The newcomer having replied with humble submission that he is willing to comply with all, the hedge pope places a crown of laurels on his head, whereupon all the Bentvueghels present cry out "Viva, viva, viva our new brother ...", as he is then called upon initiation.' This was known as the christening, and De Bruyn says that 'the misuse of the word [...] sometimes gave offence to the clergy'. There then followed a banquet at the new member's expense. 'Having thus passed the night in merriment, as day was breaking the company made its way to the Tomb of Bacchus [a sarcophagus near Sant'Agnese] to besprinkle the same, as the common saying is, it being situated a good hour from the city.'

The Bentvueghels took great pride in their parties, as shown by the large number of drawings and even paintings made of them (*figs. 38, 39*). Those scenes and written accounts tell us a fair amount about the social behaviour of Dutch painters in Rome. Alongside all the merriment and amusement, it is not without significance that here, far from home and in a very different world, there was a rite of passage into the painter's profession. What makes it all the more intriguing is that back in the world of the Dutch Golden Age, which became such an ineradicable historical episode precisely because of the talents of painters, there was no such sacralisation of the artist's calling.

1 See Van der Woude 1991, p. 301, for calculations of the number of paintings produced.
2 Cornelis de Bie, who lived in the southern Netherlands, did devote some space to sculptors in his *Gulden cabinet* of 1661.
3 This might give the impression that there was a wealth of literature about painting, but in fact little was written down in the 17th century. One certainly would have expected more discussion, and have hoped that some other biographer had filled the gap between Van Mander (1604) and Houbraken (1718-1721). The point, though, is that far more attention was devoted to painting than to the other arts.
4 Huygens 1987 (1631), p. 70.
5 David Beck 1993 (1624), pp. 82 and 54 respectively.
6 Samuel Sorbière, Lettre IV à Monsieur de Bautru, Ms. Z.2184, Bibliotèque Nationale, Paris; quoted from Floerke 1905, p. 164.
7 Mundy 1925.
8 Evelyn 1935, p. 39. Sorbière, too, believed that the Dutch bought paintings for speculative reasons.
9 De Vries 1991, p. 273.
10 These figures were calculated by Marion Boers-Goosens, who is preparing a dissertation on the art market in Haarlem; quoted in Sluijter 1999, p. 137, note 19.
11 Bok 1994, pp. 168-177.
12 De Lairesse 1740, p. 233.
13 The definition is from Lourens & Lucassen 1994, p. 41.
14 Van Mander 1604, fol. 251v (in the biography of Pieter Vlerick, the fulmination against the guilds taking up more than a page).
15 Goeree 1670, p. 15.
16 See Muller 1880, pp. 69-84.
17 Houbraken 1718-21, vol. 1, pp. 242ff.
18 The original is lost but the composition is known from a drawing by Mattheus Terwesten now in the Rijksprentenkabinet, see Schapelhouman 1986.
19 Houbraken 1718-21, p. 244.
20 The proposals are published *in extenso* in Miedema 1980, vol. 1, doc. A42, pp. 91-135.
21 For a reproduction and transcription see Miedema 1980, vol. 1, doc. A80, pp. 171-178. It is possible that the coats of arms were those of the professional groups who were obliged to attend the funeral of a guild member. That would mean that a tinsmith had to go to a painter's funeral, but not vice versa.
22 The museum in Strasbourg used to have another portrait of the syndics of the Amsterdam goldsmiths' guild by Thomas de Keyser, but it was destroyed by fire in 1944. No other examples are known.
23 The Rijksprentenkabinet has a drawing of the group portrait by the 18th-century Haarlem artist Wybrand Hendriks with annotations identifying the sitters and stating who painted whom. See Miedema 1980, vol. 1, p. 300, note 154.
24 Here I am following Panhuysen 1996, p. 6, who made this suggestion after studying the drapers' guilds in Amsterdam and Haarlem.
25 This interpretation of self-portraits was put forward by Ernst van de Wetering in his essay in the catalogue of the exhibition *Rembrandt by himself*, Van de Wetering 1999-2000, pp. 26ff.
26 See the travel account published in Hoogewerff 1919.
27 'Pour scavoir donc parler de ce noble mestier, il faut avoir esté à la boutique disputé avec les maistres, veu le traint de pinceau', manuscript in the Koninklijke Bibliotheek, Brussels, published in Merrifield 1967, vol. 2, p. 769. See pp. 825ff. for the 11 examples of 'la façon de parler des beaux tableaux'.
28 Since there are seascapes on the wall and Codde was a figure painter it is unlikely that this is his own studio.
29 Quoted by De Jager 1990, p. 71 (and note 45) in his interesting comparative study of the contracts of painters' and goldsmiths' apprentices.
30 De Jager 1990, p. 75 and notes 93-100, gives the following figures. For a one-year contract the tuition fees and lodging expenses came to an average of 82 guilders, for a two-year contract 611/2 guilders, and for a three-year contract 29 guilders.
31 This was the conclusion reached by Montias 1982, pp. 161ff, in his study of Delft.
32 Miedema 1987, p. 19, even goes so far as to say 'Ik denk dat ik hierover kort kan zijn: over het hoe en wat van het vakonderwijs aan schilders in de 16de en 17de eeuw weten we niets' ('On this point I can be brief: we know nothing about the how and the what of the professional training of painters in the 16th and 17th centuries'). Van de Wetering 1997 is less pessimistic, and presents numerous specific facts and hypotheses about the training given in Rembrandt's workshop.
33 This is the suggestion put forward in Van de Wetering 1997, pp. 53-74.
34 Raupp 1984, p. 199, doubts that the young woman is a pupil, but suggests that she may be the personification of the art of drawing and is teaching the painter. This seems unlikely to me. In the first place, she is not taking her supposedly inspirational role very seriously, and secondly, what she is drawing has little relevance to what he is painting. A third point is that as a type she resembles the girl in Jan Steen's *Drawing lesson* in the Getty Museum, where there is no question there of who is teaching whom. That picture, too, is often taken as a sort of allegory, but that seems far-fetched to me, given the girl's realistic dress and blue apron.
35 They are identified from the title page of the book; see Bok 1994, p. 181.
36 Van Hoogstraeten 1678, p. 345.
37 See exhib. cat. Amsterdam 1997, pp. 247-252.
38 In 1642, for instance, a group of Haarlem painters called them rogues because of the high prices they charged, which 'extinguished the love of art in many a bosom'. For the document see Miedema 1980, vol. 1, doc. A120, pp. 246-253.
39 On shops selling silver and gold see cat. Amsterdam 1999, p. 9.
40 Described in Lunsingh Scheurleer 1942, p. 39.
41 The thesis that this manner of painting was adopted for economic reasons was first proposed by Montias 1987; see also Sluijter 1999.
42 For the document see Miedema 1980, vol. 1, doc. A120, pp. 246-253; for a commentary see De Marchi & Van Miegroet 1995, pp. 458-460.
43 See Ter Molen 1992 for a detailed discussion of this print.
44 See Montias 1987 and Chong 1987-88, p. 116.
45 See Montias 1982, p. 292ff.
46 Briels 1987, p. 13.
47 Sluijter 1999, p. 118.
48 Sluijter 1999.
49 See Montias 1982, pp. 288ff.
50 This emerges from Brulez's study *Cultuur en getal* of 1986, which is based on the thousands of biographies in Thieme-Becker. However, that lexicon was published so long ago that Brulez will have missed the many pieces of information about mobility and motives which have been unearthed since then. All the same, it is telling that the conclusion to be drawn from Table 8 on p. 42 is that in the period 1600-1650 the mobility of 'visual artists' from the Netherlands (excluding the southern Netherlands) was the highest in absolute terms. The small Dutch Republic was good for 22.6% of the total number of mobile artists in Europe. The French, Italians and Germans accounted for the highest absolute numbers in the period 1650-1700, but given the far greater number of artists in those large countries, the Dutch were still the most travelled in relative terms.
51 See Gerson 1942, pp. 543-545.
52 See Scholten 1993, pp. 198ff.
53 Gerson 1942.
54 Huygens 1987, pp. 84-97.
55 De Bruyn 1698, pp. 6ff.

Detail of fig. 40 ▸

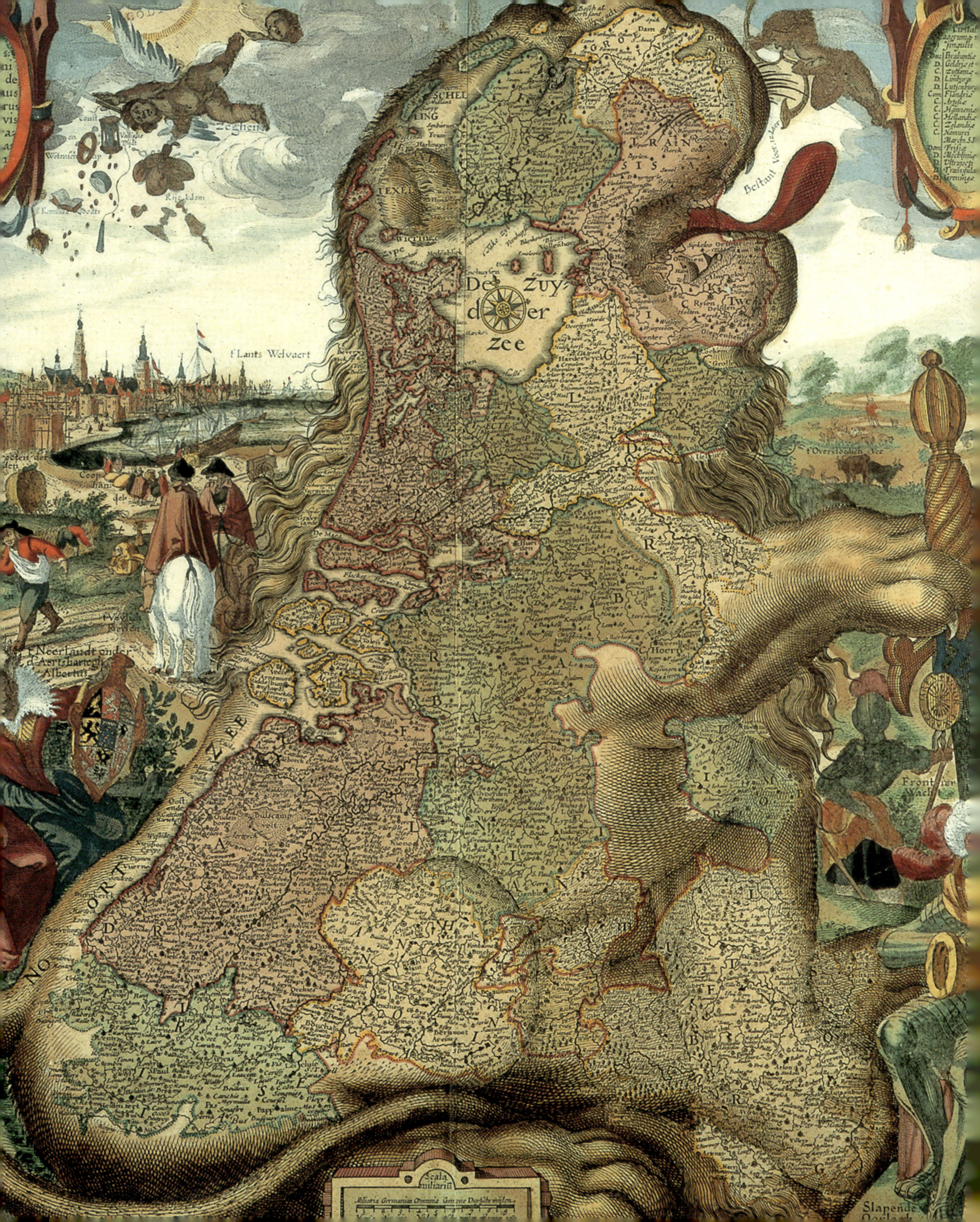
De Zuy der zee
t'Lants Welvaert
TEXEL
NOORT ZEE
Scala
Slapende

The Republic of the Seven United Provinces in the 17th century

WAR

When Jan Pieterszoon Sweelinck, Amsterdam's official organist, travelled to Antwerp in 1604 to discuss the construction of a new harpsichord for the city with Ruckers, the famous firm of instrument makers, the situation in the fledgling Republic of the Seven United Provinces was still very fluid.

In the north, Willem Lodewijk of Nassau, the stadholder of Friesland and Groningen, had brought the city of Groningen under his authority only ten years previously. The army of the Republic, which he and his cousin Prince Maurits had swiftly transformed from a ragtag collection of mercenaries and civic militias into a professional fighting machine, conducted campaign after campaign against the Spanish troops in Overijssel and east Gelderland. In the south, Brabant, Limburg and Zeeuws-Vlaanderen were a permanent theatre of war, and would remain so for years to come (*fig.* 40). The struggle raged on, and many people feared for their lives and property. At sea, privateers from Dunkirk inflicted heavy losses on the Dutch fishing and merchant fleets. An attempt to take Dunkirk became bogged down near Nieuwpoort in 1600. Ostend fell into Spanish hands in 1604, the year of Sweelinck's journey, as Antwerp itself had done back in 1585.

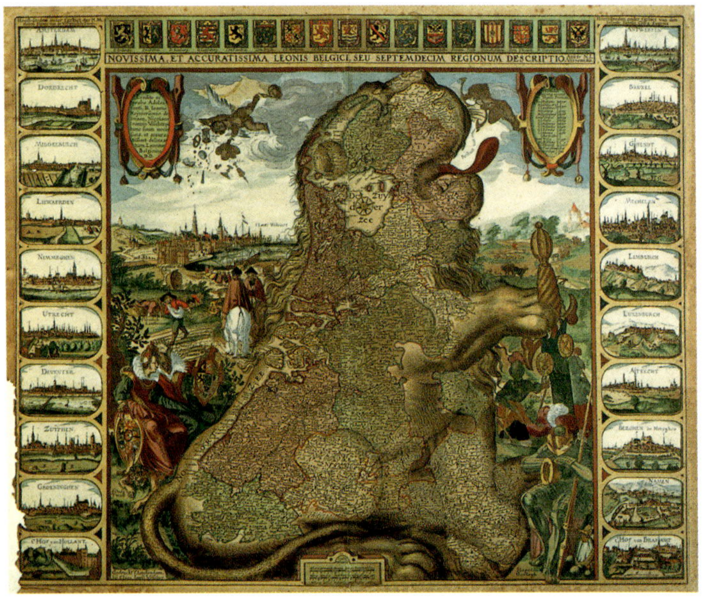

fig. 40 Claes Jansz Visscher's 'Lion map' (Leo Belgicus) of 1609, an allegorical print of the Twelve Years' Truce (1609-1621) showing all 17 provinces, 1609; coloured etching and engraving, 47 x 57.2 cm. Rotterdam, Stichting Atlas van Stolk

At first sight the future appeared far from secure when Sweelinck went on his mission, but already there were signs that change was in the air.

In 1597, Cornelis de Houtman returned from the East Indies after a successful voyage round the Cape of Good Hope, in seas controlled by the Portuguese. The Dutch East India Company (VOC) was founded in 1602 as a trading conglomerate which, with the aid of the States-General in The Hague, combined the initiatives of enterprising merchants from the various cities so as to trade from a position of strength in those parts of the Far East which were in the grip of the Spanish and Portuguese.

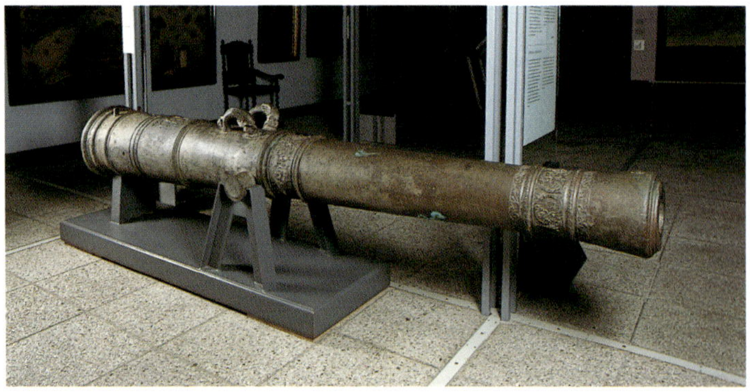

fig. 41 Cannon from the Dutch East Indiaman *Witte Leeuw* which sunk off St Helena in 1613 in a battle with Portuguese ships. Cast by Henricus van Meurs, c. 1600; bronze. Amsterdam, Rijksmuseum

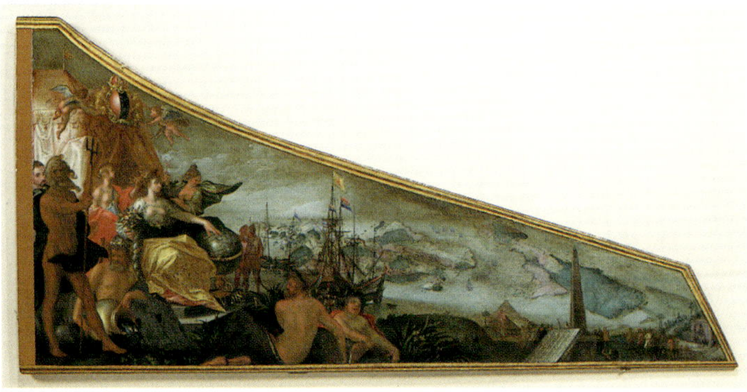

fig. 42 Pieter Isaacsz, assisted by Karel van Mander, *Allegory of Amsterdam as the centre of world trade*, 1606; oil on panel, 79.4 x 165 cm. The painting is on the lid of the city harpsichord of Amsterdam. Amsterdam, Rijksmuseum

Self-confidence had never been higher, particularly among the trading elites of Holland and Zeeland. The route to Asia lay open, and soon these merchants would be as rich as their Iberian competitors (*fig.* 41).

This background explains the *Allegory of Amsterdam* which Pieter Isaacsz painted in 1605 on the inside of the lid of the harpsichord delivered by Ruckers. It is a scene that proudly proclaims an optimism and a self-confidence bordering on recklessness. 'Exclusam hesperia perituram Hispane putasti me? Frustra', runs the first line of the poem inscribed on a tablet in the painting. 'Did you think that I, barred from the Spanish west, would be lost? Wrong'. Amsterdam had the world at its feet, and was not going to let any Spaniard get in its way (*fig.* 42).

The people of Amsterdam were not the only ones who saw prosperity beckon. Thousands flocked to the cities of Holland and Zeeland from the southern Netherlands, Scandinavia, Germany, Poland, France and Scotland. The first waves consisted of those fleeing war or religious persecution (1618 saw the start of a war that ravaged Germany for 30 years), but the later ones came looking for work. And work there was in abundance—in the towns and cities, in the countryside, on the battlefield. The prosperity of the Republic was powered by a wartime economy, and so it was for a long time to come.

The entire 17th century, in fact, was marked by violence. The original enemy was Spain, but after the two sides signed a peace treaty at Münster in 1648 [48] the Republic found itself confronted with two mighty opponents, France and England, which proved a constant menace on land and sea. Many lives were lost in both the Americas and Asia in conflicts with the same foes as in Europe, as well as with the native populations and the climate. The spices were dearly bought. The other side of the coin was that war provided work and income. At the height of the fighting, the arms trade and industry, in which men like Louis de Geer and Louis Trip made fortunes, accounted for 5% of the Republic's gross national product—the same share as that of the VOC.

ECONOMY

The untold thousands who settled in the Republic were determined to succeed. They were not just the poor but, certainly in the early stages, skilled craftsmen, merchants and intellectuals, many of them from the southern Netherlands and France. They brought not only their labour, skills and capital, but networks of contacts with business associates throughout Europe. That colourful world came together in the Republic, where it was concentrated in a few cities in the west of the country.

The influx of people and the upturn in economic activity forced the cities to expand enormously and very rapidly. The harbours in

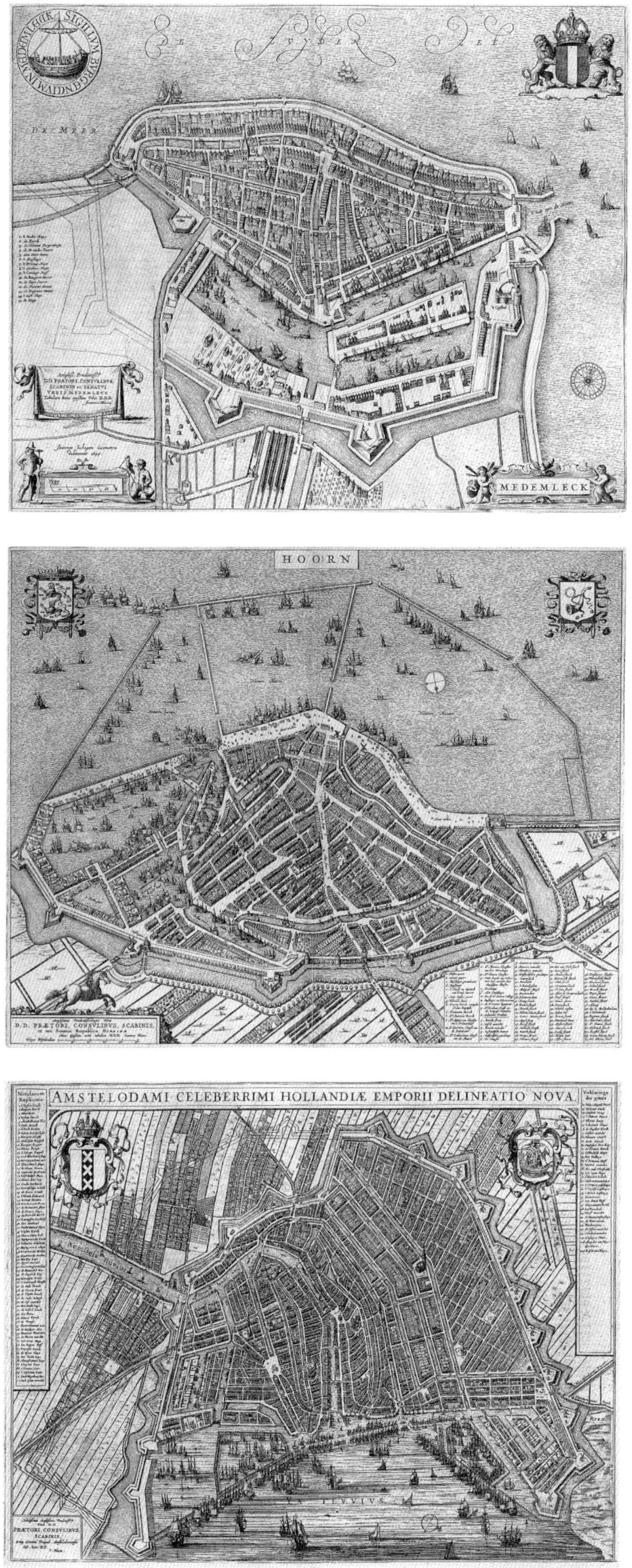

fig. 43 Three maps from the *Stedenatlas* by Joan Blaeu: Medemblik, 1649; Hoorn, 1652; Amsterdam, 1649. Amsterdam, Rijksmuseum, Rijksprentenkabinet

12 port cities were enlarged 21 times between 1600 and 1650, despite the fact that 10 of them had already increased their capacity 17 times in the preceding 25 years. Amsterdam's population grew from 50,000 in 1600 to 200,000 in 1660, and the same pattern was repeated in industrial cities like Leiden and Haarlem (*figs.* 43a-c).

Accounts of the Republic's prosperity often stress the importance of maritime trade. The success of the herring fishery and the Baltic traffic, which for good reason were known as the basic trade, were already making a substantial contribution to the country's coffers in the 16th century, and this grew in the following century as trade routes were extended to the Mediterranean, the Atlantic and the Indian Ocean. The agrarian sector was less spectacular, and wrongly receives less attention, but market-oriented, intensive agriculture, horticulture and livestock farming provided a solid basis for economic success. It was a sector that had been a leading exporter since the middle ages, for it produced more than was needed for domestic consumption (*fig.* 44). Prudent water management and short lines of communication with the urban markets ensured that the Republic was never struck by famine in the 17th century, thus strengthening the nation's sense of security. Land was reclaimed with the aid of massed arrays of windmills, increasing the acreage available for cultivation.

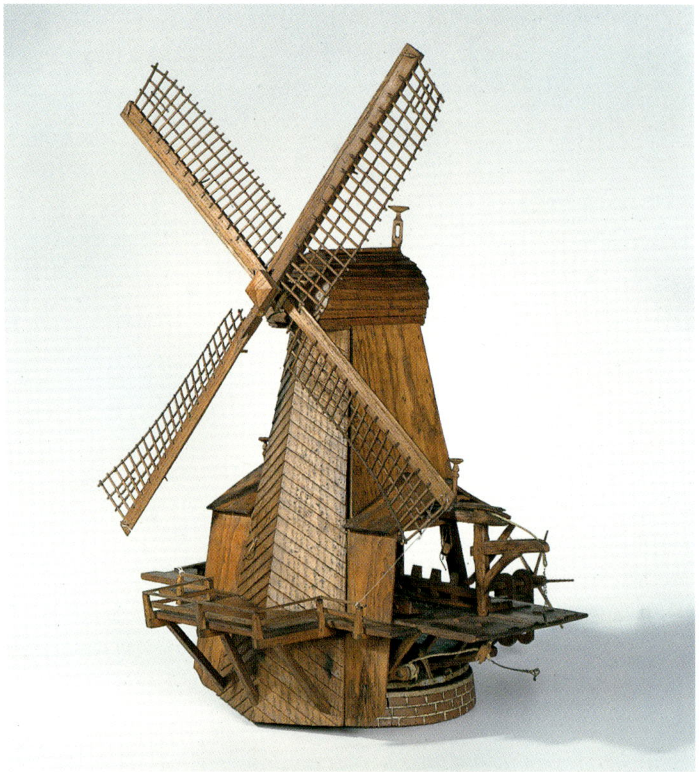

fig. 45 Model of a post sawmill, 17th century; oak. Amsterdam, Rijksmuseum

Important factors in entrepreneurship other than labour are sources of energy, speed of trade operations and inventiveness. Immigration had provided a large labour pool. The guild organisations, which dominated the urban economies in the middle ages, were no longer so powerful in the 17th century, but they still provided an organisational structure for many occupations. They were also extremely important from a social point of view, serving as meeting-places and centres of mutual support for their members.

Energy came from the intensive use of wind power. Industrial windmills dotted the skylines of all the towns and cities, and visitors to the Zaan region just to the north-west of Amsterdam could see at least 128 of them at work in 1630 (*fig.* 45). Watermills ensured that the water table in low-lying areas was kept far enough below the surface to allow cattle breeding and agriculture to continue undisturbed.

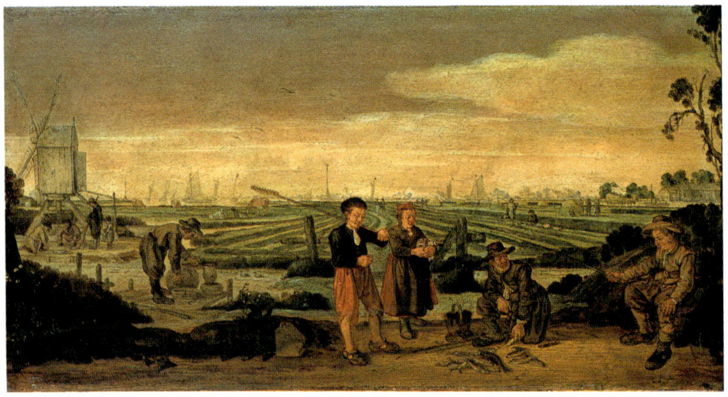

fig. 44 Arent Arentsz, called Cabel, *Fishermen and farmers with a Dutch polder landscape in the background*; oil on panel, 27 x 52 cm. Amsterdam, Rijksmuseum

In addition to wind there was peat, which was used as fuel and had been a major energy source since the 16th century. Peat extraction took place on such a large scale that it was eventually prohibited in the west of the country, because the inland lakes left behind by the diggings were beginning to present very real dangers to the local population. It then shifted to the more sparsely populated northern and eastern provinces.

Speed of trade and the efficient use of manpower were ensured by a transport infrastructure of tow-barges and passage-boats, which evolved between 1620 and 1650. The digging of canals combined with passage-boats plying the inland waterways created a network linking the towns and villages in the west and the centre of the country. Fixed timetables meant that markets could count on regular supplies, that merchants could rely on news reaching them swiftly and reliably, and that appointments could be made, orders placed and accounts settled. The tempo of work and business increased considerably. As the English ambassador, Sir William Temple noted in 1673 in his *Observations upon the United*

Provinces of the Netherlands: 'One horse shall draw in a boat more than fifty can do by cart', and 'by this easie way of travelling, an industrious man loses no time from his business, for he writes, or eats, or sleeps while he goes; whereas the time of labouring of industrious men, is the greatest native commodity of any countrey'. In 1665, there was a total of 658 kilometres of towpath canals.

The Republic's mobile society, which was constantly receiving fresh impulses from its immigrants and foreign contacts, was a breeding ground for inventiveness and the development of fresh ideas. The practical man was gradually edged aside by the scholar, and here military and civilian technology marched side by side. The scope was limitless: fortifications, urban development, mechanical engineering, arms technology, cartography, mathematics and physics, philosophy, law. People like Simon Stevin, Petrus Plancius, Willibrord Snellius, Hugo Grotius, Spinoza and Cornelis Drebbel set out to couple theory with practice (*fig. 46*). In the period 1590-1670 an average of 50 patent applications a year were submitted to the States-General (up to 1639 it was actually over 75 a year), but that figure dropped to below 25 after 1670.

All in all, the 17th century, and particularly its second half, was a time of relative prosperity and security for the inhabitants of the Dutch Republic.

The country was awash with money, as was demonstrated by the tulip craze, when enormous sums were paid for single bulbs, only for many people to be left bankrupt when the bottom dropped out of the market in 1637. However, although there was plenty of money, it was very unfairly distributed by our standards. Many people had no income at all, or only a very small one. They were either unable to work, had to rely on odd jobs, or were seasonal workers, not just in agriculture and the construction industry, but in the fisheries, shipping and the army as well. This meant that for long periods they had no money coming in at all. For large sections of the population the churches provided a social and economic safety net, caring for the disadvantaged and providing financial support.

Above the group of people temporarily or permanently dependent on charity was a very motley and relatively broad central group consisting of soldiers, craftsmen, farmers shopkeepers, fishermen, barge skippers and other self-employed people. A paucity of archival sources makes it almost impossible to say how large this group was, but it has been calculated in a study of the country village of Graft in the province of North Holland that 16% of the inhabitants could be described as impoverished in 1680, while 4% were indigent, 68% 'self-supporting' and 12% prosperous. This is just an example; there were pronounced local differences throughout the Republic. People with property, be it a house, a shop, a ship or a piece of land, had a cushion to protect them from setbacks and could tide themselves over lean periods, but most people lived around the poverty line. Although the better-off in the propertied group could permit themselves certain luxuries, buying books, furniture and the occasional map, print or painting, their

fig. 46 Willem van Swanenburg after Jacques de Gheyn II, *The land yacht designed by Simon Stevin in which Prince Maurits sailed along the beach from Scheveningen to Petten in 1602*; engraving, 68 x 148 cm. Amsterdam, Rijksmuseum, Rijksprentenkabinet

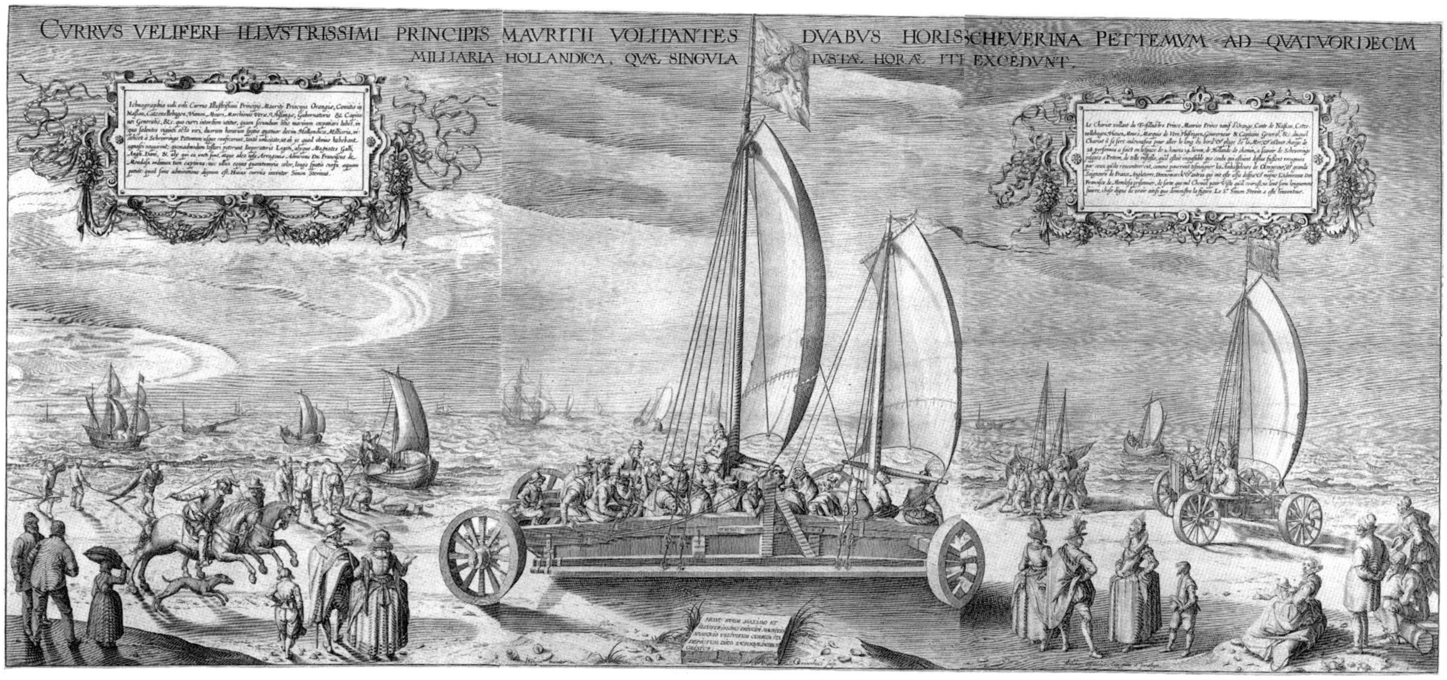

incomes bore no relation to those of the small, prominent group of fabulously wealthy merchants and industrialists who formed the top layer of society. Most of them had made their fortunes in the first few decades of the 17th century, and increasingly they coalesced into an oligarchy of the rich. They surrounded themselves with luxury, and built country houses on the banks of the rivers Vecht, Spaarne and Kromme Rijn in which their lavishly decorated 'pleasure yachts' were moored. They patronised artists and amassed collections of curiosities, porcelain, weapons and other luxury items. They bought up the lordships of manors or shires, which enabled them to emulate the great aristocratic landowners in the eastern provinces. They divided up the administrative posts between them, and public offices, most of which could be farmed out, provided not only money but power. These regents built up extensive client networks, making groups of people socially and economically indebted to them. Some of their wealth flowed back to the poorest in society, perhaps prompted by a religious sense of duty. By supporting or founding charitable institutions they joined the civic authorities, the church and the guilds in the upkeep of the existing system of welfare for the needy, such as orphans, widows and the elderly.

Although this social safety net was better than those elsewhere in Europe, all the inhabitants of the Dutch Republic, rich and poor alike, lived at a time of patchy medical knowledge, poor hygiene and an often monotonous diet, which ensured that invalidity and death were always close acquaintances.

Although it is often not recognised as such, the level of education and literacy in a society is an important factor in economic life. They help determine an individual's ability to run a business, introduce new developments and communicate efficiently and swiftly. Both training and literacy were well advanced in the Republic, and by the second half of the 17th century roughly 75% of the men and 50% of the women could sign their names. Literacy was also higher than in many other European countries. Going by the impressive and unique production of printed matter in the form of books, newsletters, pamphlets and leaflets, there was clearly a sizable market. The printing press thus became an instrument for the rapid dissemination of knowledge and art.

GOVERNMENT

There was really only one element of Dutch society that lagged behind the tumultuous developments on the socio-economic and intellectual fronts, and that was the country's political structure. The Dutch Revolt was largely directed against the Habsburgs' monarchical policy of administrative centralisation, and was driven by a religious fervour and readiness for self-sacrifice which was in fact also targeted against an absolute power: that of the pope in Rome.

The success of the Revolt gave birth to a decentralised state that was held together by a military pact: the Union of Utrecht. The Union dated from the early days of the Revolt (1578), and quite understandably it did not resolve constitutional issues. Practice was to provide a *modus vivendi* in the form of a republic, however hesitantly adopted (*fig. 47*). It led to a form of government with a decentralised and multi-layered decision-making process which was controlled by a small group of solid citizens with vested interests. It should be remembered that politics was not a profession at this time. Offices were filled by rotation. Right up to the very highest organs of the state it was burghers who exercised power and unscrupulously used their influence to further their business interests. Indeed, those interests were paramount. At the end of the 16th century, the number of members of the Rotterdam town council was increased from 24 to 32, 'for they are engaged on maritime affairs and trade, and consequently are often away from home'. These officials were constantly meeting each other in all

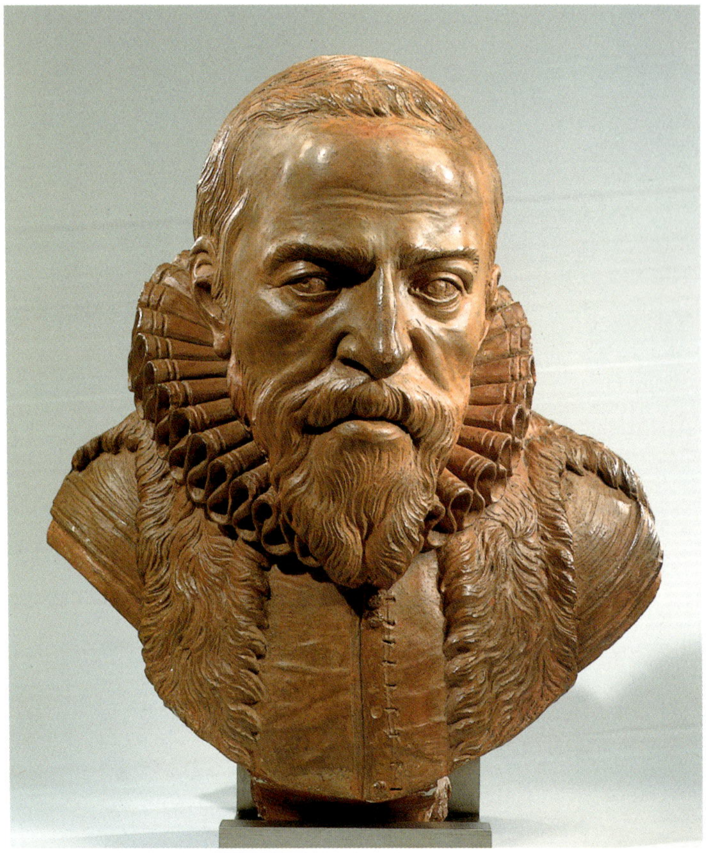

fig. 47 *Johan van Oldenbarnevelt (1547-1619), Pensionary of Holland and one of the founders of the Republic of the Seven United Netherlands,* second half of the 17th century; terracotta, h. 40 cm. Amsterdam, Rijksmuseum

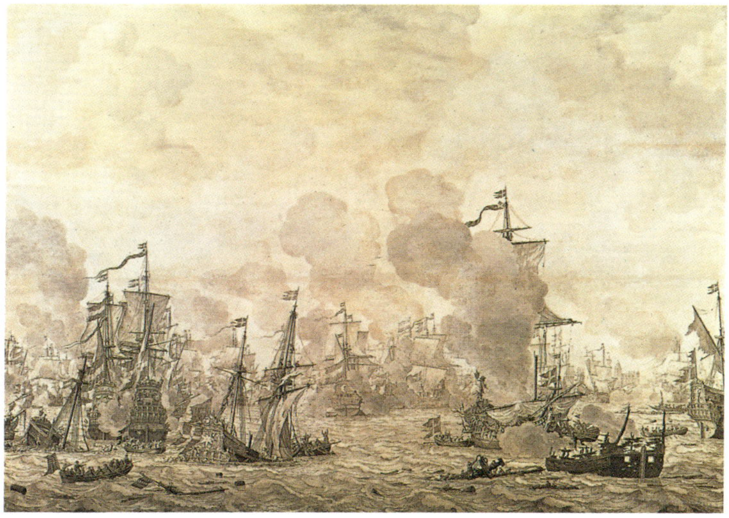

fig. 48 Willem van de Velde the Elder, *The Battle of the Sound in the Fourth Northern War between a Dutch fleet under the command of Jacob Wassenaar van Obdam and the Swedish fleet, 8 November 1658*; pen and ink on panel, 97.5 x 141 cm. Amsterdam, Rijksmuseum

sorts of administrative bodies and societies, ranging from chambers of rhetoric to the civic guard. Power was wielded in the same way in the east of the country, but not so much by a burgher elite as by the great aristocratic landowners.

The States-General was the supreme governing body of the Republic, and was composed of delegates from the provinces. The captured regions of North Brabant and parts of Limburg, known as the Generality Lands, were governed directly by the States-General. The provinces were administered by the provincial States assemblies, which in turn consisted of delegates from the towns and cities that were entitled to vote. The burgomasters and the city councils were chosen by the prosperous citizens and appointed by the stadholder.

The latter, who was originally the military representative of the absent ruler, was a unique figure in the Republic. He derived his power and authority from the Union treaty, his aristocratic birth and, if he was a member of the House of Orange, from his status as the ruling prince. There were several stadholders at any one time during the years of Habsburg rule, but with the outbreak of the Revolt that power was concentrated in two places, with the result that there were two stadholders' courts in the 17th century: in Leeuwarden and The Hague. The main influence of the members of the Nassau family of Friesland and Groningen was at a provincial and local level, and their rank as counts did not give them the international stature that the stadholders of Holland enjoyed as princes of Orange. Their possession of the principality of Orange made them members of the international, royal elite, and the fact they were also stadholder of the richest provinces in the Union was an added bonus. Moreover, as Captain-General and Captain-Admiral the stadholder was the supreme commander of the Republic's army and navy, which was no sinecure in so violent an age. The princes of Orange worked hard to strengthen their position on the domestic and foreign fronts through their networks of clients and relatives. The stadholders of Friesland also made a point of being seen at the court of the Oranges and of ensuring that the family ties were maintained.

The political system of the Republic was rooted in consensus. Consultation was a fact of life. Decisions were taken after extensive 'deliberation'. The memory of that discussion model lives on today in the Dutch saying 'op zijn elf en dertigste' (at its eleven and thirtieth, meaning: at a snail's pace), referring to the talks that the Frisian delegates had to hold with the province's 11 towns and 30 districts before they could adopt a standpoint in the States assembly. In practice, though, power lay with those with the biggest purse, that is to say the representatives of the province of Holland, which provided more than half the Republic's budget. In the course of the 17th century the Pensionary of Holland grew to become the most influential politician and administrator in the Republic, and the counterpart of the most important servant of the States-General, the stadholder.

The stratified decision-making process entailed inevitable delays in arriving at political resolutions. Initially that did not present too much of a problem. In the first half of the century, Germany was being torn apart in a murderous war of religion. The same applied to France, and England had its Civil War. In effect, the Republic had only Spain to deal with, but that all changed in the second half of the century, when Louis XIV ascended the throne of France, and England and Sweden finally had their hands free. The impunity with which the Dutch sailed the seas was a thing of the past, and this led to new military confrontations (*fig. 48*).

The political system in the Republic created acute internal political tensions on several occasions. The first came during the Twelve Years' Truce with Spain, when the foreign menace receded for a while. The conflict was originally a religious one, with the strict Calvinists winning a Pyrrhic victory over the moderates with the resolutions of the Synod of Dordrecht but failing to turn the Republic into a theocracy. From the political point of view the matter reached its dramatic climax with the execution of the elder statesman Johan van Oldenbarnevelt, when the stadholder, Prince Maurits, abandoned his former teacher and fellow architect of the Republic to the executioner's sword. Stadholder Willem II's attack on Amsterdam in 1650 and the subsequent Great Assembly in the Knights' Hall in The Hague also brought about little change (*fig. 49*). Holland and Zeeland merely left the stadholderate of their provinces vacant, only filling them again in 1672. It was probably a blessing for the Republic that the formidable figure of Johan de Witt was Pensionary of Holland during the minority of Willem III, and that he was given a free hand to run the country. Under his rule the Dutch Republic emerged as a major European power, both economically and militarily.

With the construction of Amsterdam's new Town Hall (1648-1654) (*fig.* 50), that masterly creation of Jacob van Campen and the ultimate expression of civic power, the author of the verse on Pieter Isaacsz's harpsichord lid was proved right. Inlaid in the floor of the building's Civic Hall is a map of the world, putting it literally at the feet of the citizens of Amsterdam, while outside, on the pediment stands the figure of Atlas with the earth on his shoulders.

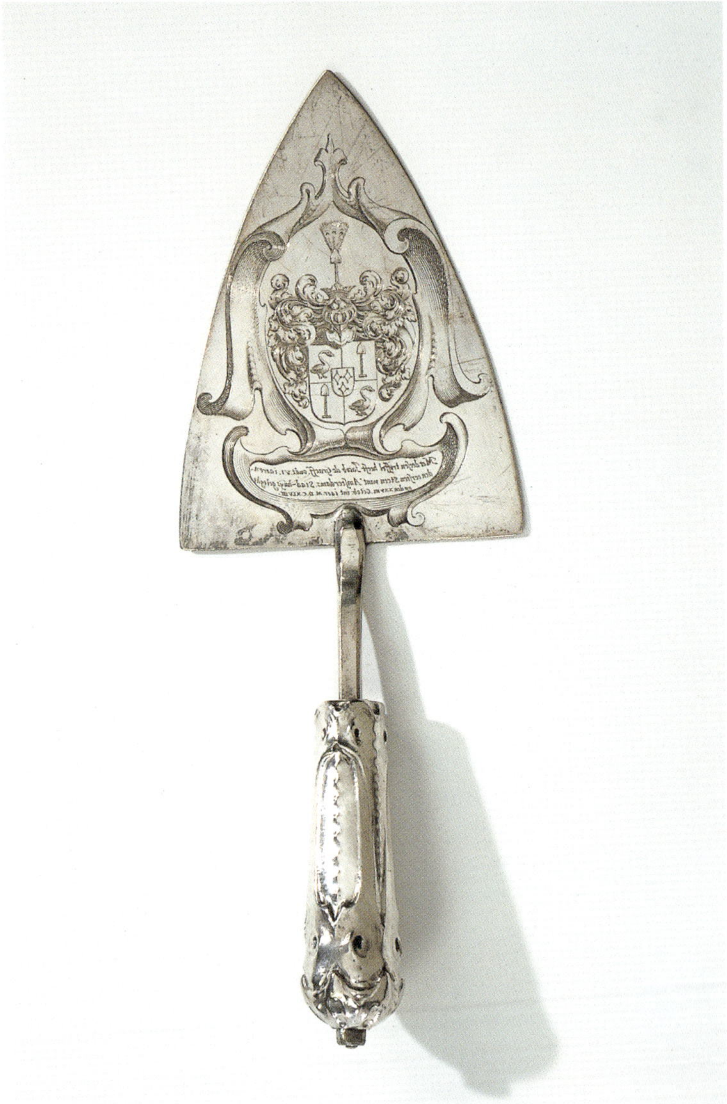

fig. 50 Johannes Lutma (attributed to), *Trowel commemorating the laying of the first stone of Amsterdam Town Hall by the four burgomaster's sons on 28 October 1648*; silver, 27.8 x 11 cm. Amsterdam, Rijksmuseum

LIMITS TO GROWTH

However, the Dutch Republic was not unassailable. That emerged in 1672, when the great European powers joined forces and attacked, threatening to overwhelm the country. This cost the De Witt brothers their lives (*fig.* 51). The French armies were only forced back by deliberately flooding the countryside, while the 'wooden wall' at sea under the command of Michiel de Ruyter managed to prevent the combined Anglo-French fleet from invading. Admirals became the heroes of the people (*fig.* 52). The crisis gave Willem III a leg up into the saddle. He was appointed stadholder, and became a European leader with a royal touch, championing the politics of balance of power and Protestantism. His marriage to Mary Stuart brought him the throne of England in 1688, which put the crown on the royal ambitions of the House of Orange (*fig.* 53).

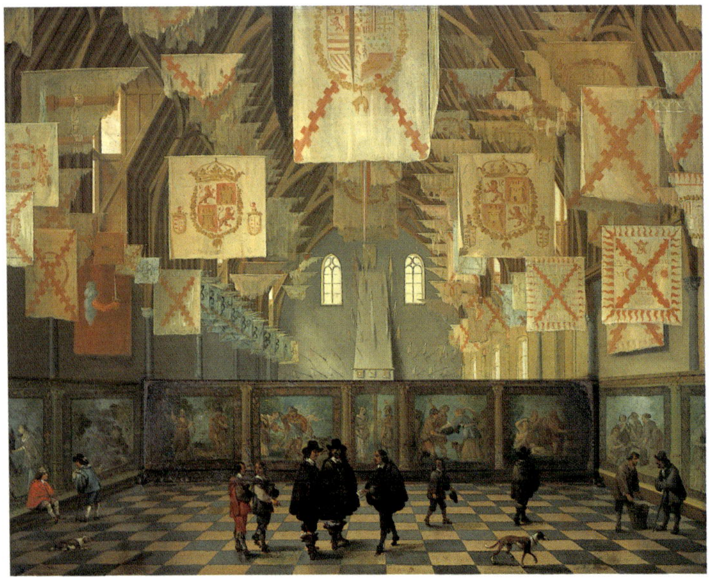

fig. 49 Dirck van Delen, *The great hall of the Binnenhof in The Hague during the Great Assembly of the States-General in 1651*; oil on panel, 52 x 66 cm. Amsterdam, Rijksmuseum

Overseas expansion had reached its limits around the middle of the century. The Republic scored its greatest successes in the Far East. The Dutch East India Company had seized the monopoly of the spice trade by force, and had a far-flung network of trading posts throughout Asia. The VOC was a major presence in inter-Asian trade, alongside the Chinese, Indian and Arabic traders. Its settlement on the small island of Deshima in the Bay of Nagasaki was the only European factory allowed to trade with Japan. In 1640 the company drove the Portuguese out of Ceylon and set up trading posts around the coast. In the Indonesian archipelago, Batavia (modern Jakarta) grew to become an Asian centre of trade and

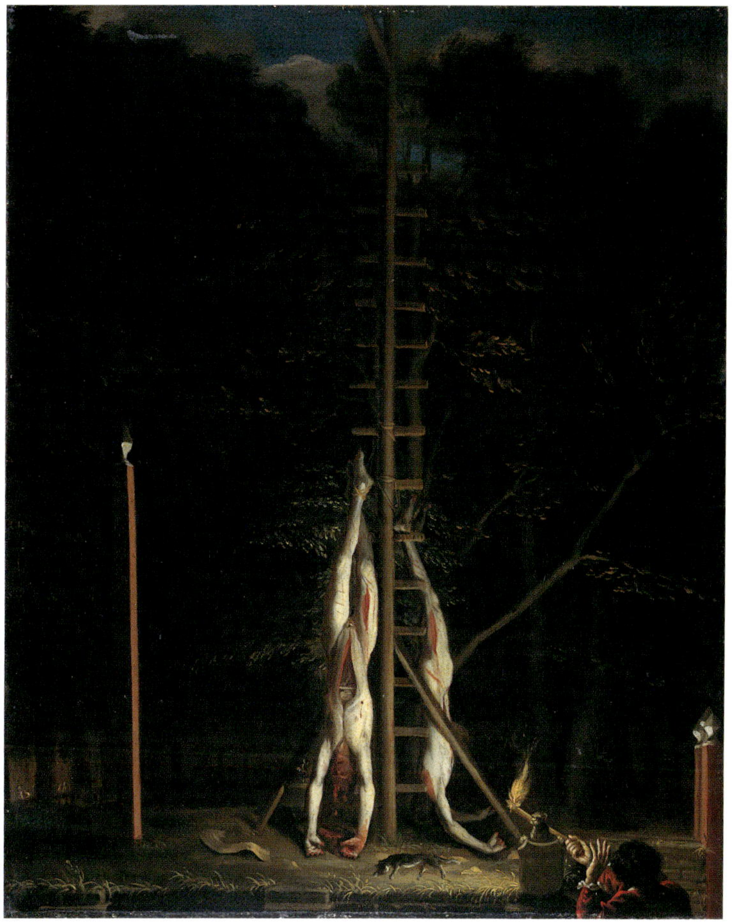

fig. 51 Jan de Baen, *The corpses of the De Witt brothers, Jan and Cornelis, hanging on the Groene Zoodje on the Vijverberg in The Hague*, 1672; oil on canvas, 69.5 x 56 cm. Amsterdam, Rijksmuseum

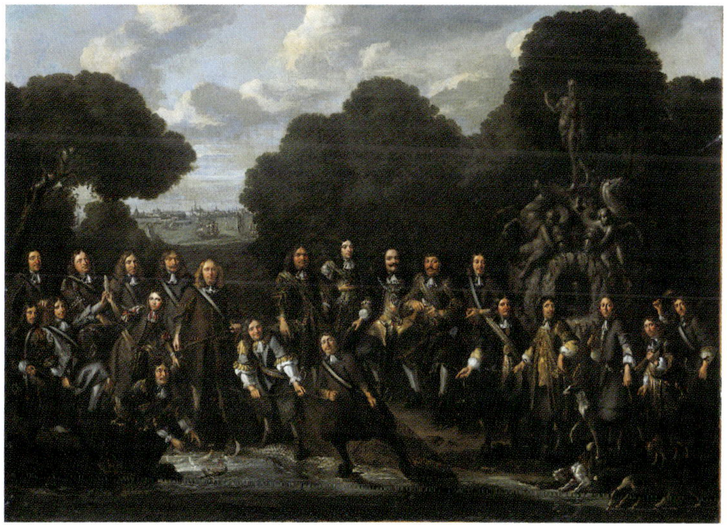

fig. 52 Willem Eversdijck (attributed to), *Allegory of the flowering of the Dutch fishery after the Second Anglo-Dutch War (1665-1667), with Dutch admirals, among them Michiel de Ruyter, hauling in the full nets*; oil on canvas, 114 x 162 cm. Amsterdam, Rijksmuseum

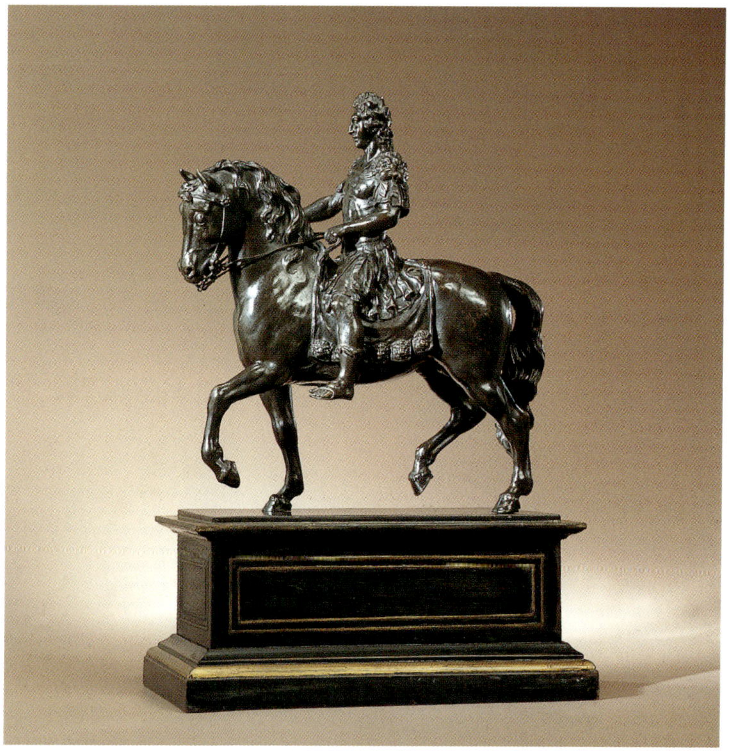

fig. 53 Michael Rysbrack, *Equestrian statue of King-Stadholder Willem III*, second quarter of the 17th century; bronze, h. 37 cm. Amsterdam, Rijksmuseum

industry, a cosmopolitan city where all the peoples of Asia met. The Cape of Good Hope became a permanent staging post for the VOC ships from 1652.

The Dutch were less successful in America and Africa. The West India Company (WIC) was founded in 1621, and combined trade with military adventurism. Initially it had everything its own way against the Portuguese in Brazil, but was evicted in 1654, which led to its bankruptcy in 1674. The second WIC, which was formed the following year, concerned itself with trade alone. There was difficulty establishing settlements in North America, and when New Amsterdam was captured by the English the Dutch turned their attention to areas in South America, Surinam among them. This was chiefly because of the lucrative sugar plantations and slave trade, which the WIC had been finding highly profitable since its conquest of parts of the Brazilian coastal regions. When Brazil was lost, new markets were sought and found in the Caribbean and Surinam. In order to ensure plentiful supplies of slave, the WIC had built or captured several forts on the coast of modern-day Ghana, and one of them, San Jorge d'Elmina, became one of the main slave trading posts on the west coast of Africa.

The overseas territories brought prestige to the Dutch Republic, but at the same time made it essential for its public figures to tread the international stage in order to protect the country's interests. The Republic's diplomatic contacts extended from the Muscovite court of the Russian tsar to the Ottoman sultan in Constantinople, the rulers of the countries of North Africa, the Japanese shogun in Edo, the Chinese emperor in Peking and the maharajahs of India. Anyone seeing the 'privy cabinet' of the States-General, in which the correspondence with foreign rulers was stored, will immediately realise how limited those contacts really were.

No matter how far-flung its interests, the central concern was always the situation in Europe, where it became increasingly difficult to continue functioning as the marketplace of the continent, and where the traditional mainstays of the Baltic trade, the Mediterranean trade, the North Sea fishery and whaling were constantly under pressure (*fig. 54*). The political equilibrium was delicate, and continually had to be maintained by military action, mainly at sea and on France's northern border, in the southern Netherlands. The scale of these military operations grew explosively, putting a severe strain on the financial investments that had to be made in order to continue as an actor on the European stage. Political and economic competition from neighbouring European powers grew, and the consequences were felt throughout society. In hindsight it can be seen that unbridled growth found its limits in the third quarter of the century. That is not to say that prosperity evaporated, but gradually the cost of maintaining its status as a world power became too much for the flourishing Republic of the stadholder-king.

FURTHER READING

Algemene Geschiedenis der Nederlanden, vols. 5-9, Haarlem 1979-80; Van Deursen 1991; Gaastra 1991; Israel 1995; De Vries & Van der Woude 1995; Frijhoff & Spies 1999

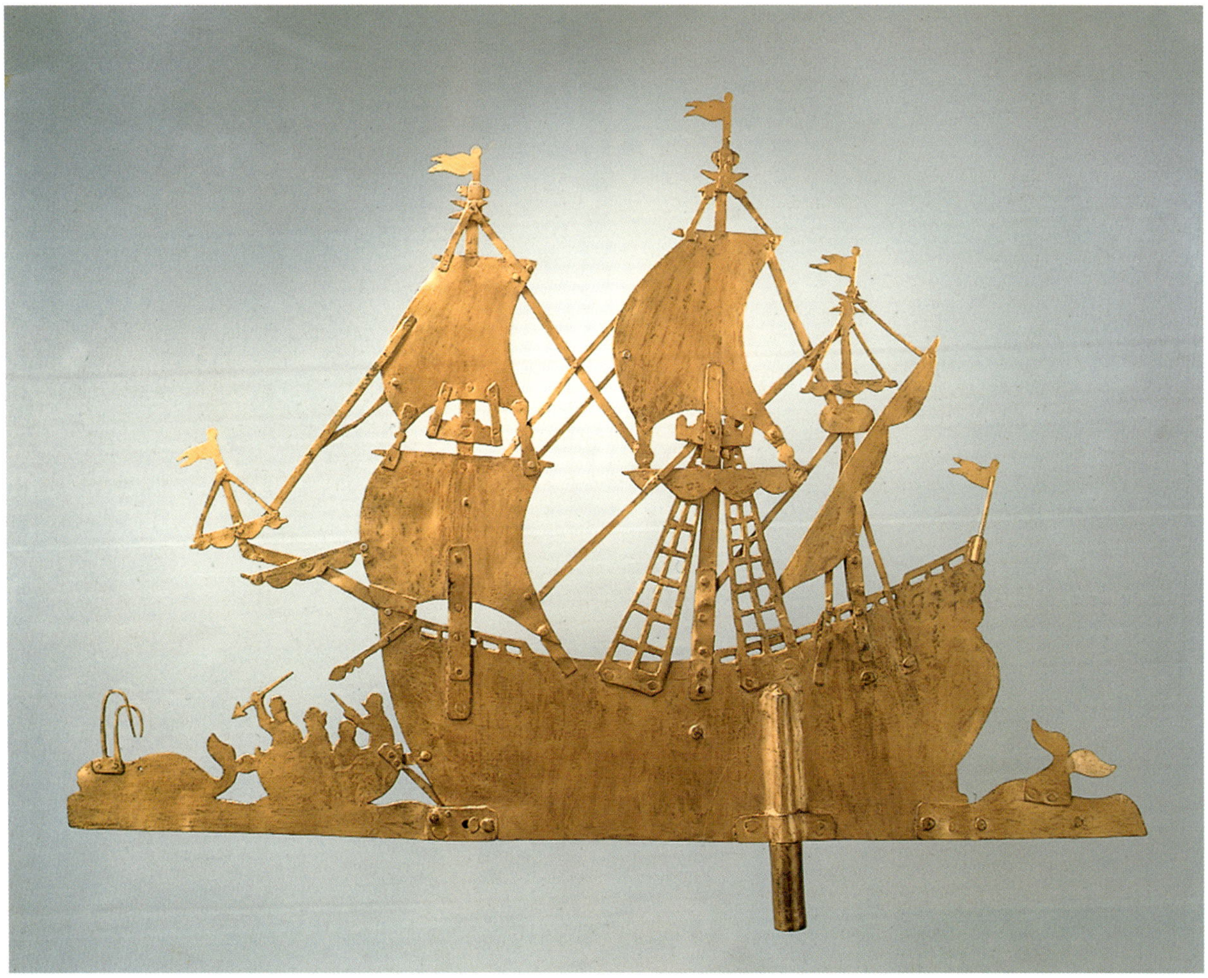

fig. 54 Weathervane in the form of a whaler flanked by two whales being hunted by whalers in a boat; gilt metal. Amsterdam, Rijksmuseum

Detail of [82] ▸

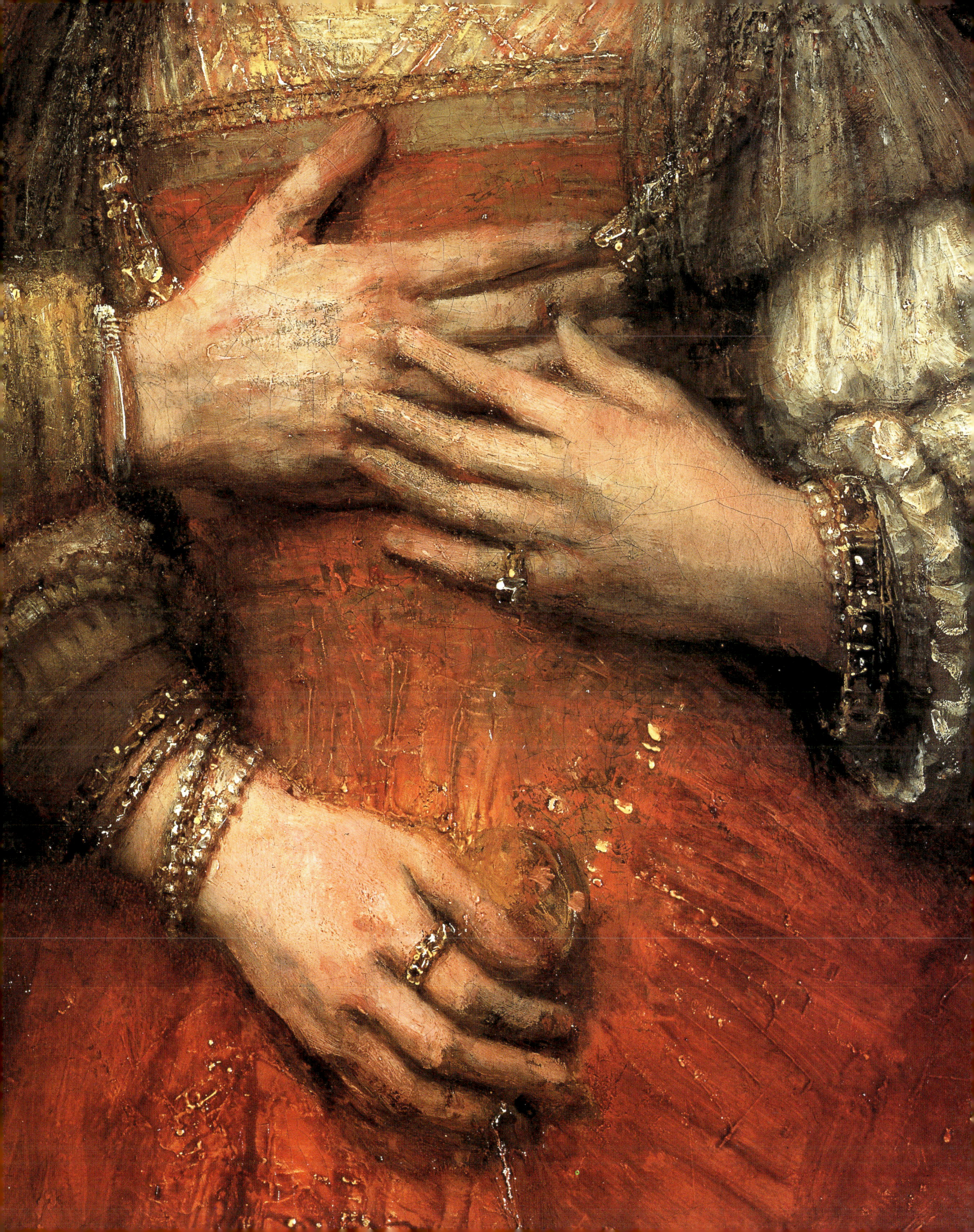

Paulus van Vianen (Utrecht c. 1570-Prague 1613)

1 *Ewer and basin with episodes from the stories of Diana and Callisto, and Diana and Actaeon, 1613*

Silver, ewer: h. 34 cm, w. 17.4 cm, d. 12 cm; basin: h. 6.4 cm, w. 52.3 cm, d. 40.5 cm
On the front of the basin: *PV* and *1613*
Bought from the artist by Nicolaes Snouckaert van Schauburg; acquired in 1947
Inv. no. BK-16089

The silver ewer and basin decorated with mythological scenes are the most important work that Paulus van Vianen ever produced. The silversmith, who hailed from Utrecht, made the ensemble one year before his death in Prague, where he had been working since 1603 as court goldsmith to Emperor Rudolf II. The latter had little time for affairs of state, concentrating instead on his patronage of the arts. By getting the most outstanding artists of the day to come and work for him, Rudolf turned the castle in Prague into an international centre of the arts and sciences. Practitioners of the 'applied' arts, Paulus van Vianen among them, were treated as the equals of sculptors *[see 2]* and painters, practitioners of the fine arts.

The ewer and basin are embellished with scenes based on the *Metamorphoses* of the Roman poet Ovid (43 BC - AD 18). Both of them involve Diana, the goddess of the hunt. The upper surface of the basin shows the goddess spattering the hunter Actaeon with water so that he begins turning into a stag as punishment for coming across Diana and her nymphs bathing. Van Vianen had already depicted this episode in 1610 on a small gold cup. Actaeon has been fully transformed into a stag on the underside of the basin, where he is killed by his own hunters and hounds. The ewer depicts the story of the nymph Callisto. She had become pregnant by Jupiter, who had disguised himself as Diana in order to gain access to her. On one side of the ewer she is turned into a she-bear as punishment for breaking her vow of chastity, and on the other she comes within a hair's-breadth of being killed by her son Arcas. Jupiter stayed his hand, though, and turned her and her son into stars in the sky.

One characteristic of Van Vianen's work is the subtle depiction of the landscape setting. His virtuoso embossing and chasing technique enabled him to invest the almost flat relief with a great sense of depth, and with his delicate engraved work he even managed to achieve an atmospheric perspective derived from the arts of drawing and painting. Van Vianen used this method of suggesting depth time and again in the drawn sketches he made of the countryside around Prague. He used some of those studies, either wholly or in part, in the silver plaquettes that were his main medium.

The story of Diana and Actaeon gave Van Vianen the opportunity to depict a large number of nude figures in varied poses. What is striking is that the stances and gazes of the nymphs on the front of the basin lead the viewer's eye to the main scene, which in a typically Mannerist inversion is not in the foreground but on the third or fourth level back *[see also 3]*

In addition to this pictorial quality, the ewer and basin are highly ornamental. The rim of the basin is divided into sections by flaccid, fluid ornaments: masks, bats' wings and forms resembling bones and sinews. Paulus van Vianen played a key role in the development of this anti-classical form of ornamentation, which has been known since the 19th century as the auricular style. In the course of the 17th century it was to stamp its mark on the decorative arts in the Dutch Republic, especially on silver. The foot, handle, spout and cover of the ewer, and the feet of the basin, are fashioned as three-dimensional auricular ornaments. One year after this ewer and basin were made, Adam van Vianen stole a leaf from his younger brother's book when he created the most extreme manifestation of this style *[5]*.

It is not just the superbly executed scenes that proclaim this to be an autonomous work of art; the design of the ewer and basin demonstrates that they were never intended to be used. The foot of the ewer is too small and narrow to support it when full, the handle is too high for pouring, and the basin too shallow to hold water. The status of an autonomous work of art is heightened by a *trouvaille* on Van Vianen's part. He made the basin from two sheets of silver of the same size, which he fastened together with decorative bolts. The use of two sheets enabled him to emboss a second scene on the underside. This made the ensemble unsuitable for placing on a buffet as a decorative showpiece.

The two pieces were probably made for Nicolaes Snouckaert van Schauburg (1568-1635), who held high positions at the court of Rudolf II.

LITERATURE

Ter Molen 1984, vol. 2, no. 19; exhib. cat. Amsterdam 1993-94, no. 190

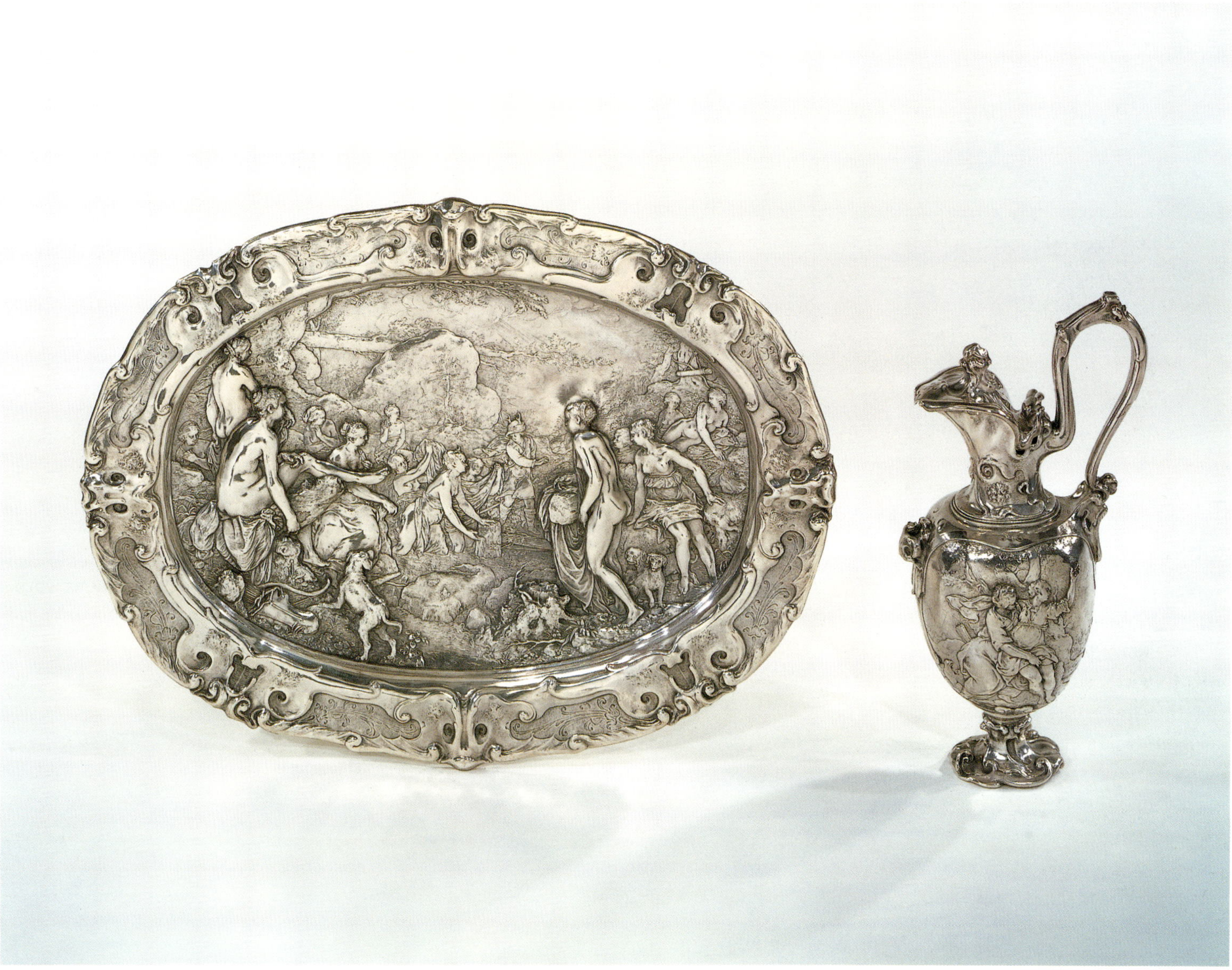

Adriaen de Vries (The Hague 1556-Prague 1626)

2 *Bacchus discovering Ariadne on Naxos, c. 1610*

Bronze, 52.5 x 42 cm
Donated by the N.V. Internationale Antiquiteitenhandel in 1935
Inv. no. BK-14692

After fleeing Crete with Theseus, Ariadne, the daughter of King Minos, fetched up on the island of Naxos. There she fell into a deep sleep, only awakening when she was discovered by the god Bacchus. He married her, and from then on the fair Ariadne was a member of his entourage. The story, first related in the *Eikones* of Philostratus the Elder, inspired this relief by Adriaen de Vries.

The sculptor chose the moment when Bacchus, accompanied by a satyr as his torchbearer, discovers Ariadne in bed. The young nude god comes rushing in and tears back the curtain from the bed, watched by Cupid, who is seated by the bed. Beside the little god of love is an owl, symbolising nighttime. Lying in the foreground are Ariadne's slippers, which stand for the power of woman. In a striking break with tradition, De Vries decided to set the scene in a bedroom rather than out of doors. Here he was resorting to a pictorial formula that was favoured by the northern Mannerists for several stories about the classical gods, such as Vulcan surprising the adulterous Mars and Venus in bed, Jupiter and Danae, and Cupid and Psyche. The main source of inspiration for the composition must have been the work of Bartholomeus Spranger, for there is a remarkable resemblance to Hendrick Goltzius's print of *Mars and Venus* of 1588, which is based on an invention by Spranger. The original model for the reclining Ariadne is found in a bronze composition by Giambologna, who was De Vries's teacher when he first went to Italy. The latter's main innovation was the introduction of the dynamic Bacchus, who dominates and orders the picture space. His prominent, diagonal placement gives the scene a Baroque sense of drama and concentrates all the elements of the composition on the actual discovery of Ariadne, which is the crux of the story.

Adriaen de Vries, born to an apothecary in The Hague, studied in Florence and worked in Milan, Turin, Rome and Augsburg before arriving in Prague in 1602 to enter the service of Emperor Rudolf II as court sculptor. The *Bacchus and Ariadne* relief dates from his Prague period, at a time when he was at the height of his fame and was regarded as one of the pre-eminent sculptors of his day.

The relief must have been made around 1610, for in style it is closely related to other works from those years, such as the relief of *Rudolf II as patron of the arts*, which is dated 1609, and *Vulcan's forge* of 1611. The influence of De Vries's *Bacchus and Ariadne* can be detected in the late work of the silversmith Paulus van Vianen, most notably in his plaquette of *Mercury and Argos* of 1610, both in the soft modelling of the embossed silver and the dramatic, diagonal positioning of the male nude.

Although the style, date and subject of the relief would seem to indicate that it was commissioned by Emperor Rudolf II, it is not listed in the inventory of the imperial *Kunstkammer* of 1607-1611, nor in later ones. The patron must therefore be sought in the immediate vicinity of the Prague court, probably among the Bohemian or German nobility.

LITERATURE
Cat. Amsterdam 1973, no. 205; exhib. cat. Amsterdam 1993-94, no. 181; exhib. cat. Amsterdam/Stockholm/Los Angeles 1998-99, no. 26

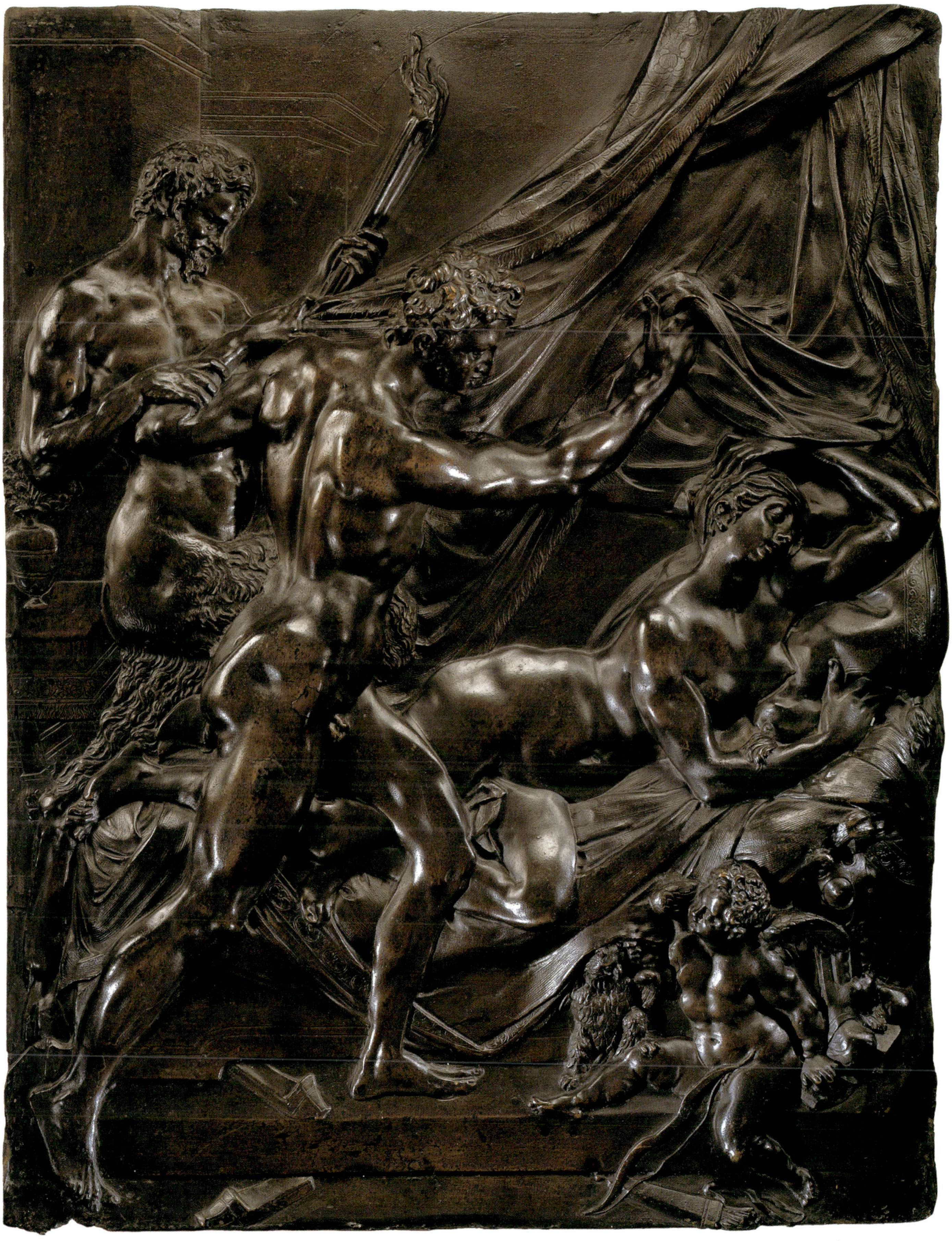

Workshop of François Spiering (Antwerp c. 1650-Delft 1631)
after a design by Karel van Mander (Meulebeke 1548-Amsterdam 1606)

3 *Tapestry with the story of Cephalus and Procris, c. 1610*

Wool and silk on a woollen warp, 345 × 520 cm
At lower centre: FRANCICVS SPIRINGIVS FECIT
Acquired in 1954 with the aid of the Commissie voor Fotoverkoop
Inv. no. BK-1954-69-B

This is one of a series of tapestries known in the 17th century as the 'poetic fables of Diana'. They depict mythological scenes in which Diana either plays a key role or is given a moralistic function. One has to study the tapestry closely in order to make out the tragic love story of Cephalus and Procris as related in Ovid's *Metamorphoses*. The two female figures in the centre are the goddess Diana and Procris, a princess. The beginning of the story is shown in the background above them. Cephalus, nurturing seeds of suspicion planted in his mind by the frustrated Aurora, goddess of dawn, has disguised himself as a suitor to test the fidelity of his wife Procris by showering her with gifts. Overwhelmed by the presents her resolve wavers, and Cephalus casts off his disguise (also shown in the background at the top). Procris flees from him (centre right) and joins Diana and her nymphs (on the left and right of the tapestry). While she is with Diana, Procris is given a hunting dog and a spear (far right), which she in turn gives to Cephalus (not shown) after she has returned home on Diana's advice. Nor does the tapestry show the dramatic end to the tale. Procris, in her turn, now starts to doubt Cephalus's fidelity (again it is a third party who awakens these suspicions), and pays for it with her death, for Cephalus kills her by accident with Diana's spear.

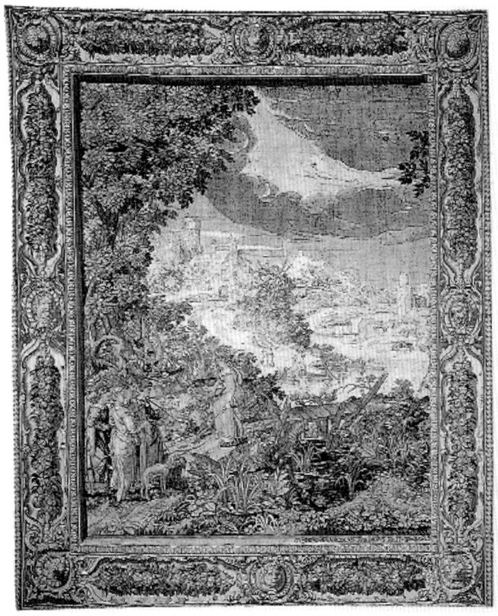

3a François Spiering, *Tapestry with the story of Cephalus and Procris from the small Diana series*, Delft 1613. Private collection

François Spiering made several sets of Diana tapestries during his career. The series from which the Rijksmuseum work comes was designed by Karel van Mander, a Flemish artist who, like Spiering, emigrated to the northern Netherlands. Spiering settled in Delft in 1582, Van Mander in Haarlem the following year. The latter, in his *Wtleggingh op den Metamorphosis* of 1604, describes Diana's parting gifts to Procris of a spear and a dog as the symbols, respectively, of the triumph of reason and of the faithfulness of an honourable wife. He also warns against searching for what one does not wish to find by listening to the insinuations of others, namely supposed infidelity. In Ovid, and on the tapestry, Diana stands for marital fidelity, for she is ordering Procris to return to her husband. Viewed in this light it is interesting to note that Spiering made at least two of his Diana series for newly-weds: one in 1613 for Elizabeth, the daughter of King James I of England, who had just married Elector Frederick V of the Palatine, and the other in 1620 for King Gustav II Adolf of Sweden on the occasion of his marriage to Maria Eleanora of Brandenburg.

The tapestry with the story of Cephalus and Procris comes from the so-called large Diana series. François Spiering also wove a smaller series after different designs. He signed both with his full name. The scenes in the first are in the fairytale style of late 16th-century Brussels tapestries, while the second presents a more contemporary picture of the Dutch landscape [3a].

LITERATURE

Exhib. cat. Amsterdam 1993-94, no. 78

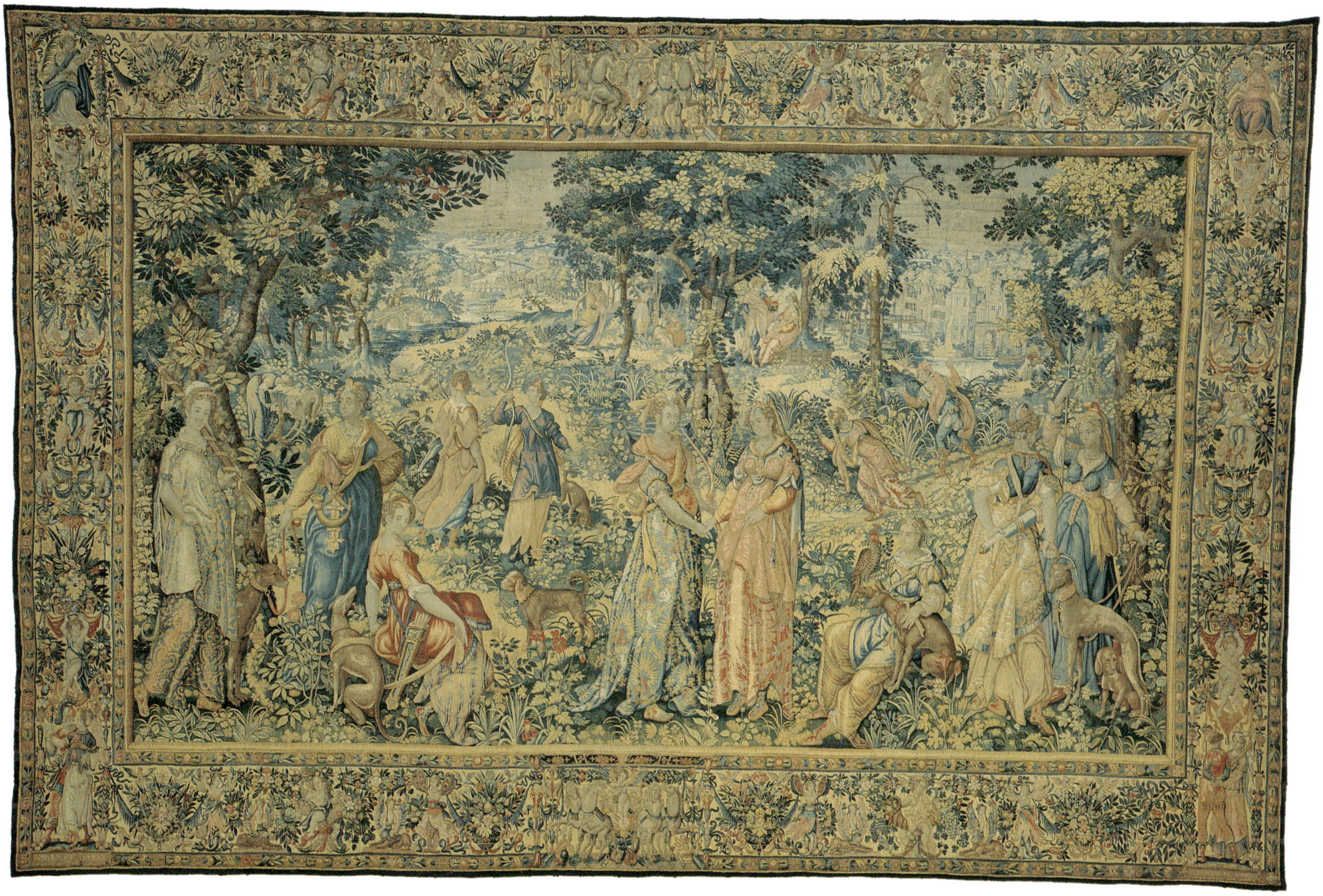

Hendrick de Keyser (Utrecht 1565-Amsterdam 1621)

4 *Portrait of Vincent Coster, 1608*

Marble, h. 75 cm
On the back: *HDK* and *F.AO 1608*
Purchased in 1900 with the aid of the Vereniging Rembrandt
Inv. no. BK-NM-11452

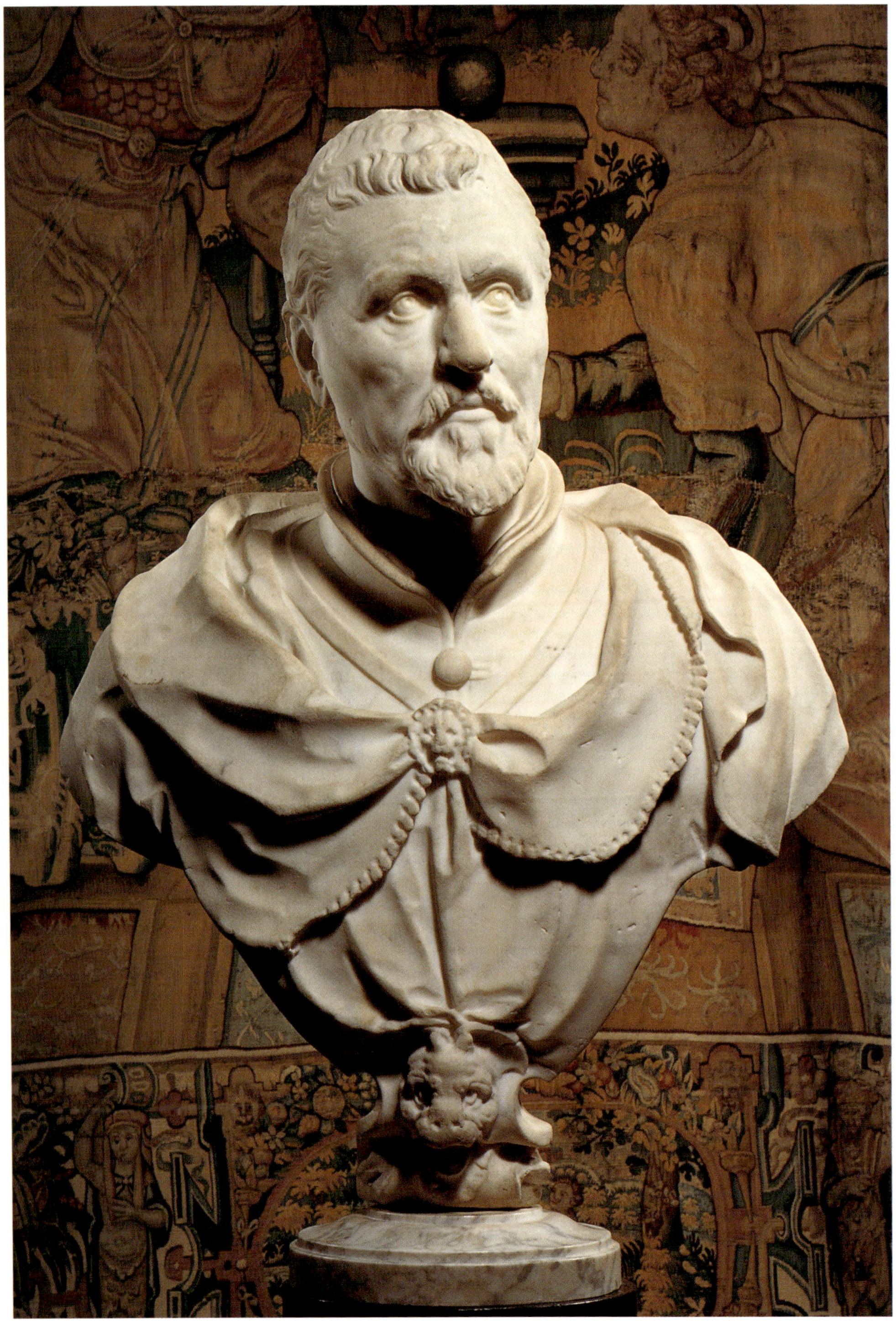

Vincent Coster (1553-1608/10), a wealthy Amsterdam vintner and wine-gauger, took an unusual step when he commissioned Hendrick de Keyser to sculpt his portrait. He was breaking with decorum, which decreed that portrait sculpture was reserved for sovereigns and holders of high office. The result is one of the earliest civilian portrait busts to be made in the Netherlands, and a clear sign of the growing self-assurance of the Dutch burgher class at the beginning of the 17th century. It was executed in white marble, a medium that was very rarely used by Dutch sculptors at the time, who generally worked in sandstone or the more costly alabaster. Hendrick de Keyser knew that he was breaking new ground, for in a petition of 1612 he asserted that he was responsible for introducing Carrara marble in the Netherlands, '[...] since no one in these parts has so far done work in marble of any merit, save he, the petitioner alone'. Coster's bust is indeed the earliest known marble portrait in the northern Netherlands.

The white marble gives the portrait a classical air, which is reinforced by the clothing. The elegantly draped toga evokes associations with male portraits from Roman times. Only the termination of the bust in a grotesque mascaron betrays the early 17th-century date of the work. All in all, this portrait reflects both Coster's aspiration to compete with the highest echelons of society and De Keyser's Classicist leanings.

In 1986, a fragment of a terracotta bust bearing Hendrick de Keyser's monogram was discovered by chance during restoration work on Prinsengracht in Amsterdam. Although it lacked the head it was possible to identify the sitter. That bust, too, was once a complete portrait of Vincent Coster. The location of the find provided the clue, for the fragment was fished out of the canal opposite the site of a well-known 17th-century tavern and pleasure garden known as Het Oude Doolhof (The Old

Maze), the owner of which was none other than Vincent Coster. Since it is known that he also asked De Keyser to make a terracotta portrait of him, it can safely be assumed that this fragment is what remains of it. The less ambitious execution suggests that the terracotta was made a few years before the marble. It presumably stood in or near Coster's pleasure garden, where other sculptures were on display in the 17th century.

LITERATURE
Cat. Amsterdam 1973, no. 224; exhib. cat. Amsterdam 1993-94, no. 59; cat. Amsterdam 1995a, no. 9

Adam van Vianen (Utrecht 1568/69-Utrecht 1627)

5 *Covered ewer, 1614*

Silver-gilt, h. 25,5 cm
On the underside: *A.D.Viana.FE.A° 1614*
Made for the Amsterdam silversmiths' guild; in the guild's possession until 1821, then in a Scottish private collection; acquired in 1976 as a donation from the Prins Bernhard Fonds, the Vereniging Rembrandt and the Commissie voor Fotoverkoop
Inv. no. BK-1976-75

5a Detail of the inner vessel with lizards

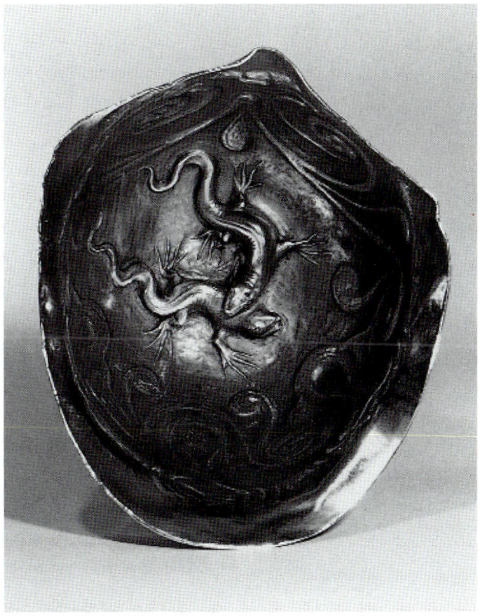

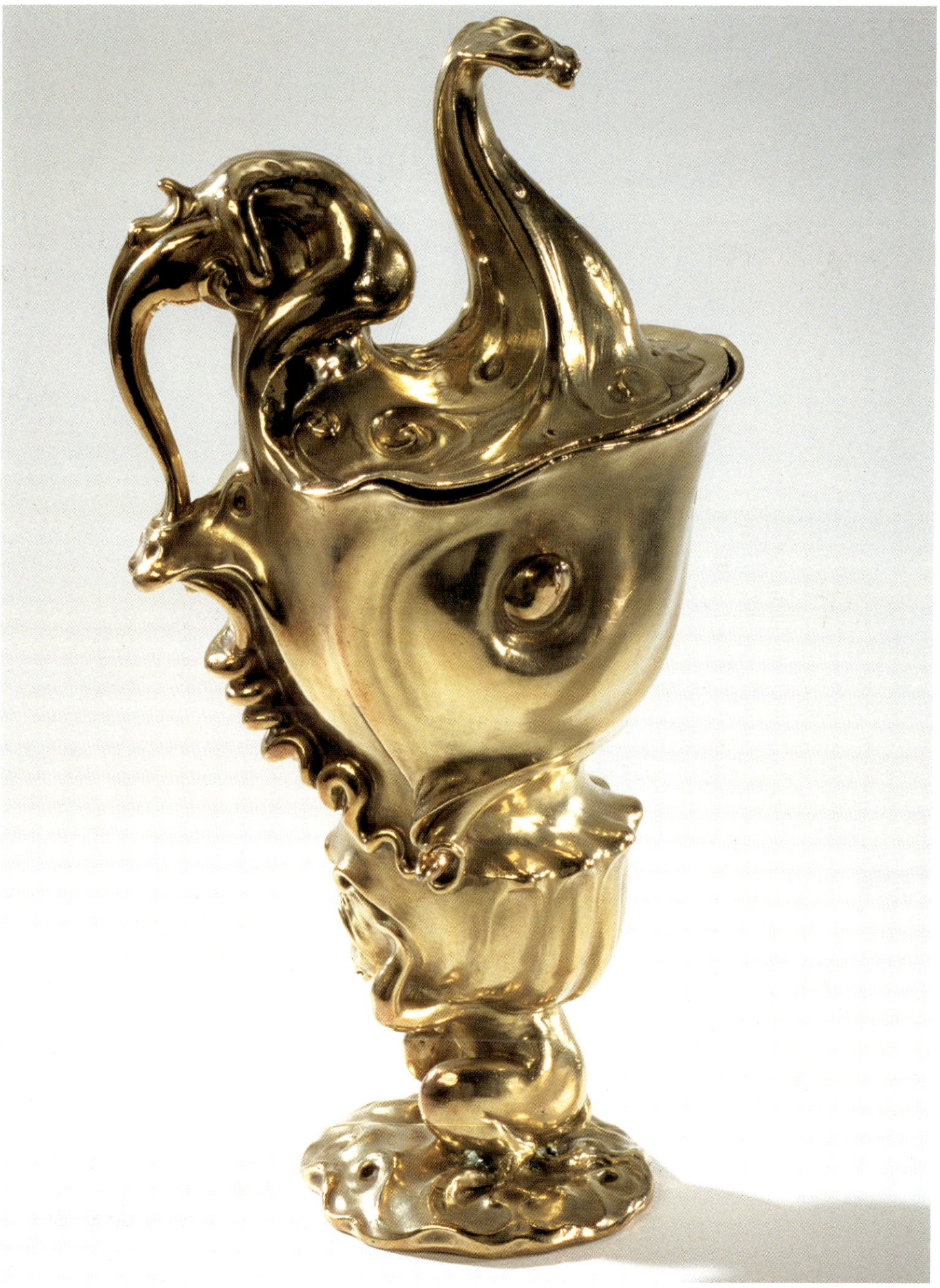

The ewer is the most extreme example of the so-called auricular style, an anti-classical form of design with a flaccid, fluid appearance comprising fantastic sea-creatures and human body parts like bones, ears, sinews and folds of skin. It had previously been used chiefly for border decoration [1], but here the object as a whole has been conceived as a single, uninterrupted ornament.

Adam van Vianen made the ewer in memory of his younger brother Paulus, who had died in Prague in 1613. Adam, who worked in Utrecht, was commissioned to produce this remarkable piece by the Amsterdam silversmiths' guild. The fact that the largest and foremost silversmiths' guild in the Dutch Republic paid homage to someone who had worked abroad for almost all his career testifies to Paulus van Vianen's fame. He was evidently held in such high regard in the Netherlands that the commission to honour his memory was not awarded to a member of the Amsterdam guild but to his own brother, Adam, in Utrecht.

Judging by the unique, unorthodox appearance of the ewer, Adam was given great freedom to honour his brother as he wished. This enabled him to produce a manifesto enshrining the artistic heritage of the Netherlands' most important silversmith. Unlike his brother, Adam had worked until then in a fairly traditional style in which the auricular ornament played only a minor part. This unique commission would have stimulated him to vie with his brother's work. The result is an almost abstract monument of viscous, flowing and intertwining forms from the midst of which creatures emerge: a monkey crouching on the foot, the handle in the form of a woman whose hair arches down into the nostrils in a monster's head, and a sea-snake rearing up from the cover. A surprise awaits within, for two startled lizards adorn the inner vessel [5a]. The fact that Van Vianen signed his ewer shows that he regarded it as an autonomous sculpture, and the same applies to all his later work.

Adam van Vianen was greatly admired for this piece, which must have been on display in the guild's chambers in the city's Weigh-House. It features in dozens of paintings, almost always as part of a biblical or mythical trove of treasure. Pieter Lastman was the first to depict it in his *Crucifixion* of 1615 [5b]. There it is not gilt, and thereafter it was sometimes shown with gilding and sometimes without, which makes it impossible to know precisely when it was applied. The ewer became even more celebrated in 1650, when it was depicted in the *Constighe modellen* published by Adam's son Christiaen (c. 1600/05-1667) —a collection of prints with designs and sketches of finished works by Christiaen and his father.

Quite apart from its artistic merits, the ewer was being praised at an early date for its technical virtuosity, for almost all of the body is 'raised' from a single piece of silver. In 1675, Joachim von Sandrart stressed this aspect of the Utrecht master's craftsmanship in his three-volume *Teutsche Academie*.

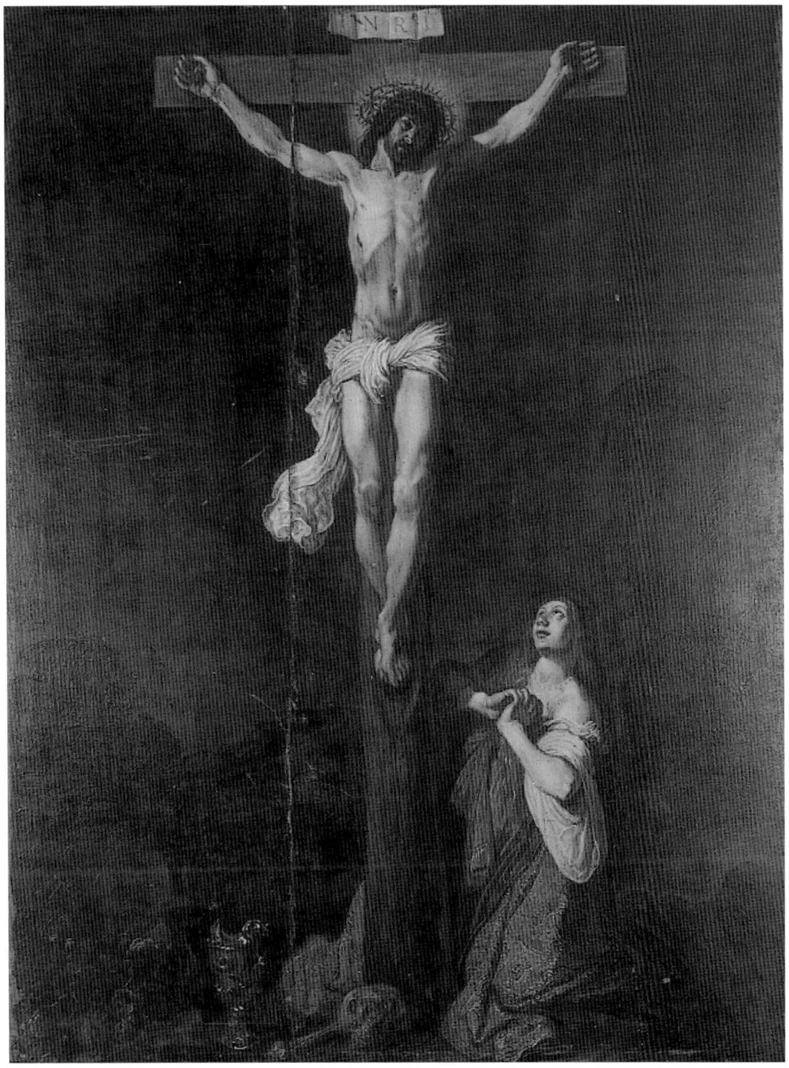

5b Pieter Lastman, *Crucifixion*, 1615; oil on panel, 50 x 39 cm. New York, private collection

LITERATURE

Ter Molen 1984, vol. 2, no. 409; exhib. cat. Utrecht 1984-85, no. 61; Baarsen 1989a; exhib. cat. Amsterdam 1993-94, no. 112

Detail of [6] ▸

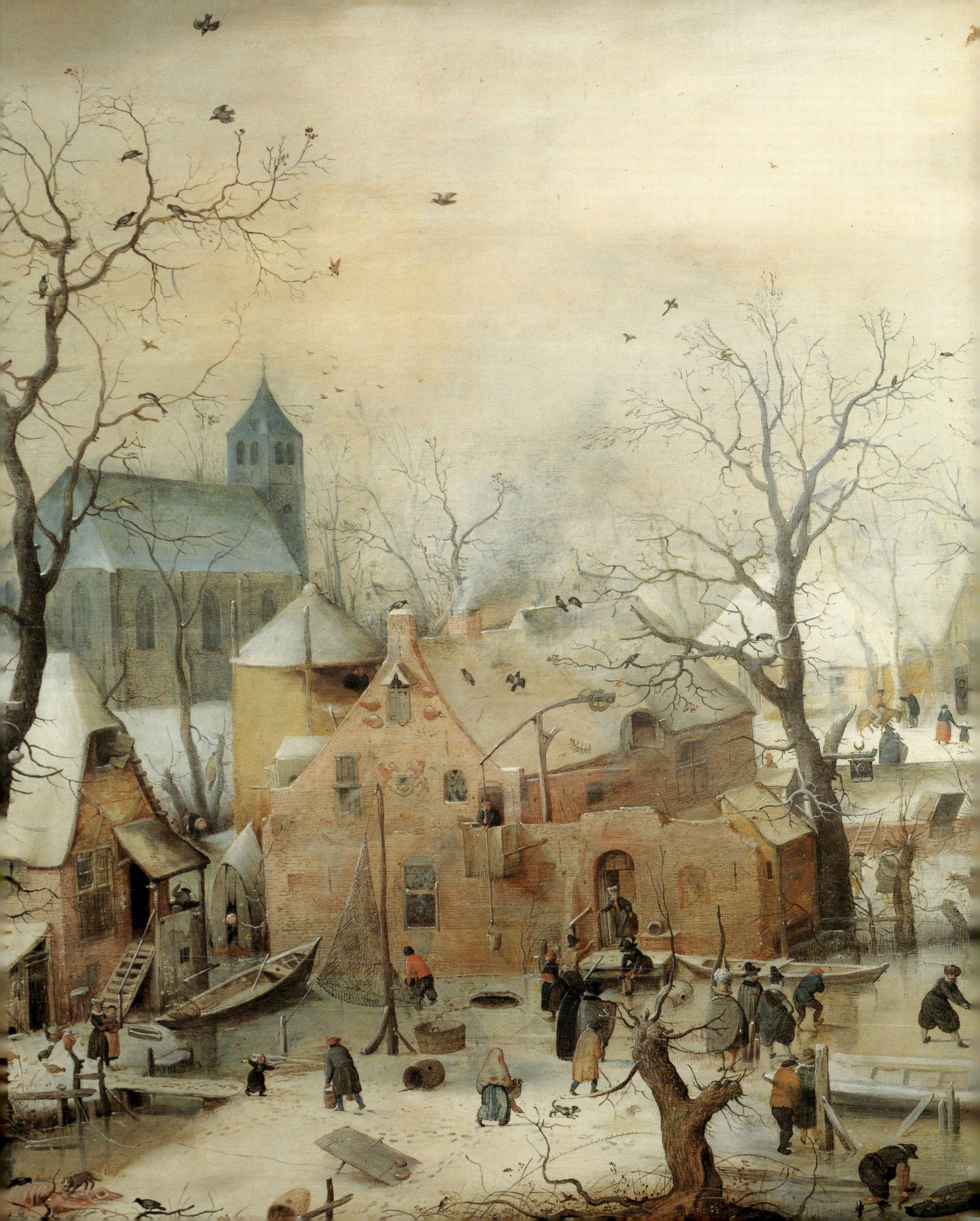

Hendrick Avercamp (Amsterdam 1585-Kampen 1634)

6 *Winter landscape with skaters, c. 1609*

Oil on panel, 77.5 x 132 cm
At right on the wooden shed: *HAENRICVS AV* (*HA* in ligature)
Purchased in 1897 with the aid of the Vereniging Rembrandt
Inv. no. SK-A-1718

Hendrick Avercamp was one of the first Dutch painters to specialise in a particular genre. By 1610 he had discovered the world of the winter landscape, which he always depicted with a hazy vista in the distance, the weather not too cold to prevent scores of people coming outdoors to indulge in winter pastimes. The large painting in the Rijksmuseum is one of his earliest works, and must have been painted shortly before 1610. He chose a high horizon, which enabled him to include the buildings on either side of the frozen river or waterway as well as a mass of people, from carefree skaters to miserable wretches scrabbling for the basic necessities of life. Avercamp arranged the buildings superbly, with farmhouses to the left and right of the frozen water, the Halve Maan (Half Moon) inn on the left with a haystack and the village church beyond, and in the middle distance a small castle. The recession into depth is subtly controlled by two elements running parallel to the picture plane: the narrow rowing-boat in the foreground, and further off the wooden posts marking the course of the now icebound ferry. The balanced distribution of the figures and buildings across the whole width of the picture is typical of Avercamp's early work. Later in his career he devoted more attention to the figures, for which he often made closely observed studies before inserting them in far more tautly organised compositions. The odd way of rendering reflections in the ice, many of which are indicated with delicate, horizontal dashes, also shows that this is an early work. Another strange feature is the high hill in the background with a windmill perched on top—a distinctly alien element in a scene which is otherwise so very Dutch. It is evidence that the young artist was still searching for his form.

Pieter Bruegel the Elder is often cited as the source of inspiration for this painting, and rightly so. Bruegel, too, employed a high horizon in order to give himself as much space as possible for his children's

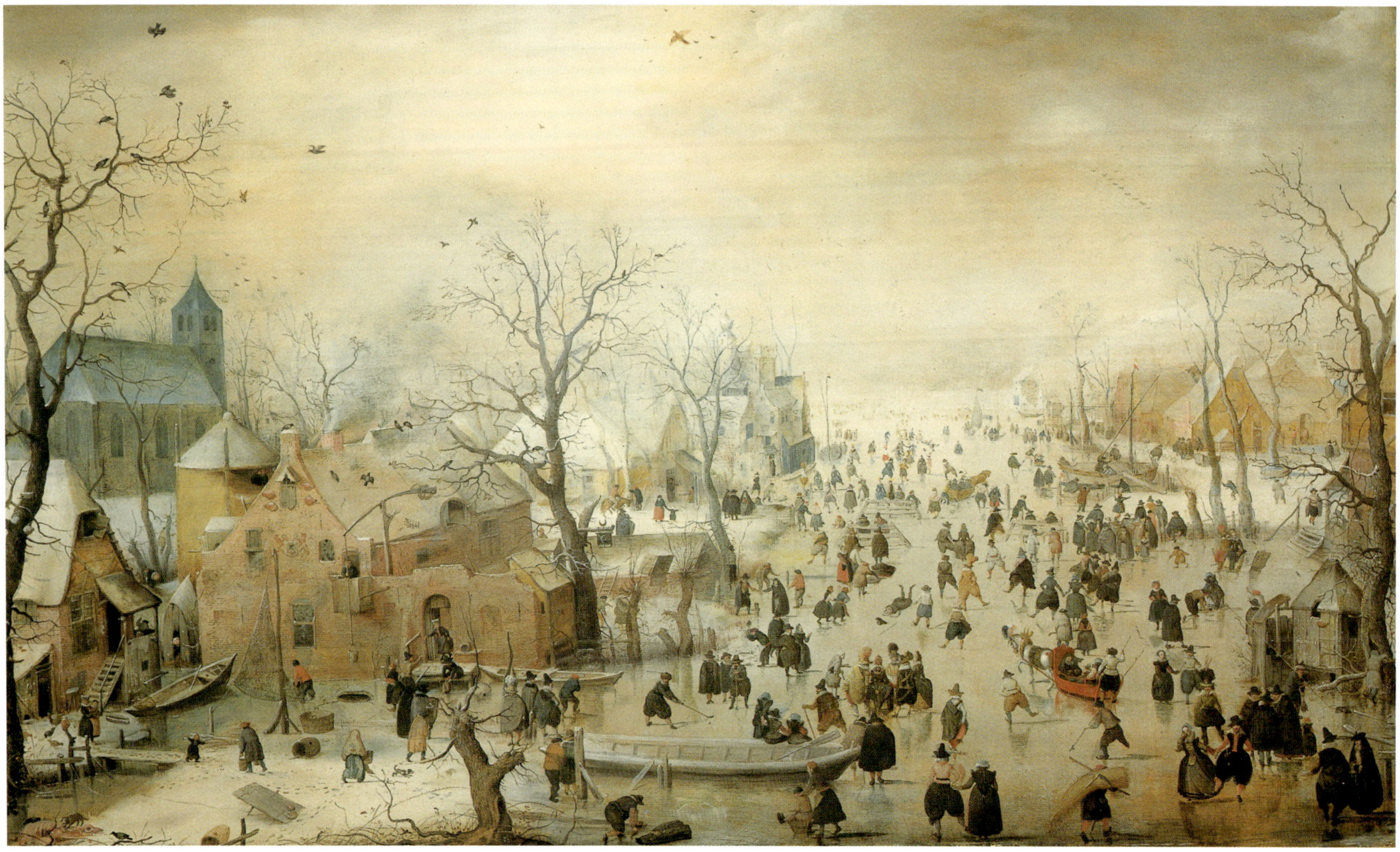

games, for instance, or for his proverbs, or for a Flemish winter landscape with the Massacre of the Innocents. Avercamp also borrowed the splendid, silhouetted trees from Bruegel, along with the motif of the bird-trap—the old door in the left foreground propped up on a stick tied to a piece of string, under which food has been scattered [*6a*]. It is not certain how the model for this reached Avercamp. Bruegel's painting dates from 1565, but Avercamp could also have seen this detail in a work by Pieter Brueghel the Younger, who painted several repetitions of his father's composition. The earliest of them dates from 1601, not long before Avercamp presented his own view of winter in this painting. The elder Bruegel died in 1569, when his sons were still very young children. The work of both Pieter Brueghel the Younger and Hendrick Avercamp belongs to the artistic fashion usually referred to as the Bruegel Revival.

LITERATURE

Exhib. cat. Amsterdam/Boston/Philadelphia 1987-88, no. 5; exhib. cat. Amsterdam 1993-94, no. 305

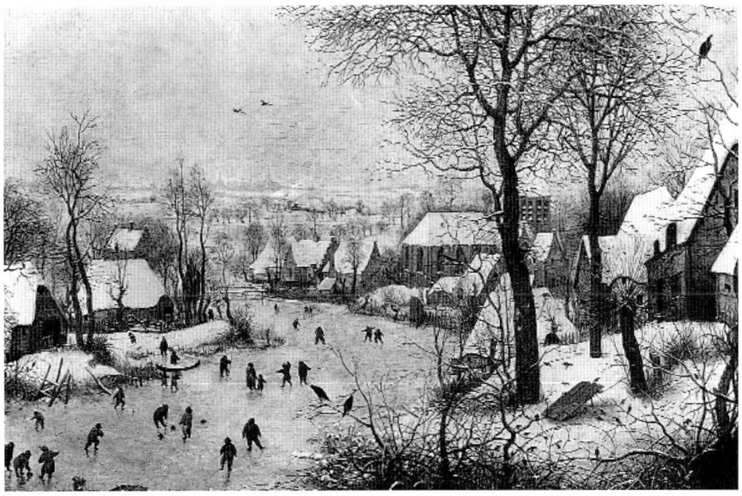

6a Pieter Bruegel the Elder, *Winter landscape with skaters and bird-trap*, 1565; oil on panel, 38 x 56 cm. Brussels, Koninklijke Musea voor Schone Kunsten

Adriaen van de Venne (Delft 1589-The Hague 1662)

7 *The harbour of Middelburg, 1615*

Oil on panel, 64 x 134 cm
At lower centre: *AV VENNE 1615* (*AV* in ligature)
Bequeathed in 1898 by D. Franken Dz
Inv. no. SK-A-1775

Historically important events are not always recognised as such by contemporary observers, just as developments considered momentous at the time are downgraded by later generations. Historians were writing back in classical times, with varying degrees of awareness of their own bias, but the visual depiction of historical events only began in the Renaissance, and became increasingly commonplace in the 17th century. Initially attention focused on battles and peace treaties, but then the repertoire was expanded with subjects from a mythical past which were believed to be true, such as the breaking of the chains across the mouth of the port of Damietta by crusader ships from Haarlem, or the story of the Batavian insurrection against the Romans. In 17th-century Dutch art there are quite a few sea and land battles, as well as a number of receptions or departures of important personages. Some events were portrayed remarkably soon after they had happened, but in other cases there were considerable delays. For instance, the Battle of Gibraltar in 1607 was regarded as the turning-point of the Dutch struggle against Spain, but most of the depictions date from many years later.

The painting by Adriaen van de Venne, commonly known as *The harbour of Middelburg*, records an event which was certainly considered important at the time, but unfortunately we are not sure what it was. For a long time it was thought to be the departure of Elector Frederick V of the Palatine in 1613, but a few years ago it was suggested that it was the departure of the English governor of Vlissingen, Den Briel and Fort Rammekens in 1616. The latter theory was demolished soon after it was launched when the painting was restored and its date was revealed as 1615. Since then, the elector's departure in 1613 leads the field as the most likely subject.

Frederick's visit to Middelburg was certainly regarded as a festive occasion by the Zeelanders at the time, but today most people are unaware of the historical context. During the Twelve Years' Truce, King James I of England tried to strengthen the ties with several continental powers. As part of his diplomatic offensive he bestowed the Order of the Garter on Prince Maurits of the Netherlands and Elector Frederick of the Palatine. Maurits's duties prevented him from travelling to London to attend the ceremony, and Frederick received the insignia in his stead. Frederick sailed back to Middelburg, where he was welcomed by Maurits, who was his uncle. Maurits had a special connection with the province of Zeeland. His main role in the province of Holland was as commander-in-chief of the

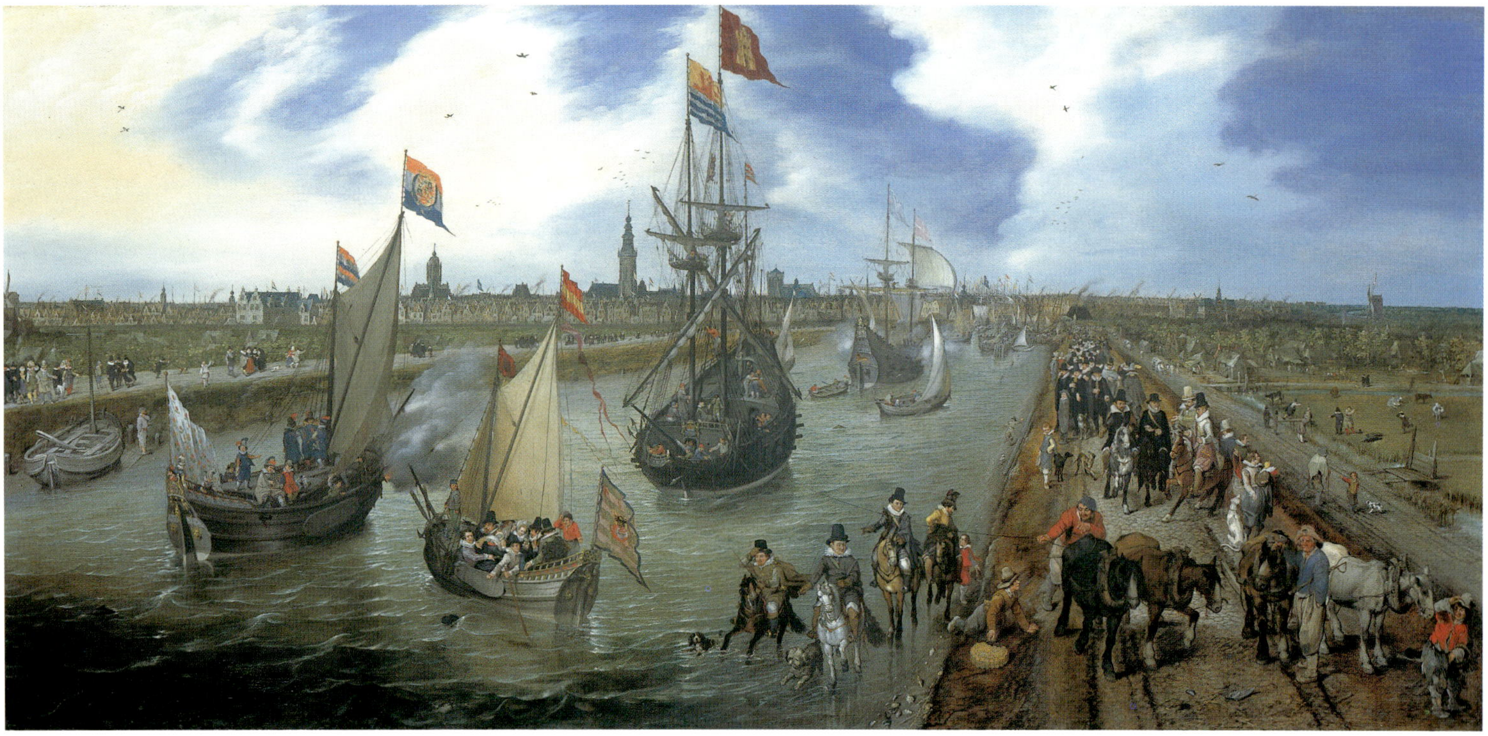

Republic's army, but in Zeeland he was also the Marquess of Veere and Vlissingen. There, in other words, he was not just the highest-ranking military officer but also the premier noble. Receiving the Order of the Garter represented international recognition both for him and for Zeeland.

In addition to depicting a historical event, *The harbour of Middelburg* tells us a surprising amount about 17th-century life. There are vessels of every description on the water, some of them rendered in great detail. There is the graceful skyline of Middelburg itself, and on the right Van de Venne provides a glimpse of land management with a view of a 17th-century polder. Above all else, though, there is the cross-section of the population of the city, from the highest to the lowest: grand gentlemen on horseback, beggars, horse-drivers and boys throwing stones into the water. This motley array is channelled into a disciplined compositional scheme by the taut lines of the embankments running beside the waterway.

At the beginning of his career, Van de Venne was a follower of the famous Antwerp painter Jan Brueghel, who painted landscapes with views of villages in addition to the flower still lifes for which he is famous. A slightly earlier painting shows Van de Venne still working entirely in Brueghel's style [*7a*]. The special feature of the works he made between 1614 and 1620 is that he turns the landscape into a vehicle for historical scenes. His most notable work in this respect is *Fishing for souls* (*fig.* 85) in the Rijksmuseum. *The harbour of Middelburg* unites landscape, cityscape, genre scene and historical event in a surprisingly matter-of-fact way.

LITERATURE

Bol 1989, pp. 50-53; Kluiver 1995

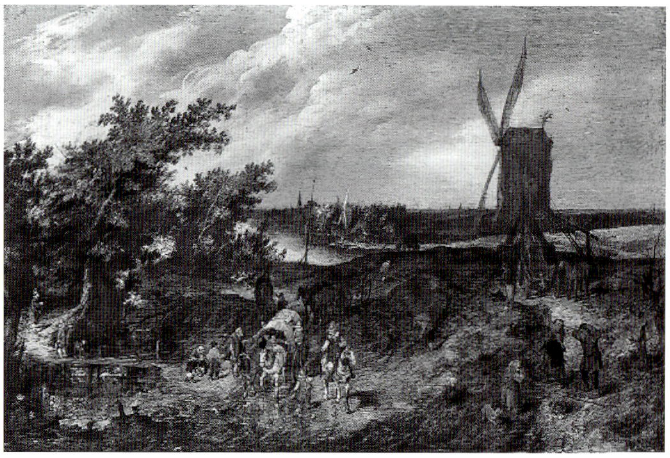

7a Adriaen van de Venne, *Summer landscape*, 1614; oil on panel, 42.2 x 68 cm. Berlin, Staatliche Museen, Preussischer Kulturbesitz

Esaias van de Velde (Amsterdam 1587-The Hague 1630)

8 *The ferryboat, 1622*

Oil on panel, 61.5 x 113 cm
At lower right: *E.V. VELDE 1622*
Purchased in 1885
Inv. no. SK-A-1293

Ferryboats feature in many 17th-century Dutch paintings. In landscapes by Jan van Goyen and Salomon van Ruysdael (the Rijksmuseum has a painting by each with a ferryboat) they are often present almost as a matter of course. It is to this motif that this painting owes its popular name, which it has had since it entered the museum. The artist has graphically illustrated the crossing of this stretch of water. The boat is being poled along by ferrymen and contains travellers, two cows, and a horse hitched to a two-wheeled cart. People are waiting on both banks, a rider is heading off out of the picture, and there is the customary inn. However, the painting's attraction lies not in the almost systematic depiction of the activities associated with a river crossing, which are all parallel to the picture plane. It is to the view into the distance, the stretch of the Dutch countryside, that the painting rightly owes its fame. The eye is led from the inn with the tall tree in the left foreground to the landing-stage on the far bank, which is also beside a tall tree, and then back across to the other side where a small church and a mill are reflected in the water.

The entire scene is executed in a restrained palette of earth colours, saturated green, with some blue and whitish pink tints for the sky and the mirror-smooth water. This muted colour scheme and the broad, panoramic format of the painting has become more pronounced since a strip at the top some 14 centimetres wide [*8a*]was covered over by a new frame, possibly in 1988. It consists chiefly of sky and is not autographed, but was very probably added late in the 17th century. This also shows that the original horizon was not set low down at all but was in fact quite high

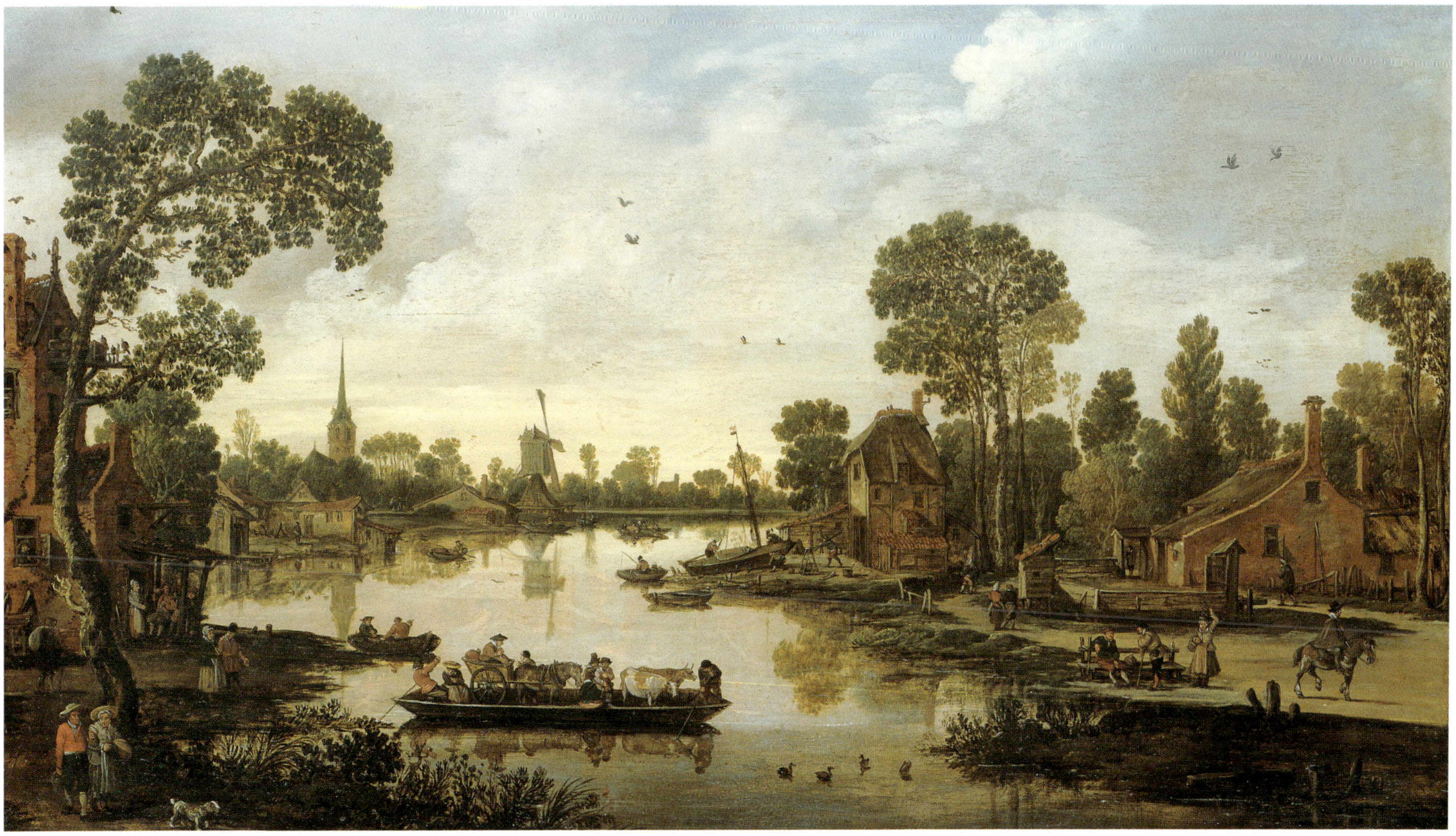

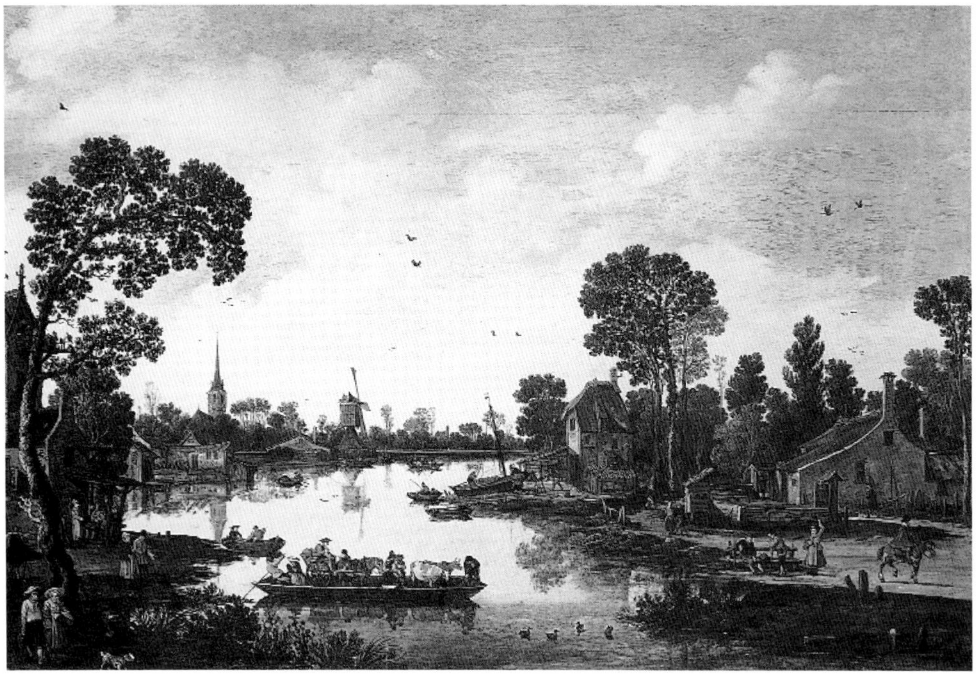

8a *The ferryboat* with the 14 cm strip of blue sky added to the top in the 17th century

in order to show as much as possible of life in this corner of the countryside.

The ferryboat has often been cited as an early example of the love that Dutch painters had for their own country, as the prototype of the painted Dutch landscape. The amazing beauty of peaceful water in this boggy but very green landscape—water, moreover, in which the world is reflected and across which the boat is being sedately punted—shows that the artist had discovered the beauty of his own surroundings. This becomes all the more apparent when one compares this landscape with the lush fantasies painted before this period, such as Joos de Momper's *River landscape with wild boar hunt*, which can be dated around 1610 [8b]. Yet there is a sense of detachment about the scene, and that is precisely because of the rather high vantage point. It is as if the viewer first has to get past the ferryboat in order to appreciate all the beauty of the Dutch countryside. In its sweep the painting also differs from the extremely simple drawings and prints of the Dutch landscape that were so popular in the second decade of the century. Comparison with an etching by Claes Jansz Visscher [9] makes it clear that the direct approach is indissolubly bound up with a certain simplicity of motifs and composition. Van de Velde himself excelled in small, uncluttered works. Their compression is well illustrated by his *Dune landscape* of 1629—a little painting in which even nothing is too much, a small masterpiece of simplicity. Van de Velde created a complex masterpiece with his *Ferryboat* in which he may not have done full justice to the essence of his talents but in which he demonstrates that he can draw the viewer irresistibly into the world of the Dutch lowlands of his day.

LITERATURE

Exhib. cat. Amsterdam/Boston/Philadelphia 1987-88, no. 106

8b Joos de Momper, *River landscape with wild boar hunt*, c. 1610; oil on panel, 61.5 x 113 cm. Amsterdam, Rijksmuseum

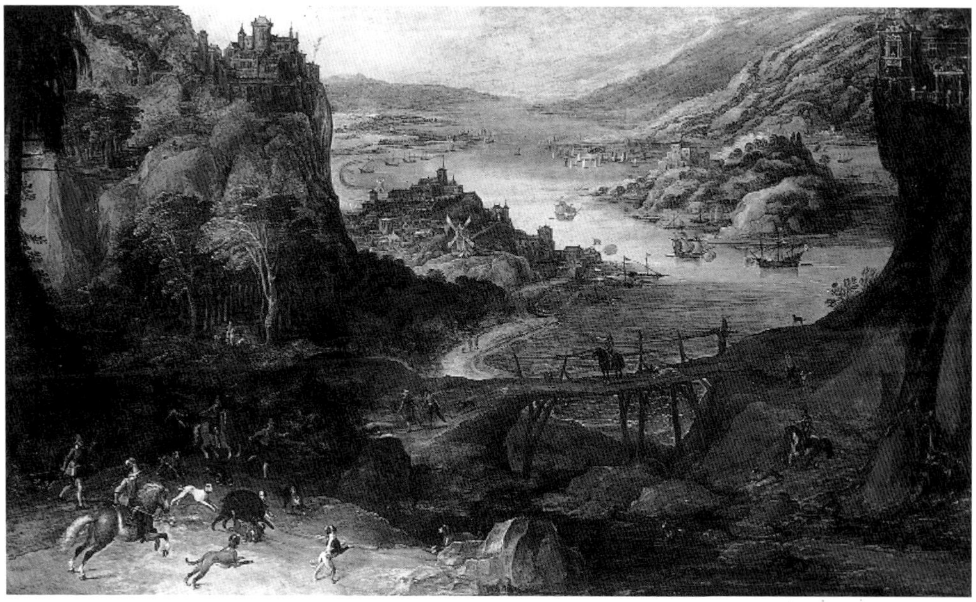

Claes Jansz Visscher (Amsterdam 1586/87-Amsterdam 1652)

9 *Jan Deyman's country house and orchard, c. 1608-1609*

Etching, first state of five, 15 × 20.8 cm
From the second state, in the lower left corner: *CIV*
Purchased in 1888
Inv. no. RP-P-1888-A-12755

Claes Jansz Visscher started out as an etcher working for various print publishers, making prints after designs by David Vinckboons and other artists, as well as helping in the production of maps. He was also a keen draughtsman whose early drawings are related to those by Vinckboons, both in the types of figure and rendering of the countryside. His landscapes, however, soon became more open and simpler in their composition under the influence of a series of 16th-century etched views of peasant villages based on drawings by the so-called Master of the Small Landscapes. In 1612 Visscher actually copied those landscapes in etchings which he published with a title page attributing the designs to Pieter Bruegel. That series played a key role in the development of the direct, faithful depiction of the Dutch countryside, to which Visscher's own drawings and etchings made an important contribution.

While out on his drawing expeditions, Visscher must often have found himself near the country estate of the Amsterdam merchant Jan Lamberts Deyman depicted in this etching. It probably lay to the west of Amsterdam on the Spaarndammerdijk or the Haarlemmerweg. He also drew the estate from another angle using the same

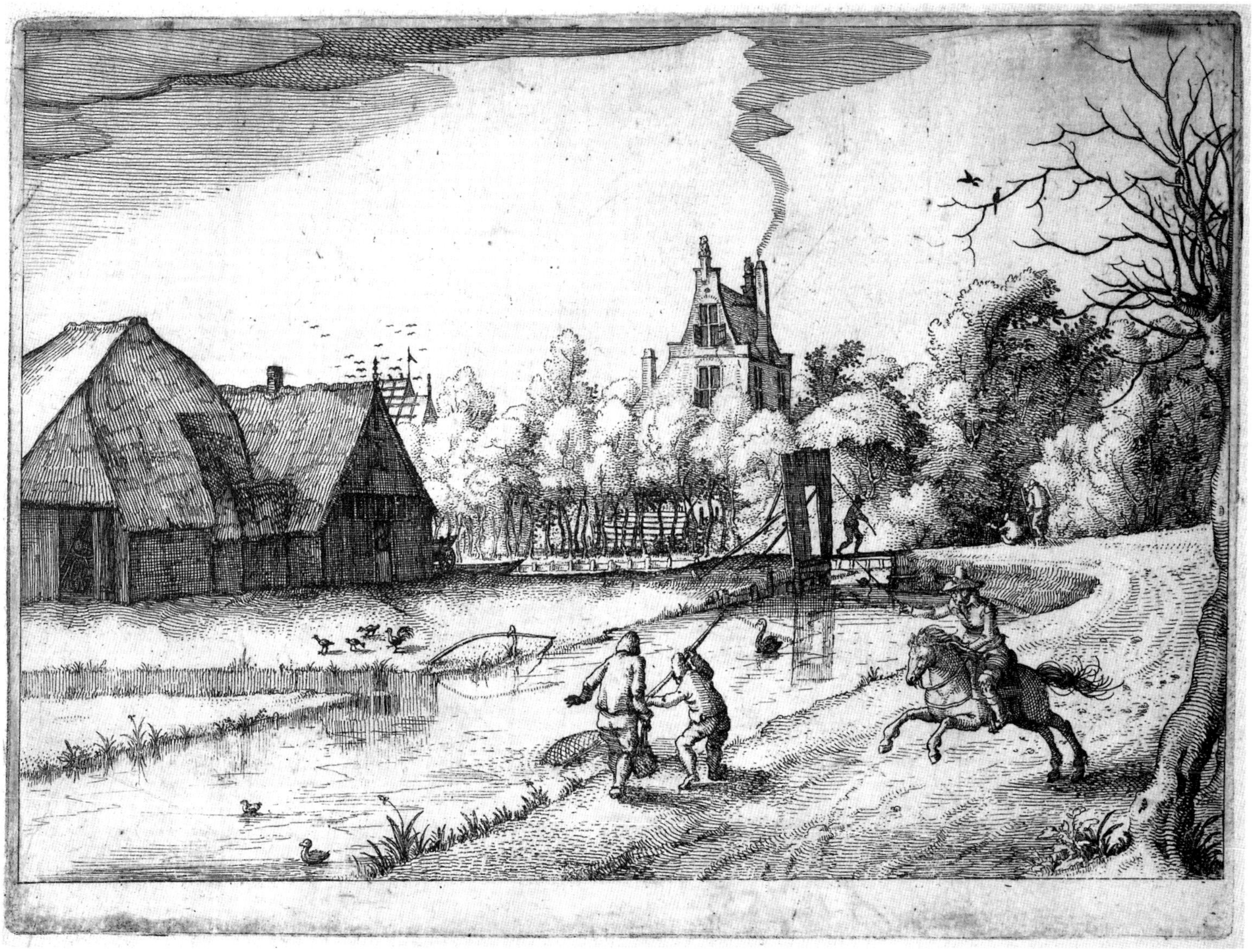

technique as the preparatory study for this print: pen and brown ink with a grey wash [9a]. The etching is in the same direction as the drawing, so Visscher evidently felt it important to produce a print that was topographically accurate. The drawing also helped him with the correct distribution of light and shade and with details like the gateway and the thatched roofs on the left. The careful drawing was probably made with the print in mind, for another one done with the pen over a black chalk sketch is in a far freer, almost calligraphic style [9b].

Visscher enlivened the etching by populating the landscape with all sorts of figures and poultry. The two fishermen may be an allusion to his name—a visual pun which he often included in his landscapes. He borrowed the horseman from a free etching by Antonio Tempesta, an Italian artist much admired in the Low Countries, in a series which he had copied in 1609.

This is a proof impression, *avant la lettre*. Visscher published it in 1612 as one of a suite of six prints, adding his monogram and the identification of the location: 'IANDAIMEN BOGAERDT, Onderweghe[n] SLOTERDYCK'.

LITERATURE

Hollstein 195; Meischke 1978, p. 105; exhib. cat. Amsterdam 1993-94, no. 325; cat. Amsterdam 1998, under no. 393

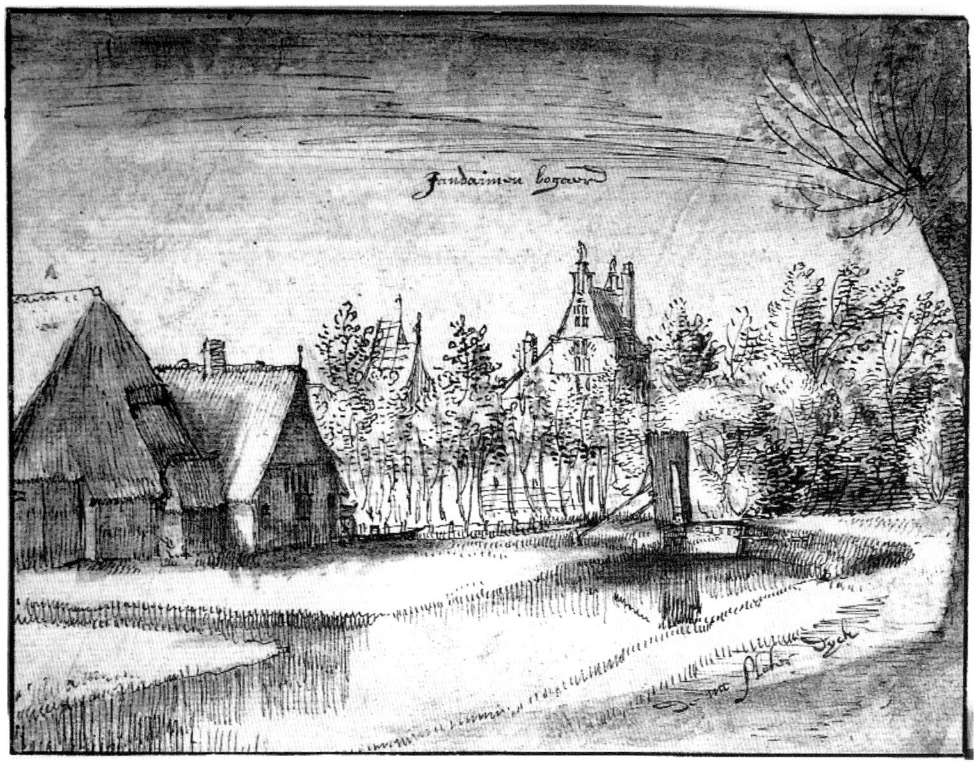

9a Claes Jansz Visscher, *Jan Deyman's country house and orchard*, c. 1608; pen in brown, grey wash, 14.4 x 19.1 cm. Haarlem, Rijksarchief

9b Claes Jansz Visscher, *Jan Deyman's country house*, c. 1608; pen in brown over a sketch in black chalk, 10.8 x 16.4 cm. Paris, Fondation Custodia (F. Lugt Collection)

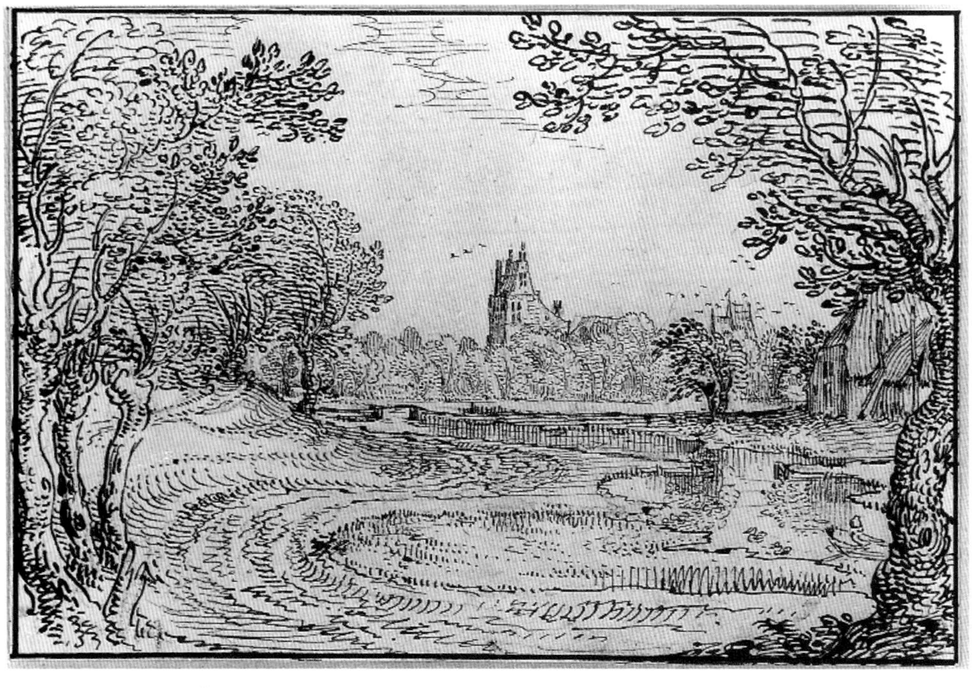

Hercules Segers (Haarlem 1589/90-The Hague between 1633 and 1638)

10 *Mountain valley with fenced fields, c. 1620-1630*

Etching and drypoint, in blue on white paper, brush in pink and blue,
second state of two, 22.2 x 48.3 cm
From the collection of Pieter Cornelis, Baron van Leyden; purchased by King Louis Napoleon in 1807 and transferred to the Rijksmuseum in 1816 after a period in the Koninklijke Bibliotheek in The Hague
Inv. no. RP-P-OB-840

From time to time one comes across a 17th-century evocation of an artist's qualities which really hits the nail on the head. One such comes in Samuel van Hoogstraeten's account of Hercules Segers: 'of a reliable and firm attentiveness, assured in his drawing of landscapes and terrains, pleasing in elegant mountains and grottoes, and pregnant of whole provinces, to which he gave birth along with boundless spaces'.

It is very possible that Van Hoogstraeten got to know Segers's art in the house of his teacher Rembrandt, for the inventory of the latter's possessions shows that he had quite a few of Segers's works in his collection. Rembrandt must have been fascinated by the unusual, experimental nature of Segers's prints and his capricious paintings, although few people shared that interest, according to Van Hoogstraeten. Segers is believed to have died completely destitute, and his art only came to be appreciated after his pitiful death. In 1678, when Van Hoogstraeten's book appeared, that was already a fact.

Segers's etchings occupy a relatively isolated position in 17th-century printmaking. They are printed in colour (often on prepared paper) and are worked up with the brush, which turns them almost into paintings. The texture of the paper of this *Mountain valley with fenced fields* makes it look as if it was printed on canvas, an effect which Segers probably achieved by putting a piece of linen in the press along with the paper, as was done by some 16th-century artists for chiaroscuro woodcuts. Segers reduced the cut of his compositions for each impression and coloured them differently. There are five other impressions of this particular etching, each one differing from the others in some way. All six are trimmed within the platemark, and all are in different colours. Van Hoogstraeten was probably referring to this practice when he spoke of Segers's approach as 'printing paintings'. The copperplate must have measured at least 28.6 x 51.6 cm, which happens to be almost the size of one of his paintings.

The world Segers depicted is decidedly outlandish. He dreamed up unusual structures and was inventive in the creation of tone. Sometimes he deliberately left excess ink on the plate, in other cases he added accents with the brush. Here the rocky

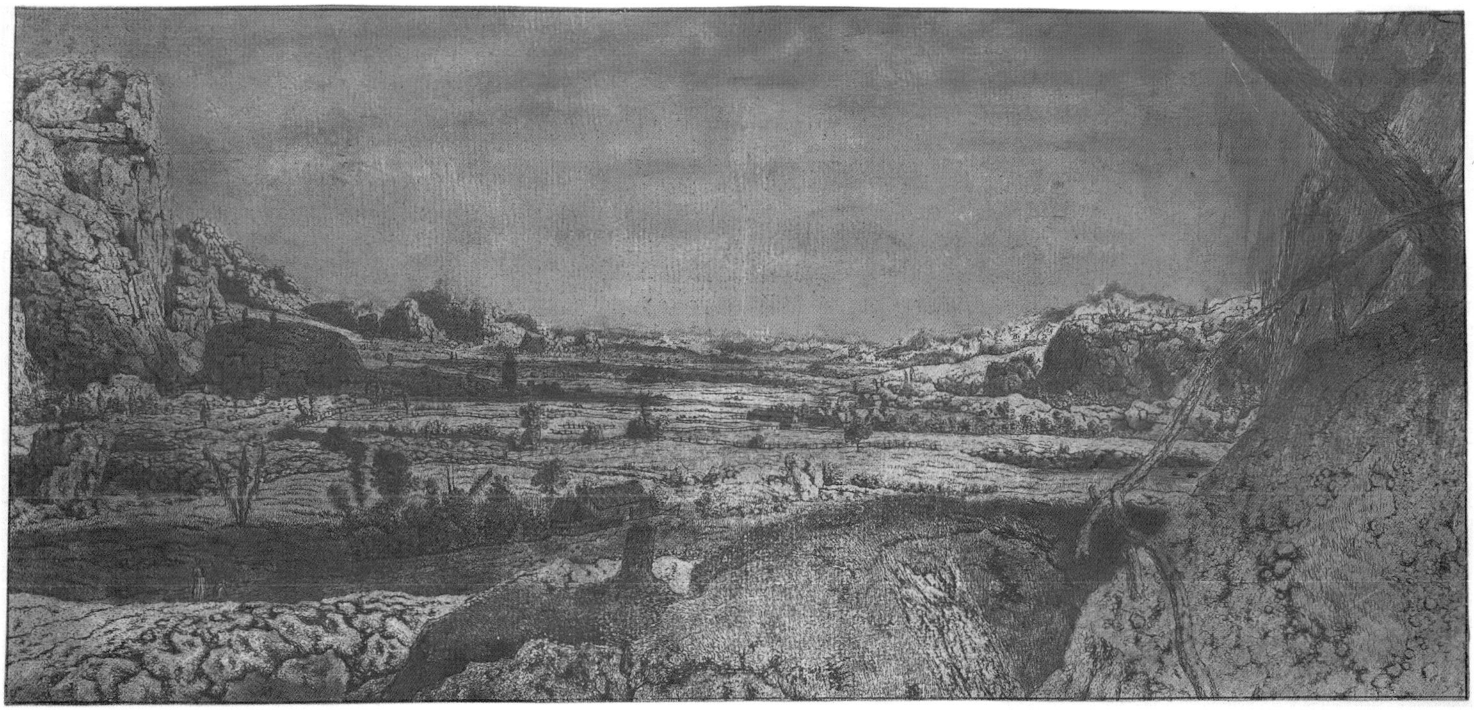

ground has a nervous pattern which most closely resembles the surface of the brain. The visionary landscape is not completely desolate. On the left there are two figures walking, and traces of habitation can be found throughout the scene. The viewpoint is high, with the result that we appear to be descending a mountainside on a path with a wooden rail running beside it. Our eyes are drawn almost 'a whole province' into the scene, and once again the artist demonstrated his ability to 'give birth to boundless spaces'.

The extent to which Segers transformed impressions taken from the same copperplate in order to make them unique is shown by a comparison of this atmospheric sheet, which has been worked up in various ways, with an impression in black ink on snowy white paper that was cropped far higher up, just below the platemark [10a].

LITERATURE

Hollstein 6; Haverkamp Begemann 1973, no. 6 IId; exhib. cat. Amsterdam 1993-94, no. 347; exhib. cat. Amsterdam 2000c, no. 41

10a Hercules Segers, *Mountain valley with fenced fields*, c. 1620-1630; etching in black ink, framing lines with the brush in grey, 28.6 x 47.3 cm. London, British Museum

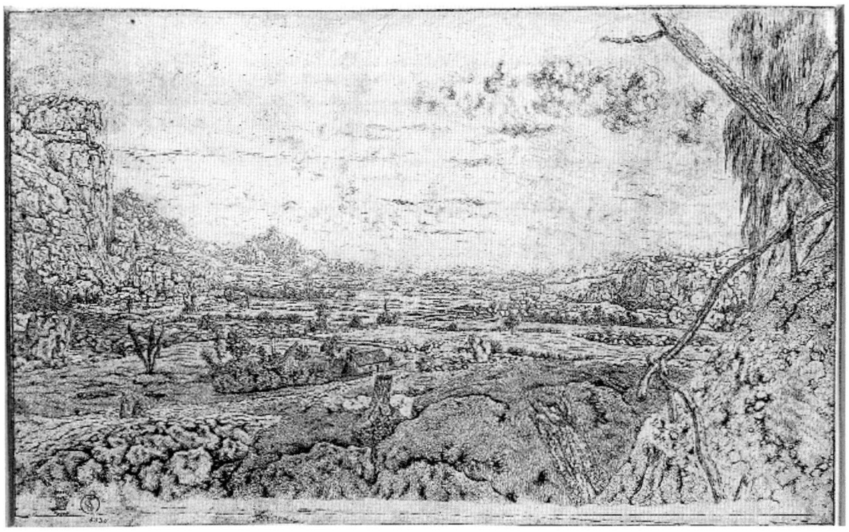

Pieter Lastman (Amsterdam 1583-Amsterdam 1633)

11 *Orestes and Pylades disputing at the altar, 1614*

Oil on panel, 83 x 126 cm
On the altar: *Pietro Lastman fecit 1614*
In various collections, including those of Reinier van der Wolf (1657-1676), Jan Six (1702) and G.G. Taets van Amerongen (1805); purchased in 1908 with the aid of the Vereniging Rembrandt
Inv. no. SK-A-2354

Pieter Lastman was in Italy from 1602 to 1607, and like many artists who went there he was doubtless impressed not only by the remnants of classical civilisation but also by the large history paintings by 16th-century Italian masters. He was also inspired by the small cabinet paintings of the German painter Adam Elsheimer (1578-1610), who worked in Italy. All these influences come together in *Orestes and Pylades disputing at the altar*. In addition to such obvious classical motifs as the rotunda in the background there is the many-figured composition itself, in which Lastman reduced the large-scale Italian model to a smaller format midway between a large Italian history piece and an Elsheimer cabinet picture. Although executed several years after his return from Italy, he signed it with the signature he had used there: Pietro Lastman.

Orestes, son of the hero Agamemnon, was accompanied by his loyal friend Pylades on an expedition to Tauris to steal a statue of the goddess Artemis and bring it back to Greece. They were taken prisoner before they could do so, and it was decreed that one of them was to be sacrificed to Artemis. Each was prepared to die to save the other, and that is the moment depicted here. To the left of the altar the two young men are outdoing each other in nobility of character. Iphigenia, high priestess of the temple dedicated to Artemis, stands in the right foreground holding a letter which the one who escaped death was to take back to Argos. The statue of Artemis is being borne in procession in the background. The story goes on to relate how Iphigenia realised at the last moment that Orestes was her brother, and with a ruse the three of them managed to escape, taking the statue with them.

Lastman's contemporaries undoubtedly recognised his skill in depicting stories of this kind. His convincing portrayal of the emotions of the heroes would have gained him a reputation as a good history painter. Rembrandt, who was his pupil for a while, later overshadowed him completely in this respect, which may be one reason why Lastman, once so celebrated, faded into obscurity. There is an allusion to that fall from grace in a poem which Joachim Oudaen wrote about the painting around 1657, when it was in the collection of Reinier van der Wolf:

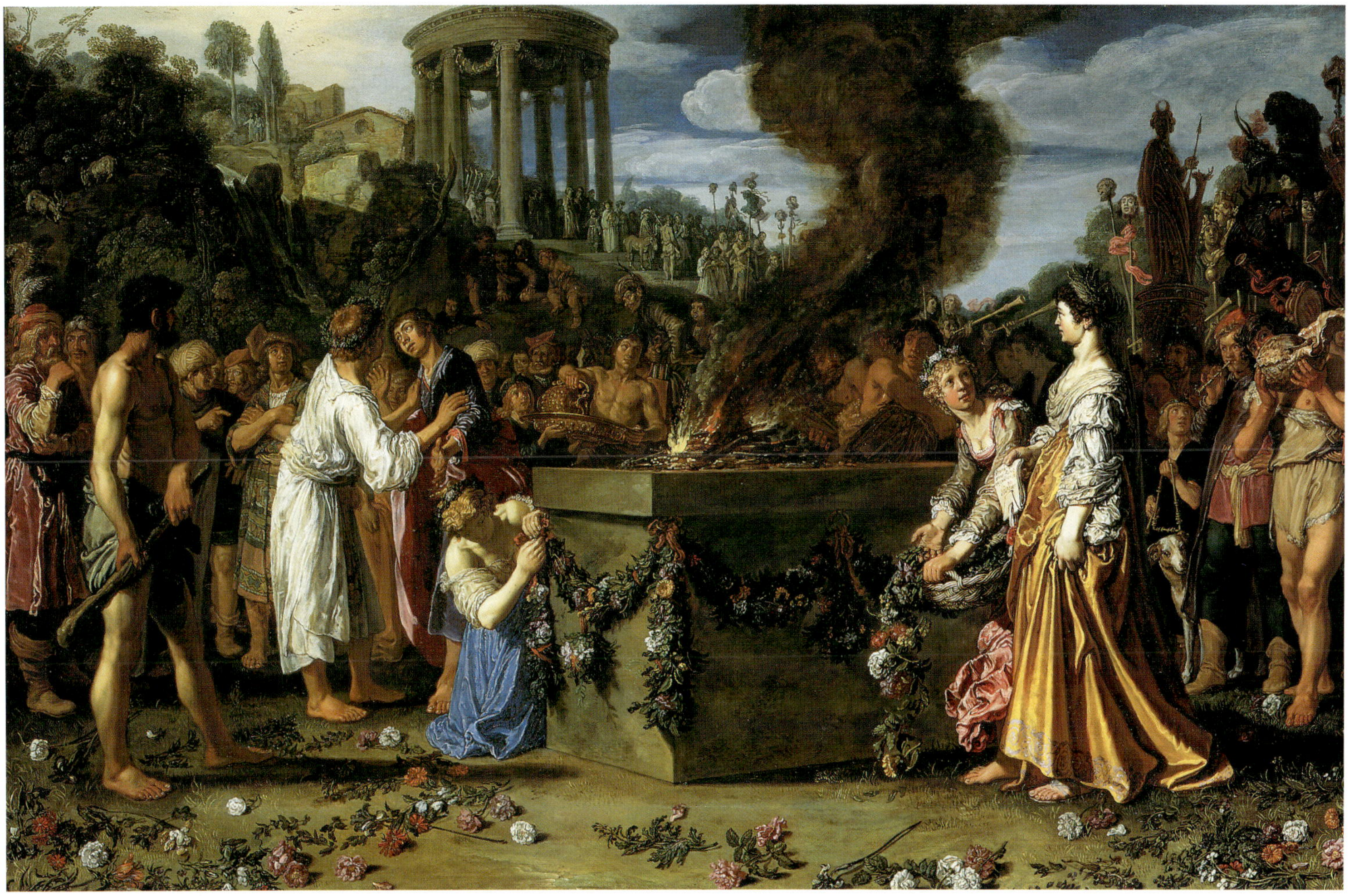

Van der Wolf, so wealthy in art,
Although oblivion overtook the name
Of this famed artist who so fitly
Painted the loyal rivalry with which
Two friends loved each other
To the point of death at the altar.

Oudaen also mentions a painting of the saints Paul and Barnabas at Lystra as being the companion piece of *Orestes and Pylades*, although by then it was in the collection of the Amsterdam merchant Jan Six [*11a*]. The two works certainly have the same dimensions, and are a match as regards subject and composition. Moreover, the Six painting is also dated 1614 and bears the same Italianised signature: 'Pietro Lastman'.

LITERATURE

Exhib. cat. Amsterdam 1991a, no. 7; exhib. cat. Amsterdam 1993-94, no. 248

11a Pieter Lastman, *Sts Paul and Barnabas at Lystra*, 1614; oil on panel, 89.6 x 123.6 cm. Present whereabouts unknown

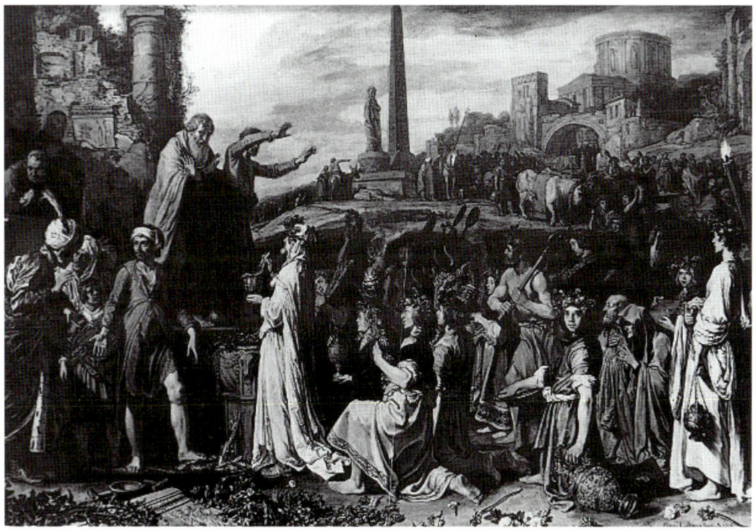

Hendrick Goltzius (Mühlbracht 1558-Haarlem 1617)

12 *Lot and his daughters, 1616*

Oil on canvas, 140 x 204 cm
At lower left: *HG 1616*
Acquired in 1976 with the aid of the Vereniging Rembrandt, the Rijksmuseum-Stichting, the G.H. van Sant Bequest and the Dutch government
Inv. no. SK-A-4866

Having gained an unrivalled reputation as an engraver, Hendrick Goltzius decided to try his hand at painting. He was over 40 when he struck out on this new path, and by the time he died on 1 January 1617 he had built up a sizable painted oeuvre. *Lot and his daughters* was completed just before his death.

Goltzius depicted the biblical story (Genesis 19: 16-18, 24-26, 30-38) in a remarkably evocative way. He shows Lot as a randy old man who cannot resist the temptations of drink and beautiful women. The artist concentrated on rendering the female nude in accordance with his own ideals of beauty, which are presented quite comprehensively in the figures of the two women. At the same time, he relates the story in a rather old-fashioned way as a simultaneous narrative, with different episodes combined in a single canvas. On the right are the burning cities of Sodom and Gomorrah, in the centre Lot's daughters are plying him with drink, and on the left they succeed in seducing him, which was the object of the exercise.

The story was well-known to Goltzius's contemporaries as a classic tale of disaster in which everything that can go wrong does so, even for those who had found favour with God. Lot, who was a nephew of Abraham's, lived with his wife and two daughters in Sodom, a sink of corruption like its twin city Gomorrah. They were so sinful that God decided to destroy them. In a preceding episode (Genesis 18), God had visited Abraham with two angels, and their conversation was of great importance for the story, and for the meaning of this painting. After hearing about the planned destruction of the two cities, Abraham asked how many righteous men had to live there if divine retribution was to be averted. God eventually agreed that the cities would be spared if ten righteous men could be found there. The two angels then went to Sodom, where they were received by Lot. It turned out that there were only four pious people there: Lot, his wife, and his two daughters. They were warned to leave the city, and above all not to look back. As they fled, Lot's wife could not resist the temptation to look, and was turned into a pillar of salt (on the far right in the painting, in front of the burning cities). In their refuge in the wilderness, Lot's daughters decided to seduce their father so that they would not remain childless. So even the last surviving inhabitants of Sodom and Gomorrah were not faithful to God. Their descendants, the Moabites and Ammonites, were to become involved in a war with Abraham's seed, the people of Israel.

Goltzius was not the kind of person to neglect the inner meaning of a work. This particular story, of course, contains very clear warnings: about disobedience to God,

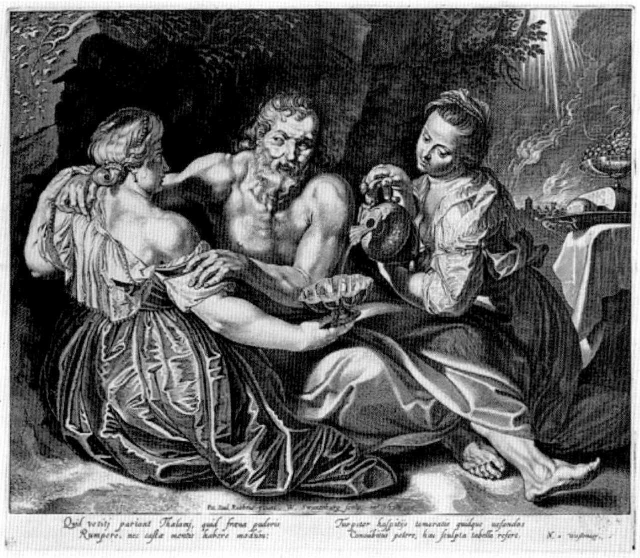

12a Willem van Swanenburg after Peter Paul Rubens, *Lot and his daughters*, 1612; engraving, 31.4 x 37.7 cm. Amsterdam, Rijksmuseum, Rijksprentenkabinet

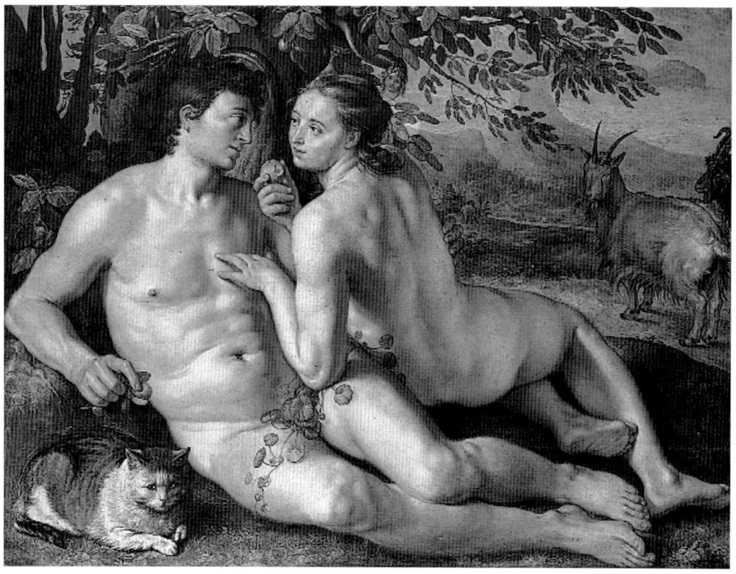

12b Hendrick Goltzius, *The Fall of Man*, 1616; oil on canvas, 104.5 x 138.5 cm. Washington, National Gallery of Art

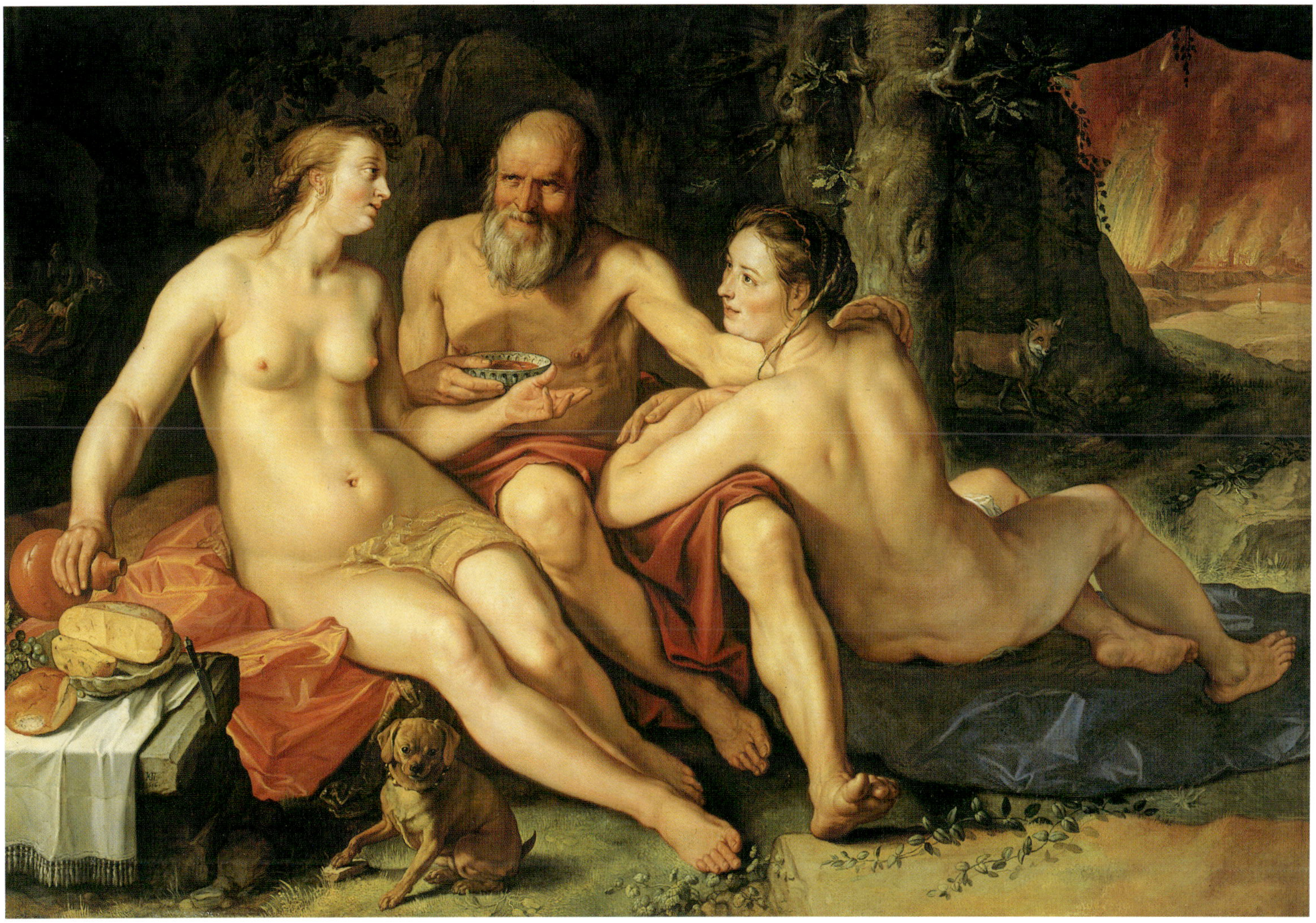

drunkenness, and the wiles of women. The animals in the painting highlight the aspects that Goltzius wanted to stress. The dog in the foreground stands for vigilance, for the lesson to be learned by sinful man when alerted by its barking. The fox in the background symbolises guile, in this case the wiliness of women against which man should be on his guard. Goltzius undoubtedly had yet another purpose, namely to perfect his skill at depicting the human body. His composition broadly follows that of a painting by Peter Paul Rubens, now in Schwerin, which was copied in a print by the Leiden engraver Willem van Swanenburg [*12a*]. Goltzius evidently saw few problems in following Rubens's design. By replacing the latter's clothed figures with imposing nudes he made it clear how he had improved on his model. The importance he must have attached to practice and improvement is demonstrated by a slightly smaller painting of 1616, *The Fall of Man* [*12b*], in which he placed Adam and Eve at the moment of temptation in exactly the same poses as Lot's two daughters. The simplification of the composition and the more pronounced confrontation of the ideals of male and female beauty suggest that the Washington painting was a further step in Goltzius's development.

LITERATURE

Van Thiel 1989a; exhib. cat. Amsterdam 1993-94, no. 217

Hendrick ter Brugghen (Utrecht or The Hague 1588-Utrecht 1629)

13 *Doubting Thomas, c. 1622*

Oil on canvas, 108.8 × 136.5 cm
Purchased in 1956
Inv. no. SK-A-3908

The most important of the Dutch artists who took their lead from Caravaggio (1573-1610) and his Roman followers at the beginning of the 17th century came from Utrecht. Gerard van Honthorst [14], Dirck van Baburen (c. 1595-1624) and Hendrick ter Brugghen, who came back to Utrecht in 1615 after spending years in Italy, were the leading lights of the Utrecht Caravaggisti, as they are known. What is remarkable, though, is that Caravaggio's influence on Ter Brugghen's work only reached its peak around 1620-1622. We can assume that the immediate success of paintings by Honthorst and Van Baburen, who returned from Rome in 1620 and 1621 respectively, renewed his interest in the work of the great Italian master.

It is clear, at any rate, that the *Doubting Thomas* is based squarely on Caravaggio's painting of the same subject, which is now in Potsdam but was then in the famed collection of the Marchese Giustiniani in

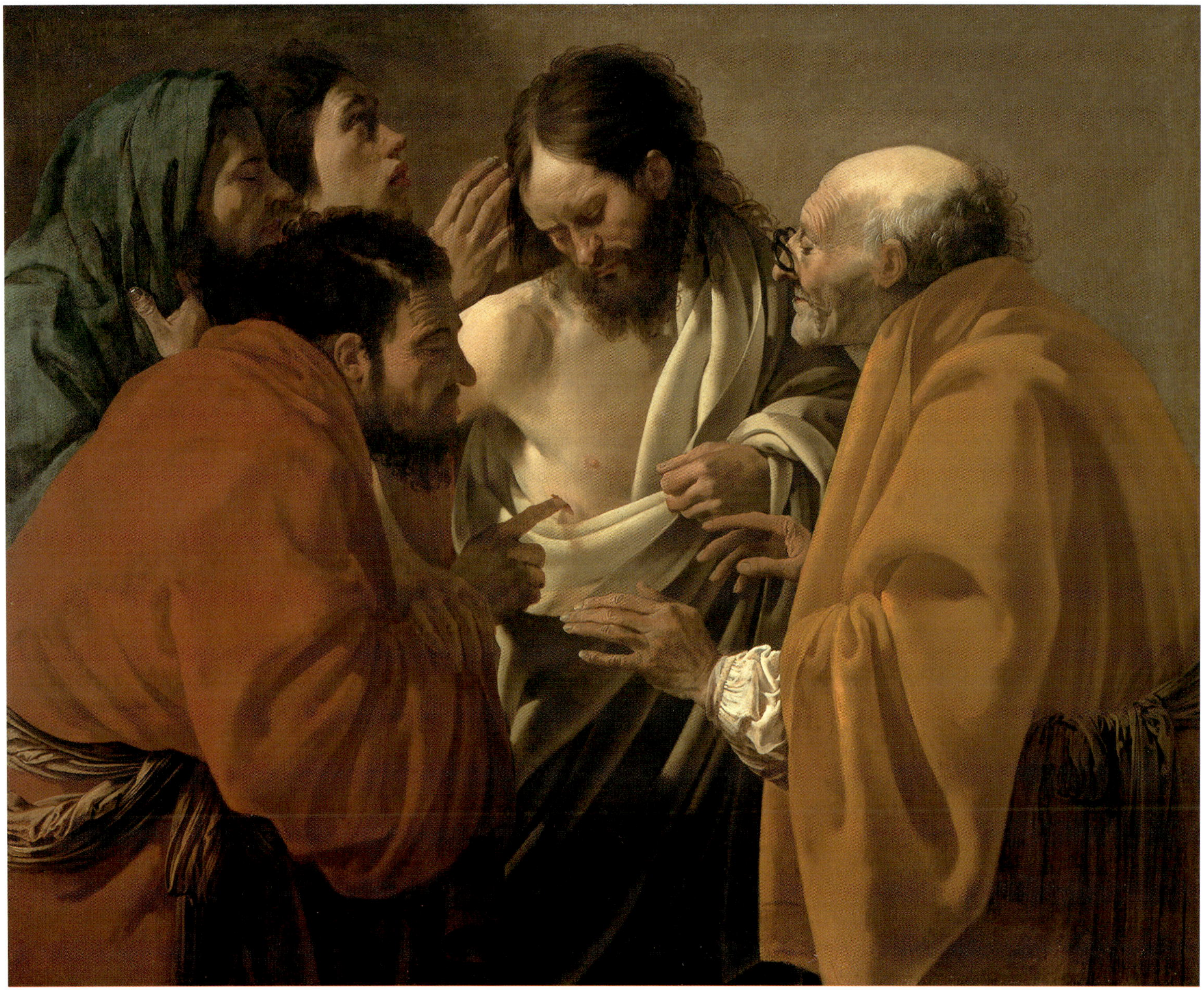

Rome. The composition, reversed left for right and comprising a few half-length figures, leaves little doubt about this borrowing. Like Caravaggio, Ter Brugghen concentrated on the subtle interplay of hands, which demands the viewer's attention. The apostle Thomas, whose hand has been clasped by Christ, pokes a finger in the wound in Christ's side in order to satisfy himself that it is indeed the risen Christ standing before him (John 20:24-29). Thomas had not been present when Christ first showed himself to his disciples, and refused to believe what they told him. Eight days later Christ again appeared, and this time the doubting Thomas was with them. Christ said: 'Reach hither thy hand, and thrust it into my side'.

When Rubens was on a diplomatic mission to the Dutch Republic in 1627 he visited several artists, in Utrecht and elsewhere, and is supposed to have said that he had met only one true painter in the whole country: Hendrick ter Brugghen. That was certainly not the prevailing view at the time, although today Ter Brugghen is indeed regarded as the greatest of the Caravaggisti. The muted pastel shades and the melting brushwork display his talent and exceptional feeling for colour to the full. The bespectacled old man on the right was Ter Brugghen's own invention. This secondary figure features in several of his works, and appears to have been borrowed from 16th-century, southern Netherlandish paintings in the manner of Marinus van Roemerswaele and Jan van Hemessen.

LITERATURE

Exhib. cat. Utrecht/Braunschweig 1986-87, no. 12; exhib. cat. San Francisco/Baltimore/London 1997-98, no. 5

Gerard van Honthorst (Utrecht 1590-Utrecht 1656)

14 *The merry fiddler, 1623*

Oil on canvas, 108 x 89 cm
In the centre, on the parapet: *GHonthorst. fe. 1623*
Purchased in 1824
Inv. no. SK-A-180

Leaving aside the obvious references to drink and music, the most eye-catching feature of this lively painting is the game that Honthorst is playing with the viewer with the aid of this troubadour. The artist has shattered the two-dimensional nature of the picture by fooling the viewer into believing that this merry figure has just

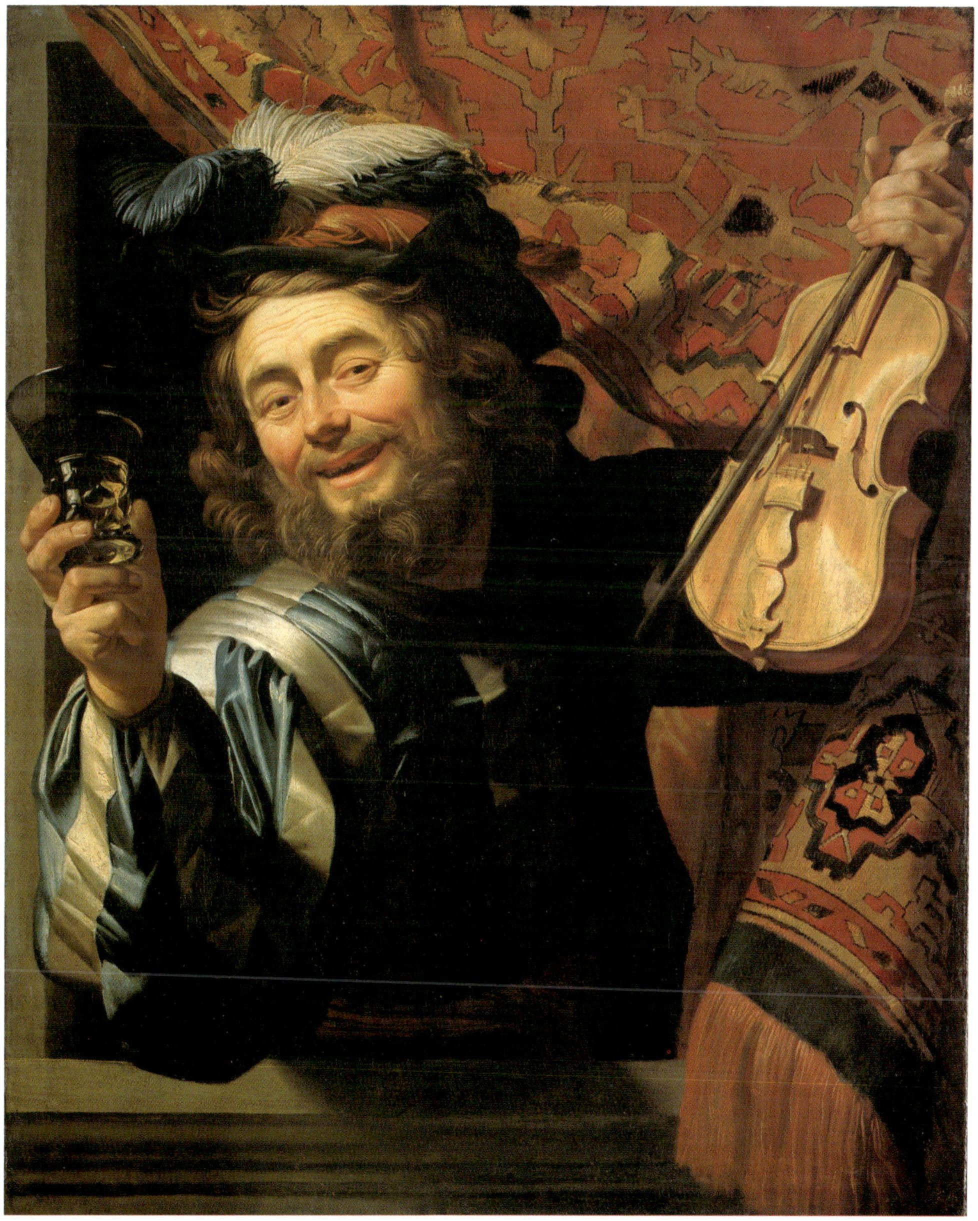

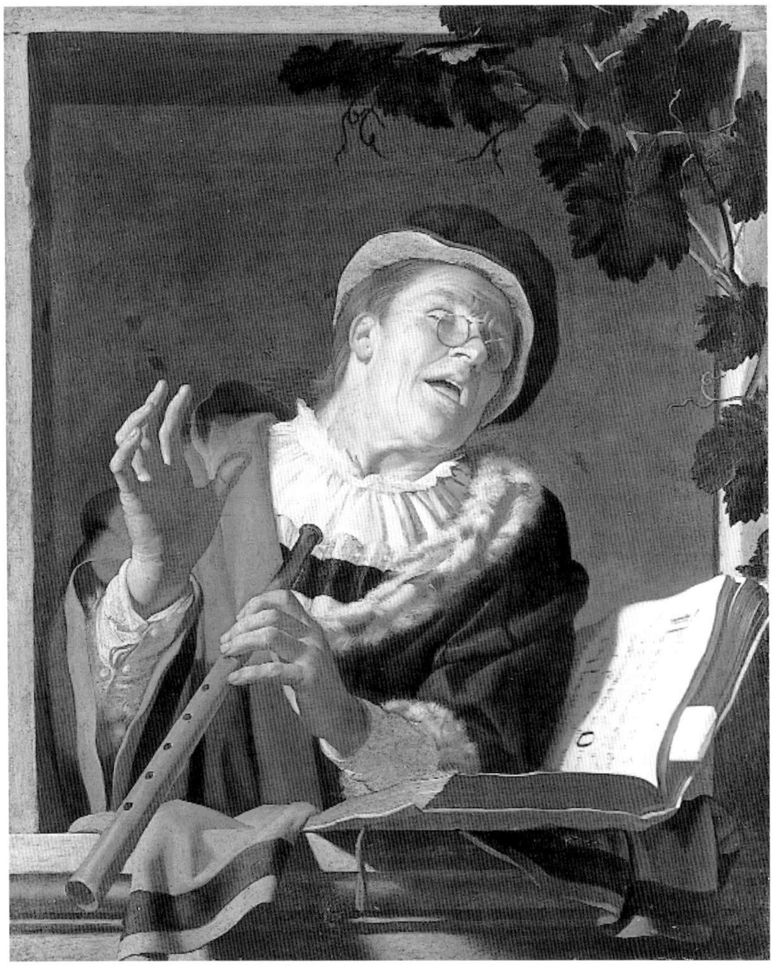

14a Gerard van Honthorst, *Flute player*, c. 1623; oil on canvas, 107.5 x 85.5 cm. Schwerin, Staatliches Museum

pulled back the curtain and popped out of the niche in order to raise a glass to us in a hand that appears to be reaching out of the picture.

This device betrays the Dutch origins of the Caravaggist Honthorst, who returned from Rome to Utrecht in 1620. The interplay of light and shade, the closely observed wrinkled brow, crow's feet around the eyes, and the gap between the front teeth may have been inspired by the realism in the work of Caravaggio and his followers, but the deliberate creation of the illusion that this man could shake our hand, as it were, was a self-imposed task mainly set by northern artists. None of Honthorst's Italian models ever succeeded in achieving such a great sense of depth.

Several lifesize half-lengths had already been produced in the Netherlands, but Utrecht Caravaggisti like Honthorst, Hendrick ter Brugghen and Dirck van Baburen made them a stock element in their repertoires. Seldom, though, are their works as startling as this *Merry fiddler*. Only Honthorst's *Flute player* in Schwerin [14a] has a comparable illusionistic effect, and since it has almost identical dimensions and the same stone niche it is regarded as the companion piece to the *Merry drinker*.

The illusionism would have been vitiated for viewers in Honthorst's day by the outlandish cut of the man's costume, which is probably based on an Italian fashion, while his grimace and rather over-exuberant pose give the scene a slightly grotesque air. These elements were thus the ones that other painters swiftly reduced to more acceptable proportions, particularly Frans Hals, whose half-lengths from the early 1620s still have unusual costumes and plumed hats, but whose *Merry drinker* of around 1628-1630 [29] represents a great leap forward towards an utterly convincing live snapshot. All these works, with the possible exception of the *Merry drinker*, are genre scenes. There are even earlier examples of illusionistic half-lengths in portraiture, among them Werner van den Valckert's *Portrait of a man with ring and touchstone* dated 1617 [20], although that picture lacks the informality so typical of the work Frans Hals was producing a few years later.

Finally, there is the question of whether Honthorst intended there to be a little more to the painting than just a merry musician raising his glass. It is unlikely that he stands for one of the five senses, because he could be interpreted as either Taste or Hearing, and there is no evidence to support an identification of the figure with the visual type of the rhetorician.

LITERATURE

Exhib. cat. Philadelphia/Berlin/London 1984, no. 48; exhib. cat. Utrecht/Braunschweig 1986-87, no. 64; Judson & Ekkart 1999, no. 241

Netherlands or Germany

15a *Roemer with the motto of Prince Maurits, 1606*

Clear green glass with diamond-point engraving, h. 11.2 cm
A.J. Enschede Bequest, 1896
Inv. no. BK-NM-10754-47

15b *Roemer of green glass, engraved by Anna Roemers Visscher, 1621*

Clear green glass with diamond-point engraving, h. 13 cm
J. Kneppelhout Bequest, 1886
Inv. no. BK-NM-8188

The small *roemer* with its milled foot-rim, two rows of thorn prunts and the slightly flared bowl is a type of drinking glass that was very common in the last quarter of the 16th and beginning of the 17th century. The scene engraved on the bowl, though, is rare, and consists of the arms of Prince Maurits, his heraldic motto *Je maintiendray Nassau*, and his emblem of a felled orange tree with the motto *Tandem Fit Surculus Arbor* (In time the sapling becomes a tree). The Rijksmuseum has another, large *roemer* of this kind which is painted in gold and also dates from 1606.

The withered tree felled to the ground symbolises the tragic murder of William the Silent in 1584. His eldest son, Filips Willem, was in exile in Spain at the time, and his youngest son, Frederik Hendrik, had only just been born. The hopes of the fledgling Republic were pinned on the young and little-loved Maurits. The three oranges on the shoots springing from the felled tree stand for William the Silent's children. Maurits took this device as his emblem and combined it with the above motto.

Two ideas underlie the device and the motto, first that a rash, callow youth (which is how Maurits was seen at the time) can grow into a wise and able man, and secondly that even a tree-trunk that is almost dead can send out fresh shoots which will continue the family line, in which people have placed their hopes.

The manner of engraving, with the areas within the outlines being filled with parallel hatching, is typical of early northern

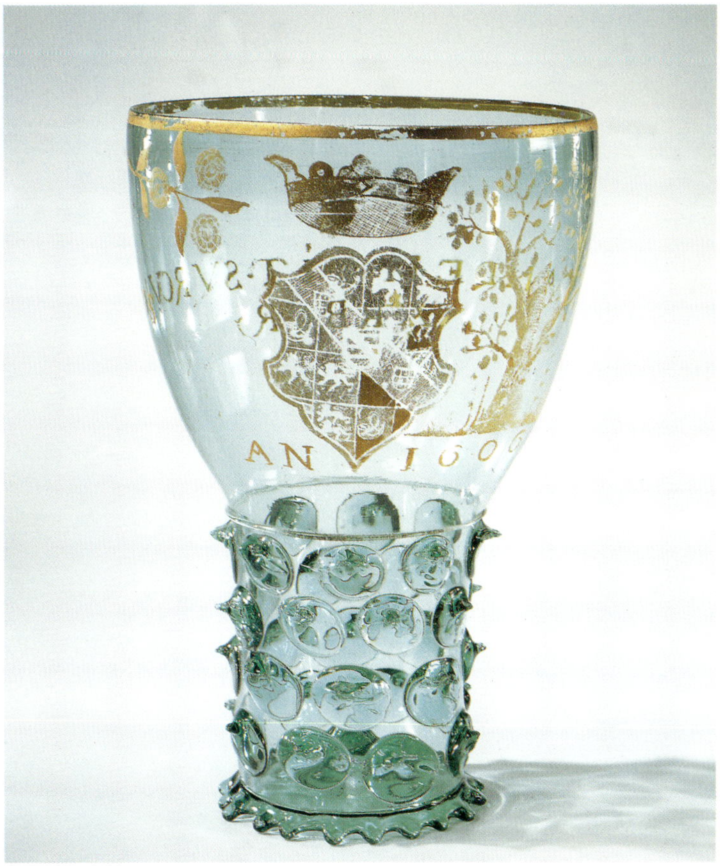

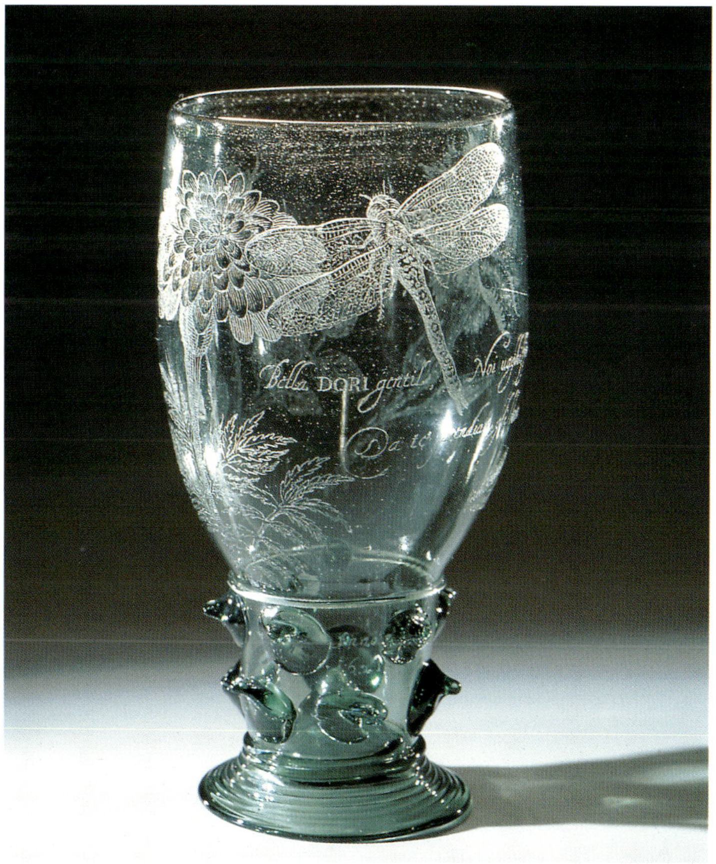

Netherlandish diamond-point engraving. It was a technique developed in Venice in the second half of the 16th century, and once it was over its peak there it had a second heyday in the Dutch Republic in the first half of the 17th century.

This kind of small *roemer* is of a slightly later date than the one with Prince Maurits's coat of arms. The milled foot-rim has been replaced by a coiled foot constructed from a thread of glass wound around a wooden mould. The prunts, though, are of the same type. The bowl is taller and more elegant, and has a sharply flared wall.

The engraving, which is delicate and of very high quality, is an early work by Anna Roemers Visscher (1583-1651) executed in the old Venetian manner. Anna and her sister Maria Tesselschade (1594-1649), who was also a skilled glass engraver, belonged to the cultural elite of their day, and were on friendly terms with the poet and playwright Pieter Cornelisz Hooft and Constantijn Huygens, the secretary of Stadholder Frederik Hendrik. It is known from contemporary written sources that Anna engraved several glasses for Huygens.

The bowl of this one is decorated with a shell, a dragonfly, an African marigold, a wild rose, a carnation and the inscription *Bella DORI gentil, Noi uaghi fiori/ Da te prendiam gli honori* (Beautiful, graceful Doris, it is only from thee that we, beautiful flowers, derive the honour of our fame). Engravings from Adriaen Collaert's *Florilegium*, published in Antwerp in 1590, served as the models for the flowers, while the dragonfly was copied from Nicolaes de Bruin's *Volatilium* of 1594, also published in Antwerp.

LITERATURE

Ritsema van Eck 1980, pp. 162-164; cat. Amsterdam 1993a, no. 400; Smit 1990, p. 44; cat. Amsterdam 1995b, no. 13

Johannes Sijmonsz van der Beeck, called Torrentius

(Amsterdam 1589-Amsterdam 1644)

16 *Still life with flagon, glass, jug and bridle, 1614*

Oil on panel (oval), 52 x 50.5 cm
On the bridle: T or JT (in ligature) *1614*
In the collection of King Charles I of England in the 17th century; acquired in 1918 with the aid of the Vereniging Rembrandt
Inv. no. SK-A-2813

As far as we know, this magnificent still life is the only surviving painting by Johannes Sijmonsz van der Beeck, better known as Johannes Torrentius (*torrens* = *beek*, or brook in English). He was a controversial artist who was accused of blasphemy and producing pornographic pictures. The latter led to him being sentenced to 20 years in prison in 1628 (after a trial during which he was tortured in an attempt to extract a confession), and many of his paintings were publicly burned. Torrentius was released in 1630 on the intercession of Charles I of England, who once owned this painting, and entered the king's service. He produced nothing during his time in England, though, and returned to the Netherlands shortly before his death.

16a Claes Jansz Visscher, *Elck wat wils* (To each his own). Illustration from Roemer Visscher, *Sinnepoppen*, Amsterdam 1614

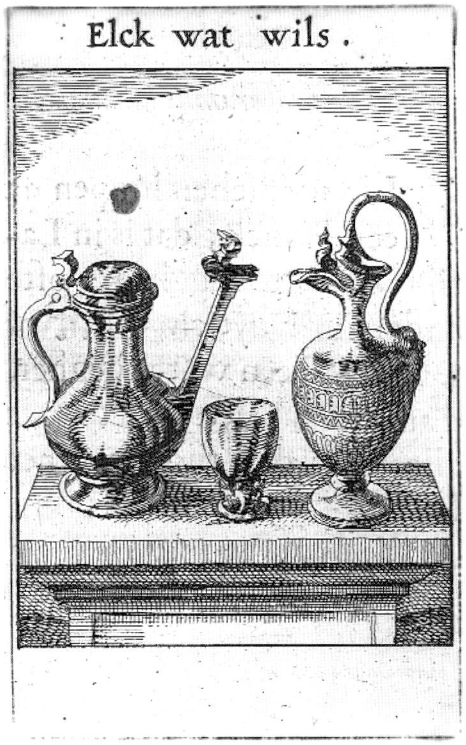

It is ironic that this unambiguous allegory of and plea for moderation and temperance is now the only surviving work by an artist who was accused of excesses of every kind. The similarity to an emblem with the same message and made in the same year is unmistakable [*16a*]. The question is whether the painter or the poet came up with the idea, or whether it was a joint effort. The wine from the flagon can be diluted, or 'tempered', with water from the jug, and thus alludes to the virtue of moderation. The meaning is perfectly clear even without the supporting evidence of the emblem. The perspectively perfect bridle at the top refers to the need to hold oneself in check, while the lines of verse set to music speak for themselves: 'wat bu-ter maat be-staat, int on-maats qaat ver-ghaat' (Those who know no moderation will perish in evil dissipation). This exhortation to be moderate does not apply just to drink and tobacco, but is undoubtedly used in a wider sense.

With its simple composition seen from below, which is what gives it its monumental air, this work of 1614 bears little resemblance to other still lifes from the opening

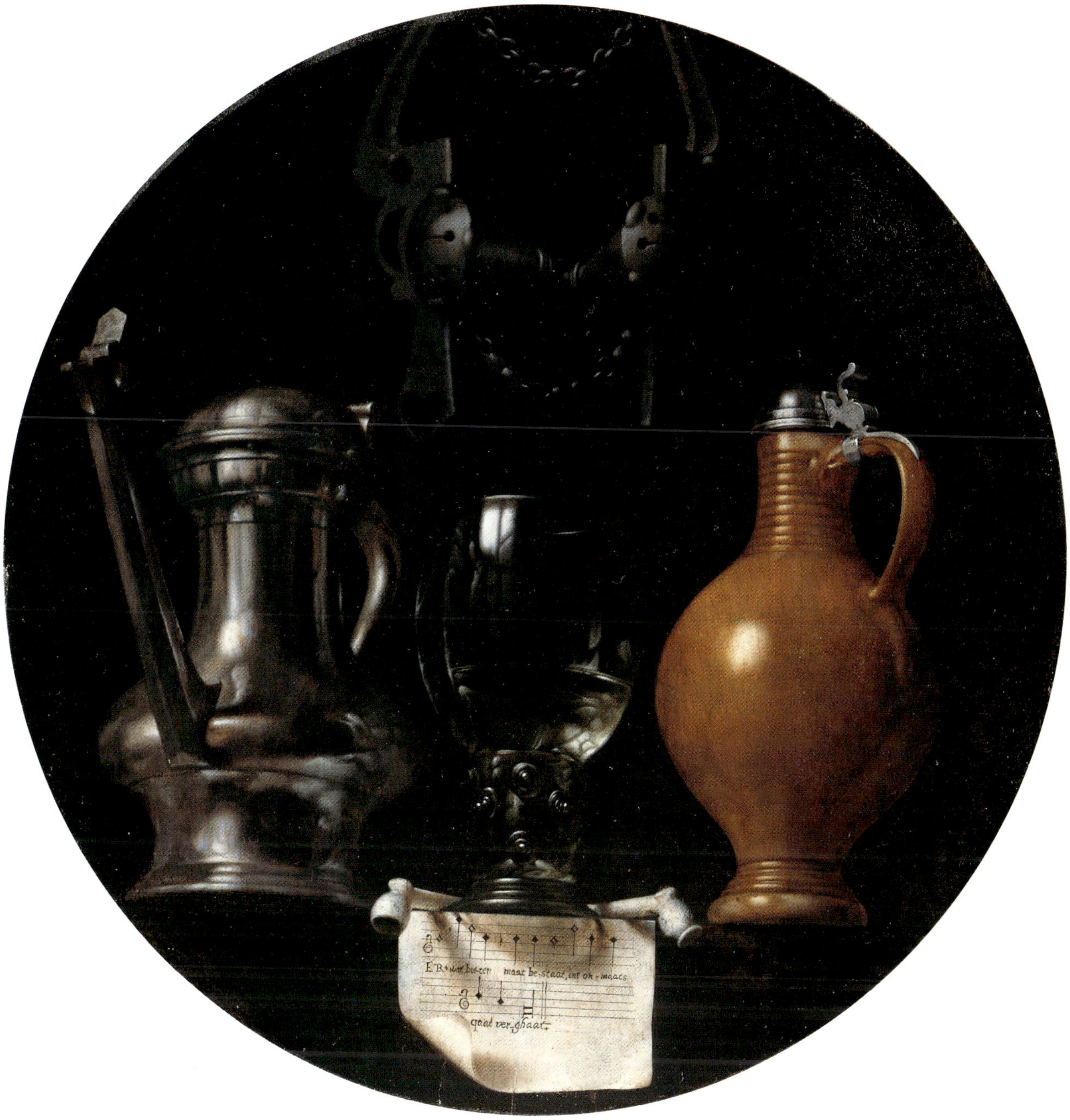

decades of the 17th century, such as the far more elaborate compositions of Nicolaes Gillis and Floris van Dijck, all of which actually adopt a high vantage point [18]. By placing the objects in such a tantalising way on the edge of the ledge, as if the slightest touch would knock them off, Torrentius succeeded in creating a convincing *trompe-l'oeil* effect that is reinforced by the masterly imitation of the textures of the different objects and the effective rendering of the shadows, such as the transparent one cast by the foot of the glass onto the sheet of music below.

Constantijn Huygens relates in his autobiography that Torrentius had once asked if he could see his camera obscura. During the demonstration Torrentius feigned total ignorance of the apparatus, which made Huygens suspect that he used it surreptitiously in order to 'conjure up' such deceptively lifelike scenes. Huygens was surprised that so few artists used a camera obscura, but perhaps he did not realise that being able to project something does not mean that you can also paint it. The refinement of Torrentius's handling of paint betrays his painterly skill, and it is that, coupled with a thorough knowledge of the effect of light, that is ultimately indispensable, with or without aids. According to Huygens, all sorts of stories were doing the rounds about the magical effect of

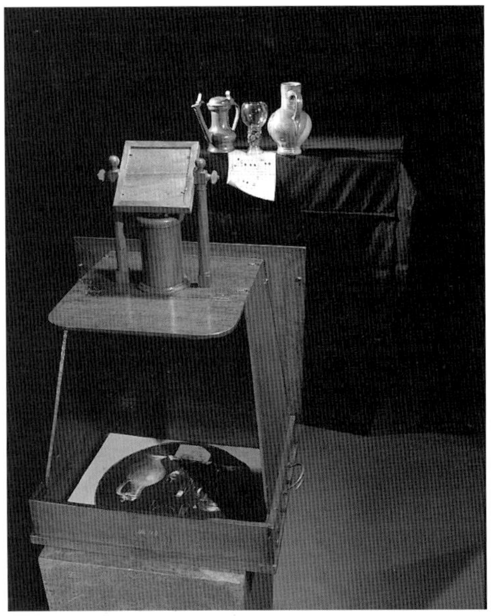

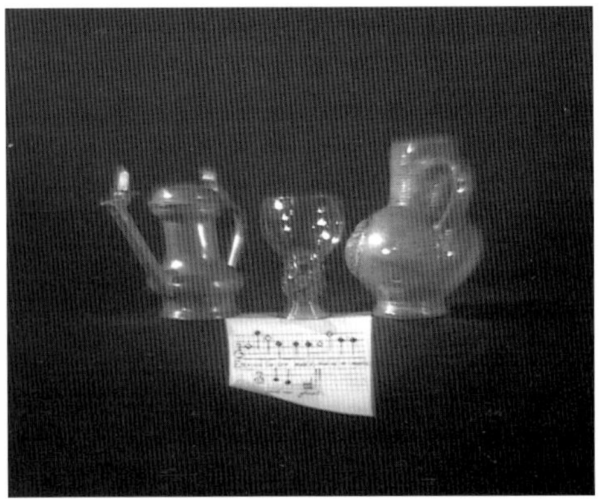

16b and 16c Photographs of an installation with a camera obscura and a re-creation of Torrentius's still life

Torrentius's paintings, as if the artist commanded a mysterious technique. Huygens, though, attributed it solely to the use of the strictly scientific instrument of the camera obscura, and an experiment has shown that Huygens's suspicions were probably well-founded [*16b, 16c*].

LITERATURE
Exhib. cat. Amsterdam 1993-94, no. 277; Brown 1997; exhib. cat. Amsterdam/Cleveland 1999-2000, no. 11

Passchier Lammertijn (Courtrai ? c. 1562-Copenhagen 1621)

17 *Tablecloth with a banquet on a table, 1604*

White linen damask, 5-shaft satin, l. 417.9 cm, w. 213.2 cm
Donated by the heirs of F.M.J. Helmer in 1990
Inv. no. BK-1990-15

With the arrival of southern Netherlandish immigrants in the northern provinces at the end of the 16th century, Haarlem gained not only a number of outstanding painters but some highly qualified craftsmen as well. The city had long been famed for its linen bleach-works, and their standard improved when a group of specialist southern Netherlandish yarn bleachers settled there. Immigrant weavers simultaneously raised Haarlem linen damask to an amazingly sophisticated technical and artistic level. It was as a result of these developments that the Haarlem linen bleacheries and damask weaving shops were hymned at length in a panegyric written about the city in 1628 by Samuel Ampzing, a local preacher.

The best-known linen weaver and merchant in the group was Passchier Lammertijn, who was registered in Haarlem as a tablecloth merchant in 1586, only one year after the fall of Antwerp. He grew to become a supplier of table linen to an illustrious clientele that included the Haarlem city authorities and the States-General in The Hague, which presented Lammertijn's costly linen to European rulers. In 1619 he went to Copenhagen, possibly at the invitation of King Christian IV, who had founded a silk factory called Kongelig Majestaets der nederlandske Manufaktur og Silkevaerk the previous year. Lammertijn referred to himself in Denmark as a *bomside* weaver, or bombasine weaver. He was not at the factory long, for this virtuoso weaver from Haarlem died in November 1621.

The tablecloth that entered the Rijksmuseum in 1990 has a pattern of a banquet laid out on a table in the central panels, as do two colourful silk tablecloths in the Kremlin Treasury, and another of linen damask in Rosenborg Castle in Copenhagen. Woven into the borders of all four pieces are various coats of arms. On this, the earliest, which is dated 1604 and was woven in Haarlem, they are those of France and Navarre, which in combination with the motto shows that they were designed for Henri IV of France.

The central panel contains saucers, plates and dishes laden with shellfish, fish and poultry, pies and fruit, along with knives and forks for eating this delicious repast. Scattered between the dishes are flowers and twiglets, individual pieces of fruit, some of which have been cut open, and the occasional butterfly. The horizontal borders of all four surviving cloths have scenes of farming, hunting and shipping, but they are not identical. The Amsterdam banquet piece is the only one to bear Passchier Lammertijn's initials, which are modestly relegated to a bag in the border with the views of life on the farm.

17a Vault mosaic with drinking vessels, birds and twigs, c. 320-330. Rome, Santa Costanza

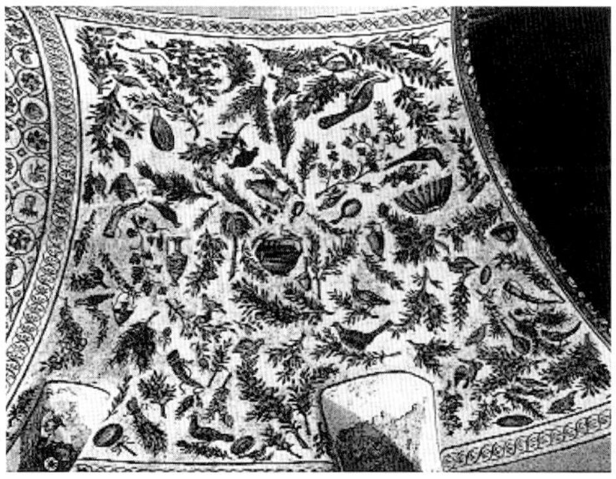

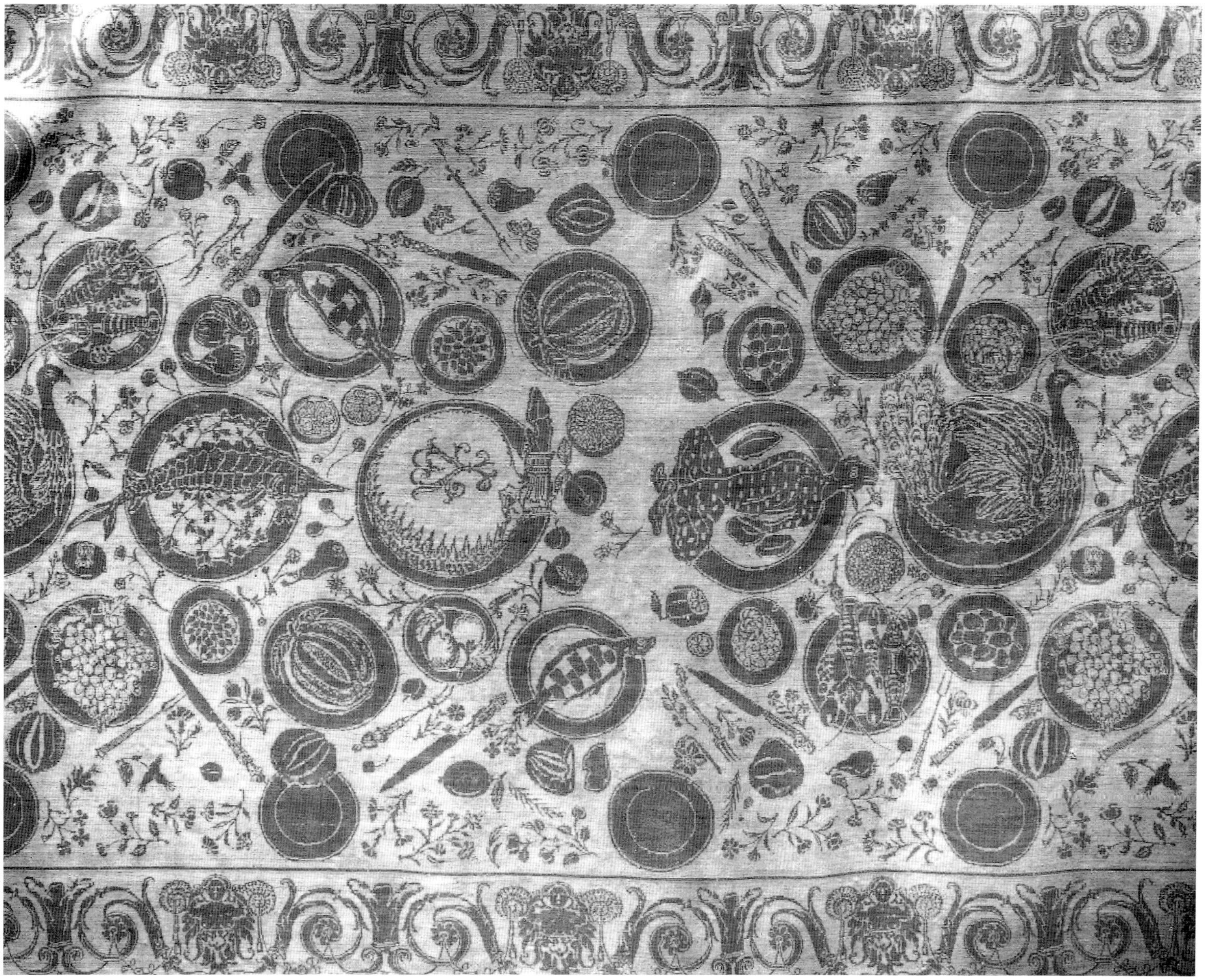

detail

While the border scenes look like they were chosen from a grab-bag of Dutch prints, the composition of the banquet itself appears to be original. Haarlem artists of the early 17th century painted still lifes with well-laid tables which were known as banquets or breakfast pieces, like the linen damask tablecloth, but they never show the meal vertically from above [*see 18*]. One wonders whether Lammertijn got in touch with the painter Karel van Mander for help with the pattern on the tablecloth. The latter also lived in Haarlem and was a fellow immigrant from the southern Netherlands, and according to his biography published in 1616-1618 he also designed linen damask. Van Mander had been to Rome as a young man, and like so many northerners he undoubtedly visited Santa Costanza. There, executed around 320-330 on the vault in the early Christian mausoleum, is a mosaic with a scattered pattern of vessels, birds and twigs similar to that on Lammertijn's damask [*17a*]. It is not inconceivable that Van Mander designed or proposed a pattern for Lammertijn which had a classical origin and also echoed the painted Haarlem banquet pieces.

LITERATURE

Burgers 1999; Paludan 1999

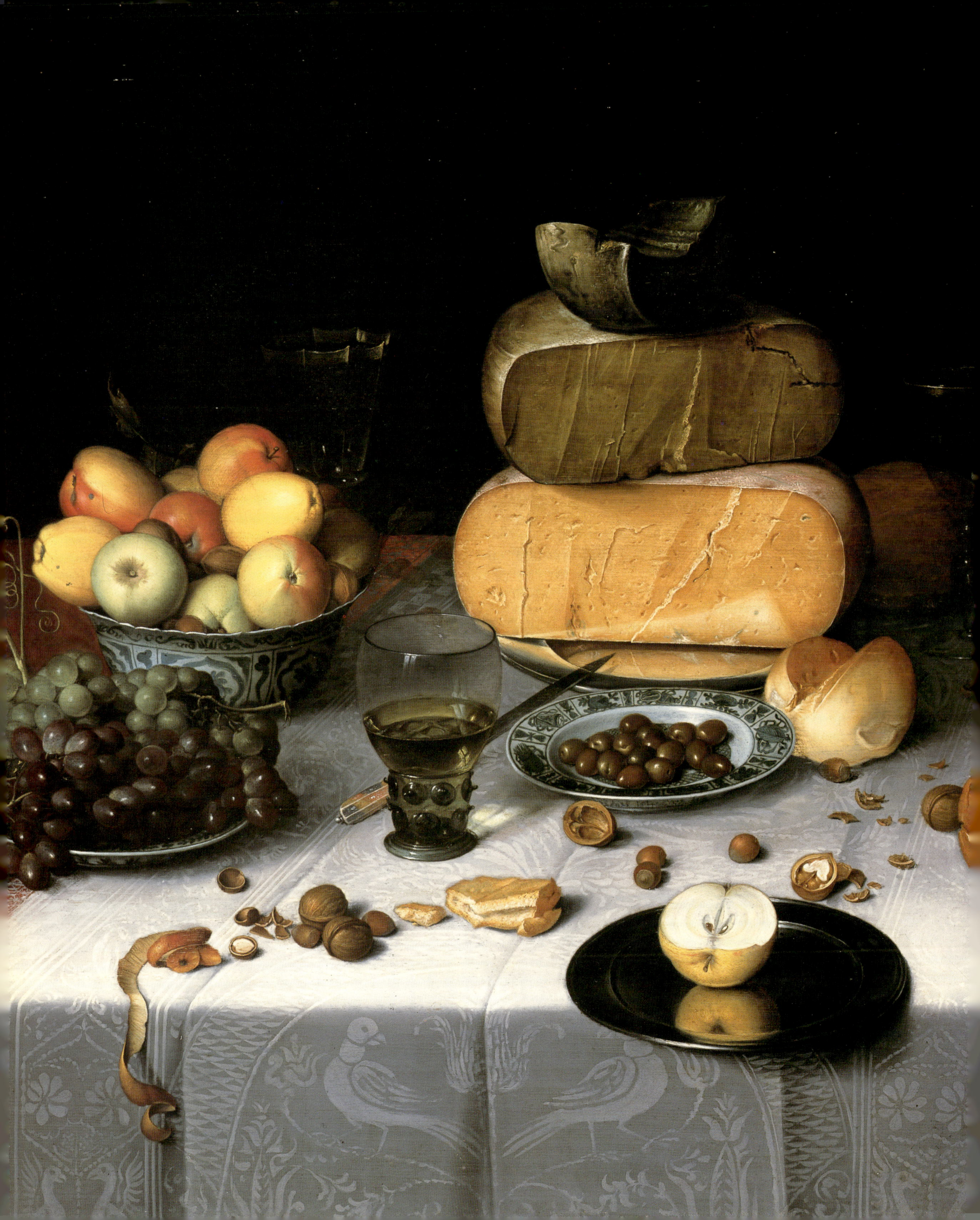

Floris van Dijck (Haarlem 1575-Haarlem 1651)

18 *Laid table with cheeses and fruit, c. 1615*

Oil on panel, 82.2 x 111.2 cm
Purchased in 1982 with the aid of the Vereniging Rembrandt and the Rijksmuseum-Stichting
Inv. no. SK-A-4821

Floris van Dijck stands at the beginning of the Dutch still-life tradition. He was a true specialist. His entire oeuvre, consists of no more than a dozen paintings of food carefully arranged on tables seen slightly from above. Although there is almost no development to be traced in his oeuvre, which spans the period 1610-1622, each of his paintings stands out for the extreme precision and evident pleasure with which the artist showed off his skill at imitating textures of different kinds. He was superb at capturing the crispness of bread, the crumbliness or creaminess of cheese, or the differences in colour and translucence of glass. The hard relief on the stoneware flagon is brilliantly done, as are the subtle colour differences of the decoration on the Wanli porcelain. Apples are in a variety of colours, with the stalk foreshortened, or cut in two and reflected in a pewter plate. The peel from an apple is draped almost deliberately over the edge of the table—a device that would become famous with the lemon peel that features in so many still lifes. The motif of a plate jutting out over the edge of the table is executed with great elan, and it too was to become very popular [*see 34 and 35*].

As with the apples, there is a great variety of colour throughout the picture, and it is accentuated by the red and white damask

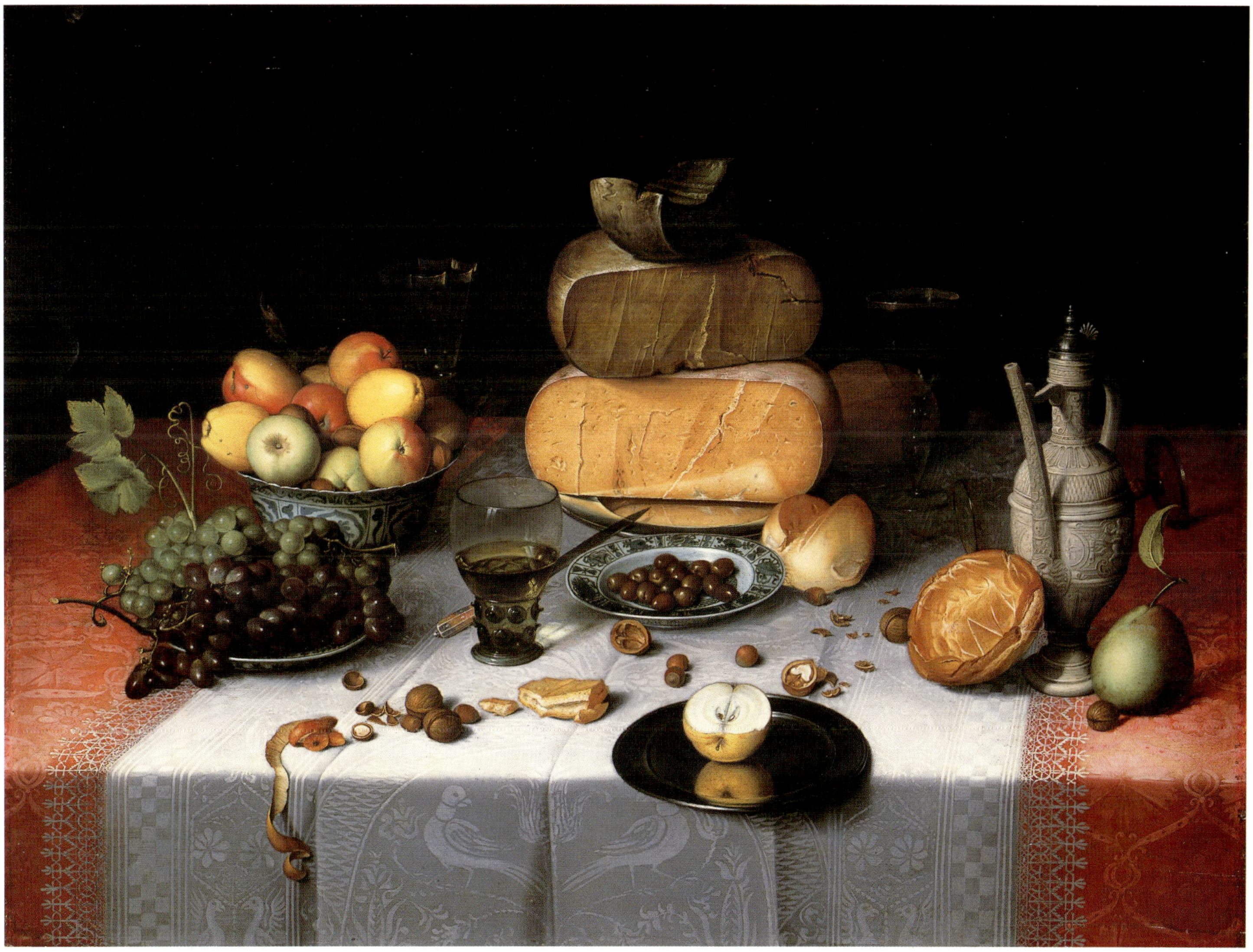

tablecloth, the sheen of which varies depending on the pattern woven into it. Floris van Dijck lived in Haarlem, like Passchier Lammertijn [*see 17*], a leading manufacturer of this kind of damask, and perhaps he deliberately set out to paint a famous local craft product. The colour is drained from the painting in the background, for all that can be seen beyond the table is a dark space.

Van Dijck wrestled with two opposing aims. In addition to depicting everything as faithfully as possible, he must also have felt the need to create an ordered composition. He opted for a symmetrical arrangement, with the objects divided up into groups, which he composed with both care and hesitation. The latter is well illustrated by the objects grouped around the spouted flagon on the right. The walnut is just touching the pear, and the pear in its turn overlaps only a very small part of the foot of the flagon. The bread roll is jokily placed against the ewer in such a way that it looks as if the bearded male head at the base of the spout is taking a bite out of it. The roll only covers a very small part of the ewer, but is positioned so as to cast a largish shadow, greatly enhancing the sense of depth in the painting.

The type of still life made by Floris van Dijck is sometimes called a 'display banquet', which is an apt name for these paintings in which everything has to be shown off to its best advantage. Such carefully arranged, laid tables seen a little from above were painted in both the Dutch Republic and Flanders in the early decades of the 17th century, among others by Osias Beert and Nicolaes Gillis.

LITERATURE

Exhib. cat. Amsterdam 1993-94, no. 276; exhib. cat. Amsterdam/Cleveland 1999-2000, no. 10

Amsterdam

19 *Triangular salt with cover, 1618*

Silver, parcel-gilt, h. 30.2 cm
Marked with the Amsterdam assay office mark and the year letter H (1618)
Purchased in 1988 with the aid of the Ministry of Welfare, Health and Cultural Affairs, the Vereniging Rembrandt and the Rijksmuseum-Stichting
Inv. no. BK-1988-15

Salt had been regarded since the middle ages as an exceptional product that both healed and purified, and as a costly condiment it had traditionally been given pride of place on the dining table. This ornate silver specimen with its cover demonstrates that the object's ceremonial significance was still current in the early 17th century. It is the earliest known salt of its kind, and the only one still to have its cover. Surviving specimens and paintings show that the type had a brief flowering in various cities in the northern Netherlands. It seems that similar salts were being made in the southern Netherlands in the same period. A note of 1622 by the Antwerp notary G. van den Bossche records that the local goldsmith Abraham Valcq 'certifies that he made for Sr. Luis Clarisse a silver salt with a pepperbox on top and three small gilt drops hanging from the salt, and that on the bottom of the base is the assay mark of Antwerp'. The 'three gilt drops' very probably hung from the corners of a triangular salt. The one in Amsterdam also has drops hanging from the supports, which are in the form

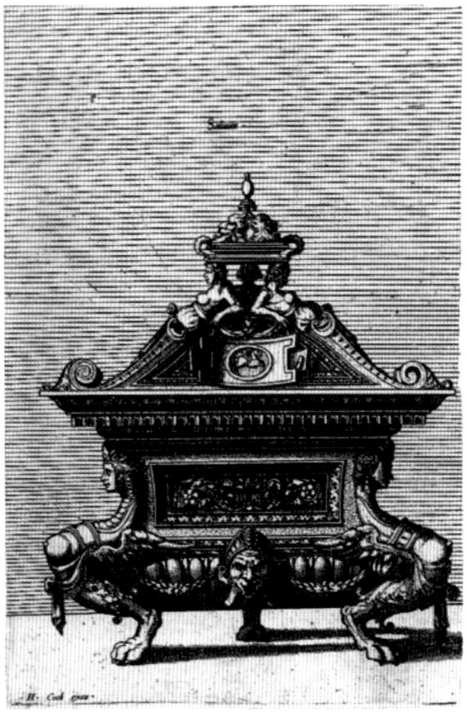

19a Lucas or Johannes Doetecum after Hans Vredeman de Vries, *Design for a salt*, 1563; engraving, 20.1 x 12.6 cm. Amsterdam, Rijksmuseum, Rijksprentenkabinet

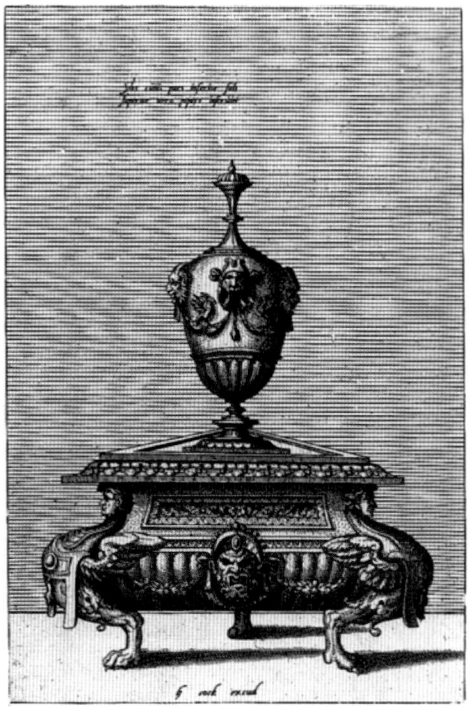

19b Lucas or Johannes Doetecum after Hans Vredeman de Vries, *Design for a salt*, 1563; engraving, 20.5 x 13.9 cm. Amsterdam, Rijksmuseum, Rijksprentenkabinet

of chimerical creatures. The 1661 estate inventory of the Antwerp corn merchant Guillaume Blommaert lists two more: 'silver salts [...], triangular with three columns standing in the middle, in the one the figure of Caritas and in the other the figure of Fides, the sides gilt'. These, too, may have been made in Antwerp. Although they are related to the one in Amsterdam, their supports took the form of columns.

The triangular salt had its origin in specimens from the Italian Renaissance which were interpreted by Hans Vredeman de Vries (1527-1604) in various engravings of 1563 [*19a, 19b*]. De Vries was working in Antwerp at the time, so it is possible that salts of this kind were first made there. Be that as it may, the one made in 1618 is so far the earliest to have come down to us.

The Amsterdam salt is partly old-fashioned in style and partly innovative. In its composition of several elements it is closely related to silversmithing practice of the second half of the 16th century. Much of the ornamentation also had its origins in that period, most notably the cast elements and the stamped borders. The embossed components, the masks and the putti in particular, are of a more fluid and organic design with early traces of the avant-garde auricular style, which only caught on properly in Amsterdam in the 1630s.

LITERATURE
Baarsen 1989b; exhib. cat. Amsterdam 1993-94, no. 101; cat. Amsterdam 1999, no. 6

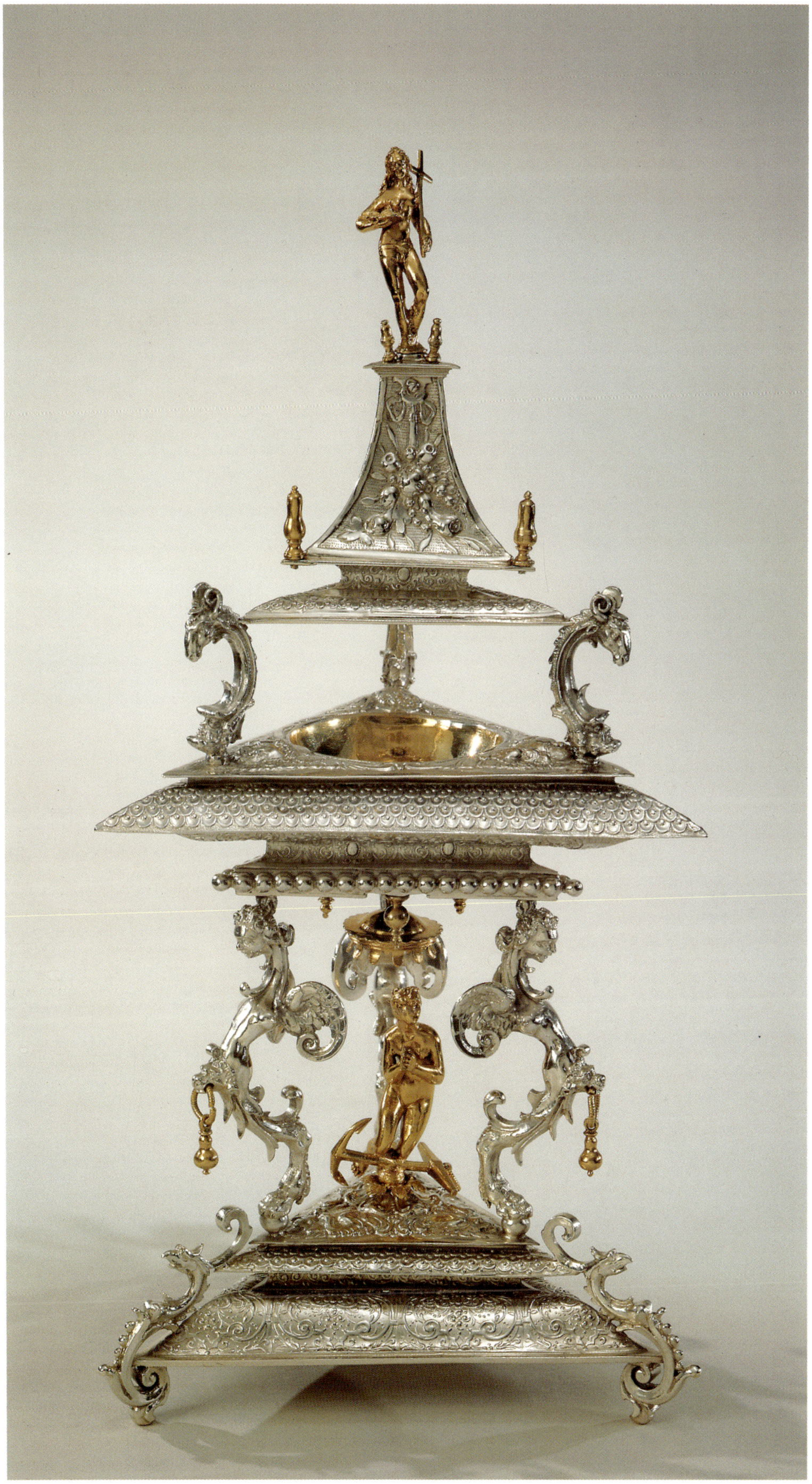

Werner van den Valckert (The Hague ? c. 1585-Amsterdam 1627/28)

20 *Portrait of a man with ring and touchstone, 1617*

Oil on panel, 65 × 49.5 cm
On the touchstone: *W v Valckert fe 1617*
Probably by descent in the sitter's family; purchased in 1957 from the estate of Antoon van Welie
Inv. no. SK-A-3920

This portrait displays Van den Valckert's polished painting technique to perfection. The painting is so well preserved that it could have left the artist's studio yesterday, allowing the viewer to enjoy his refined handling of paint to the full. In the black of the costume, for example, both the matt and the shinier textures of the various pieces of clothing are utterly convincing, while the marvellous sheen on the skin of the face and hands was achieved with considerable *sfumato*—the technique of softening outlines in order to bring about imperceptible transitions between areas of colour. However, Van den Valckert was well aware that too much refinement could leave the scene looking flat, so he brought the sitter's wispy hair to life with a few deft highlights, while the more striking touches that capture the fluffiness of the ruff heighten the liveliness of the scene as a whole.

That vivacity, however, is chiefly due to the illusionistic effect of the man leaning out of a niche, which recedes slightly on the left. His right hand appears to be projecting out of the picture, and the viewer's eyes are automatically drawn to the attribute he is displaying. The gold ring, together with the touchstone which he is holding in his left hand, are the clues to his profession and official function.

It seems very likely that this is the Leiden goldsmith Bartholomeus Jansz van Assendelft (1585-1658), for it was recently discovered that Van Assendelft was an ancestor of a 19th-century owner of the portrait, Frans de Wildt. A convincing reconstruction of the line of descent ties the painting to Van Assendelft. It is the attributes of the gold ring and touchstone that identify the sitter as a goldsmith, the latter object referring more specifically to the function of assayer. In 1617, Van Assendelft took on his first administrative post as assayer in the Leiden goldsmiths' guild, so it is more than likely that he decided to have himself portrayed in that capacity the very same year. This, together with the reconstructed provenance, forms the basis for the identification of the sitter. That, though, leaves the question of why a goldsmith in Leiden would choose to have his portrait painted by an Amsterdam artist. The explanation lies in the very probable ties of friendship between Van Assendelft's teacher, Frans Bastiaensz van Mieris (an uncle of the painter Frans van Mieris, who moved from Leiden to Amsterdam), and Werner van den Valckert. It would have been his teacher, then, who suggested Van den Valckert's name. Comparison of this portrait with the much stiffer ones being produced by Van den Valckert's contemporaries Michiel van Mierevelt and Cornelis van der Voort shows that he had not made a bad choice. Only Frans Hals was to surpass Van den Valckert in the decade to follow. He did so not only by putting his sitter's in more informal poses but also by abandoning the painterly refinement that was so popular at the time for a radically different, looser manner [*see 29*].

LITERATURE

Van Thiel 1983a, pp. 155-156, 180, no. 11; exhib. cat. Amsterdam 1993-94, no. 267; Ekkart 1999

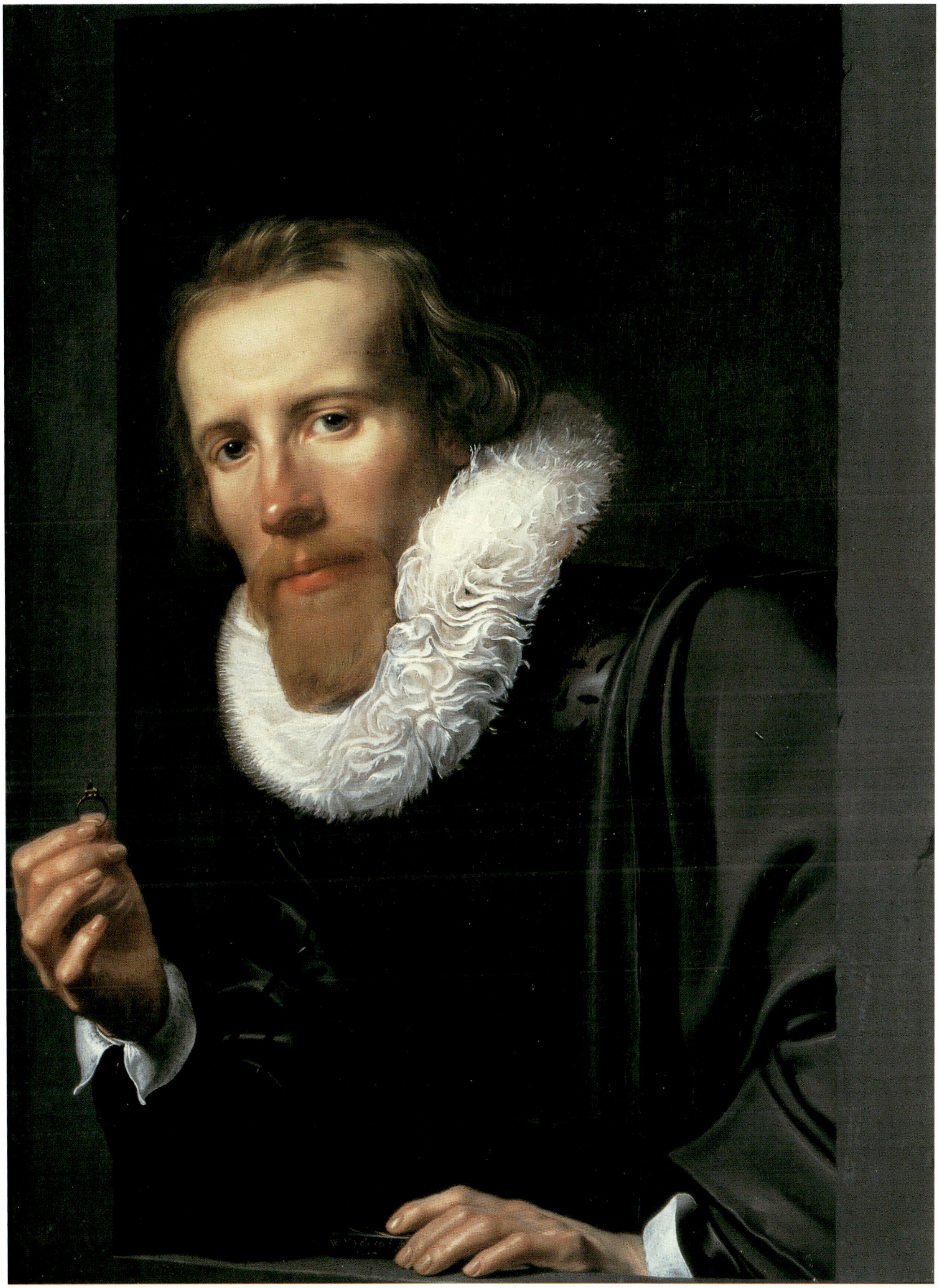

David Bailly (Leiden 1584-Leiden 1657)

21 *Self-portrait, c. 1625*

Brush in black and grey, heightened with white bodycolour, on light brown paper, 16.4 x 12.2 cm
From the collections of drawings of Cornelis Ploos van Amstel (1800), D. Versteegh (1823) and F. Adama van Scheltema (1912); purchased in 1912
Inv. no. RP-T-1913-11

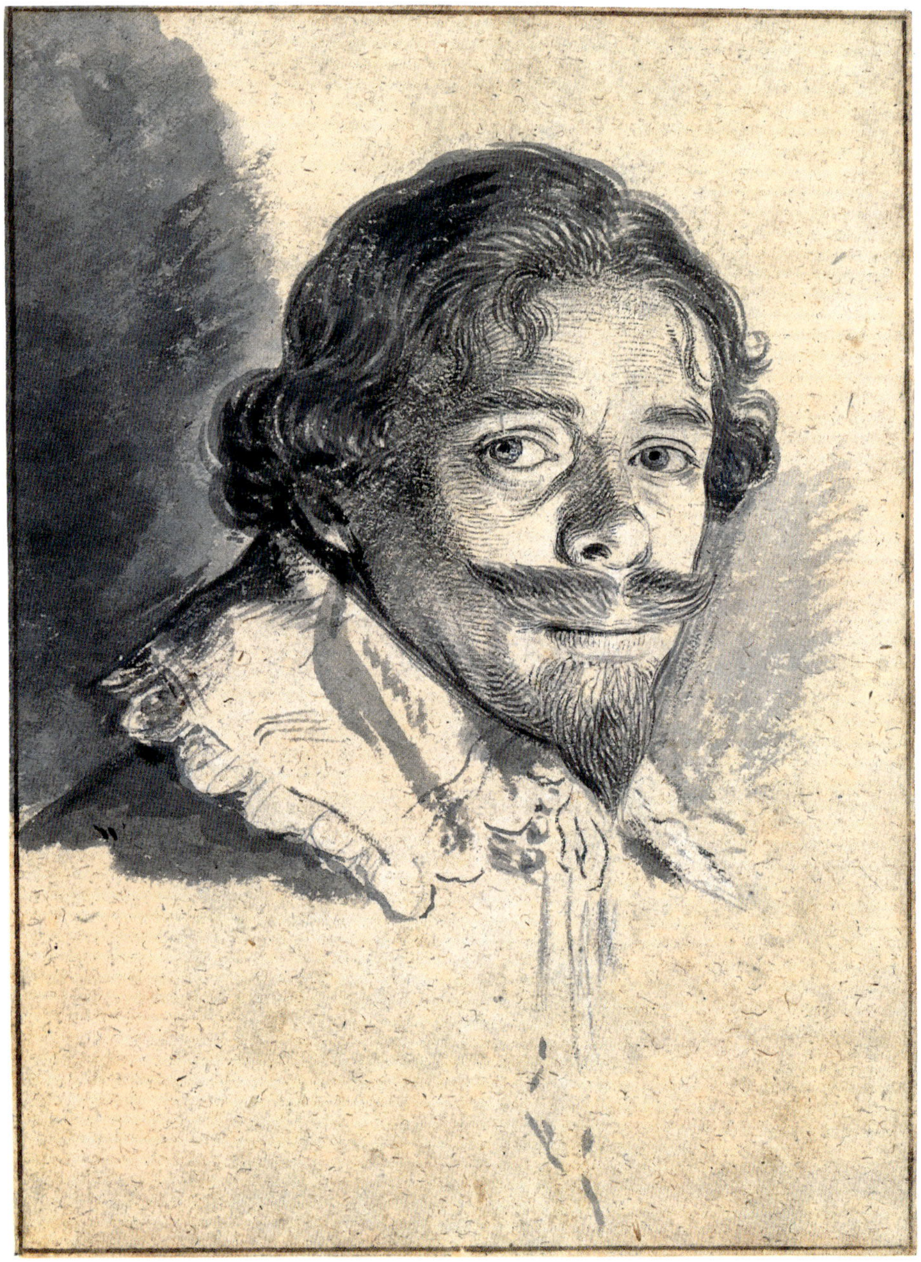

This drawing was reproduced from time to time in old books about the history of Dutch literature because it was thought to be a portrait of the poet and playwright Gerrit Adriaensz Bredero. Such mistaken identifications are not uncommon, but this one was widely believed and took a very long time to correct. The sheet was described as the portrait of Bredero in the auction catalogue of the collection of Ploos van Amstel in 1800. The myth may have been created by Ploos van Amstel himself, for he has been caught out more than once 'christening' the portraits in his collection with more imagination than hard evidence.

In 1801, J. de Frey made an etching after Bailly's drawing that bears the inscription 'De Poëet G.A. Brederode'. More than 80 years later there was a major reprint when it served as the frontispiece of the 'Bredero album'—a supplement to the second volume of *Oud Holland*, a periodical devoted to the history of Netherlandish art and culture. It was not until the 1950s that the story was finally laid to rest.

This is not the celebrated writer of farces and love poems at all, but the painter David Bailly. That is immediately clear from a comparison with a second drawing by Bailly, also in the Rijksmuseum [*21a*], which very probably came into the possession of the collector Sybrand I Feitama in 1686 and has long been recognised as a self-portrait. The two drawings are obviously of the same man and must have been made at about the same time, for the hairdo and cut of the beard are almost identical.

However respectable, such an old tradition cannot be automatically accepted as conclusive proof. Fortunately, though, there is a third portrait of Bailly. He was a member of the Leiden civic guard, and was immortalised as its standard-bearer in the *Portrait of seven officers of the orange-white-green company of Captain Harman Brosterhuysen* painted by Floris van Schooten in 1626. The story goes that Bailly was so unhappy with Van Schooten's work that he decided to paint

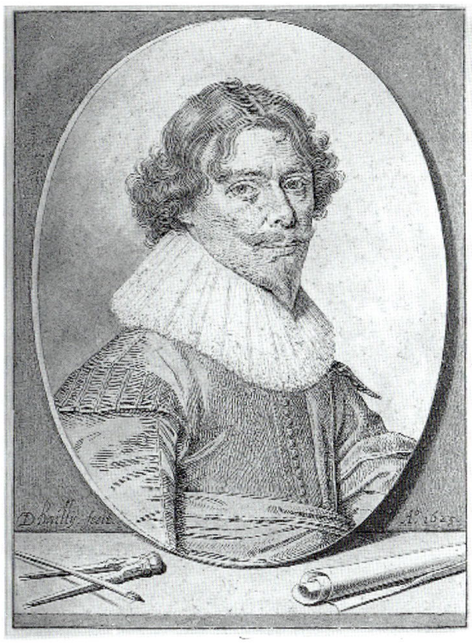

21a David Bailly, *Self-portrait*, 1625; pen in brown, brush in grey, 18.3 x 13.7 cm. Amsterdam, Rijksmuseum, Rijksprentenkabinet

his own likeness in the group portrait. True or not, the men in the painting and the two drawings are patently one and the same person.

This self-portrait is in a category of its own within Bailly's drawn oeuvre. All his other known drawings are meticulously executed with the pen in a style that imitates the lines of an engraving. Dramatically lit from below, this self-portrait done solely with the brush is an adventurous exception to those worthy but not very exciting works.

LITERATURE

Cat. Amsterdam 1998, no. 27

Northern Netherlands (?)

22 *Ruff: fraise à la confusion, c. 1615-1635*

Cambric, linen and floss silk, neckband 38 cm, w. 13 cm
From the collections of Jonkvrouw C.J.A. Warin, Nederhorst den Berg (1902), and of Miss H. Rahusen; on loan since 1923
Inv. no. BK-NM-13112

Fashionable young Frenchmen began wearing the *fraise à la confusion* in the first decade of the 17th century in a reaction against the highly starched ruff with its regular flutings, which originated in Spain. The new type, to which little or no starch was applied, falls in supple, disordered folds on top of and beside each other. That informal look was achieved by ruffling or folding a long strip of an extremely fine quality cambric to a neckband fitting the circumference of the wearer's neck. This new fashion was introduced into the northern provinces by emigrants from the southern Netherlands, many of whom looked to France for new ideas.

Although at first worn only by the young in the Dutch Republic, it soon became widely accepted. Petrus Scriverius, for instance, a 50-year-old historian and poet from Haarlem, had his portrait painted by Frans Hals in 1626 wearing a *fraise à la confusion* with fashionable, tufted edges, while in 1633 Rembrandt painted the 76-year-old Remonstrant preacher Johannes Wtenbogaert in a similar ruff.

The one in the Rijksmuseum consists of twelve strips of cambric of varying lengths

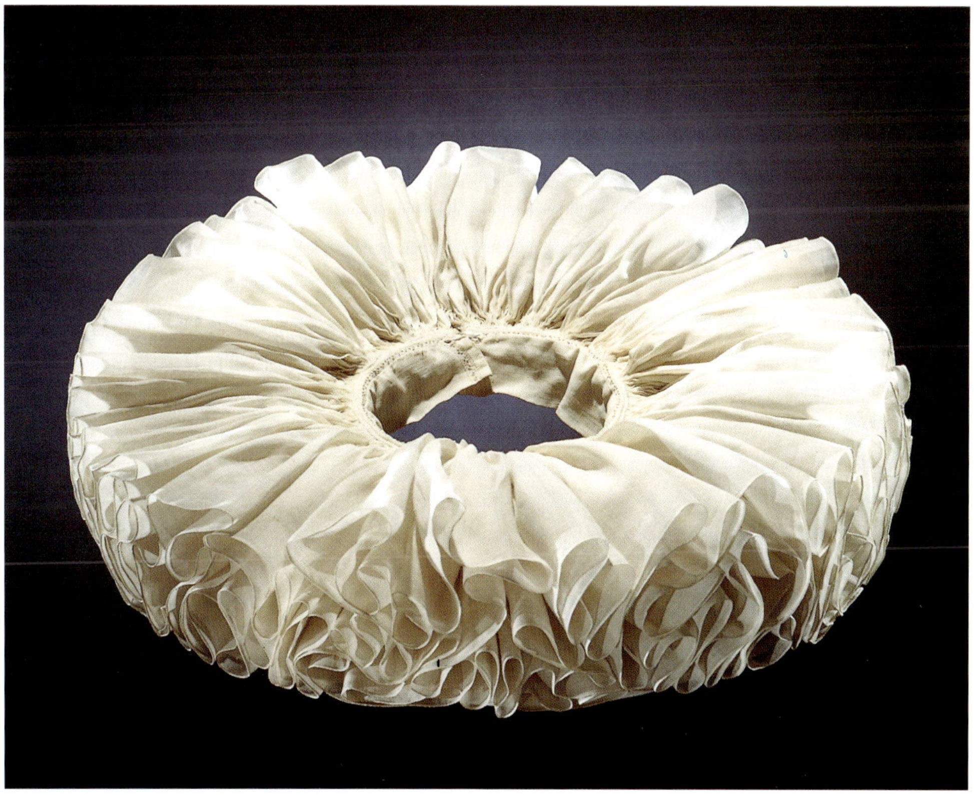

which together make up a total of some 19.5 metres. The strips, which are 13 centimetres wide, are sewn with hundreds of tiny flat pleats to a double neckband 38 centimetres long. The neckband, the inside of which is marked 'CY' with red silk, is decorated with back stitching and French knots. The cambric strips are finished with a delicate rolled edge.

This type of ruff can only be made from extremely thin linen batiste. The northern Netherlands, and Haarlem in particular, was known for its linen-weaving shops, which were famed far beyond the borders of the Republic. The standard of workmanship was very high, largely thanks to the influx of immigrants from the southern Netherlands who had settled in and around Haarlem. Those weavers introduced 'camerix doek', or cambric, which was the finest quality of linen and was woven from the softest and longest flax fibres.

LITERATURE

Arnold 1973, pp. 109-124

Northern Netherlands

23 *The wedding gloves of Johanna le Maire, 1622*

White chamois, satin, silk, floss silk, freshwater pearls, gold thread, gilt (?) metal, l. 24 cm
Made for the wedding of Johanna le Maire and Pieter van Son in June 1622; from the collection of E.G. Coles (c. 1880); purchased in 1978
Inv. no. BK-1978-48

It is very rare for an object to be preserved together with a painting in which it is depicted. That was the case until 1978 with the gloves of Johanna le Maire of Amsterdam, who on 14 June 1622 married Pieter van Son of Breda in the Nieuwe Kerk in Amsterdam. The couple were painted by Nicolaes Eliasz, called Pickenoy (c. 1591–c. 1654), following the custom in wealthy 17th-century circles of sitting for one's portrait shortly before or after getting married [23a-b].

In many of those portraits the husband or wife (or both) holds a pair of beautifully embroidered gloves, which gradually came to be known as bridal gloves. The reason is that after signing the antenuptial contract before a notary, the betrothed couple not only exchanged the usual marriage pledges like a ring and wedding medal but also showered each other with ornately decorated gloves, lace ruffs, cuffs and handkerchiefs, a fan, key-chain and a 'wedding gown' or 'bridegroom's shirt'. These were all put on display in a wicker basket decorated with flowers and bows in the bride's house during the 'sitting in state', which was a sort of reception for the friends and acquaintances of the couple and their parents. On the wedding day the servants ceremoniously carried the basket to the newlyweds' home, but the bride was by

23a Nicolaes Eliasz Pickenoy, *Portrait of Pieter van Son*, 1622; oil on panel, 105 x 78 cm. Amsterdam, Rijksmuseum

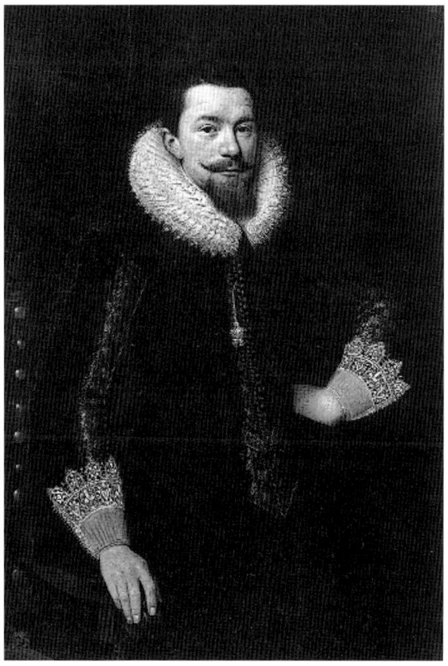

23b Nicolaes Eliasz Pickenoy, *Portrait of Johanna le Maire*, 1622; oil on panel, 105 x 78 cm. Amsterdam, Rijksmuseum

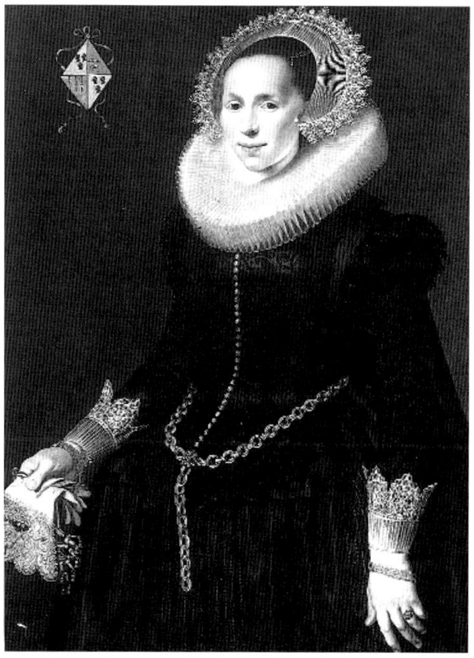

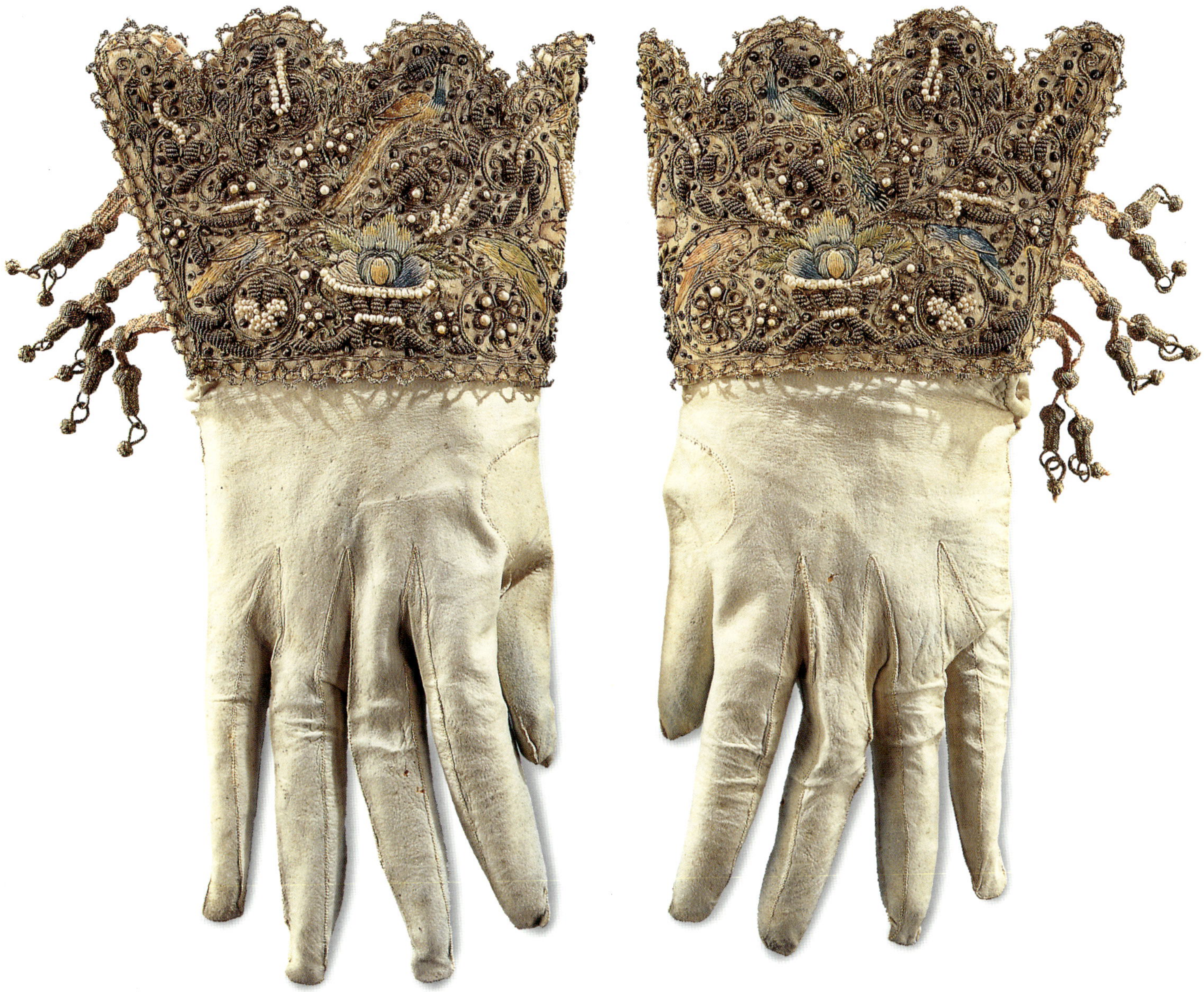

then wearing her gloves, one of which she removed when the couple gave each other their right hand to solemnise the marriage.

Not surprisingly, the embroidery of such special gloves contained numerous allusions to love and matrimony. In this case the cuffs are lined with red silk which has faded to pink, and the centrepiece on the outside is a heart made of pearls pierced with arrows of gold thread. Below it are two clasped hands standing for marital fidelity and the shaking of hands during the wedding ceremony. Above the heart is a peacock as a symbol of the married state (Concord) and faithfulness. The partridge alludes to fertility, and so does the pomegranate embroidered amidst a bowl of fruit. The violet refers to the loss of virginity, while the rose represents all-conquering love.

On 7 July 2000 the Rijksmuseum was able to buy the portraits of Johanna le Maire and Pieter van Son at Christie's in London, reuniting the gloves and portraits after 22 years, ensuring that they will remain together for the enjoyment of generations to come.

LITERATURE
Du Mortier 1984; Du Mortier 1989

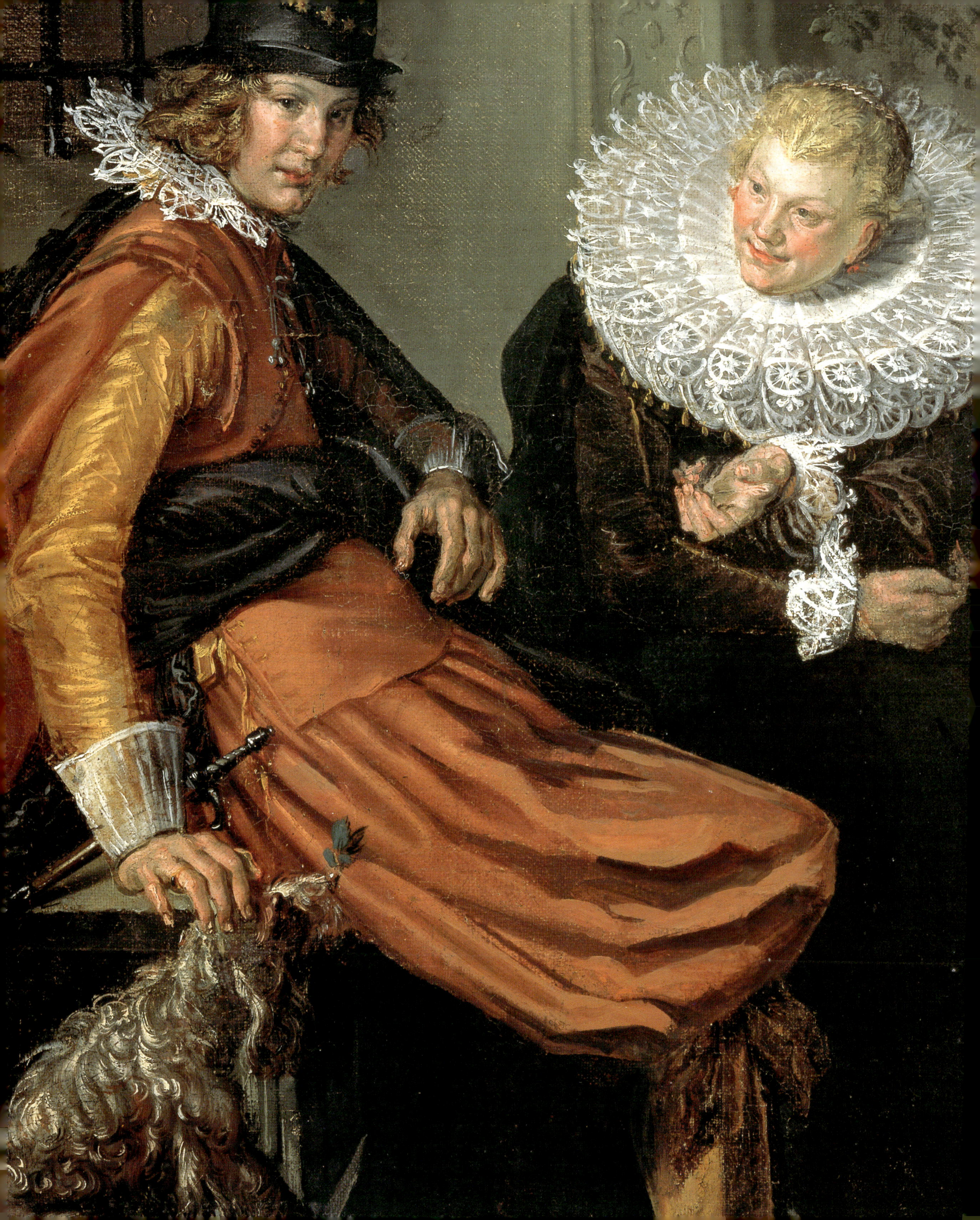

Willem Buytewech (Rotterdam 1591/92-Rotterdam 1624)

24 *Dignified couples courting, c. 1618*

Oil on canvas, 56 x 70 cm
From the collection of J. van der Linden van Slingelandt, Dordrecht (1785, as Frans Hals); acquired in 1926 with the aid of the Commissie voor Fotoverkoop
Inv. no. SK-A-3038

There are ten paintings currently attributed to Willem Buytewech. Until the beginning of the 20th century they had been regarded as works by Frans or Dirck Hals. Not one of them is dated or signed, but the similarities to Buytewech's surviving drawings (some 125 in all) and prints (32) led to their reattribution. The kinship with his graphic oeuvre shows that they were made between c. 1616 and 1624.

Buytewech was called 'witty Willem' in the 17th century, undoubtedly because of his brisk and lively portrayals of ingeniously chosen subjects, for the word witty (Dutch: *geestig*) was probably being used in the sense of the inventiveness and ingenuity of his style and choice of subject, although his work is also witty in the modern sense of humorous.

The *Dignified couples courting*, as this painting is known, also displays his 'witty' take on life. We are in a courtyard in the company of four fashionably dressed figures. The artist's dashing brushstrokes capture their poses perfectly, and their sumptuous attire is depicted with equal virtuosity. At first sight this appears to be

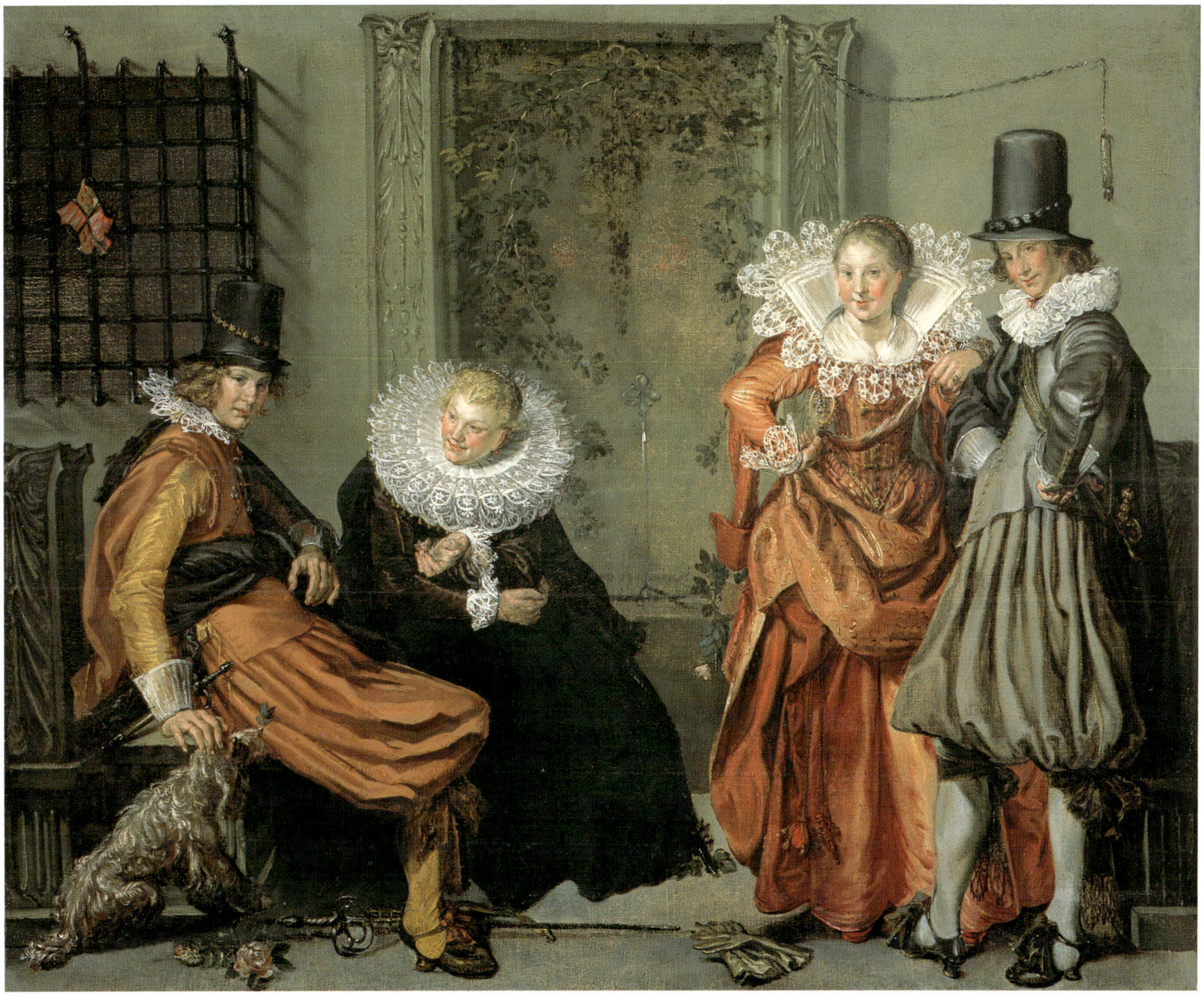

an innocent scene of two dandies and two ladies, all in luxurious garb. However, it looks very much as if the real subject is love. The clues include the fountain, which often stands for the springs of love, and the two rosebuds which the seated woman is holding. She proffers them to the man beside her, and although he is gazing out of the picture, apparently ignoring her, he is going to have to choose one of the rosebuds in the end, namely either her or the standing lady—although the latter seems to have made up her mind already. Whichever rose the seated youth chooses, his partner can manipulate the result, for she has her arms crossed and if needs be can switch left for right.

Should a deeper significance be attached to the almost invisible spider's web surrounding the coat of arms on the trellised window? It is, after all, a perfectly plausible place for a web, and may have been added as a true-to-life detail. It has nevertheless been associated with an emblem published in 1618 in the first edition of Jacob Cats's *Sinne- en minnebeelden*. Cats warns the reader in his accompanying text not to remain dangling in 'Venus's net'. The question, though, is whether 'witty Willem' was really so ingenious as to warrant searching for underlying meanings in details of this kind.

LITERATURE

Exhib. cat. Amsterdam 1976, no. 10; exhib. cat. Amsterdam 1993-94, no. 297

Pieter Codde (Amsterdam 1599-Amsterdam 1678)

25 *Gallant company, 1633*

Oil on panel, 54 x 68 cm
At upper centre: *PC 1633*
On loan from 1974; purchased in 1986 with the aid of the Vereniging Rembrandt and the Rijksmuseum-Stichting
Inv. no. SK-A-4844

Pieter Codde is best known for his paintings of elegant companies in interiors, most of which are quite small, although he did produce history paintings and probably started out as a portraitist. In the second quarter of the 17th century he concentrated on meeting the demand for paintings of interiors peopled with elegant figures. His attention to detail and meticulous technique ensured that his work stood out from that of contemporaries working in the same genre. This *Gallant company* is an undisputed high point in his oeuvre. The sparsely furnished interior is enlivened by the presence of four women and two men, all of them very smartly dressed. The entire scene is built up with closely packed silver-grey and brownish tints, as can be seen in the subtle gradations of colour in the figures' dress, which Codde set down on the panel with the utmost delicacy. The resulting tonality is beautiful, and is a facet of the work which can still be appreciated to the full because the painting is so exceptionally well preserved.

It looks an innocent enough scene at first sight: six people gathered together in a fairly simple room containing only a table and a bed. The man in the foreground is carrying a brace of partridges, while the one who has just entered is presenting a hare to the woman with her back to us. It is on account of these details that the scene is also known as *The return of the hunters*. However, the improbability of certain elements in the scene make it clear that there is more going on than that title would suggest. It is not very likely, for instance, that the men would have been out hunting in their Sunday best, and it is equally implausible that they would be received in a bedroom where a woman is attending to her toilet to a lute accompaniment. Codde's contemporaries would have interpreted this as a scene with a double meaning, for 'hunting the hare' and bird-catching were also synonymous with love-making in the 17th century. So this is not about hunting the game on display, but on chasing women. The bed and the musical instruments also allude to the figures' frivolous intentions. Codde's delicate brush may initially give the impression of complementing the refinement seemingly displayed by this elegant company, but it soon becomes clear that the real subject of the picture is considerably less genteel. The scene contains a lesson about man's futility in pursuing nothing but sensual pleasure.

LITERATURE

Exhib. cat. Amsterdam 1976, no. 13; Van Thiel 1989b

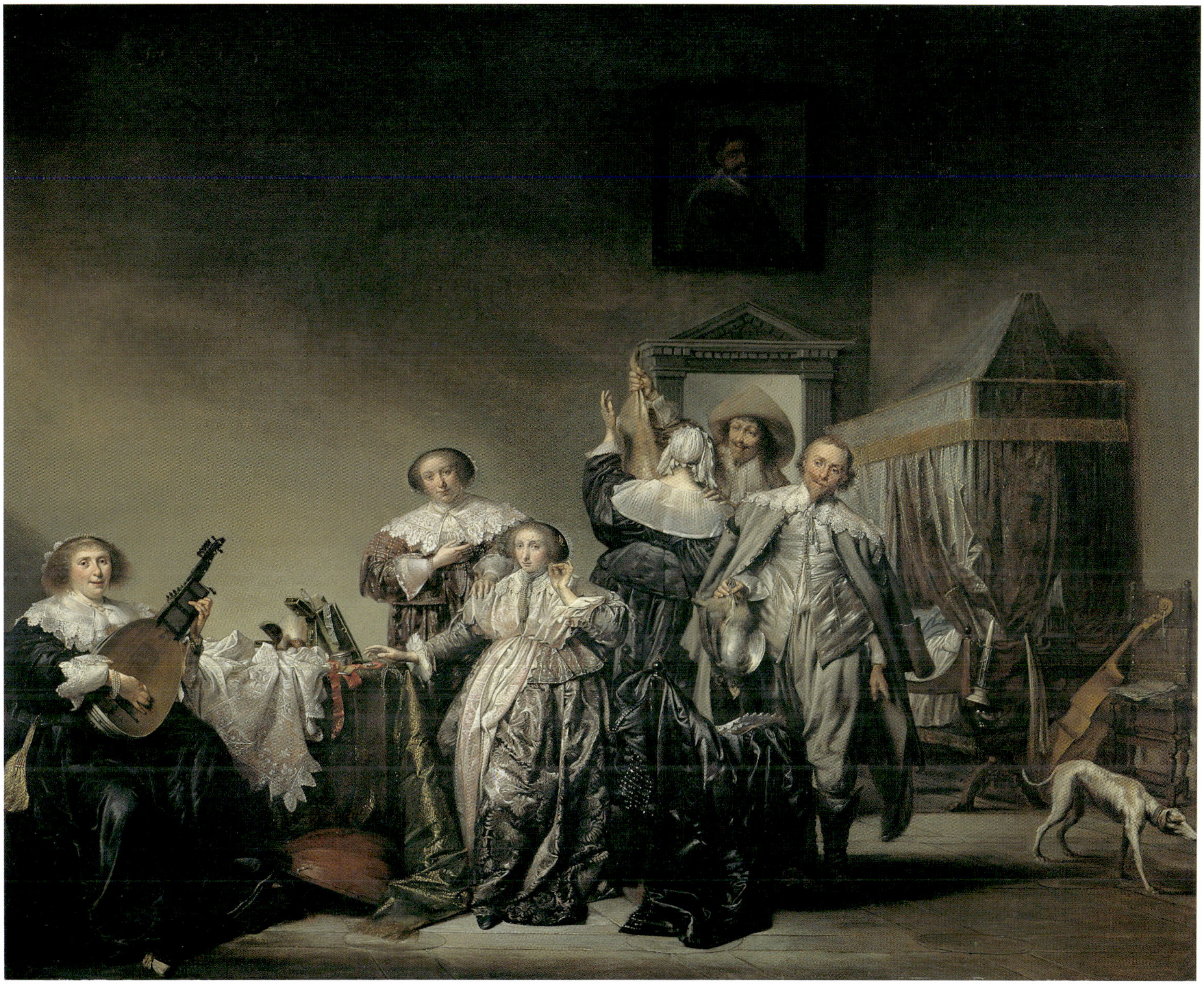

Northern Netherlands

26 *Armchair, c. 1600-1625*

Rosewood and ebony, upholstered with velvet and leather,
h. 131.5 cm, w. 64 cm, d. 61.5 cm
Purchased in 1947
Inv. no. BK-16019

Since time immemorial a seat been intimately connected with the status of its user. A king had his throne, the master of the house his chair (with or without arms). By taking his place in it he proclaimed his ownership of the house, his position as the supreme authority in his own immediate world. If an honoured guest came calling, he might be offered the chair as an exceptional mark of respect. The probate inventories of countless 17th-century houses speak of a single 'man's chair', meaning the principal one. Often, too, there was a 'woman's chair', which would usually have been smaller and slightly less imposing.

It is perfectly understandable that people wanted a chair with such weighty connotations to look grand. This particular one is among the most stately and costly Dutch 'men's chairs' to have survived from the early 17th century. The dignified shape with a straight, upholstered back, a rectangular, upholstered seat, and straight legs joined with rails, was derived from 16th-century Spanish models. They became so prominent in the young Dutch Republic that master chair-makers were commonly referred to as 'Spanish chair-makers', which even became their official name within their guild. The unusually high back of this specimen is crowned with two lions facing each other, the traditional symbols of rulers, both holding an empty armorial shield.

The chair stands out not just for its form but for its workmanship as well. It is made of rosewood with decoration in ebony—two types of tropical wood that were rare and extremely expensive in the early 17th century, shortly after the foundation of the Dutch East India Company. The hard wood, which is difficult to work, is ornately carved. Each arm ends in a volute with a fish-like monster covered with an acanthus leaf. One particularly striking feature is the high openwork upper stretcher running around all four sides and decorated with a strapwork pattern which is a typically northern, sharply and delicately detailed variation on Spanish models. Similar stretchers are found in a few chair designs by Crispijn de Passe the Younger, which were published in Utrecht in 1621 [*26a*]. Even the back is richly decorated [*26b*], showing that the chair was not intended to be placed against a wall but was meant to stand free, probably at a table or by the hearth.

The costly, green velvet upholstery seems to be original. Tacking stitches ensure the even distribution of the seat padding. The upholstery is finished with ornamental brass nails in three sizes, which are arranged in decorative patterns that echo the ebony discs applied to the wooden parts. These ornamental nails are yet another sign of Spanish influence. The fringe has been replaced. It is most unusual for a chair of this age to have survived with

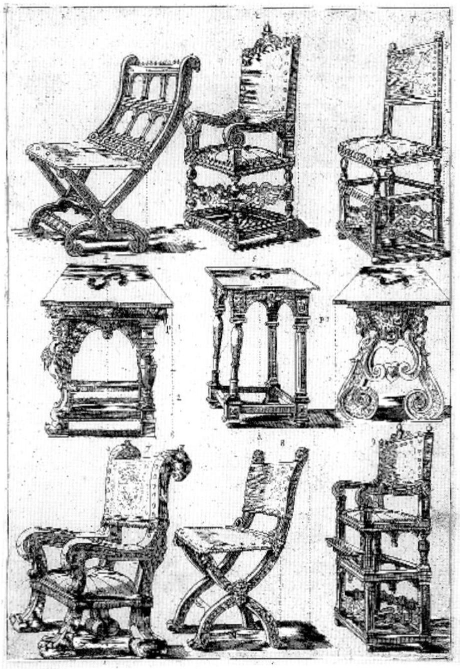

26a Crispijn de Passe the Younger, *Furniture designs*; engraving from *Schrenwerckers Const...*, Utrecht 1621. Amsterdam, Rijksmuseum, Rijksprentenkabinet

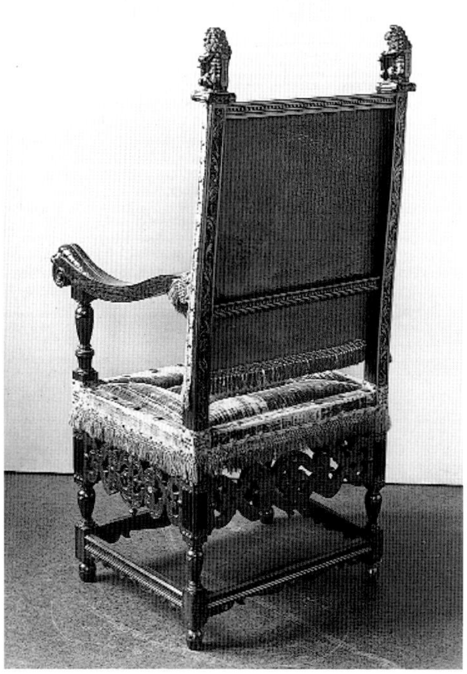

26b Back of the armchair

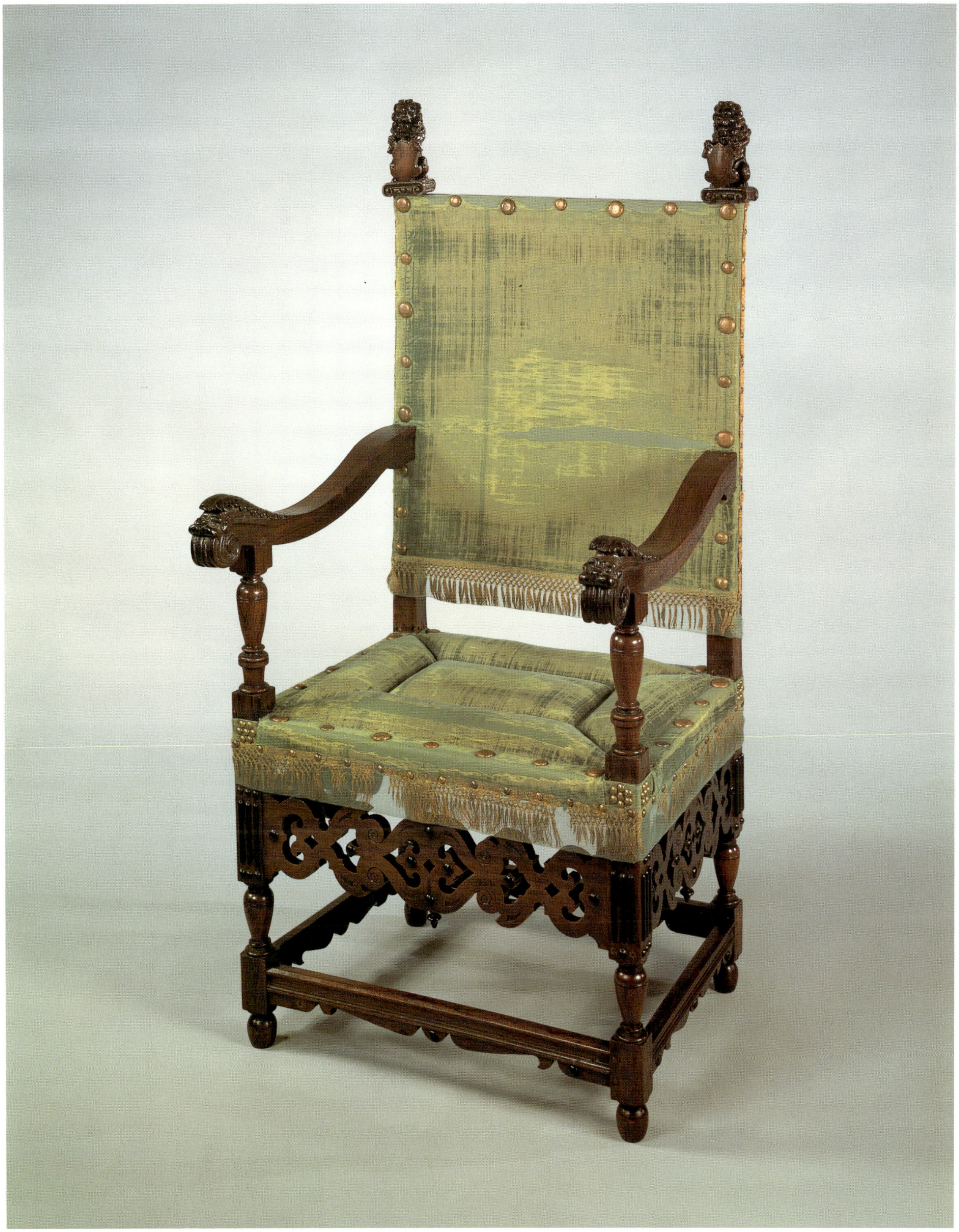

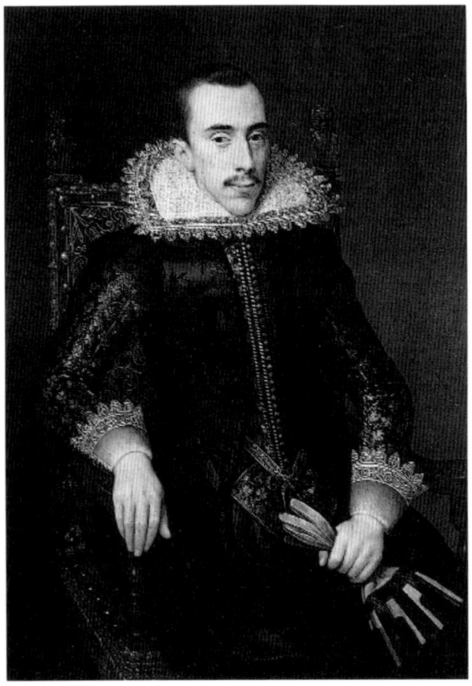

26c Salomon Mesdach (attributed to), *Portrait of a man from the Boudaen Courten family*, 1620; oil on panel, 96 x 70 cm. Amsterdam, Rijksmuseum

its original upholstery. Sadly, nothing is known of its history before it appeared on the art market in 1947.

A portrait of 1620 shows a man of the Boudaen Courten family of Zeeland seated in a very similar chair, although the back appears to be a little lower [*26c*]. The green upholstery of his chair is embroidered with a pattern of foliage and flowers. That splendid piece of furniture is as clear an indication of the sitter's high standing in society as his strikingly ornate dress.

LITERATURE

Cat. Amsterdam 1952a, no. 186; cat. Amsterdam 1993b, no. 2; exhib. cat. Amsterdam 1993-94, no. 74

Northern Netherlands

27 *Cupboard, c. 1630-1650*

Oak and ebony, h. 212 cm, w. 160 cm, d. 78 cm
Purchased in 1900
Inv. no. BK-NM-11448

If a chair is the mark of a person [*see 26*], a cupboard proclaims the status of the house. Both items derived their importance chiefly from their 'contents'. With a chair it was the person who sat in it, with a cupboard it was more literally the objects it contained. The most magnificent cupboard in the house was reserved for costly linen and other textiles. These often formed the bulk of the trousseau that a woman brought to a marriage, and embodied the prosperity of the household, a prosperity that was promulgated by the cupboard. It is not surprising, then, that great care was lavished on it. The linen cupboard was the most ornately decorated and monumental piece of furniture in most early 17th-century middle-class households.

A linen cupboard was probably often bought or received as a present on the occasion of a marriage, as must have been the case with this one. Aptly for a marriage cupboard, it is carved with scenes illustrating typically male and female virtues. St George is slaying the dragon and rescuing the maiden in a medallion in the left-hand section of the frieze. Its counterpart on the right shows the Roman hero Marcus Curtius. According to the legend, a chasm suddenly opened in the Forum in Rome, and an oracle declared that it would only close again if the city's most precious possession was sacrificed by casting it into the gaping maw. Feeling that that priceless asset was valour, Marcus Curtius donned full armour, mounted his horse and leapt into the chasm, which duly closed behind him. Counterpointing these examples of male courage and resolve are scenes extolling the virtue of female chastity. The six reliefs on the doors depict episodes from the story of the chaste Susanna. The upper section is divided into two by three female caryatids symbolising Faith, Charity and Hope, the theological virtues which everyone was expected to honour. This iconographic programme gives the cupboard a markedly didactic nature alongside its function as a showpiece. The Dutch had been familiar with such 'sermons in wood' on church furnishings since at least the 16th century, but now the Christian virtues were being promulgated in the home.

It was essential that the form of a cupboard should not be so eye-catching as to detract from the various messages conveyed by its decoration. The type that evolved in the early 17th century consequently remained almost unchanged for several decades. The purchaser of a cupboard of this kind was interested not in modish innovation but in the values of a traditional bearer of meaning. It shares that aspect with the graphic models from which the carved scenes were taken. The episodes from the story of Susanna on this cupboard, which can be dated roughly to 1630-1650 on the evidence of its decoration, are based on prints after Maarten van Heemskerck that had been executed back in 1563. Needless to say, the customer did want his cupboard to be as beautiful as possible. This one is superbly proportioned, and has carvings of the highest quality and rhythmic accents in ebony. Only the most expensive cupboards had caryatids, and the costliest of all had a further three on the lower section. It is to these figures that such pieces of furniture owe their modern Dutch name of *beeldenkasten*.

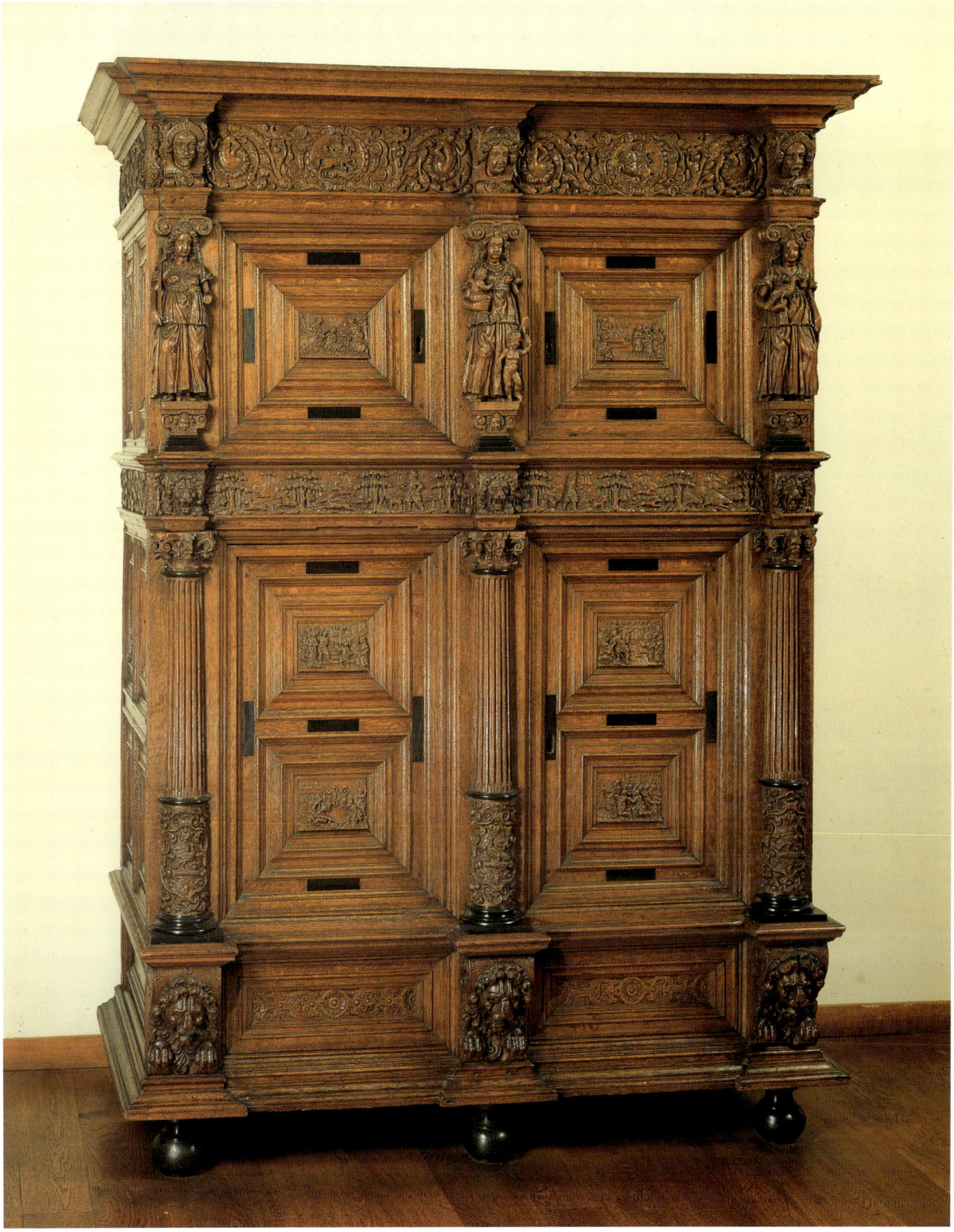

LITERATURE

Cat. Amsterdam 1952a, no. 101; cat. Amsterdam 1993b, no. 9

Frans Hals (Antwerp 1582/83-Haarlem 1666)

28 *Marriage portrait of Isaac Abrahamsz Massa and Beatrix van der Laen, 1622*

Oil on canvas, 140 × 166.5 cm
From the collection of Jan Six (1702); purchased in 1851 at the sale of the Hendrik Six van Hillegom Collection
Inv. no. SK-A-133

The man and woman in this portrait are presented to us in a highly unusual way, not in the centre of the picture but to the left of it, seated companionably side by side beneath a tree and looking out at the spectator with engaging smiles. Frans Hals must have known them well, for seldom did a couple allow themselves to be portrayed so informally in 17th-century Dutch painting. They are also shown full-length, a mode of presentation that was usually reserved for the very highest in the land.

The sitters are the Haarlem merchant Isaac Massa and his wife Beatrix van der Laen, the daughter of a former burgomaster of the city. They married in 1622, and undoubtedly had themselves painted by Hals the same year to mark the occasion. Numerous elements in the painting allude to that festive event. Of particular significance are the large spear thistle in the lower

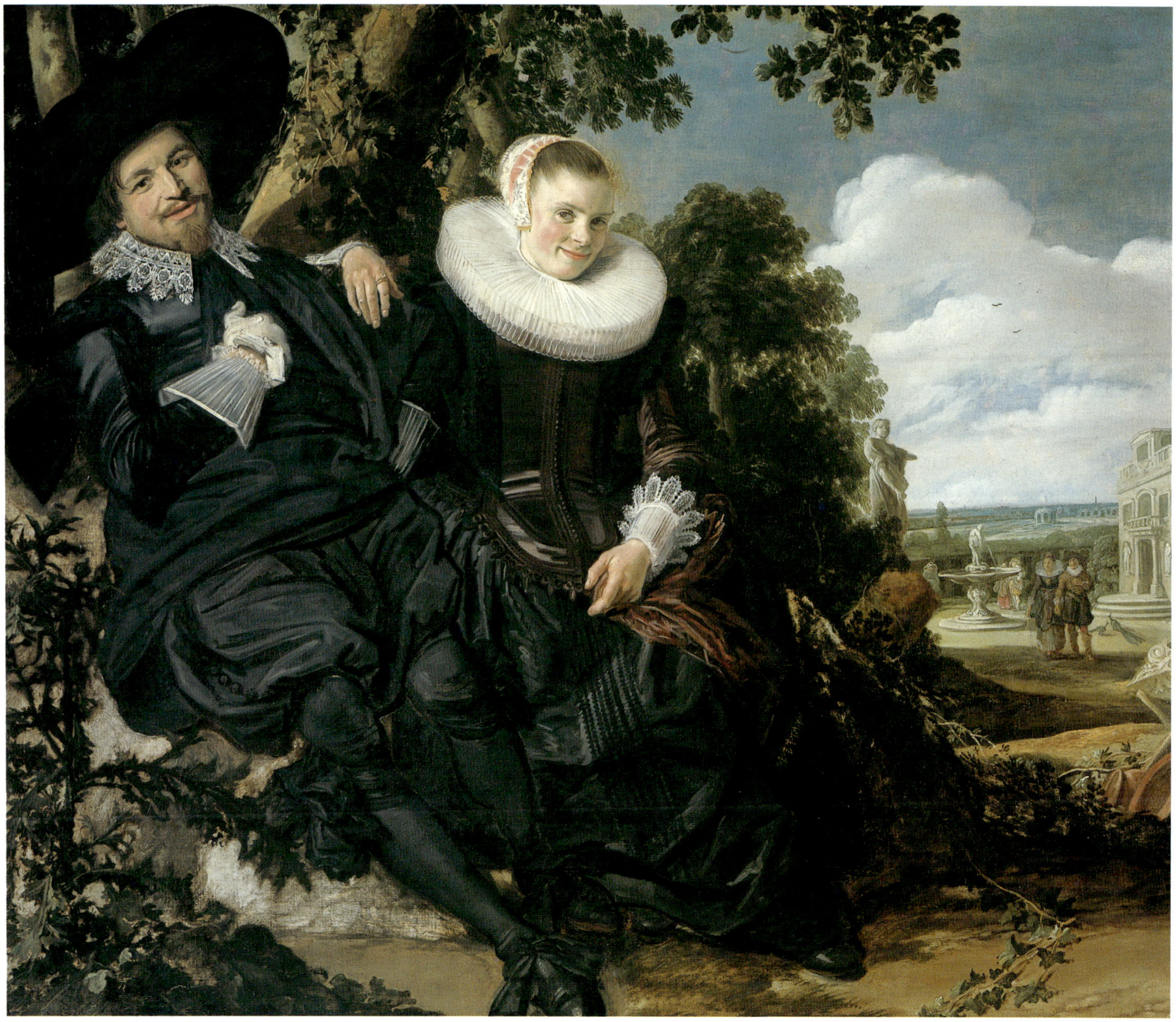

left corner, the ivy at lower right and the tree between the newly-weds. The latter is a familiar symbol of love, matrimony and mutual fidelity. The ivy has a very similar connotation, for it had symbolised love and devotion since classical times. The spear thistle stood for marital fidelity, and this was reflected in its popular name of Man's Fidelity, or *Männertreu* in German. The background, too, is laden with meaning. Peacocks strut and two couples walk arm-in-arm in a park landscape in a reference to the Garden of Love—an allegorical motif known since medieval times that centred around the themes of love, marriage and fruitfulness. Massa occupies the hierarchically superior position on the right (left to the viewer) of his wife, but it is she who catches the most light, which falls from the left. This is almost always the case with double and paired portraits, and it was also recommended to painters in numerous treatises.

Frans Hals must have known Isaac Massa well. There were certainly a number of personal ties between the two families at a later date, and Isaac had himself painted by Hals on at least two other occasions. Frans Hals was Haarlem's most successful portrait painter between 1620 and 1650, and his fame spread far beyond his adopted city. People from Amsterdam, Utrecht and The Hague had themselves immortalised by him, which he did in his own inimitably dashing yet unerring way.

LITERATURE

De Jongh & Vinken 1961; Slive 1970-74, vol. 3, no. 17; exhib. cat. Haarlem 1986, no. 20; exhib. cat. Washington/London/Haarlem 1989-90, no. 12

Frans Hals (Antwerp 1582/83-Haarlem 1666)

29 *The merry drinker, c. 1628-1630*

Oil on canvas, 81 x 66.5 cm
Far right of centre: FH
Purchased in 1816 at the Dowager C.P. Baron van Leyden van Warmond sale at Leiden
Inv. no. SK-A-135

It was the Utrecht Caravaggisti, as they are known, who introduced the Dutch Republic to the genre of evenly-lit paintings with just a single, lively, half-length figure holding a musical instrument, a glass or some other object. Another typically Caravaggesque touch is the old-fashioned dress worn by someone like Gerard van Honthorst's *Merry fiddler* [14], an earlier work in the genre here echoed by Frans Hals with this *Merry drinker*. One difference, though, is that this man's costume is what would actually have been worn in Holland around the end of the 1620s. In addition, the figure looks far more like a portrait than do the gleeful characters painted earlier in Utrecht. However, the light tonality dominated by yellow and brown ochres does display an unmistakable debt to the way in which the Caravaggisti coloured their protagonists.

It was also in this kind of painting of half-length figures that Frans Hals developed his distinctive broad manner of painting, in which he permitted himself great technical licence. *The merry drinker* shows off his virtuoso technique to the full. He applied the touches, dabs and strokes to the canvas rapidly and without hesitation, flawlessly modelling the hands, head and clothing in a single pass. He painted the laughing man in a very lively fashion, and seemingly without effort. It is hardly surprising to learn, then, that at the beginning of the 19th century *The merry drinker* was regarded as a mere sketch, an unfinished painting.

Hals depicted numerous fisher children and young, laughing boys in the same manner. Such swiftly executed genre pieces were evidently very popular with his contemporaries. Most of them were repeated several times, probably by pupils or followers, in the same period as the original. There are six early copies of *The merry drinker*, for instance.

Although Frans Hals applied a smooth finish to his portraits of the 1620s, particularly in the faces, he occasionally showed off his incredibly free technique in those of the 1630s. It is not surprising that at first he reserved his spontaneous brushwork for genre scenes, for they were not painted on commission, which meant that he did not have to take a client's wishes into account.

Genre-like scenes disappeared from Hals's oeuvre after 1640, and as far as we know he only painted portraits from then on. It is not clear why he stopped producing this kind of work for the open market, but one suspects that by then, when he was at the height of his fame, he could make a very comfortable living from portraiture alone.

LITERATURE

Slive 1970-74, vol. 3, no. 63; exhib. cat. Washington/London/Haarlem 1989-90, no. 30

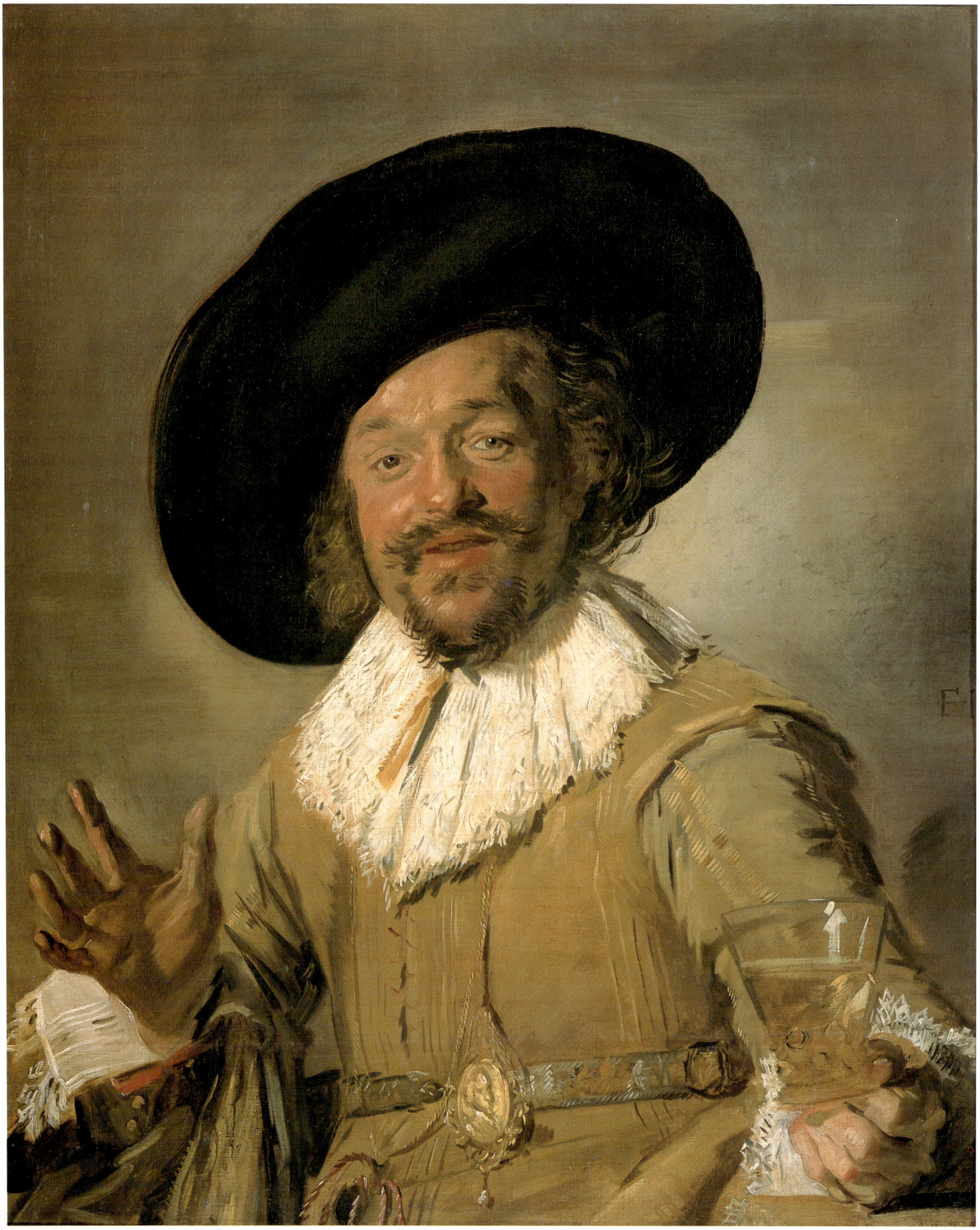

Rembrandt Harmensz van Rijn (Leiden 1606-Amsterdam 1669)

30 *Self-portrait as a young man, c. 1628*

Oil on panel, 22.6 × 18.7 cm
On loan from 1960 to 1971 from D.H. Cevat (Guernsey), from whom it was purchased in 1977 with the aid of the Vereniging Rembrandt, the Prins Bernhard Fonds, the Stichting VSB Fonds and the Commissie voor Fotoverkoop
Inv. no. SK-A-4691

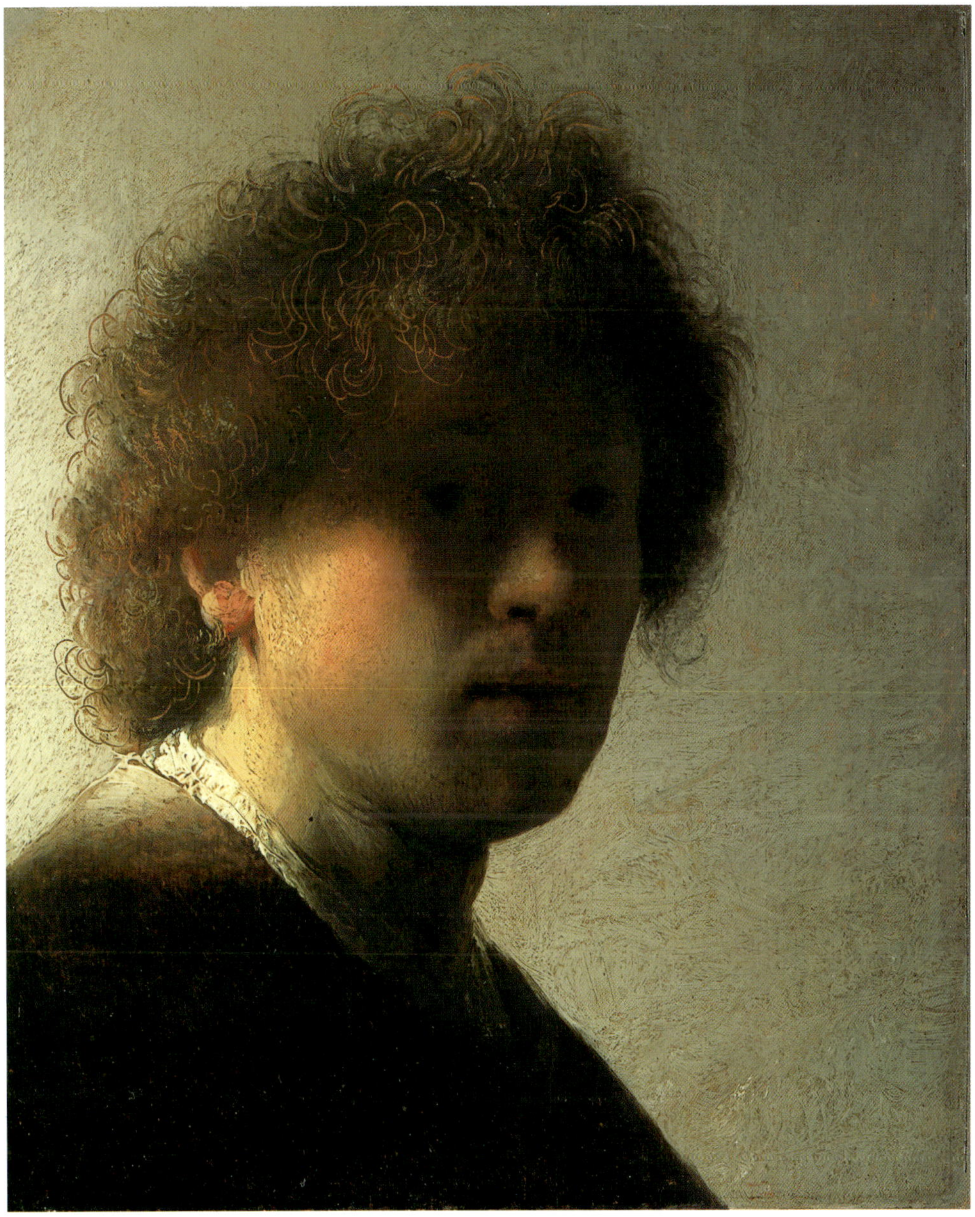

It is impossible to say how many self-portraits Rembrandt made, for any estimate depends on the definition of what does and does not belong to his oeuvre. Leaving aside the drawings and prints, the most rigorous scholars only admit a total of around 45, while others accept more than 60. All in all, with the drawings and prints included, Rembrandt must have recorded his own likeness at least 85 times. Whatever the true totals, he certainly depicted himself more often than any other 17th-century artist.

The self-portraits served various purposes. Some of them show him playing a role: as a hunter holding up a bittern (in the painting in Dresden), or as the Prodigal Son (with Saskia, also in Dresden), as one of those who crucified Christ (in the *Raising of the Cross* in Munich), as a member of the civic guard (in *The night watch*) or as the apostle Paul (in the late self-portrait in the Rijksmuseum, *fig.* 11). On several occasions he posed as an artist: confidently aware of his place in the pantheon of great masters (competing with Titian in his self-portrait in London's National Gallery), or as a painter in his studio (in the large self-portrait in Vienna, or the painting in Kenwood House).

Early on in his career, Rembrandt used the self-portrait to experiment with facial expressions or to explore the effect of light and shade. He must have been 22 years old when he made this small painting in which most of his face is shrouded in shadow. The best-lit areas are the ear and parts of the right cheek and the nose. They are painted with very few colours, but Rembrandt mixed them in such a way as to create the impression that there are more. The difficulty with the darker passages was to give shape to the face using very limited means. The eyes are particularly impressive, for unlike most self-portraits the artist is not looking out at the spectator. This is a difficult trick to pull off. When an artist looked into the mirror while painting his self-portrait he saw his reflection facing him head-on. By painting a likeness that does not look out of the picture he is presenting an image of himself that he cannot actually see. Rembrandt then made things even more difficult for himself with the lighting he chose. Eyes are obviously an essential part of the face in portraits, but here Rembrandt had to strike a delicate balance between the expressiveness of the face and the minimal depiction of the shadowed eyes.

He also conducted a marvellous experiment in the rendering of his shaggy, curly hair. He first painted an underlying layer in various colours, and after applying the hair in brown paint he took a sharp implement (probably the handle of his brush, but possibly a pointed piece of wood) and scratched in the curls, revealing the underlying colours. It is a simple but effective trick, and he was clearly delighted with the effect.

LITERATURE

Bruyn *et al.* 1982-89, vol. 1, no. A 14; Chapman 1990, pp. 22-24, 34, 37, 38, 71; exhib. cat. London/The Hague 1999-2000, no. 5

Rembrandt Harmensz van Rijn (Leiden 1606-Amsterdam 1669)

31 *Portrait of Johannes Wtenbogaert, 1633*

Oil on canvas, 130 x 103 cm
At upper right: *Rembrandt. ft./ 1633*
Commissioned by Abraham Anthonisz Recht; from the collections of Manfrin, Venice (until 1856), Baron Mayer de Rothschild, Mentmore (until 1977), Earl of Rosebery (1992); acquired in 1992 with the aid of the Vereniging Rembrandt, the Prins Bernhard Fonds, the Stichting VSB Fonds, the Rijksmuseum-Stichting, the Dutch government and numerous companies and private individuals
Inv. no. SK-A-4885

This painting is a record of a very special event, the meeting between two of the most remarkable figures in Dutch history: the elderly and combative Remonstrant preacher Johannes Wtenbogaert (1557-1644), whose fame must have been at its height at the time, and the up-and-coming painter Rembrandt van Rijn, who stood on the threshold of celebrity. We are well informed about the genesis of the portrait, for Wtenbogaert noted in his diary that he posed for Rembrandt in Amsterdam on 13 April 1633. The finished painting was not for Wtenbogaert himself but for one of his most loyal followers, the Amsterdam merchant Abraham Anthonisz Recht (1588-1664).

Johannes Wtenbogaert, who was born in Utrecht in 1557, went to Geneva in 1580 to study theology, and there forged a friendship with Jacobus Arminius (1560-1609). After serving as a preacher in Utrecht from 1584 to 1590 he was called to the ministry in The Hague in 1591, thanks to the support of Prince Maurits and Johan van Oldenbarneveldt, Advocate of Holland (1547-1619). He was made tutor to Frederik Hendrik, the future stadholder, and accompanied Prince Maurits as army chaplain on his campaigns of 1599 and 1600. Wtenbogaert was appointed court preacher to the prince in 1601.

He soon rose to head the religious faction urging tolerance in the many dogmatic disputes that erupted around this time, and it was under his leadership that the so-called Remonstrance was drawn up on 14 January 1610. This declaration, signed by 44 preachers, argued among other things that the state, as an impartial authority, should act as the guardian of freedom of conscience. It was a theological document, but it took on a political significance and sharpened the divisions in the conflict between the Remonstrants and Counter-Remonstrants, the supporters of two Leiden professors of theology, Jacobus Arminius and Franciscus Gomarus (1563-1641) respectively. Events took a fateful turn for the Remonstrant party when Prince Maurits openly sided with their foes in 1617. Maurits had Johan van Oldenbarneveldt arrested in 1618, tried for treason and executed. Other supporters of the libertarian cause, among them the jurist Hugo Grotius, were imprisoned. Wtenbogaert had already fled the country, first to Antwerp and then to Rouen. When Maurits died in April 1625, he secretly returned to the Republic, settling in Rotterdam in 1626. In 1629 he moved back to his former house in The Hague, dying there in 1644.

Rembrandt depicted the venerable preacher standing by a table on which there is a black hat in front of open book with handwritten pages. Wtenbogaert, who was 76 at the time, is shown three-quarter length. He is making a gesture associated with eloquence with his left hand and holds his gloves in the other. Rembrandt

Detail of [31] ▸

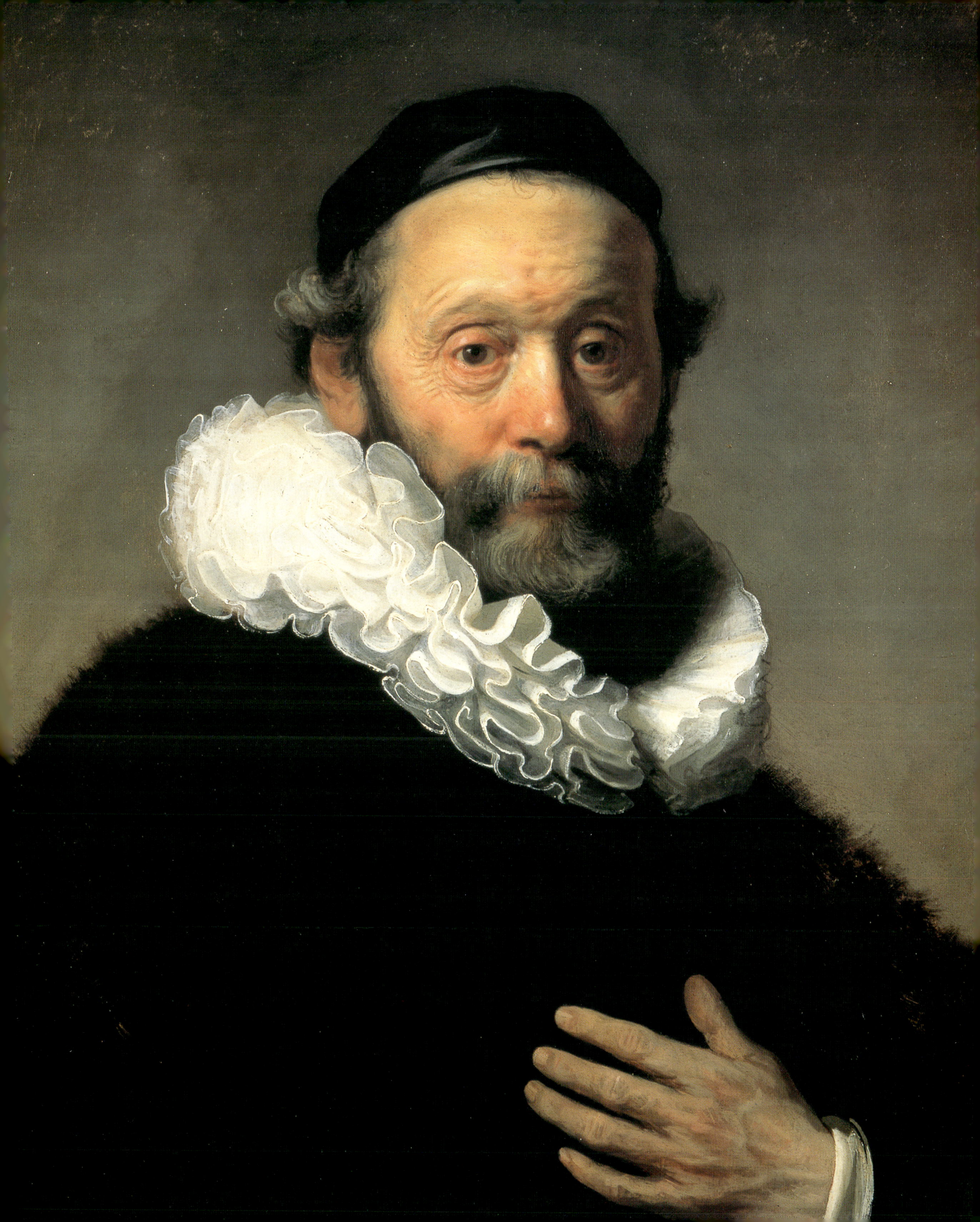

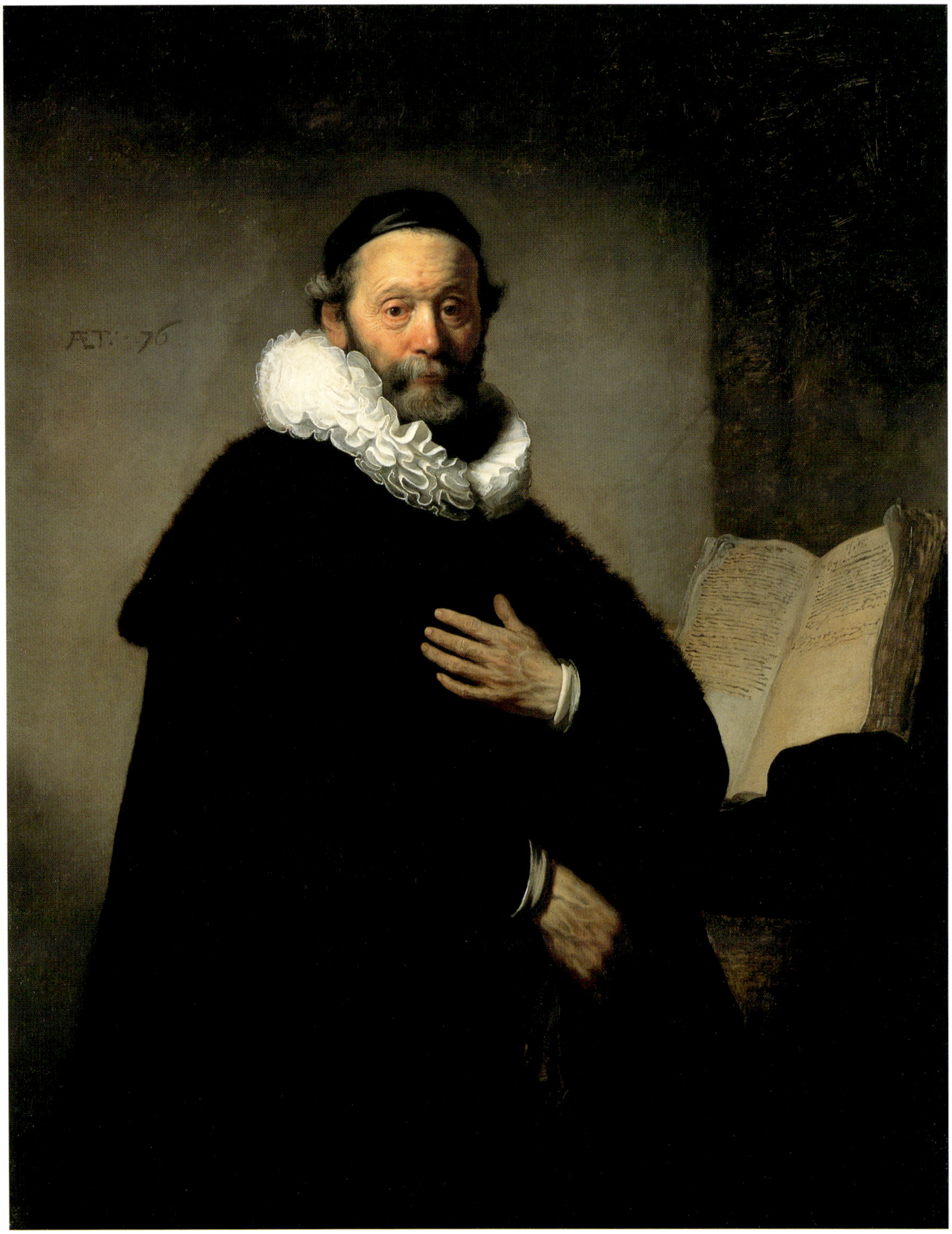

introduced a modicum of action in his portraits from the early 1630s in order to bring out the vivacity of his models. The illusion of restrained action and movement is achieved here through the dignified pose of the preacher, whose body is turned to the right but whose expressive gaze is directed straight at the viewer. It is as if he has turned away from his writings for a moment to look out at us.

LITERATURE

Bruyn *et al.* 1982-89, vol. 2, no. A 80; Kloek 1992; Bijl *et al.* 1994

Govaert Flinck (Cleves 1615-Amsterdam 1660)

32 *Isaac blessing Jacob, 1638*

Oil on canvas, 117 x 141 cm
The signature and the date 1638 disappeared when the painting was restored at the beginning of the 20th century
Purchased in 1808 at the sale of the collection of Gerrit van der Pot van Groeneveld, Rotterdam
Inv. no. SK-A-110

One of the benefits of the Reformation was that the Old Testament was translated into Dutch, making it accessible to broad swathes of the population for the first time. Many editions were lavishly illustrated, and this in turn led to the popularity of Old Testament scenes in 17th-century Dutch painting. The burgher class, brought up within this literary and visual tradition, must have regarded such pictures as desirable objects for decorating their homes while at the same time testifying to their Christian beliefs. In Amsterdam, anyway, Old Testament scenes were extremely popular in the circle formed by Rembrandt, his pupils and his many followers, and that is certainly true of the blessing stolen from Isaac (Genesis 27:1-29), the subject of this painting by Govaert Flinck. The 17th-century viewer was undoubtedly familiar with the story and thus knew, along with two of the protagonists, that the aged patriarch was being deceived.

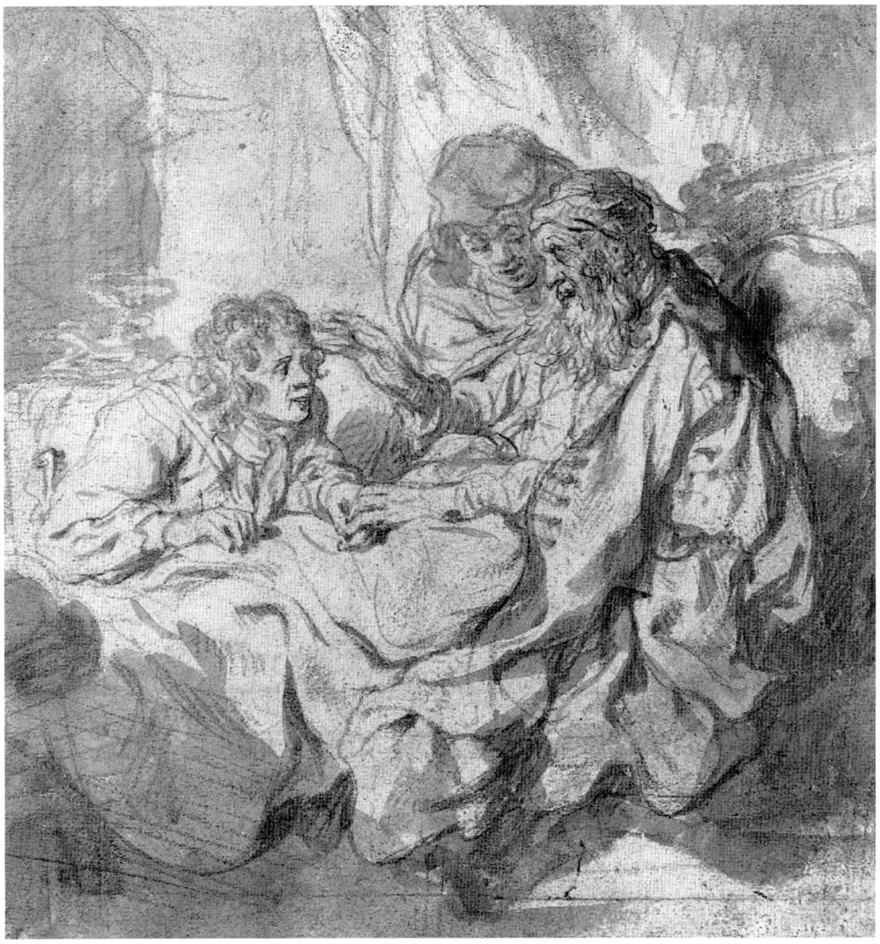

32a Govaert Flinck, *Isaac blessing Jacob*; red and black chalk, grey wash, 19.2 x 18.9 cm. Rotterdam, Museum Boijmans Van Beuningen

Jacob, urged on by his mother Rebecca, misled his father Isaac by disguising himself as his elder twin brother, Esau, in order to receive the blessing due to the firstborn. He put on Esau's clothes, and Rebecca completed the imposture by having him cover his hands and smooth neck with the skins of two goat kids which she had just slaughtered, so that he would feel as hairy to the touch as his brother. The blind Isaac has already raised his right hand but has a moment of doubt, and to reassure himself that it is his eldest son he reaches out and touches the hand of Jacob, who gazes up at him timorously. Rebecca looks on intently to see if her plan will work.

Govaert Flinck, who was a Mennonite, tells the biblical story with a great sense of drama and acute psychological insight. He also gave it careful thought, for he drew a preparatory study [*32a*], which is a rarity in his oeuvre. He focused on the psychological interaction by showing the figures in close-up, demonstrating that he was a worthy pupil of Rembrandt, with whom he studied for a while around 1633. There are no known paintings by Rembrandt of this subject, although there are some drawings. Several other Rembrandt pupils depicted the same scene, among them Gerbrandt van den Eeckhout and Jan Victors.

LITERATURE

Exhib. cat. Amsterdam 1991b, no. 1

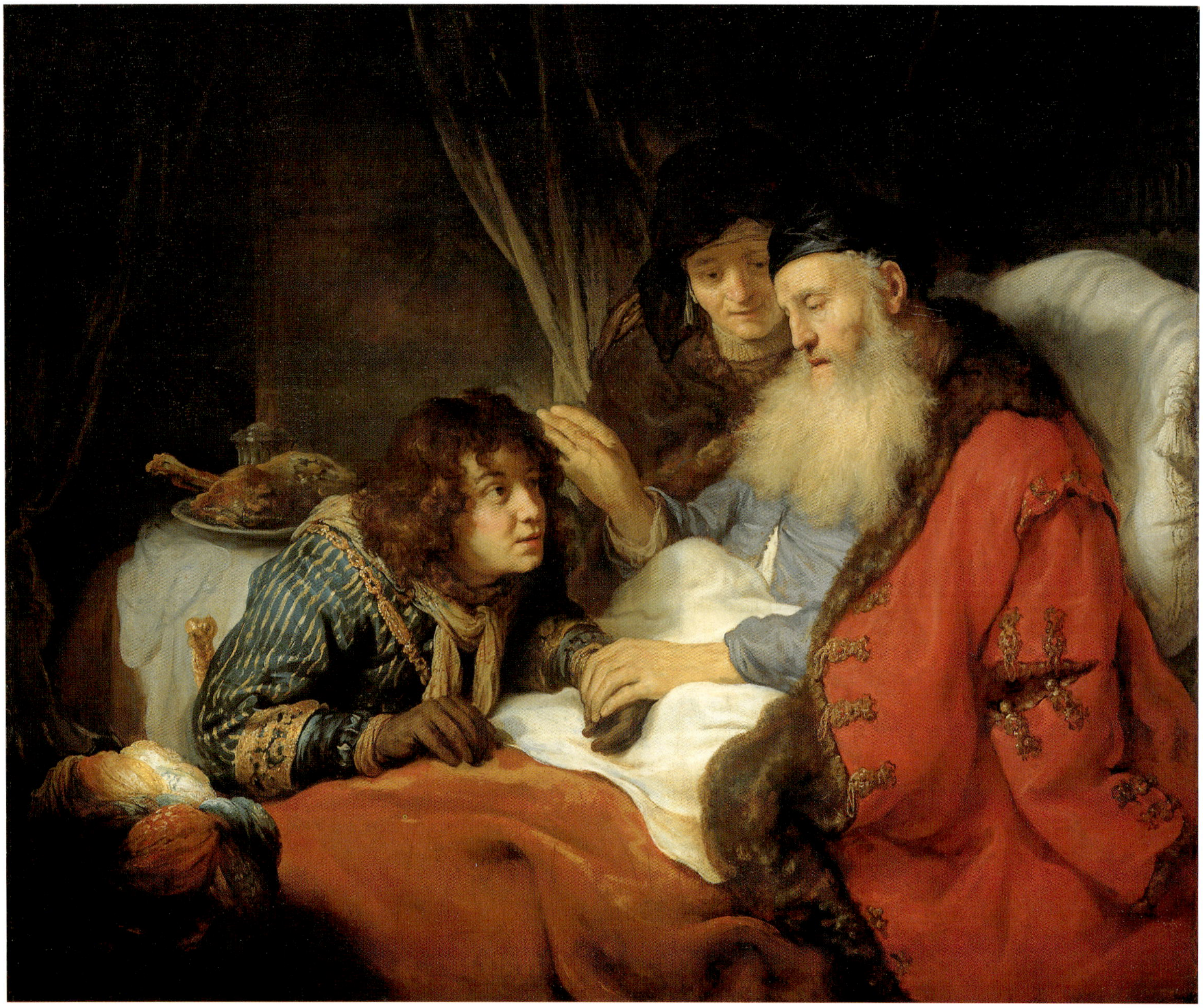

Johannes Lutma (Emden 1587-Amsterdam 1669)

33 *Two salts, 1639*

Silver, parcel-gilt, h. 24.2 cm, w. 12 cm
Both with the Amsterdam assay office mark, the year letter H (1639), and the maker's mark of a heart in an escutcheon (Johannes Lutma)
From the collection of W.J.R. Dreesmann, Amsterdam; purchased in 1960 at the sale of his collection
Inv. nos. BK-1960-13a/b

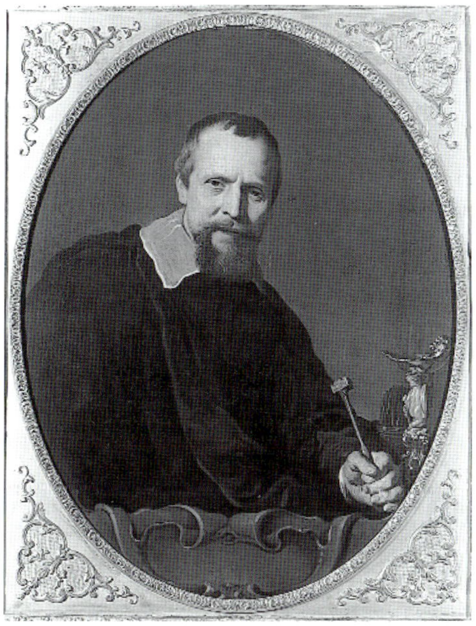

33a Jacob Backer, *Portrait of Johannes Lutma*, c. 1639; oil on panel, 91 x 71 cm. Amsterdam, Rijksmuseum

Johannes Lutma must have regarded these salts as a high point in his oeuvre, for around 1650 he had a very similar one included in his portrait, which was painted by Jacob Backer (1608-1651), a pupil of Rembrandt's [*33a*]. The salts are from a series of four, the two others being in the Amsterdams Historisch Museum.

The triangular foot, which is entirely covered with auricular decoration, and the stem in the form of a human body, were both devised by Adam van Vianen [*see 5*], but despite this influence Lutma's salts have a very different look. In contrast to Van Vianen, who raised the silver from a single sheet, Lutma's pieces are composed

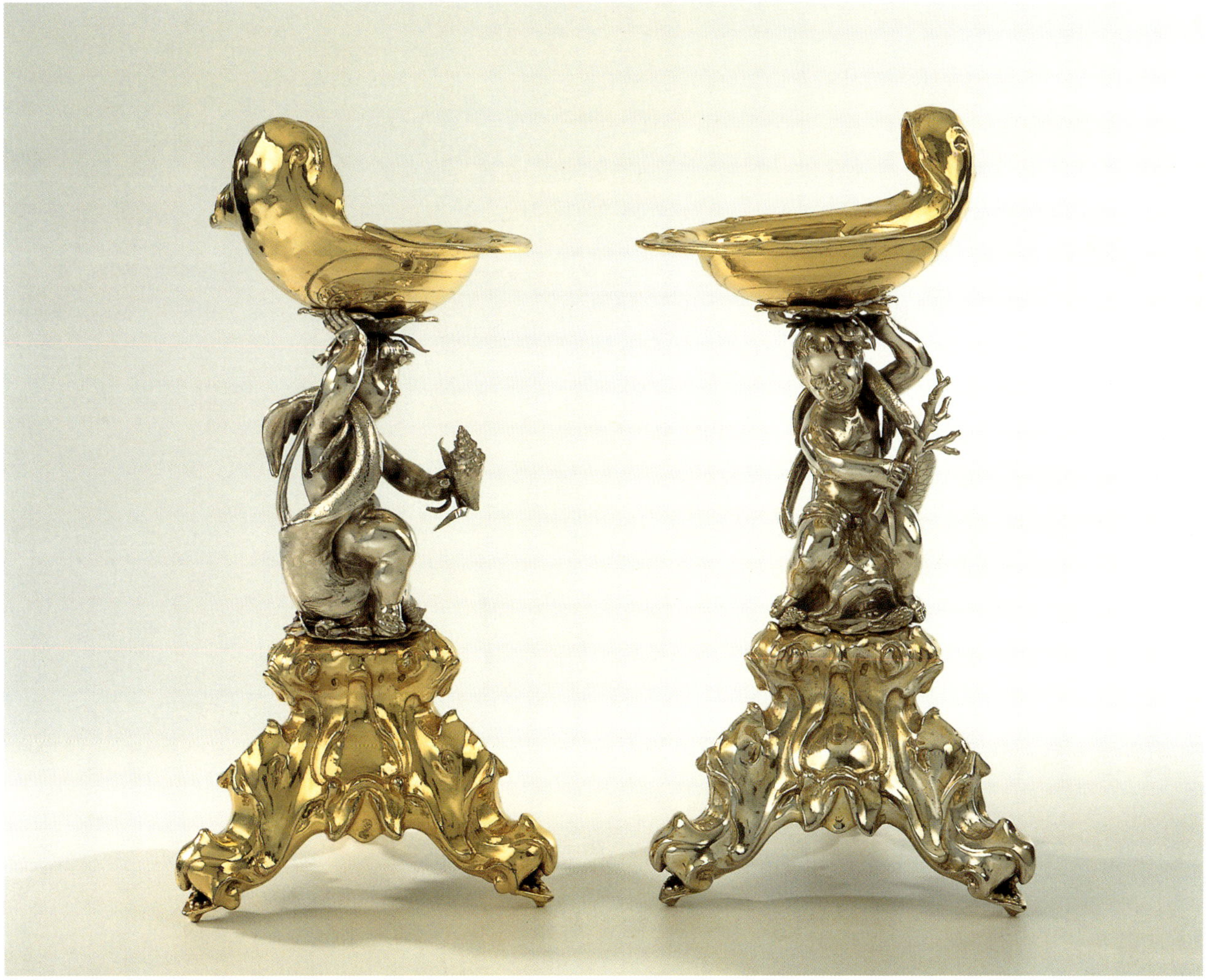

of separate elements, which is why there is no continuity between foot, stem and salt-well, as there is in Van Vianen's silver. The feet and stems of the Lutma salts, however, were not embossed but cast separately, and thus operate as two distinct formal elements. The contrast is accentuated by the fact that the surfaces of the foot and the well are gilt, while the stem is a matt white.

There was a practical reason for casting the parts separately. Not only did it make it relatively easy to produce several salts, but the parts could also be used for other types of object. This is illustrated in a still life by Willem Kalf containing a glass-holder, the stem of which is closely related to those of the salts [67]. Interestingly, the glass-holder in the painting is fully gilt, but that was probably artistic licence on Kalf's part. Standing beside the glass-holder is a ewer made in 1632 by Christiaen van Vianen (c. 1600/05-1667), now in the Victoria & Albert Museum in London. It is clear from the painting that these silver objects were well known in their day.

Probate inventories and depictions in paintings show that glass-holders were very common in the first half of the 17th century. They had a decorative or ceremonial function, with the glass being inserted into the holder to create a more imposing sort of drinking vessel. They gradually fell out of fashion as the century passed and were melted down, and nowadays they are extremely rare. Kalf's still life is the only evidence we have that Lutma also made glass-holders.

LITERATURE

Exhib. cat. Amsterdam 1984-85, no. 28; cat. Amsterdam 1999, no. 10

Pieter Claesz (Berchem 1597/98-Haarlem 1660)

34 *Still life with turkey pie, 1627*

Oil on panel, 75 x 132 cm
On the blade of the knife: *PC Ao 1627*
From the collection of Count J.C.N. van Lynden, Sint-Michielsgestel; purchased in 1974 with the aid of the Vereniging Rembrandt, the Prins Bernhard Fonds and the Commissie voor Fotoverkoop
Inv. no. SK-A-4646

Unlike Floris van Dijck [18], Pieter Claesz shows one of the sides of this laid table. That, and the suggestion of light falling on a wall behind it, gives the painting a more spacious look. The light also makes a *roemer* of white wine gleam, as well as casting a superb shadow with yellow highlights. The suggestion of space around the table is heightened by the reflection of a window in the pewter jug. This mirroring of light can be seen in six different forms in the ornate shape of the jug. Reflected on its round belly is the table with the cut loaf of bread and the plate with the lemon slices, together with a vague outline of the painter at his easel.

This is a far more bravura piece than Van Dijck's, and is painted with a more dashing, sometimes almost coarse brush. Instead of Van Dijck's costly, crisply ironed damask, Claesz typically covered his table with a rough rug with a white tablecloth on top, the creases and folds which articulate it and cast shadows that give it an elegant look. With his brisk manner of working, Claesz allows suggestion to play a much greater role than the meticulous Van Dijck. He also abandoned the orderly

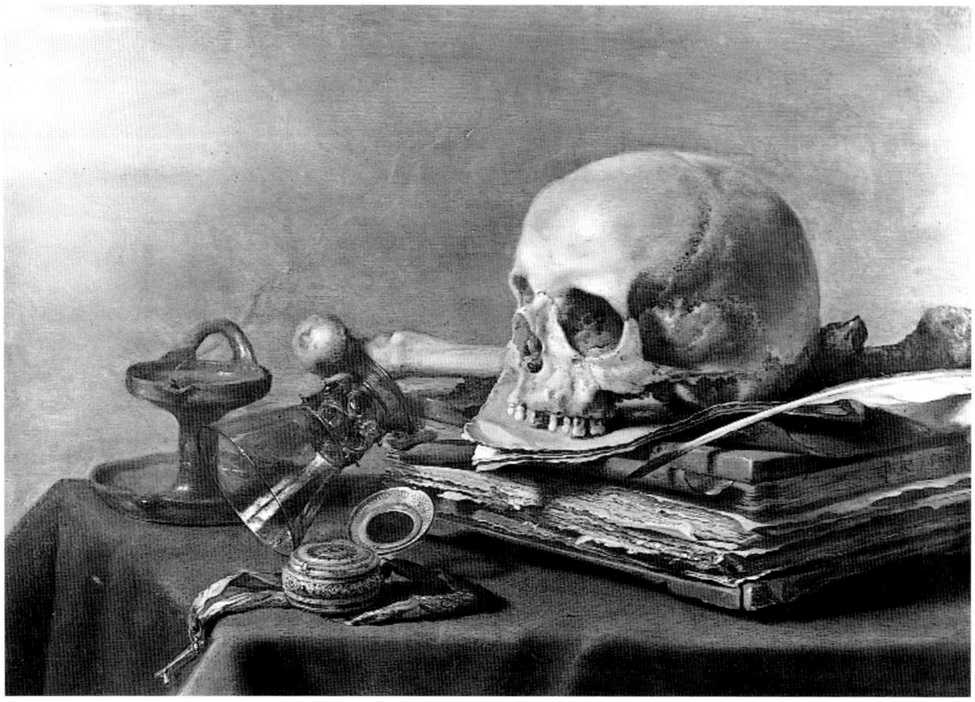

34a Pieter Claesz, *Vanitas still life*, 1630; oil on panel, 39.5 x 56 cm. The Hague, Mauritshuis

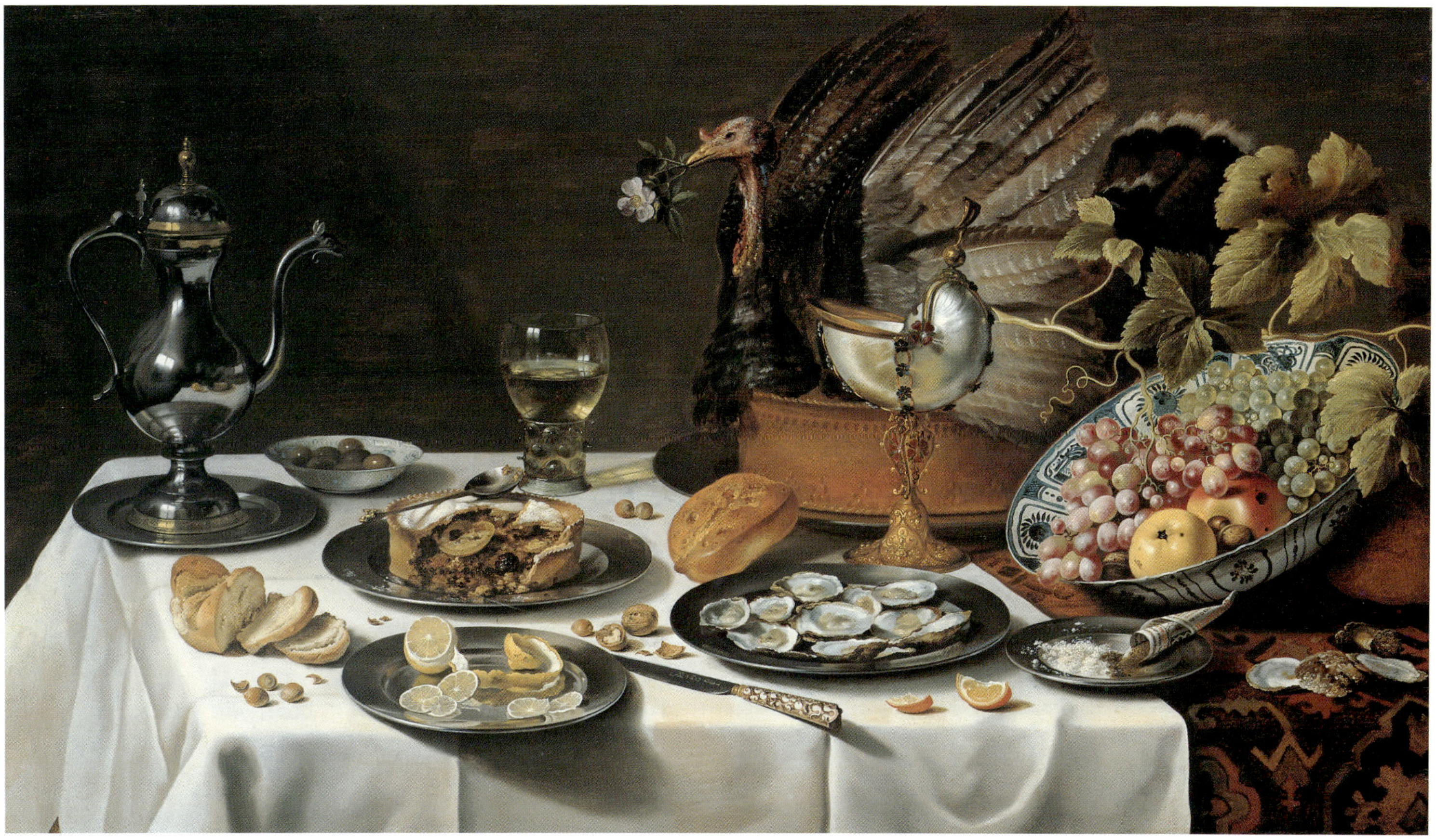

arrangement of the objects, although the scene is still thoughtfully composed. It is no coincidence that the fabulous animal on the spout of the jug is looking directly at the head of the turkey. Pieter Claesz had far less trouble with overlaps. The apples in the bowl on the right are half hidden by the bunches of grapes, and the bowl itself is leaning against a loaf of bread. The bowl and the vine leaves in turn partly block our view of the turkey pie. The wealth of colour is retained, and is exploited in the turkey's gaudy neck and the sprig of wild rose in its beak. The nautilus cup with its ornate foot and the inlaid handle of the knife contribute to the overall colourfulness of the scene.

Husk and content were also a motif in Floris van Dijck's painting, witness the apple cut in two, but for Pieter Claesz they became an important device for creating a variety of shapes: lemons, peeled and sliced, a page torn from an almanac and rolled up to hold pepper on a plate next to a scattering of sea salt, half and whole hazelnuts and walnuts, an opened pie, and the insides and outsides of oyster shells.

The *Still life with turkey pie* dates from 1627, and immediately precedes an impressive series of simple yet refined compositions in which Pieter Claesz discovered his great strength shortly before 1630. They are small works with relatively few objects subtly arranged and lit *[34a]*. In this painting, fine and imposing though it is, Claesz was above all trying to find an answer to the showpiece banquets of an artist like Floris van Dijck, although he did not really succeed in distancing himself from them.

LITERATURE
Van Thiel 1975

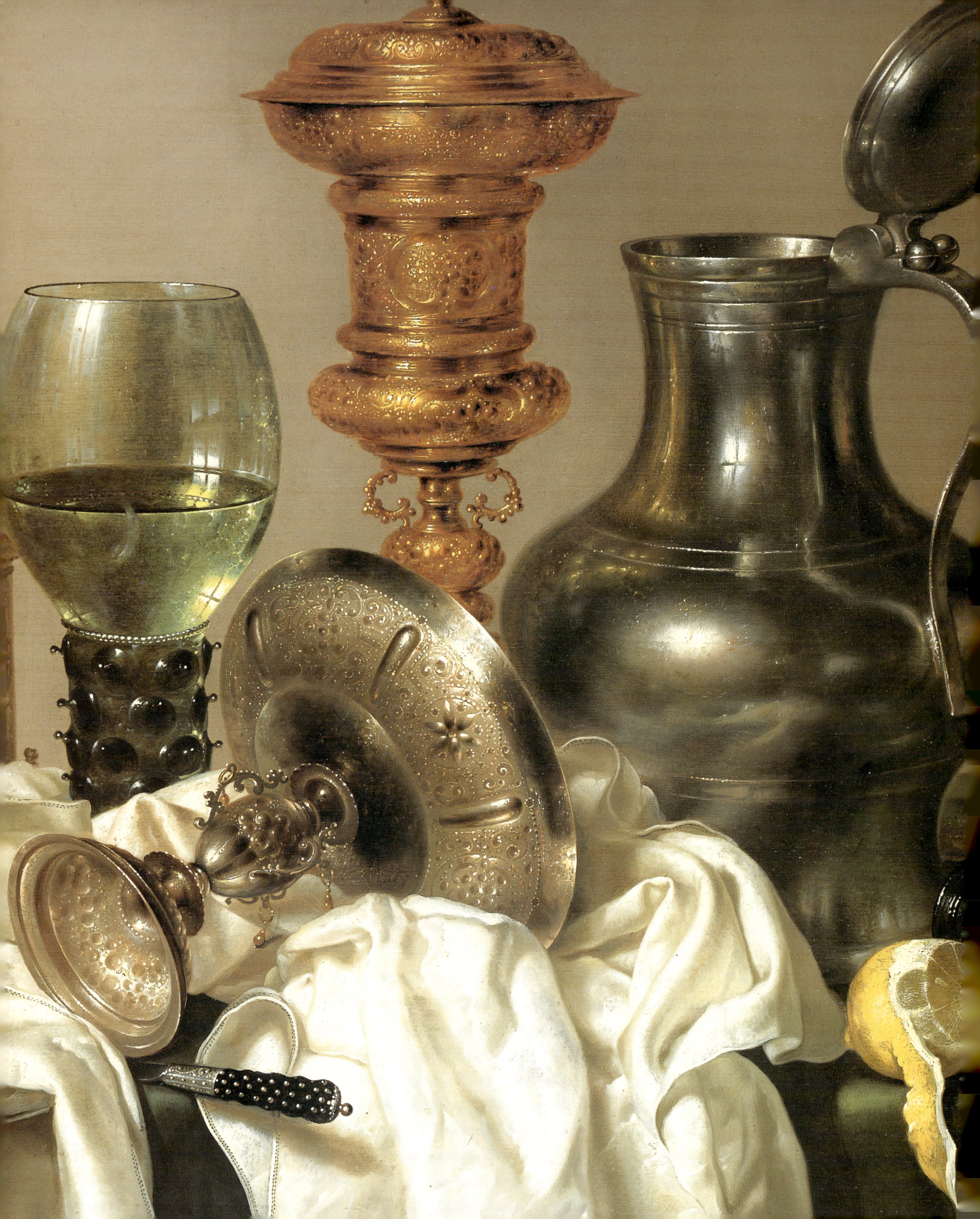

Willem Claesz Heda (Haarlem 1593/94-Haarlem 1680)

35 *Still life with gilt goblet, 1635*

Oil on panel, 88 x 113 cm
On the edge of the tablecloth on the right: *HEDA 1635*
Purchased in 1984 with extra funds from the Ministry of Welfare, Health and Cultural Affairs, and with the aid of the Vereniging Rembrandt
Inv. no. SK-A-4830

Willem Heda, like Pieter Claesz [34], excelled in seemingly straightforward still-life compositions which prove on closer examination to be arranged with remarkable discrimination. This particular painting, though, is one of the largest and most complex works from his finest period, around the mid-1630s.

Heda was an absolute master of grey tones, and in this painting he showed off his dazzling skill to the full. A silver *tazza*, a pewter jug, a cylindrical salt with a mound

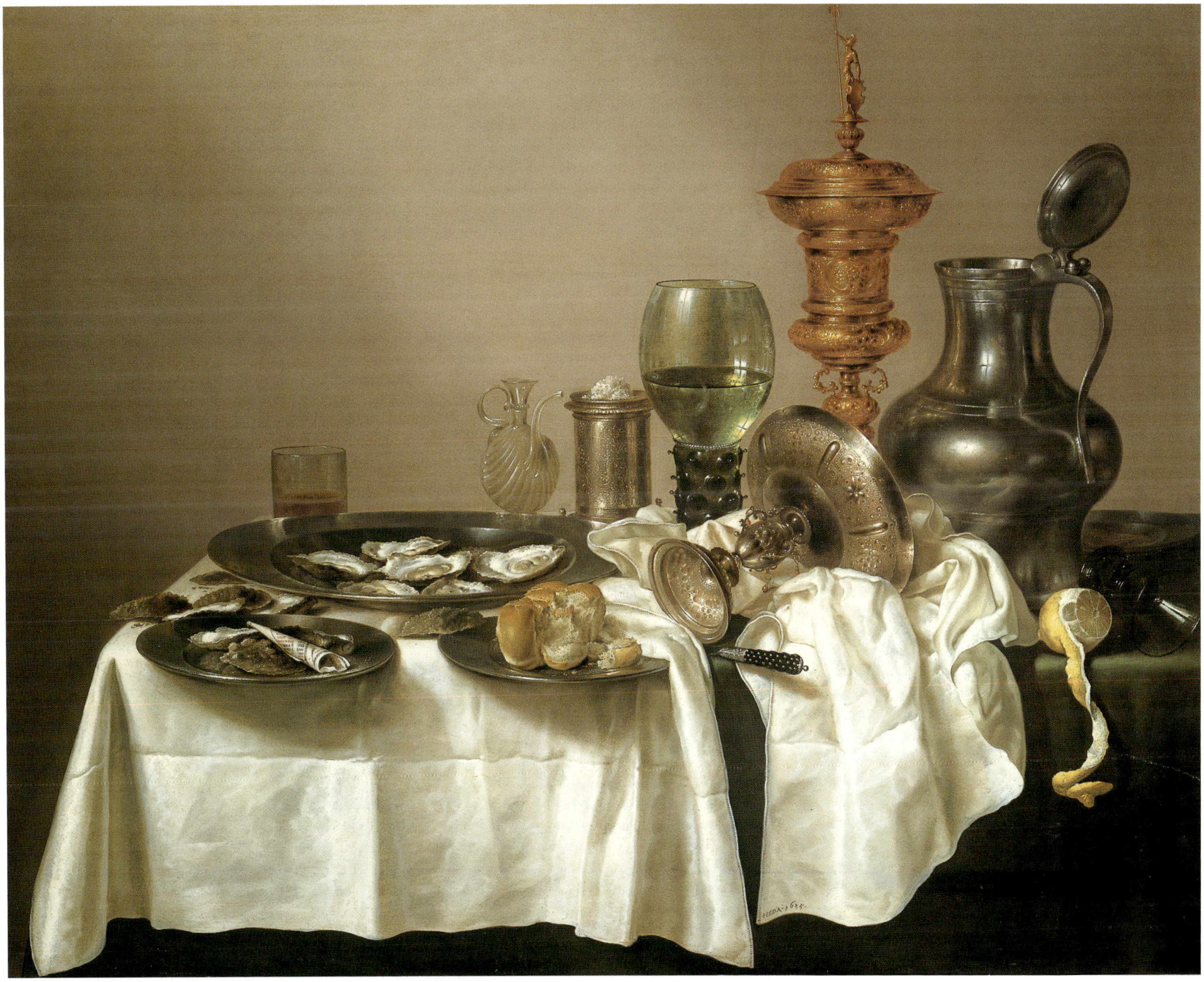

of sea salt on top, a glass oil with a spout, and pewter plates with oysters. Most of the objects are in varying shades of grey, sometimes tending towards blue, occasionally towards brown. Together they form an intriguing silhouette against a brown-grey background with a vague suggestion of light source falling on it. The elegantly decorated *tazza* is one of the high points, lying on its side to provide a view of the inside of the foot with its plain, unchased silver. Heda could use whites and greys alone to depict a tablecloth, smooth with taut folds or crumpled up and wrinkled, or for example a window reflected in the pewter jug. The interplay of reflected light is done with great delicacy on the jug, the light gleaming on edges and the reflection of the handle creating a subtle colour shift on the body of the jug.

Heda used a richer palette in this ambitious painting than he did in his simpler works, which are often misleadingly labelled 'monochrome' because of the limited range of colours. The palette is indeed restrained compared to the two works by Floris van Dijck and Pieter Claesz [18, 34], but the bright yellow of the lemon, the red liquid in the glass on the left, the green glass of the *roemer*, the red and brown of the gilt copper, ornamental goblet with yellow accents, and the golden brown loaf of bread do make this the most exuberant work of Heda's 'monochrome' period. He was not looking for garishness in those colours but for sensitive or interesting contrasts, as can be seen from the one between the subdued green of the tablecloth and the harsh blue-green of the fallen *berkenmeier* on the far right.

Heda shows far less of the tabletop than Van Dijck and Claesz do. In Claesz's case one gets the impression that the artist wanted to allow us to chart the precise positions of the objects, but Heda freely shows the side of the table, while the low vantage point and sheer number of objects hide its surface. Heda's solution, however, is remarkably effective in conveying the suggestion of an over-laden table. The two plates perilously close to the edge and the shadows they cast on the tablecloth below are extremely important for imparting a sense of depth. They and the numerous overlaps make it clear that there is space on and around the table.

LITERATURE
Klock 1989a

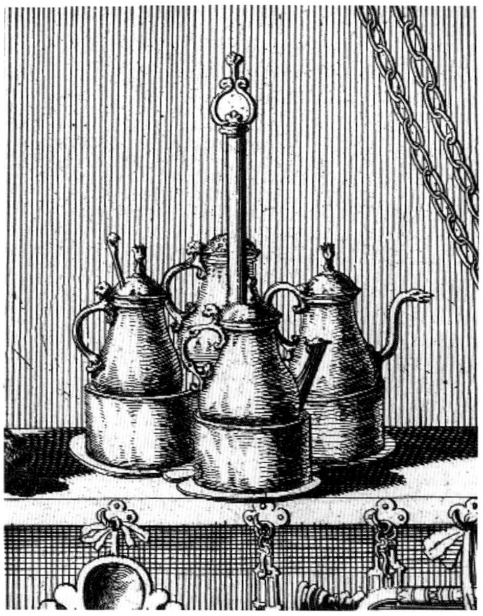

36a Anonymous artist after Jan Luyken, *Print advertising the Durgerdam lottery* (detail), 1688; etching, 58.2 x 51.5 cm. Amsterdam, Rijksmuseum, Rijksprentenkabinet

Anthonie Grill (Augsburg 1609-Sweden 1675), attributed to

36 *Cruet-stand, 1642*

Silver, with traces of gilding, holder h. 27.1 cm
Marked on the underside of the stand and on the foot-rims of the oil cruet, the two shakers and the salt with the Amsterdam assay office mark, the year letter L (1642) and the maker's mark of a stork between the letters AG (attributed to Anthonie Grill)
Purchased in 1997
Inv. no. BK-1997-1

For centuries the salt had taken pride of place on the table [*see 19*], but here it is a far more modest piece that is just one part of a set consisting of a small cruet for oil, two shakers, probably for different kinds of pepper, and a small goblet for the salt. This set is the earliest known form of a silver ensemble made in the Netherlands for secular use. The silversmith was meeting a demand for new sorts of utensil prompted by the import of spices from the Orient that got under way in the early 17th century.

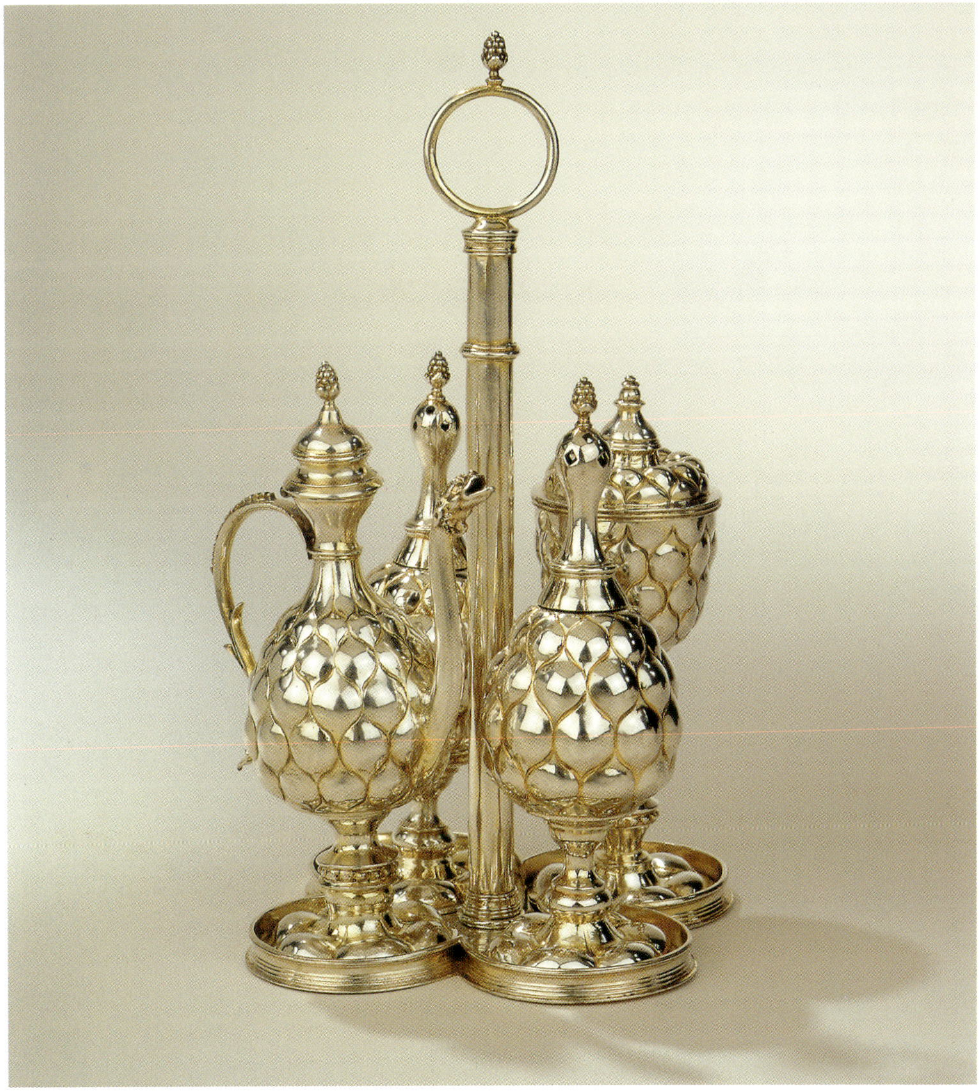

This is the only known cruet-stand of its type. A similar one, with containers of a different shape, is depicted in an anonymous print after Jan Luyken [*36a*] that was published to advertise a lottery of silver objects held in the village of Durgerdam, near Amsterdam, in 1689. It was the third prize, and is described as 'a silver cruet-stand worth 130 guilders including cost of manufacture'. It consists of a lobed base with holder on which four one-handled bottles stand. Two of them have spouts and probably held oil and vinegar, the third was for mustard and the fourth for pepper. Cruet-stands of this kind must also have been in use in the southern Netherlands in the same period. The inventory of the silverware belonging to Jan Lindemans of Antwerp, who died in 1664, lists 'a set in six parts, namely an oil bottle, vinegar bottle, pepper pot, sugar shaker and salt, a crown with a Bacchus on top'. What is interesting about that stand, which may have been made in Antwerp, is the inclusion of a sugar shaker. The 'crown' may have been the carrying-ring.

The fir-cone shape of the Amsterdam cruets is probably connected with the Augsburg origins of the silversmith, Anthonie Grill, for it had been in widespread use in that region since the early 16th century. Grill and his brothers Andries and Johannes settled in Amsterdam before 1630, and it is possible that they and other German silversmiths who had moved to Amsterdam introduced this design into the Dutch Republic.

LITERATURE
Cat. Amsterdam 1999, no. 12

Cornelis van Poelenburch (Utrecht c. 1594/95-Utrecht 1667)

37 *Figures beneath the arches of a classical ruin, c. 1620-1625*

Verso: part of the Colosseum
Pen in brown, brush in brown and some grey, over traces of a sketch in black chalk, 42.7 x 38.5 cm
At lower right: CP
From the collection of Jacob de Vos Jbzn, Amsterdam; acquired with the aid of the Vereniging Rembrandt in 1884
Inv. no. RP-T-1884-A-293

'It seems to me that that century [the 17th] had no regard for artists if they had not seen Rome for themselves', wrote Arnold Houbraken in his biography of Cornelis van Poelenburch. And indeed, a seemingly endless stream of Dutch painters went south throughout the 17th century. Many felt that their training was only complete after a stay in the Eternal City. Some remained just a few months in Italy, others spent years there, and a handful settled permanently in the land of Raphael, Michelangelo and the classical artists.

Cornelis van Poelenburch was certainly in Rome in 1617, for in that year he wrote a poem in Italian in the *album amicorum* of the Frisian painter Wybrand de Geest, who arrived in the city in December 1616. Further testimony to Poelenburch's stay comes in the form of drawings with autograph annotations like 'in roomen' (in Rome), 'buyten roomen' (outside Rome) and 'in tievele' (in Tivoli). Dated drawings with inscriptions of this kind survive from the period 1619-1623.

Poelenburch's Italian drawings from the first half of the 1620s are characterised by a lavish use of the brush in dark brown ink and close attention to the rendering of light and shade. Those are also features of this large view of the dark vault of a classical ruin. It is drawn on a sheet of Italian paper which is very large indeed by Poelenburch's standards, and seems to have been drawn in Rome in the early 1620s.

At first sight one could be forgiven for thinking that Poelenburch drew the interior of a large cave. Only on closer inspection does one discover a partially overgrown arch of masonry as well as other irregular remnants of brickwork. It is not certain where the artist drew this gloomy vault. It could be part of the ruins of the imperial palaces on the Palatine, or of one of the thermal bath complexes, or the ground floor of the Colosseum. The latter suggestion is perhaps nearest to the mark, given the view of the Colosseum from the southwest on the back of the sheet. Poelenburch occasionally used motifs from his collection of drawings in the landscape backgrounds of his paintings, and that was the case here. Exactly the same fragment of the Colosseum appears in the background of his *Martyrdom of St Lawrence* in Kassel, which is dated around 1622-1624. The echoes of Poelenburch's stay in Italy continued reverberating in his paintings, not so much in his choice of subject, although classical ruins do regularly crop up in his landscapes, as in the warm, Mediterranean sunlight that bathes his scenes.

Cornelis van Poelenburch enjoyed great fame in his own lifetime. Collectors vied with each other to buy his small landscapes with biblical, mythological or historical scenes painted on copper or panel, and would have agreed with Houbraken 'that he outdid his contemporaries not only in feeling, softness and fine outlines, but also in the pleasing choice of subjects, the ingenious incorporation of ancient ruins, naturally coloured landscapes, and tenuous, bright skies'.

LITERATURE

Cat. Amsterdam 1998, no. 266

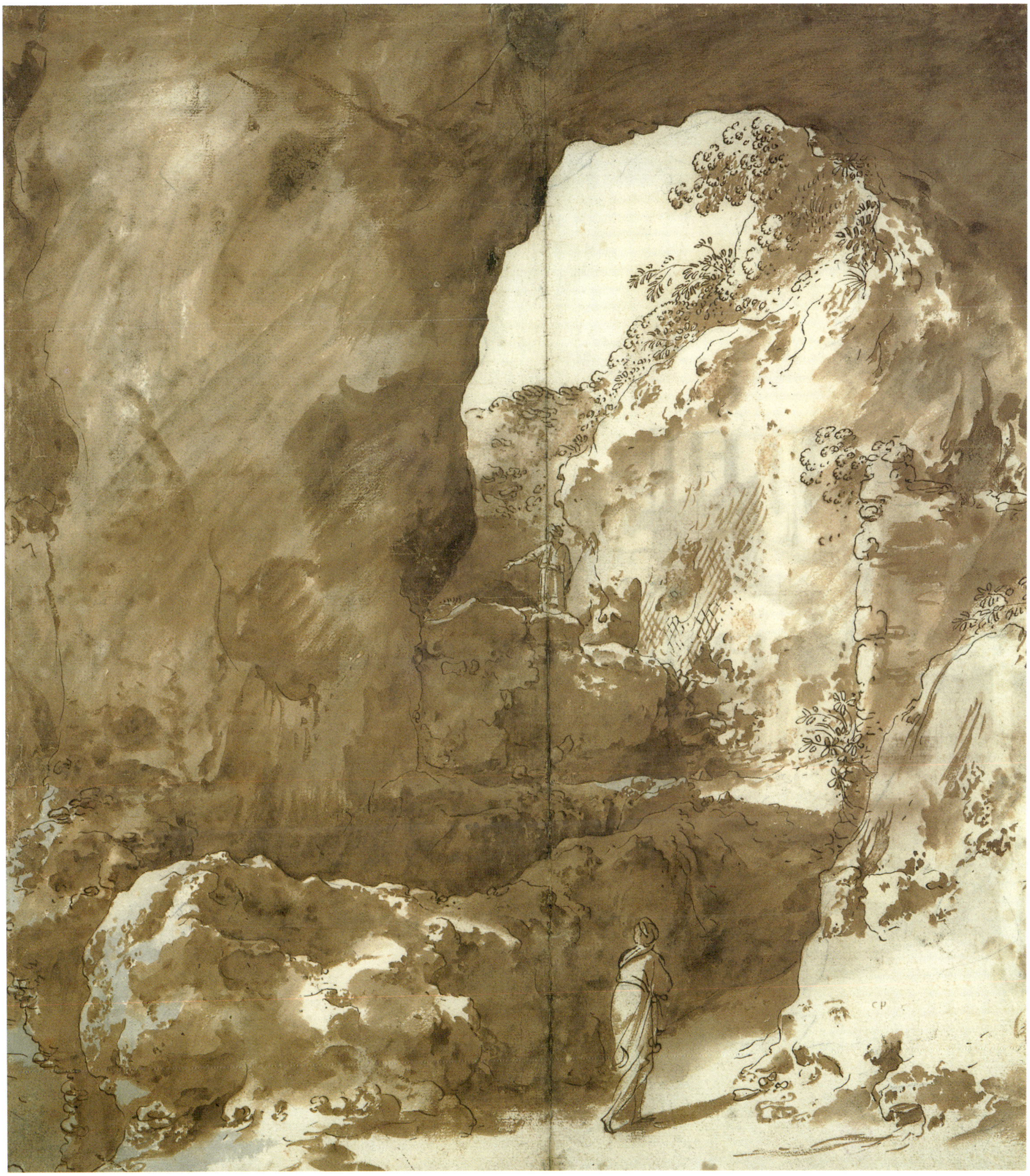

Rembrandt Harmensz van Rijn (Leiden 1606-Amsterdam 1669)

38 *The stone bridge*, *c. 1638*

Oil on panel, 29.5 x 42.5 cm
In various collections, including that of the Marquess of Lansdowne, Bowood (1883); purchased in 1900 with the aid of Dr A. Bredius and the Vereniging Rembrandt
Inv. no. SK-A-1935

There are only a few known landscape paintings by Rembrandt, which makes it all the more remarkable that the first Rembrandt bought by the Rijksmuseum just happened to be one of them. It is fortunate that it caught the purchaser's eye, for it is not really a work that one would immediately associate with the prevailing view of a master whose portraits and biblical scenes were imbued with a deeply felt humanity. What is abundantly clear to anyone, though, is that this landscape is, at the very least, a haunting scene, and as such it must have fitted in with the Romantic notion of Rembrandt's artistry.

He has depicted a moment when the sun is still just able to pierce through a gap in the clouds, lighting up the stand of trees in the centre in an almost surrealistic way and giving the distinctively Dutch polder landscape an air of looming menace. The reality, both literally and figuratively, is less spectacular. In Rembrandt's day, for example, one would not have come across a stone bridge in a stretch of countryside like this, for as a rule they were only found in towns. On top of that, Rembrandt very probably took earlier models as the basis for his visionary conception of the landscape. It has been argued convincingly that the inspiration for the scene came from a landscape etching of 1616 by Jan van de Velde [*38a*], which shows once again that Rembrandt always took account of the tradition within a particular genre. This of course does not alter the fact that he opted for an extremely dramatic mood, but in that respect too he must have been drawing on the work of other masters, such as Hercules Segers. Rembrandt owned several paintings by Segers, and it is generally believed that one of them was the work now in Florence [*38b*].

It was only quite late in his career that Rembrandt developed an interest in landscape as a more or less independent genre. He made his earliest dated landscape etching in 1641, for instance, and it was not until the 1640s that he made landscape drawings with any regularity. In his painted oeuvre, the *Landscape with the Good Samaritan* in Cracow is dated 1638, and *The stone bridge* must have been executed around then or a little later. Dendrochronological examination has revealed that the panel could not have been painted before 1638.

It has been claimed that this landscape and the one in Cracow really expound a Christian moral, with the man on the far left with his staff over his shoulder being a symbol of mankind making its way to the church representing salvation on the right. Such an explanation is not really convincing. It is more the drama of nature that has been elevated to a subject in its own right than the drama of man's existence on earth.

38a Jan van de Velde, *Skaters on a river*, 1616; etching, 12 x 18.8 cm. Amsterdam, Rijksmuseum, Rijksprentenkabinet

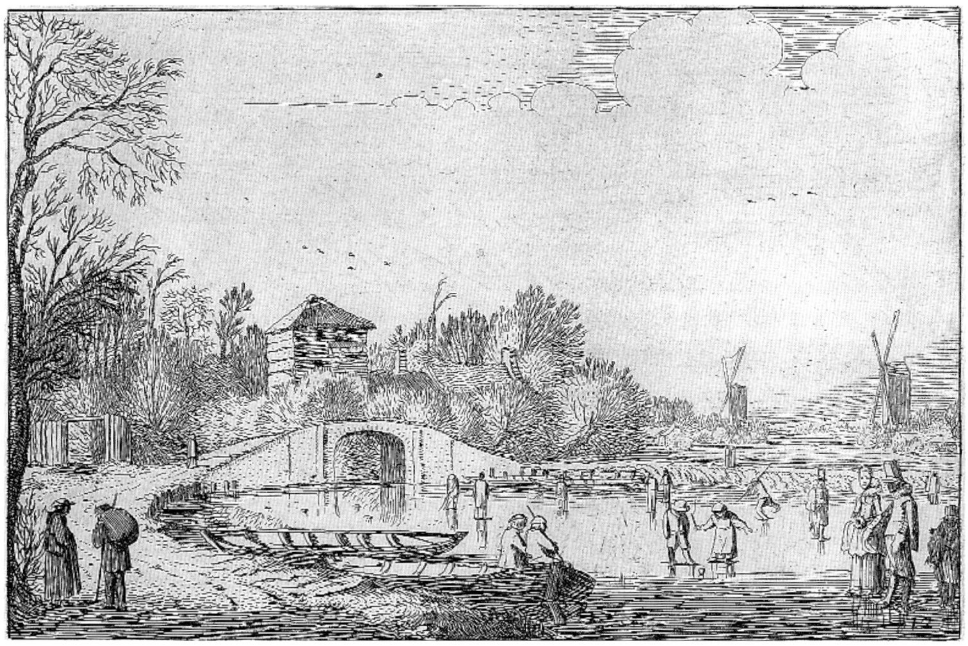

LITERATURE

Bruyn *et al.* 1982-89, vol. 3, no. A 136; exhib. cat. Amsterdam/Boston/Philadelphia 1987-88, no. 76; Schneider 1990, no. 1; exhib. cat. Berlin/Amsterdam/London 1991-92, no. 31

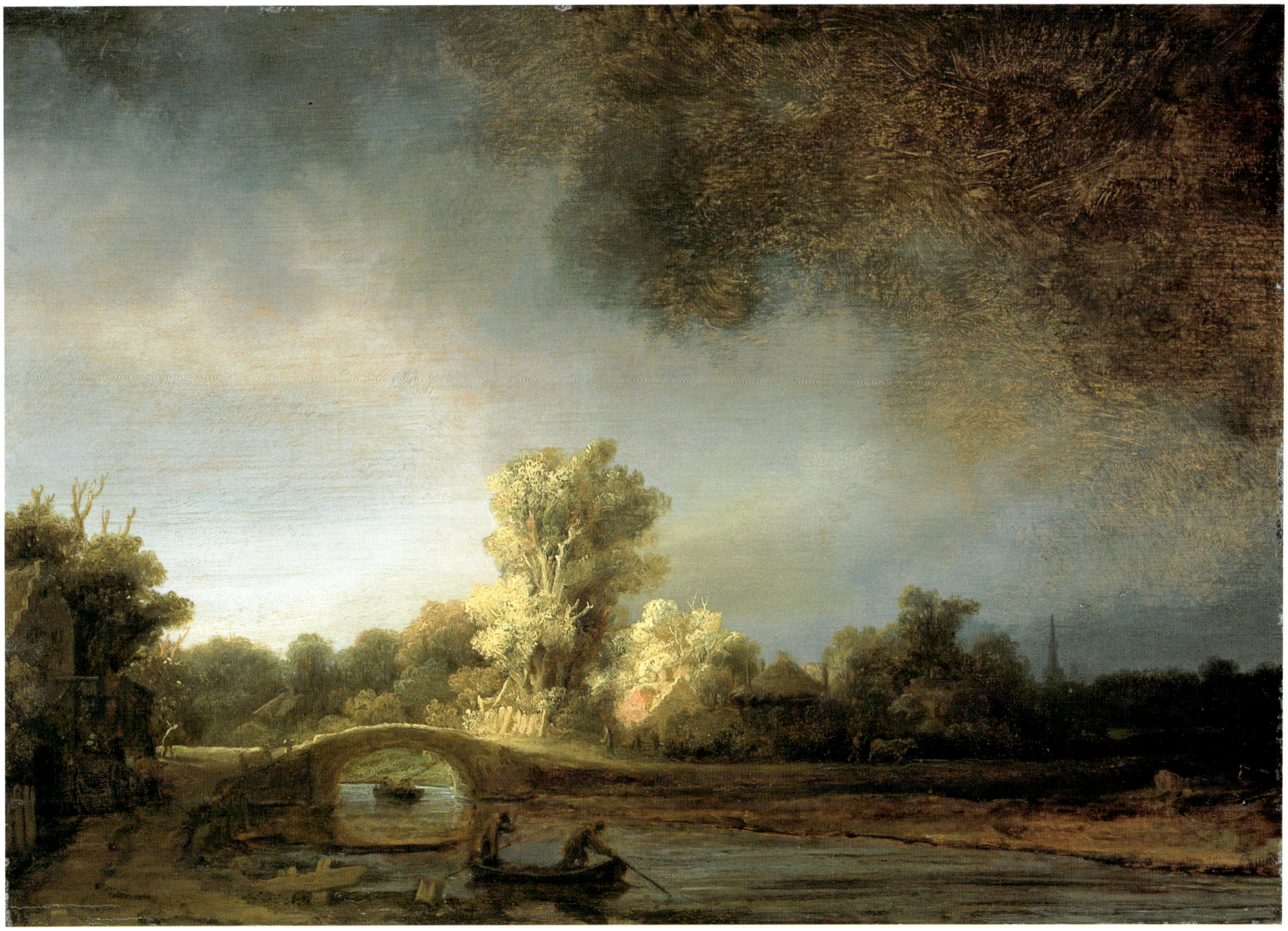

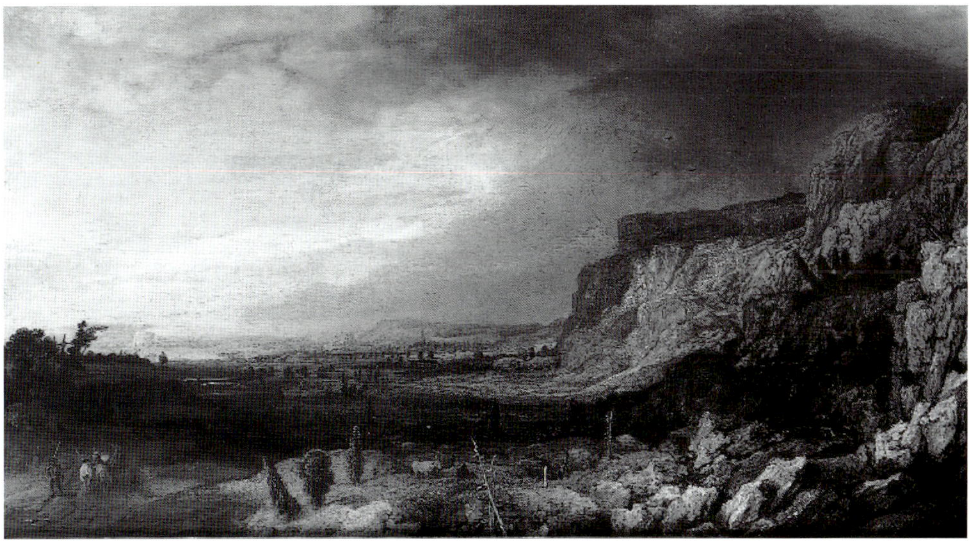

38b Hercules Segers, *Mountain landscape*, c. 1630-1635; oil on canvas transferred to panel, 55 x 100 cm. Florence, Galleria degli Uffizi

Jan van Goyen (Leiden 1596-The Hague 1656)

39 *Landscape with two oaks, 1641*

Oil on canvas, 88.5 x 110.5 cm
At lower centre: *ivG 1641* (*iv* in ligature)
Bequeathed in 1870 by L. Dupper Wzn, Dordrecht
Inv. no. SK-A-123

Two travellers are resting by a pair old oaks ravaged by wind and weather on a hillside overlooking a plain that stretches to the far horizon. A shaft of sunlight pierces the heavy overcast to illuminate the area in front of the trees at a point that must be regarded as the heart of the painting. The men are wearing remarkably colourful garb, the seated one in a blue coat and yellow trousers, his companion in a red jacket and brown trousers. Only on looking more closely does one spot a third wayfarer, a man in a green jacket who is heading off down the hill.

It is not the travellers who are the main subject of the painting but the twisted trunks of the oaks standing out starkly against the sky. Their lonely, elevated position in the landscape suggests that their shapes are due to lightning strikes. Although their battered look recalls the Dutch saying that old age brings infirmity, Van Goyen's main emphasis is on their green foliage, on the resilience of old trees which manage to survive despite their vulnerability.

Van Goyen undoubtedly got his inspiration for this painting on a trip to the eastern Netherlands, where similar views can be found near a town like Nijmegen. He made many such expeditions, filling sketchbooks along the way with masses of black chalk drawings to serve as models when he returned home. He did not usually aim for topographical accuracy in his paintings, so these two oaks should not be seen as portraits of trees, however attractive that idea might be.

The following year, 1642, Jan van Goyen again painted an old oak tree, this time by the waterside [*39a*]. There, too, the contrast between the contorted shape of the trees and the sky behind them is a key element of the painting. The oaks in the painting of 1641 may have been blasted as a result of their lonely position high up on a hill, but the oak in the 1642 picture is endangered by its proximity to water—a vulnerability which has been associated with the theme of death never being far away. That seems to be contradicted by the impressive age of the trees and the vitality of their young shoots. It is undeniable, though, that Van Goyen exploited the pictorial potential of the trees to the full. He graphically captured their writhing shapes with a wealth of yellows, ochres and greens, and an occasional touch of pink. His main inspiration, then, was probably the pictorial attraction of the aged trees.

39a Jan van Goyen, *An old oak by the waterside*, 1642; oil on panel, 65 x 58 cm. Private collection

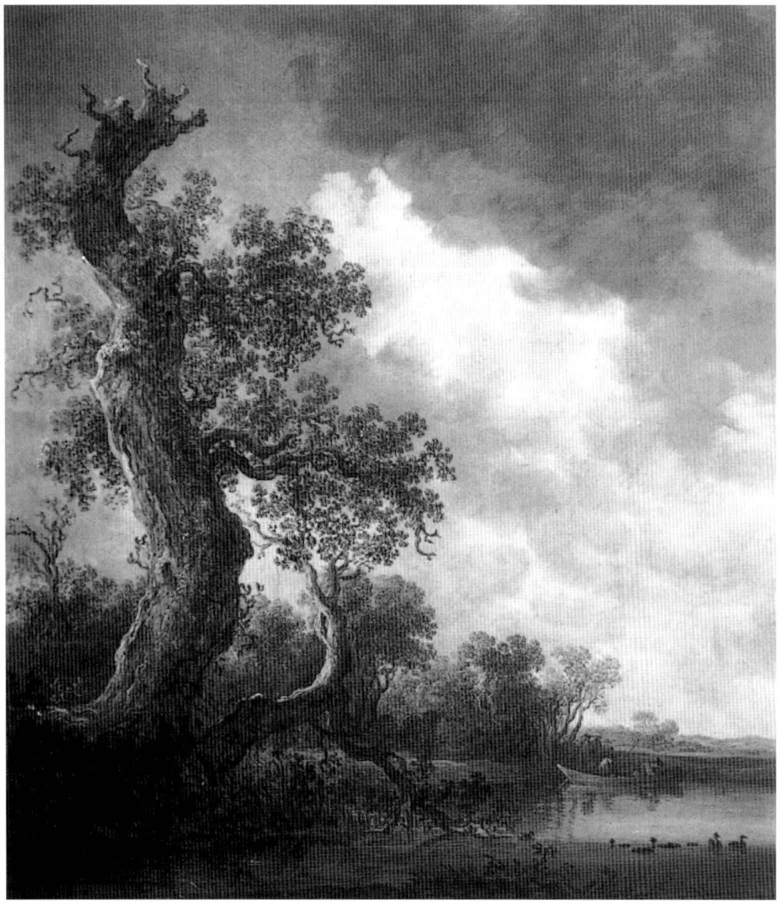

LITERATURE

Beck 1972-87, vol. 2, no. 1144; exhib. cat. Leiden 1996-97, no. 23

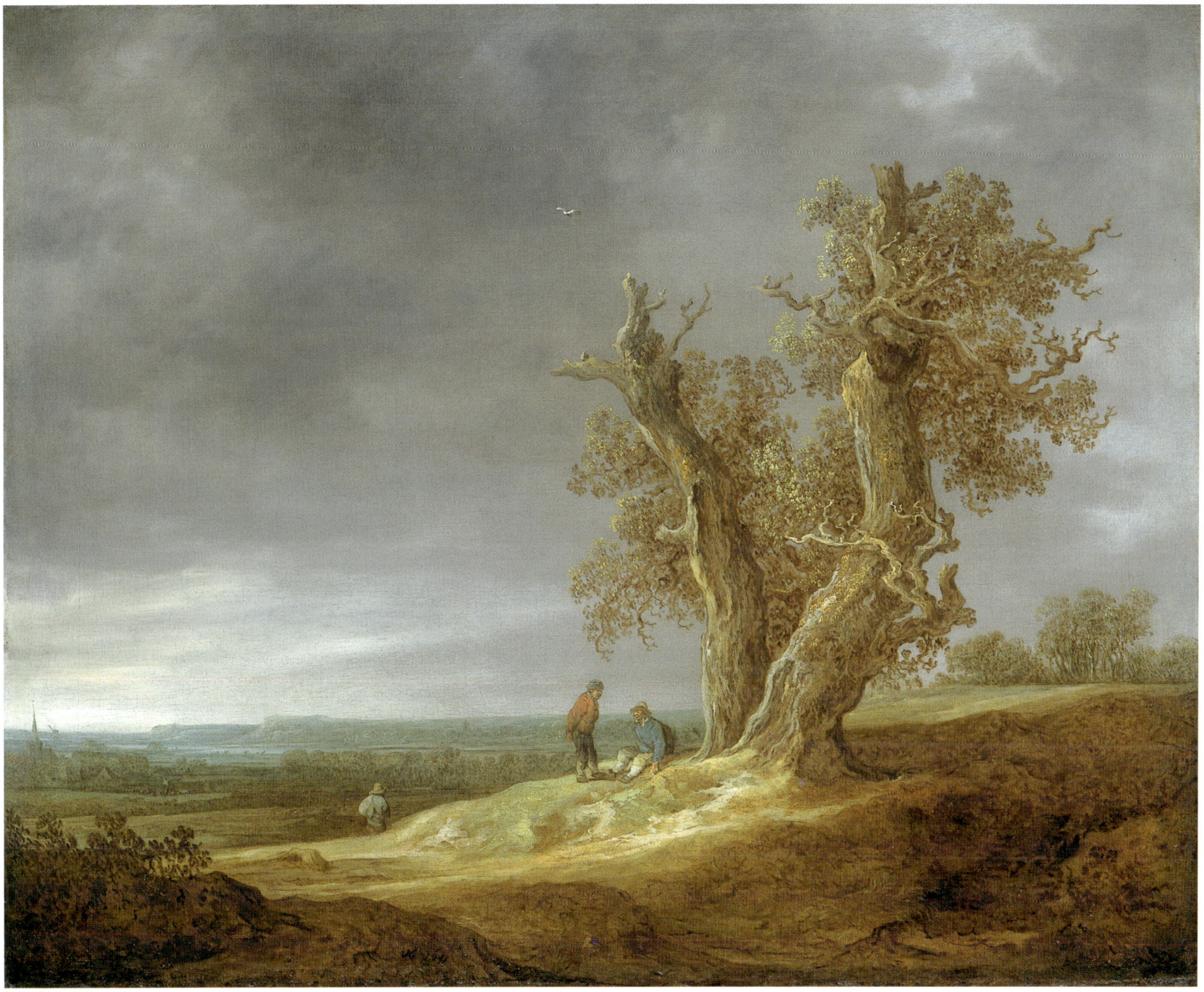

Aert van der Neer (Amsterdam 1603/04-Amsterdam 1677)

40 *River view by moonlight, c. 1645*

Oil on panel, 55 × 103 cm
At lower centre: *AV* DN
From the collection of Jonkheer Jan Six van Hillegom, Amsterdam (1928); presented in 1936 by Sir Henry Deterding
Inv. no. SK-A-3245

There is a tale that Aert van der Neer, who was an innkeeper, saw some of his customers painting and decided that surely it could not be all that difficult to paint a moonlit landscape. You just took some yellow, some brown and some blue and, lo and behold you had captured the mood of a moonlit night. The truth is that Van der Neer was first and foremost a painter, and that he eventually went bankrupt after opening an inn to earn a living. His early work, which followed the examples of Jan van Goyen [39] and the Camphuysen brothers, is fairly colourful, more so in fact than that of his models. His development as an artist is the complete reverse of what the anecdote suggests: he gradually discovered that his strength lay in toning everything down.

The simplicity of the palette makes this painting a marvel. The moon illuminates a landscape with a muddy track running past a few houses on which two waggoners are being bothered by dogs as they make their way home. A couple of fishermen in their boats are taking advantage of the peaceful moonlit night, and a handful of sailing boats have been severely delayed by the lack of wind. The painter worked with the minimalist palette described above. The landscape was painted with dark brown over an underlying layer of light ochre which is left uncovered in the areas where the moonlight falls. A lead-grey area on the left gives the suggestion of a dark pool, which takes on a sense of depth from the presence of some ducks, themselves no more than a few touches of colour. The underlying layer is covered with blue for the night sky and for the parts where it is reflected in the water, with some added white for the vista lit up by the moon. The silhouettes of houses, windmills, trees and fishing boats combine to make a simple but highly evocative compilation of elements.

Van der Neer also employed a few rather rough-and-ready but extremely effective technical tricks, the first of which was scratching into the wet paint. On the left he took a pointed implement, perhaps the handle of his brush, to remove the wet paint and reveal the light underlayer. He used it to depict a fence and a few tall posts by the side of a cottage. In the left foreground he set down a low fence of long

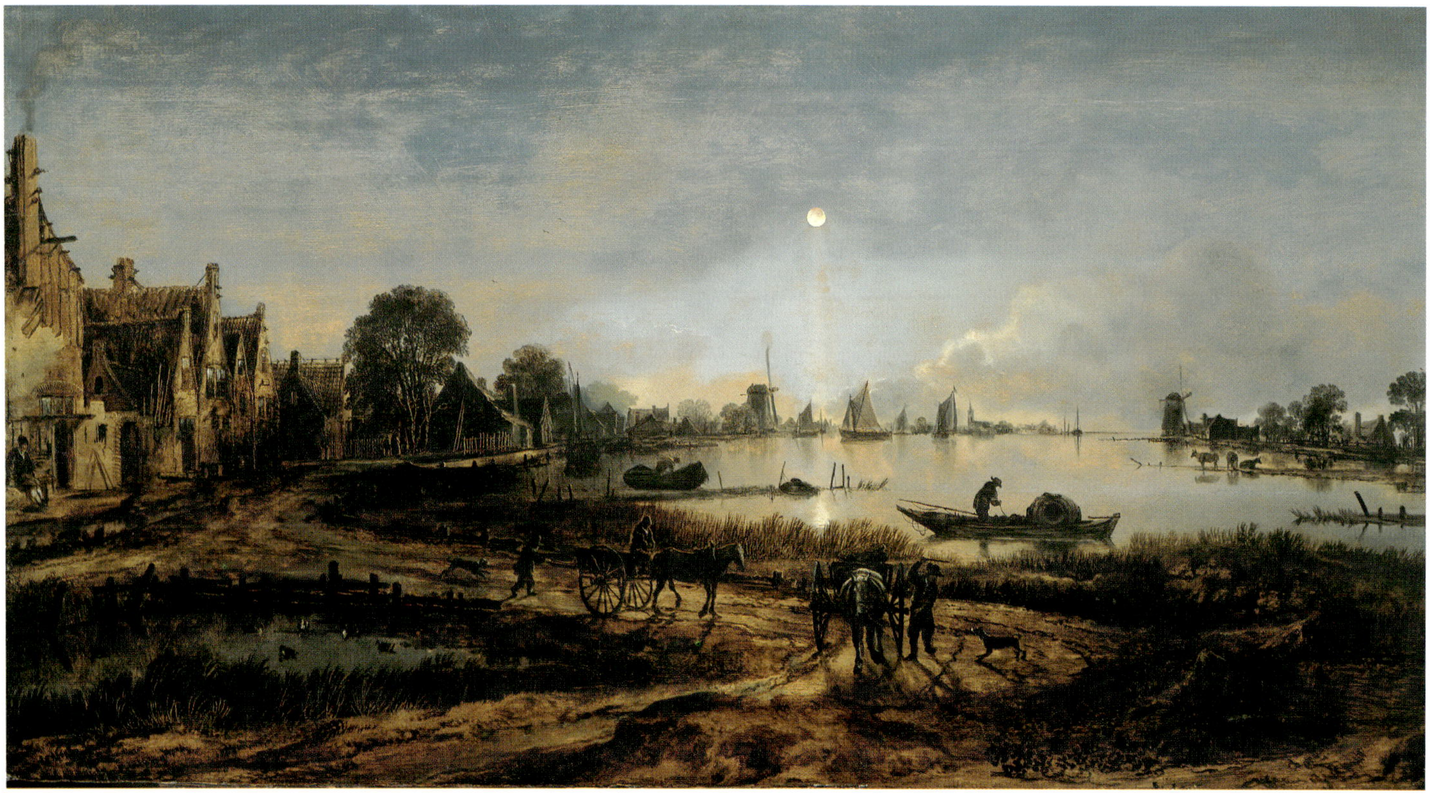

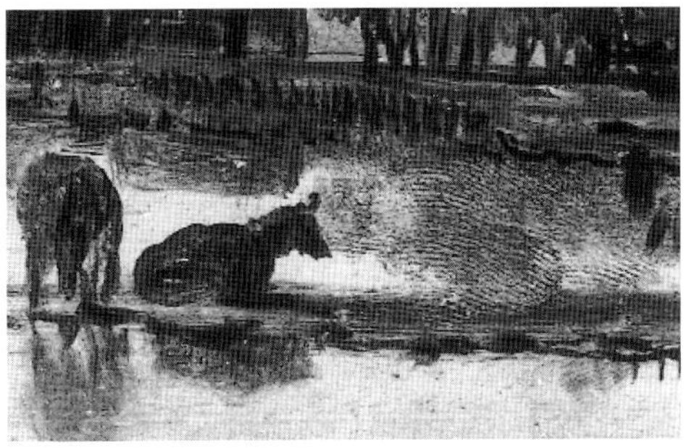

40a Detail of the *River view* with Van der Neer's fingerprint by one of the sail arms of the windmill

planks with a few broad strokes of dark brown paint which he then scratched, this time with a fairly blunt implement, using the bared underlayer to render the moonlight shining through the gaps in the fence. The outlines of the man on the cart, his horse and the cartwheels were highlighted by scratching in the paint, creating a very forceful, backlit silhouette. That the artist was merely interested in effects is clear from the foreshortened horse in the centre. The harness at its breast was depicted by scratching away the paint, but the illuminated length running along its flank was indicated with dark paint. Here Van der Neer was not motivated by what would have been illuminated in reality but by the effect of contrasts that he was seeking.

He also used his fingers in a few places. For the plume of smoke rising from the chimney on the left he put some black paint on his fingertips and smeared it onto the panel. When he realised that he had made one of the sail arms of the windmill in the centre a little too long, he wiped the excess off with his finger, leaving a clearly visible fingerprint.

LITERATURE

Bachmann 1982, p. 103; Zeldenrust 1983

Jan van de Cappelle (Amsterdam 1626-Amsterdam 1679)

41 *The home fleet saluting the state barge, 1650*

Oil on panel, 64 x 92.5 cm
At lower left: *jvcapel 1650*
Purchased in 1803 by the Nationale Konst-Gallerij in Huis ten Bosch
Inv. no. SK-A-453

Van de Cappelle was a rich man. He died leaving several properties, a yacht, and the sizable sum of 90,000 guilders. His money came from a profitable paint factory, a family business which he probably only ran on his own for the last five years of his life. It can be assumed, then, that he had quite a lot of time on his hands to indulge his passion for painting. Gerbrandt van den Eeckhout, a pupil of Rembrandt's, wrote that Jan van de Cappelle 'taught himself [how to paint] for his own pleasure'.

It is clear from Van de Cappelle's oeuvre that he took his example from Simon de Vlieger, which is confirmed by the numerous works by that marine artist in his stunning art collection, which also included paintings and drawings by Rembrandt, Rubens, Hals, Van Dyck, Brouwer, Segers and Avercamp. Van de Cappelle had 16 paintings by Jan Porcellis and 10 by Jan van Goyen. In addition to 9 paintings by De Vlieger he owned no fewer than 1,300 of his drawings (as well as more than 400 by Van Goyen, nearly 900 by Avercamp and around 500 by Rembrandt).

This breathtaking *tour de force* of 1650 was inspired by a painting that De Vlieger made in 1649, which is now in Vienna [41a]. De Vlieger more or less introduced this

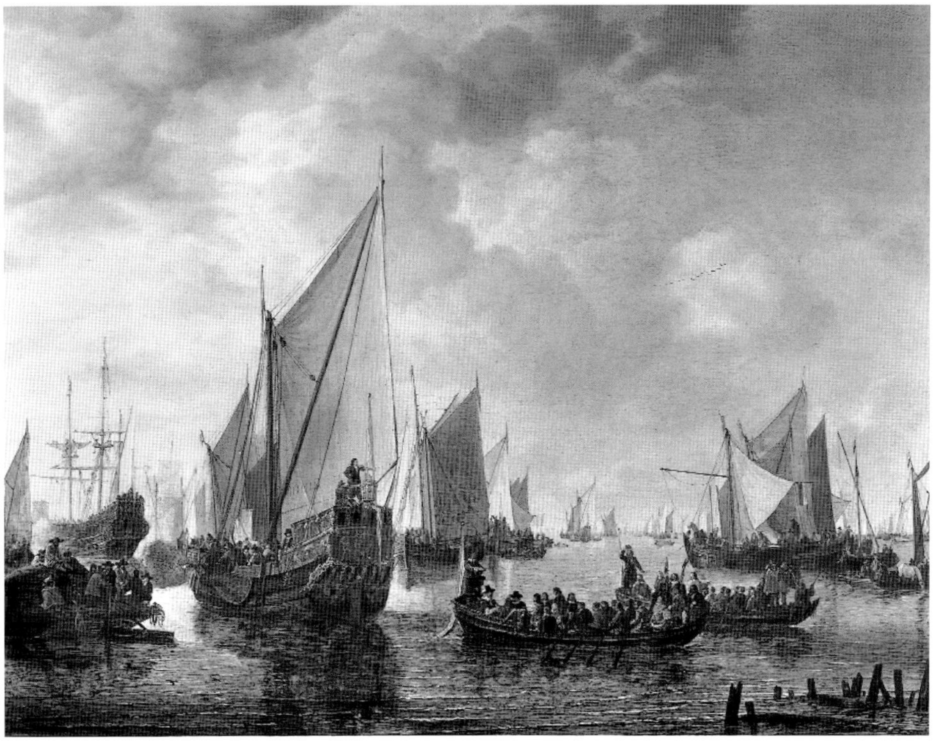

41a Simon de Vlieger, *Prince Frederik Hendrik disembarking at Dordrecht*, 1649; oil on panel, 71 x 92 cm. Vienna, Kunsthistorisches Museum

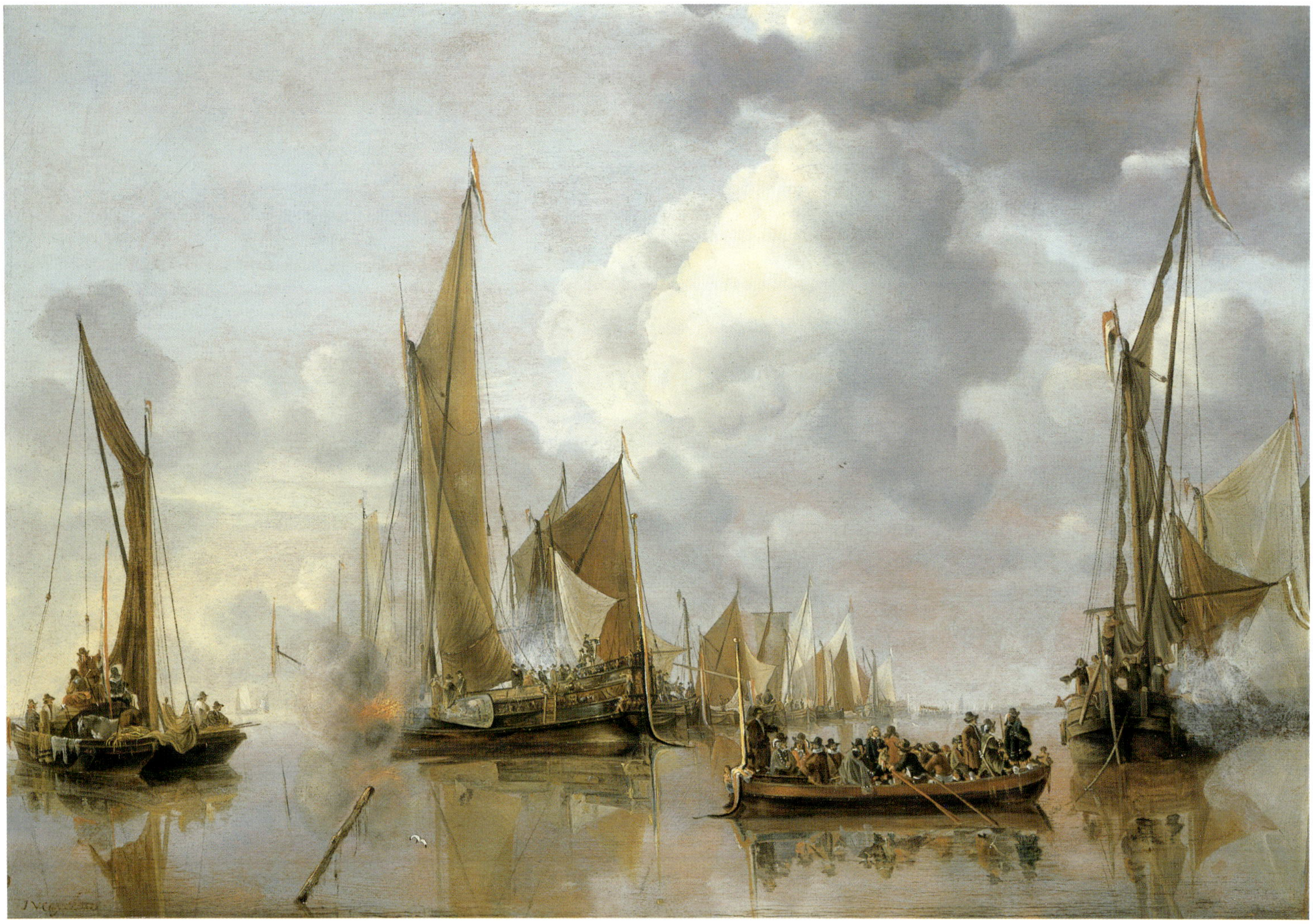

genre in marine art, although it is little more than a variant within the established tradition of recording important events at sea. It was a popular practice, and Karel van Mander wrote in his *Schilder-boeck* of 1604 that the public took 'great pleasure in these little ships, there being much seafaring in Holland'. The compositions of the paintings by De Vlieger and Van de Cappelle are almost identical. An almost endless line of ships extends from the left foreground to the horizon just to the right of centre, while the ship on the right serves to create the effect of a vista through the middle. The left and right halves of both paintings are linked by a gig crammed with passengers, probably dignitaries who are about to board or have just disembarked from one of the ships. The paintings also have many details in common, like the trumpeter on the stern of the ship on the left which is firing a salute, as it is in De Vlieger's painting. Van de Cappelle departed from his model by giving his picture a more serene and calm mood. He did so not only through a more precise depiction of his ships but above all through the superb reflections in the calm water—a motif designed to impart a sense of monumentality to the scene which he exploited better than De Vlieger. In addition, he bathed his seascapes in a marvellous, golden orange glow, particularly in his later work, abandoning De Vlieger's more monochrome, silver-grey approach.

Van de Cappelle, like De Vlieger, was a superb painter of clouds. The dark passages in the sky in this work act like a repoussoir, accentuating the endless sweep of the overarching heavens and seemingly pushing the horizon even further back. Van de Cappelle used this device on several occasions, and not surprisingly it was something else that he had borrowed from De Vlieger. Above all, though, Van de Cappelle is the painter of the calm mood, and one can well imagine this man of leisure making the studies he needed from his yacht. His estate contained 798 of his drawings, but only a handful survive today.

LITERATURE

Russell 1975, pp. 21-23, and p. 63, no. 17

Pieter Saenredam (Assendelft 1597-Haarlem 1665)

42 *The interior of the Church of St Odulphus in Assendelft, 1649*

Oil on panel, 50 x 76 cm
At the bottom of the choirstall on the left: *dit is de kerck tot Assendelft een dorp in hollandt van pieter saenredam, dese geschildert int jaer 1649. den 2 October* (This is the church at Assendelft, a village in Holland, painted by Pieter Saenredam on the 2nd of October in the year 1649)
From the collections of Jeronimo de Bosch, Amsterdam (1812), Jeronimo de Vries (1848) and Adriaan van der Hoop; bequeathed by the latter to the City of Amsterdam, 1854; on loan to the Rijksmuseum since 1885
Inv. no. SK-C-217

Pieter Saenredam's earliest dated painting, the *Interior of the Church of St Bavo in Haarlem* of 1628, shows that he had already broken with the tradition of the fantasy architecture piece. It was a genre that arose in Antwerp at the end of the 16th century, and was still being practised by several of Saenredam's contemporaries in the northern Netherlands. He also abandoned the custom of using the architectural space as a mere backdrop to religious or secular subjects. Instead he painted the 'portrait' of a

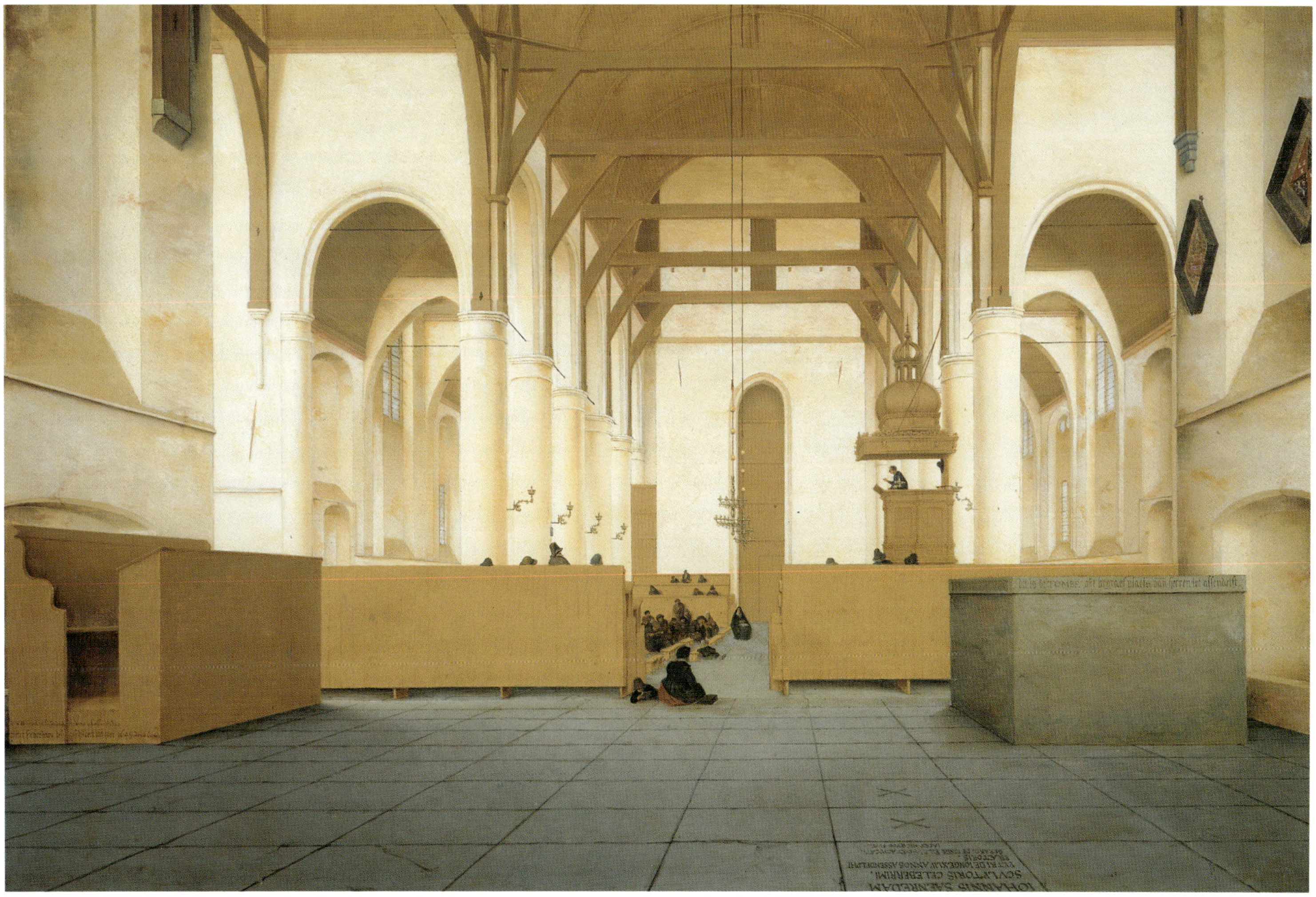

building for the sake of its intrinsic qualities. The sole purpose of the few people in his paintings appears to be to indicate the scale.

That staffage takes the form of a congregation listening to a sermon in this *Interior of the Church of St Odulphus in Assendelft* of 1649. The uncluttered, carefully planned composition combined with the meticulous manner of painting and the refined use of colour, with the tone being set by a mellow brown, make this one of Saenredam's finest works. The church undoubtedly held a special significance for him, for it stood in his birthplace and was where his father, the engraver Jan Saenredam, was buried in 1607. His gravestone is clearly marked with the inscription (viewed upside-down) at lower right, which opens with the words IOHANNIS SAENREDAM/ SCVLPTORIS CELEBERRIMI ([Here lies] Johannes Saenredam, celebrated engraver). That stone, incidentally, is now all that remains of the church, which was demolished in the 19th century.

When Saenredam decided to paint the interior of a church he first made a detailed sketch on the spot. He then took it back to his Haarlem studio, where he worked it up into a perspectival construction drawing which was the same size as the projected painting. This was then transferred to a panel and the painting executed in oils. Many years could pass between the initial sketch and the finished painting. The first sketch for the choir of the Assendelft church is dated 9 August 1633, and the construction drawing 9 December 1643. Interestingly, in an annotation on the latter sheet Saenredam states that he had executed the painting on a panel made from a single plank, obviously so that the surface would not be disfigured by an unsightly glued join.

LITERATURE

Schwartz & Bok 1989, no. 19; exhib. cat. Rotterdam 1991, no. 16

Frans Hals (Antwerp 1582/83-Haarlem 1666) and Pieter Codde (Amsterdam 1599-Amsterdam 1678)

43 *The company of Captain Reynier Reael and Lieutenant Cornelis Michielsz Blaeuw, known as 'The meagre company', 1637*

Oil on canvas, 209 x 429 cm
To the right of centre: *A° 1637*
Painted for the Crossbowmen's Hall, Amsterdam; moved to the old Town Hall, successively in the Great Chamber of the Council of War and the Burgomasters' Chamber; on loan from the City of Amsterdam since 1885
Inv. no. SK-C-374

Jan van Dyk, the compiler of a list published in 1758 of the paintings in Amsterdam's Town Hall, remarked of this civic guard piece that the guardsmen 'are so thin and slender that one could rightly call them the meagre company', and the painting has been known by that name ever since. The company is that of the two gentlemen seated on the left: Captain Reynier Reael and Lieutenant Cornelis Michielsz Blaeuw. The names of the other guardsmen are not known.

Various archival records supply a fair amount of information about the genesis of this civic guard piece. Frans Hals, who lived in Haarlem, accepted the prestigious Amsterdam commission in 1633. That year, and possibly in 1634 as well, he worked on the group portrait in Amsterdam, but by 1636 he had still not honoured a promise of 1635 to finish the painting. Reael and Blaeuw enlisted the help of a lawyer, who wrote to Hals in an attempt to force him to complete the picture within 14 days, failing which the principals would get another painter to complete it, demand repayment of money already advanced and sue for damages for default. Hals then informed them that initially it had been agreed that the work would be painted in Haarlem, and that it was only later that he had consented to sketch the heads in Amsterdam and complete the picture in Haarlem. However, he had been unable to get all the guardsmen together in Amsterdam. Reael and Blaeuw replied that they had agreed to pay 66 guilders for each portrait instead of 60 if he painted his subjects entirely in Amsterdam. Hals, however, insisted that the work had to be done in Haarlem, and that he would come to Amsterdam to paint the few members of the company who refused to go there.

There are no documents detailing what happened next, but the result shows that Hals missed out on the remarkably high fee of 1,056 guilders, because his patrons turned to another artist. We would be completely in the dark as to his identity but for another 17th-century source. According to a list made in 1653 of the works hanging in the headquarters of the various Amsterdam civic guard companies, the work was painted by Frans Hals and then finished by Codde ('Francois Hals geschildert ende bij Coode voorts opgemaeckt').

It is fascinating to see how Pieter Codde, who generally worked on a small scale with a delicate brush [see 25], adapted to Hals's style for the occasion. Nevertheless, it is patently obvious who painted what. Hals's broad brush is instantly recognisable in the figures of the standard-bearer on the far left and the man seated beside him, and a comparison between them and the man in the middle shows that Codde could not match the evocative brushwork of his colleague from Haarlem. It is also clear that Hals could give a sublime rendering of a man with his hand on his hip, whereas

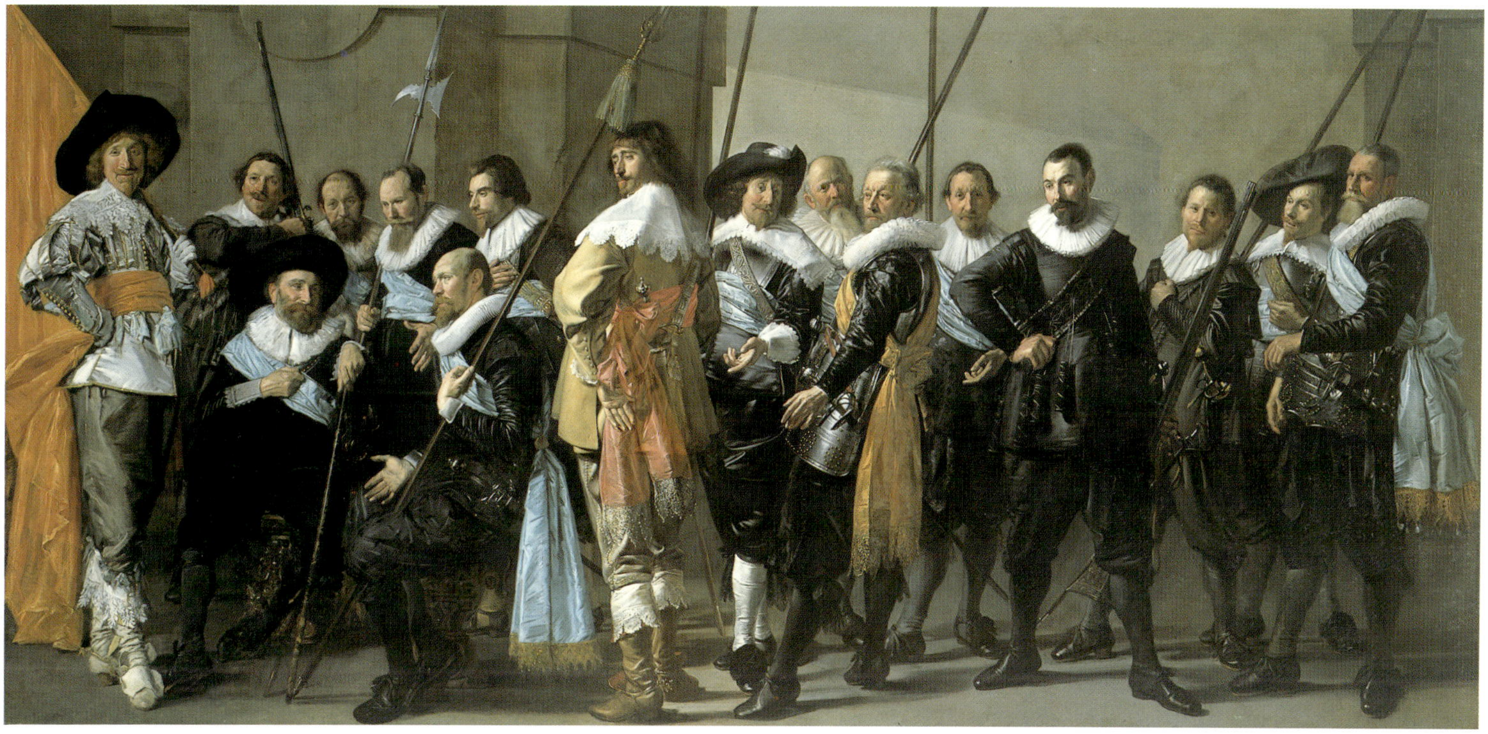

Codde's central figure adopts an almost impossible pose. Codde tried to imitate Hals's brisk brush in the lace collars and ruffs, but a comparison between those worn by the two seated men reveals who had the better and more telling touch.

It is not clear why the guardsmen chose Pieter Codde to finish their group portrait. It is possible that he belonged to Captain Reael's company, for he certainly lived in the city district from which its members were recruited. Moreover, the notary who drew up the inventory of Codde's estate in February 1636 was the one who wrote the letters to Hals in the spring of that year, which might explain how Codde was introduced to his patrons.

LITERATURE

Slive 1970-74, vol. 3, no. 80; exhib. cat. Washington/London/Haarlem 1989-90, no. 43

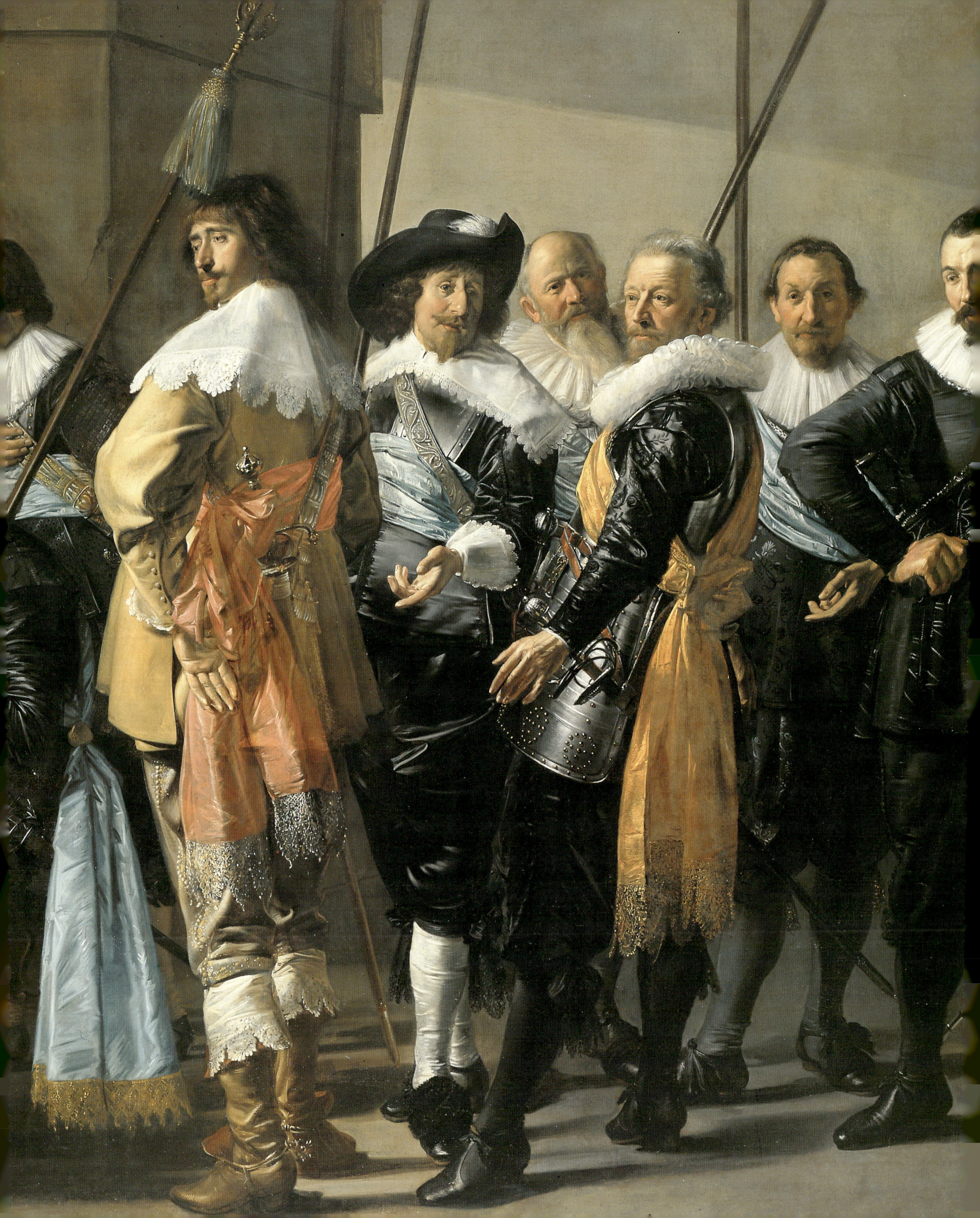

Rembrandt Harmensz van Rijn (Leiden 1606-Amsterdam 1669)

44 *The company of Captain Frans Banning Cocq and Lieutenant Willem van Ruytenburgh, known as 'The night watch', 1642*

Oil on canvas, 363 × 437 cm
At lower left: *Rembrandt f 1642*
Painted for the Great Hall of the Calivermen's guildhall in Amsterdam; from 1715 in the Small Chamber of the Council of War in the Town Hall; on loan from the City of Amsterdam since 1808
Inv. no. SK-C-5

The group portraits of neighbourhood watches composed of civilians, known as civic guard pieces, are among the most remarkable products of Dutch art, with *The night watch*, Rembrandt's world-famous masterpiece, being the odd one out within the genre. Civic guard portraits are a visual reflection of the fragmentation of power in the Dutch Republic and of the high pretensions of the cities. The latter already contributed on a *pro rata* basis to the upkeep of a central, standing army under the command of the stadholder, but for their own defence they also organised bodies of volunteers who would take up arms in times of need. Civil militias of this kind did not exist in neighbouring countries, where power was wielded from the centre. Each city in the Republic ran its civic guards along quite strict lines, and only men who could pay for their own equipment could join. The civic guard officers had their portraits painted in many of the towns. This singular state of affairs was thus documented in a large number of civic guard pieces, 57 of which have survived from Amsterdam alone. As a result, the Netherlands not only has a visual record of these urban militias but also thousands of faces of men prominent in urban life.

The guardsmen, who paid for their individual portraits out of their own pockets, would have wanted to look their best in these group scenes, and it is this that makes *The night watch* such a contradictory painting. It is not an orderly gathering of guardsmen in serried rows but a lively depiction of an obscure incident in which the individuals are subordinated to the whole. In other words it is a superb but utterly atypical specimen of the genre. Part of the fame of *The night watch* can be put down to the need to recognise a great master's largest painting as being his most important work, but in part it is also due to the admiration for this cross-grained example of a cultural and historical phenomenon which is so typically Dutch: the civic guard piece.

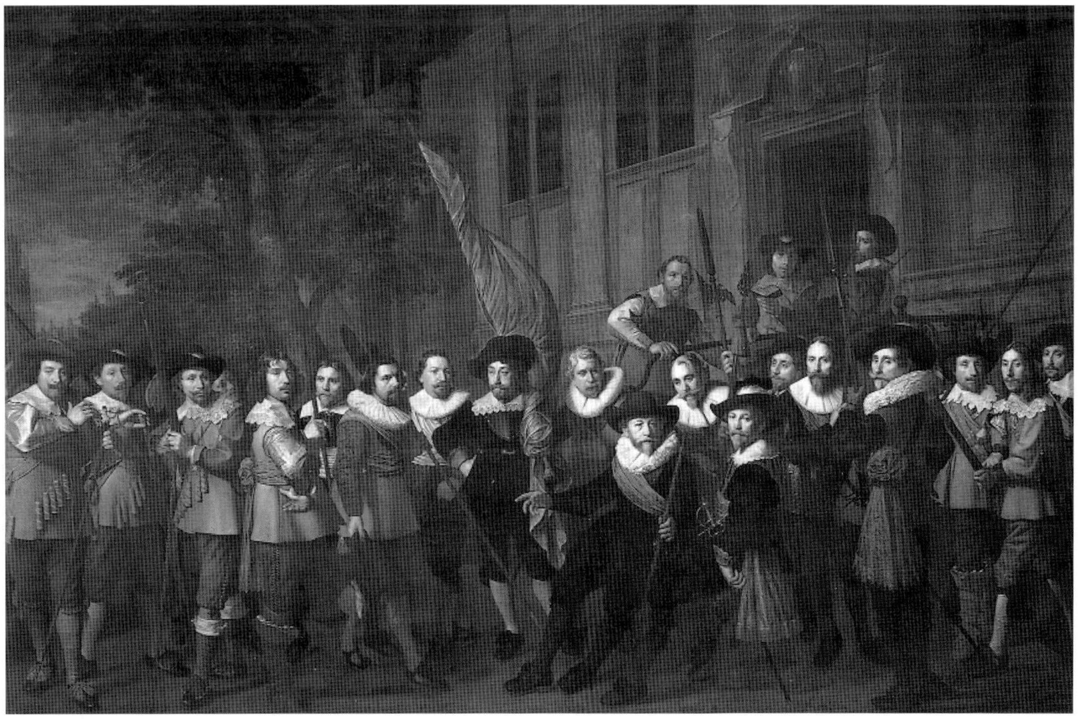

44a Nicolaes Eliasz Pickenoy, *The company of Captain Jan Claesz Vlooswijck and Lieutenant Gerrit Hudde*, 1642; oil on canvas, 340 × 527 cm. Amsterdam, Rijksmuseum

◂ Detail of [43]

The taut composition of the traditional civic guard portrait, with the sitters neatly depicted one beside the other, was no longer considered satisfactory in the 17th century. Instead the men were shown arranged informally around a table, or with some on a dais, in attempts to break the rigid pattern while at the same time portraying each person to the best possible effect. Pickenoy's large group portrait, which like Rembrandt's was painted in 1642 for the Great Hall of the Calivermen's guildhall [*44a*], speaks volumes in this respect. All the heads are there, down to the finest detail, and most of the bodies as well. It is a worthy effort, extremely well executed, and all the participants would have been satisfied, but it is probably fair to say that none of them was particularly excited by the work as a whole, for it is rather lifeless. The Rembrandt is quite the reverse. The key features of *The night watch* are powerful chiaroscuro effects and bustling, almost chaotic activity.

An early source explained this by saying that the captain is ordering his lieutenant to march the company out, so the men emerging from a gateway are on the point of forming ranks before marching off. The moment is comparable to an orchestra awaiting the arrival of the conductor: everyone is trying out his instrument, and the result is cacophony.

A critique of *The night watch* appeared at an early date. Samuel van Hoogstraeten, a pupil of Rembrandt's, gave his ideas about the painting in his *Inleyding tot de hooge schoole der schilderkonst* of 1678. He argues that compositions should be lively before going on to say: 'It is not enough for a painter to place his figures side by side in rows, as one sees all too often in the guard guildhalls here in Holland. [...] Rembrandt paid very good heed to this in his painting in the guildhall in Amsterdam, devoting more attention to the grand design he had chosen than to the individual likenesses he was commissioned to make'. He also called the painting 'picturesque in conception, smooth in its modulation [from foreground to background]' and 'powerful', but would have preferred Rembrandt to have made it a little lighter. Van Hoogstraeten, in other words, shared all the considerations, amazement, admiration and critical attitudes that the painting still appears to awaken in viewers today.

The composition and the distribution of light and shade can still be described as sensational. The captain of the guard, Frans Banning Cocq stands in the centre with almost all the other figures apparently whirling in chaos around him. Standing to the right of him is Lieutenant Willem van Ruytenburgh, who is much smaller but whose illuminated clothing give him a very prominent place in the composition. As a result of the visual rhyme of Banning Cocq's silhouetted glove and the shadow of the left hand on Van Ruytenburgh's jerkin, and of the outstretched hand and the protruding partisan held by Van Ruytenburgh, these two very contrasting figures nevertheless form a unit. On the right, a large number of pikemen are being held back by another whose pike bars their way. An officer makes a gesture to indicate that the company will shortly be moving off. Behind the lieutenant is a dwarfish figure, evidently a guardsman, who is loading his musket at what is quite clearly not the appropriate moment. To the left of the main group another man is priming his weapon, which shows that Rembrandt had no idea how much it weighed, for it is impossible to hold one of those heavy firearms with one hand while carrying out the delicate task of charging it with powder with the other. Behind this man is one of the strangest figures in the scene: a brightly lit girl with a dead bird dangling at her side. She is the group's mascot, for these calivermen had a cock's claw blazoned on their coat of arms. Between her and Banning Cocq is a guardsman who is invisible apart from his magnificent breeches and a helmet decked with oak leaves. The ensign behind him is looking up at the standard, seemingly oblivious to the pandemonium around him. The painting depicts an action which is given a heightened sense of drama by the fall of light. It would not be surprising if some of the guardsmen were unhappy with Rembrandt's decision to make the parts of the scene subordinate to the whole, certainly if one examines some of the heads more closely, and it is also understandable that not everyone would have been able to appreciate the qualities of the military activity. However, it is precisely because he sinned against rules of every kind that Rembrandt once again arouses our wonderment.

LITERATURE
Haverkamp Begemann 1982; Bruyn *et al.* 1982-89, vol. 3, no. A 146; exhib. cat. Haarlem 1988, pp. 94-95, 97-99

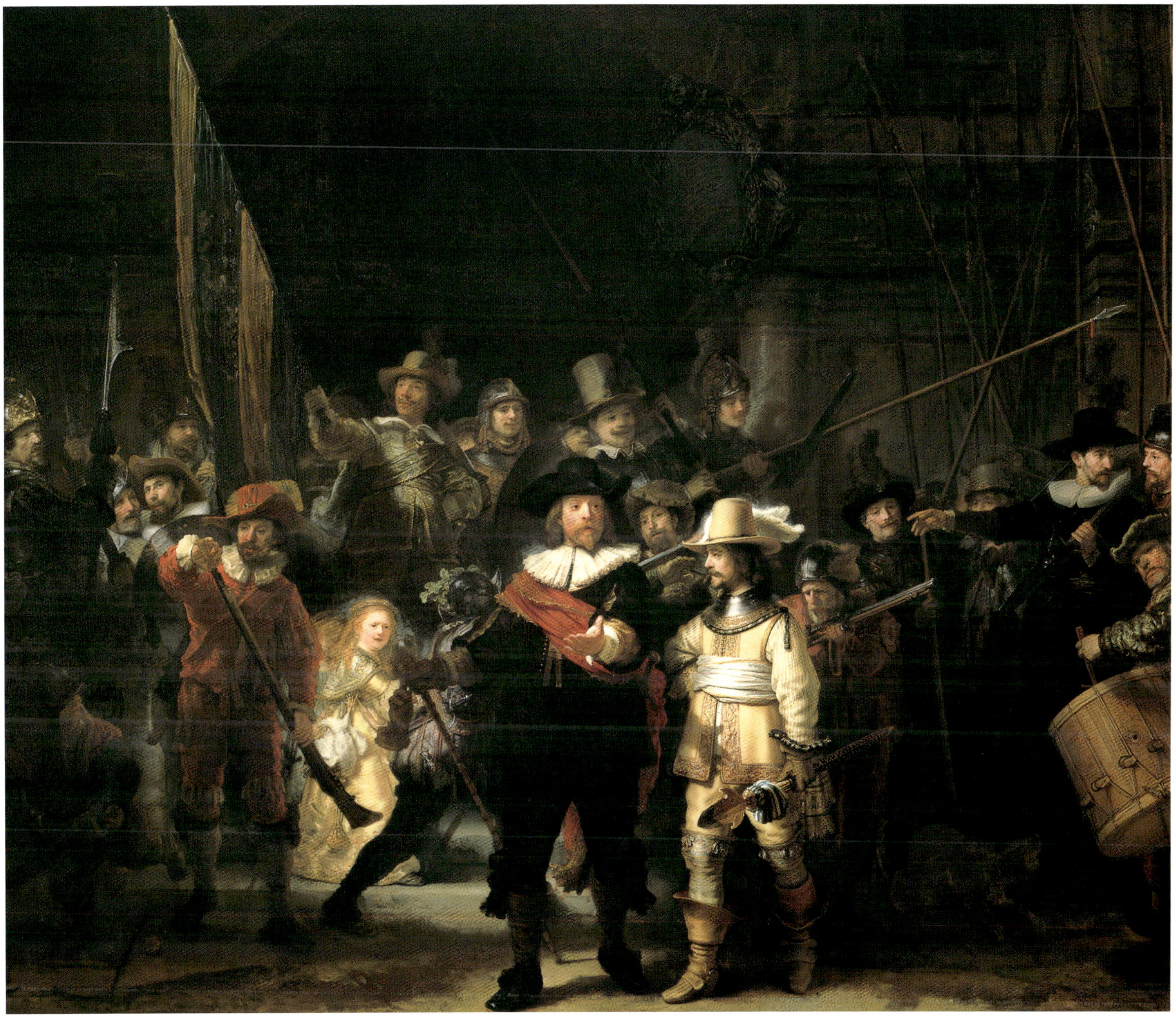

Johannes Lutma (Emden 1587-Amsterdam 1669)

45 *Ewer and basin, 1647*

Silver, ewer h. 50.4 cm; basin diam. 74.5 cm
Marked on the neck of the ewer and the underside of the basin: Amsterdam assay office mark, year letter Q (1647) and the maker's mark of a heart in an escutcheon (Johannes Lutma)
Probably made for the States assembly of the province of Holland as a gift for Admiral Maarten Harpertsz Tromp; purchased in 1895 from Mrs C.W. Steinmetz-van den Bogaert, one of Tromp's descendants
Inv. no. BK-NM-10244

Lutma's monumental and exuberantly decorated ewer and basin were probably presented by the States of Holland to Maarten Harpertsz Tromp (1598-1653) in gratitude for his role in the capture of Dunkirk in 1646. From 11 September to 7 October of that year the town had been besieged and then taken by the French, with Tromp lending a helping hand at sea. The action resulted in a far safer passage through the Straits of Dover, where the Dutch mercantile fleet was constantly being harried by privateers.

Maritime heroes who performed outstanding services for the Dutch Republic were usually honoured with gold chains and a medal by such august bodies as the States-General, the Dutch East India Com-

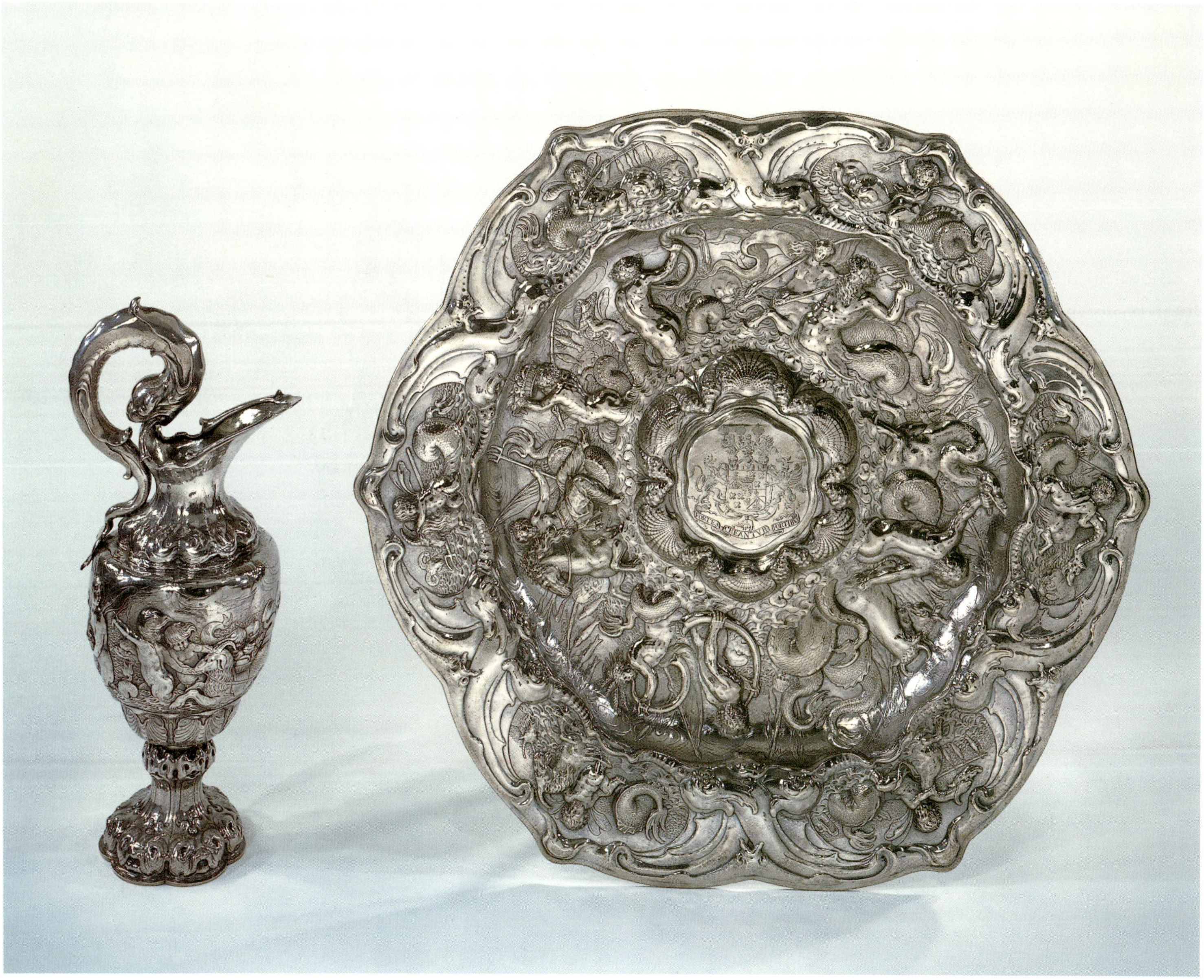

pany or the Admiralty, but on this occasion the choice fell on a monumental showpiece in silver, a ewer and basin made by Amsterdam's leading silversmith, Johannes Lutma. The size of the pieces gave Lutma the opportunity to use his speciality, auricular ornamentation, in its most luxuriant form. The basin, moreover, provided him with a surface for a very prominent scene, and one which is perhaps an allegory of the victory of Tromp and his men over the privateers. Neptune, ruler of the oceans, and his sea-gods are safeguarding the fruits of the sea and the land from the attacks of rapacious sea-monsters. The theme of Neptune as ruler is combined with Ceres, goddess of the harvest on land, who is depicted on the ewer with ears of corn and a sickle as her attributes. Mounted on her triumphal chariot she makes her way past menacing sea-creatures while nymphs and children bear fruits of the sea and fish. The complex mythological scene, with its great variety of poses, allowed Lutma to show off his compositional talents. His mastery as a silversmith is particularly evident in the rendering of the different kinds of skin of the animals, which are executed in various delicate chiselling techniques.

The detachable boss in the middle, known as an umbo, bears the coat of arms of Cornelis Tromp (1629-1691), the son of Maarten Harpertsz. It probably replaced his father's arms when he inherited the ewer and basin. The escutcheon is adorned with the Danish Order of the Elephant, so could not have been executed before 1676, when that honour was conferred on him.

LITERATURE

Cat. Amsterdam 1952b, no. 121; exhib. cat. Amsterdam 1984-85, no. 38; cat. Amsterdam 1999, no. 14

Herman Doomer (Anrath c. 1595-Amsterdam 1650), attributed to

46 Cupboard, c. 1640-1650

Oak veneered with ebony, kingwood, rosewood and pseudo-acacia (?), inlaid with mother-of-pearl and ivory, h. 218 cm, w. 196 cm, d. 84 cm
Probably by descent in Herman Doomer's family; from the collections of Sir Glynne Welby (Denton Manor, Lincolnshire) and L.J.L. Wittop Koning; purchased in 1975 at an auction in Amsterdam
Inv. no. BK-1975-81

Herman Doomer was one of the first Amsterdam ebonists, a new group of cabinetmakers who specialised in making pieces of furniture in ebony, and more generally of items made or veneered with hard, tropical types of wood. Since this required very special skills, the ebony workers were recognised as a distinct group within the cabinetmakers' guild in 1626, and had their own masterpiece test. Tropical woods were very expensive, and working them made higher demands of the craftsman, so ebonists doubtless enjoyed a higher status than ordinary cabinetmakers and joiners. Doomer was the most famous of them all.

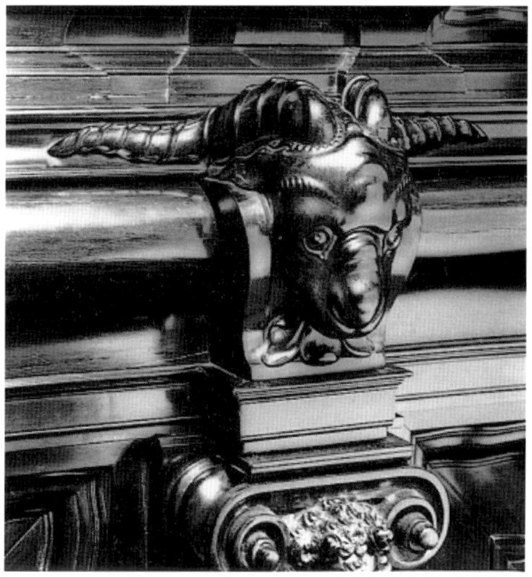

46b Detail of the cupboard

46a Rembrandt, *Portrait of Herman Doomer*, 1640; oil on panel, 75 x 55.3 cm. New York, Metropolitan Museum of Art

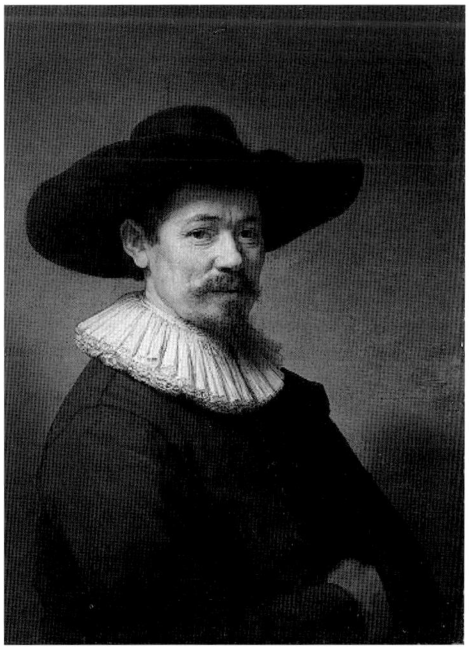

He was born in Anrath in Germany and moved to Amsterdam around 1613, where he soon prospered. The best-known evidence for this is provided by the portraits that Rembrandt painted of him and his wife in 1640 [*46a*]. Doomer bought several houses in Amsterdam and assembled a not inconsiderable collection of paintings.

This exceptional cupboard is a magisterial display of his skill, and at the same time a demonstration of the potential of the furniture-maker's art which had never before been seen in Amsterdam. The form is extremely intricate, with a recessed upper section and turned columns. The working of the ebony is amazingly skilful, particularly the sculpted work [*46b*]. The exterior is inlaid with superb mother-of-pearl flowers which stand out sharply against the dark background. On opening this heavy black cupboard one is confronted with a surprisingly colourful interior comprising not only ebony but other kinds of wood as well [46c]. The piece as a whole is conceived as an exceptionally large display piece of virtuoso cabinetmaking. The central panel of the upper section opens downwards to reveal a compartment decorated with more mother-of-pearl flowers, and with a perspective view with mirrors at the back. This is clearly no ordinary storage cupboard.

Doomer probably did not make this *tour de force* on commission, for it was still in his widow's possession on her death in 1678. The investment in time and materials must have been so great that a regular craftsman, however successful, would have been hard put to justify it. One of Doomer's motives in making the piece was probably to demonstrate that he had risen above the status of craftsman. In the process he took the ebonist's art to such heights that no buyer could be found for his masterpiece in the whole of Amsterdam, rich mercantile city though it was. One person who would definitely have appreciated the cupboard on its merits was Rembrandt, Doomer's greatest fellow artist and the painter of his portrait.

LITERATURE

Cat. Amsterdam 1993b, no. 16; Baarsen 1996

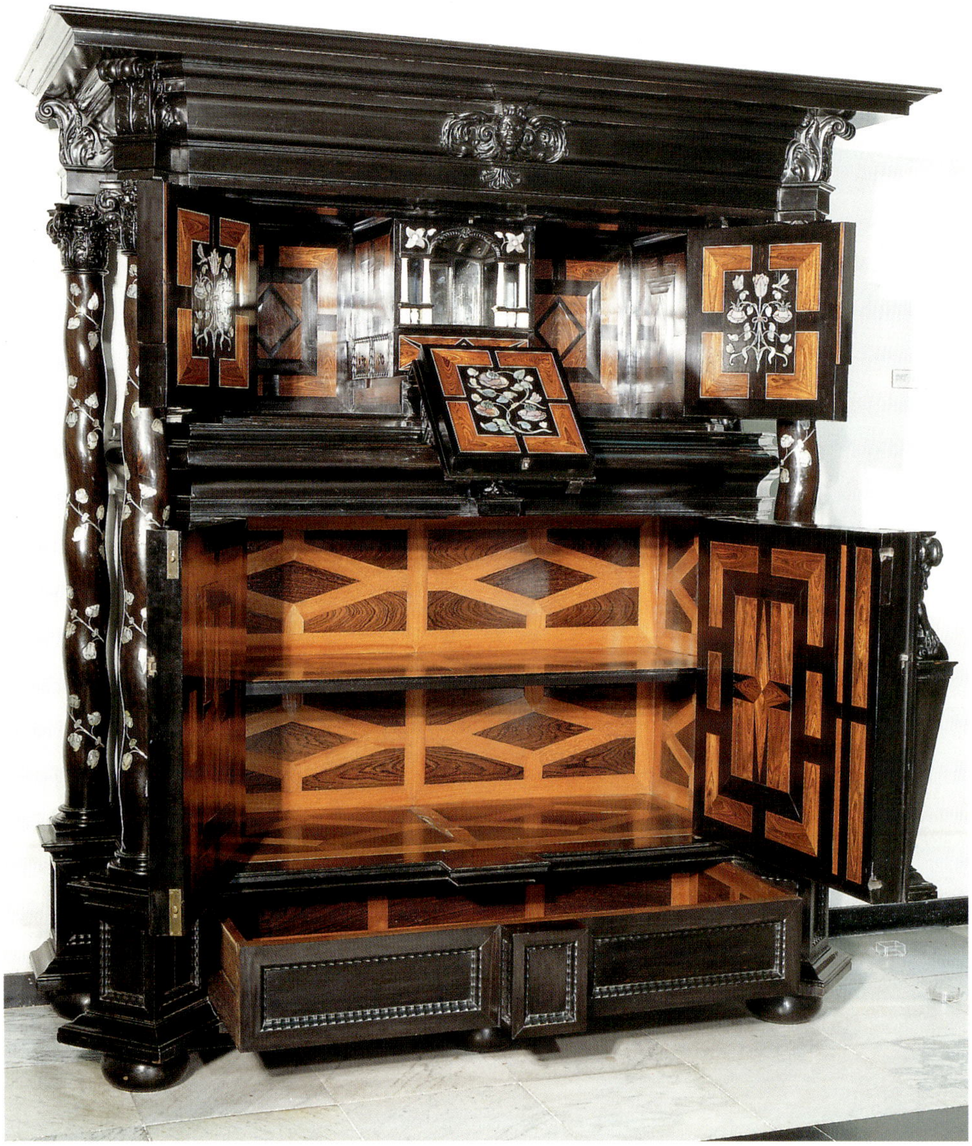

46c The interior of the cupboard

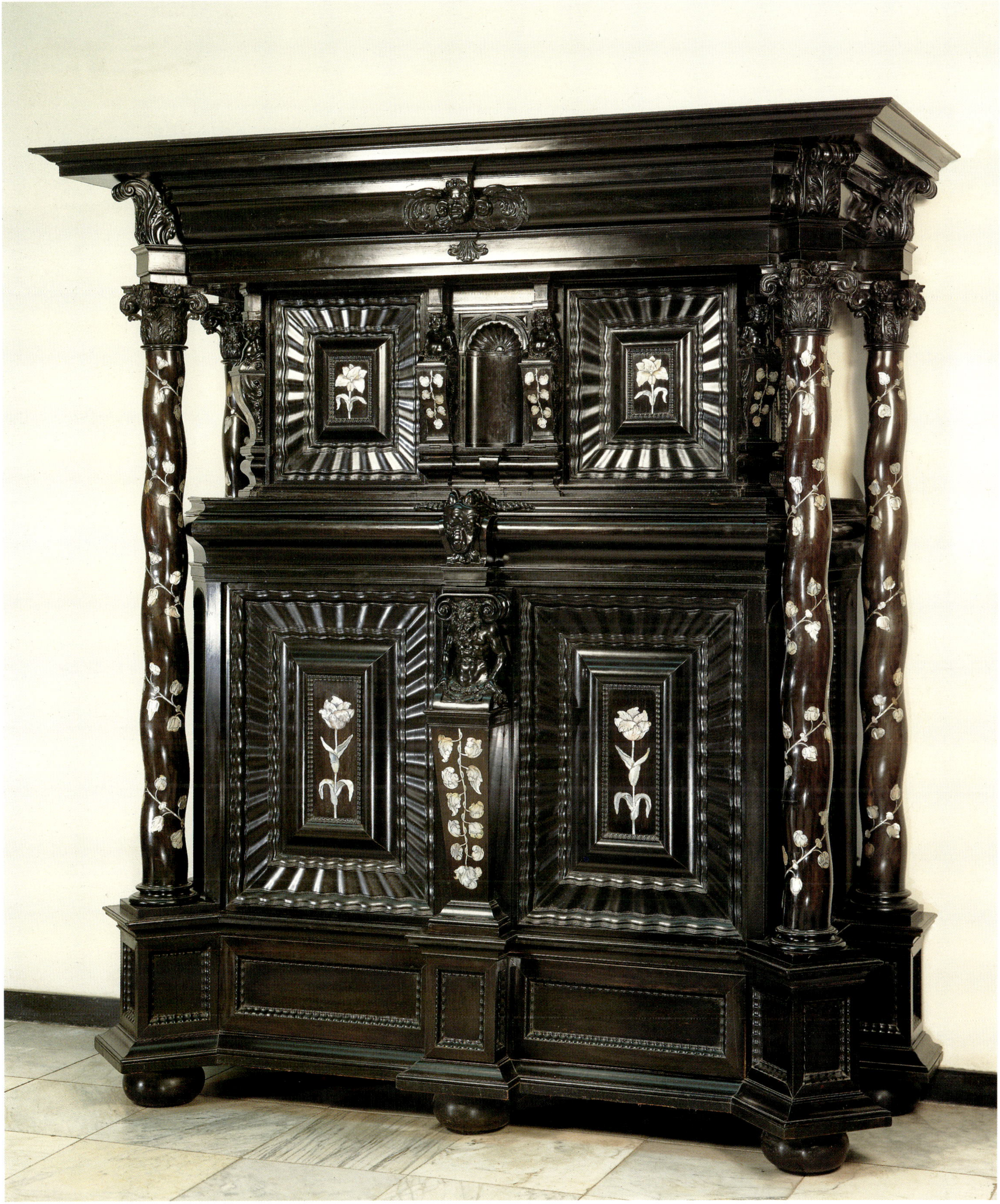

Dirck van Rijswijck (Cleves ? 1596-Amsterdam after 1679)

47 *Tabletop, c. 1650-1660*

Touchstone, inlaid with mother-of-pearl, in an ebony border, diam. 138.5 cm
In Van Rijswijck's house around 1664; then owned by Gerard Jonckheer, Rotterdam (1710), the heirs of the bailiff De Groet (1762) and J. van Kuyk, Delft (1819); purchased from the latter's heirs in 1904
Inv. no. BK-NM-1916

The year 1660 saw the publication of a poem by Joost van den Vondel, 'Op de toetssteene feesttafel der Goden' (On the touchstone banqueting table of the gods), which was devoted to this tabletop. 'The table, the octagon' stood 'in Rijswijck's house' at the time, in order to 'Invite the gods/ From their high thrones/ To the nacreous feast for the eyes'. Dirck van Rijswijck's house stood in Amsterdam's Berenstraat between Prinsengracht and Keizersgracht, and the tabletop was on display there for a long time. Melchior Fockens, in his *Beschrijvinge der wijdt-vermaarde koopstadt Amstelredam* of 1662, and Filips von Zesen, in the *Beschreibung der Stadt Amsterdam* of 1664, both reported that it could be seen there. Neither could find words enough to express their admiration of this masterpiece. Von Zesen even wrote a long Latin poem about it, complete with German translation.

There were clearly few works of art in Amsterdam that were as famous as this tabletop. Van Rijswijck's distinctive inlay work of mother-of-pearl had been exciting admiration for years. Vondel had hymned another of his works back in 1654, a 'table wreath' made for Gerard Hulft. The poet praised the incredible virtuosity with which the artist achieved a deceptively naturalistic effect using two simple materials, dull touchstone and the inside of a shell, and he specifically stated that no pigments had been used. The ingenuity with which Van Rijswijck employed the colour and markings of the various pieces of mother-of-pearl recalls the way Florentine artists incorporated different types of stone in their *pietre dure* panels. It is not surprising, then, that Cosimo III de'Medici, heir to the Grand Duchy of Tuscany, took great pleasure in inspecting Van Rijswijck's work when he visited Amsterdam in 1667. It also reminded his contemporaries of Japanese lacquer-work inlaid with mother-of-pearl—giving it an exotic dimension that would only have made it more attractive.

The tabletop is the largest surviving work by Van Rijswijck. He made a large number of smaller panels in the same technique which were very popular with the many Amsterdam collectors who had a love of exotic materials and artistic rarities. This tabletop was evidently too large and too regal in appearance for the Amsterdam collectors. Like Doomer's showpiece cupboard [*see 46*], this high point of Van Rijswijck's oeuvre found no buyer. He kept it in his house, where, as a costly attraction, it undoubtedly helped him sell many of his smaller works. A second, equally large tabletop, now lost, probably entered the collection of Frederick Willem, Elector of Brandenburg (1620-1688), and was certainly in the Prussian royal collections in the 18th century.

LITERATURE

Cat. Amsterdam 1952a, no. 306; cat. Amsterdam 1993b, no. 15

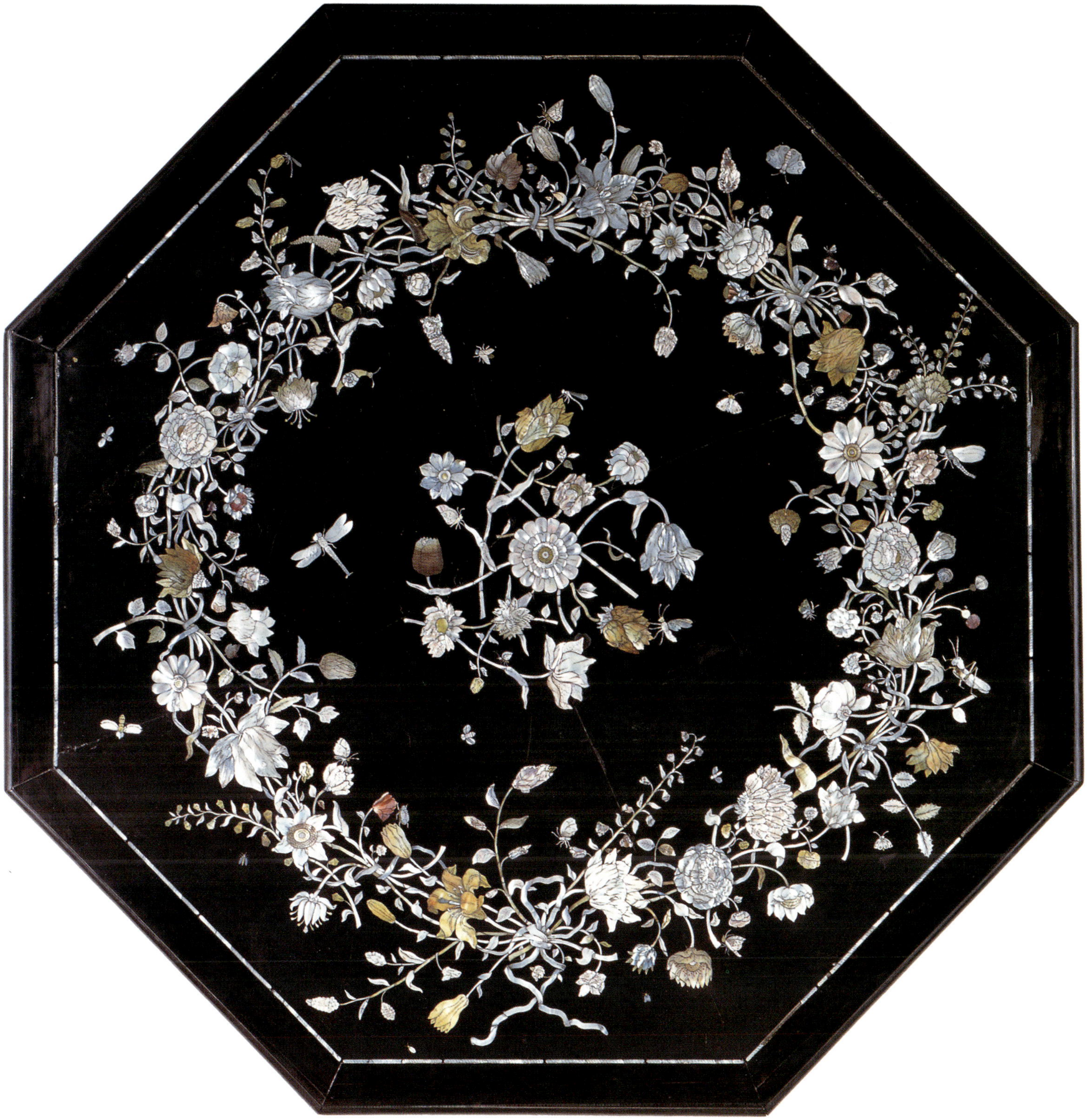

Bartholomeus van der Helst (Haarlem 1613-Amsterdam 1670)

48 *The celebration of the Peace of Münster in the headquarters of the crossbowmen's civic guard (St George's guard) in Amsterdam, 1648*

Oil on canvas, 232 x 547 cm
At lower centre: *Bartholomeus van de Helst fecit A° 1648*
Painted for the Calivermen's guildhall; from 1715 in the Town Hall; on loan from the City of Amsterdam since 1808
Inv. no. SK-C-2

Whereas Rembrandt attempted to breathe new life into the civic guard piece with his *Night watch* [44] by trying out a completely different formula, Bartholomeus van der Helst sought perfection six years later while remaining within the traditional programme. He succeeded so well that the debate about the relative merits of his and Rembrandt's paintings, which both hang in the same gallery in the Rijksmuseum, continues even today. In the first place, Van der Helst adhered far more closely to the terms of his commission, and managed to portray all the sitters convincingly and recognisably. He gave the scene the liveliness which must have been Rembrandt's principal goal by depicting the men in a great variety of poses and with a wealth of colour. Nowhere, though, do his artistic ideas get in the way of his chief aim: to paint good portraits. For the composition he used the device of grouping the guardsmen around a table—an arrangement which had been introduced back in the 16th century and was mainly used in the 17th century for group portraits of regents and small gatherings of civic guard officers. Back in 1533 Cornelis Anthonisz had depicted guardsmen at a meal [48a], in which he resolved the classic problem of how to depict those with their backs to the painter by simply not allowing anyone to sit on his side of the table. Van der Helst did place the superior officers in front of the table, but with their backs to the other participants. An artful pattern of human interaction (the officers shake each other's hands, remove their hats, are distracted) disguises the fact that the poses of some of the men verge on impoliteness towards the others. The composition is perfectly understandable to the modern viewer, who is familiar with the staged group photograph.

In other respects, too, it is clear that Van der Helst paid equal attention to all parts of the scene. Whether it is the face of the standard-bearer in the middle, the yellow stockings of the man standing on the left or the plumed hat of the man on the right, everything is depicted with the greatest of care. The artist took great pains over the imitation of the different materials. The rich, black attire of the captain, his iron cuirass with the reflection, the guild's silver drinking-horn in his hand, the gold embroidery on the costume of the lieutenant sitting across from him—everywhere there is a concern for the rendering of textures. At times one wonders whether the artist could not just as well have been a still-life painter, and that does not just apply to the wine-cooler in the left foreground or the food on the table. In this regard, too, Van der Helst seems to have set out to paint a true masterpiece, displaying all his skills to the full. The aspect of unity, which Rembrandt sought in spectacular chiaroscuro effects in his *Night watch*, was of secondary importance to him.

48a Cornelis Anthonisz, *The banquet of File H of the Amsterdam crossbowmen (the 'Copper-coin banquet')*, 1533; oil on panel, 130 x 206.5 cm. Amsterdam, Amsterdams Historisch Museum

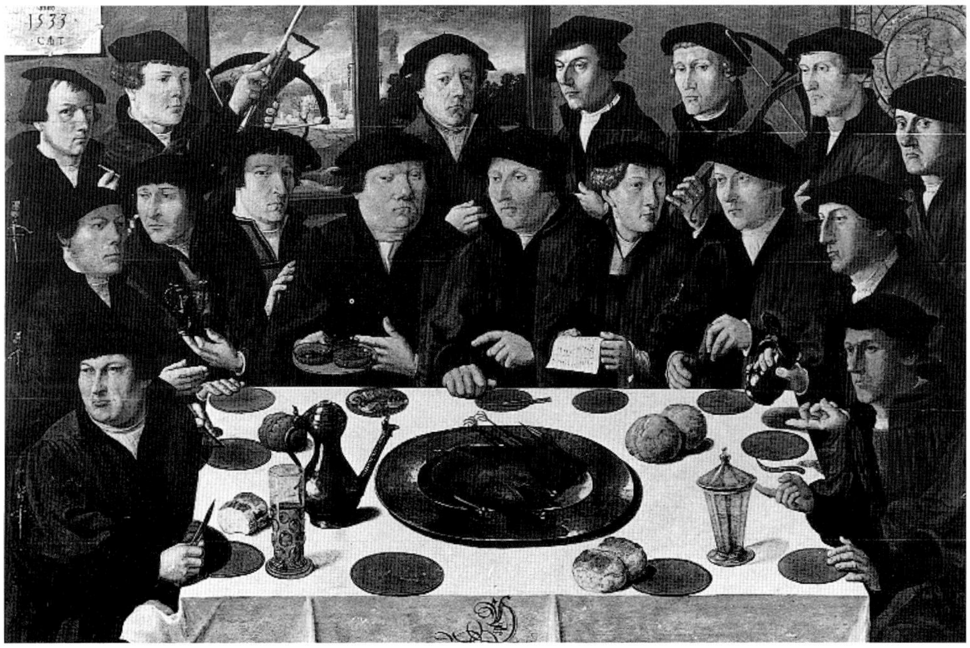

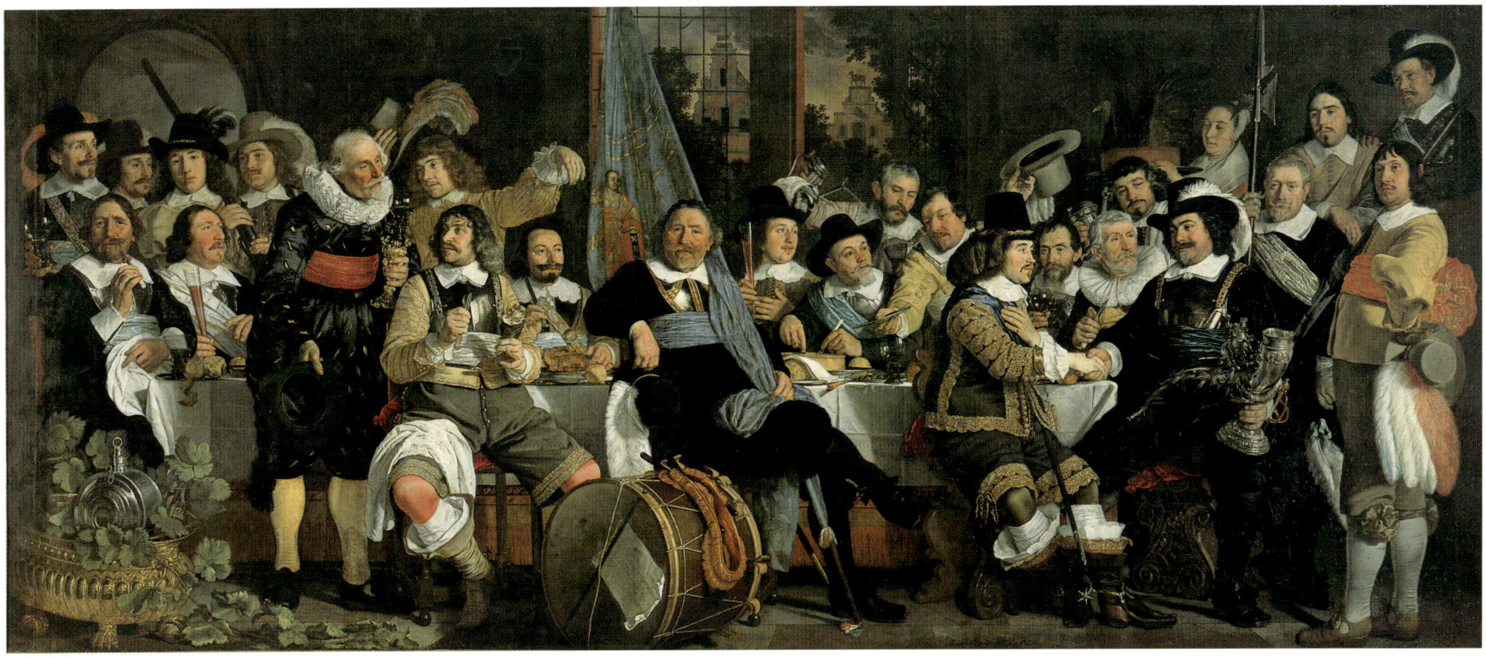

The main aim of Bartholomeus van der Helst was to record this gathering of civic guardsmen by painting good likenesses of them. There is a list of the names of the men who are depicted here under the command of Captain Cornelis Jansz Witsen and Lieutenant Johan Oetgens van Waveren, the two men shaking hands on the right. Unfortunately, it is not known which name belongs to which face, apart from Jacob Banning, the standard-bearer seated in the middle, and Christoffel Poock, the guild steward with the spouted flagon on the right. Nor are the names known of the servant pouring a drink in the centre background or of the serving-maid behind Poock in the right background.

The men have gathered to celebrate the signing of the Treaty of Münster, which brought the Eighty Years' War to an end. Not only did it close a terrible chapter of bloodshed (the treaty also concluded the Thirty Years' War which had torn Germany apart), but it also meant that the whole of Europe now recognised the Republic of the Seven United Provinces as a sovereign state. The piece of paper painted beneath the cord of the drum contains the evidence that this feast of St George's civic guard is indeed connected with that historic event. On it is a poem written by Jan Vos (1620-1667), one of the poets who wrote works hailing the peace. The poem renounces guns and swords, and the drinking-horn of St George becomes a symbol of peace.

Bellona reviles blood, aye Mars curses the clangour
Of coercive metal, and the sword cleaves to the scabbard.
So now brave Witsen offers noble Van Waveren
The horn of Peace for the eternal covenant.

LITERATURE

De Gelder 1921, pp. 1-10, 64-81, 230-234; exhib. cat. Haarlem 1988, no. 189

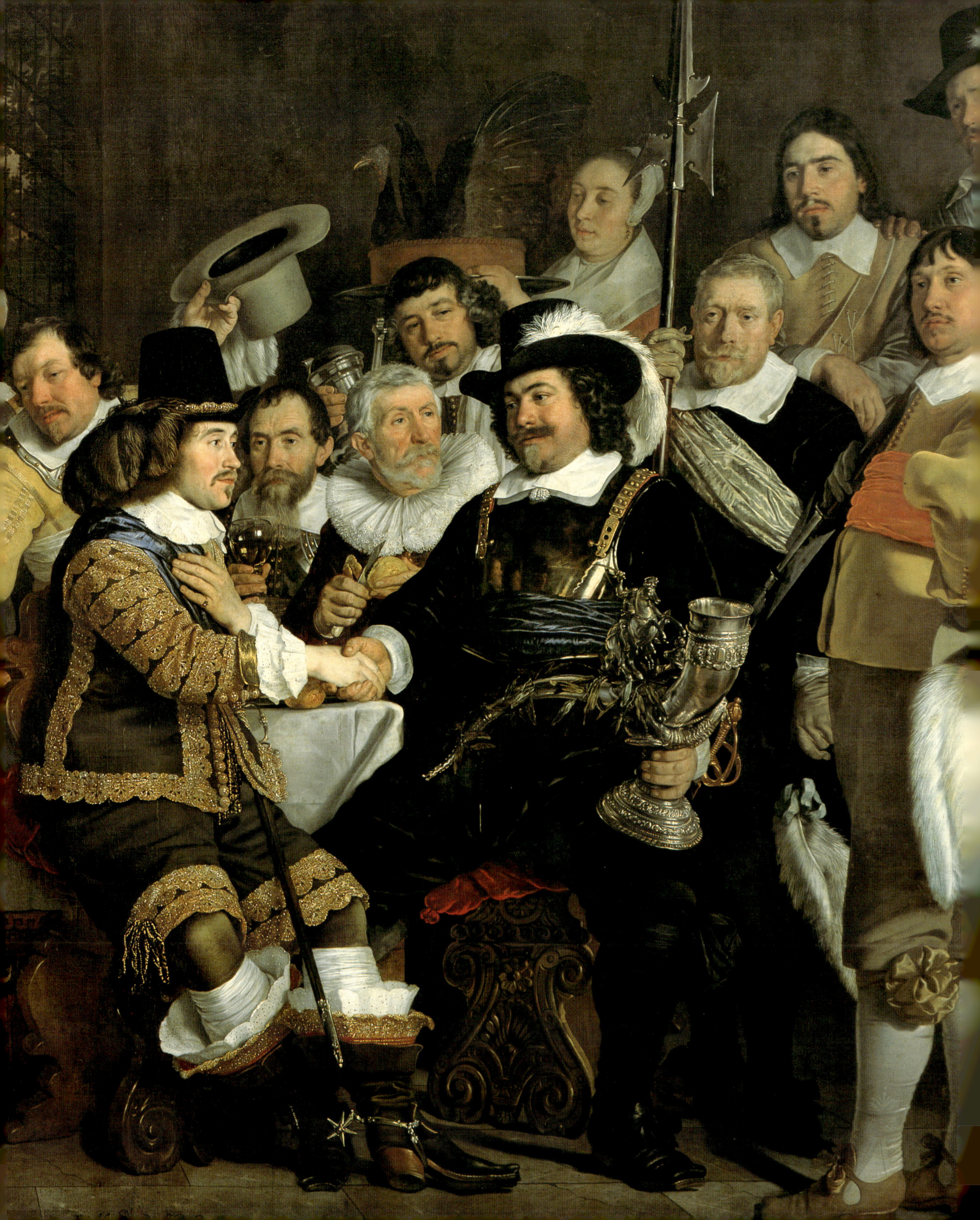

Johannes Verspronck (Haarlem c. 1607-Haarlem 1662)

49 *Portrait of a girl dressed in blue, 1641*

Oil on canvas, 82 x 66.5 cm
At lower left: *J.VSpronck An° 1641*
From the Augusteum, Oldenburg, as part of the collection of Duke Peter Friedrich Ludwig of Oldenburg (since 1805); purchased in 1922 by M.P. Voûte Sr, Amsterdam, and loaned to the Rijksmuseum; acquired from M.P. Voûte Jr in 1928 by the Vereniging Rembrandt and donated to the State for installation in the Rijksmuseum
Inv. no. SK-A-3064

Verspronck's portrait of this girl is an undisputed high point in his oeuvre of around 100 paintings, almost all of them skilful, meticulously executed portraits. A member of the wealthy burgher class who wanted his 'picture taken' would have found Johannes Verspronck a good photographer. For a more bravura, ingenious likeness he would have turned to another Haarlem artist: Frans Hals. It is thought that Verspronck may have studied with Hals, but if he did he certainly worked in an extremely sober variant of his teacher's style.

Verspronck's portraits are all cast in the same mould: the subject is seen from the side in front of a subtly lit, light brown or greyish background with the head turned towards the viewer, usually with the trace of a smile playing around the corners of the mouth. It is always clear, too, that the elegantly dressed sitters had to radiate a kind of dignity, their cool reserve announcing that they were not to be trifled with. It has been said, not unwittily, that one could hold a conversation with them that would be as genteel as it was shallow. There is clearly no lack of dignity in this girl's portrait. Her dress makes her look like an adult but in fact she is probably no more than ten years old, far younger than most viewers probably realise.

This is one of the few portraits by Verspronck with a range of colour that goes further than the blacks, greys and browns of most of his portraits, so it is not surprising that this unidentified young lady has come to be known as 'The blue girl'. In addition to the unusual colour scheme there is the evocative young face, which is anything but lifeless despite the meticulous way it is painted. It has an immediate appeal, so much so that some writers succumbed to the temptation of psychological speculation. Frederik Schmidt-Degener, director of the Rijksmuseum at the time, wrote in 1928 about his recent acquisition that the girl's face has a hint of 'shyness at having her portrait painted, but a slight twist at the corner of the mouth betrays her inner pleasure in the novelty of the occasion'. Others were struck by the artist's psychological perception, and felt that Verspronck 'already saw the woman in this self-assured child'.

Two superb paintings by Verspronck in Enschede are believed to be of the girl's parents, for they have a shared provenance and identical dimensions [*49a, 49b*]. Somehow, it seems, this particular family led the artist to outdo himself.

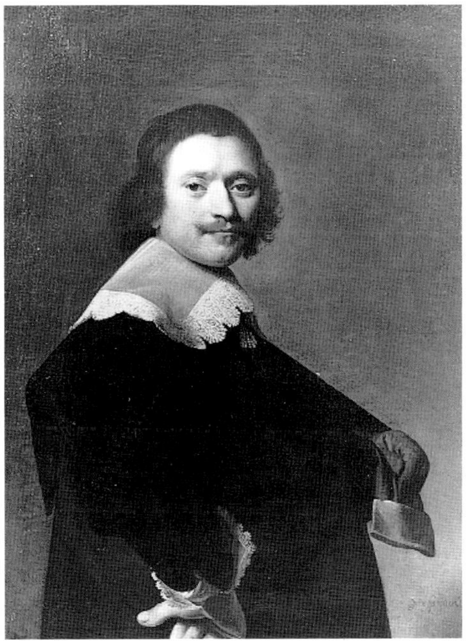

49a Johannes Verspronck, *Portrait of a man*, 1641; oil on canvas, 82 x 66.5 cm. Enschede, Rijksmuseum Twenthe

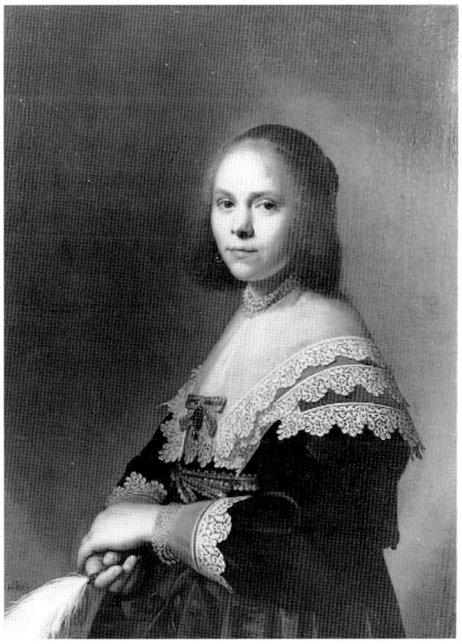

49b Johannes Verspronck, *Portrait of a woman*, 1640; oil on canvas, 82 x 66.5 cm. Enschede, Rijksmuseum Twenthe

LITERATURE

Ekkart 1979, no. 33; Van Thiel 1983b; exhib. cat. Haarlem/Antwerp 2000-2001, no. 38

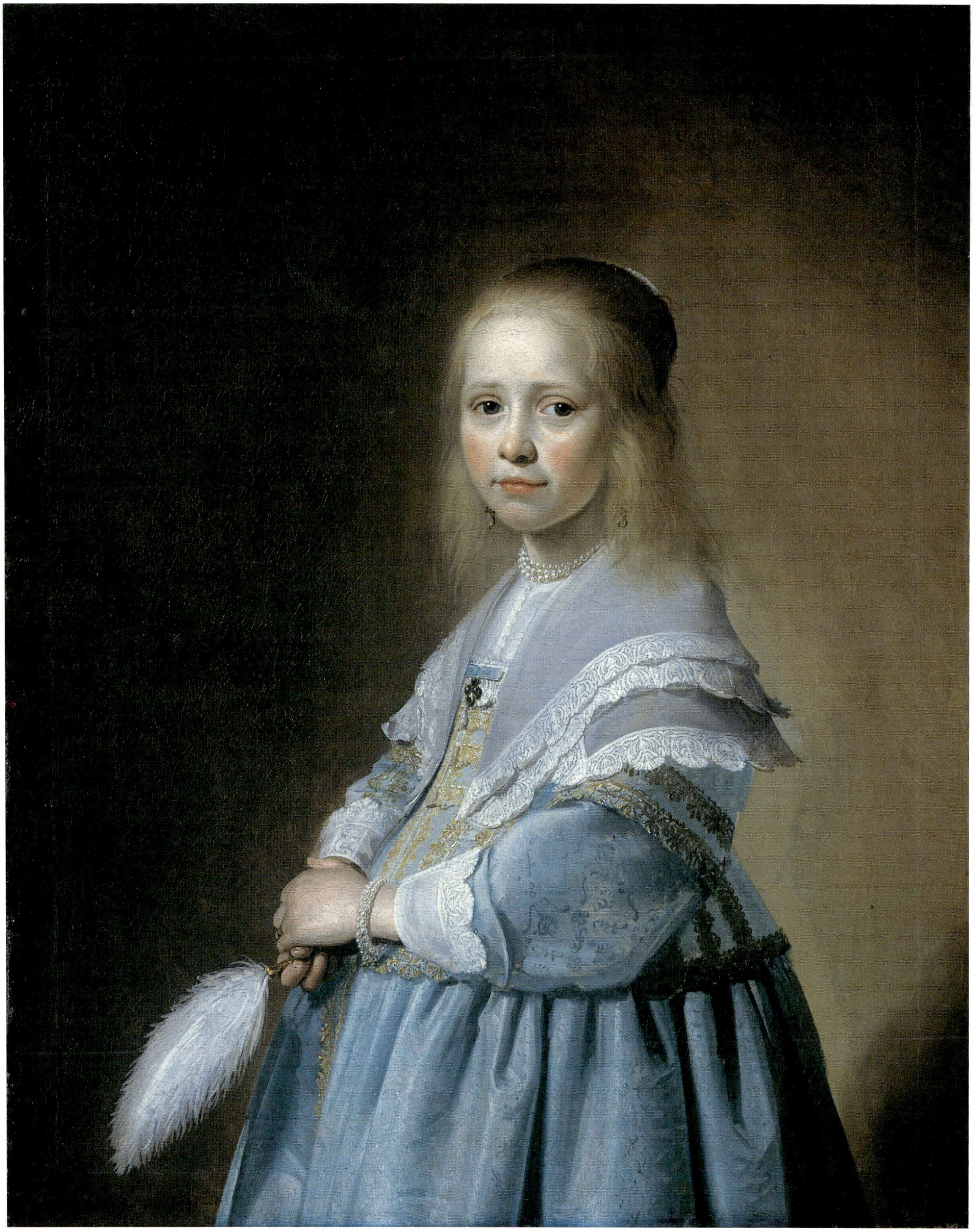

Rembrandt Harmensz van Rijn (Leiden 1606-Amsterdam 1669)

50 *Three women and a child by a doorway, c. 1645*

Pen in brown, 23.3 x 17.8 cm
From the collection of Jacob de Vos Jbzn; acquired with the aid of the Vereniging Rembrandt in 1885
Inv. no. RP-T-1889-A-2056

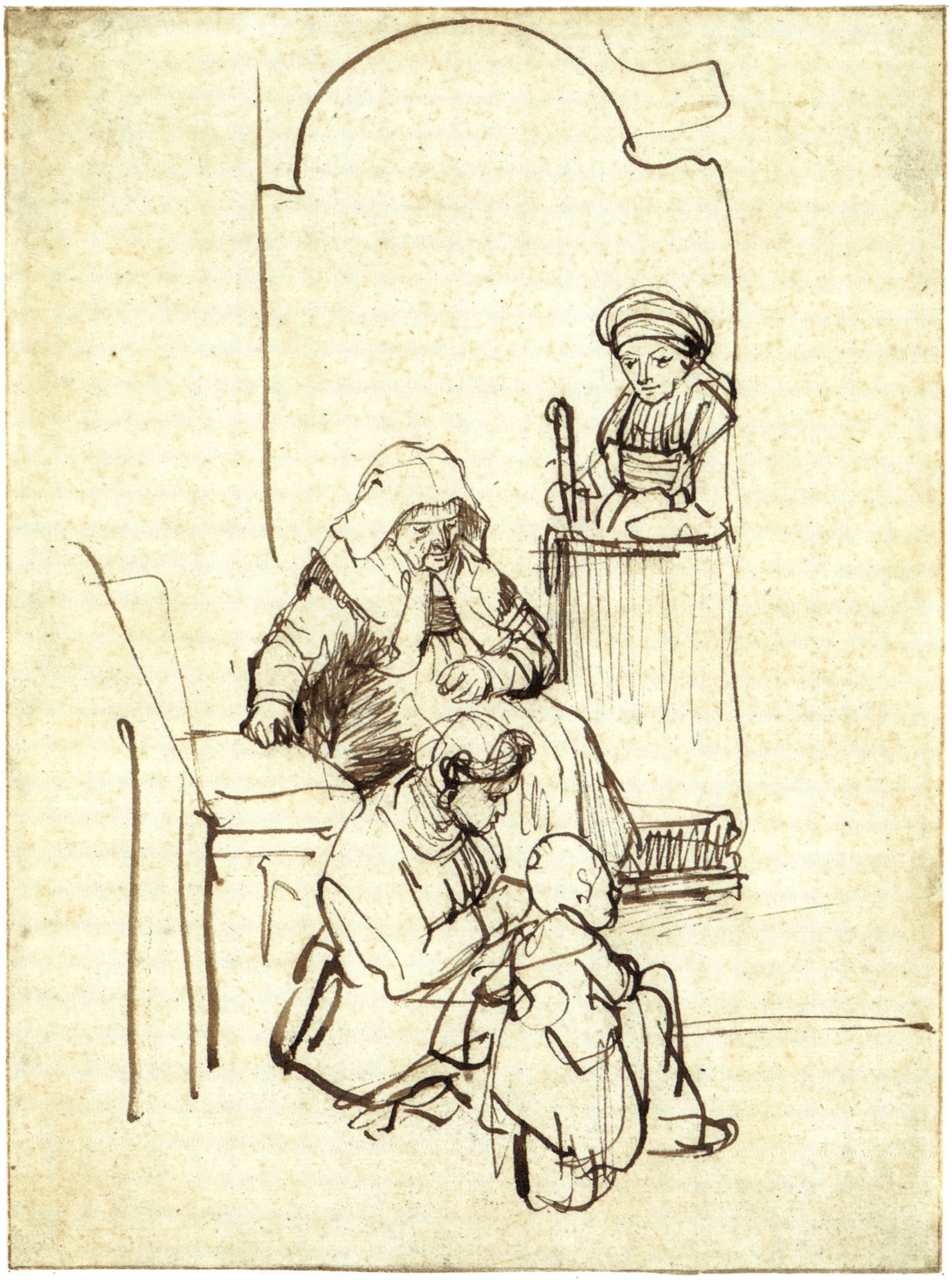

In the estate left on the death of Jan van de Cappelle, marine painter and one of the greatest Dutch 17th-century art collectors, [*see* 41], was a portfolio 'containing 135 drawings of the life of women with children by Rembrandt'. This may very well have been one of them, for the subject certainly matches the inventory description. In the 1630s Rembrandt drew many studies of mothers (and grandmothers) with children coping with the mundane events of everyday life: a child frightened by a dog, a bawling infant being picked up by its mother in an attempt to soothe it, a woman carrying her snoozing child upstairs. Rembrandt clearly observed these little scenes in his own immediate circle; the only question is whether he drew them from life or later, from memory. Perhaps he did both. Some drawings of figures in action simply could not have been made on the spot, but others, like this serene group of three women and a child, could well have been done from life.

The scene revolves around the figure of an old woman seated on a low chair or stool. She is outdoors, in front of a doorway with an arched top. Sitting at her feet is a much younger woman busy with her needlework, beside whom is a standing child seen three-quarters from the back and with its head turned away from us. A third woman is looking on from inside the house, leaning her left arm on the half-door.

What is always so fascinating about Rembrandt's draughtsmanship is the way in which he suggests forms without actually describing them, creating an evocation with his highly personal penmanship which sometimes approaches Japanese calligraphy. This is superbly illustrated by the small group of the seated woman and child in the foreground. Strictly speaking, the lines do not depict anything, nor do they record the forms, but taken together they create a perfect illusion of form, volume and space. Another striking feature is the way Rembrandt carefully detailed the old woman's face with a very fine pen. Her figure is the only one with shaded passages, which are done with a tangle of hatchings. The result is to fasten the viewer's attention on her, the pivotal character in this domestic scene.

The drawing comes from the famous collection of Jacob de Vos Jbzn. There were more than 60 drawings listed as Rembrandts in the De Vos sale catalogue in 1883, and the Teyler Museum in Haarlem made the highest bid at the auction, paying the princely sum of 5,200 guilders for a view of a city wall. The *Three women and a child by a doorway* fetched far less, for it was tucked away in a lot consisting of 15 drawings labelled 'School of Rembrandt', which was sold for 480 guilders—a real bargain, as it turned out. The *City wall* has long since been rejected as a work by Rembrandt, but the lot of 15 sheets proved to contain two autograph drawings of the highest quality.

LITERATURE
Cat. Amsterdam 1985, no. 27

Artus Quellinus (Antwerp 1609-Antwerp 1668)

51 *Portrait of Andries de Graeff, 1661*

Marble, h. 75 cm
On the plinth: AND.DE.GRAEFF.COS.AMST.A.QVELLINO.F.CIƆIƆCLXI
Purchased in 1817
Inv. no. BK-18305

The Antwerp sculptor Artus Quellinus was enlisted to come to the north and work on the decoration of Amsterdam's new Town Hall, now the Royal Palace on Dam Square. His stay in the city from 1650 to 1663 provided a major impetus for the development of Dutch sculpture. Not only did he produce work of the highest quality himself, he also trained a generation of gifted sculptors who stamped their mark on sculpture in the Republic after 1650—among them Rombout Verhulst, Bartholomeus Eggers and Artus Quellinus II.

The initiative for building a grand civic palace which would proclaim Amsterdam's fame and might was taken by several humanist members of the city government who had an internationalist outlook. Their main source of inspiration was the glory of classical Rome, and they too profited from presence of this modernist sculptor in Amsterdam by ordering marble portrait busts of themselves, thereby demonstrating their Classicist taste on a more personal level. Some of those portraits have a Baroque grandeur that was unusual in the Netherlands, and thus epitomise the cultural aspirations of the patrons. That is certainly true of the 1661 portrait of Burgomaster Andries de Graeff (1611-1678).

The bust's sense of a moment frozen in time demonstrates Quellinus's familiarity with the latest developments in Italian Baroque sculpture. In Italy, and particularly in Rome, sculptors like Bernini and Algardi had developed a new portrait style in the first half of the 17th century in which refined stylistic devices were used to enhance the naturalism of sculpted portraits. The aim was to compensate to some extent for the monochrome nature of the material, be it stone, bronze or terracotta, which made it very difficult for sculptors to rival painters in power of expression. The devices included turning the face sideways to give it an 'unposed' look, and portraying the sitter's lips slightly parted, as if he had been turned to stone in mid-sentence. Improvements were also made to the modulation from bust to plinth, which was usually very unnatural. Now it was carefully concealed by draperies, such as a cloak draped around the shoulders and the chest.

Quellinus had picked up modernist tricks of this kind during his stay in Italy, and tried them out in this bust of Andries de Graeff, which he turned into an imposing and monumental portrait of the burgomaster by including his right arm. De Graeff appears to have been turned to stone just when he was coming to meet the viewer. The play of light and shadow in the folds of the cloak, the wig, and the delicate decoration of the lace collar give the bust an added sense of depth and naturalness. The burgomaster has been immortalised as if he were a Roman consul—an allusion also made in the Latin inscription on the plinth.

LITERATURE
Cat. Amsterdam 1973, no. 301; cat. Amsterdam 1995a, no. 18

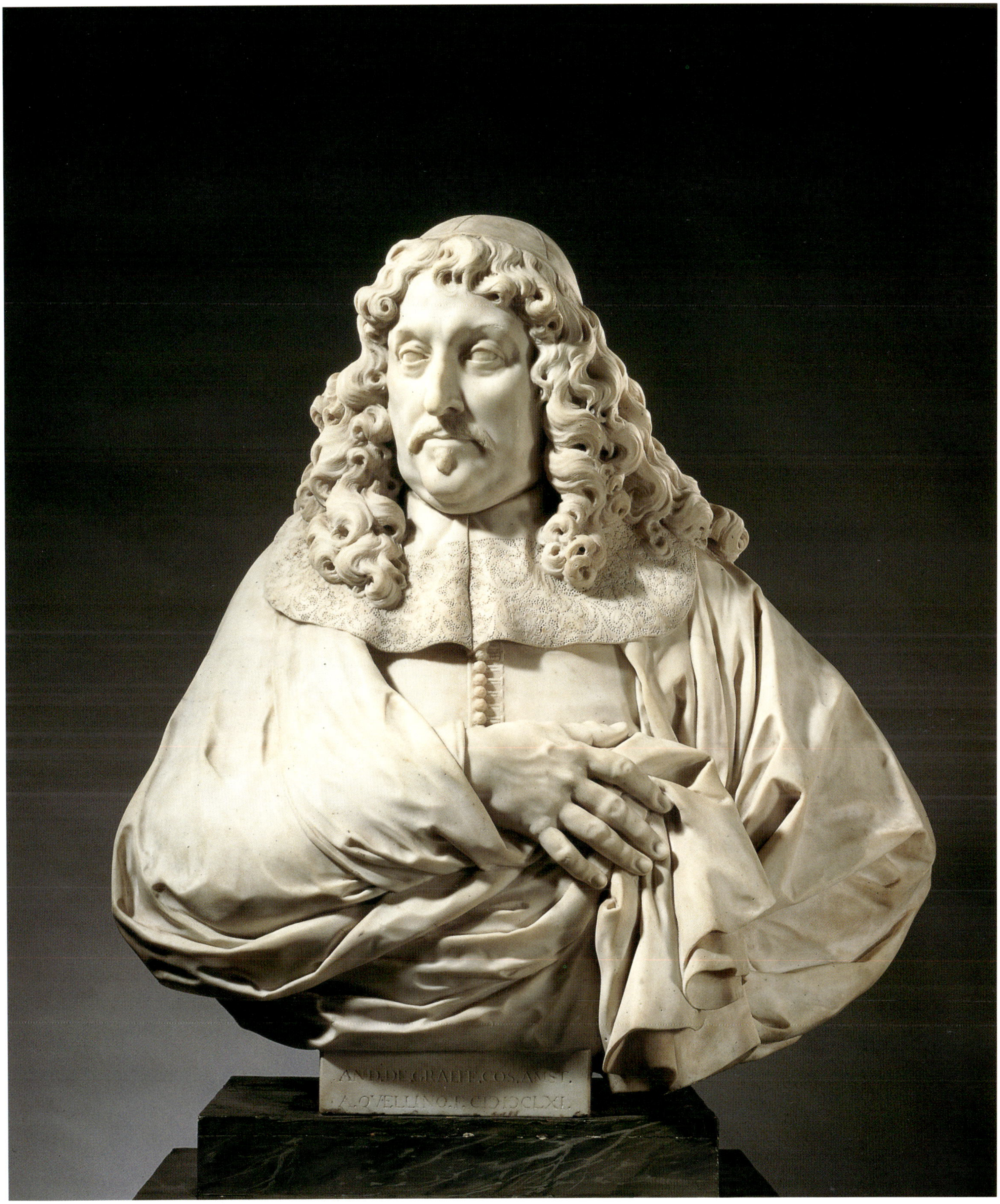
AND. DE GRAEFF. COS. AMST.
A. QVELLINO. F. CIƆIƆCLXI.

Artus Quellinus (Antwerp 1609-Antwerp 1668)

52 *The judgement of Brutus: Justice, c. 1651-1654*

Terracotta, 73 × 83 cm
From the Art Chamber in the Town Hall; transferred to the Oude Mannenhuis in 1837 with the Rijksacademie voor Beeldende Kunsten; on loan from the City of Amsterdam since 1887
Inv. no. BK-Am-51/21

Amsterdam's new Town Hall was officially inaugurated on 29 July 1655, seven years after work had started on the grandiose project, the likes of which had never been seen in the Dutch Republic. It was not actually finished in 1655, but by 1662 the roof had been completed and most of the rooms were ready. In its scale and wealth of decoration, no grander structure had been erected in the Netherlands since the building of the Gothic cathedrals. The Town Hall was expressly designed to proclaim the civic pride of Amsterdam and its city fathers, and at the same time reflected the city's great flowering as a trading metropolis.

The Antwerp sculptor Artus Quellinus was contracted to supply the sculpted decoration for the facades and the many rooms in the building, and from 1650 to 1663 he headed a workshop in Amsterdam. Working closely with Jacob van Campen, the architect responsible for the project, and the burgomasters who made up the building committee, his large shop shaped the sculptural programme for the Town Hall.

Although little is known about the division of labour within the workshop, it can

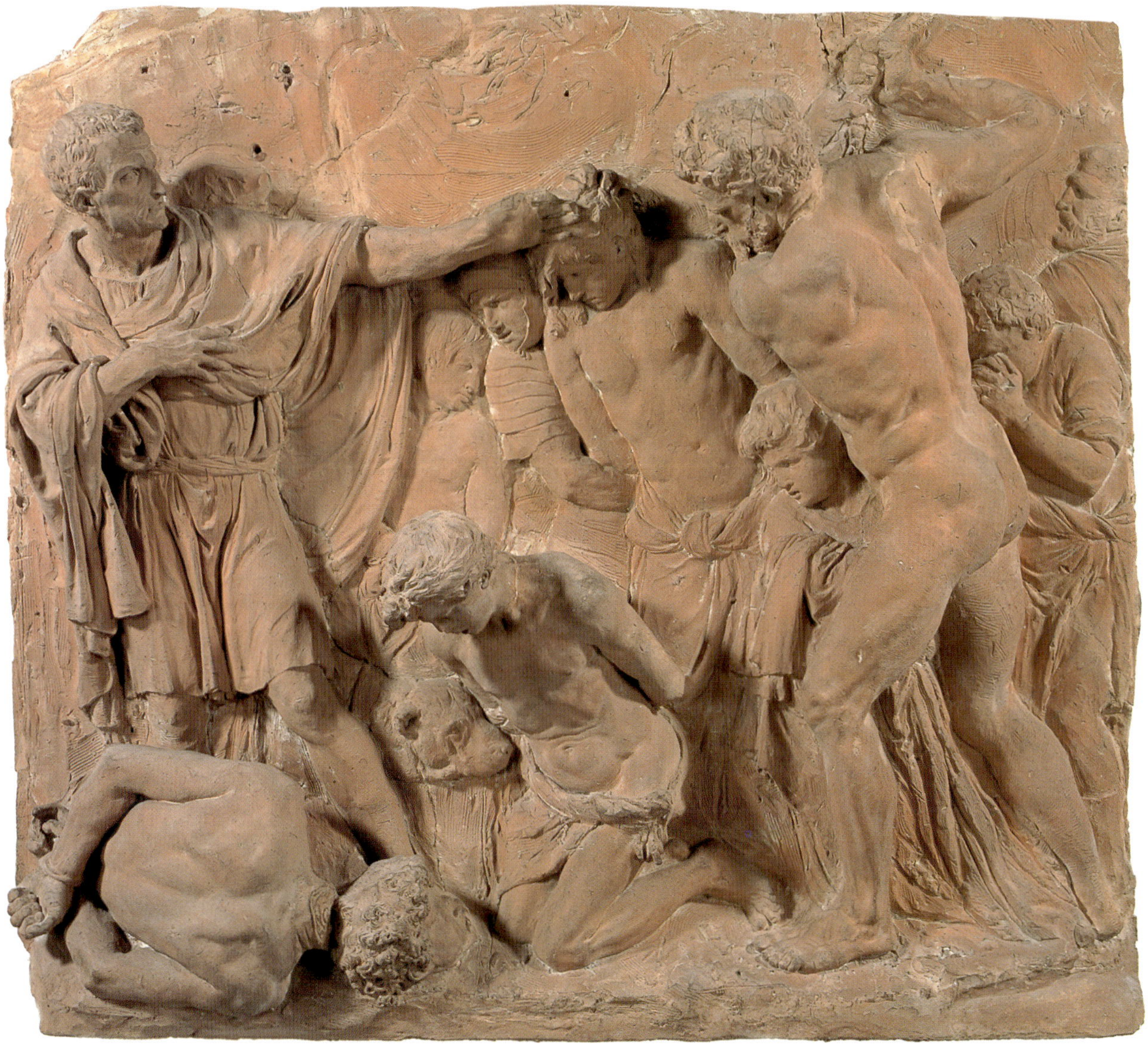

be deduced from the many surviving designs and sketches in fired clay that terracotta models like this one played an important part in translating the ideas of Van Campen and Quellinus into marble. That does not mean, however, that Quellinus made all the terracottas himself. Several replicas of those designs, for example, suggest that there was a market for 'souvenirs' of the building, and they were undoubtedly made by workshop assistants.

The terracotta design for the marble relief with the Judgement of Brutus, which was one of the three classical scenes of justice in the Tribunal, shows the composition almost complete. The main actors in the drama are fully detailed, but the background is still sketchy. Several motifs found in the finished marble are missing, among them the faces of a number of background figures. That the relief is a 'work in progress' is immediately evident. The background contains numerous traces of the sculptor's modelling implements, such as the lines incised and combed in the wet clay. These are the initial indications of drapery folds or the outlines of background motifs. Small holes made in the clay with a stylus are probably measuring points which the sculptor could use to scale up the model when carving the marble. It is likely that Quellinus made this composition in 1651, for in the Town Hall accounts there is an invoice in his handwriting dated 24 October 1651 for: 'First, the design modelled in terracotta for the judgement of Junius Brutus', for which he was paid 200 guilders.

LITERATURE

Fremantle 1959, pp. 157-164; cat. Amsterdam 1973, no. 279; cat. Amsterdam 1995c, pp. 48-51 and no. 91

Jan Asselijn (Dieppe c. 1615-Amsterdam 1652)

53 *The threatened swan, c. 1650*

Oil on canvas, 144 × 171 cm
At lower right: *JA*
Purchased in 1800 at the sale of the collection of Jan Gildemeester Jzn
Inv. no. SK-A-4

Although Jan Asselijn is known chiefly for his sun-drenched Italianate landscapes he also painted several impressive animal pieces. His best-known work in that genre is without question this large and stunning *Threatened swan*. The bird, seen almost frontally with outstretched wings and curved neck, has rounded on a dog in the water on the left which is approaching the swan's nest. It is above all in the imitation of textures that Asselijn demonstrates his great mastery. Deceptively lifelike feathers glide through the air or float on the water, large water droplets which have rolled off the bird's wet webbed feet lie on the ground, and the numerous shades of white in the depiction of the swan are a marvel.

In 1800 this was the first work to be purchased by the still highly nationalistic Nationale Konst-Gallerij, the forerunner of the Rijksmuseum. It was undoubtedly bought because of its supposed political and symbolic connotations, which are due to the inscriptions on the painting. Below the swan are the words DE RAAD= PENSIONARIS (The Pensionary), one of the eggs in the nest is labelled HOLLAND, and the legend above the dog's head pro-

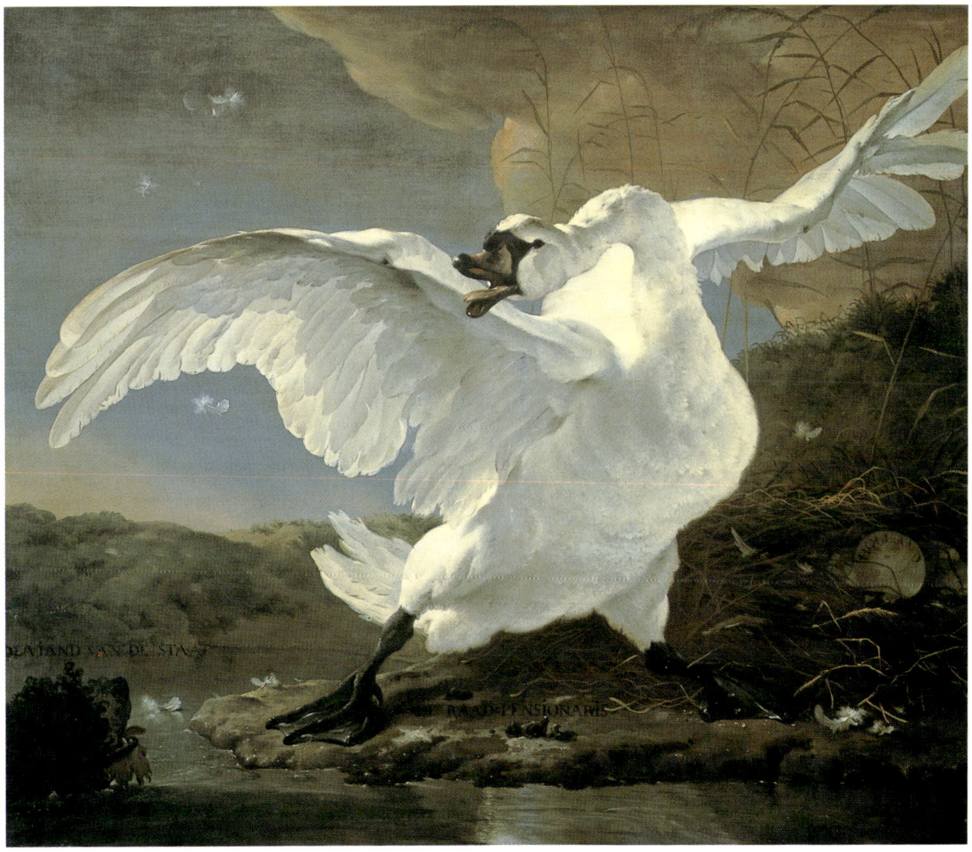

claims it to be DE *VIAND VAN DE STAAT* (The enemy of the state). The Pensionary in question is Johan de Witt (1625-1672), and the amusing combination of word and image is an emblematic reference to his vigilance in defending the Republic against its many enemies during his term of office.

The problem is that Jan Asselijn died in 1652, a year before De Witt became Pensionary, so he could not possibly have painted the inscriptions. They were probably added in the mid-18th century, when a pamphleteering war broke out between the rival factions supporting the States assemblies and the House of Orange—a conflict that has gone down in Dutch history as the 'De Witt War'. A swan was the obvious choice to symbolise the Pensionary, for in addition to alluding to his surname (Witt means 'white'), his family had itself adopted the swan as its symbol.

Those later inscriptions seem to have altered the meaning of Asselijn's painting for good. Their insertion a century after the painting was made changed it from a realistic picture of animal life into a political allegory. Just how long-lived that misunderstanding was is demonstrated by the fact that when the Nationale Konst-Gallerij made its first purchase, so many years later, it did so precisely because of the painting's supposed nationalist credentials.

LITERATURE

Cat. Amsterdam 1976, p. 89

Paulus Potter (Enkhuizen 1625-Amsterdam 1654)

54 *Cows in a meadow by a farm, 1653*

Oil on canvas, 58 x 66.5 cm
On the fence on the left: *Paulus Potter: f: 1653*
Bequest of Jonkheer J.S.H. van de Poll, 1880
Inv. no. SK-A-711

Paulus Potter portrayed six cows and two sheep in a meadow lined with pollard willows beside a farmhouse. Some of the meticulously detailed animals have sought the shade under the trees. The long shadows show that a hot summer's day is drawing to a close. A peasant woman is milking a cow on the right, while a hunter with his gun on his shoulder approaches with his dog. The view through the trees to the horizon is coloured with the golden light of the sun reflected in a body of open water. The artist has superbly captured the mood of a peaceful, languid late afternoon.

Scenes of herdsmen with cattle had been popular in Dutch painting since the 1620s, when they were painted mainly by the first generation of the so-called Italianates, of whom Cornelis van Poelenburch [37] and Bartholomeus Breenbergh were the leading lights. They placed their figures and animals in hilly, idealised landscapes, sometimes accompanied by classical nymphs and gods. Potter, though, transported his pastoral from that ideal vision of Arcadia to the 17th-century Dutch countryside. There is little sign, though, of the poverty-stricken conditions under which countryfolk had to

54a Paulus Potter, *Farmhouse near The Hague*, 1647; oil on panel, 39.7 x 50.2 cm.
Chester, Eaton Hall, The Duke of Westminster

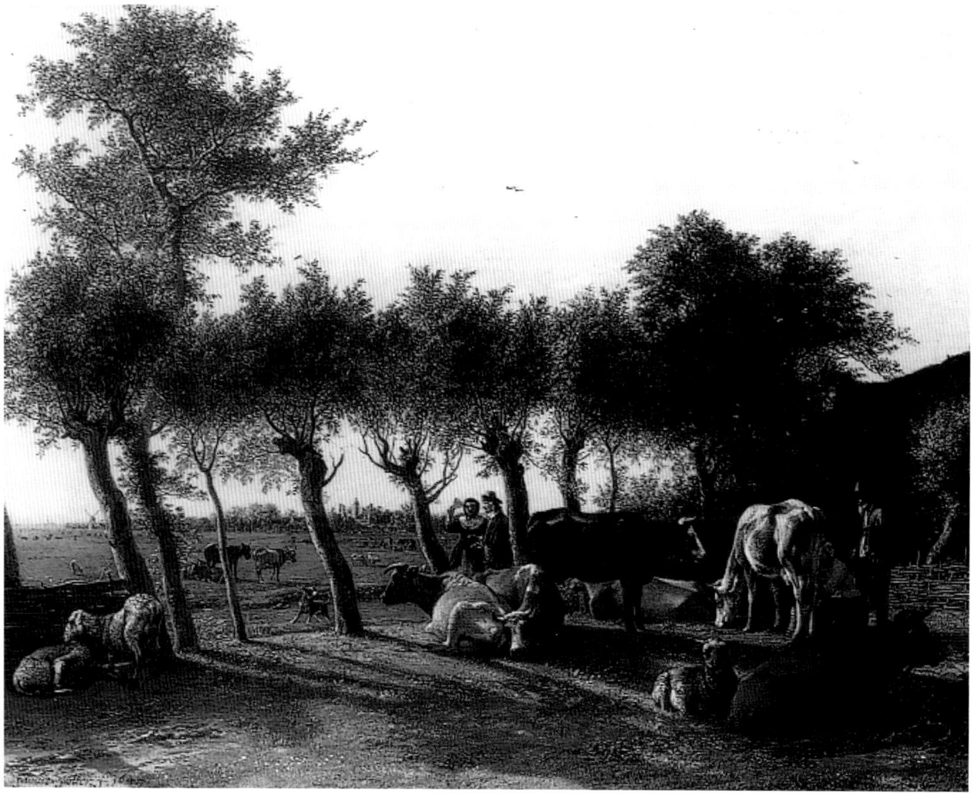

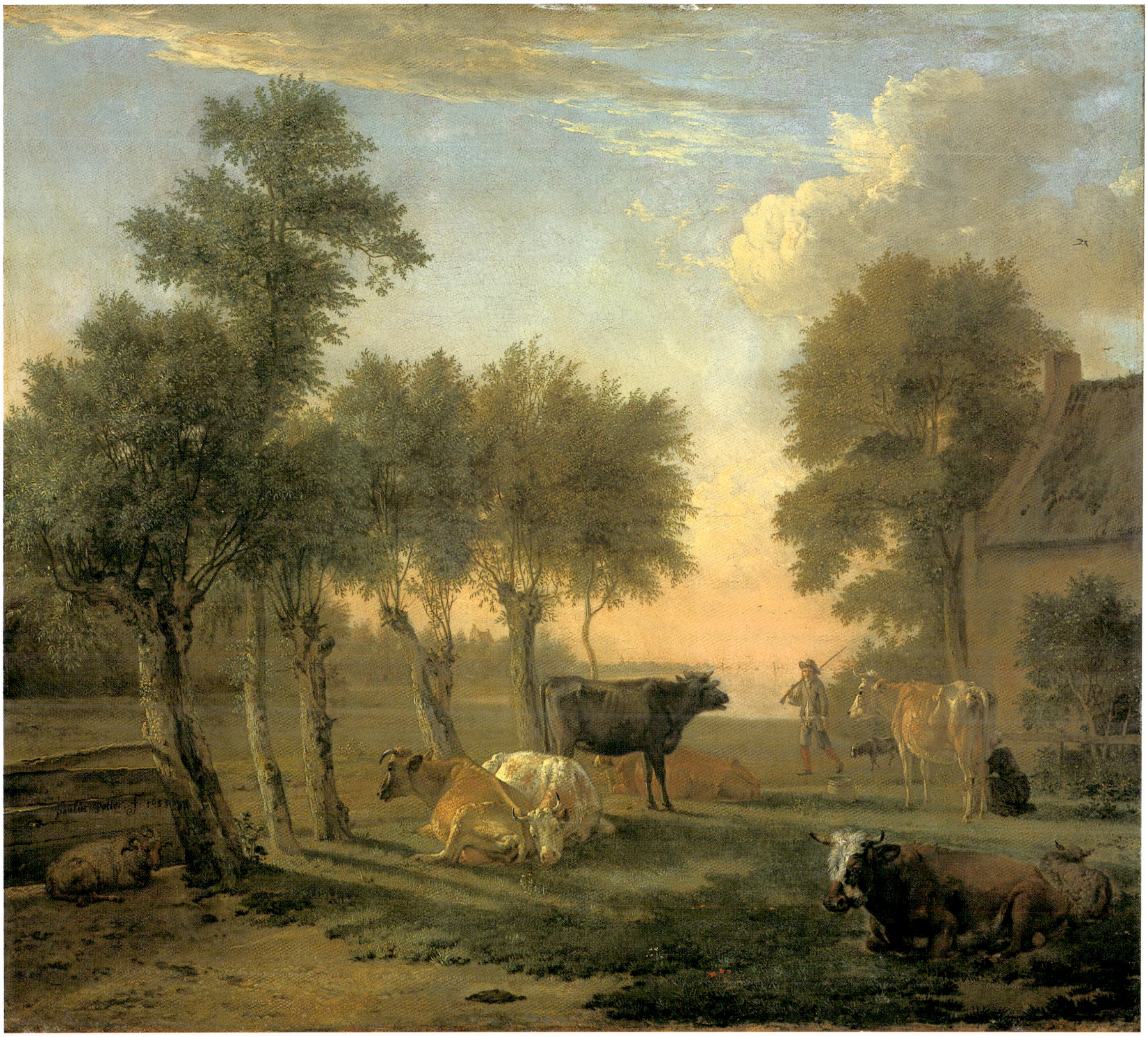

live, or of the harsh, grinding labour with which they struggled to keep their heads above water. Quite the reverse; the artist is presenting us with a true Dutch Arcadia.

The style and subject are typical of Potter's oeuvre, whose main claim to fame is his lifesized *Young bull* of 1647, the scale of which is distinctly atypical, for he usually painted his animals in a landscape in a handier format. Paulus was the son of Pieter Potter, a specialist in landscapes and still lifes and his son's first teacher. The pupil's exceptional talent was apparent at an early age, and he was only 22 when he painted the *Young bull*, his masterpiece. Dating from the same year is an earlier and slightly smaller variant of the picture in the Rijksmuseum, which also shows cows and sheep resting in a meadow with a row of pollard willows and a farmhouse [54*a*]. The two cows lying on the ground in the centre of the composition are identical in both paintings, and were evidently based on a drawing, probably done from life, which Potter kept in his studio among his stock of models.

LITERATURE

Exhib. cat. The Hague 1994-95, no. 30

Jan Both (Utrecht c. 1615-Utrecht 1652)

55 *Italian landscape with draughtsman, c. 1650*

Oil on canvas, 187 x 240 cm
At lower centre: *JBoth f.*
Bought from John Smith of London by Adriaan van der Hoop in 1834; bequeathed by the latter to the City of Amsterdam, 1854; on loan to the Rijksmuseum since 1885
Inv. no. SK-C-109

In addition to painters like Jan van Goyen and Salomon van Ruysdael, who took the Dutch landscape as their subject, there was quite a large group of artists who specialised in southern, Italian landscapes in the first half of the 17th century. Most of these so-called Italianates had lived in Italy for varying lengths of time. One of the best known was undoubtedly Jan Both, who worked there from 1638 to 1642. He made the trip with his older brother Andries (1612/13-1642), and when the latter drowned in Venice Jan returned to his native Utrecht, where he continued his successful career. He had already made his name in Rome, where he had sold work to several Roman prelates and the King of Spain.

The Dutch and Flemish artists working in Rome in the 17th century formed a society called the Bentvueghels. Whenever a new painter arrived from the north he was inducted into the society during a boisterous parody of a christening party at which the wine flowed freely, and was given a Bentvueghel nickname, which was usually a less than flattering allusion to his appearance or character. Jan and Andries Both are documented at a gathering of artists in Rome in 1638, but their nicknames are not known.

There are surviving depictions of members of the society going out together to draw and paint the countryside around Rome, and this picture by Jan Both also includes a draughtsman. Although drawing outdoors was a common practice at the time, painting landscapes directly from nature must have been highly unusual. Only very rarely did Both and his colleagues depict a specific topography. Almost all their works are quite obviously imaginary compositions, and this *Italian landscape with a draughtsman* is no exception. It shows a waterfall and a small gorge overgrown with bushes and trees close to a country road with a bridge which has just been crossed by a travelling party consisting of a carriage drawn by two horses and two heavily laden horses led by grooms. By the side of the road are three groups of two figures each, all wearing rather rustic garb. Judging by their poses and the sheet of paper held by one of them they are artists surveying the countryside. Opening up on the right is a broad view of the Roman *campagna*. Both painted the scene with remarkably light, bright colours, and exploited the effect of the sunlight to the full. He also shows that he had an eye for the decorative qualities of jagged rocks and woodland. It was here, above all, that his great originality lay, and his example was followed by artists like Adam Pynacker and Aelbert Cuyp [*see 56, 57*].

LITERATURE

Exhib. cat. Utrecht 1965, no. 56; exhib. cat. Amsterdam/Boston/Philadelphia 1987-88, no. 15

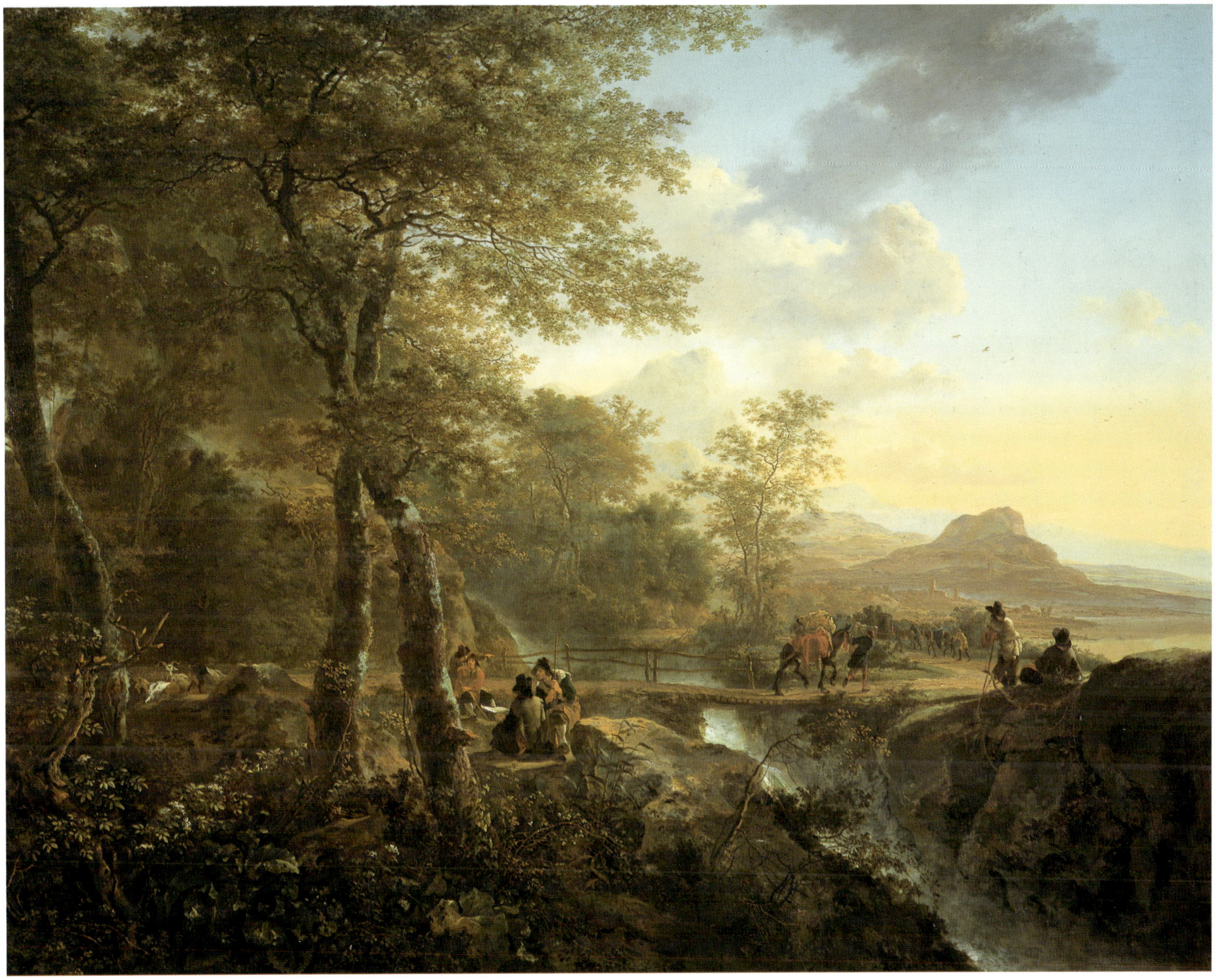

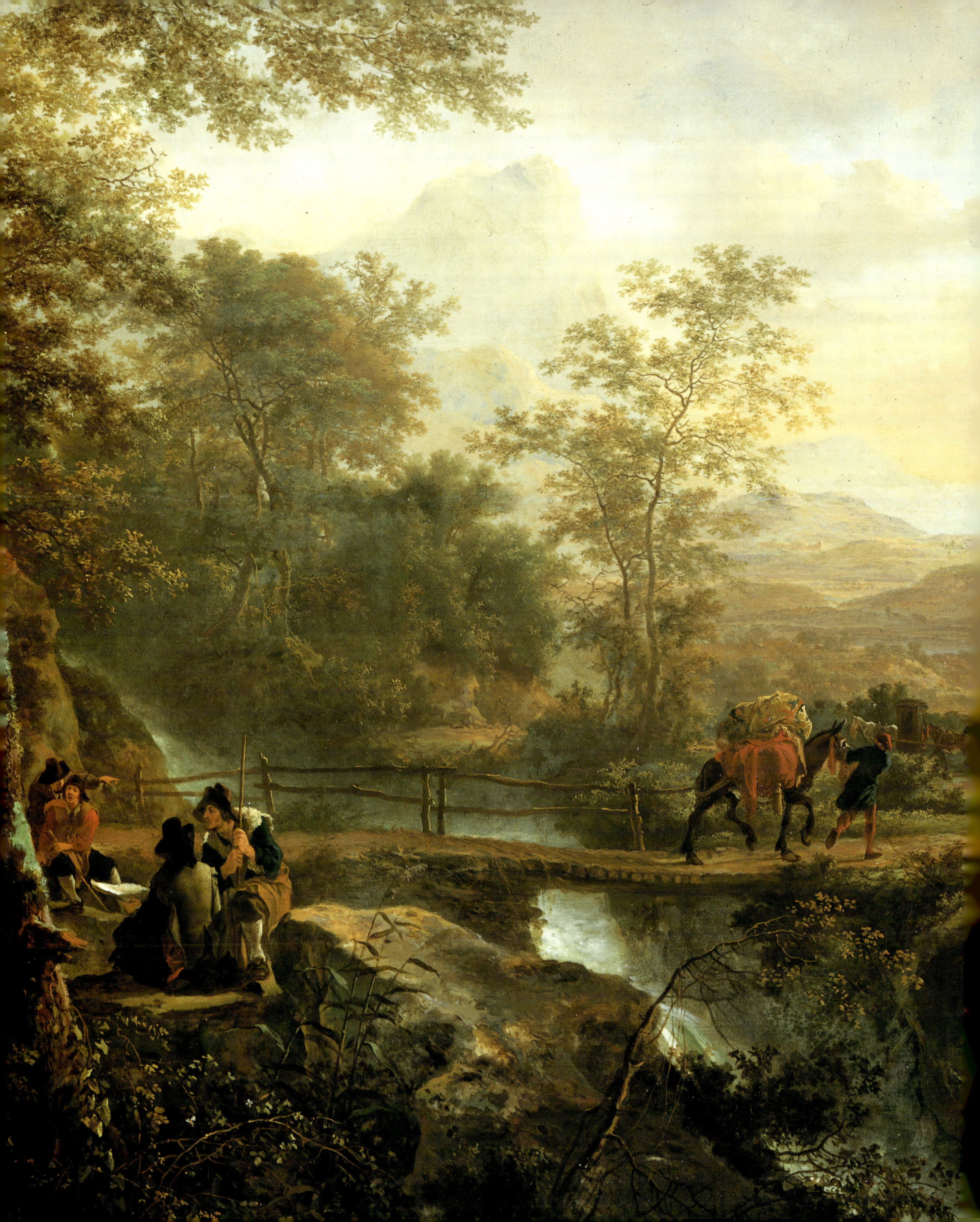

Adam Pynacker (Schiedam c. 1620-Amsterdam 1673)

56 *Boatmen moored on a lake shore, c. 1660*

Oil on canvas on panel, 97.5 × 85.5 cm
At lower left: *APijnacker*
Purchased in 1808 at the G. van der Pot van Groeneveld sale, Rotterdam
Inv. no. SK-A-321

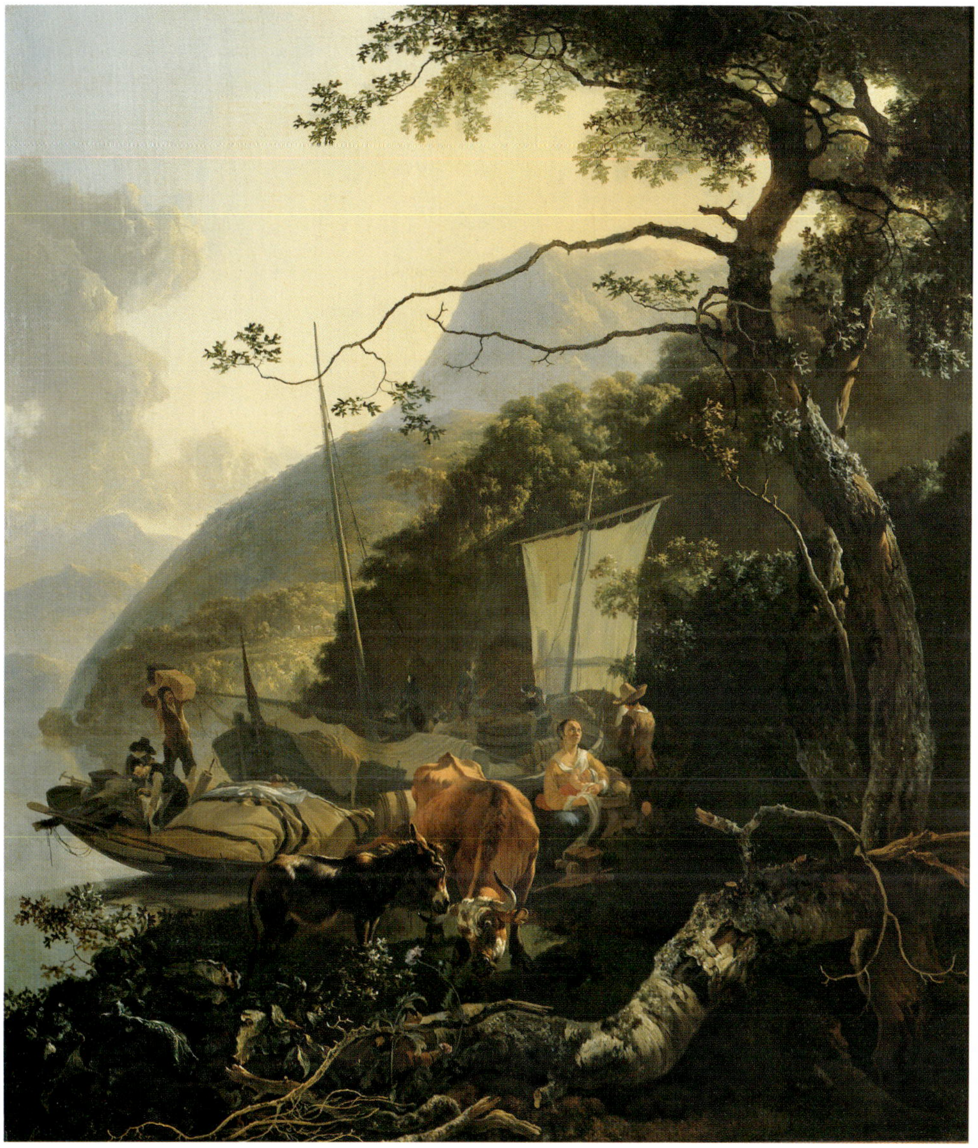

Lying by the shore of a mountain lake with a magnificent view on the left are two fully laden boats. Men on the one nearest the viewer are busily loading or unloading their cargo. The other boat contains several passengers, and its hoisted sail indicates that it is about to depart. In the centre of the composition are a man and a woman with a child in her arms—a group reminiscent of the Holy Family on their flight to Egypt. In front of them stand an ox and an ass, while the immediate foreground is closed off by a broken tree limb with numerous branches, twigs and foliage, and at far left by large cabbage leaves. A tall tree cuts off the composition on the right like a stage-flat. The backlit branches and their leaves stand out sharply against the light yellow background. The dress of the figures, the type of boat, the light palette and the bright sunshine identify this as a southern landscape, but there is no need to search for a specific location, for this is an imaginary scene. The motifs are variations on a Mediterranean theme, and were taken from sketches and drawings which the artist had brought back with him from Italy.

It is believed that Adam Pynacker spent several years in Italy around 1645, although there is no documentary evidence to prove it. His main employment there was probably as an agent for his father, a wine merchant who had his own fleet of ships. Pynacker the artist was fascinated by the writhing shapes of gnarled trees, interweaving branches and the foliage of undergrowth. This extremely fluid interplay of lines is echoed in this particular painting by the rather nervous approach to the composition as a whole, with its numerous modelling touches and dabs of the brush. This application of the paint, together with the many catchlights and heightenings in the sky, the foliage of the tree on the left and the vegetation in the foreground give the picture great liveliness and tension, which are features of Pynacker's work of the 1660s.

◂ Detail of [55]

The agitated ox with its bulging eyes appears to be expressing that tension in a way that is more just symbolic.

The rather complex, restless composition with its many contrasts detracts from the realism of the scene. Moreover, there is so much detail that the effect of it being 'just like the real thing' is almost lost. This development towards an unnatural-looking, mannered sort of Italianate landscape can also be seen in the work of a master like Nicolaes Berchem from the end of the 1660s.

LITERATURE

Exhib. cat. Utrecht 1965, no. 116; exhib. cat. Amsterdam/Boston/Philadelphia 1987-88, no. 66; Harwood 1988, no. 74

Aelbert Cuyp (Dordrecht 1620-Dordrecht 1691)

57 *River landscape with horsemen, c. 1655*

Oil on canvas, 128 x 227.5 cm
At lower centre: *A. cuyp*
From the collection of Edmund de Rothschild, England; purchased in 1965 with the aid of the Vereniging Rembrandt, the Prins Bernhard Fonds and the Commissie voor Fotoverkoop
Inv. no. SK-A-4118

Two horsemen wearing cuirasses and orange sashes which identify them as Dutch army officers have halted to water their horses on the bank of a river flowing through a landscape bordered by high hills. A herdsman in a bright red coat with his dog lying at his feet stands watching them from a little way off. His herd, numbering just four cows, is not in the least bit interested and looks the other way. The road the riders have travelled runs past a farmhouse with a stone front wall and a large, lopsided barn with a thatched roof. A covered cart pulled by a white horse has halted by a trough in front of the farmhouse. A peasant couple stand between the cart and the house. Approaching on foot between this little scene and the foreground is a wayfarer. The road evidently leads to a village or small town with a church with a tall spire. Further to the left, in the far distance, are the towers of a ruined castle.

Aelbert Cuyp saw similar ranges of hills as a young artist on a couple of journeys along the Rhine near Wageningen, Nijmegen and Cleves, and he was obviously impressed by their steepness, accustomed as he was to the flat countryside and water back in his native Dordrecht, for he recorded them in a slightly exaggerated form in drawings [57a]. When he used them a few years later for this painting he made them part of a mood landscape. The sun is low in the sky, creating a warm light and casting long shadows. The riders are resting, the cattle listless. The cloud formations point to a hot day that may yet end with a violent thunderstorm.

Cuyp built his composition up very carefully indeed. The rhythm of the overgrown fingers of land stretching out into the water on the left, which are cleverly anticipated by a silhouetted branch and its reflection, is varied on the right by the rhythm of the steep hillsides. That in turn is echoed by the sloping roof of the barn, while the stone front of the farmhouse is repeated in the house a little further up the hill. The long shadows cast by the horsemen intersect a small stream. If the painting is viewed simply as a flat surface, the righthand rider is very close indeed to the church spire, but the suggestion of a road running past the farmhouse and the great

57a Aelbert Cuyp, *River landscape*; black chalk and pencil, 16.5 x 24.8 cm. Present whereabouts unknown

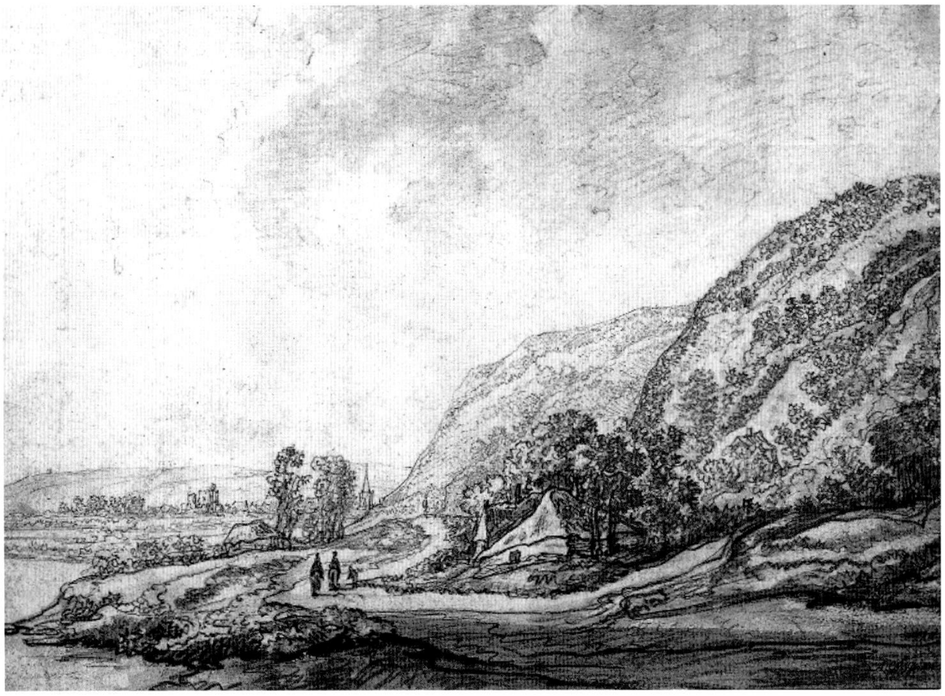

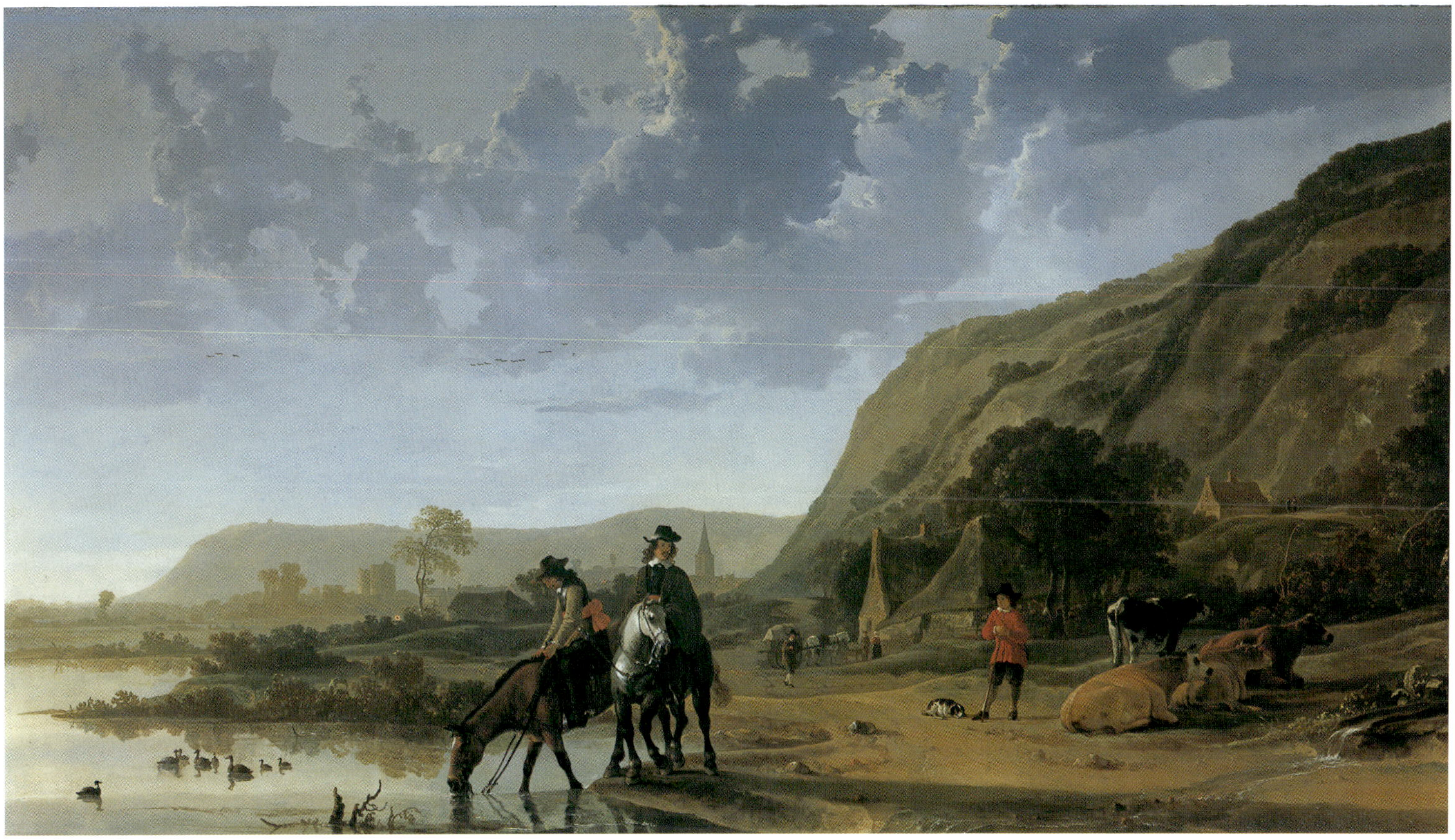

difference in intensity between the boldly brushed horseman and the hazy atmosphere around the spire ensure that the distance between foreground and background is utterly convincing.

Cuyp borrowed the golden light in the painting from Jan Both [55] and his friends, painters who had been to Italy and had fallen under the spell of its hilly landscapes and hazy vistas. Those artists, the Italianates, took their lead in turn from the work of Claude Lorrain, although by and large they paid less attention to the classical architecture that played such a prominent role in his landscapes. Aelbert Cuyp never travelled much further than Cleves, but with this monumental version of the Rhine landscape bathed in a golden light he nevertheless succeeded in telling a magnificent story of horsemen from far-places on a warm summer evening.

LITERATURE

De Bruyn Kops 1965; exhib. cat. Dordrecht 1977-78, no. 34

Aelbert Cuyp (Dordrecht 1620-Dordrecht 1691)

58 *View of Arnhem, c. 1645-1650*

Black chalk, brush in yellowish green and grey, gum arabic, 19 x 48.6 cm
Purchased in 1900
Inv. no. RP-T-1900-A-4379

In an age when every journey was a laborious and often hazardous undertaking, the close at hand could very quickly seem very far away indeed. Artists from the province of Holland wishing to see something other than the flat polder landscape around their birthplaces did not need to travel any great distance (to our 21st-century eyes, at least) to find themselves in surroundings that differed vastly from what they had left behind. One popular trip took them eastward along or on the great rivers to Cleves in Germany. Many of them must have made that journey, for there are many surviving views of cities along the route, the favourites being Rhenen, Arnhem and Nijmegen. Aelbert Cuyp must have been one of those eager travellers, for in the collection of the Amsterdam printroom alone there are views of all the above places.

The *View of Arnhem* shows the city from the north-west. The most prominent building among all the towers and spires is the Great Church of St Eusebius just to the left of centre. Its tower may provide a clue to the date of Cuyp's Rhineland journey. The city authorities of Arnhem decided shortly after the Treaty of Münster (1648) that the unfinished church tower had to be completed, and they also ordered that it at last be given a carillon and a clock. The tower in this drawing still lacks its top, which suggests that Cuyp visited the city before the beginning of the 1650s. However, one has to tread cautiously here, for 17th-century artists sometimes left things out of their drawings on purpose. The most famous example is Rembrandt, who made a drawing of the Montelbaan Tower in Amsterdam without the superstructure added to it by Hendrick de Keyser at the beginning of the century. But even if one assumes that Cuyp drew exactly what he saw before him, that does not say all that much about the date of this particular sheet. A large drawing of this kind, carefully worked up with watercolour, would undoubtedly have been made in Cuyp's studio on the basis of a far less detailed travel sketch. And there is indeed a smaller view of Arnhem in the printroom of Leiden University, which may well have been the model for the Amsterdam drawing.

Many of Cuyp's drawn landscapes have banks of clouds which look rather stiff and stereotype. There is a suspicion that these are latter additions, possibly ordered by an 18th-century collector who felt that his landscapes were 'incomplete' unless they had a scudding rack of cumulus. This

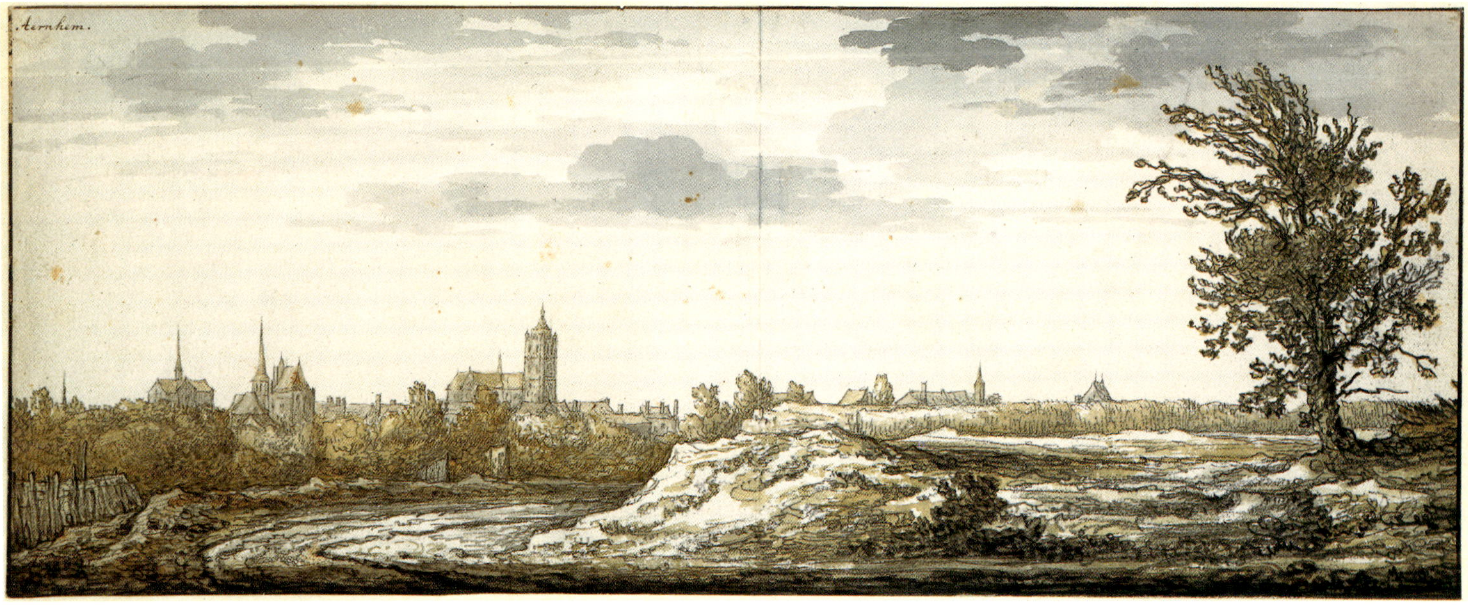

‘finishing’ of drawings was common practice in the 18th century, and was not frowned upon at all. In fact, artists like Dirck Dalens II and Isaac de Moucheron must have earned some of their daily bread working up and ‘finishing’ old drawings.

LITERATURE

Exhib. cat. Amsterdam 1987, no. 39

Northern Netherlands

59 *Layette cupboard, c. 1650-1675*

Oak and walnut, h. 178 cm, w. 119 cm, d. 57 cm
Purchased in 1985
Inv. no. BK-1985-10

A host of customs, many unknown in other countries, surrounded the birth of a child to a prosperous 17th-century Dutch family. One was the presentation of the newborn’s layette in a rectangular basket, usually of wickerwork and lined with fabric. The term *luiermand* (layette basket) gradually came to be used not just for the basket but for the baby’s outfit as well, and a special piece of furniture was introduced to house it: the layette cupboard. The one in the Rijksmuseum is typical in being a fairly small cabinet standing on a table-shaped support. It contained very few separate compartments, so had plenty of room for the clothes. There is little to distinguish the exterior from that of an art cabinet on a base, and 17th-century estate inventories repeatedly reflect a confusion about its rightful name. They also suggest that once a child had grown up the layette cupboard was moved from the lying-in room to the living quarters or a reception room.

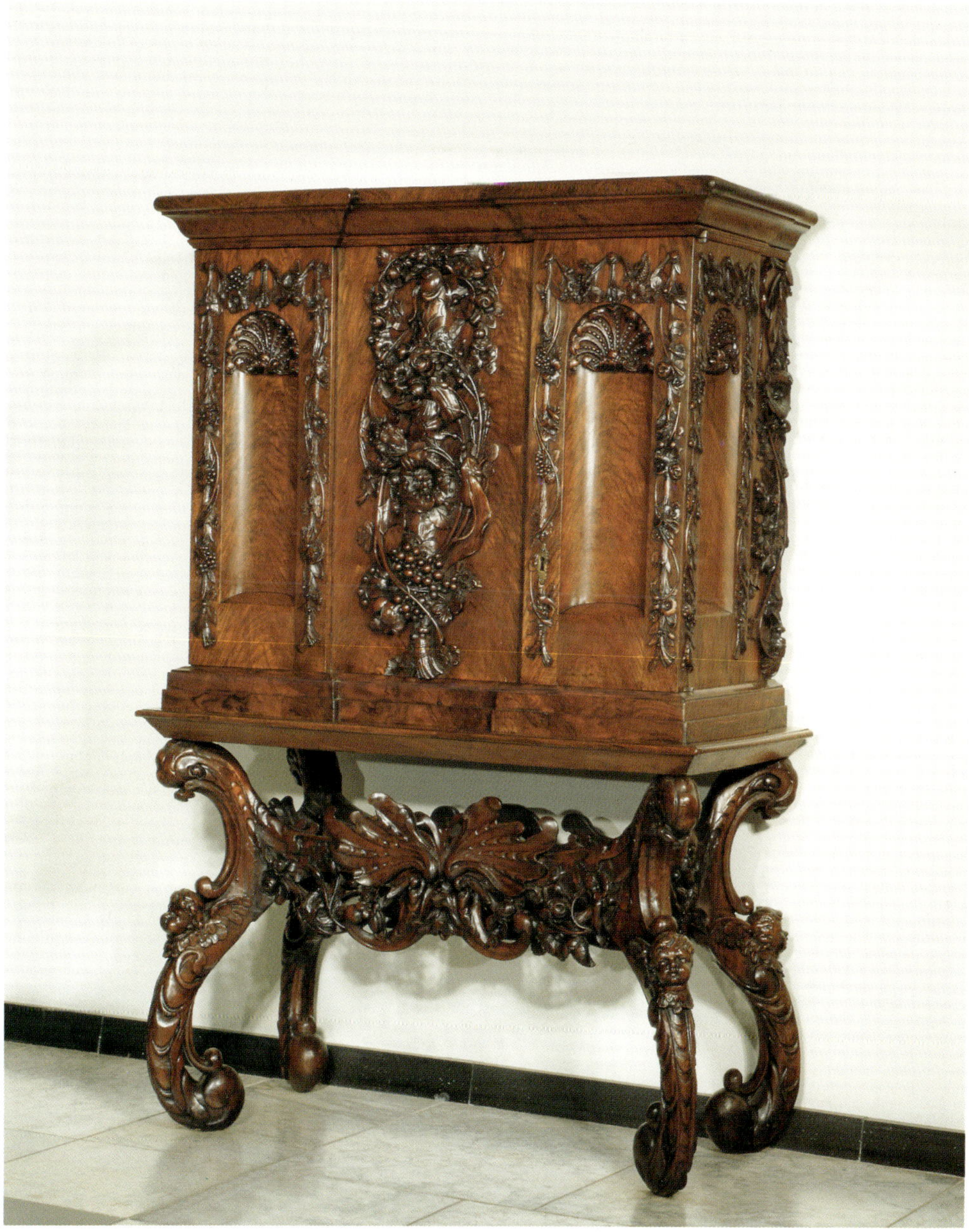

There is a similar cupboard in a private Dutch collection which has a central festoon composed not of flowers and fruit but of various objects associated with infancy, such as nappies, a cradle, clothing and a jingler. The function of that particular cupboard is beyond doubt, and although the carved decoration of the one in the Rijksmuseum lacks such specific allusions, other similarities show that it was indeed used for the same purpose. The decoration is remarkable for its high quality, fashionable nature and the contrast between the cupboard and its stand. The latter, with its flaccid, almost fluid legs and the grotesque mask shape in the middle is a splendid example of the use of auricular ornament in furniture. This was a style that evolved at the beginning of the century in silverware [*see 1, 5*], but only came into widespread use in furniture after 1650. The Amsterdam artist Gerbrandt van den

Eeckhout (1621-1674) published a series of designs for tables in an extreme version of the auricular style in 1655.

The luxuriant festoons on the cupboard itself are related to that style, but this upper part as a whole is an example of Dutch Classicism, which had its heyday around 1650. With its preference for clearly articulated forms and harmonious proportions it was diametrically opposed to the anti-classical auricular style, but elements of both are combined in many of the most ornately carved pieces of furniture from the third quarter of the 17th century. Seldom, though, is the result so effective as in this layette cupboard, which appears to be proclaiming that a new member has been born to a family which held the arts in high regard.

LITERATURE

Baarsen 1989c; cat. Amsterdam 1993b, no. 18

Frans Post (Leiden c. 1612-Haarlem 1680)

60 *View of Olinda, Brazil, 1662*

Oil on canvas, 107.5 x 172.5 cm
In the left foreground: F. Post/1662
Purchased in 1880
Inv. no. SK-A-742

Frans Post was the son of the glass painter Jan Jansz Post and a younger brother of the architect Pieter (1608-1669), whose buildings include the Mauritshuis in The Hague. In 1636 Frans went to Brazil as a member of an expedition headed by the owner of that house, Johan Maurits, Count of Nassau-Siegen. An enterprising military man, Johan Maurits had been appointed governor of Brazil by the directors of the Dutch West India Company, and he insisted that he be accompanied not only by the customary soldiers and merchants, but also by scientists and artists who would study the flora and fauna of the new colony and record them in drawings and paintings. Another painter on the expedition was Albert Eckhout (c. 1610-1665), and he and Post were the first European artists to set eyes on the New World. Unfortunately, only seven of the landscapes which Post painted in South America have survived. In 1679, Johan Maurits gave that group, or part of it, to Louis XIV of France.

Post continued painting Brazilian and West Indian scenes after his return to Haarlem in 1644. There was evidently a market eager for scenes of life in faraway places. The muted colour schemes and often rather naive nature of his early landscapes executed in Brazil now made way for more skilfully composed scenes with greater colour contrasts.

This *View of Olinda* of 1662 is certainly one of them, although the degradation of the yellow in the mixture of yellow and blue used for the green has unfortunately led to the blue becoming more pronounced than the artist intended. Olinda had been the capital of Pernambuco province in the days of Portuguese rule. The Dutch captured it in 1630 and burned it to the ground. On the left are the slightly fanciful remains of the cathedral, which in reality did not stand in lonely isolation out in the countryside. Post depicted it on several occasions, usually seen from the right, which means that he used drawings he had made on the spot and kept in his studio for inclusion in his compositions as the mood took him. This is well illustrated by the animals in the foreground, which are too large compared to their surroundings. The painter's drawings evidently did not contain enough information for him recall the correct scale of certain motifs. Interestingly, the painting is still in a 17th-century frame of carved limewood, which was originally gilt. Its decoration matches the exoticism of the painting, consisting as it does of a festoon of tropical insects, reptiles and flowers and fruits found in Brazil.

LITERATURE

Sousa-Leao 1973, no. 36; exhib. cat. Amsterdam 1984, no. 46; exhib. cat. Amsterdam/Boston/Philadelphia 1987-88, no. 72

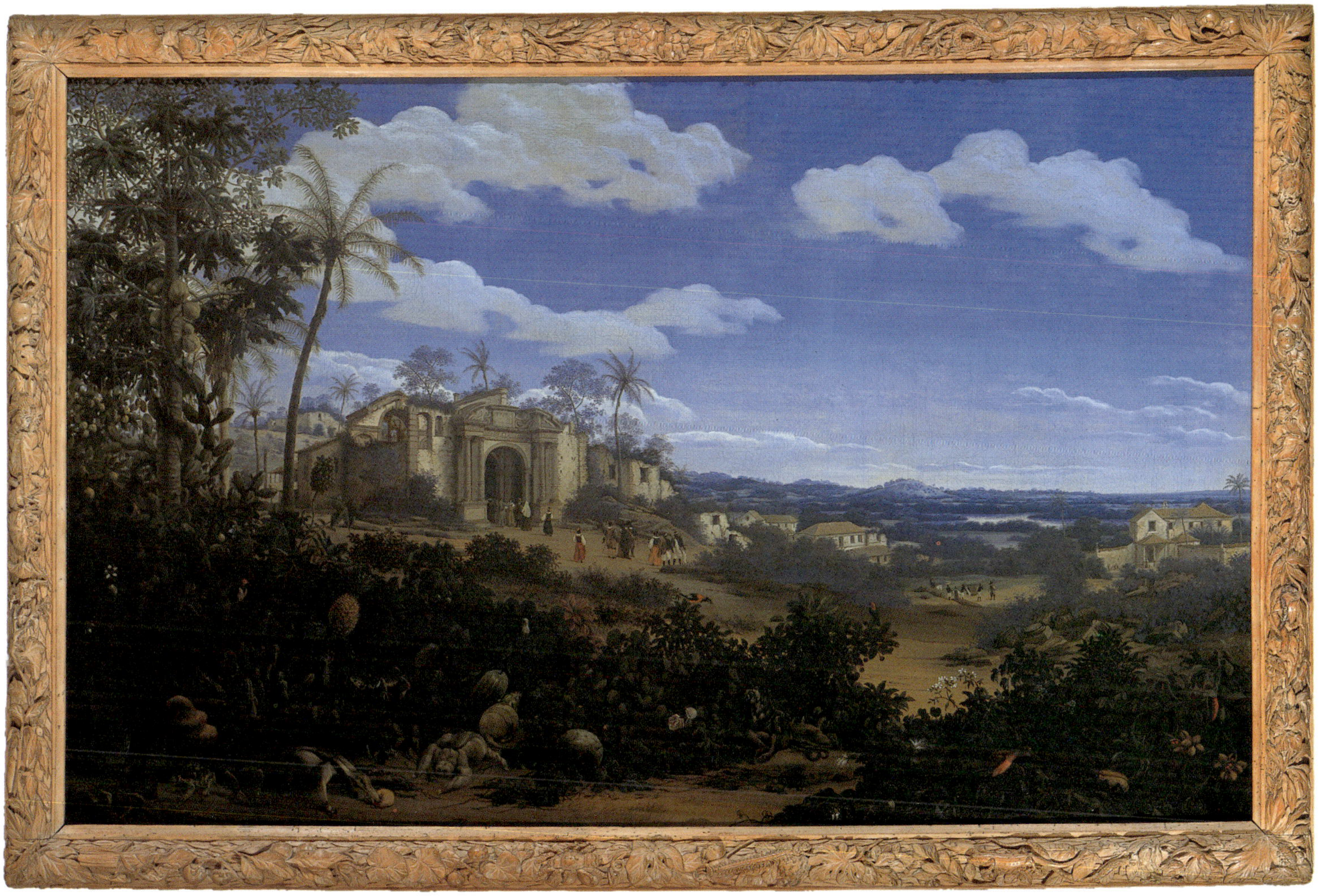

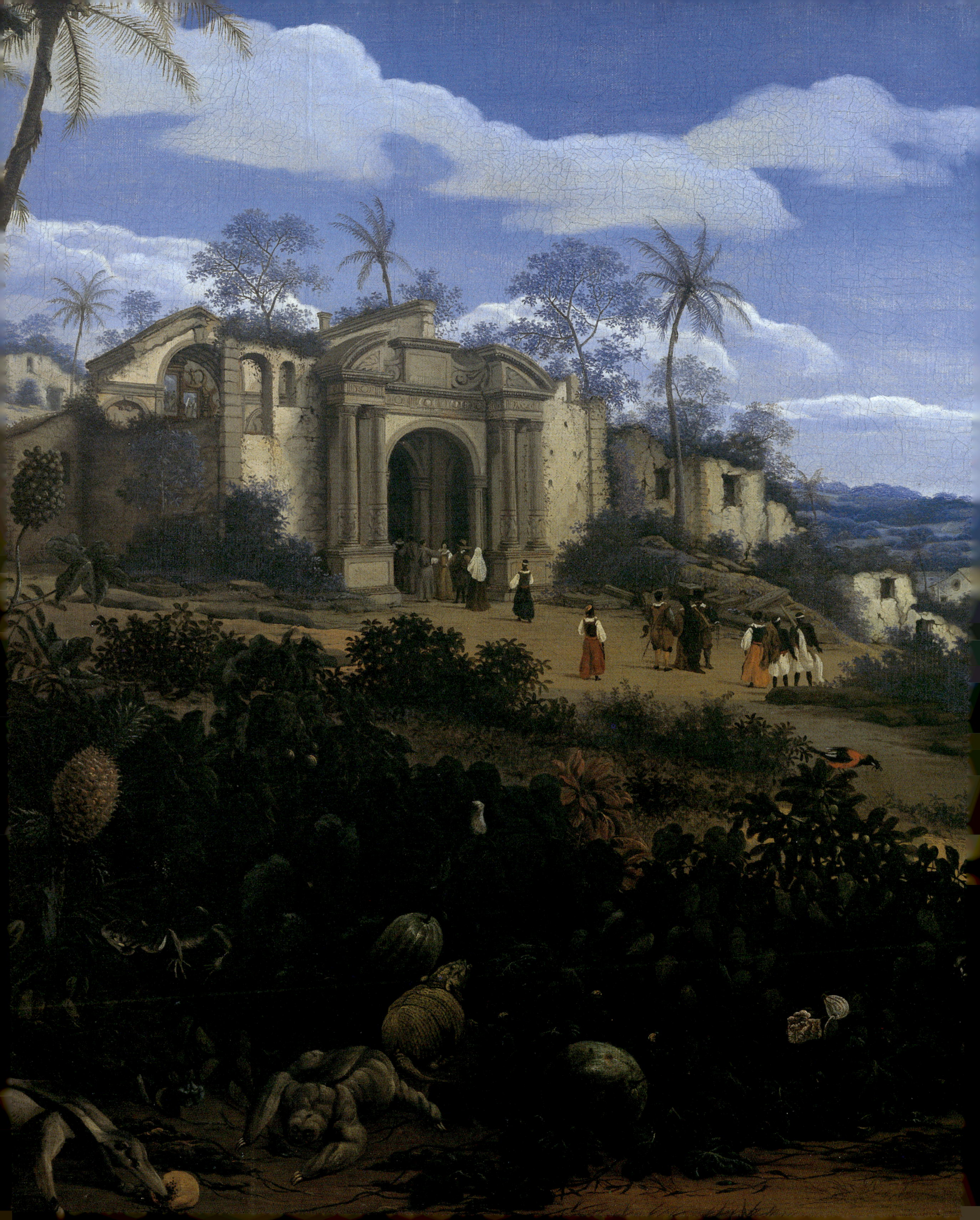

Philips Koninck (Amsterdam 1619-Amsterdam 1688)

61 *Panorama with farmhouses along a road, 1655*

Oil on canvas, 133 x 167.5 cm
On the wall of the cottage on the left: *P. Koninck 1655*
From the collection of the Earl of Derby, Knowsley Hall (since the late 18th century); purchased in 1967 with the aid of the Vereniging Rembrandt, the Prins Bernhard Fonds and the Commissie voor Fotoverkoop
Inv. no. SK-A-4133

If the term 'abstraction' could be applied to any 17th-century landscape paintings then it is to those by Philips Koninck. Basically, many of them consist of little more than two horizontal strips, the lower one containing a panoramic view of a flat stretch of countryside, the one at the top a cloud-filled sky majestically spanning the earth as far as the horizon. That is the case with this *Panorama with farmhouses along a road*, which is one of the artist's most beautiful works.

Viewed close up, the landscape is composed of a seemingly infinite number of dabs of paint which were applied to the canvas with a rather coarse brush in an apparently arbitrary way. Only when one steps back three or four metres does everything come into focus. Clumps of trees emerge, streaks of light and dark brown paint placed at right angles to each other turn out to be buildings or even complete towns. The light and dark passages in the countryside indicate the areas bathed in sunshine or overcast, while even lighter passages prove to be bodies of water. Only

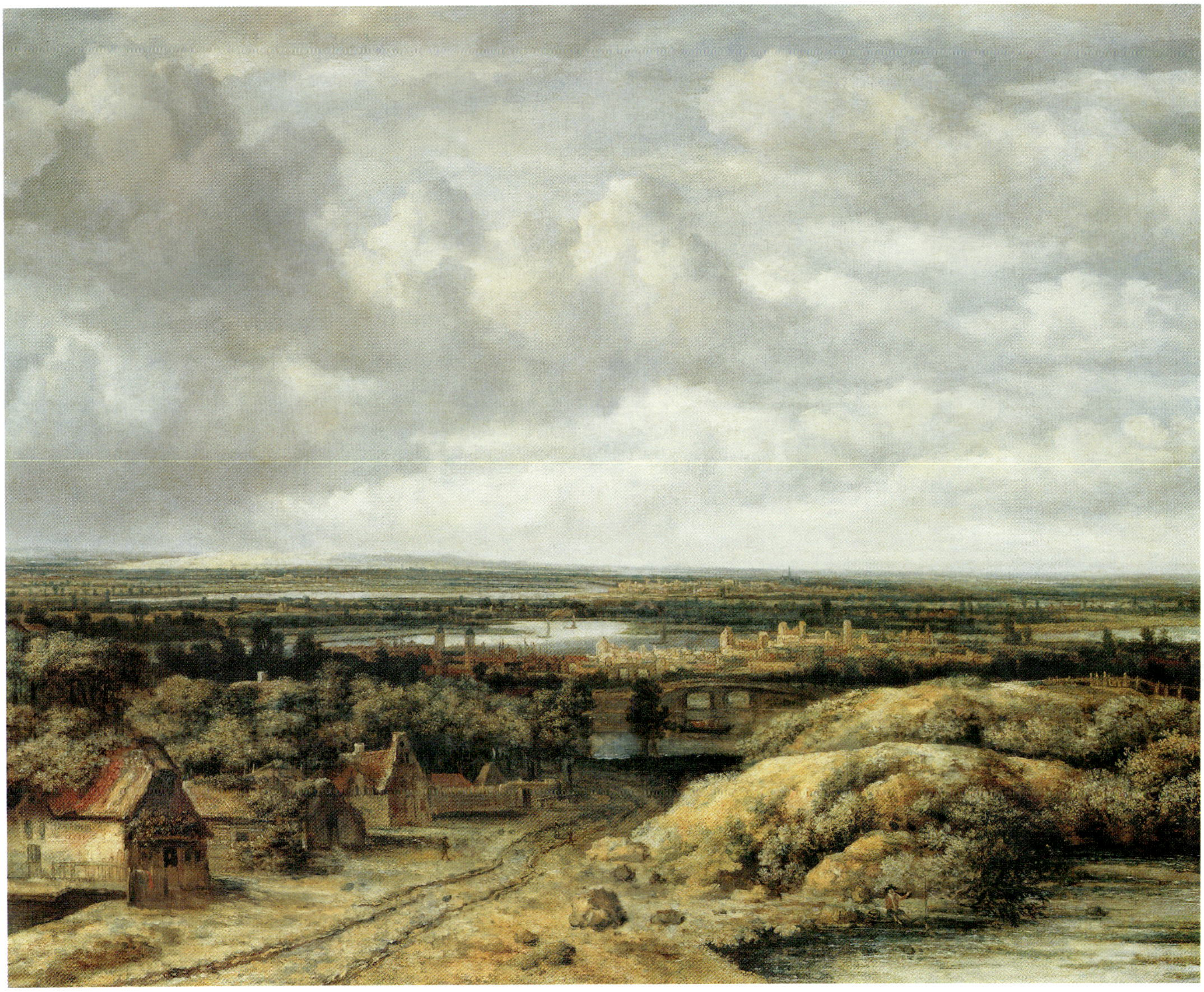

◂ Detail of [60]

the details in the immediate foreground, such as the cottages and the handful of figures, remain identifiable when seen from close to, but that does not apply to the different kinds of vegetation, which again have to be viewed from a distance to make any sense.

So some credence can be attached to Houbraken's statement in his *Groote schouburgh der Nederlantsche konstschilders* (1718-1721) that Koninck was a pupil of Rembrandt's—an assertion as yet unsupported by any hard evidence. If true, he probably studied with the great master after 1641, when he returned to Amsterdam after a period in Rotterdam. He also looked to the example of Hercules Segers, who likewise emphasised the vastness of the countryside in his paintings and prints [*see 10*]. Koninck found his own style in the 1650s, and began painting his distinctive panoramic views with meandering rivers. The technique is reminiscent of Rembrandt, but the structure of the composition, however indebted to Segers, is immediately recognisable as Koninck's own work, chiefly because of the seemingly simple device of dividing the canvas rigidly into two more or less equal horizontal bands.

There are similar panoramas in the drawn oeuvre of Koninck, some of recognisable locations, but that is not true of the paintings. The one in the Rijksmuseum may look a little like Koninck's drawings of the Gelderland countryside, but this particular view will not be found there. Koninck's painted landscapes simply do not exist, however lifelike they may appear.

LITERATURE

Gerson 1936, no. 26; Van Thiel 1967; exhib. cat. Amsterdam/Boston/Philadelphia 1987-88, no. 53

Jacob van Ruisdael (Haarlem 1628/29-Amsterdam 1682)

62 *The windmill at Wijk bij Duurstede, c. 1670*

Oil on canvas, 83 x 101 cm
At lower right: *Ruisdael*
Bought by Adriaan van der Hoop from John Smith in 1833; bequeathed by Van der Hoop to the City of Amsterdam, 1854; on loan to the Rijksmuseum since 1885
Inv. no. SK-C-211

The windmill at Wijk bij Duurstede is one of Jacob van Ruisdael's most famous and best-loved paintings—it is one of the best-loved works in the whole of the Rijksmuseum, come to that, although it is not entirely clear why. It undoubtedly has something to do with the need to have an acknowledged masterpiece by a celebrated painter in a national museum. On top of that, it combines several typically Dutch motifs in a monumental way: water, towering skies and a windmill spotlit by the sun.

The mill that stands out so magnificently against the lowering clouds is a powerful symbol of man's struggle against the elements. Mankind itself is also present in the shape of numerous small figures, but even the most prominent of them, the three women on the right, look puny beside the majestic mill, the river flowing past the bank reinforced with revetments, and the mighty heavens. The precise location is the confluence of the rivers Rhine and Lek. The sluicegate on the right blocks off the entrance to the Kromme Rijn, once the most important arm of the Rhine but by Ruisdael's day no more than a watercourse draining excess rainwater from the land between Wijk and Utrecht, which was closed off at high tide, as it is here. The ships on the water look vulnerable, their sails not yet filling with the wind which the menacing weather in the distance will surely bring.

Ruisdael was a master of the imaginary landscape, but this is a reasonably accurate picture of Wijk bij Duurstede, with the tower of the town church on the right, and further off, to the left of the mill, the castle that was the summer residence of the bishops of Utrecht until well into the 16th century. Standing on its walls were two corn-mills. This, the westerly one, was demolished in the 19th century. All that Ruisdael left out were the town walls and the Vrouwenpoort (Ladygate), which would have been roughly on the spot where the three women are standing. Those omissions accentuate the height of the mill.

It is far from certain that Ruisdael intended this to be anything more than an evocative and topographically recognisable landscape, although there are indications that some of the motifs could have had a more symbolic connotation for 17th-century viewers. In earlier paintings, a windmill often stood for the pointlessness of human endeavours, while castles might allude to Martin Luther's famous line: 'A safe stronghold our God is still', which is based on a passage in one of the psalms but recurs in several variants throughout the Bible. The two discarded millstones in the right foreground have been construed as Vanitas motifs, Ruisdael may have given them such prominence, moving them from their logical position at the foot of the mill, in order to remind the viewer that life is short.

LITERATURE

Exhib. cat. The Hague/Cambridge 1981-82, no. 39; exhib. cat. Amsterdam/Boston/Philadelphia 1987-88, no. 88; Walford 1991, pp. 150-151

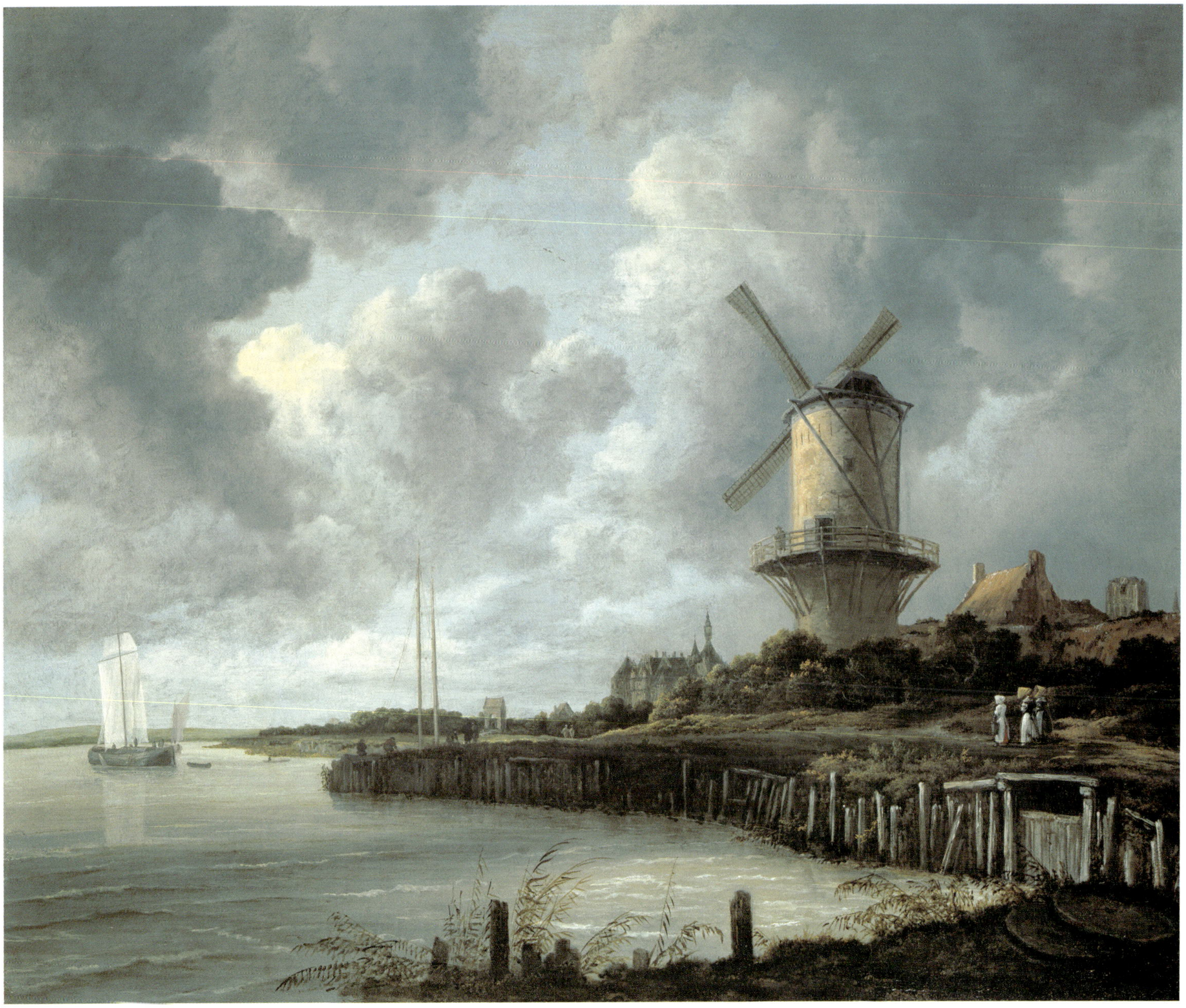

Jacob van Ruisdael (Haarlem 1628/29-Amsterdam 1682)

63 *Landscape with waterfall, c. 1670*

Oil on canvas, 142 x 195 cm
At lower right, on a rock: *JVRuisdael*
Bequeathed by Adriaan van der Hoop to the City of Amsterdam, 1854;
on loan to the Rijksmuseum since 1885
Inv. no. SK-C-210

The tone in Ruisdael's large *Landscape with waterfall* is set by just one small part of the painted surface. Our gaze is immediately drawn to the serene landscape with the small church in the distance, we should beware against giving it all our attention, for the waterfall in the foreground extends across the full width of the picture, and the painter gives us no guarantee at all that we are standing safe and sound on dry land.

There are various contrasts like that between the peaceful vista and the roiling waterfall, one being the placid lake held back by the rocky barrier of the falls. Ruisdael cleverly gave it a great sense of recession into depth by showing a shepherd with his flock crossing a ford in the distance. Another device that enhances the sense of spaciousness is found in the trees in the right middleground. At first sight they appear to form a wood, but it is one in which the background light penetrates between the tree-trunks. It cannot be very deep, in other words, and it seems that there are several paths leading to a broad expanse of countryside beyond, some of which are being used by travellers. The small vista to the left of centre reveals not only the small church and two windmills but a rolling cultivated landscape with sheaves of corn. This gives a clue to the season: summer is coming to an end so this may be August, the harvest month. The contrast between the agricultural land and the rough terrain around the waterfall was undoubtedly of the artist's devising.

This is an imaginary landscape, composed in the studio with the aid of motifs studied in the east of the Netherlands and around Bentheim in Germany, an area which was a rich vein of inspiration for Ruisdael.

The broad view of this stretch of countryside is at the expense of the attention to detail which Ruisdael displayed in his early years. Then he would record the details of an elderberry bush or of a dead tree-trunk, but now he is more concerned with the wood as a whole and with the decorative placement of a tree-trunk that has fallen into the water. He had also lost the fascination with the rampant vegetation in a wood that is so characteristic of his etchings [63a]. In its place came an interest in contrasts and compositional arrangement.

The subtle structure of the picture is governed by the two views leading off into the distance. One runs across the rocks of the waterfall, through the half-toppled birch on the right to the path through the trees and ultimately to the distant but invisible background. Once out of the wood, the path must cross the watercourse that emerges from behind the trees and spills into the lake before tumbling over the waterfall. Ruisdael's masterly compositional touch is also evident in the interplay of forms between the trees and the clouds, which appear almost to comment on the foliage of the trees.

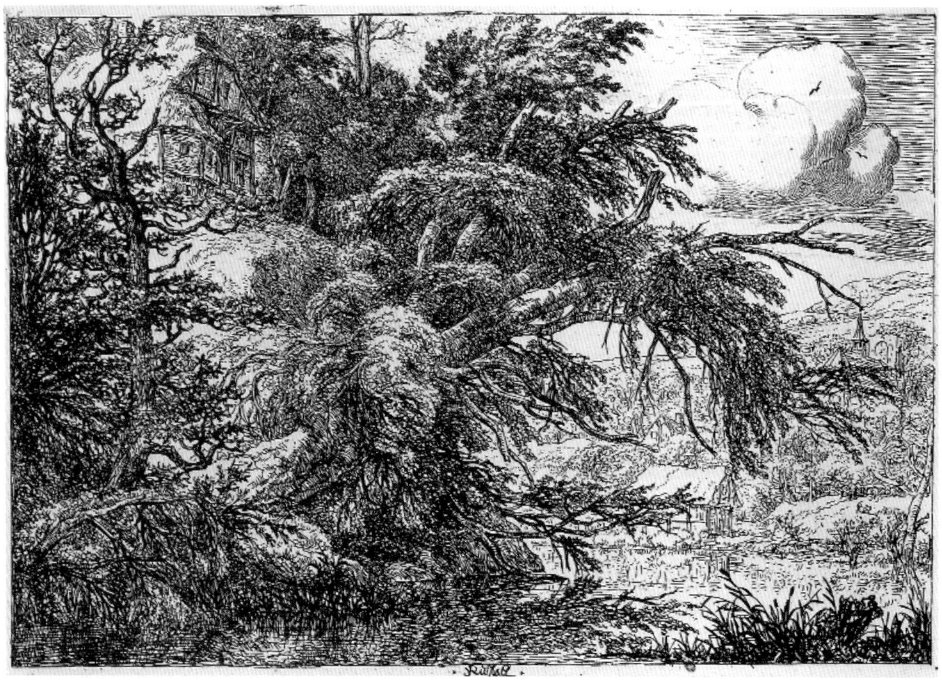

63a Jacob van Ruisdael, *Cottage on a hill*, etching, 19.4 x 27.9 cm. Amsterdam, Rijksmuseum, Rijksprentenkabinet

LITERATURE
Walford 1991, pp. 143-145

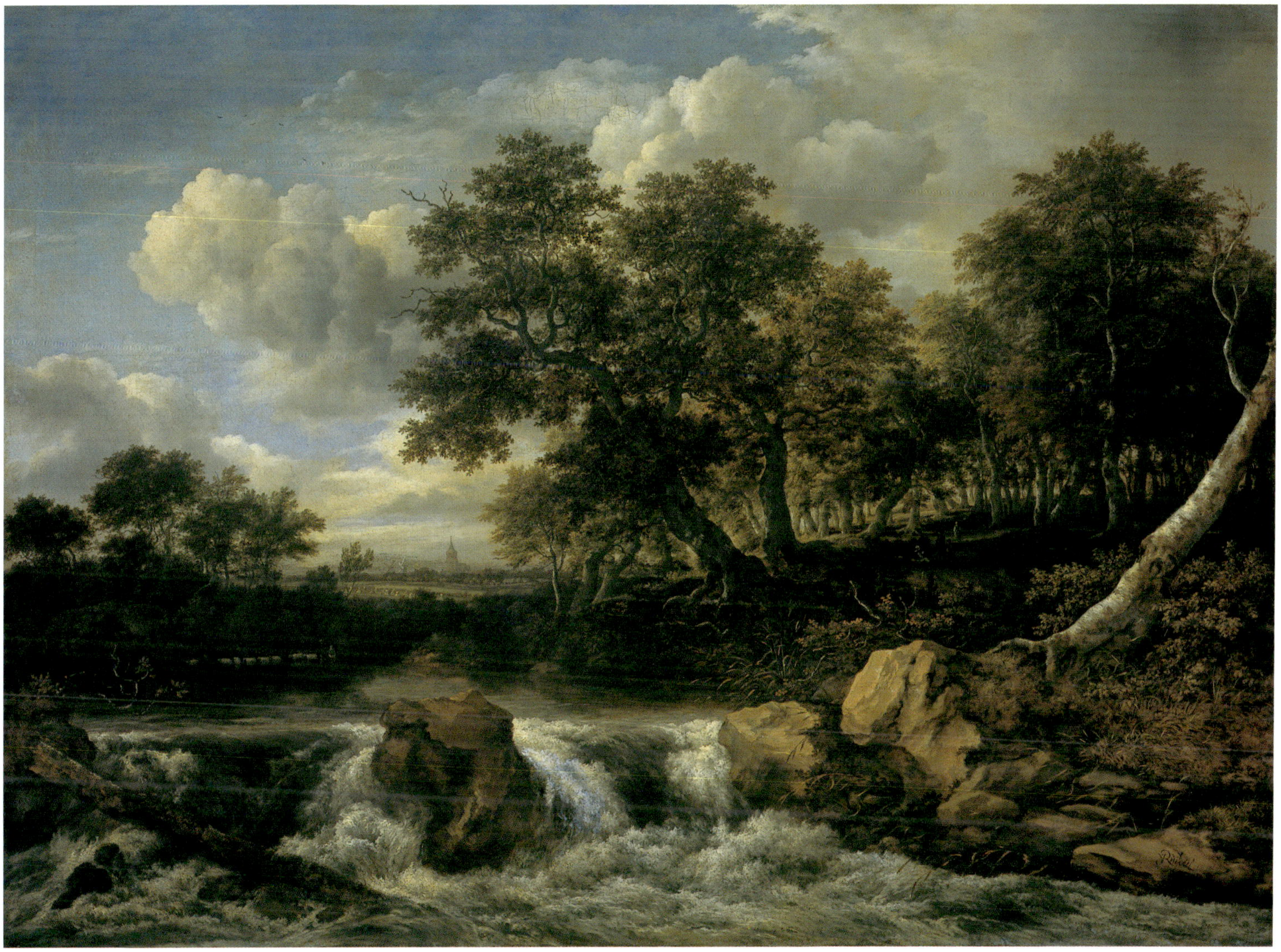

Meindert Hobbema (Amsterdam 1638-Amsterdam 1709)

64a *A watermill, c. 1664*

Oil on panel, 62 x 85.5 cm
At lower left: *m.hobbema*
Bequeathed by Adriaan van der Hoop to the City of Amsterdam, 1854; on loan to the Rijksmuseum since 1885
Inv. no. SK-C-144

64b *A watermill, c. 1666*

Oil on panel, 60.5 x 85 cm
At lower left: *m.hobbema*
Bequest of L. Dupper Wzn, 1870
Inv. no. SK-A-156

These are two views of one and the same watermill, as can be seen from the identical construction of the mill itself, the barn and the surrounding landscape, although there are a few minor differences. It appears to be an oil-mill, judging by the large barrels outside. Interestingly, the mill is shown from two different angles, the emphasis in the frontal view being on the falling water and the stream, while the other scene examines the timber chute and wheelwork. Hobbema based both paintings on one or more drawings which he clearly made on the spot. Other drawings from the same session were preliminary studies for several other paintings, one of them dated 1664.

Meindert Hobbema produced more than 30 paintings of watermills, more than

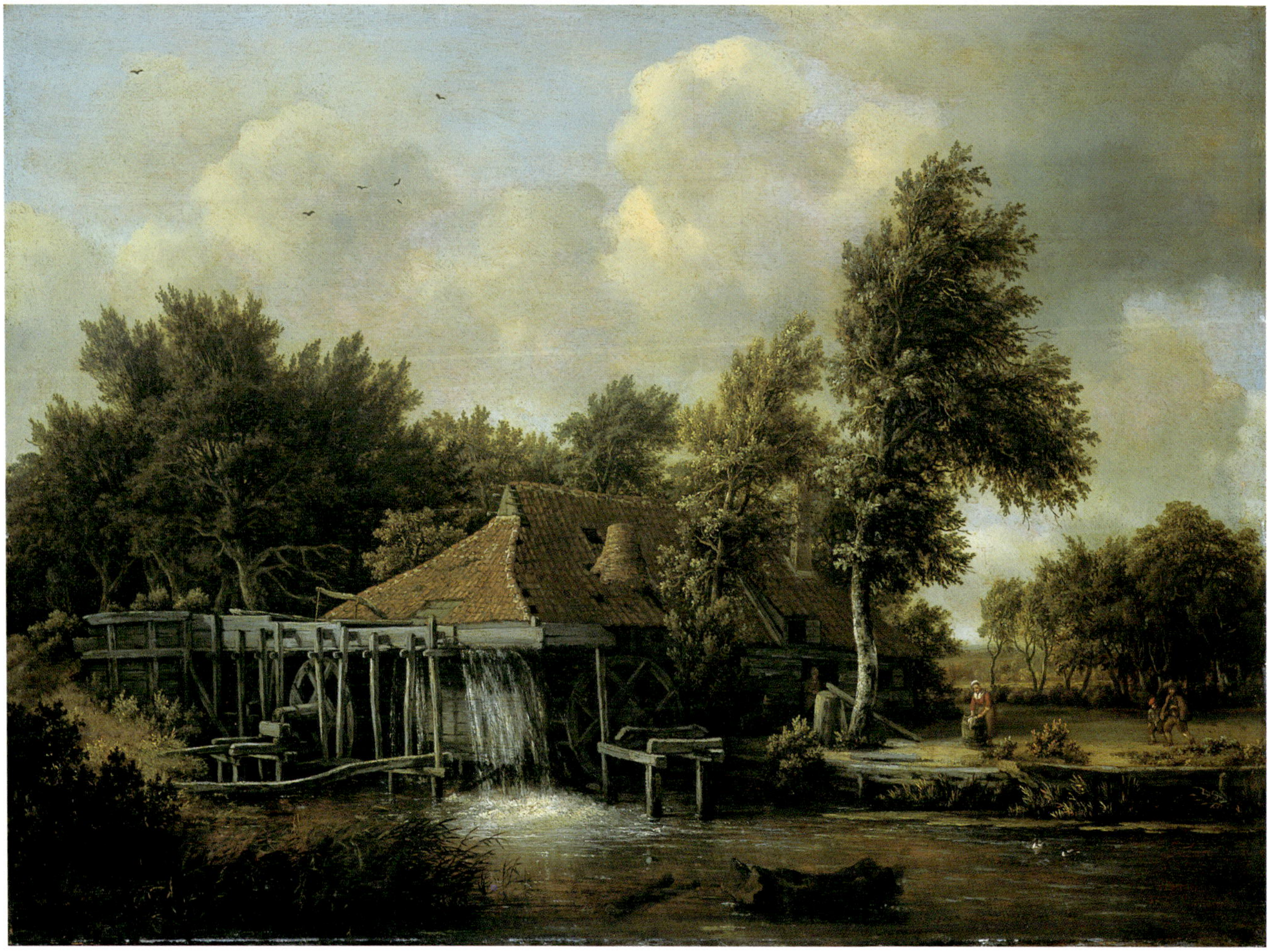

any other Dutch painter, so his name will probably be linked with the subject for all time. His interest in it was undoubtedly fired by his teacher Jacob van Ruisdael, who began painting watermills in 1653 after discovering their artistic potential during a study trip to Bentheim, just over the border in Germany. On a visit to the Singraven estate near Denekamp he must have become fascinated by the complex of watermills there, which he drew and reproduced in several of his paintings. Hobbema, too, depicted the mills near Singraven on more than one occasion.

At the beginning of the 1660s, Ruisdael and Hobbema went on a study trip together through the provinces of Gelderland and Twenthe, where there were many watermills. It was on that journey that they must have studied the unidentified one in the two Rijksmuseum pictures, for there are several drawings of it by both artists, which they used as the basis for paintings back in their Amsterdam studios.

The two in the Rijksmuseum are undated, but on the evidence of the annual growth rings in the oak panels they were most likely painted between 1662 and 1668, the one from the Van der Hoop Bequest probably predating the other by a year or two. Hobbema had been an established artist for some years by then, and was the height of his powers. In 1668 he was appointed a wine-gauger in Amsterdam, the official who checked the size of wine barrels for excise purposes—a post which he occupied until his death. One consequence of his appointment was a sharp drop in his artistic output after 1668, although he never abandoned the brush altogether nor did his powers decline, as shown by *The avenue at Middelharnis* (London, National Gallery), which is one of his most popular paintings.

LITERATURE

Broulhiet 1938, nos. 17, 20; Giltay 1980

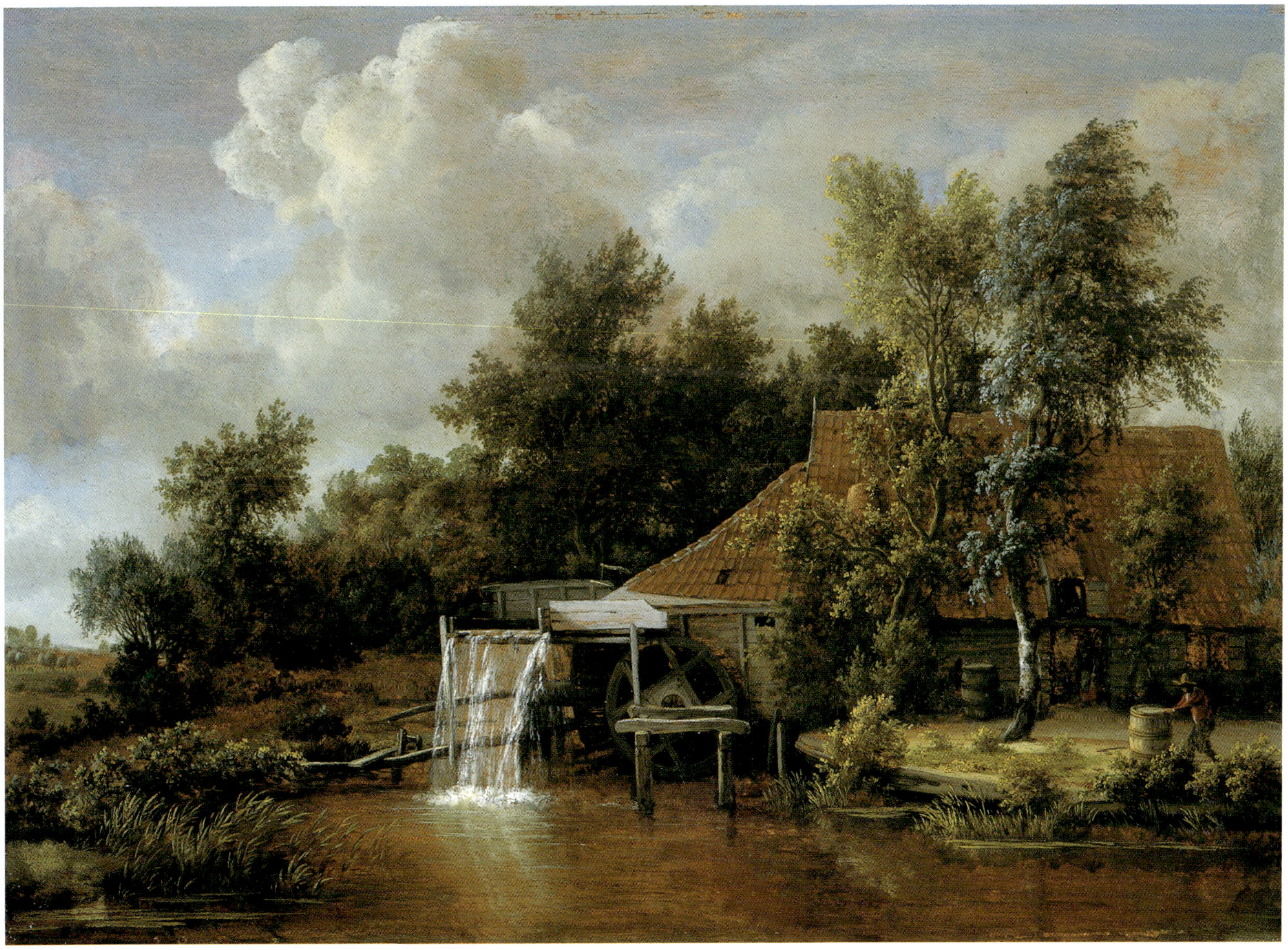

65 *Tablecloth with Flora in a cartouche, c. 1660-1680*

Tapestry, wool and silk, l. 194 cm, w. 275 cm
Donated by A.J. Enschedé to the Koninklijk Oudheidkundig Genootschap, 1859; on loan to the Rijksmuseum since 1885
Inv. no. BK-KOG-41

Floral tablecloths were a typically northern Netherlandish genre in tapestry-making, and generally date from the second and third quarters of the 17th century, most of them being woven in Delft and Gouda. Smaller numbers were manufactured in other towns with tapestry workshops, such as Amsterdam and Schoonhoven. Like Turkish rugs, they were laid over heavy oak tables in Dutch households.

Most Dutch floral tapestries survive in the form of tablecloths, but they were also used as chimneypiece valances, blankets, as the upholstery for chairs and benches, and for loose cushions. The regents' room of the Deutz almshouse in Amsterdam has a floral tablecloth and two armchairs and eight chairs covered with a matching floral tapestry [*65a*]. Agneta Deutz (1633-1692), who was extremely wealthy, bequeathed the ensemble, which originally numbered 12 chairs and came from her house on Keizersgracht (No. 121) to the almshouse she founded, which was built in 1694/95.

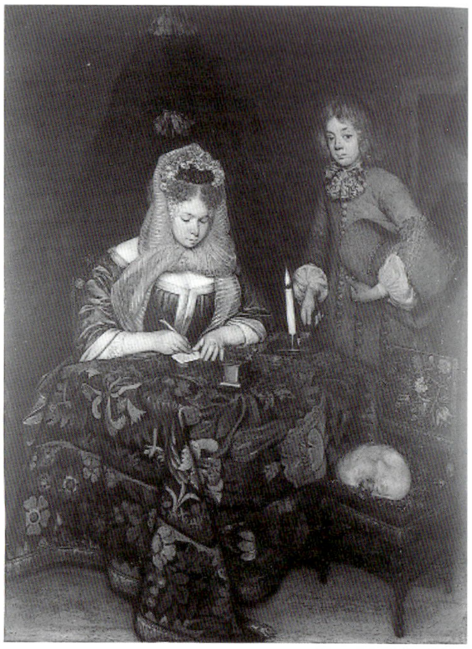

65b School of Gerard ter Borch, *Woman writing*, c. 1685; oil on canvas, 65 x 50 cm. USA, private collection

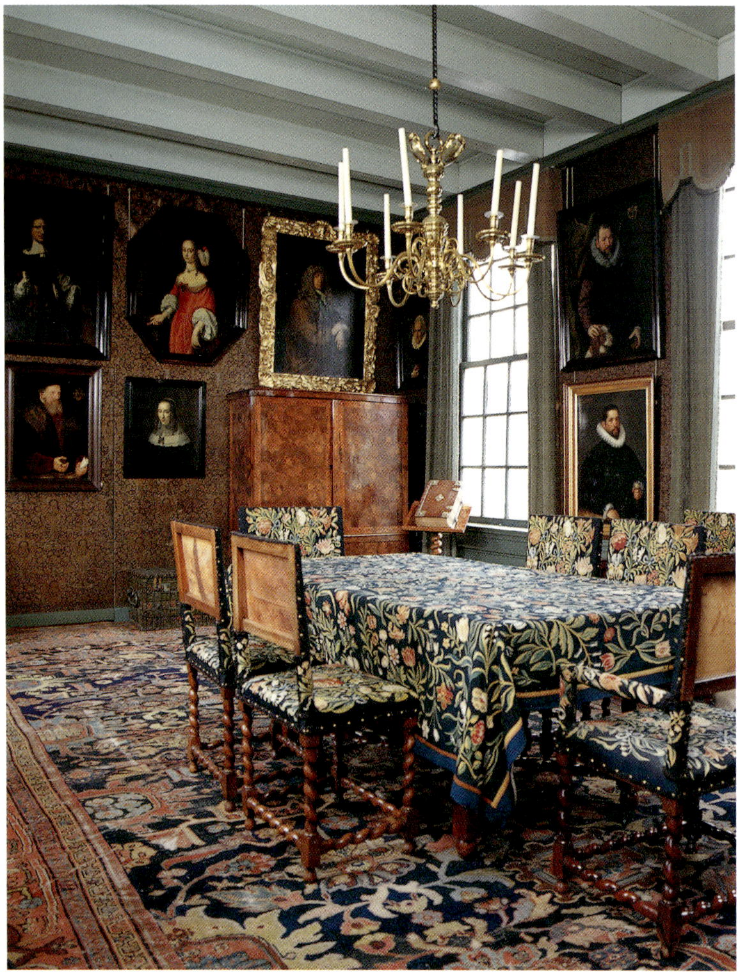

65a The regents' room of the Deutz almshouse in Amsterdam in its present state

Archival documents like estate inventories and commissions from weavers sometimes contain information about the use of floral tablecloths. It is known, for example, that the tapestry weaver Pieter van der Cracht, whose shop had branches in Schoonhoven and Amsterdam, supplied a number of tapestry blankets, a tapestry tablecloth and upholstery for chairs, all with a floral pattern, to the residents of a building in Rapenburg (No. 61) in Leiden. Similarly flowery furniture could be found in the assembly rooms of the civic authorities. In Delft in 1661 and 1662, for example, the burgomasters ordered a tablecloth and a large number of chairs upholstered with floral tapestries from the weavers Abraham Goosensz and Maximiliaan van der Gucht, who headed workshops in Gouda and Delft respectively.

In addition to documents, 17th-century genre paintings are an interesting source of information about how tapestries were

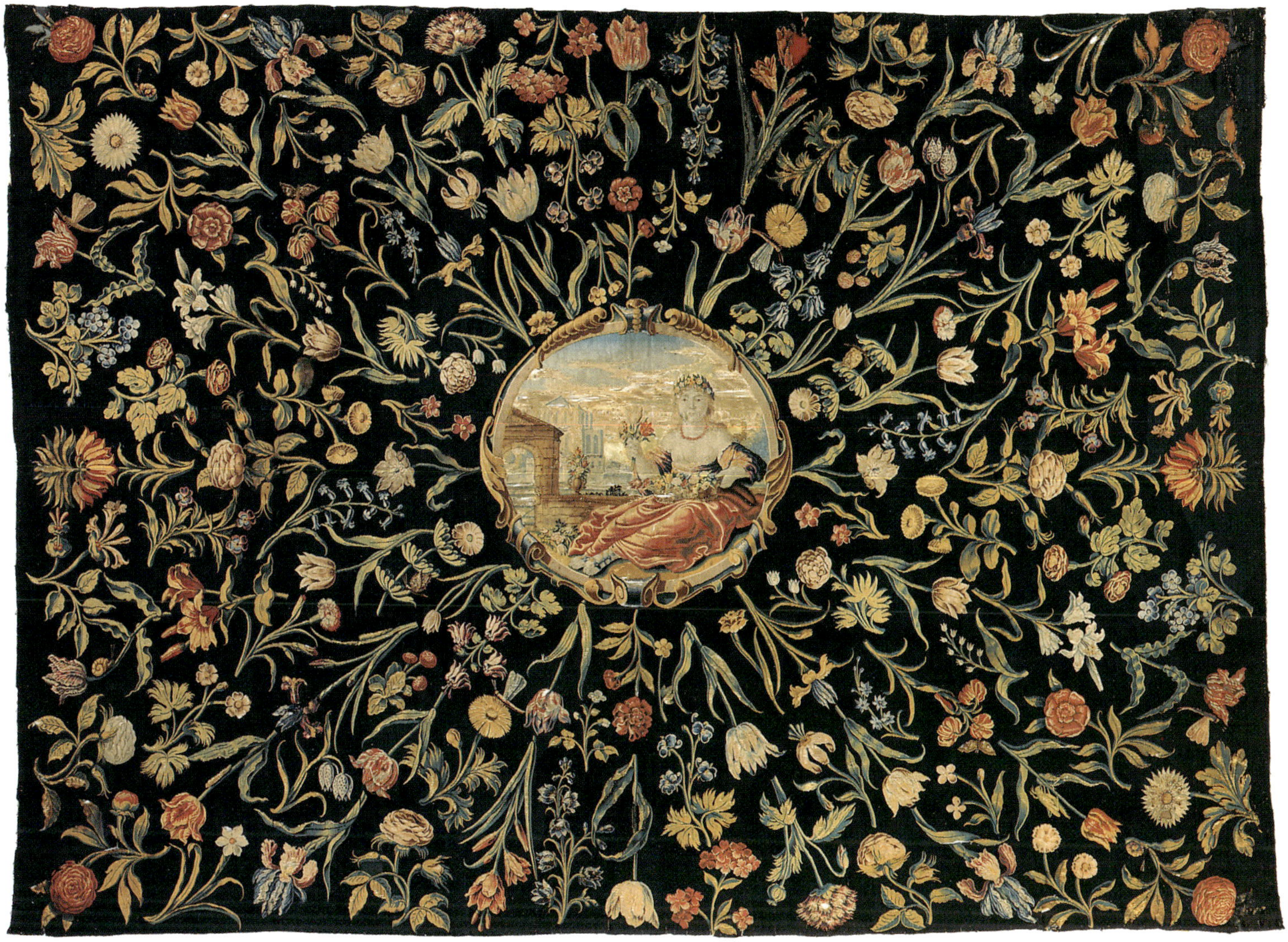

used. Some do feature floral specimens, but more often it is a Turkish or Persian rug. However, their presence in these paintings is not an indicator of their popularity in Dutch households, for painters liked depicting them in order to show off their virtuosity. What the paintings do tell us is which designs were in vogue. One of a woman writing by an artist from the school of Gerard ter Borch dating from around 1685 shows a rather outsized floral tablecloth with large flowers and a wide border. As in the Deutz almshouse, the chairs are covered with matching upholstery *[65b]*.

The tapestry in the Rijksmuseum is decorated not just with flowers. In the centre is an oval cartouche with auricular ornamentation around the personification of Flora. She is seated in a landscape with buildings in the background and has a basket of flowers on her lap. Dozens of flower and long stems fan out from this central scene to the edges of the tablecloth.

Floral tablecloths and chairs upholstered with the same material attest to the remarkable interest taken in botany in the northern Netherlands, which began in the early 17th century and led to the craze for collecting tulips in the 1630s. Flowers were found not just on tapestries but on silver, tin-glazed wall tiles, gilt leather, wood carving and painted interior decoration. The floral style lasted until the end of the century.

LITERATURE

Exhib. cat. Amsterdam 1971-72, no. 22; exhib. cat. Amsterdam 2000b, no. 134

Jan Davidsz de Heem (Utrecht 1606-Antwerp c. 1684)

66 *Festoon of fruits and flowers, c. 1660*

Oil on canvas, 74 x 60 cm
At lower centre: *J.D. de Heem P*
Purchased in 1809 with the Van Heteren Gevers Collection
Inv. no. SK-A-138

Jan Davidsz de Heem developed a type of still life around 1650 which is marked by a lavish display of highly colourful objects and an attention to even the minutest detail. Luxuriant paintings of this kind, which are usually referred to as sumptuous still lifes, were eagerly collected even in De Heem's own day, and went on to become extremely popular in the princely courts of Germany in the 18th century.

Sumptuous still lifes have never been a priority in acquisition policies in the Netherlands since 1885, when a serious start was made on purchases for the Rijksmuseum's collection. Their luxuriance and the artist's overweening display of his own abilities were considered un-Dutch. However, De Heem's works, while not fashionable, have never been cheap. Their fabulous technique and wealth of objects have always had their admirers.

Strictly speaking, the *Festoon with fruits and flowers* does not qualify as a sumptuous still life, lacking as it is in variety. It is really a limited subject which is sometimes found as just one element in a larger and more varied composition in De Heem's larger sumptuous pieces. This is demonstrated by a comparison with his lavish still life in Vienna, which is one of the finest works of its kind in his oeuvre [*66a*]. De Heem pulled out all the stops in that work, painting not only display tables but musical instruments, flowers, a parrot and a festoon of fruits as well. The latter is much more sketchily rendered than the one in the Rijksmuseum. The prime aim of the Vienna picture is to impress the viewer with the enormous variety of objects and materials, but the dominant feature of the Rijksmuseum canvas is the wealth of detail, which provides the almost endless delight of discovering a new and brilliant detail behind every piece of fruit and every flower.

De Heem did, though, introduce a certain amount of variation in the degree of detail. Some of the fruits are rendered extremely meticulously, but others are merely indicated with a few brushstrokes. This was a common device in the 17th century, and was later explained by Adrianus Wiltschut in his *Teyckenbouck* (Drawing book) of 1701. De Heem must have been one of the first painters to employ it successfully.

The *Festoon* has been in the museum's collection since the early 19th century, but until recently it was not known how it entered the museum. It turns out that it came from the art cabinet of A.L. van Heteren Gevers, the 137 paintings of which were purchased *en bloc* by King Louis Napoleon to enrich the national museum shortly before he was dethroned in 1810. In the course of time it acquired a superb 17th-century frame decorated with auricular ornamentation which probably came from one of a pair of portraits, the other frame being used for a flower piece by Abraham Mignon (1640-1679), which was only bequeathed to the museum in 1870. This turned two totally unrelated paintings into companion pieces which were hung as a harmonious decorative ensemble high above the cabinets in the museum's Department of Sculpture and Decorative Arts. This lofty position and a badly oxidised varnish made it impossible to appreciate De Heem's virtuoso display of verisimilitude. It was only when the painting was cleaned in 1992 that it was discovered to be in excellent condition, with the result that the Rijksmuseum gained a superb De Heem it barely knew it had.

LITERATURE
Exhib. cat. Utrecht/Braunschweig 1991, no. 24; exhib. cat. Amsterdam 1999, no. 6

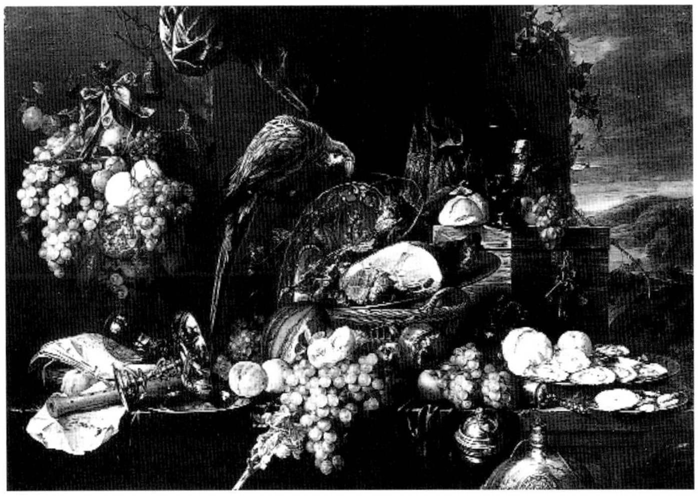

66a Jan Davidsz de Heem, *Sumptuous still life with a parrot*, c. 1655; oil on canvas, 116 x 169 cm. Vienna, Akademie der bildenden Künste

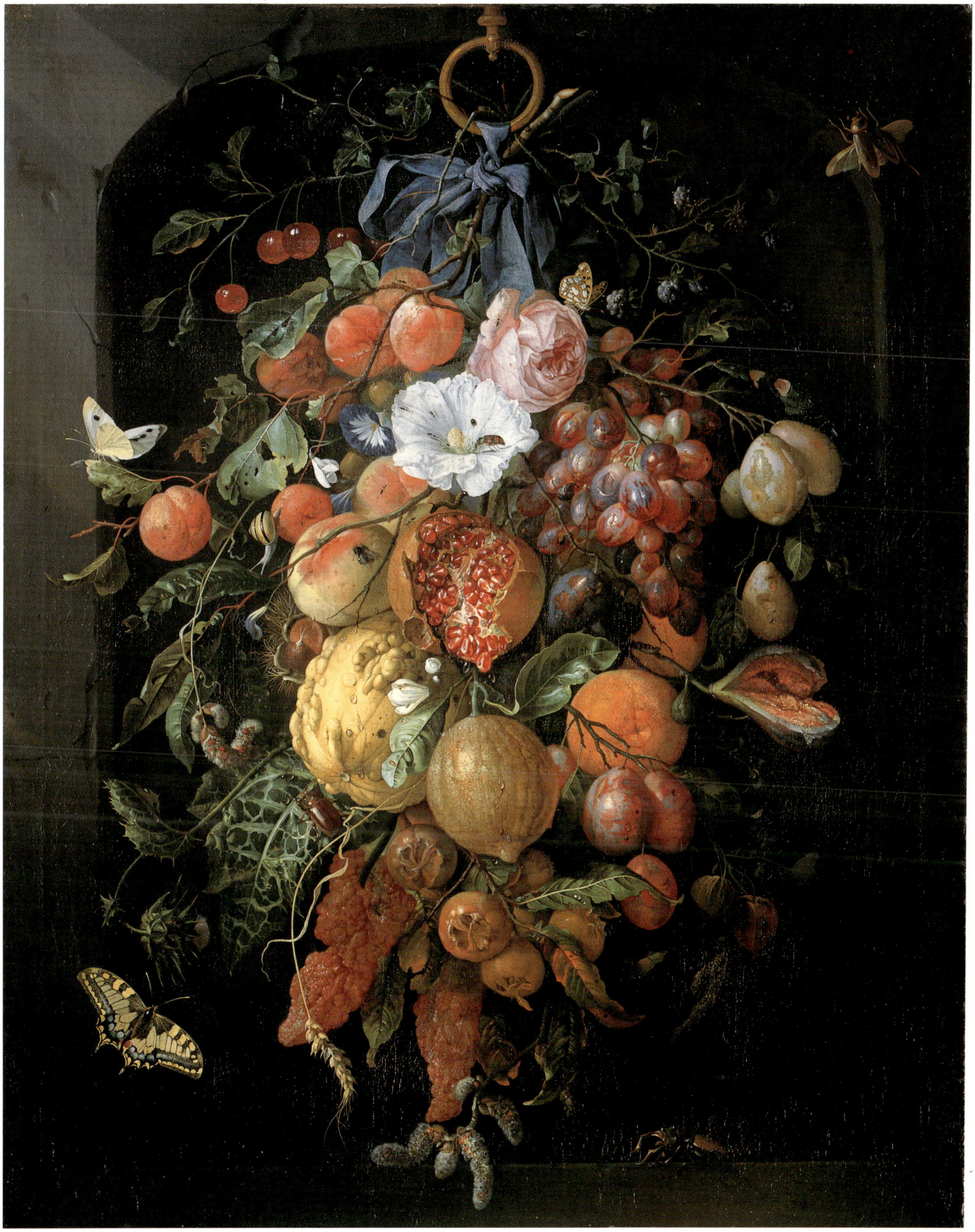

Willem Kalf (Rotterdam 1619-Amsterdam 1693)

67 *Still life with silver jug, c. 1665*

Oil on canvas, 73.8 × 65.2 cm
Purchased in 1821
Inv. no. SK-A-199

Willem Kalf arranged some costly objects and pieces of fruit as shapes that loom up out of the dark background of this still life. Although precious, the objects have to some extent been reduced to the status of props in the game the artist plays with light and reflections. Only part of the inside of the large Wan Li bowl of blue and white Chinese porcelain is visible, and almost nothing of the outside, which is in shadow. Lying on the table in front of it to the right, like a curled-up caterpillar, is a small but very expensive watch with its cover open. It is impossible to read the time. The most eye-catching elements are the subtle decoration of the gold case and the purplish pink ribbon. A knife with an agate handle is partly concealed by the leaf of the orange. The clearest view is of the jug on the left, which is clearly the work of Christiaen van Vianen, one of a family of silversmiths who became famous for their virtuoso manner of embossing in the so-called auricular style [*see 1, 5*]. Auricular ornaments are composed of undulating organic forms resembling the folds of flesh around cartilage, as found in the ear. Kalf subordinated the jug with its sinuously embossed auricular ornaments to his own fascination with reflections, such as the yellow sheen of the lemon or, even more subtly, the mirroring of the blue of the porcelain bowl in the silver straps.

What is most striking, though, is the lack of definition in the object in the centre of painting. It is a green glass of the type known as a *roemer* in a silver-gilt glass-holder designed by the Amsterdam silversmith Johannes Lutma. The glass was held by clamps, which here take the form of lion's heads. The sphere from which the clamps rise is supported by a putto who wittily turns his back on the old man on the auricular jug. The forms of the glass-holder are largely a matter of conjecture, but the task is simplified somewhat by the symmetry of the *roemer*, which was quite a common kind of glass in the 17th century. It is possible to build up a consistent and full picture of the glass-holder from other paintings and from comparable work by Lutma, but that was not what Kalf was after. Above all he wanted to render the subtle play of reflected light with gradations between green, brown and yellow for glass, gold and white wine. It is worth noting that the glass in this magnificent drinking ensemble allows the light coming from the left to fall onto the background: a niche against which the table has been placed.

The appearance of the fruit (there are a few hazelnuts in addition to the citrus fruits) has been enlivened with delicate shades of colour ranging from yellow, white, to a hint of orange. The granular surface of the peeled lemon (Kalf deliberately avoided the classic spiral of peel dangling from the lemon which was so difficult to execute) contrasts with the white pith cut at angles and with the juiciness of the fruit's flesh. The cap placed crookedly on top is a brilliantly suggestive touch.

The most recent restoration of the painting, completed in 1999, revealed that Kalf had originally envisaged a roomier composition, placing the silver jug much further to the left and facing the other way. He then changed his mind and went to the other extreme of this compact arrangement with the valuable objects all jostling for attention.

LITERATURE

Cat. Amsterdam 1999, p. 31; exhib. cat. Amsterdam 1999, no. 10; exhib. cat. Madrid 1999, p. 31; exhib. cat. Amsterdam/Cleveland 1999-2000, no. 49

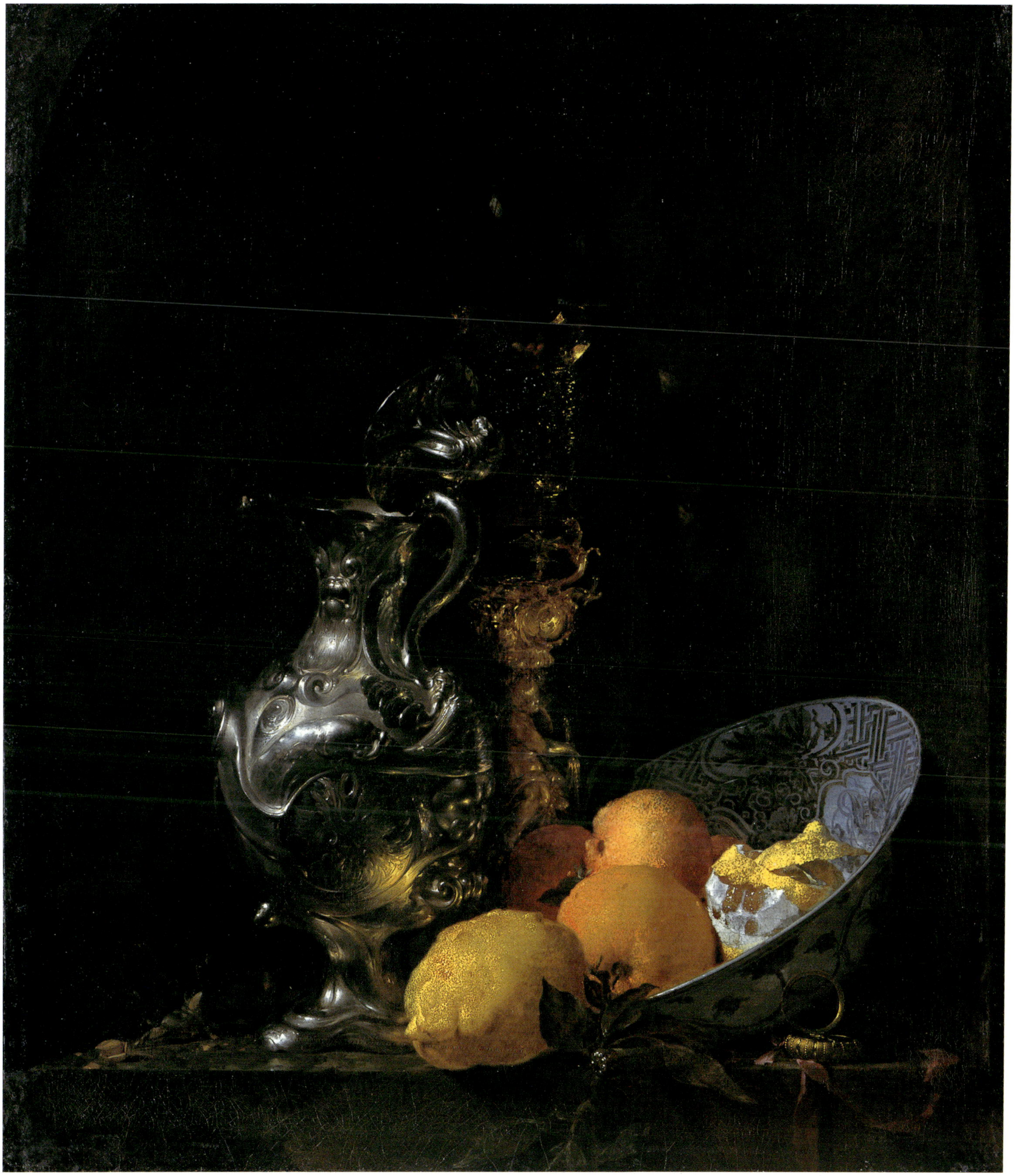

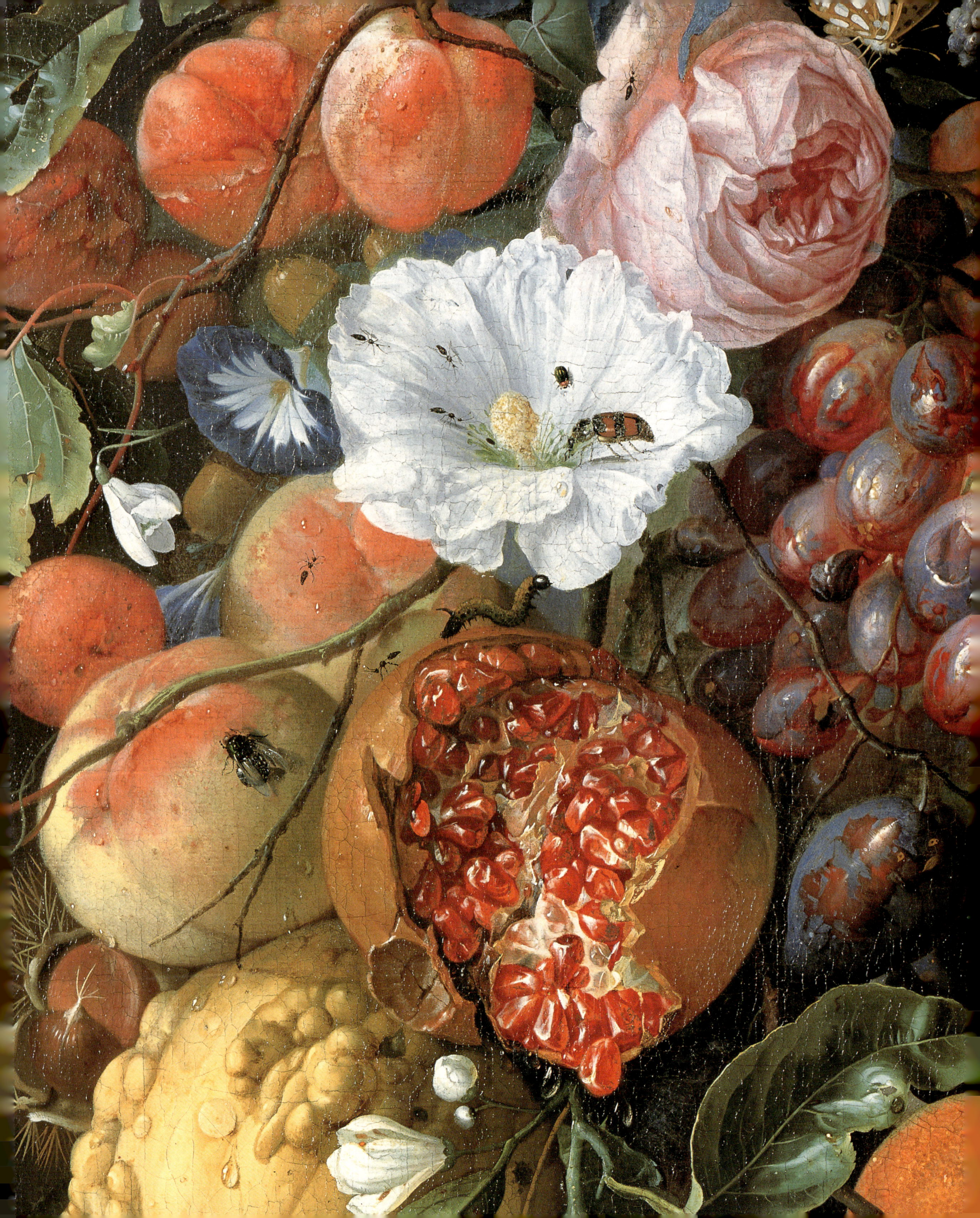

Gerloff Brouwer (Sneek c. 1627-Amsterdam 1676), attributed to

68 *Bowl, 1661*

Silver, h. 7.1 cm, ø 45 cm
Marked on the underside with the Amsterdam assay office mark, the year letter I (1661) and the maker's mark GB in an oval (attributed to Gerloff Brouwer)
From the collection of W.J.R. Dreesmann; purchased in 1960
Inv. no. BK-1960-18

This is a fine example of the luxuriant floral style that was so widespread in the Dutch decorative arts in the third quarter of the 17th century. This form of decoration, derived directly from nature, first emerged in the Netherlands around 1610 in tapestry-weave tablecloths, and as the century progressed it evolved into an almost national style in many branches of the applied arts.

There are eight reserves on the broad rim of the bowl. Reading clockwise from lower centre, the first contains a putto holding a stem with three tulips, the second a sunflower, irises, a lady's-slipper orchid, a carnation and flags, the third a putto with different kinds of garden anemone, the fourth a hollyhock, the fifth a putto with carnations, the sixth a lily and an anemone, the seventh a putto with two trumpet daffodils and an *Incomparabilis* daffodil, and the eighth a stem with columbine and lilies. The depictions of the blooms are based on prints, as undoubtedly is the central scene of a man and a woman making a garland of flowers. The lobate surrounds of the reserves on the rim is a modest form of auricular ornamentation, which was completely superseded by ornate floral decoration later in the century.

The bowl was probably used to hold fruit. A lottery print published in 1688 on the occasion of a fire in Durgerdam near Amsterdam shows a bowl similar to this one with the compartments on the rim framed by this sort of decoration. That piece is described on the print as 'a silver fruit-bowl worth 105 guilders including cost of manufacture'. There are also a number of 17th-century paintings with bowls of this kind being used for fruit, as in an interior by Frans van Mieris of 1675 [68a].

The silversmith, Gerloff Brouwer, must have been a well-known master in his day, judging by a legal document drawn up by the Amsterdam notary Crosse in 1662. It states that the silversmiths' guild of Leiden had bought 'gold and silver work' in Brouwer's shop in Halsteeg, namely 'a black enamelled hoop-ring', 'a silver cap ring' and 'a silver pendant'. Following each item are the words 'van hemzelf' (by himself), meaning that they were all made by Brouwer. He obviously produced various kinds of objects in both gold and silver which he sold in his own shop, doubtless along with the work of others silversmiths. It is fair to assume that he had a workshop on the premises, so this silver fruit-bowl must also have been made and sold in Halsteeg.

LITERATURE
Cat. Amsterdam 1999, no. 24

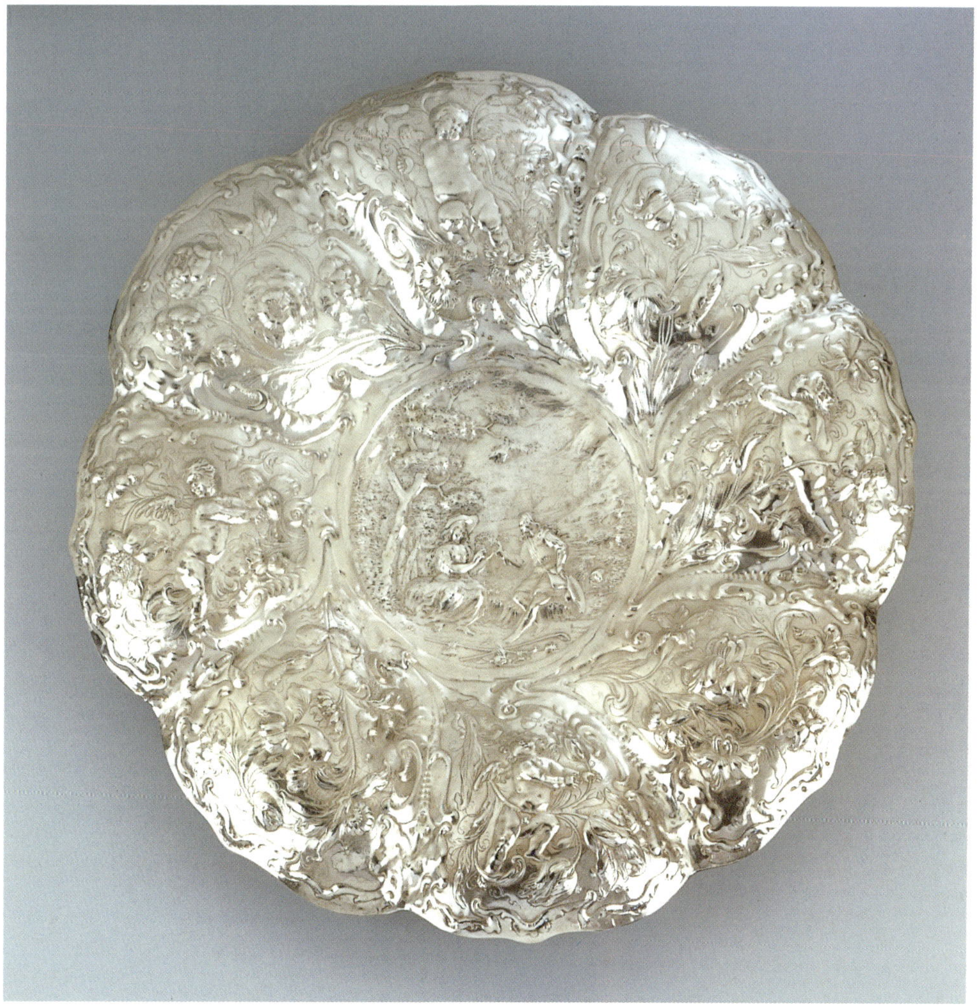

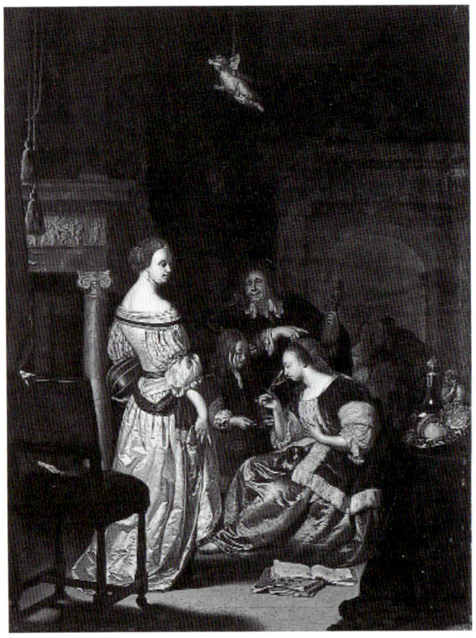

68a Frans van Mieris the Elder, *The family concert*, 1675; oil on panel, 52 x 40 cm. Florence, Galleria degli Uffizi

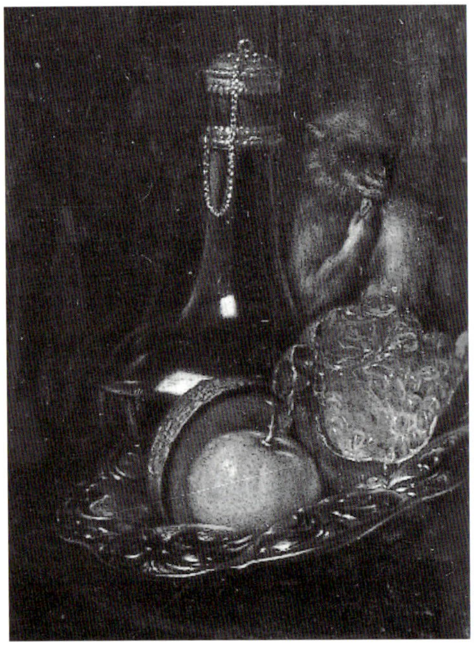

68b Detail of *68a*

Northern Netherlands

69a *Flute glass with the portrait of Prince Frederik Hendrik, c. 1650-1675*

Clear glass with diamond-point engraving, h. 36 cm
A.J. Enschede Bequest, 1896
Inv. no. NM-10754-52

69b *Dish for Joost van Heemskerk and Anna Conink, 1685*

Clear glass with diamond-point engraving by Willem Jacobsz van Heemskerk; ø 32.3 cm
From the Van Heemskerk family, Leiden; purchased by Stadholder Willem V in 1771 for the Koninklijk Kabinet van Zeldzaamheden, The Hague; in the Rijksmuseum since 1885 as part of the Nederlandsch Museum voor Geschiedenis en Kunst
Inv. no. NG-NM-764

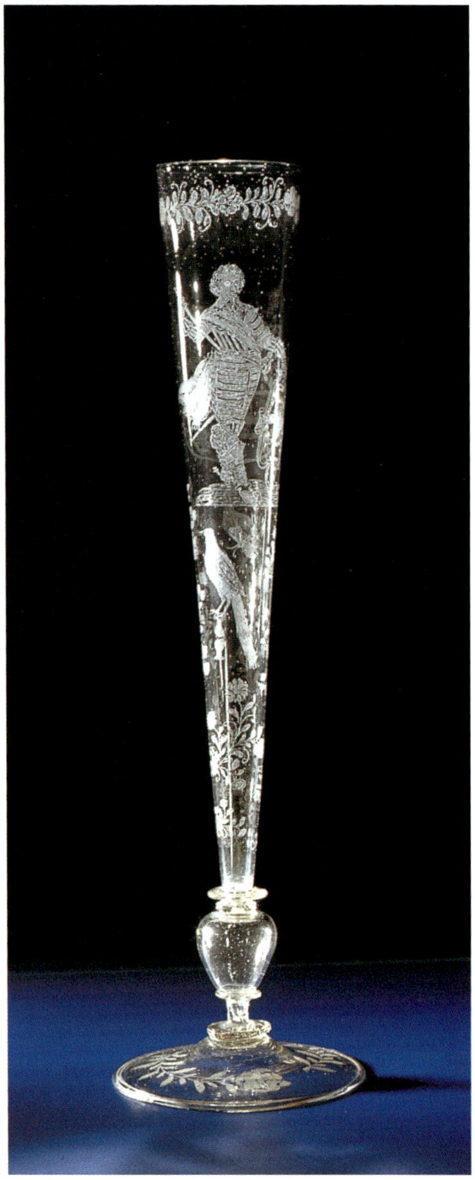

This is a good example of the type of flute glass blown *à la façon de Venise* which became fashionable in the Netherlands in the second half of the 17th century. Similar glasses were being made a century earlier in Venice, but were much smaller, around 25 centimetres in height, compared to more than 40 centimetres in the Republic. The Dutch type, which generally has a hollow, baluster stem, was produced in large numbers and features in many paintings.

Engraved on the bowl is a portrait of Prince Frederik Hendrik in full armour. He holds his commander's baton in his right hand, while his left rests on a shield blazoned with two hands clasped around seven arrows beneath a laurel wreath. Frederik Hendrik's personal coat of arms is engraved on the back of the glass. Below the portrait are two peacocks on pedestals amid a scattering of long-stemmed flowers. The rim is edged with a floral scroll.

The engraving is typical of later diamond-point work from the second half of the 17th century, with the lines no longer rigidly side by side but intersecting, creating a greater contrast between light and dark passages.

The anonymous engraver of this glass modelled his portrait on a print by Crispijn van de Queborn, which was used as the title page of Pieter Bor's *Oorspronck van s'Hertogenbosch* published in The Hague in 1630. It is interesting to see how the engraver radically simplified the print by omitting the background and various details. He also moved the laurel wreath, which two putti hold above Frederik Hendrik's head, to a rather illogical place on the shield.

The hands clasped around a sheaf of seven arrows below the wreath and with the word 'UNIO' symbolises the union of the Seven Provinces under the peaceable rule of Stadholder Frederik Hendrik.

The words engraved around the rim of this dish are 'Bestand'ge noit-besweken Trouw, Werkt lyvelijk- en ziel-behouw' (Faith, unwavering and steadfast, will make both soul and body last). In the centre is the monogram 'IVHAC' (Joost Van Heemskerk Anna Conink) beneath a crown in which the same letters are repeated. Below the monogram is the motto 'Iuste & Syncere' (Upright and sincere). On the back of the dish is the signature 'W.V.H. AEs 72 3/4 Ao1685' (Willem van Heemskerk at the age of 72 and three-quarters in the year 1685).

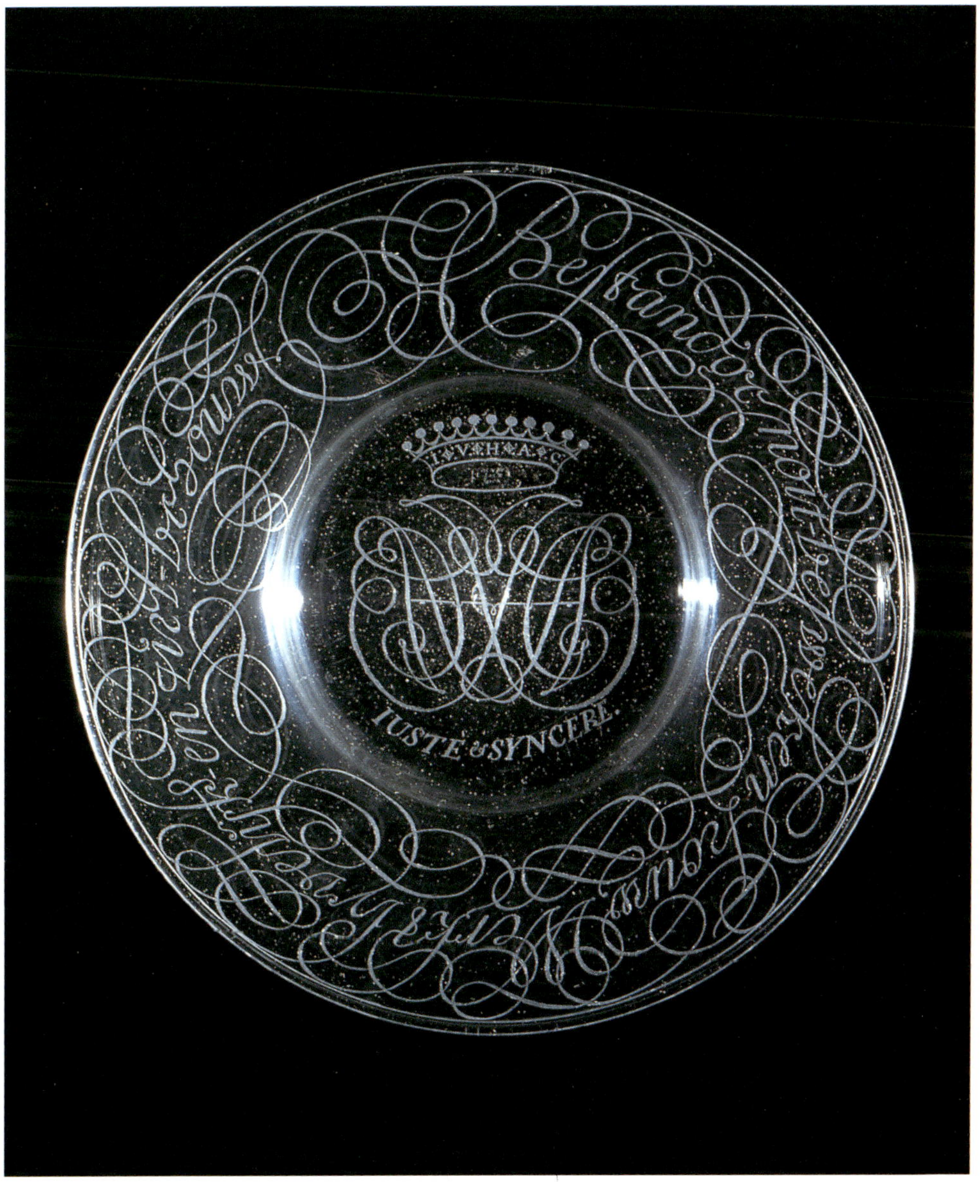

In the second half of the 17th century, Willem Jacobsz van Heemskerk (1613-1693) and other amateur glass engravers carried on the tradition of glass calligraphy introduced at the beginning of the century by Anna Roemers Visscher [*15b*] and Maria Tesselschade. Van Heemskerk, who was a cloth merchant by trade, may actually have been inspired by Maria Roemers to take up this form of calligraphy.

He engraved this dish to celebrate his son Joost's marriage to Anna Coninck in 1685. It remained in his possession until his death in 1693, and it and many other glass objects he had engraved passed by descent to his grandson Leonardus van Heemskerk, whose collection was auctioned in Leiden in 1771. Some 30 pieces were bought for the stadholder, including this dish, which was lot no. 192. The glass owned by the stadholders formed the basis for the Rijksmuseum's glass collection, so now it has 30 pieces engraved by Van Heemskerk.

LITERATURE

Cat. Amsterdam 1993a, no. 42; cat. Amsterdam 1995b, nos. 20, 87

Amsterdam

70 *Pair of candlesticks, 1668*

Silver, both h. 28.4 cm, ø 19.7 cm
Both marked on the underside of the foot-rim with the Amsterdam assay office mark, the year letter F (1668) and an unknown maker's mark
Purchased in 1968
Inv. no. BK-1968-30

These are the only surviving examples of an unusual type of candlestick. A very similar one is depicted in two paintings by Gerard ter Borch from c. 1670 *[70a]* and 1672. With their abstract decoration of gadroons and diamond-heads they are in marked contrast to the candlesticks adorned with floral motifs which were so popular in the Republic at this time. It is only the decoration of the drip-pan, consisting of eight slightly concave sections, that resembles a stylised flower. The candlesticks are related, though, to another kind produced in this period, which had a smooth concave foot and a composite rod stem. Examples of that type are depicted in an anonymous print

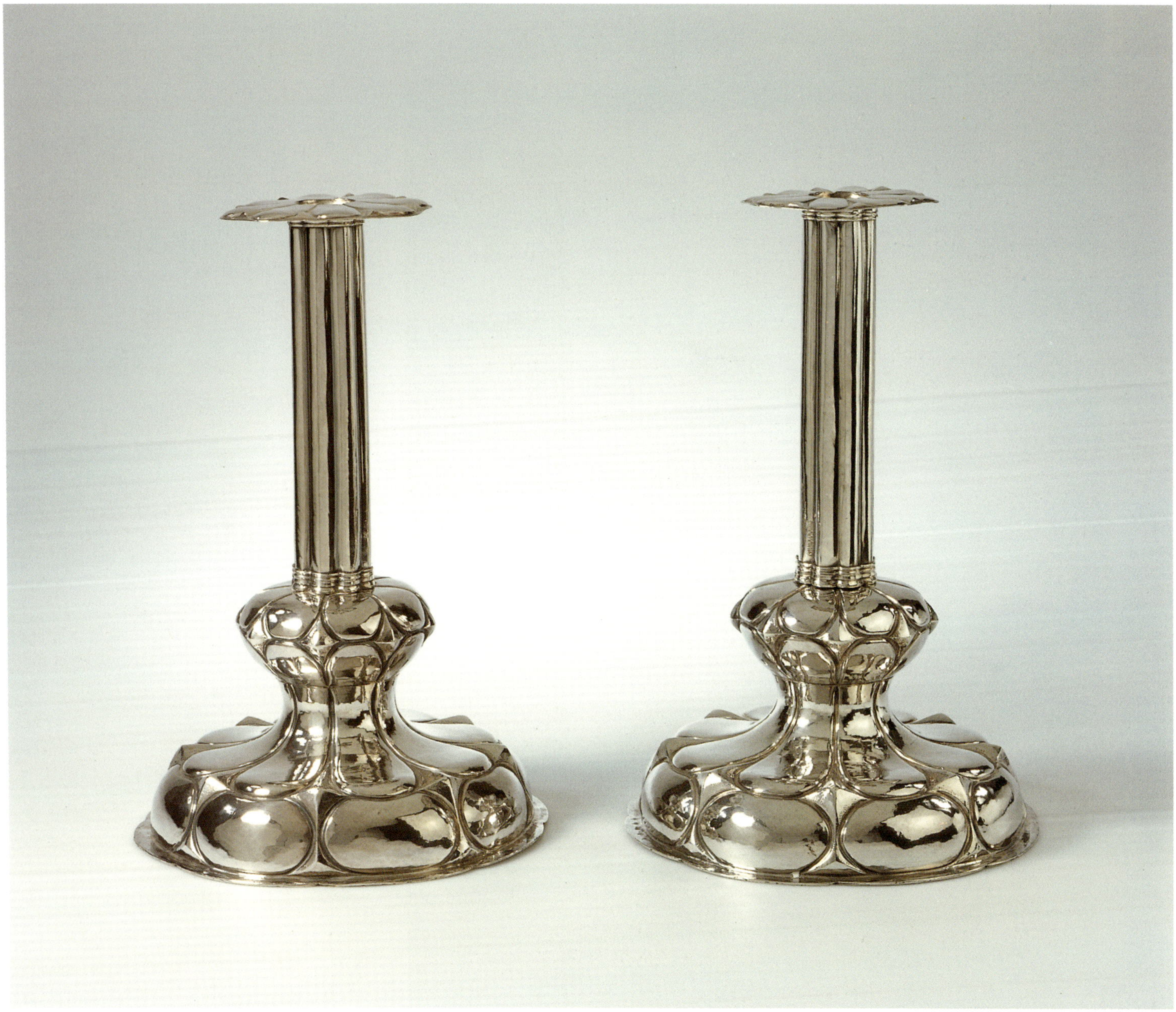

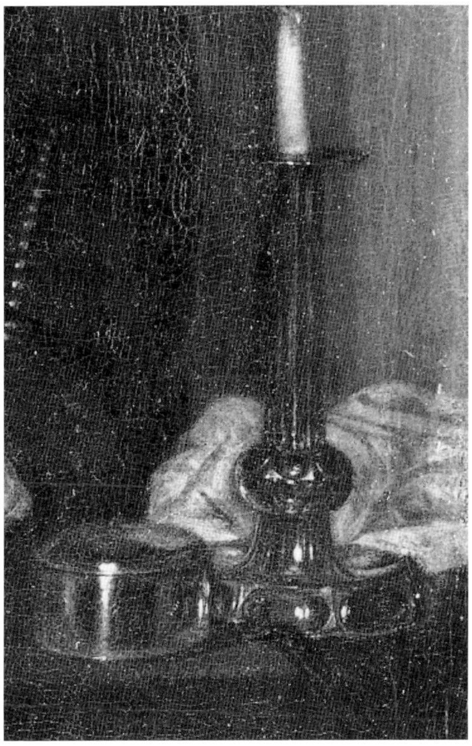

70a Gerard ter Borch, *Young woman and an officer making music* (detail), c. 1670; oil on canvas, 62 x 47.5 cm. Kassel, Gemäldegalerie Alte Meister

after Jan Luyken which was published to announce a lottery of silver objects in Durgerdam in 1689.

Although these candlesticks are the only ones of their kind, their robust, sober design gives them a distinctly Dutch look which is immediately recognisable. In the last quarter of the 17th century this indigenous form was to make way for the French court style, which set the fashion throughout Europe from then on [*see 108*].

LITERATURE
Exhib. cat. Amsterdam/Toledo/Boston 1979-80, no. 76; exhib. cat. Amsterdam 1984-85, no. 64; cat. Amsterdam 1999, no. 28

Adriaen van Ostade (Haarlem 1610-Haarlem 1685)

71 *The family, 1647*

Etching, first state of seven, 17.8 x 15.9 cm
At lower right: *Av Ostade 1647*
From the collection of Pieter Cornelis, Baron van Leyden; purchased by King Louis Napoleon in 1807 and transferred to the Rijksmuseum in 1816 after a period in the Koninklijke Bibliotheek in The Hague
Inv. no. RP-P-OB-12.742

Adriaen van Ostade left nothing to chance when he etched this scene on the plate. He carefully followed the preparatory drawing he had made, which is exactly the same size as the print [*71a*]. He reversed the design left for right, so that the impression taken from the plate would be in the same direction as the drawing. The surviving copperplate, although heavily reworked by later owners who saw money in running off yet

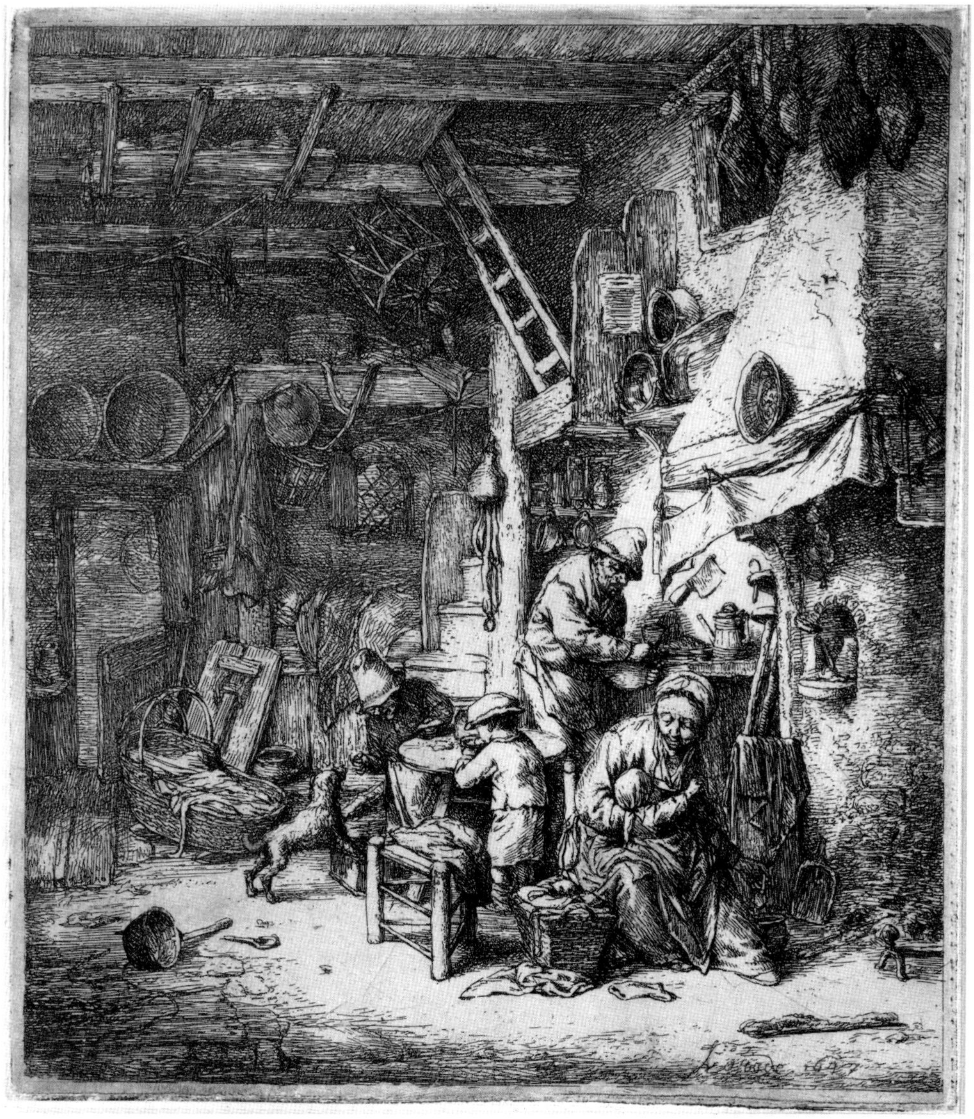

another stack of impressions, gives an idea of the care with which Van Ostade set about his task.

First he cautiously outlined the interior and the many details in the drawing with the pen before applying a wash with the brush to give a suggestion of space and to indicate the distribution of light and shade. He then took an etching needle and, referring constantly to the drawing, scratched shapes and shadowed passages in the etching ground with short strokes. In the process, dashes, dots and short lines became pots, baskets, a sieve, a cradle, a distaff, hams, a string of onions and all the other objects scattered around this room which was home to a simple village family consisting of five people and their dog.

In the 1640s, after a period in which both he and Adriaen Brouwer produced stingingly satirical tavern scenes of peasants carousing, smoking and going for each other's throats, Van Ostade started portraying the more domestic side of the life of peasants and other simple souls. Those scenes are less caricatural than his earlier work, but whether that makes them more sympathetic to the lot of countryfolk is open to question. The men and women chatting, men groping women's breasts, and drunkards are depicted in a more descriptive way, as if Van Ostade wanted to amuse the townee buyers of his paintings, coloured drawings and prints with rural comedies of manners featuring specific groups of the population.

A little later Van Ostade's depictions of peasant life became repetitive and dutiful. The etching of *The family* has an attractively picturesque look about it due to the care with which Van Ostade furnished the room. Other artists were inspired by this print until well into the 19th century, and it spawned many imitations.

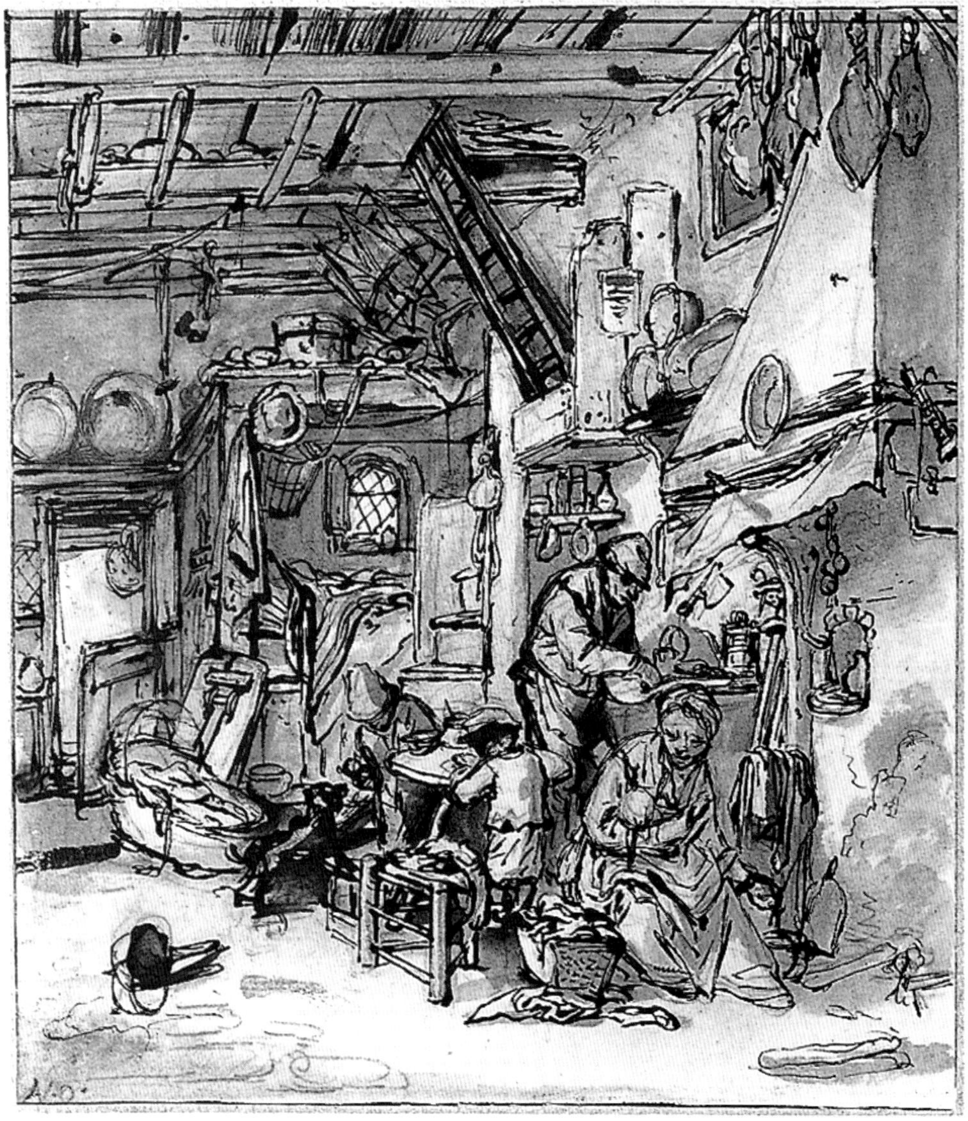

71a Adriaen van Ostade, *The family*; pen and brown ink, grey and brown wash, over a sketch in black chalk, 17.4 x 15.4 cm. New York, Pierpont Morgan Library

LITERATURE

Hollstein 46; exhib. cat. Boston/St. Louis 1980-81, no. 101; exhib. cat. Georgia 1994, nos. 111-112; exhib. cat. Amsterdam 2000c, no. 40

Detail of [72] ▸

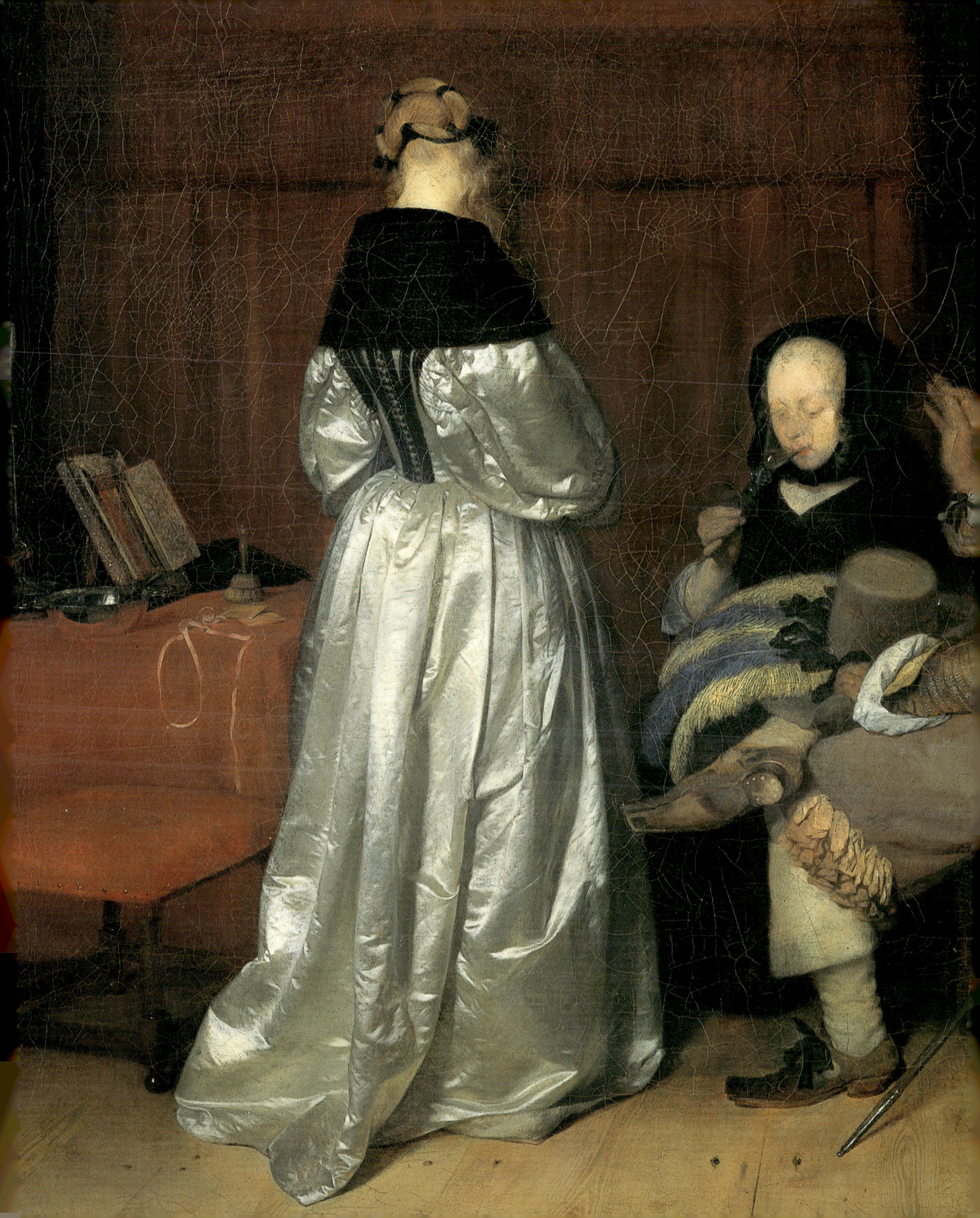

Gerard ter Borch (Zwolle 1617-Deventer 1681)

72 *Gallant conversation ('The paternal admonition'), c. 1654*

Oil on canvas, 71 x 73 cm
From the collection of Willem Lormier, The Hague (1763); acquired in 1809 with the art cabinet of Adriaan Leonard van Heteren Gevers
Inv. no. SK-A-404

At the point where many genre painters descend into unadorned anecdote, Ter Borch almost always displays his subtlety by choosing a moment that leaves us wondering about the nature of a scene. As a result, the strength of his genre works lies not just in their technical refinement but above all in their ambiguity. The state of mind of the protagonists is always well captured, yet, however contradictory it may sound, it is not easy to divine their intentions.

That is also true of this painting. A second version in the Gemäldegalerie in Berlin was copied in a print by the engraver Johann Georg Wille in 1765 under the title *Instruction paternelle* [72a]. The picture had a great reputation, and Goethe tells in his *Elective affinities* of a group of people who staged the scene as a *tableau vivant* based on Wille's print. The question is whether it is correct to give the painting the title proposed by the engraver, if only because the seated man is too young to be the father of the young lady with her back to the viewer. The word 'instruction', though, is not such a bad choice, for the young man's gesture does make it look as if he is giving an instruction or explaining something. It is not clear what it might be, or what the young woman's reaction is, thanks to the clever device of showing her from the back.

For a long time it was claimed that the man was holding a coin with which he was buying the girl's favours, making this a brothel scene. The trouble with this interpretation is that there is no coin to be seen (nor is there one in the Berlin version or Wille's engraving), and when the Amsterdam picture was last restored there was nothing to indicate that there ever had been one. All the same, there is a lot to be said for viewing this as an encounter in a brothel. The bed in the background and the table with a mirror at which the girl can do her toilet certainly give pause for thought. The seated soldier, too, looks more like a visitor than someone at home in the room. This would make the woman who seems to be staring a little sheepishly into her glass the procuress. Her gaze is another element that can be interpreted in several different ways. The title *The paternal admonition* (a stricter variant of Wille's), which had evidently become the customary one in the 18th century, made Goethe regard her as the mother who was a little ashamed about the 'father's admonition'.

The elusive nature of Ter Borch's genre scenes can be seen as his trademark. He was also unrivalled in exploiting the sheen of satin to lend lustre to his paintings, and he used it time and again. Goethe was struck by both these traits. During the *tableau vivant* the 'magnificent figure in an abundantly folded white satin dress' refused to turn around when asked to do so, for the performers had 'grasped the sense of these artistic representations too thoroughly'. Back in the early 18th century the biographer Arnold Houbraken superbly summed up the various aspects of Ter Borch's painting technique: 'He not only succeeded in imitating the essential characteristics and all the elegance in a lively manner, but also in painting the attire and exceptional stuffs according to their nature, white satin above all, so naturally, thinly and artfully that it truly appeared to be satin, and he therefore employed it in his works on many occasions'.

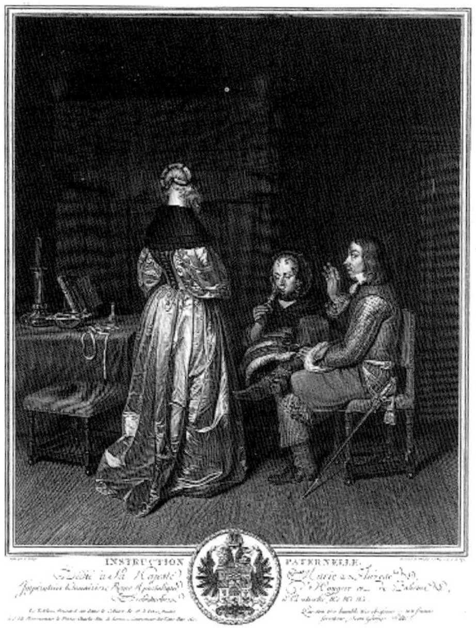

72a Johann Georg Wille after Gerard ter Borch, *Instruction paternelle*, 1765; engraving, 34 x 43.5 cm. Amsterdam, Rijksmuseum, Rijksprentenkabinet

LITERATURE

Gudlaugsson 1959-60, vol. 1, pp. 96-97, vol. 2, no. 110.I; exhib. cat. The Hague/Münster 1974, no. 32

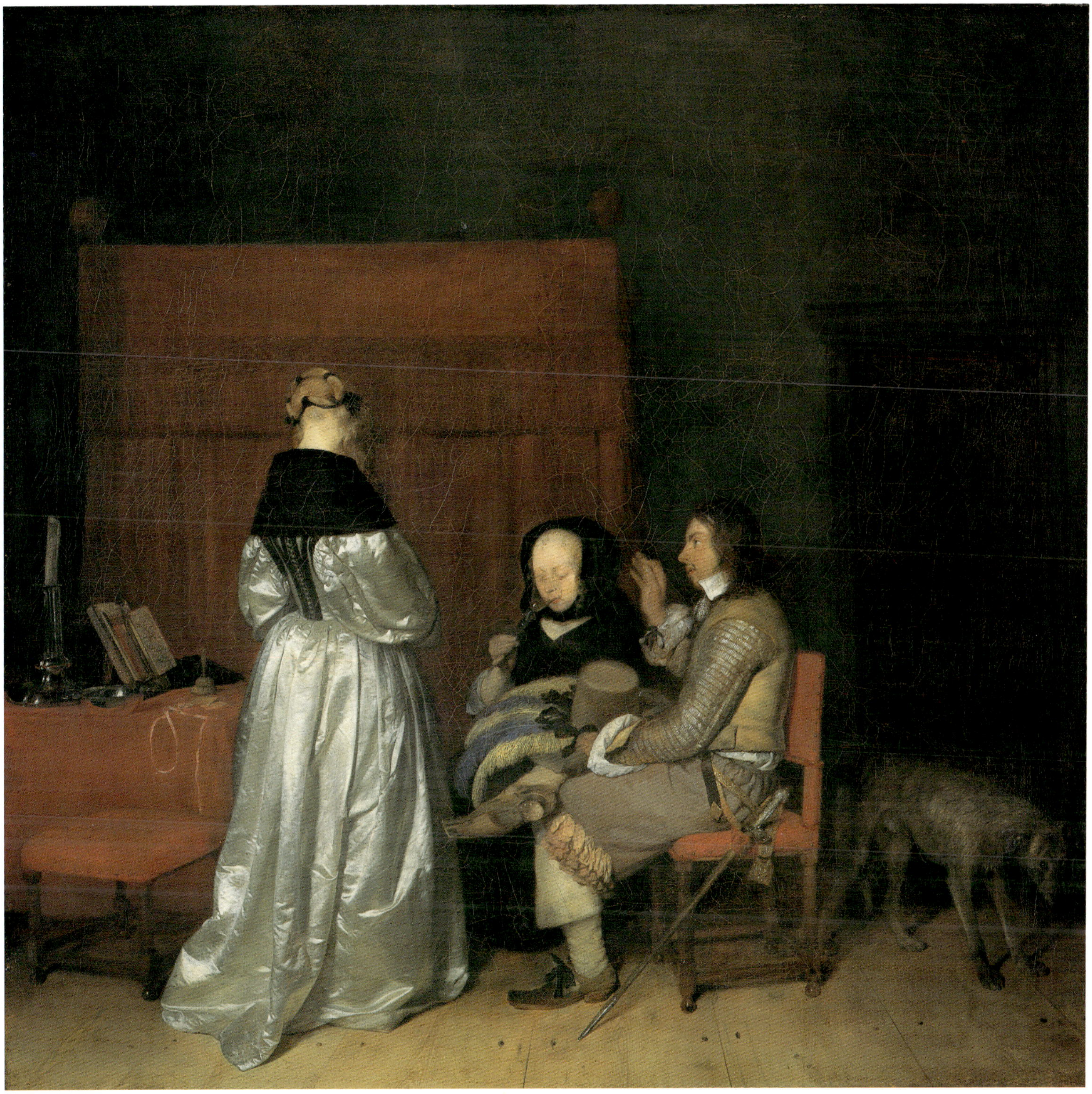

Gerard Dou (Leiden 1613-Leiden 1675)

73 *The night school, c. 1660*

Oil on panel, 48 x 37 cm
On the footstool: *Gdou* (*Gd* in ligature)
In 1665 in the collection of Dou's patron, Johan de Bye, Leiden; then in the collections of Adriaan Wittert van der Aa (1710), Pieter de la Court van der Voort and his son Allard (1766) in Leiden; purchased at the sale of the collection of Gerrit van der Pot van Groeneveld in 1808
Inv. no. SK-A-87

'Should anyone desire to have the light flame of a candle or lamp shine in his painting he should certainly satisfy that desire, taking good note of the difference between the light and that which is illuminated, just as Gerard Dou and his followers did so admirably', wrote the Rembrandt pupil Samuel van Hoogstraeten in his *Inleyding tot de hooge schoole der schilderkonst*, a theoretical treatise published in 1678. Candle-lit scenes soon came to be associated with Gerard Dou, another of Rembrandt's pupils, who began painting 'candlelights' of this kind in the late 1650s. They proved immensely popular, and as early as 1661 a mezzotint print was made after his *Girl placing a burning candle in a lantern* in the collection of Archduke Leopold of Austria [*73a*]. In 1665 Dou's patron, Johan de Bye, owned several of these nocturnes, including this *Night school*. As Van Hoogstraeten rightly observed, many imitators followed Dou's lead, among them his pupil Godfried Schalcken, who made something of a speciality of it.

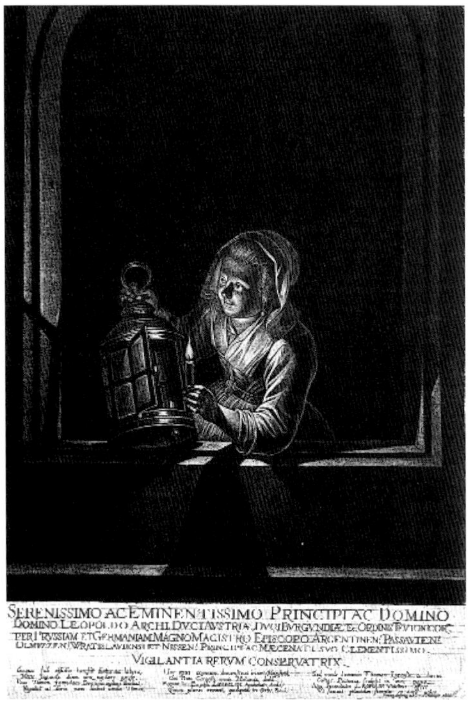

73a Jan Thomas after Gerard Dou, *Vigilantia rerum conservatrix* (Vigilance protects things); mezzotint, 51.9 x 35.6 cm. Amsterdam, Rijksmuseum, Rijksprentenkabinet

The realistic rendering of several different sources of light and their effects is no easy task for a painter. Philips Angel, who also lived in Leiden, asserted in an address to the members of the city's Guild of St Luke in 1642 that only a painter could depict 'a rainbow, rain, thunder, lightning, clouds, vapour, light, reflections [and] evening [...] none of which the sculptors can imitate'. This was one of the arguments which painters put forward in the so-called *paragone* debate, in which they vied with sculptors for pre-eminence among the arts, so Gerard Dou would have seen it as a challenge to depict an evening scene by candlelight as convincingly as possible. In this picture he very successfully captured the effect of light coming from four different directions, together with the soft glow which makes the scene just barely visible. Nor did he shy away from giving a clear view of the candles, although it would have been simpler to hide them behind another object, since depicting the actual flame is perhaps the trickiest of all. He did partially conceal one of them, showing how the flame appears when seen through the matt glass of a lantern. Moreover, the more diffuse light cast on the floor through the sides makes a fascinating contrast to the direct light falling on the floor through the lantern's open door.

That this is one of Dou's more remarkable works is a view that was shared by Johannes Meerman, Director-General of the Sciences and Arts, who reported to King Louis Napoleon in 1808 that he had succeeded in buying the famous painting for 17,500 guilders for the Koninklijk Museum (forerunner of the Rijksmuseum) at the sale of the Van der Pot van Groeneveld Collection. He added that the former owner had received an offer of 50,000 guilders for it ('on avait offert 50.000 au defunt possesseur'), implying that he had certainly not paid over the odds.

LITERATURE
Martin 1913, p. 170; exhib. cat. Leiden 1988, no. 14; exhib. cat. Amsterdam 1989-90, no. 9; exhib. cat. Washington/London/The Hague 2000-01, no. 28

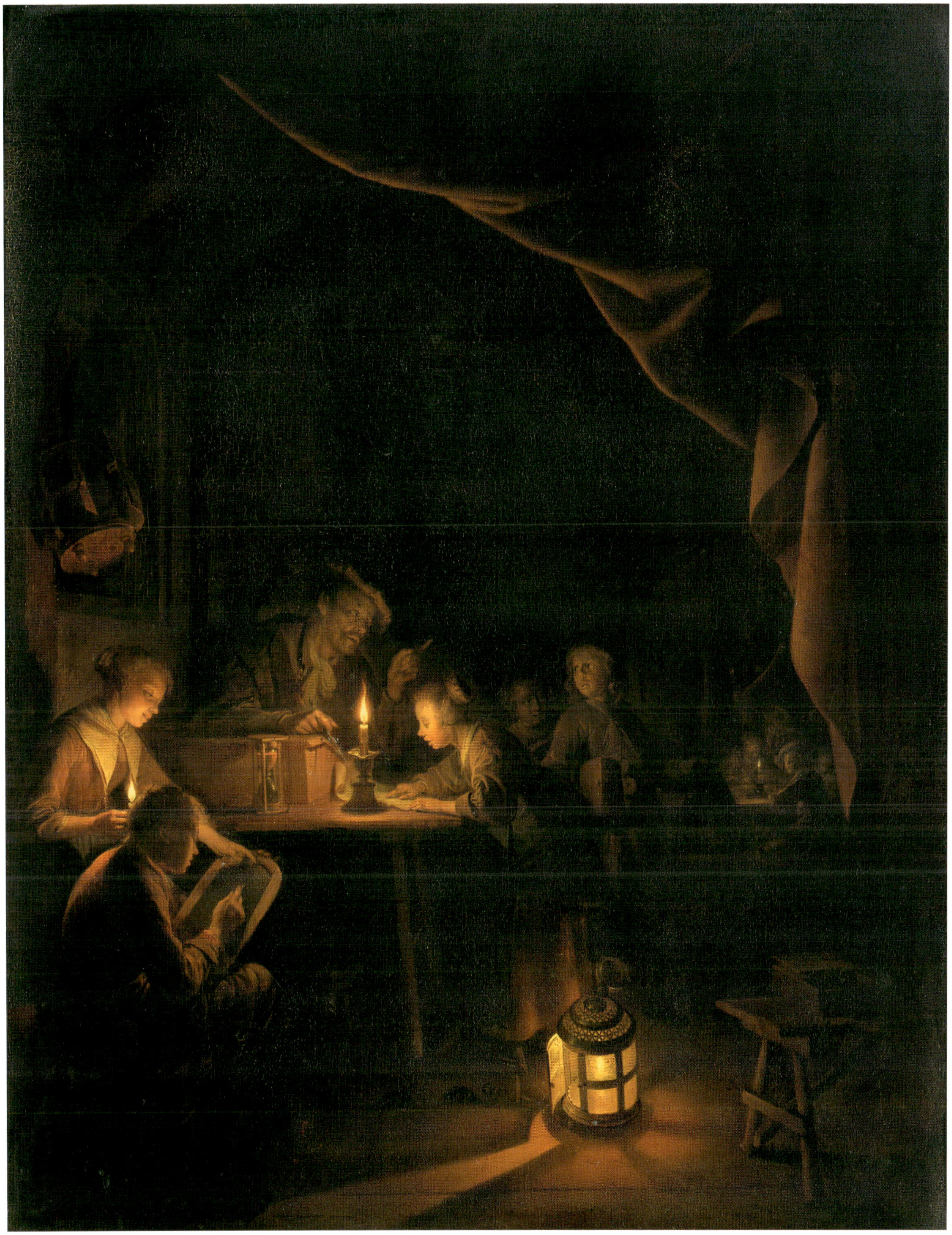

Jan Steen (Leiden 1626-Leiden 1679)

74 *The feast of St Nicholas, c. 1665-1668*

Oil on canvas, 82 x 70.5 cm
At lower right: *JSteen.* (JS in ligature)
Acquired in 1809 with the art cabinet of Adriaan Leonard van Heteren Gevers
Inv. no. SK-A-385

'Another such lifelike and ingenious painting shows a gangling young ninny who is standing there crying because he has spied a rod or cane sticking out of his shoe instead of something tasty (the painting depicts a feast of St Nicholas and can still be seen in the cabinet of Mr G. Franken in Dordrecht).' This was how Arnold Houbraken described a painting by Jan Steen in his *Groote schouburgh der Nederlantsche konstschilders en schilderessen* (1718-1721). There was indeed a painting of a feast of St Nicholas in the collection of Gillis Franken, which was sold along with the collection of Johan van der Hulk in Dordrecht on 23 April 1720, but it is not clear whether it was the one now in the Rijksmuseum. Their dimensions are different, although it is possible that a mistake of almost exactly 1 foot in the height and width was made in the sale catalogue.

Whatever the answer, Houbraken's description is remarkably apt, as telling in fact as the facial expressions Steen gave his characters. This was an aspect of his paintings that was always admired, even by those who turned up their noses at his farcical scenes. The 18th-century English painter Sir Joshua Reynolds, for example, wrote that 'if this extraordinary man had had the good fortune to have been born in Italy, instead of Holland [...], and had been blessed with Michael Angelo and Raffaelle for his masters, instead of Brower and Van Gowen, the same sagacity and penetration which distinguished so accurately the different characters and expressions in his vulgar figures, would, when exerted in the selection and imitation of what was great and elevated in nature, have been equally successful; and now he would have ranged with the great pillars and supporters of our Art'. But of course all the charm would have been lost if Steen had surrendered to that very different classical ideal, and even in the 18th century, when Classicism was by and large the prevailing fashion, there were dissident voices asserting that 'there is more historical truth in the imitation of modern life, in a piece by Van Mieris, Jan Steen or Van Ostade or others, even in the flowers of Van Huysum' than in the canonical Italian examples of history painting.

In this picture Steen very ingeniously presents both the light-hearted and the more emotional sides of the feast of St Nicholas—a Catholic feast involving the giving of presents whose current popularity, ironically, is almost solely restricted to the Netherlands, which is always regarded as a Protestant country. With a clever arrangement of his figures, Steen lets three separate groups tell their own stories. The mother, for instance, is clearly delighted with her little daughter, who has received a St John the Baptist doll and a pail full of other presents. The small boy in the middle is laughing about the shoe containing a birch held by the maidservant, which belongs to the inconsolable lad on the left. Two boys and the youngest member of the family are waiting expectantly by the fireplace, which is evidently where St Nicholas deposited the presents even then. Meanwhile, grandfather looks on genially as the din rises around him, while grandmother seems to have something hidden away in the bedstead. Steen accompanies all these goings-on with a sublime rendering of textures. The mother's jacket and the still-life details with traditional sweetmeats like gingerbread and spice biscuit are superb examples of his masterly way with the brush.

LITERATURE

Boer 1994; exhib. cat. Washington/Amsterdam 1996-97, no. 30; Westermann 1997, pp. 155-156

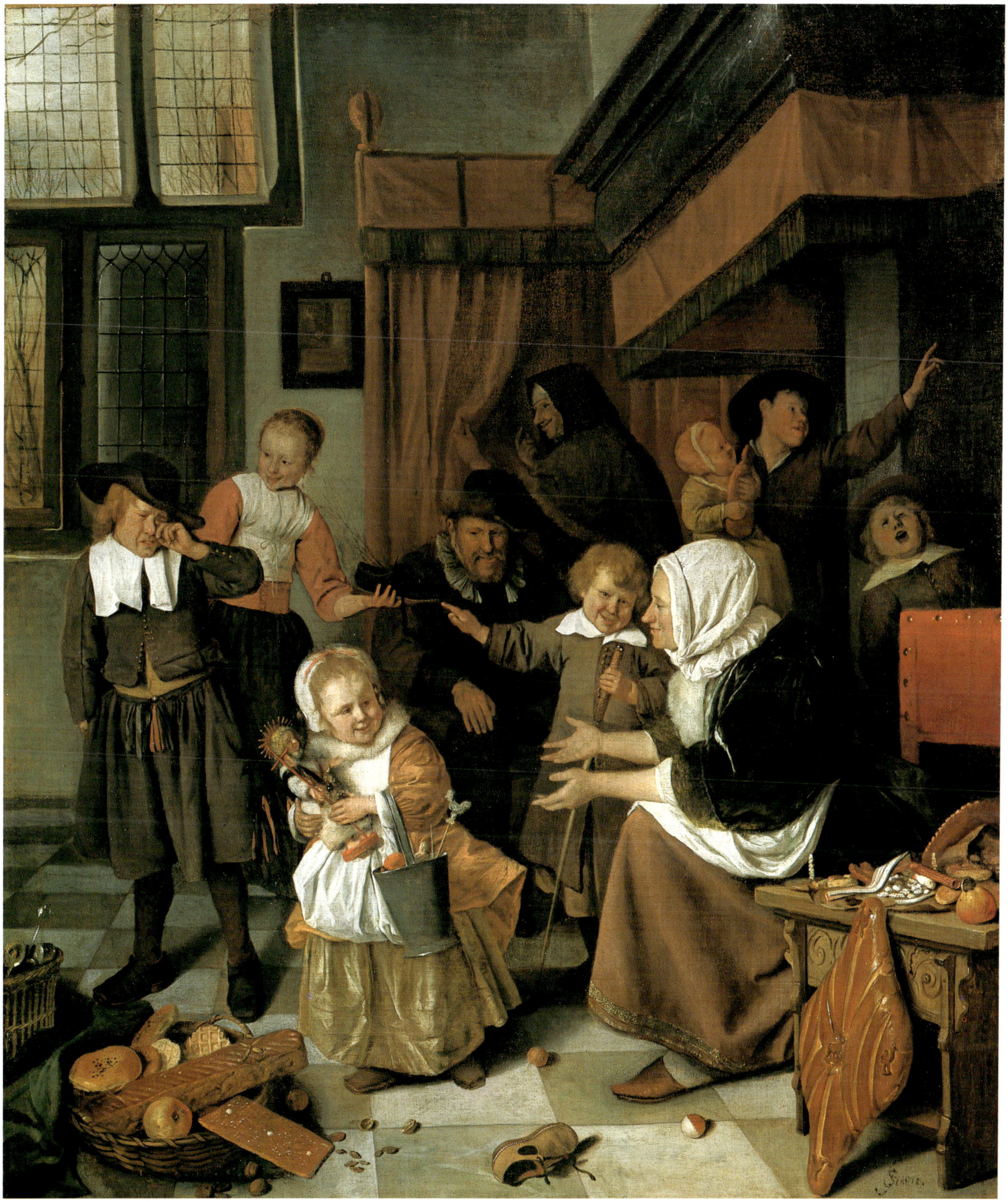

Gabriel Metsu (Leiden 1629-Amsterdam 1667)

75 *The sick child, c. 1660*

Oil on canvas, 32.2 x 27.2 cm
Above the map: *G. Metsue*
From the collections of Goll van Frankenstein, Amsterdam (1833), Steengracht (1913) and Huldschinsky, Berlin (1928); purchased in 1928 with the aid of the Vereniging Rembrandt
Inv. no. SK-A-3059

Although Gabriel Metsu was probably a pupil of Gerard Dou, his brushwork was more fluid and broader than that of the Leiden painters who prided themselves on their high, enamelled finish [*see 73 and 102*]. He was clearly influenced by their work, as he was by that of Gerard ter Borch, Pieter de Hooch and Johannes Vermeer. That is why he is often regarded as an eclectic master, although that does no justice to his own intrinsic qualities. It is true that his genre scenes, many of them elegant interiors, are sometimes rather fussy, but his sense of colour is almost always unerring. In a few works, such as this *Sick child*, he succeeded in rivalling Vermeer's simplicity and subtle use of colour, while at the same time approaching Ter Borch's evocative narrative manner [*see 72*].

The sick child is an exceptional picture within Metsu's oeuvre. He painted several genre scenes of women engaged on (or neglecting) their domestic tasks, but seldom do they have such a confrontational directness and power. If this picture indeed depicts the care for a sick child, then the unique design rules out comparison with any other 17th-century Dutch genre painting.

The earliest known reference to it is from 1833, when the English art dealer John Smith included it in his catalogue of Metsu's oeuvre as *The sick child*, and it is possible that he was merely repeating a title handed down for generations. The child's slack, crumpled pose and pallid face show that it is completely listless, while the fact that it is only half-dressed suggests that it has only just got out of bed. But is a sick child the real subject? The title may have been prompted by a need to weave a story around the evocative scene: the bowl of porridge is untouched, and the mother has worriedly taken her child onto her lap to comfort it. When the painting was sold shortly after the publication of Smith's book, it was praised in the catalogue of the Goll van Frankenstein sale for its 'expression of maternal tenderness and concern for the suffering child'. A little earlier in the catalogue it was remarked that the child 'appears to be out of sorts'.

It has been suggested that the painting is in fact a modernised form of Caritas, and certainly there are scenes in which feeding or caring for a child illustrates the Christian love of one's fellow man. The formal similarity to the visual type of the Pietà has led some to see a connection between the woman and child and the picture of the Crucifixion on the wall behind them, making it a possible allusion to the exemplary love and self-sacrifice of Christ. Whether the painter intended the scene to be read in this symbolical way is doubtful. His aim was a more general one, namely to portray the commendable care of a mother for her child, and that is how this picture would have been seen by his contemporaries.

LITERATURE
Robinson 1974, pp. 16, 52, 62, 194; exhib. cat. Amsterdam 1976, no. 41; Franits 1993, pp. 119-122

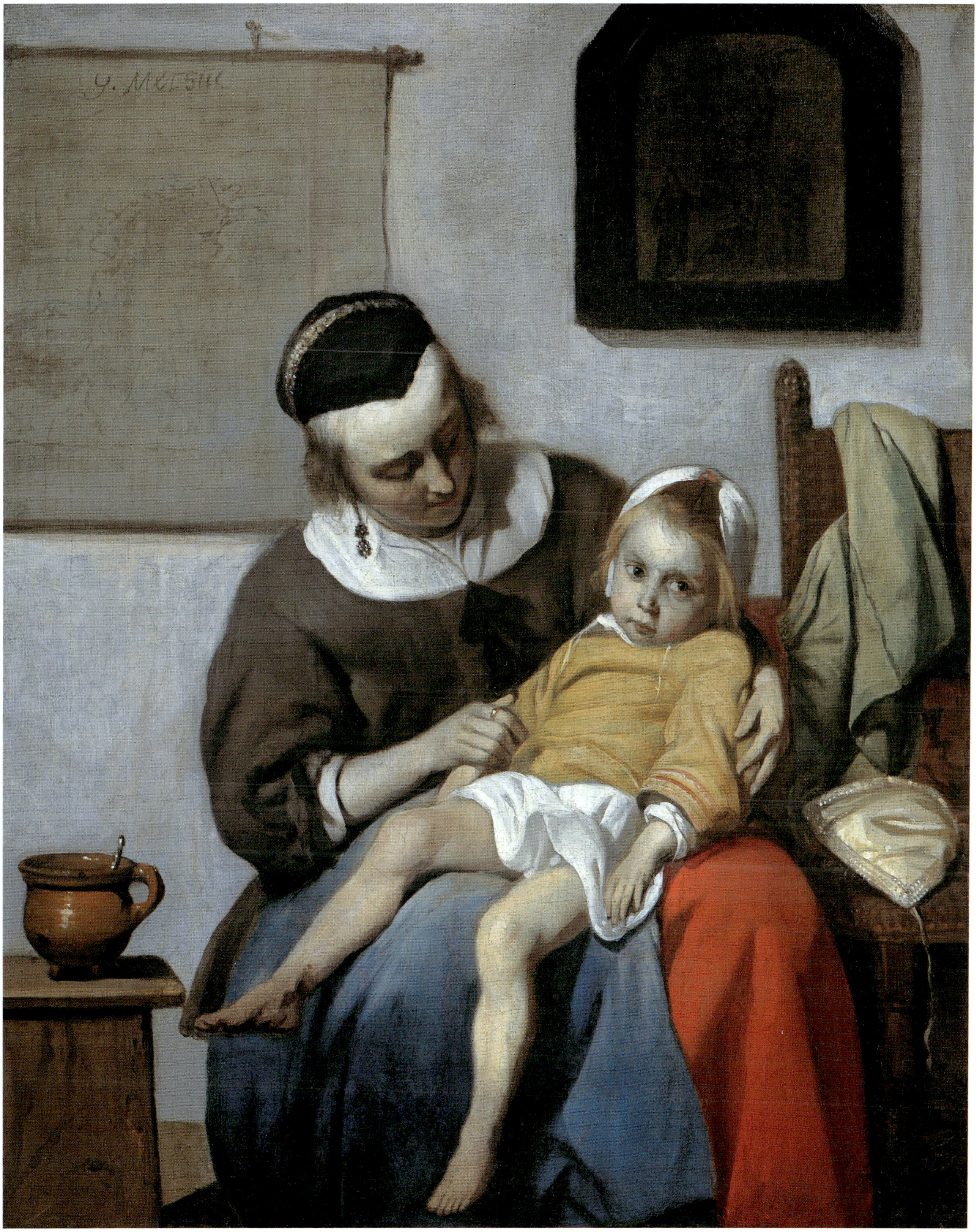

Caesar van Everdingen (Alkmaar c. 1617-Alkmaar 1678)

76 *A young woman warming her hands over a brazier, possibly an allegory of winter, c. 1645-1650*

Oil on canvas, 97 × 81 cm
At lower centre, on the edge of the table: CVE.
Purchased in 1991
Inv. no. SK-A-4878

Caesar van Everdingen and his younger brother Allart are among the finest artists ever produced by the town of Alkmaar, north of Haarlem. While Allart specialised in landscape, Caesar became a figure painter whose works are now eagerly sought after for their perfect technique and light tonality. His small oeuvre consists of portraits of individuals and groups, history paintings, and two still lifes. As a result of his collaboration with Jacob van Campen, he is counted among the so-called Haarlem Classicists—a group of artists that included such masters as Pieter de Grebber and Salomon and his son Jan de Braij. They were all history painters who set out to depict their stories in a clear-cut, straightforward way using dignified figures in a radiant and bright palette, in contrast to the low-life, half-length figures and dramatic chiaroscuro of the Utrecht followers of Caravaggio. Around 1648, all these masters (with the exception of Jan de Braij, who was still too young) were invited by Constantijn Huygens to work on the decoration of the Oranjezaal in Huis ten Bosch palace near The Hague, together with the leading artists from Antwerp. It was the most prestigious commission of the period.

The subtlety of Caesar van Everdingen's painting technique and the delicacy with which he could capture his subject is demonstrated by this scene of a young woman warming her hands over the glowing coals of a brazier standing by the edge of a table. She has caught up the hem of her greenish blue skirt and holds it over the brazier to trap as much heat as possible. The rest of her expensive attire shows that this serene woman is actually a grand lady. She is wearing a sleeveless cape of pink velvet trimmed with ermine, a white cap and a chemise edged with lace, and numerous gleaming pearls as jewelry.

In the 17th century, a figure crouched over a brazier often symbolised winter, the last of the four seasons. Because it came at the end of the year it was associated with the closing stage of a person's life, so the figure was usually an old man. Although Van Everdingen opted for a young woman instead, the scene can certainly be interpreted as an allegory of winter, the more so in that two paintings listed in the inventory of Van Everdingen's estate are referred to as 'Winter'. The other one is very probably the second version of this picture in the City Art Gallery in Southampton, England.

LITERATURE
Blankert 1991; exhib. cat. Rotterdam/Frankfurt 1999-2000, no. 28

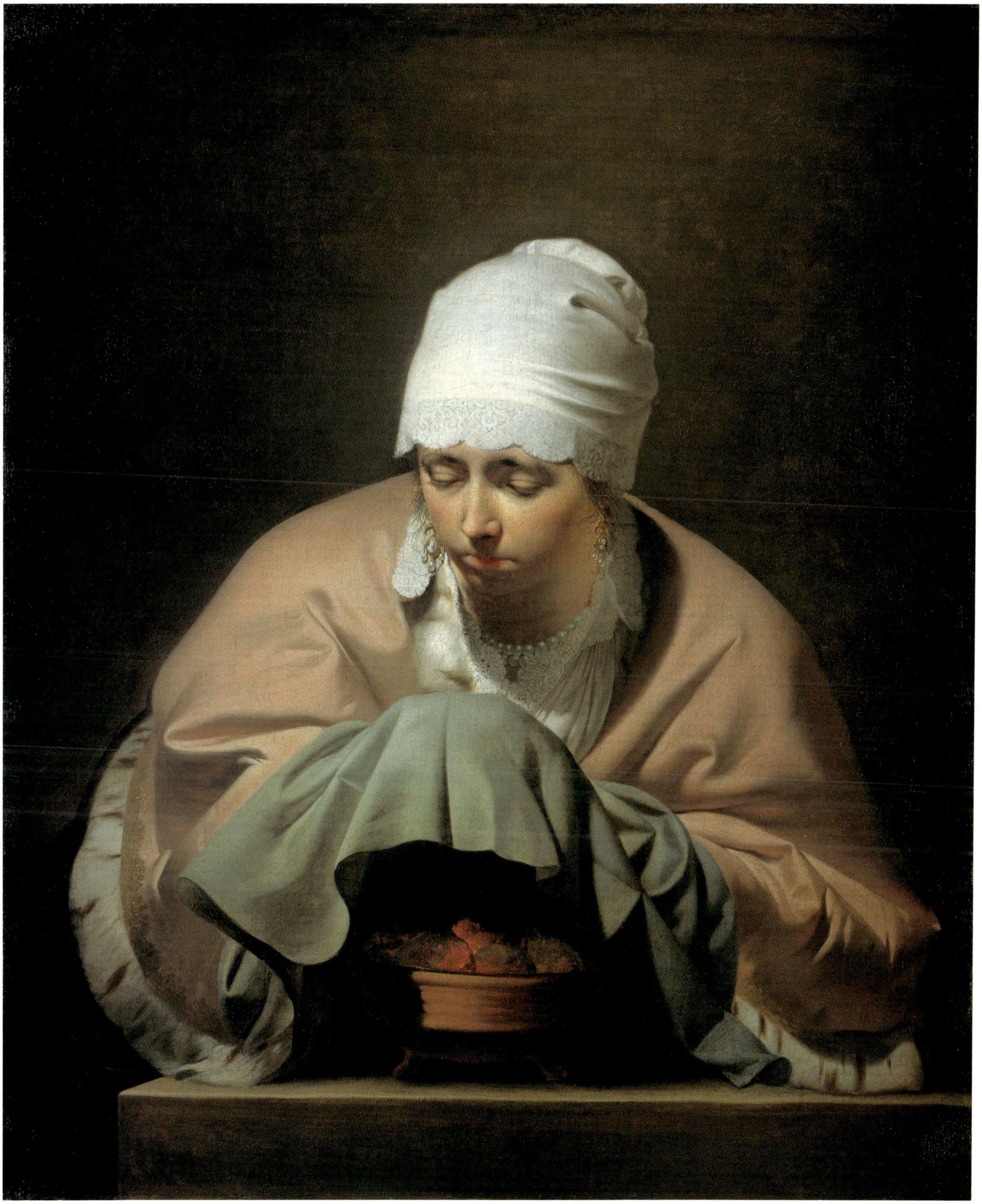

Rombout Verhulst (Mechelen 1624-The Hague 1698)

77 *Portrait of Jacob van Reygersberg, 1671*

Colour-washed terracotta, h. 55 cm
From the collection of Jonkheer D.T.A. van den Bogaerde van Terbrugge, Lord of Moergestel, Heeswijk Castle; purchased in 1896 with the aid of the Vereniging Rembrandt
Inv. no. BK-NM-10557

The portrait of the Zeeland regent Jacob van Reygersberg (1625-1675), which the sculptor Rombout Verhulst made in 1671, is the most tangible evidence of the long and close relationship between patron and sculptor. It was probably through Van Reygersberg that Verhulst won a number of major commissions in the years 1663-1671. In 1663, for instance, he delivered the monumental tomb in Katwijk for Jacob van Liere and his widow Maria van Reygersberg, a sister of Jacob's. That was followed by two memorials for members of prominent Zeeland families to which Van Reygersberg was related by marriage: for Van Gheel in Spanbroek (1668) and for Thibaut in Aagtekerke (1669). Van Reygersberg may also have been involved in the commission for the tomb of Carel Hieronymus van In- en Kniphuisen in Midwolde, which Verhulst completed in 1669. Both were fellow delegates to the States-General in The Hague, representing Zeeland and Groningen respectively. That the relationship between Verhulst and Van Reygersberg went beyond the purely professional is clear from the fact that the sculptor regularly acted as a witness to notarized documents involving the Van Reygersberg and Van Gheel families. This intimate, personal bond may have contributed to the very sensitive nature of Verhulst's portrait of his patron. The regent, who was at the height of his political and social career, is portrayed with a calm, level gaze. Although there is an almost identical marble version [*77a*], the relationship between the two is unclear. Verhulst probably made the terracotta first, 'from life', to serve as the basis for the working model in plaster. That plaster model, from which the marble was carved before it was disposed of, must have differed from the terracotta slightly, making the marble bust a little more stately and formal.

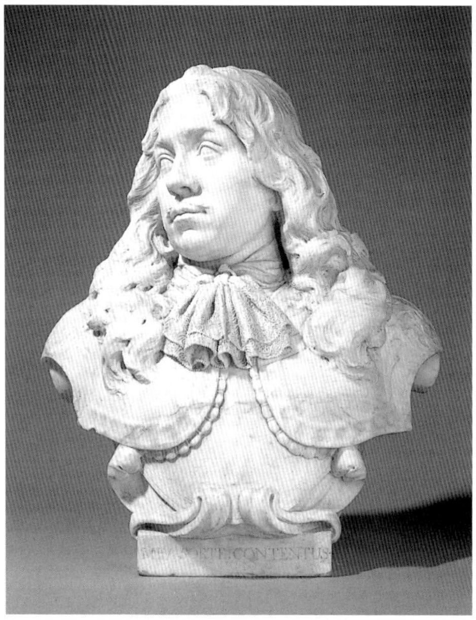

77a Rombout Verhulst, *Portrait of Jacob van Reygersberg*, 1671; marble, h. 63 cm. Los Angeles, The J. Paul Getty Museum

It is not known for whom the terracotta was made. The marble would have been a showpiece, given the costly, durable material and the inscribed plinth, and was undoubtedly for Jacob van Reygersberg himself, and it is not impossible that it was destined for a tomb, although none was ever executed. That would explain why the sculptor found such an unusual and formal solution for the termination of the bust in the form of two decorative volutes. Such a form would suit the niche architecture of a tomb.

Comparison of the marble and the terracotta is very instructive, for it reveals the sculptor's mastery in transferring all the nuances in texture and modelling from the initially pliable and soft terracotta to the hard stone. In doing so, Rombout Verhulst created one of the most successful examples of the realistic portrait style that was the fashion in the Dutch Republic in the second half of the 17th century.

LITERATURE
Cat. Amsterdam 1973, no. 314; Scholten 1991; cat. Amsterdam 1995a, no. 23

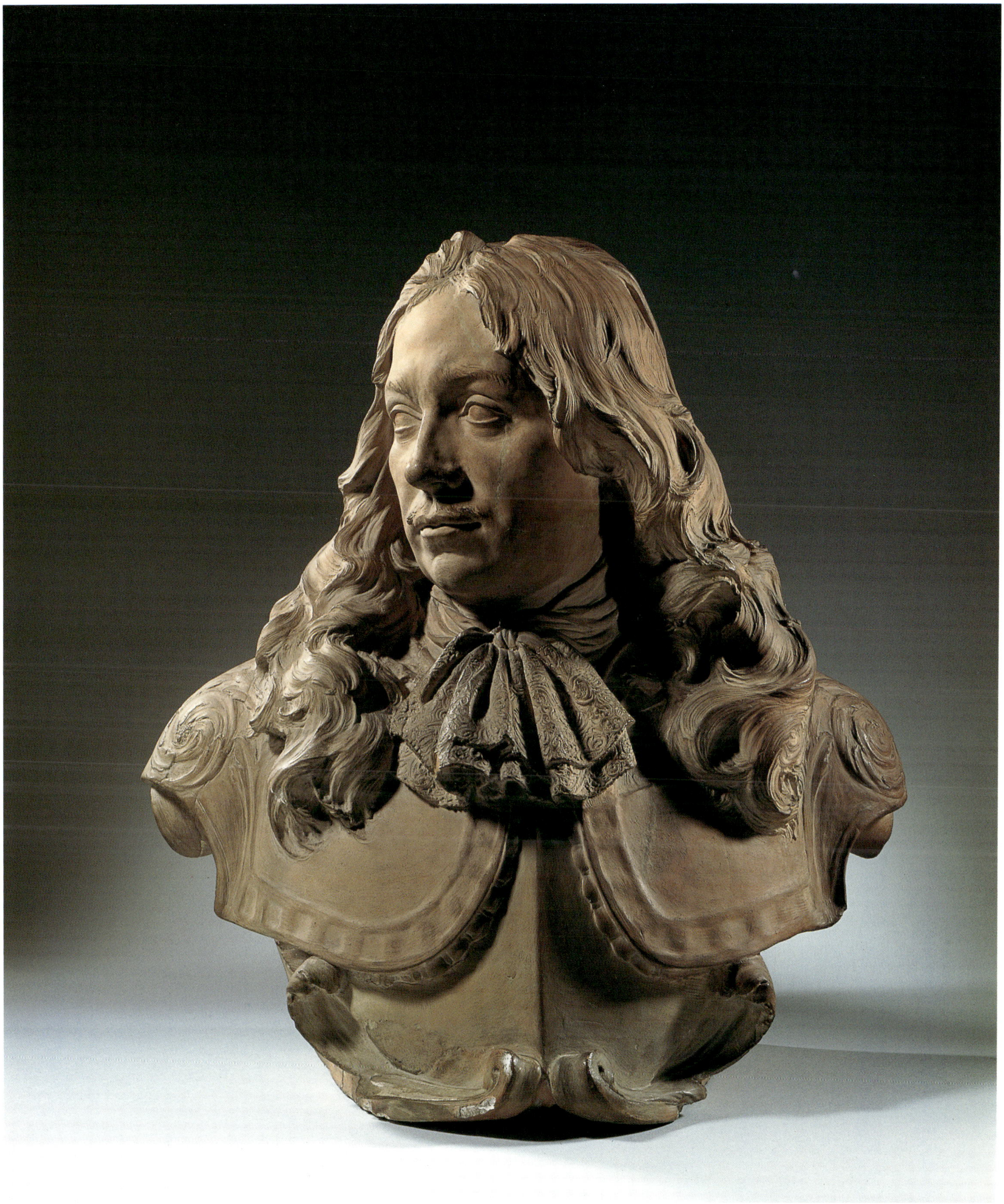

Jan de Braij (Haarlem c. 1627-Haarlem 1697)

78 *Portrait of the Haarlem printer Abraham Casteleyn and his wife Margarieta van Bancken, 1663*

Oil on canvas, 84 x 108 cm
At lower left: *JDBray 1663*
Bequeathed by F.E. Blaauw, 's Graveland, in 1939
Inv. no. SK-A-3280

This double portrait by Jan de Braij fell prey to several misunderstandings. The first was that for years the sitters were believed to be Willem Blaauw and his wife, and the painting was cherished as such by the descendants of the famous Amsterdam printing family De Blaauw, although it had not been in the family all that long. It was only in 1958 that it was discovered that the man and woman are in fact the Haarlem printer Abraham Casteleyn and his wife Margarieta van Bancken. Although a Haarlem printer certainly makes a better match with a Haarlem painter, it is above all the prominent bust of Laurens Jansz Coster, believed at the time to have been the inventor of printing from movable type, that turns the painting into a veritable celebration of Haarlem. Casteleyn was best known as the publisher of one of the earliest Dutch news-sheet, *De Opregte Haerlemse Courant*, which was published from 1656 to 1942.

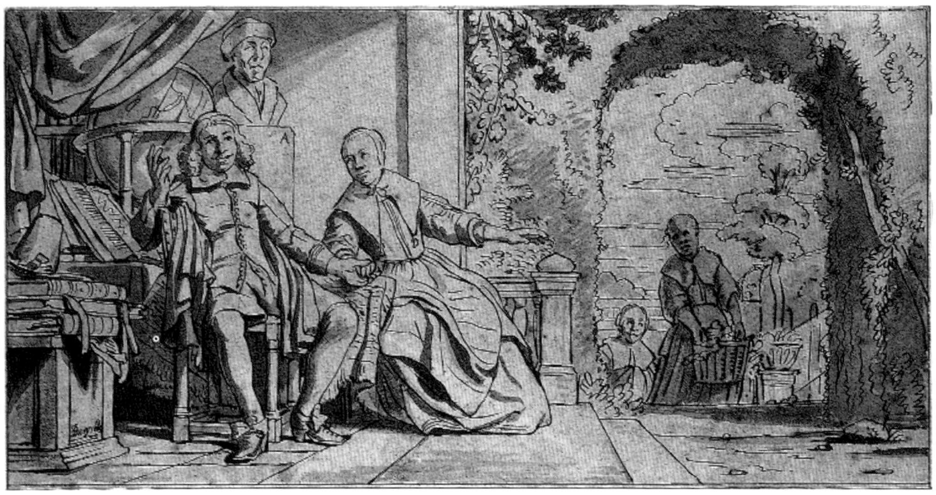

78a Jan de Braij, *Portrait of Abraham Casteleyn and Margarieta van Bancken*; pen and brush, 10.2 x 20.3 cm. Paris, Fondation Custodia (F. Lugt Collection)

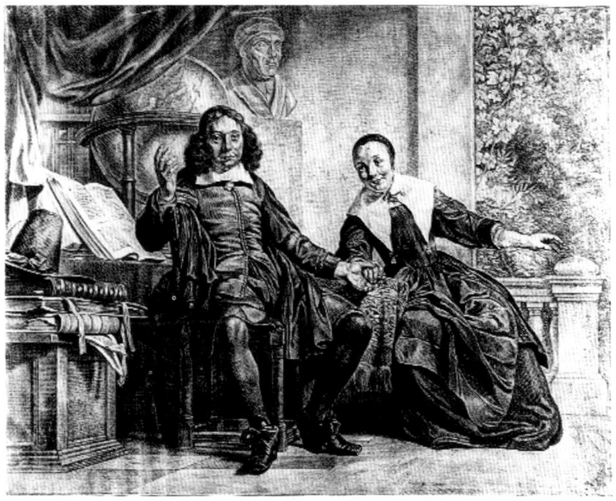

78b Jan de Braij, *Portrait of Abraham Casteleyn and Margarieta van Bancken*; black and red chalk, 36.3 x 46.4 cm. Present whereabouts unknown

The second misapprehension was brought about by an autograph drawing by Jan de Braij [78a] in which Margarieta van Bancken is pointing at an overgrown archway through which two children can be seen climbing some steps carrying produce from the garden. That drawing gave rise to the assumption that some of De Braij's painting was missing and that the large piece was all that was left. As a result, the picture had always been viewed with a mixture of admiration and disappointment. Then, when a second drawing surfaced [78b] which matched the painting in every respect, it was decided to find out what the original dimensions had been. It turned out that the artist had left grey edges unpainted on all four sides, so the painting could never have been larger. Moreover, knowledge of De Braij's use of drawings provided a fairly clear picture of the sequence of events. The pen drawing [78a] was a plan for the painting, a proposal to be shown to the patron for his approval. Part of it he rejected, and the children in the garden were omitted. One can only guess as to the reason, but perhaps they became the subject of a second painting. After completing the work De Braij made a precise copy of it in black and red chalk for his own records, as he often did. After the discovery of the four original edges the painting was cleaned and turned out to be in excellent condition. That is particularly apparent in the variety of blacks in the clothing and the luxuriance of the ivy on the right.

De Braij's modified plan, without the children and the pergola, has a remarkably

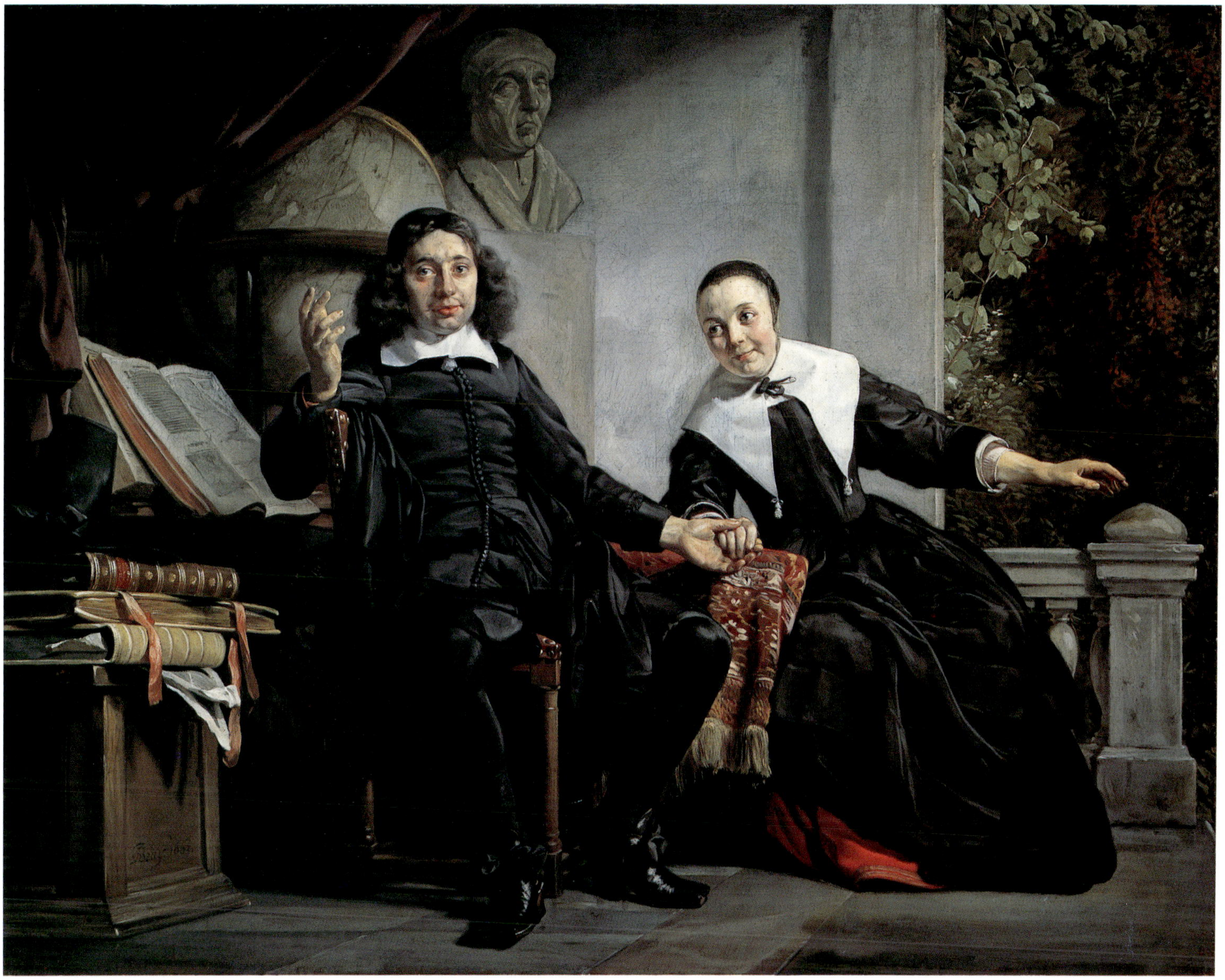

regular compositional scheme. The format of the canvas corresponds to a double golden section—two upright rectangles side by side constructed according to the ratio of the golden section. The double golden section was often used for the proportions of a painting, because the ideal proportions of the single golden section produced a format which was too oblong. In this painting the imaginary dividing line between the two rectangles runs just to the right of the pedestal with Coster's bust. As a result, the man and the woman, united though they are by their clasped hands, nevertheless inhabit worlds of their own: the woman that of the garden, the man with his books and globe that of learning.

LITERATURE

Van Hall 1958; exhib. cat. Haarlem 1986, no. 36

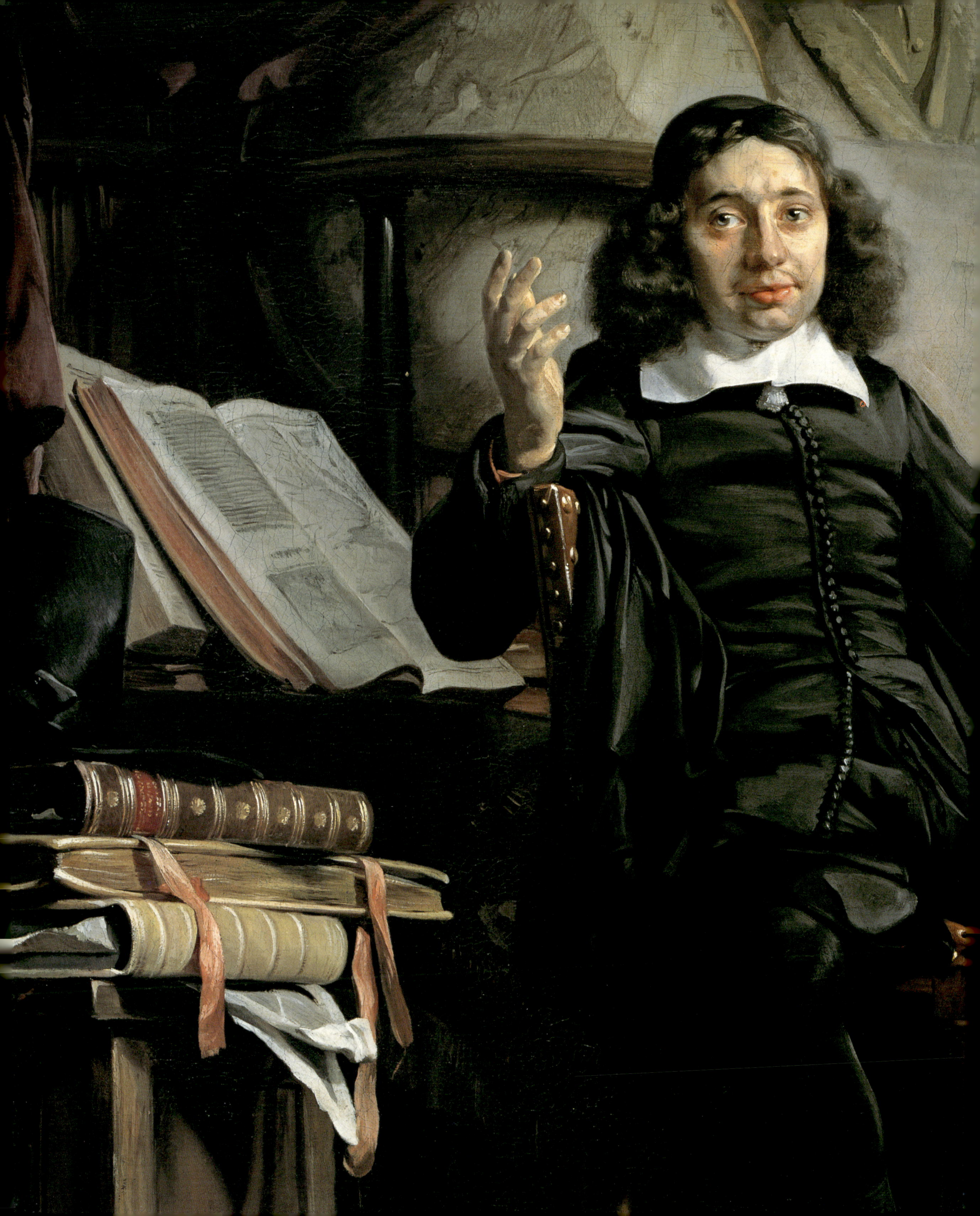

Ferdinand Bol (Dordrecht 1616-Amsterdam 1680)

79 *Self-portrait, c. 1669*

Oil on canvas, 128 x 104 cm
Bequeathed by Albertus Brondgeest in 1849
Inv. no. SK-A-42

Like his teacher Rembrandt, Ferdinand Bol painted history pieces and portraits throughout his career. He imitated the master's style until around 1650, but then switched to the more modern manner, which was based on Flemish models and can best be typified as more colourful, light and elegant. The many official commissions he received for group portraits of governing bodies and history paintings for Amsterdam institutions are evidence that he was one of the most successful artists of his day. There is little sign of that in this *Self-portrait*, for it contains not a single allusion to his career as an artist. More than that, Bol presents himself as the archetypical man of quality holding a rattan cane in his right hand as he leans nonchalantly on a statue of a sleeping Cupid. Posed in a full-bottomed wig and an expensive house-coat before a stately column on a base, it is a form of presentation which differs not one iota from the way in which Bol portrayed his rich clientele.

The canvas is still in its original lime-wood frame with auricular carving and festoons which Bol undoubtedly ordered himself. Prominent among the motifs is the sunflower, with the largest one crowning the work immediately above the artist's head. Recent research has revealed a thematic relationship between a number of the key elements, most notably the sleeping Cupid and the column in the picture, and the sunflowers on the frame. The slumbering god of love is a metaphor of the taming of carnal love, the column stands for marital fidelity and chastity, and the sunflower was a familiar symbol of honourable love. Taken together, the three

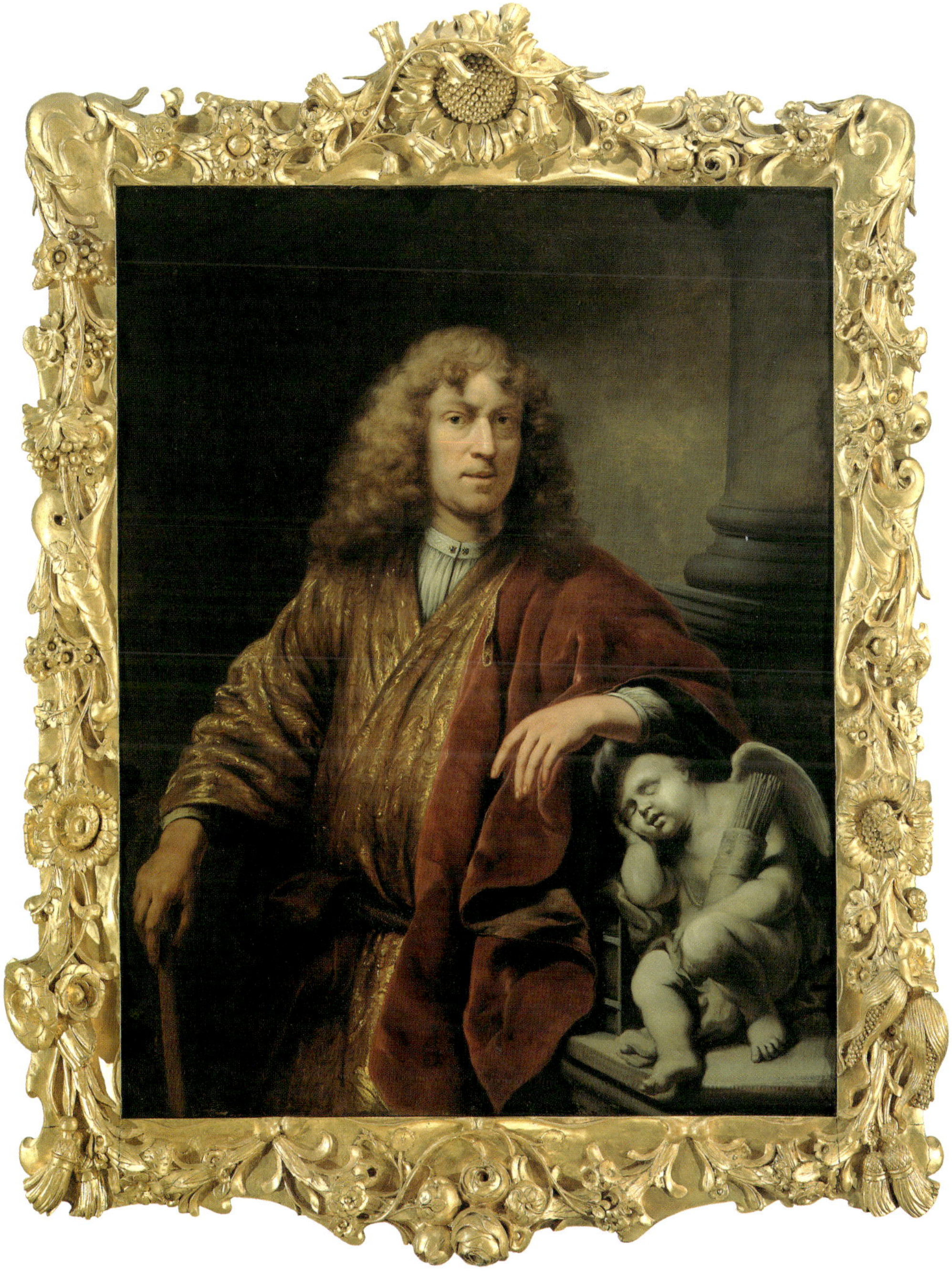

◂ Detail of [78]

motifs allude to virtuous love, the basis of a good marriage.

This investment of meaning in the *Self-portrait* closely matches the artist's personal circumstances at the end of the 1660s, when the canvas was painted. After nine years as a widower, the 53-year-old Bol married a wealthy widow of 45 in October 1669. He rarely took up the brush again after his marriage, so his presentation of himself as a fine, upstanding gentleman instead of as an artist, who was several rungs lower on the social ladder, is both understandable and full of meaning. The ethical connotations to which the various elements refer also make the painting an important personal document. It would certainly have shown his second wife that she could rest assured as to his honourable intentions.

LITERATURE

Blankert 1982, no. 103; exhib. cat. Amsterdam 1984, no. 61; exhib. cat. Haarlem 1986, no. 9; De Jongh 2000

Rembrandt Harmensz van Rijn (Leiden 1606-Amsterdam 1669)

80 *The three crosses, 1653*

Drypoint on vellum, first state of five, 38.5 × 45 cm
Beginning with the third state, left of lower centre: *Rembrandt f. 1653*
From the print collections of Wilfred Lawson (1907), Brayton Ives, New York (1915) and Bernhard Scholle, New York; bequeathed to the museum in 1961 by Mr and Mrs I. de Bruijn-van der Leeuw, Spiez
Inv. no. RP-P-1961-1196a

Rembrandt's *Three crosses* of 1653 is one of the pinnacles of printmaking. It is more like a painting than an etching. 'Hang this picture in a bright light and in such a manner that it can be viewed from a distance. It will then sparkle at its best', Rembrandt wrote in 1639 when he sent a painting to Constantine Huygens, the secretary of Stadholder Frederik Hendrik. When one views *The three crosses* from a distance in bright daylight one sees how calculating he was in this print as well. Curious as to the different effects, he made impressions on various kinds of paper and, as here, on vellum, which absorbs hardly any ink at all.

Some parts of the scene are based on other prints, but the idea for this intensely dramatic, nocturnal setting is original and came from the Bible, which says that darkness fell over the face of the earth while it was still daytime. It is as if Rembrandt's other, more peaceful etched nocturnes were merely exercises in preparation for this spectacular piece.

Christ and those nearest the Cross are brightly lit and are depicted almost entirely in outline alone, while the figures further away are done in greater detail. The man kneeling with his arms outstretched is the Roman centurion who cried out 'Certainly this was a righteous man' (Luke 23:47) and praised God when he saw the crucified Christ. The group on the right with the swooning Virgin and her mourning companions is particularly evocative.

The print was executed solely in drypoint, a technique which is only suitable for small editions. Not long after he had completed and dated the etching in the third state, Rembrandt was forced to completely rework it because the plate had become so worn. All sorts of figures were burnished out, and others were added with coarse lines in drypoint [80a]. The result was a new work of art in which the drama is orchestrated very differently, with the worn passages being concealed with a web of hatchings.

The different ways of inking the plate and the use of copious surface tone produced a number of impressions which are so dissimilar that it is hard to imagine that they all came from the same plate. It was this approach of Rembrandt's, pushing the boundaries of printmaking to the limits, that prompted 19th-century artists to hail him as a forerunner of modern art.

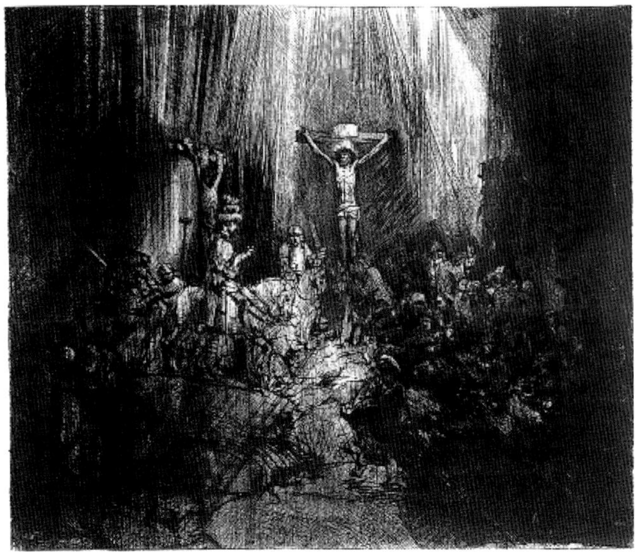

80a Rembrandt van Rijn, *The three crosses*, 1653; drypoint and burin, fourth state, 38.5 × 45 cm. Amsterdam, Rijksmuseum, Rijksprentenkabinet

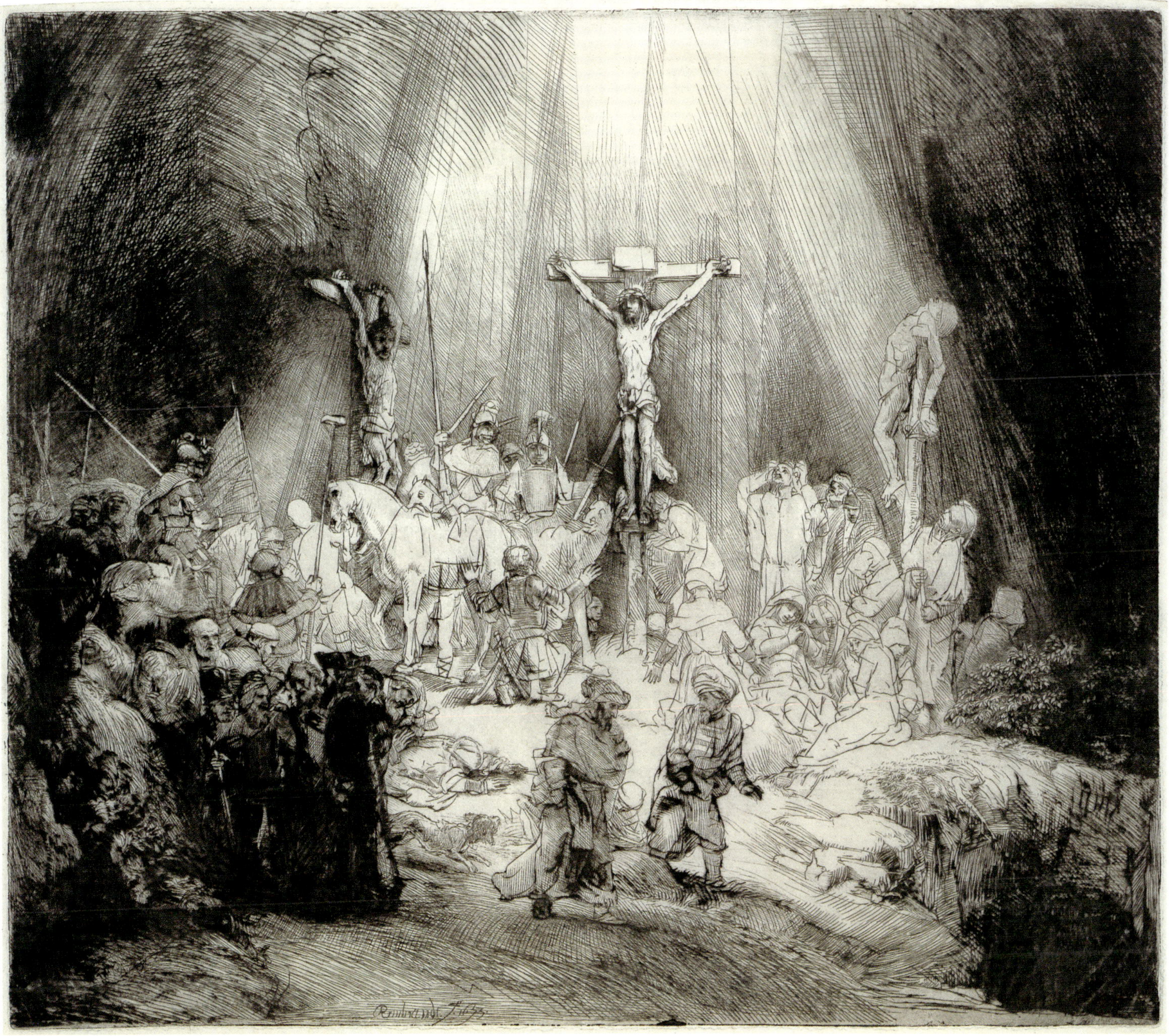

Most of Rembrandt's etchings were small enough to be preserved in albums, as they were by collectors throughout Europe in the 17th century. Larger prints like *The three crosses* must also have been hung on the walls of people's homes, and confirmation of this is found in several 17th-century inventories. One drawn up on 18 December 1665 in Amsterdam, for instance, contains the entry: 'In the inner chamber where Diderick Allewijn sleeps, three framed prints by Rembrandt'.

LITERATURE

Hollstein 78; White 1999, pp. 77-88; Luijten 2000, pp. 38-39; exhib. cat. Amsterdam/London 2000-01, no. 73

Rembrandt Harmensz van Rijn (Leiden 1606-Amsterdam 1669)

81 *The sampling officials of the Amsterdam drapers' guild, known as 'The syndics'*, 1662

Oil on canvas, 191.5 x 279 cm
In the centre, on the rug: *Rembrandt f. 1662*, and at upper right on the wall, in a later hand: *Rembrandt f. 1661*
Painted for the Staalhof, the headquarters of the drapers' guild in Staalstraat, Amsterdam; transferred to the Town Hall in 1771; on loan from the City of Amsterdam since 1808
Inv. no. SK-C-6

'Five gentlemen dressed all in black, doing nothing but sitting to have their portraits painted'. This rather dismissive view of *The syndics* was delivered in 1801 by Cornelis Sebille Roos, Inspector of the Nationale Konst-Gallerij (National Art Gallery). The painting had been offered for sale, and although the gallery decided it was not interested the work nevertheless arrived on loan seven years later in the collection which was to form the basis of the present-day Rijksmuseum. *The syndics* is unusual in several respects. The fame of many masterpieces rests on the fact they have 'something extra'. It could be said of *The syndics* that it excels in lacking anything extra at all. It is indeed above all a group portrait of five men around a table with their servant in a room with an ornate fireplace. It gives the impression of being larger than most regents' portraits, mainly because the figures are more than lifesize. It is also a portrait group in which there is an uncommon emphasis on the quality of execution. The manner is extremely forceful and is justly famed, and for some passages, such as the rug on the table, Rembrandt even used his palette knife. The climax, though, is formed by the heads, which he painted remarkably vigorously, inimitably investing them with great naturalism while using a broad brush. The main elements in this large picture are thus the portraits and the style of painting.

Rembrandt depicted the gentlemen around the table from a low vantage point, so he was evidently anticipating that the painting would be hung high up on the wall of their council chamber. Jan Wagenaar, who wrote a history of Amsterdam, must have seen *The syndics* when it was still in its original location, and in 1765 he wrote an interesting passage about the Staalhof. It contained 'a room where the five wardens of the drapery, also called syndics, in turn and one by one, appear three times a week [...] to sample and seal the blue and black cloth. Hanging in this chamber are six paintings of wardens from the 16th and 17th centuries. Each shows five wardens seated and the steward of the Staalhof standing'. Unfortunately, most of the paintings mentioned by Wagenaar can no longer be traced. The one by Pieter Pietersz [81a] is usually believed to portray six sampling officials, but perhaps there are only five, the sixth man, with the sealing-tongs, being their servant. A comparison with this work, in which all the figures are making emphatic hand gestures, shows how subtly Rembrandt depicted the hands of his syndics. It is generally assumed that his painting was finished in 1662, the year accompanying the signature (which is original), but that the sitters are the syndics appointed in 1661. This has enabled all of them to be identified, along with the servant, who is the only figure not wearing a hat. The board of wardens was a varied group containing representatives of several

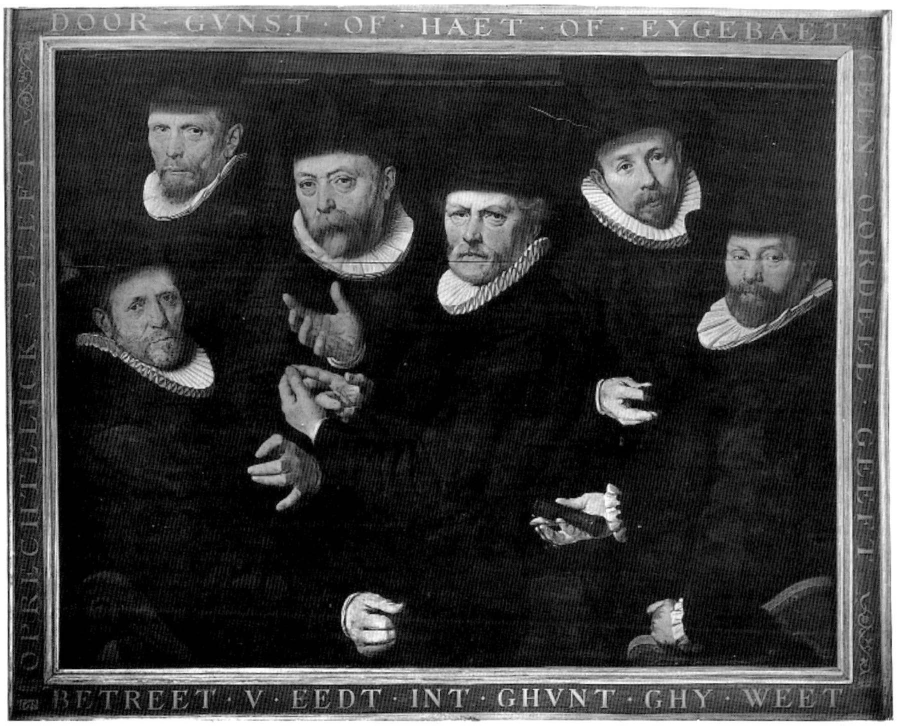

81a Pieter Pietersz, *Six wardens of the draper's guild in Amsterdam*, 1599; oil on panel, 108 x 143 cm. Amsterdam, Rijksmuseum

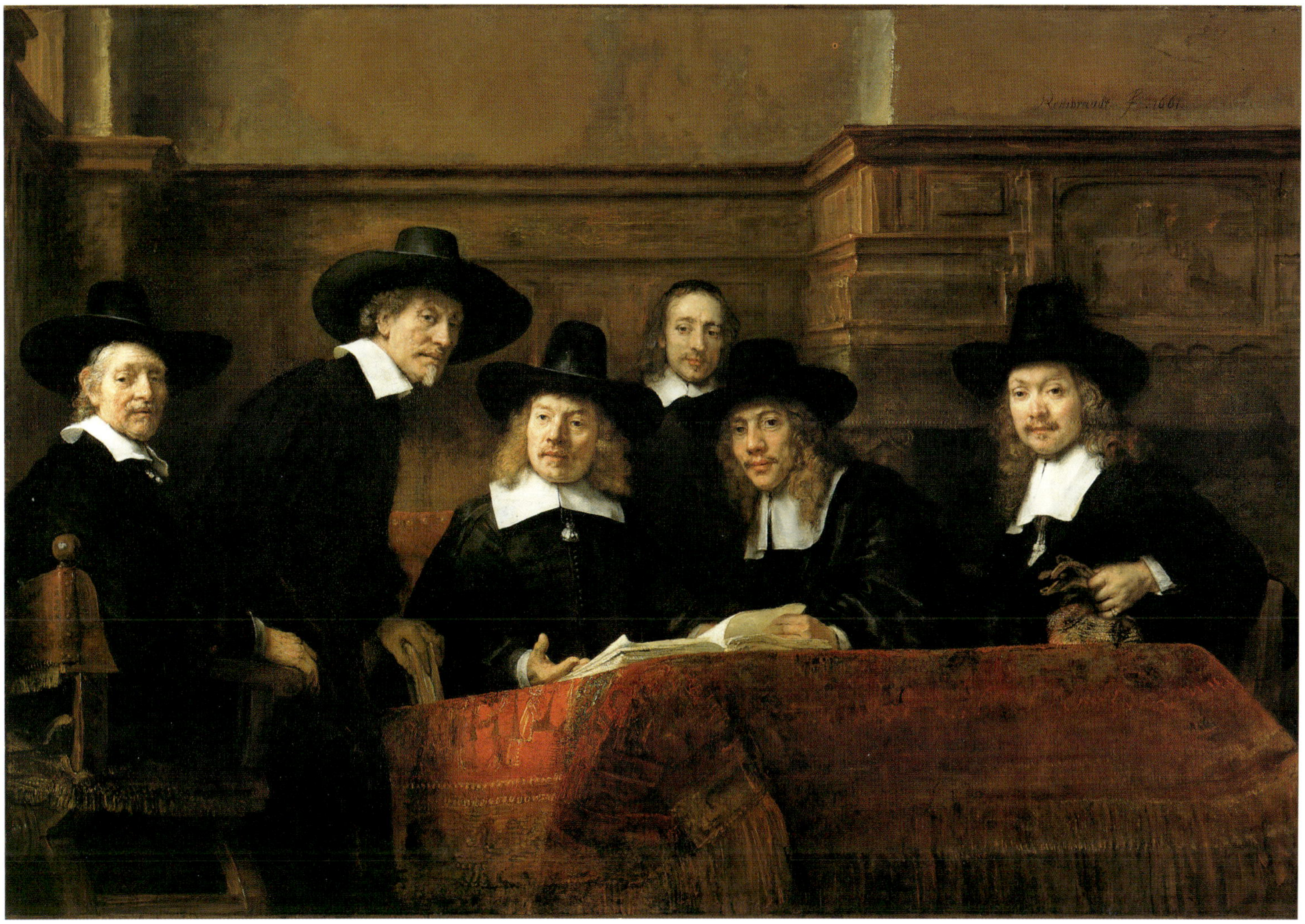

faiths, making *The syndics* an example of the tolerant coexistence that was possible in Amsterdam around 1660.

Rembrandt had trouble arranging the men around the table, and his *tour de force* of lifelike and active men around a table seen from below demanded some manipulation of the perspective. In order to appreciate this it is necessary to realise just how the men are seated. The chairman, the man behind the open book, is sitting on the short side of the table, and the two men on the right are on the long side. However, Rembrandt had great difficulty in finding a satisfactory arrangement for the two men on the left. While working on the picture he made several drawings which illustrate his search for a solution, as does the X-ray photograph of the painting. The rearmost of the two, who is the sole subject of one of the drawings, is on the point of sitting down and joining the meeting. The man in front of him has moved his chair far away from the table in order to give his neighbour room to be seated, and Rembrandt had to make his chair too high in relation to the table in order to allow him to play his full visual part in the scene. Another consequence of this solution was the great prominence given to the rug. Most of it is in shadow, but the foreshortened part, falling over the long side of the table, is fully illuminated and colours the whole painting with its intense tonality.

LITERATURE

Van Schendel 1956; Van de Waal 1956; Van Eeghen 1957; exhib. cat. Berlin/Amsterdam/London 1991-92, no. 48

Rembrandt Harmensz van Rijn (Leiden 1606-Amsterdam 1669)

82 *Isaac and Rebecca ('The Jewish bride'), c. 1665*

Oil on canvas, 121.5 x 166.5 cm
At lower right: *Rembrandt f 16..*
From the Vaillant Collection, Amsterdam (1825); bought from John Smith in 1833 by Adriaan van der Hoop; Van der Hoop Bequest to the City of Amsterdam, 1854; on loan since 1885
Inv. no. SK-C-216

When Adriaan van der Hoop recorded the purchase of this, his latest acquisition, in 1833, he described the subject as 'the Jewish bride'. He probably arrived at this identification on the basis of the woman's loose, jewel-strewn hair, for it is also found in a print by Rembrandt of Esther preparing to enter Ahasuerus's presence, which was already being called *The great Jewish bride* at the beginning of the 18th century. There is also a 'small' Jewish bride, and it seems that those two prints were responsible for many a scene of a richly bejewelled young woman with loose hair by Rembrandt or one of his followers being labelled a 'Jewish bride' from the second half of the 18th century on.

The rather puzzling name of the painting resulted in many different interpretations of the subject, but this was all cleared up when it was restored in 1992/93, for it confirmed the connection between the painting and Rembrandt's drawing of Isaac and Rebecca [*82a*]. The latter illustrates the Old Testament story of Isaac and Rebecca at Gerar in the land of the Philistines, which was ruled by King Abimelech. One day the king looked out of a window and saw Isaac caressing his wife Rebecca, whom he had passed off as his sister (Genesis 26:8).

Rembrandt's pen sketch shows the couple seated on a bench or balustrade on the left, with Abimelech looking out of the window at top right. Rembrandt derived this composition from another famous master, Raphael, who depicted the same story with the aid of his assistants in a fresco on one of the walls in the *Loggie* of the Vatican. A print of the fresco was gathered together with other Old Testament scenes and published in 1607 under the title *Historia del Testamento Vecchio*. This small volume was very popular in the Netherlands, and enabled Rembrandt to familiarise himself with Raphael's invention. X-ray photographs of the painting show that Rembrandt was initially far more faithful to the engraving, for he showed Isaac and Rebecca seated with her right leg over his left leg in a much larger composition. In the initial version Rembrandt had also painted a barred window at top right from which Abimelech spied on the couple. At a certain moment, though, Rembrandt changed his mind completely. He made the couple stand, put them in a slightly different pose and moved them to the centre of the picture, mainly by cutting off a large piece of canvas on the right. The large plant or bush was also made a good deal taller, masking Abimelech's window.

82a Rembrandt van Rijn, *Isaac and Rebecca spied upon by Abimelech*, c. 1655; pen in brown, 14.5 x 18.5 cm. New York, private collection

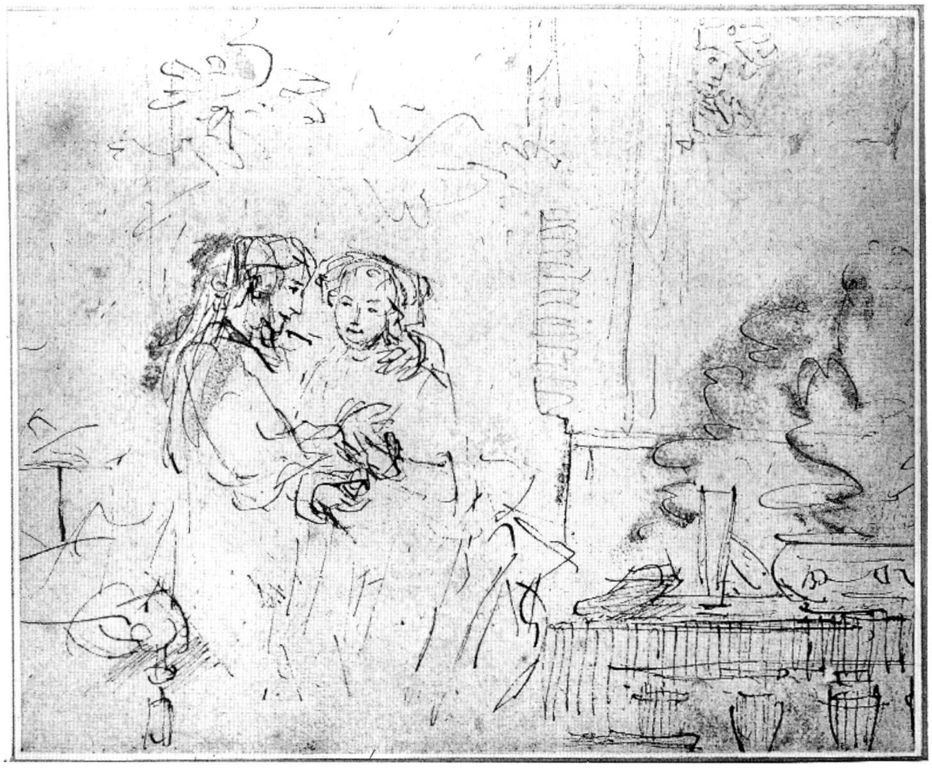

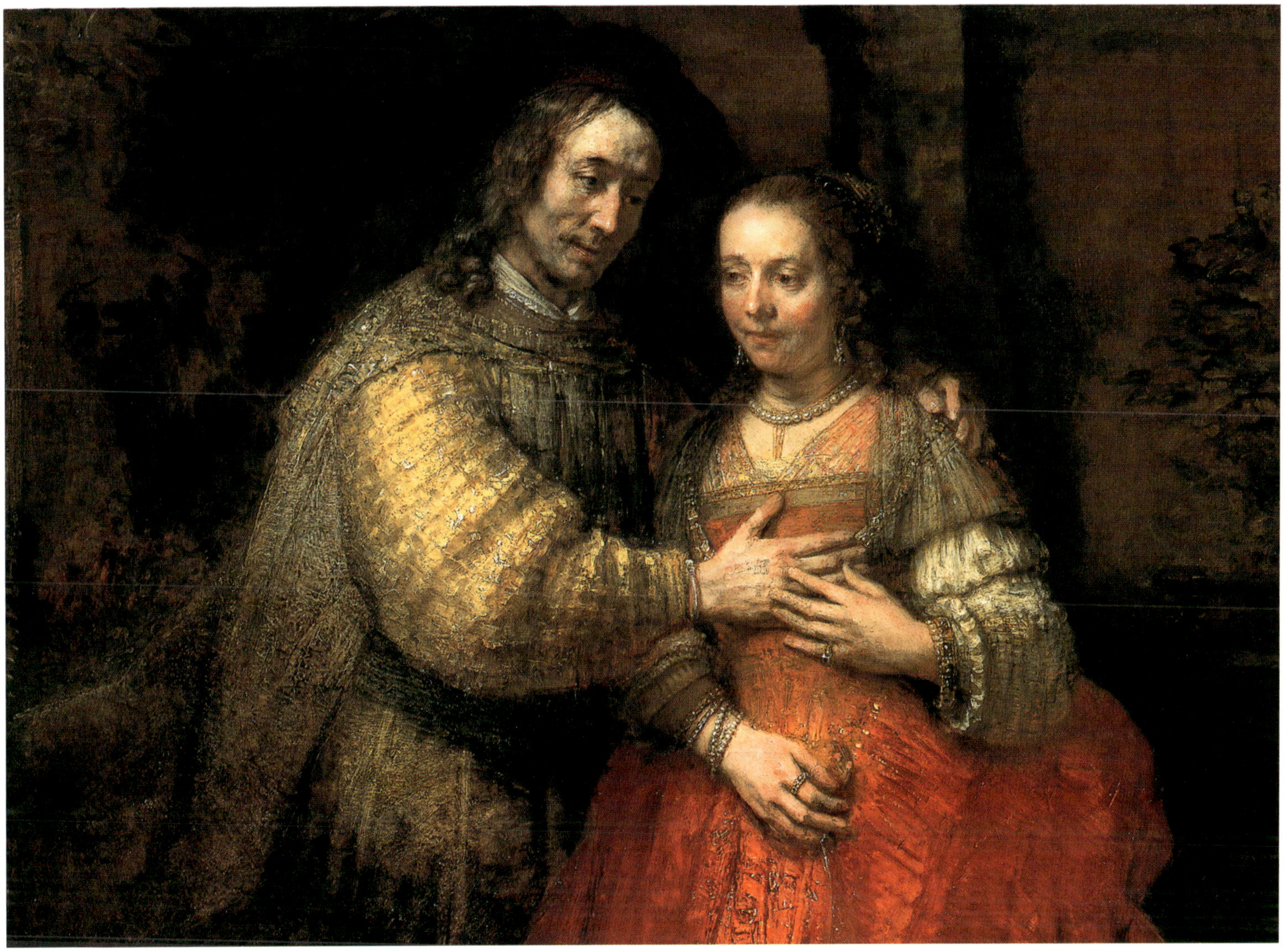

We can only guess as to Rembrandt's reasons for this drastic alteration, but what is taking place in the picture fits in perfectly with the concept of *Herauslösung* (isolation of a figure), a phenomenon often found in his work. It is the practice of lifting one or two principal characters out of their narrative context, sharpening the focus of the subject and redefining it. The story takes on a new psychological depth through this emphasis on the main actors, transforming it into a subject in its own right. In the case of Isaac and Rebecca, Rembrandt eliminated Abimelech's window, left the surroundings vague, and concentrated all the attention on the two main protagonists.

LITERATURE

Haak 1968, pp. 320-322; Van de Wetering 1997, pp. 155-160

Johannes Vermeer (Delft 1632-Delft 1675)

83 *The little street*, c. 1658

Oil on canvas, 54.3 x 44 cm
At lower left, below the window: *i VMeer* (*VM* in ligature)
From the collections of Jacob Dissius, Delft (1696), Gerrit Willem van Oosten de Bruyn, Haarlem (1800), Pieter van Winter, Amsterdam (1807), Lucretia van Winter (Six-van Winter after 1822), Amsterdam (1807-1845), and the Six family, Amsterdam (1845-1921); bought from the Six heirs by Sir Henry Deterding and donated by him to the Rijksmuseum in 1921
Inv. no. SK-A-2860

The little street is a view of part of a town, a rather unusual genre in Johannes Vermeer's oeuvre, which consists largely of virtuoso genre scenes [*see 84*]. Towards the end of the 1650s, however, Vermeer's interests shifted dramatically. This was brought about by the work of Pieter de Hooch, who was also living in Delft at the time. The latter, who was three years Vermeer's senior, began painting genre scenes set outdoors, mostly in courtyards [*83a*], and it looks as if Vermeer painted his *Little street* in creative competition with De Hooch.

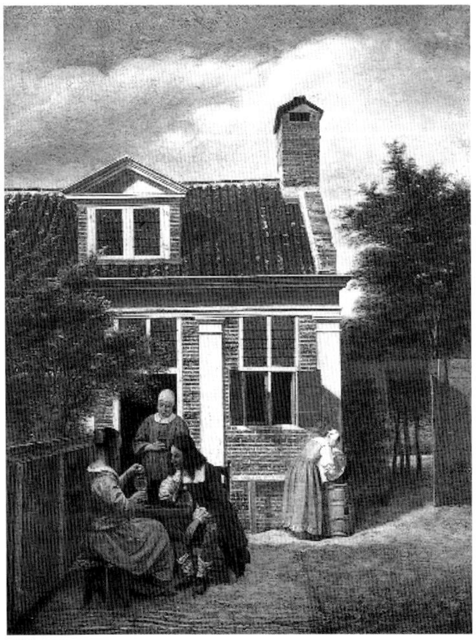

83a Pieter de Hooch, *Three women and a man in the courtyard behind a house*, c. 1665; oil on canvas, 61 x 47 cm. Amsterdam, Rijksmuseum

We are presented with an intimate view of houses with a marvellously illusionistic view down an alleyway. The delightfully light and warm palette is enlivened with touches of bright red, exactly like De Hooch's work. What is most striking though is the very different styles of the two artists. De Hooch's brush tends to be dry and draughtsmanlike, while Vermeer's is very painterly and heavily loaded with pigment. This impasto is particularly noticeable in the thick white paint at lower left, where he signed the painting. And whereas De Hooch appears to have constructed his buildings brick by painstaking brick (although it has to be said that they do look remarkably realistic), Vermeer modelled even more convincingly in an apparently loose and rapid manner. He also used his exceptional pointillist technique for the bricks and the mortar between them, with the astonishing result that he surpasses De Hooch in realism. It is here, perhaps, that the essence of Vermeer's mastery lies: he used the power of suggestion to produce a more convincingly lifelike image than his colleague ever did with his fastidious touch.

The unique naturalism of *The little street* makes it appear that the artist is giving us a random glimpse of part of his home town, which has led to many attempts to identify the houses in the painting. This was undoubtedly encouraged by the earliest known mention of it, for in an Amsterdam auction catalogue of 1696 *The little street* is described as 'A view of a house in Delft'.

But perhaps Vermeer has wrong-footed us with his seemingly photographic realism. He did not simply paint what he saw in front of him. He took a number of liberties in his only other known townscape, the *View of Delft* now in the Mauritshuis in The Hague, and employed various devices to make the image more eloquent. In other words, he often twisted reality to suit his own ends, as was pointed out long ago in connection with his interior scenes. In this he was no different from De Hooch, whose courtyards are not faithful representations of an everyday reality. Pursuing the analogy with Pieter de Hooch, there is no reason to expect Vermeer's *Little street* to be topographically accurate. That is why no one has yet come up with a convincing identification of the houses. What we see is nothing more than a fantasy based on reality.

LITERATURE

Blankert 1975, no. 9; exhib. cat. Washington/The Hague 1995-96, no. 4

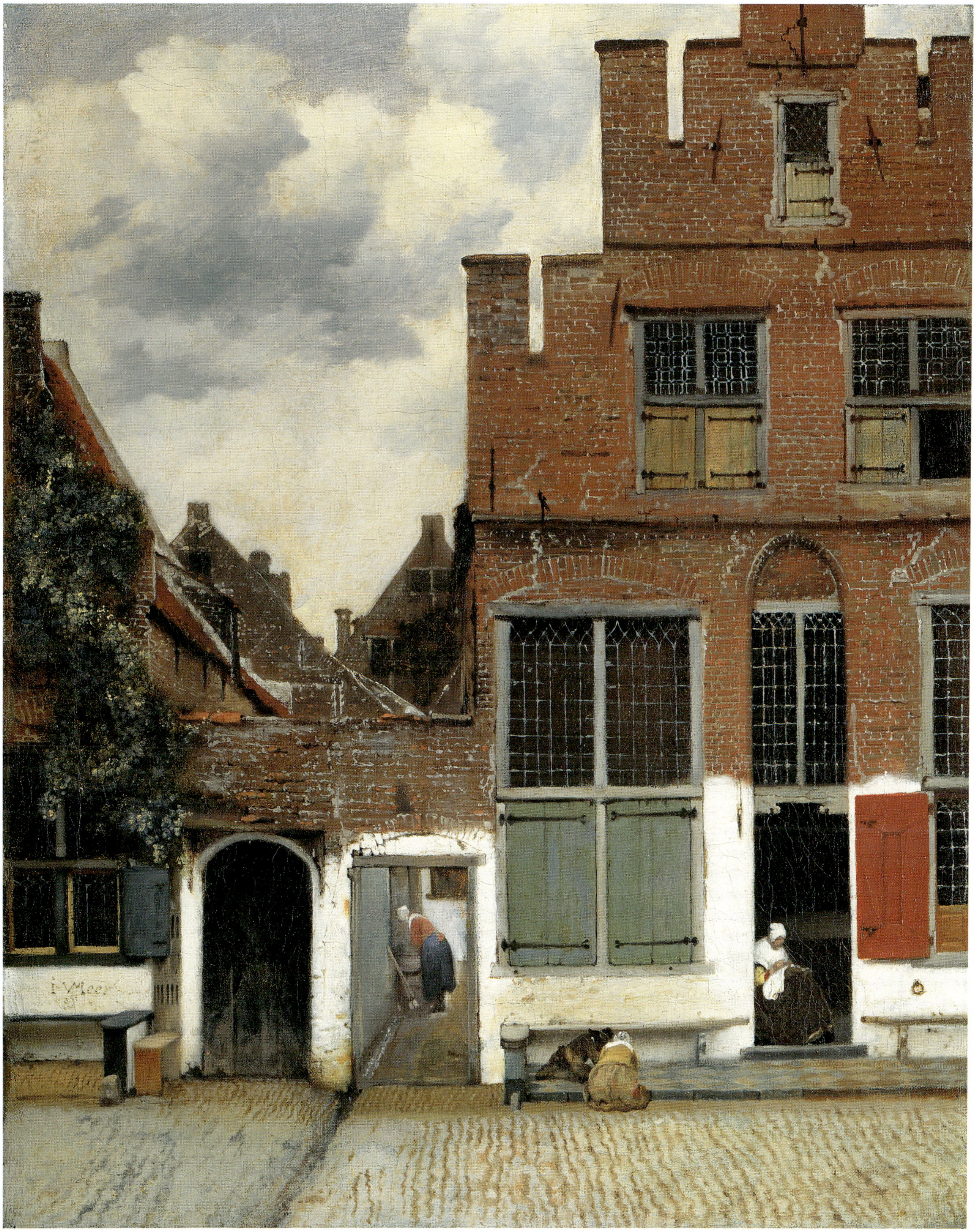

Johannes Vermeer (Delft 1632-Delft 1675)

84 *The kitchen maid*, c. 1658-1660

Oil on canvas, 45.5 x 41 cm
From the collections of Jacob Dissius, Delft (1696), Leendert Pieter de Neufville, Amsterdam (1765), Jan Jacob de Bruyn, Amsterdam (1798), Hendrik Muilman, Amsterdam (1813), Lucretia van Winter (Six-van Winter after 1822), Amsterdam (1813-1845) and the Six family, Amsterdam (1845-1905); bought from the heirs of Six van Vromade with the aid of the Vereniging Rembrandt, 1908
Inv. no. SK-A-2344

Few paintings depict 'frozen motion' so emphatically as this one. A stream of milk is being poured carefully from a jug into a bowl by the strapping young woman who stands as still as a statue. One great strength of the subject is its verisimilitude. If you are pouring something you have to stand still, you have to concentrate. In real life the controlled stream of liquid also appears immobile for a moment. The 'probable movement' in this picture stands in sharp contrast to paintings of people in motion, of action which appears to have been brought to a standstill at a random moment. We still experience the movement in Rembrandt's *Night watch* as natural, even though the group will never march off in orderly ranks. There are also paintings in which the 'frozen motion' is almost laughable, like the *Overturned bouquet* by Abraham Mignon in the Rijksmuseum, in which a cat knocks over a vase in its pursuit of a mouse. The vase is always toppling, the water spills for ever, and the cat is perpetually startled by the minor disaster it has caused. One of the great qualities of Vermeer's *Kitchen maid* is the tension between movement and concentrated composure.

Few paintings conjure up such a strong association with photography, precisely because of the frozen motion, and there is probably good reason to make that connection. In Delft, where Johannes Vermeer worked, there was extensive knowledge of optical instruments, and it has been suggested more than once that Delft painters made use of the camera obscura, a box with a tiny hole at one end through which the image of an outside scene was projected onto a piece of rectangular glass mounted in the box [*see also 16*]. The camera obscura was one of the developments that eventually led to the photographic camera. Delft artists may have found that it helped them 'see' their subjects. In this way Vermeer may have noticed the reflections of light, such as those on the maid's head and the delicate highlights playing along the top of the wicker bread-basket and the edges of the earthenware. It might also have helped him decide how to select his view of the interior. If in fact he used the camera obscura he might have had some such unexpected insight when preparing *The love letter* [*84a*]. The glass in the box would have shown him not just the young woman with the lute and the maidservant, but also the door frame, the curtain and the chair, intriguing him with the visual tension between them. It is likely that something similar occurred when he conceived *The kitchen maid*. This can be deduced from the odd shape of the table, which appears to have five sides. What probably happened is that, as in a photograph, the table stuck out too far, forcing Vermeer to truncate one corner in such a way that the viewer would not instantly be puzzled by the shape. He would have encountered the same problem when using central perspective, but had he had done so he would not have been so quick to choose this subject. As it happens, the pricked hole marking the vanishing point has now been discovered, but that does not necessarily invalidate the suggestion that he might have shaped his ideas about painting with a camera obscura. Even if he used it he would still have needed the framework of central perspective to order his observations on the canvas.

84a Johannes Vermeer, *The love letter*, c. 1668; oil on canvas, 44 x 38.5 cm. Amsterdam, Rijksmuseum

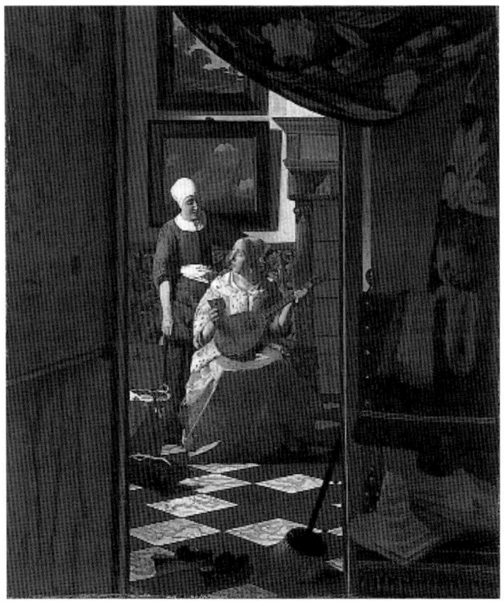

LITERATURE
Blankert 1975, no. 7; exhib. cat. Washington/The Hague 1995-96, no. 5

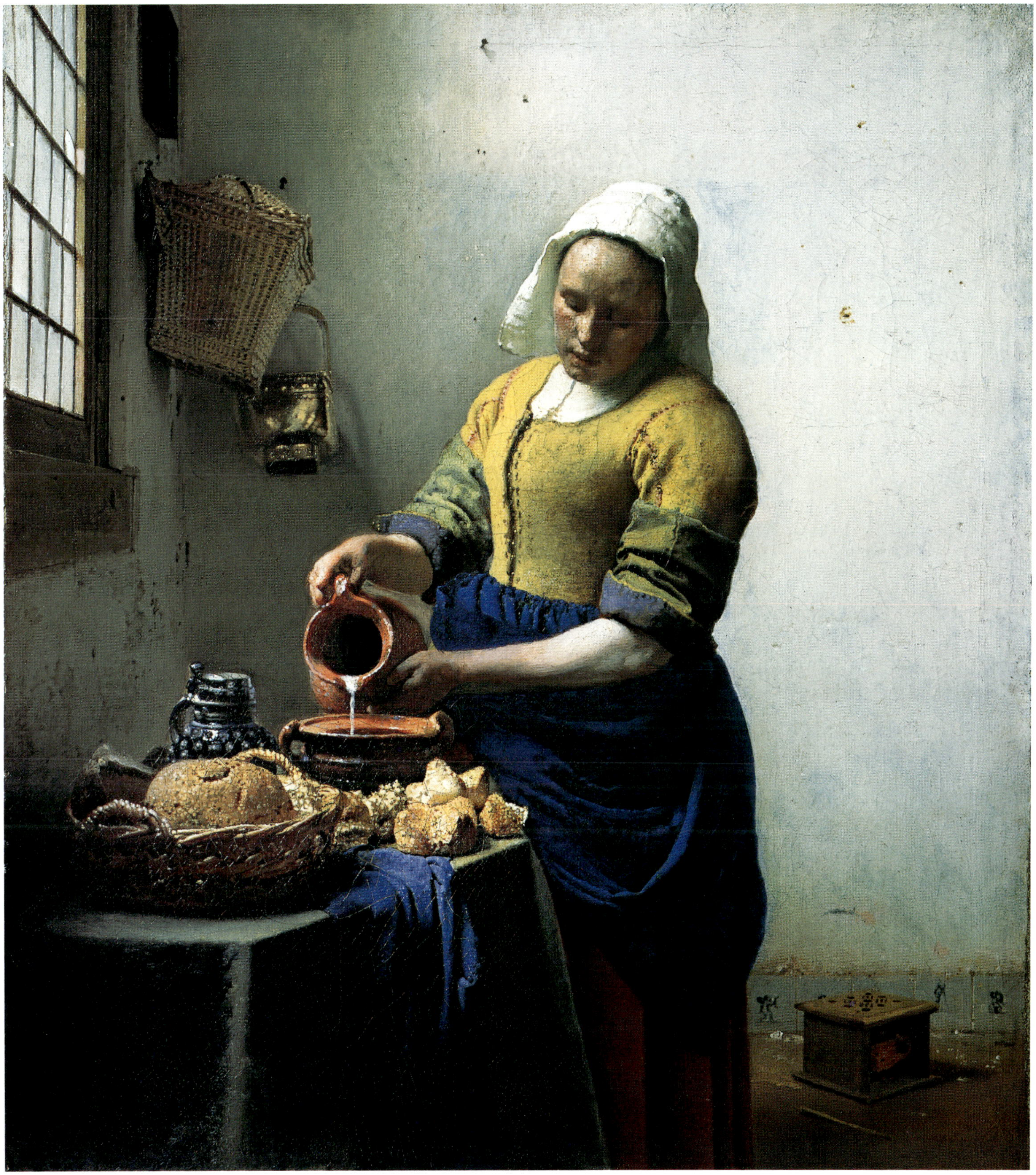

Pieter de Hooch (Rotterdam 1629-Amsterdam 1684)

85 *Interior with women by a linen cupboard, 1663*

Oil on canvas, 70 x 75.5 cm
On the stairs: *P D HOOCH/1663*
From the collections of Baron Lockhorst, Rotterdam (1726), Johannes Rendorp, Amsterdam (1794), and the family of Jan Six, Amsterdam (1833-1928); purchased by the Vereniging Rembrandt for the City of Amsterdam; on loan to the Rijksmuseum since 1928
Inv. no. SK-C-1191

Pieter de Hooch, who started his career in Delft, began by painting soldiers playing cards and drinking in rather shabby interiors. After the mid-1650s, he exchanged those cluttered barrack-rooms for the meticulously depicted homes of the prosperous burgher class. From then on his pictures generally show the interiors or courtyards of the canalside mansions which he could see all around him in Delft and later in Amsterdam, to which he moved around 1660. The perspective view is usually carefully constructed, and there is often a vista leading the gaze through several rooms at once. The question is whether those houses actually existed, and whether the artist always painted real interiors and courtyards.

A typical example of De Hooch's work is this *Interior with women by a linen cupboard*, which offers the viewer rather more than an interior depicted in strict accordance with the laws of perspective. It also shows that De Hooch could make his vistas more convincing by allowing the fall of light to contribute to the atmospheric sense of depth in a painting. The foreground is lit by warm sunlight, which bathes the first room in a gentle glow. The antechamber or hall, on the other hand, has the cool light of a room situated on the shadowed side of the house, while the house across the canal visible through the open door in the background is in bright sunshine. The artist also allowed light to fall down the staircase, although this reveals how artificial the scene is, for this seems a highly illogical place to find daylight. However, without it this corner of the room would be far too dark, so the artist took the liberty of suspending reality for a moment.

Just as orderly as the distribution of light over the various rooms is the arrangement of the figures within the scene. Their actions are blameless, although it does seem that the little boy has been allowed to disturb the peace of this well-tended room by playing the ball-game *kolf* without fear of a reprimand. The domesticity of the scene is epitomised by the way in which the woman is taking the neatly folded linen from the patient maidservant and putting it away in the magnificent linen cupboard.

However beautiful De Hooch's painting is, the inevitable comparison with Johannes Vermeer puts him in the shade. Both painted comparable scenes, but Vermeer permeated his with an indefinable, hushed mood, while those by De Hooch generally suffer under a surfeit of anecdote. In addition, his figures are often more wooden, as they are in this picture, so that they could be described diplomatically as mirroring too faithfully the 'rectilinear' nature of the scene. All the same, works by the two artists were often confused in the 19th century, with the English connoisseur and art dealer John Smith suggesting in 1833 that the then relatively unknown Vermeer may well have been a pupil of De Hooch's. Given that the two of them tackled the same pictorial problems at more or less the same time, it must have been more a question of each influencing the other.

LITERATURE
Cat. Amsterdam 1976, p. 287; Sutton 1980, no. 52; exhib. cat. Delft 1996, pp. 154-155

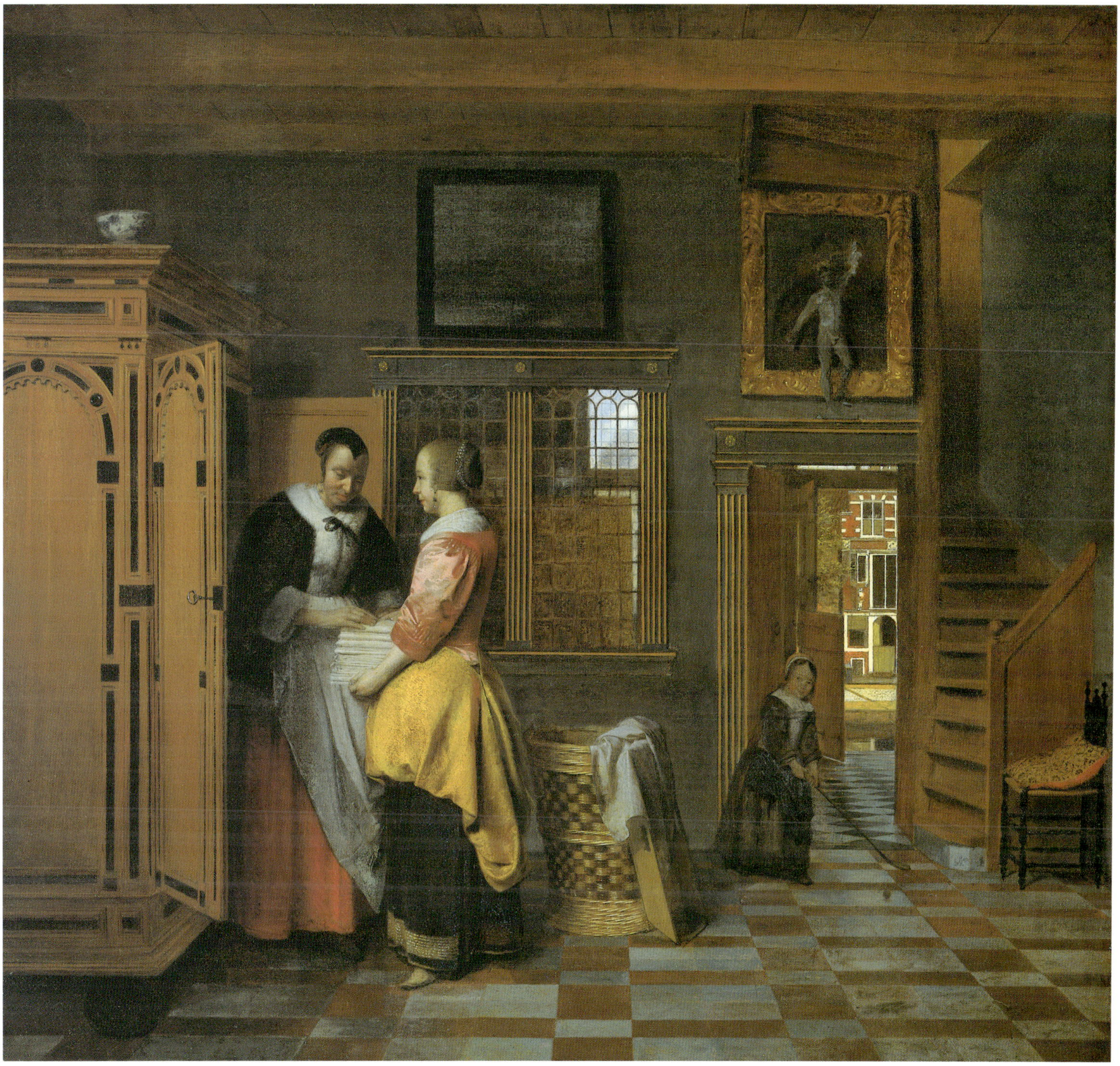

Ambrosius van Swol (active in Utrecht c. 1640-1680), attributed to

86 *The rat-catcher, c. 1660*

Boxwood, h. 30,5 cm
On top of the plinth, at the front: *A.V.S.*
Purchased in 1876 by the Nederlandsch Museum voor Geschiedenis en Kunst in The Hague; in the Rijksmuseum since 1885
Inv. no. BK-NM-2926

Judging by the number of works that have survived, *Kleinplastik* must have enjoyed something of a heyday in 17th-century Holland, yet only a few of the names of the makers of cabinet sculpture are known. Among the ranks of the wood-carvers were a number of very talented artists who produced beautiful frames for paintings and mirrors, as well as carved work on furniture and church furnishings. A few of them also made small, individual scenes for art cabinets. One of the most prominent was Albert Vinckenbrinck of Amsterdam, quite a few of whose surviving reliefs and free-standing figures survive. His *magnum opus* is the ornate pulpit of 1649 in the Nieuwe Kerk in Amsterdam. This boxwood figure of a rat-catcher and his young assistant has also been attributed to him, but that is now disputed.

The subject typifies the Dutch love of genre scenes. Similar rat-catchers are found in prints by Rembrandt, Joris van Vliet and Cornelis Visscher. They were probably a familiar sight in the cities of the day, and on the evidence of his unusual garb this particular one might come from eastern Europe. The small group appears to have been inspired by Rembrandt's etching of 1632 (B. 121), which also shows a rat-catcher and a young assistant in a similar arrangement and poses [*86a*].

The piece is monogrammed *A.V.S.* and bears the coats of arms of the cities of Utrecht and Amersfoort. For a long time the monogram was interpreted as an abbreviation of 'Albert Vinckenbrinck Sculpsit', although later it was suggested that it belonged to Albert's son Abraham. Both readings are dubious, because Vinckenbrinck the Elder invariably signed with the monogram ALVB, while his son is not known to have used a monogram. In fact, the high quality of the small group actually militates against an attribution to Vinckenbrinck, because he was not very good at carving figures.

The recent rediscovery of the wood-carver Ambrosius van Swol, whose activity is documented between 1643 and 1679, provided a good candidate for the Monogrammist A.V.S. Van Swol worked in Utrecht, the coat of arms of which is on the base of the group. He must have had something of a reputation in his day, for an inventory of 1669 speaks of 'a celebrated sculptor called Ambrosius' in connection with a carved and gilt picture frame which still survives and provides the best evidence of his skill. That Van Swol could also carve figures emerges from the mention of 'The five senses, and eight pieces of the same with pleasing little men and women, fashioned by Master Ambrosius' in the collection of Petronella Oortmans-de la Court, a wealthy merchant's widow. The fact that Van Swol's work was in this famous art cabinet, along with the ivory *Mars* by Van Bossuit [*103*] is yet another indication of the reputation he had back in the 17th century.

LITERATURE
Cat. Amsterdam 1973, no. 251; Bok 1991; Bok 1996; exhib. cat. Amsterdam 1997, no. 66

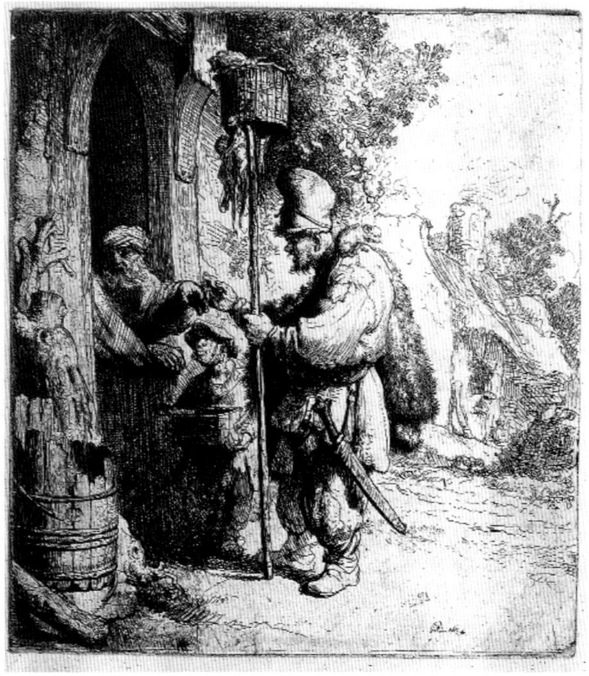

86a Rembrandt, *The rat-catcher*, 1632; etching, 13.9 x 12.4 cm. Amsterdam, Rijksmuseum, Rijksprentenkabinet

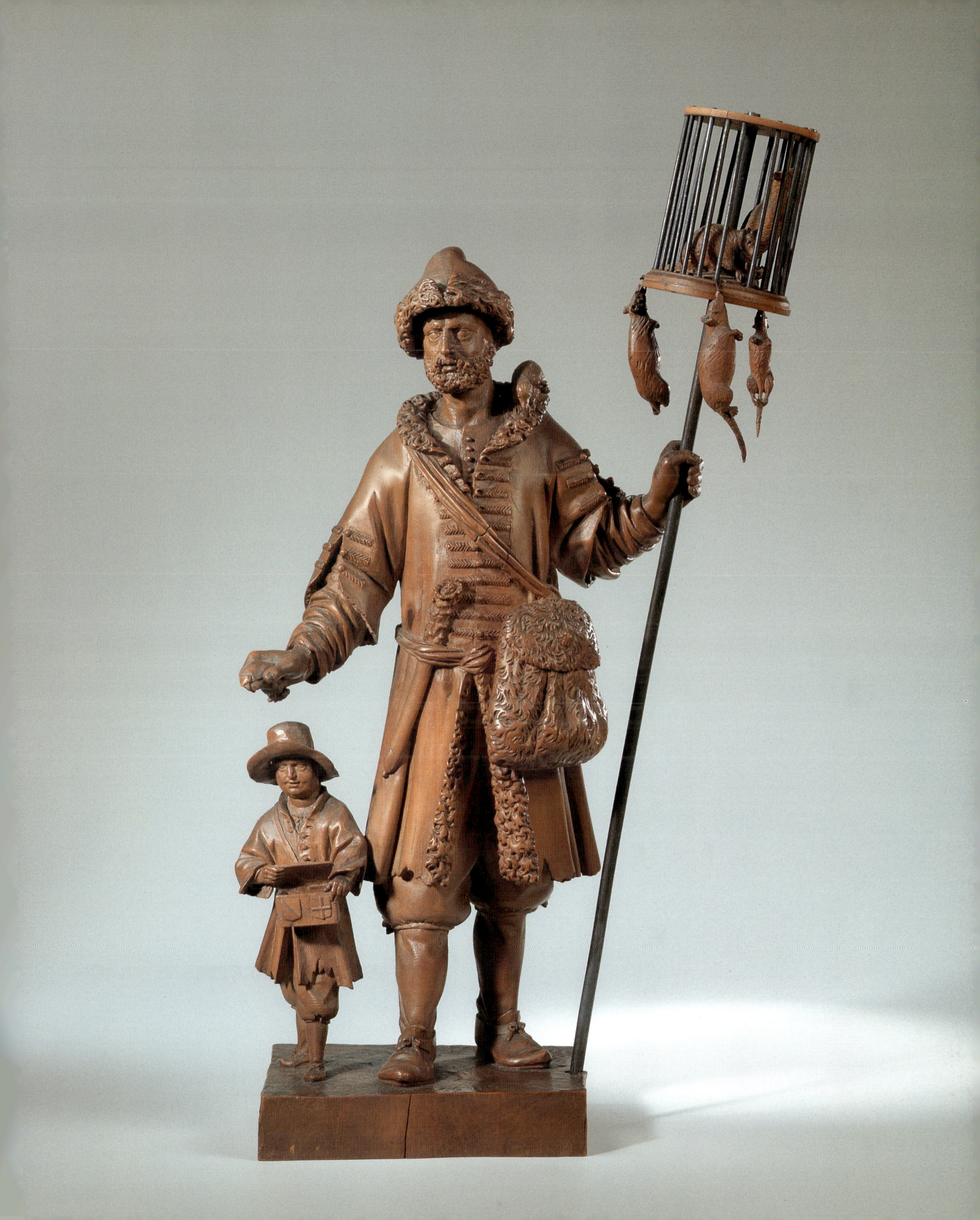

Pieter Xaverij (Antwerp 1647-Leiden c. 1680)

87 *Two laughing jesters, 1673*

Terracotta, h. 45 cm
On the front of the plinth: P.R. *XAVERI INVE 1673*
Purchased in 1882 by the Nederlandsch Museum voor Geschiedenis en Kunst in The Hague; in the Rijksmuseum since 1885
Inv. no. BK-NM-5667

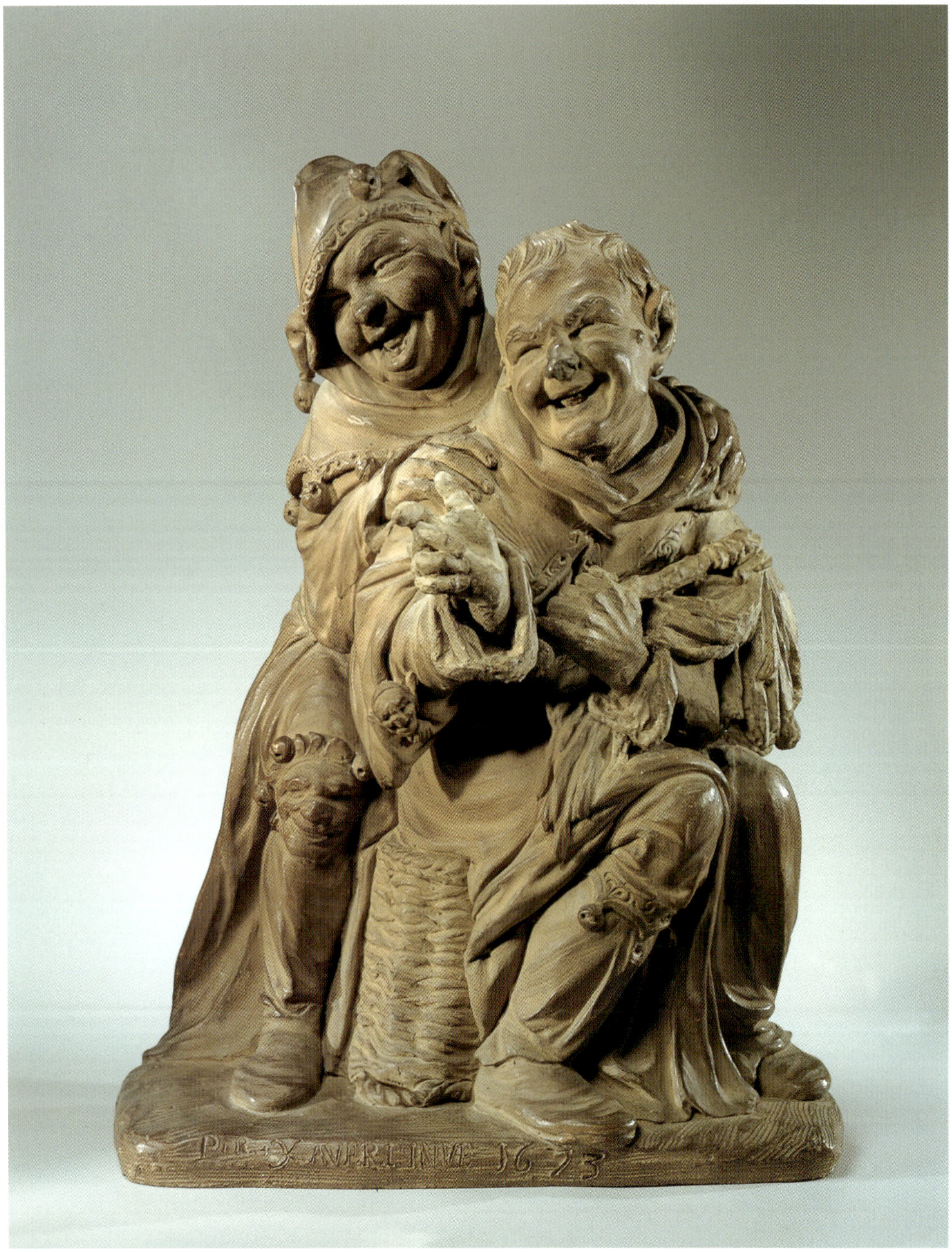

Modelling in clay was not a genre much practised in the 17th-century Netherlands. Sculptors generally did so during the preparations for a statue in stone or bronze, and although collectors were interested in such models in fired clay or terracotta they were generally not made for sale. However, there was one sculptor who is a notable exception to this rule, and that was Pieter Xaverij, who worked almost exclusively in clay. In the short time that he was active in Leiden he made a number of terracotta statues which were expressly intended as true cabinet sculptures.

Xaverij came from Antwerp and probably settled in Leiden shortly before 1670, the year in which he is first recorded there. In June he enrolled as a student of mathematics at Leiden University, and in November he married a woman from the city. The year 1670 was also the date of his earliest known statue, a terracotta figure of King David. He is last mentioned in Leiden in 1674. All his known works are dated in the period 1670-1673. It is not clear whether he was a professional sculptor or a student who made statuettes as a sideline in order to supplement his income.

Some of Xaverij's small terracottas depict crafts, although it is not always clear precisely which ones. He also made several mythological and biblical scenes which clearly betray his Flemish origins. A group of bacchantes, in particular, could have walked straight out of a work by Rubens. What is remarkable and innovative is Xaverij's tendency to make ensembles from three or more individual pieces which together form a single composition.

Another part of his oeuvre consists of comic or farcical genre scenes which are clearly designed to play on the viewer's emotions. It is likely that he was inspired in his choice of subjects by stage plays or Dutch painting and printmaking, in which genre scenes abounded, although no direct models for his compositions have yet been identified.

The *Two laughing jesters* belongs in this humorous category. It shows two seated 'buffoons' who appear to be speaking directly to the viewer. Their garish attire, complete with fool's caps, bells on their trouser-legs and a fool's staff stuffed up a sleeve, unmistakably identify them as scoffers from the topsy-turvy world with a licence to poke fun at all and sundry. Jesters in art often play the part of the revealer of truths, not seldom in situations with erotic overtones. It is not known who or what these two jesters are mocking with their provocative gestures. It is possible that the group was originally one of a pair, although as early as 1771 it was in a Leiden collection as a self-contained work. Perhaps Xaverij intended the viewers to be the targets of the jesters' ridicule, and it would have been up to them to decide which mirror was being held up to their faces.

LITERATURE
Staring 1927, no. 4; cat. Amsterdam 1973, no. 327

Frederik van Frytom (? c. 1630-Delft 1702), attributed to

88 *Dish with a landscape, c. 1680*

Faience painted blue in the glaze, ø 39 cm
On loan from Eugène Albert Garnier-Heldewier from 1877; purchased from his estate in 1962
Inv. no. BK-NM-3310

This hallmark piece had been in the Rijksmuseum on loan for almost a century when it was finally purchased in 1962. In 1877 the Belgian owner, Eugène Albert Garnier-Heldewier, evidently felt that it deserved to go on public display in the Netherlands. Objects from the second half of the 17th century with such a delicate European style of decoration were regarded even then as the finest and most desirable products of Delft faience ware.

That industry went through a period of explosive growth after 1650, not just in the number of factories but also in their size, and a considerable division of labour was introduced within the larger ones. It was the painters who gave the pieces their distinctive appearance, so they probably had

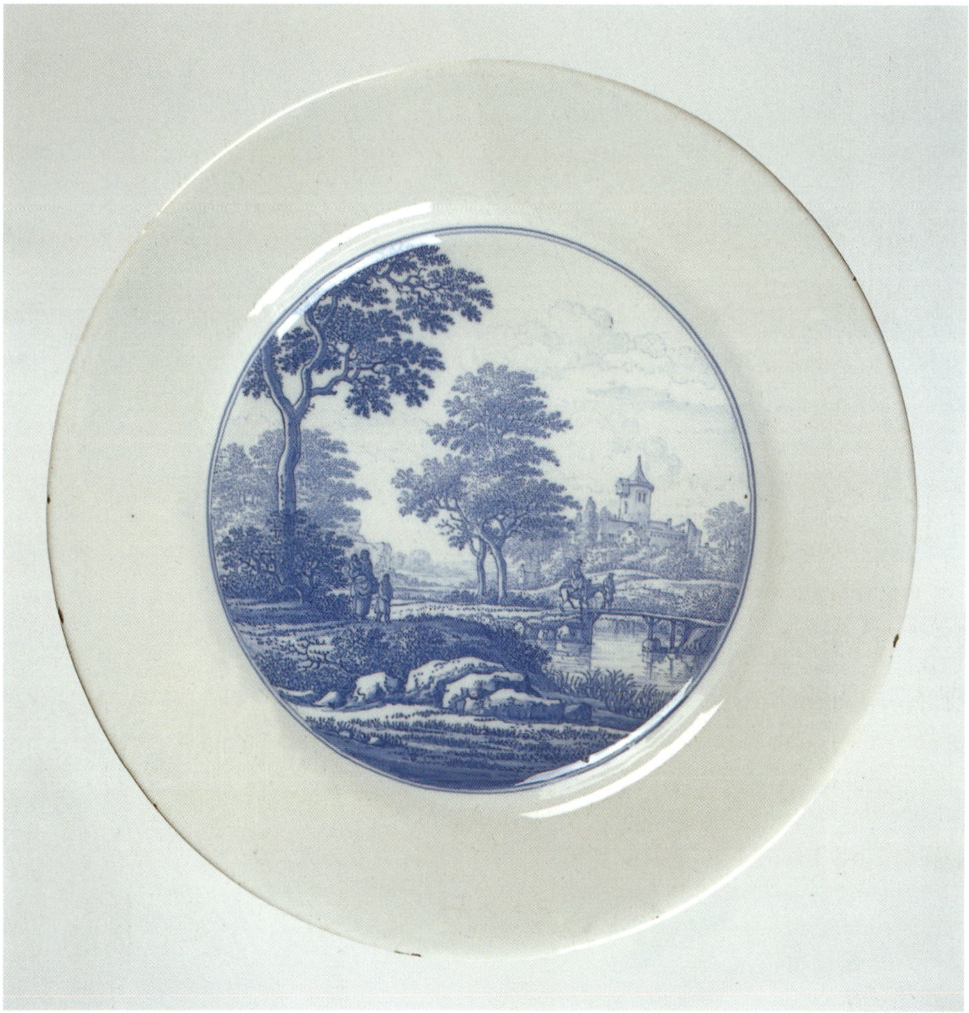

the greatest standing, although very little is known about their training, the opportunities they had to stamp their own personality on the painted work within the constraints of the craft, or, for instance, who supplied the designs and who then made the sponge for pouncing. The vast majority of faience painters have remained anonymous, no matter how important they were in the production process, with the result that most delftware can at best only be attributed to a particular factory.

The Guild of St Luke, to which all the owners of the faience factories belonged along with many of their employees, had drawn up strict rules designed above all to guarantee the high quality of the products. For example, everyone was obliged to work in the factory, and the painters were forbidden to work at home, presumably to prevent them moonlighting.

There were, of course, exceptions to this rule, and ironically this allowed one painter, Frederik van Frytom, to escape anonymity. It is not known where or precisely when he was born, but he married in Delft in 1652, which would put his age around 20. He never joined the guild, and probably worked independently for different faience producers. He occupied the post of 'guild servant' for a few years towards the end of his life, so the fact that he worked from home, outside the jurisdiction of the guild, was presumably not held against him.

Van Frytom signed the occasional special piece of delftware, enabling us to form some idea of his style. A group of plates, dishes and plaques has been attributed to him on the basis of his distinctive technique and 'handwriting'. He used the white ground of this dish in a very special way by setting down this broad, hilly landscape in delicate outlines with different shades of blue, and above all with thousands of minuscule dots. He gave the scene a superb sense of depth by painting the hills on the horizon with a very pale blue which almost fades into the background. In doing so, Van Frytom raised the craft of faience decoration to new heights.

LITERATURE

Vecht 1968, p. 64

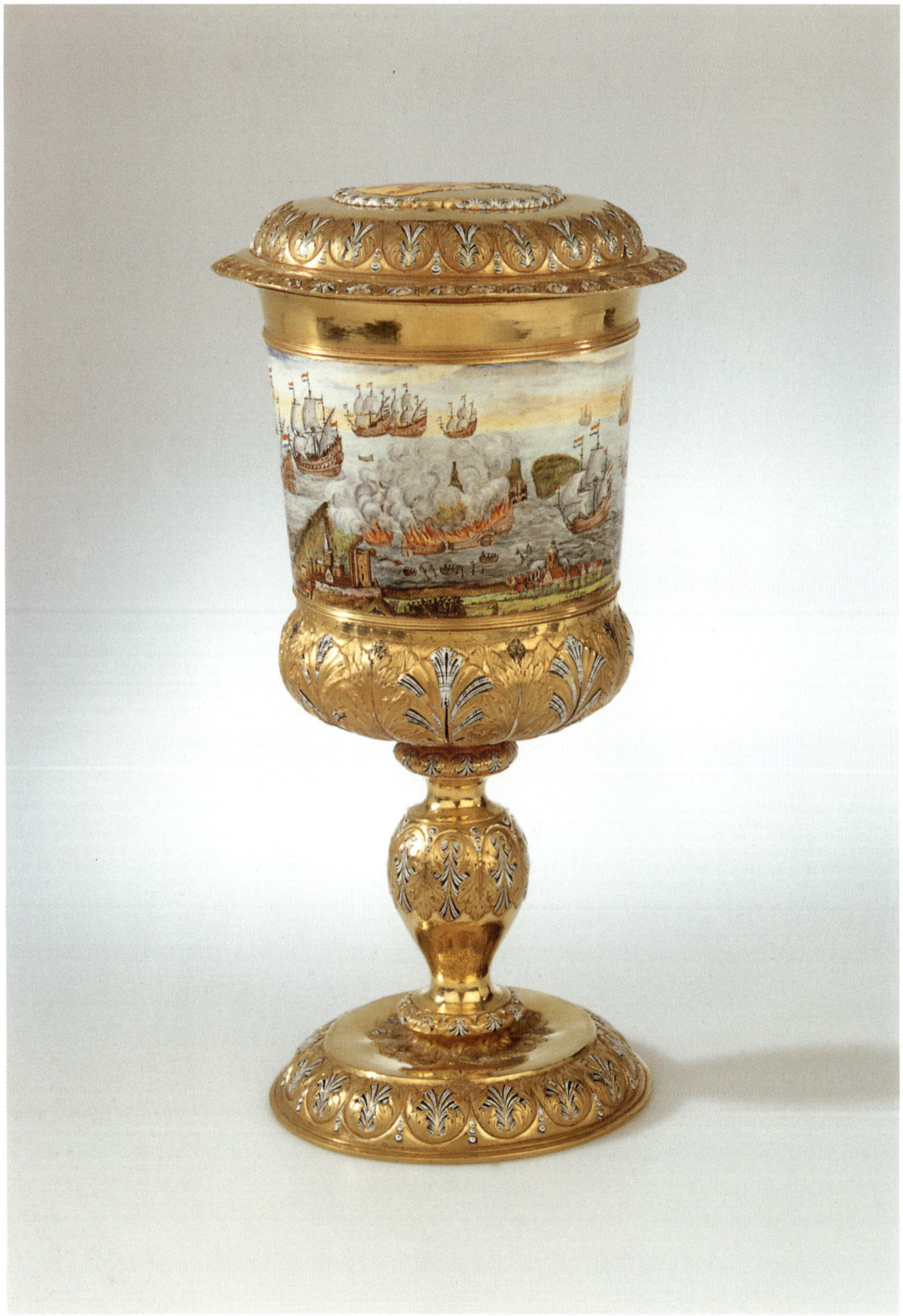

Nicolaas Loockemans (?-The Hague 1673)

89 *Covered goblet, 1667*

Gold and enamel, h. 30 cm, ø 15 cm
Marked on the bowl with the Hague assay office mark of the Dutch lion, the year letter Q (1668), and the maker's mark of a crowned anchor (Nicolaas Loockemans)
Made for the States assembly of the province of Holland, which presented it to Admiral Michiel Adriaansz de Ruyter on 7 November 1667; Von der Goltz Bequest, 1893
Inv. no. NG-NM-9659

On 7 November 1667, the Dordrecht regent Cornelis de Witt presented this goblet to Michiel de Ruyter during a banquet to honour the admiral for his daring and successful raid on the English naval base at Chatham, which was decisive in turning the tide of the Second Anglo-Dutch War of 1665-1667 in the Republic's favour. Two other people who had sailed with De Ruyter also received goblets. One was Cornelis de Witt himself, who accompanied the expedition as the representative of the States of Holland, and Lieutenant-Admiral Willem Joseph van Gendt, who was De Ruyter's second-in-command. The first of those two goblets is now in the Louvre, while the second is lost.

The commission for all three went to Nicolaas Loockemans, a Hague goldsmith whose maker's mark is stamped on the two surviving specimens. He was paid 1,000 Flemish pounds, equivalent to 6,000 guilders. The enamelling was probably assigned to a specialist, as yet unidentified.

The historical events are depicted in an unbroken series in multicoloured enamel around the conical body of the goblet. The sequence begins with 'Fort Shirenasse'. Sheerness on the Isle of Sheppey in the Thames estuary was bombarded by the Dutch and captured, and the Dutch flag can be seen flying within its walls. On the left is the town of 'Queenborow' (Queensborough) with De Ruyter's fleet off the coast. One of his ships is on the point of cutting the chain stretched between a small island in the river Medway and the mainland near the town of 'Chettam' (Chatham), beside which a number of English ships are going up in flames. The panorama ends with the town of 'Rochester' [*89a*].

The States' decision to honour De Ruyter with this gift and its reasons for doing so are recorded in an inscription on the inside of the bowl. In translation it reads: 'Compendious extract, 2 July 1667. The States [of Holland] approves the proposal of the delegates that Lieutenant-Admiral De Ruyter, having commanded the nation's fleet during and pertaining to the famous exploit of the 21st, 22nd and 23rd of July on the rivers of London and Rochester, shall be presented with a gold goblet on which the aforesaid exploit is to be limned, that it be a memorial in his family and for posterity. Corresponds in essence with the resolution of the States. Herbert van Beaumont'.

So the scenes on the body of the goblet were intended to keep alive the memory of the historic victory over the English fleet, and when the goblet was presented to De Ruyter it was thus suggested that it was a matter of commemoration and honour. Another very important factor was the pecuniary value of the gift, which was made of gold, the most costly of the precious metals. Handing over money to a high-ranking official was considered dishonourable and was therefore camouflaged. It was for that reason that individuals who had served the Republic with distinction were often rewarded with objects made of gold and silver by bodies like the States-General, the Admiralty, the Dutch East India Company and, as in this case, by the States assembly of one of the provinces. Those objects could always be melted down and turned into hard cash, if need be.

LITERATURE
Cat. Amsterdam 1952b, no. 161; exhib. cat. Amsterdam/Vlissingen 1957, no. 181; exhib. cat. The Hague 1967, no. 56

89a Daniel Veelwaard after Abraham Teerlink, *Copy of the scene on the goblet presented to Cornelis de Witt by the States of Holland*, c. 1800; engraving, 24.8 x 48 cm. Amsterdam, Rijksmuseum, Rijksprentenkabinet

Willem van de Velde the Elder (Leiden c. 1611-London 1693)

90 *The Battle of Livorno, c. 1654*

Pen and ink on a white prepared ground, 114 x 160 cm
On a floating barrel at lower right: *W.V. Velde*
From the Tromp family; purchased for the State Archives, c. 1863; transferred to the Nederlandsch Museum voor Geschiedenis en Kunst, The Hague, in 1875; in the Rijksmuseum since 1885
Inv. no. SK-A-1364

Willem van de Velde the Elder, whose son Willem the Younger was the finest Dutch marine painter of the 17th century, specialised in pen paintings—scenes drawn with the pen on a support prepared with a white ground. In his early years he drew naval battles and ship portraits with the pen on vellum. When he began to find that support too cramped he developed a similar technique for canvas and panel, producing works which most closely resemble paintings in black and white, with the difference that they were done not with a brush but with the pen alone. He was particularly sought after by senior naval officers keen to have a memento of a victory at sea, and by government bodies looking for gifts for admirals who had distinguished themselves in battle.

This particular work was probably ordered by Cornelis Tromp, son of the famous admiral Maarten Harpertsz Tromp [*see* 45]. Cornelis was an irascible man who was never happier than when in the thick of battle, and like his father he became a celebrated admiral. Although only a captain at the time, he played a key role in the Battle of Livorno (1653) during the First Anglo-Dutch War. His ship was moored in Livorno harbour as part of the Dutch fleet. It had been captured from the English shortly before, and one evening when the crew was ashore the English boarded and retook it, humiliating Tromp in the process. This was a violation of the neutrality of the Tuscan port, and the English were forced to put to sea. The Dutch, under the command of Jan van Galen, saw their opportunity and defeated the English fleet before reinforcements could arrive. Admiral Van Galen was killed in the battle, and Cornelis Tromp, who had fought where the action was fiercest in his new ship the *Halve Maan*, claimed the victory as his.

The young Tromp probably had this painting made on his return to the Netherlands, telling Van de Velde all about the battle and asking for the *Halve Maan* be shown in the centre of the fray. Although the facts about the Battle of Livorno are pretty straightforward, it is depicted here from the viewpoint of just one of the combatants. The victory gave the Dutch mastery of the Mediterranean for a while, thus safeguarding their trade with the Near East. A painting of the same subject by Reinier Nooms [*90a*] was made as an overmantel for the Amsterdam chamber of the Levant Trade, as it was called, and the focus there is on the political and economic consequences of the battle.

Van de Velde's pen painting is in a frame of ebony veneer with gilt appliqués. In a cartouche at the bottom are figures and letters identifying the ships. At the top of the frame is the coat of arms awarded to Maarten Tromp after the Battle of the Downs in 1639, which was later borne by Cornelis. Three other paintings in the Rijksmuseum, also once owned by the Tromp family, have frames with similar decoration. All three are of sea battles in which Maarten Tromp took part, among them the Battle of Scheveningen of 1653, at which he was killed. Although that painting was executed in 1657, and those of the battles of Dunkirk and the Downs in 1659, years after the events, it is likely that this undated *Battle of Livorno* was made in or very shortly after 1653. The other three can be regarded as works commemorating Maarten Tromp.

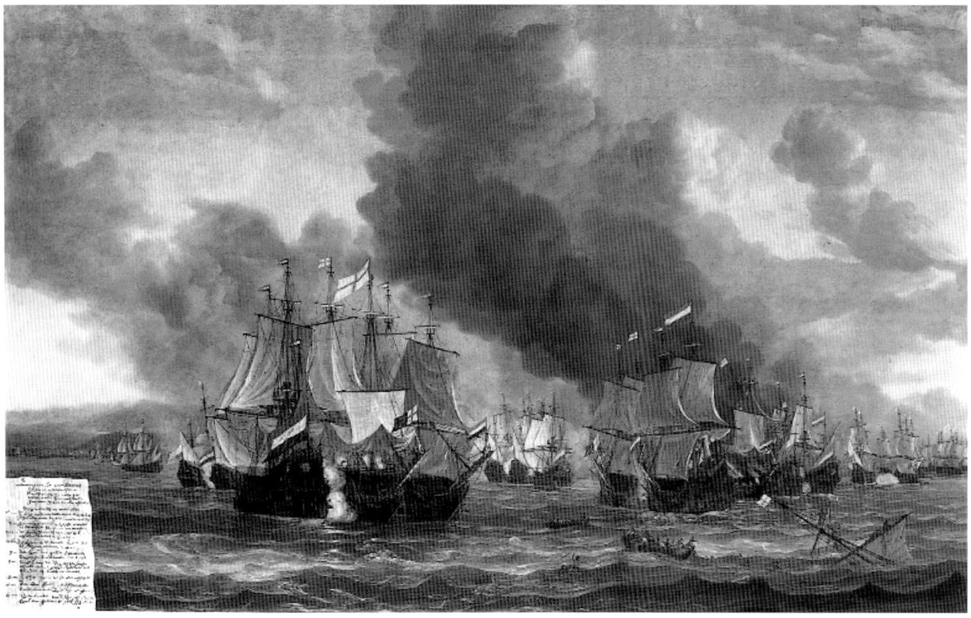

90a Reinier Nooms, *The Battle of Livorno, 12 March 1653*; oil on canvas, 142 x 225 cm. Amsterdam, Rijksmuseum

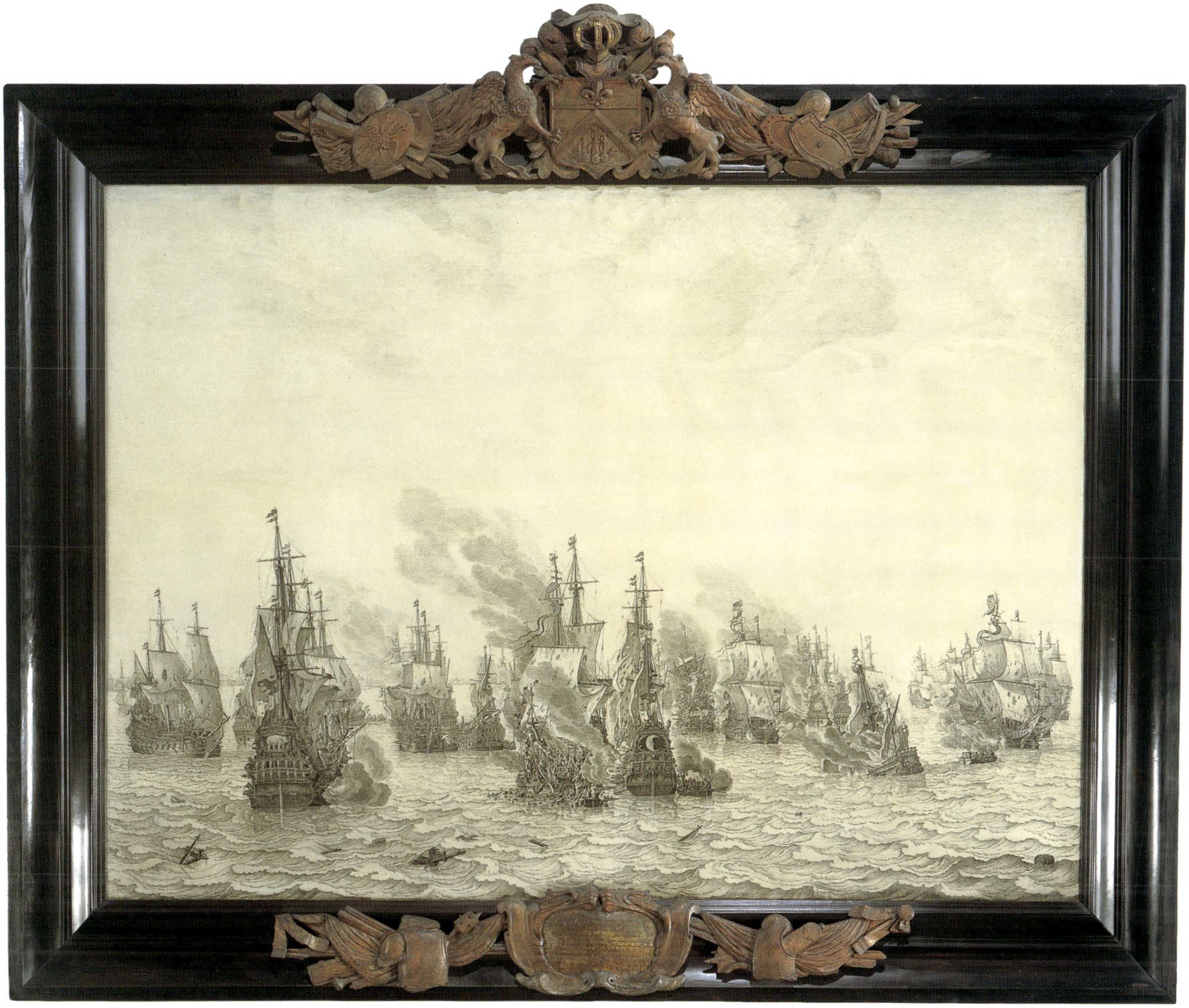

LITERATURE

Exhib. cat. Amsterdam 1984, no. 42; Robinson 1990, vol. 1, no. 337

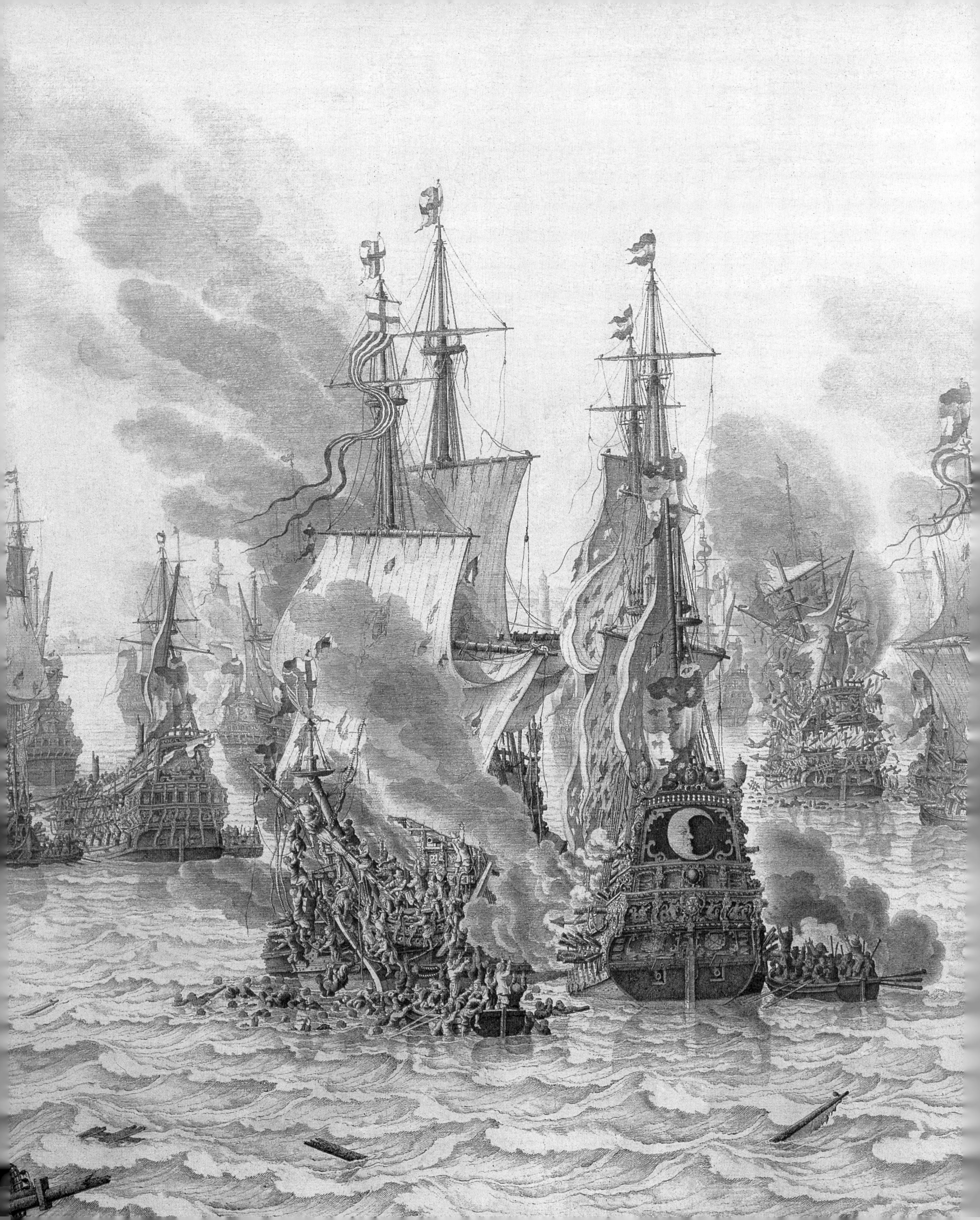

Willem van de Velde the Younger (Leiden 1633-London 1707)

91 *The taking of the English flagship the Royal Prince during the Four Days' Battle, 11-14 June 1666, 1666*

Oil on canvas, 58.5 x 81 cm
At lower right, on a piece of driftwood: *W.V.V.*
Purchased in 1808 at the G. van der Pot van Groeneveld sale, Rotterdam
Inv. no. SK-A-438

Like his father [*90*], the young Willem van de Velde specialised in paintings of ships and battles at sea, but whereas his father elected for the extreme precision of a draughtsmanlike technique, he preferred colour and a method that allowed him to depict the mood of the day, the lead-grey smoke of battle or clouds against a blue sky in stormy weather. The young artist worked for the same group of patrons as his father but supplied them with a different kind of product. His work displays great variety within the limitations of the genre, ranging from small, subtly executed pieces like this one, to a monumental view of IJ Sound in Amsterdam (*fig. 16*), now in the Amsterdams Historisch Museum, and from a single ship on mirror-smooth water to dramatic fires at sea and raging storms. Willem van de Velde the Younger was an absolute master at capturing the state of

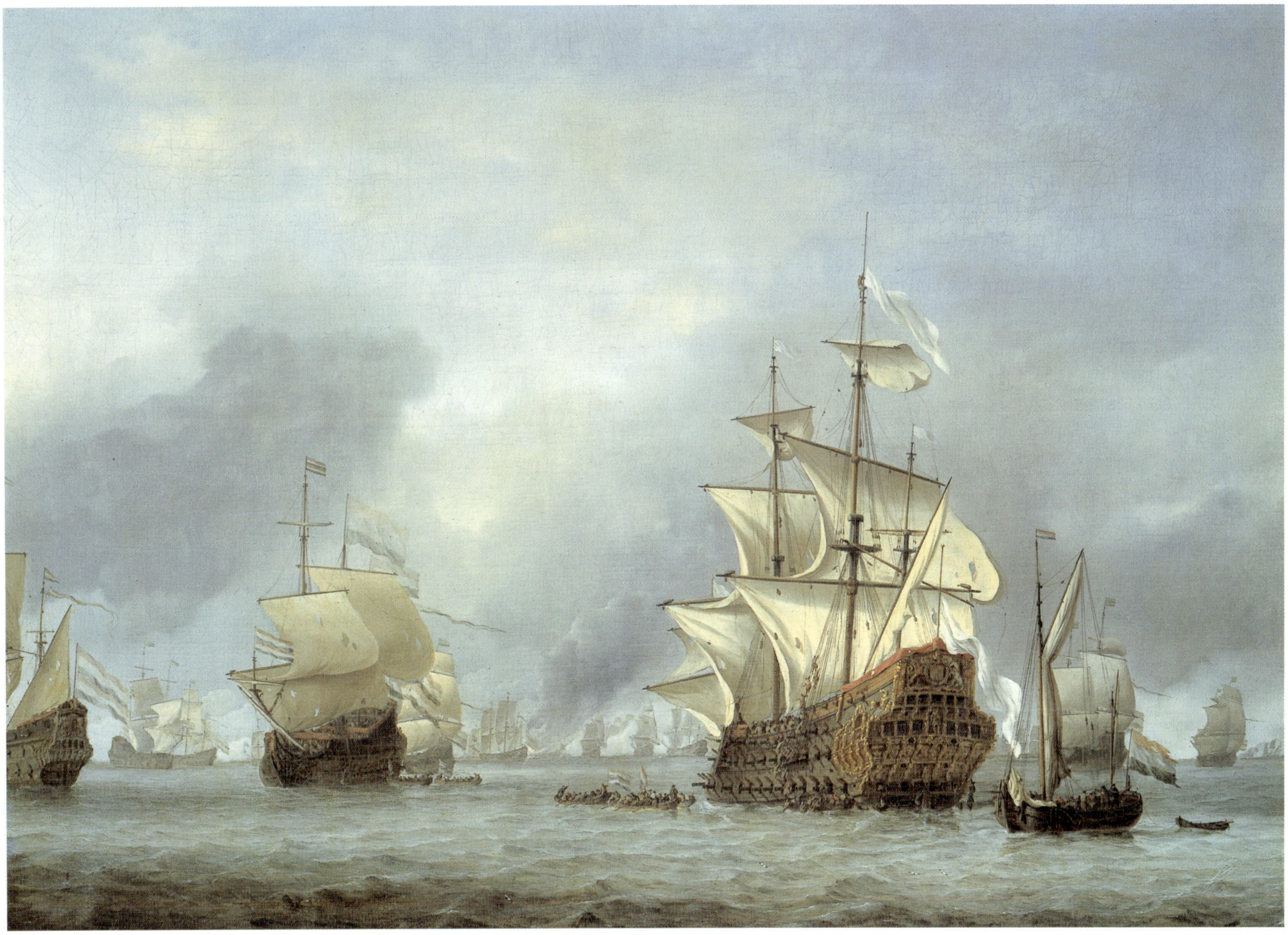

◂ Detail of [*90*]

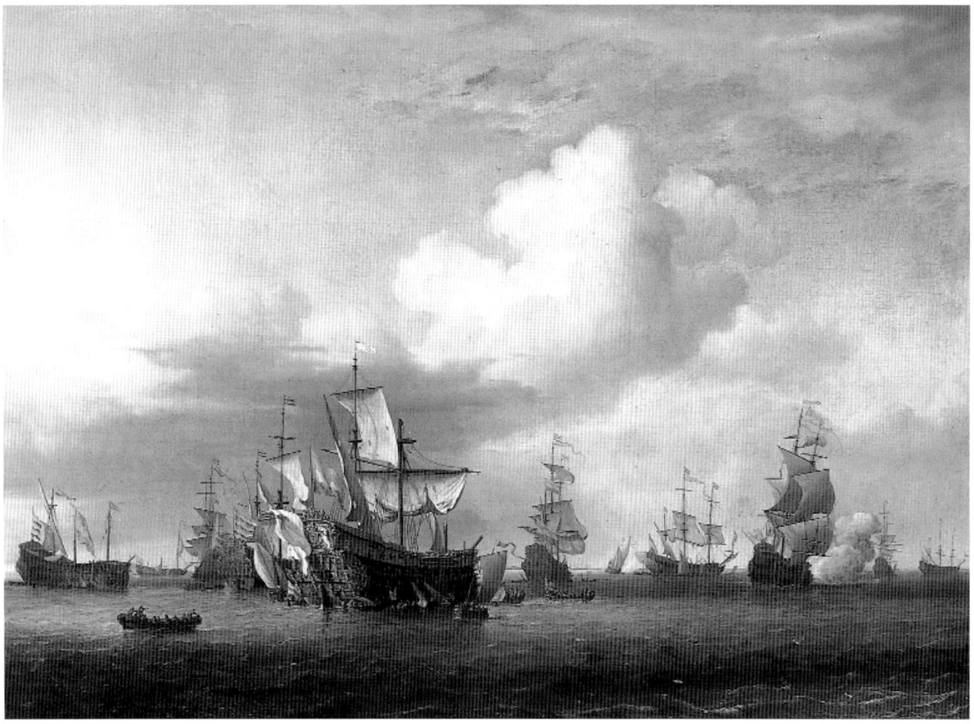

91a Willem van de Velde the Younger, *The four captured men-of-war, Swiftsure, Seven Oaks, Loyal George and Convertine, brought into the Goereese Gat after the Four Days' Battle, 11-14 1666*, 1666; oil on canvas, 58 x 81 cm. Amsterdam, Rijksmuseum

the weather or the fall of light at evening. In 1672 both father and son left Holland for England, where they hoped to find wealthier clients for their work. *The taking of the Royal Prince* and *The captured men of war brought into the Goereese Gat* [*91a*], which form a pair, depict episodes from the Second Anglo-Dutch War (1665-1667). They would have been made not long after the Four Days' Battle, and certainly before the Van de Veldes left for England in 1672.

Of all the engagements between the Dutch and English fleets in the course of the 17th century, the Four Days' Battle of 11-14 June 1666 (1-4 June Old Style) was one of the fiercest. With winter past, the English gathered off the coast of Kent and prepared to fall on the Dutch. A rumour then circulated that a hostile French fleet had entered the Channel—a false alarm as it turned out, but not before it was decided to divide the fleet, leaving George Monck, 1st Duke of Albemarle, with 56 ships to do battle with the full Dutch fleet of 85 sail under the command of Michiel de Ruyter. The outcome was a disaster for England. After two days of fighting Albemarle had only 16 ships left that were ready for battle, and on the third day the flagship, the *Royal Prince*, the largest of the English men-of-war, ran aground on a sandbank, where it was overpowered by the Dutch under Cornelis Tromp. Van de Velde depicted the moment when the English prisoners of war, among them Sir George Ayscue, were taken off. One telling detail is the figure of the sailor at the top of the mainmast hauling down the white pennant which was the mark of Ayscue's command of the white squadron.

Although the Dutch claimed victory, both sides had suffered severe losses. Those of the English were greater, and included the ships captured by the Dutch which are depicted in the companion piece [*91a*].

That work gives a more true-to-life version of the event, probably because Van de Velde was on the spot when the fleet sailed in and made several drawings of the scene. In that picture, too, there is a great display of flags, with the Dutch tricolour flying triumphantly over the stern of *Swiftsure* with the English coat-of-arms and above the white English flag taken from the mainmast. The darker sea and the leaden clouds capture the evening light to perfection.

Both paintings depict episodes from a naval battle which was regarded as a major historical event at the time and for long afterwards. However, there is nothing impartial about the reportage in the pictures. The unknown client chose the episodes, and must have had his reasons for doing so. Maybe he had been involved in both the fighting for the *Royal Prince* and the return of one of the ships depicted in the pendant. Despite portraying such historic events with a certain degree of artistic licence and perhaps even political interpretation, the Van de Veldes based their works first and foremost on oral reports and their own observations. They can be regarded with some justice as early war correspondents, even if they did not aspire to the reliability expected of reporters today.

LITERATURE

Boxer 1974, pp. 32-34; Robinson 1990, vol. 1, pp. 148-150, no. 109

Ludolf Bakhuysen (Emden 1631-Amsterdam 1708)

92 *Ships in distress in a raging storm, c. 1690*

Oil on canvas, 150 x 227 cm
In the blue flag: LB (in mirror image); at lower left on a barrel: L.B.
Purchased in 1988 with the aid of the Vereniging Rembrandt
Inv. no. SK-A-4856

This is a magisterial illustration of every seaman's worst nightmare. A severe storm is building up, jet-black clouds turn day into night, the wind howls in the rigging, and the waves rear up from the sea. The proud three-master with the Dutch lion on its stern is no more than a puny cockleshell in danger of being dashed to pieces on the rocky shore. Standing close to the painting one has little difficulty feeling the power and menace of the elements. However, when the artist was forced to choose between heightening the drama of the scene and the demands of the composition he made an odd sacrifice. The most prominent ship seems to be accommodating to the crests of the waves crashing over to the left. The contrast between ship and shore were important for the composition, as was their proximity. The dark clouds are coming from astern, from the left, but the flags show that the wind is coming from the right. It is blowing off-shore, in other words, the ship is in no immediate danger of running aground.

It is unlikely that Bakhuysen painted an actual shipwreck, although it has been

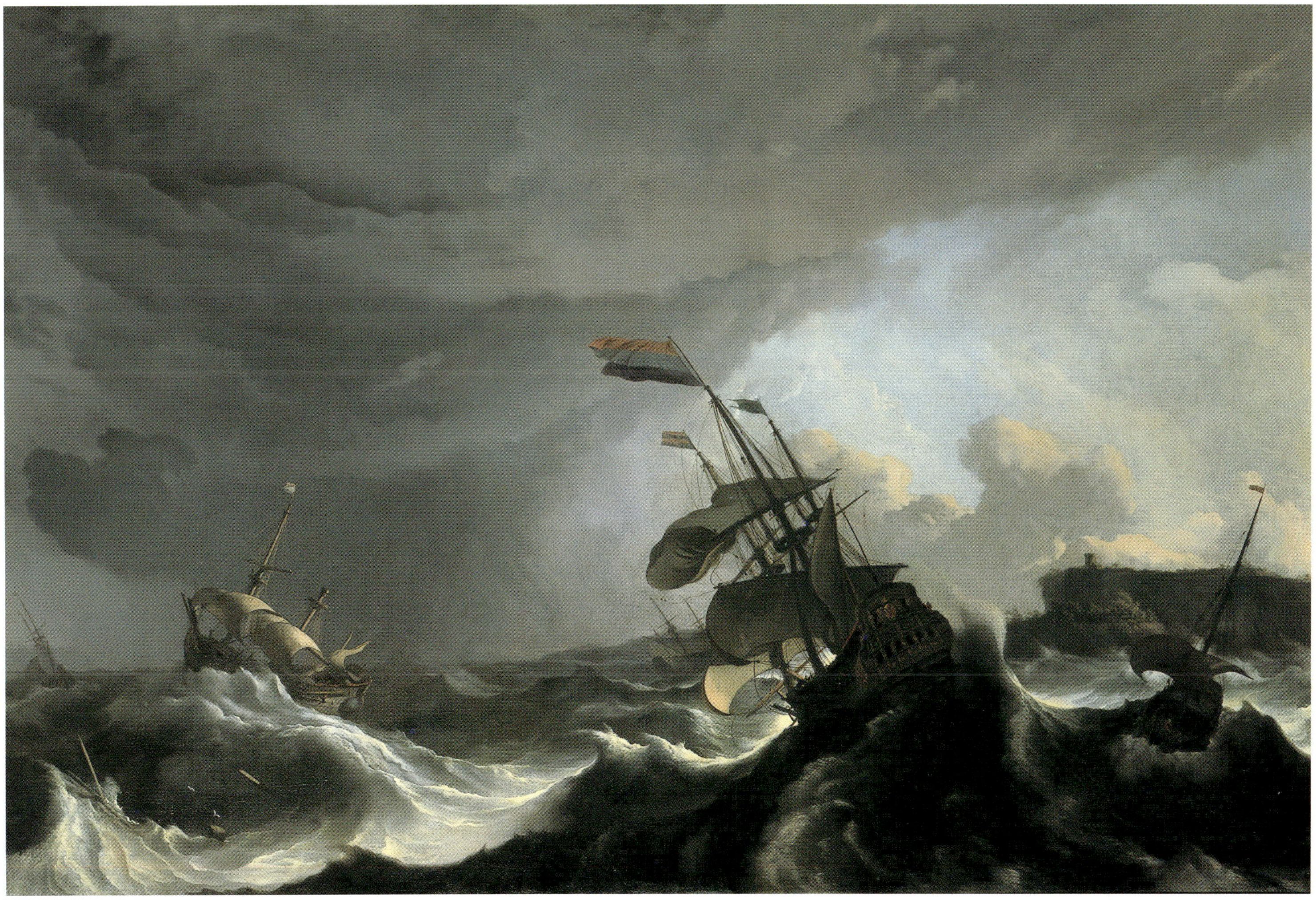

suggested that the ships are the *Hollandia* and the *Ridderschap*, which foundered off Gibraltar in 1694. They were part of a larger fleet, and it is true that there are five ships in the painting in all, but the coastline does not even faintly resemble Gibraltar, and even in the details it is impossible to say for certain that the two vessels in the foreground are the ones involved in that disaster. Moreover, the painting sits squarely in the long visual tradition of vessels in distress which runs from Pieter Bruegel via Willaerts, Porcellis and De Vlieger to Willem van de Velde the Younger and Ludolf Bakhuysen, and rarely did they depict an actual shipwreck. As a rule, paintings of this kind are more general allusions to the unpredictability of the elements and man's tenuous hold on life when assailed by the raw power of nature.

The painting must have been executed towards the end of Bakhuysen's life. Famed for his smooth technique and fine lighting effects, he must have been exploring new avenues in his old age. Part of the evidence for this comes from works of his which have been kept in the family, among them portraits, a landscape and genre paintings. In this late picture he placed his speciality, the seascape, in a different framework, seeking to tie in with an international movement represented by such artists as Salvator Rosa and Pieter Mulier, nicknamed Tempesta. It can be deduced that Bakhuysen's painting should be regarded as a 'masterpiece of old age' from its large size and the existence of a second, slightly smoother version in Raleigh, North Carolina, which is almost certainly autograph as well.

LITERATURE

Exhib. cat. Amsterdam/Emden 1985, no. S 33; Goedde 1989; De Beer 1993

Jan Hackaert (Amsterdam 1628-Amsterdam ? after 1685)

93 *Lake Zürich, c. 1660*

Oil on canvas, 82 x 145 cm
At lower right: HACKAERT
Purchased in 1897 at the G. de Clercq sale, Amsterdam, with the aid of the Vereniging Rembrandt
Inv. no. SK-A-1709

In order to round off their training, artists from the Low Countries had been travelling to Italy since the early 16th century in order to study the remains of classical Roman art. They were still doing so a century later, but now they went in search of the hilly, sun-drenched landscape that was so different from the countryside back home. Study trips of this kind were expensive, and not everyone could afford them. Others, who had set out for Rome with such high hopes, got no further than Germany, France or Switzerland for some reason, and never saw the Mediterranean.

Although Jan Hackaert is counted among the Italianate landscape painters, and his subjects and golden palette were quite clearly influenced by them, and by Jan Both [55] in particular, he never visited Italy. He did, however, travel through Switzerland on several occasions between 1653 and 1656, making detailed drawings of the countryside around Zürich, which had possibly been commissioned by the Amsterdam lawyer Laurens van der Hem. He spent the winter of 1655/56 in Zürich as the guest of a general of the artillery, Hans George Werdmüller, giving art lessons to his son.

Once back in Amsterdam, Hackaert painted this panoramic view of Lake Zürich, undoubtedly on the basis of detailed drawings which he had made on the spot, which unfortunately have not survived. This is one of the first topographical landscapes of the Alpine region. Around 1660 he painted several other Swiss

landscapes which were only recently recognised as such.

Apart from horsemen in avenues of birch trees, Jan Hackaert mainly painted Italianate landscapes. The desire to see specific locations in those works led to the identification of this as a view of Lake Trasimeno in the Italian province of Umbria, and it was not until 1972 that it was recognised as Lake Zürich.

LITERATURE

Exhib. cat. Amsterdam/Boston/Philadelphia 1987-88, no. 41

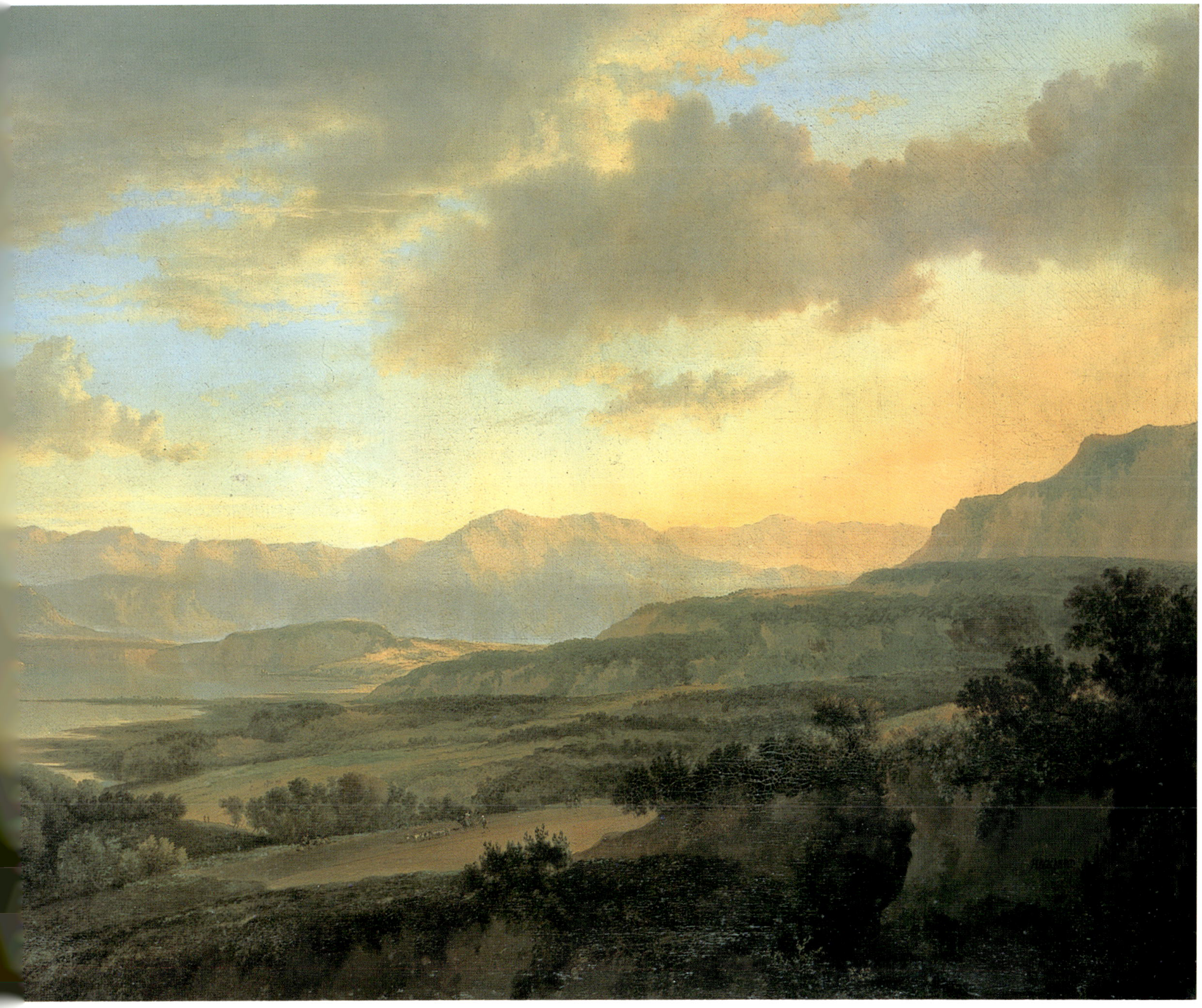

Philips Wouwerman (Haarlem 1619-Haarlem 1668)

94 *The grey, c. 1646*

Oil on panel, 43.5 × 38 cm
In the foreground: *PH W* (*PH* in ligature)
From the collections of Dirk Versteegh, Amsterdam (1823), W.P. van Lennep, Amsterdam, and Messchert van Vollenhoven, Amsterdam (1892); acquired in 1894 with the aid of the Vereniging Rembrandt
Inv. no. SK-A-1610

Everything in this painting seems to be in its preordained place. Standing slightly diagonally in the full light of day is a grey with a contrasting red saddle on its back. The rather stiffly posed animal is being led by the rein by a young man with his face averted, who together with the tree-trunk frames a view through to another trunk further along the path. A small dog in the foreground, puny in comparison to the white bulk of the horse, appears to be peering into this vista while a man emerges from behind the ridge on the right as three birds fly in perfect formation overhead. Wouwerman's masterly orchestration of this small scene has rightly made it one of the most popular in his oeuvre, above all because his 'hallmark' grey horse dominates the small panel with its monumental presence. In addition, he made superb use of transparent layers of paint, allowing the underlying ground to show through and impart a warm glow to the sky.

Wouwerman is known above all for his battle scenes, hunting parties, stables, riding schools and army camps, in all of which horses play a leading role. Many of them show an activity being interrupted, as does this early work. The horse is being given a rest from the load it has been carrying, for its rider has dismounted to shed a different kind of load out of sight on the right, which gives the averted gazes of the boy and the dog a slightly comical air.

It is a little difficult to date the works in Wouwerman's vast oeuvre, because only a few of his paintings actually bear a date. It seems very likely, though, that this one was executed around 1646, for it was undoubtedly made in the same period, perhaps even in the same year, as one in Leipzig that is dated 1646 and also shows a horse, rider and dog on a rising foreground, with a tree-trunk once again serving as a *repoussoir*. Those elements, together with the diagonal structure of the composition and the anatomy of the horse, which is excellent compared to earlier works, are the hallmarks of this period, in which Wouwerman seems to have shaken off some of the influence of Pieter van Laer, who was initially his guiding light.

Although this simple composition is far more cohesive than many of Wouwerman's paintings of battles and hunting scenes, which can be rather agitated and confused, the latter category was much sought after by wealthy collectors in the 18th and first half of the 19th century, undoubtedly because hunting was the preserve of the aristocracy. Yet it was in simpler, genre-like scenes represented by this painting that Wouwerman created his most powerful images.

LITERATURE
Duparc 1993

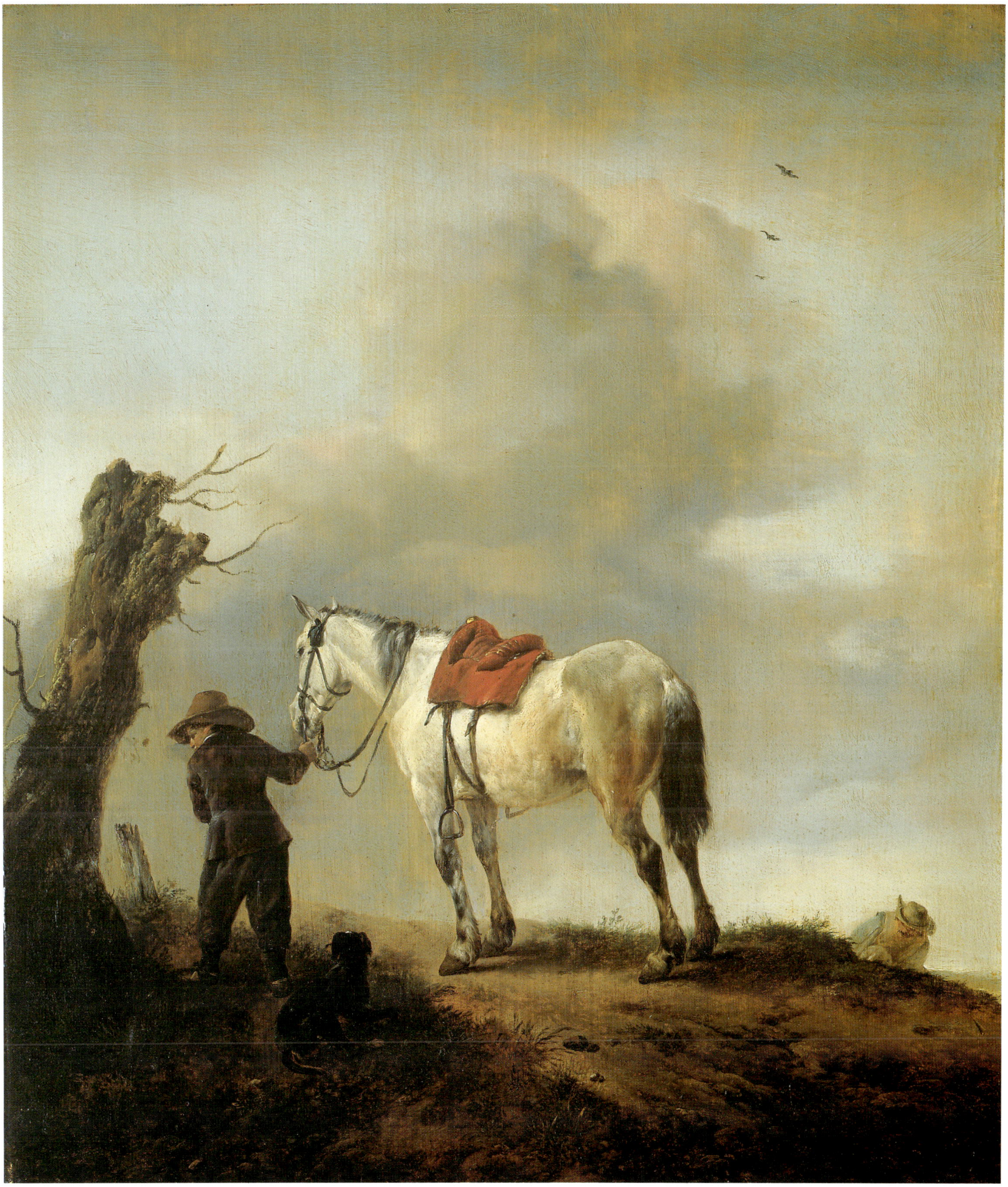

Adriaen van de Velde (Amsterdam 1636-Amsterdam 1672)

95 *The hut, 1671*

Oil on canvas, 76 x 65 cm
At lower left: *A.V.Velde. F. 1671*
From the collections of Wouter Valckenier, Amsterdam (1796) and J.A. Brentano, Amsterdam; purchased at his sale in 1822
Inv. no. SK-A-443

Unlike his elder brother Willem and their father Willem van de Velde the Elder, both famous marine artists, Adriaen chose to paint landscapes, which he did at least as well as his father and brother did in their genre. He succeeded superbly in incorporating the sun-drenched atmosphere of the Italianate painters in landscapes which did not automatically look as if they were situated in Italy, even if the motifs he used cannot always be described as purely Dutch. Adriaen was also a magnificent painter of figures and animals, which he included in his compositions in a carefully balanced way. Arnold Houbraken, the artists' biographer, wrote that 'no one [has] arisen who surpasses him in charm, clarity and pleasing selection of such objects'.

Houbraken, who probably got his information from the artist's daughter, also reported that 'Adriaen industriously drew and painted cows, oxen, sheep and landscapes, going out into the countryside daily carrying his implements, and continued doing so once a week until his death'. And indeed, a considerable number of such studies 'from life' have come down to us, and the subjects of most of them were used in his paintings. Those preliminary studies show that Adriaen usually began by making a rough composition sketch before proceeding to separate studies from the live model for the various figures, generally in red or black chalk. He also made offsets of some of those studies so that he could use them reversed left for right. Finally he made a detailed design drawing of the whole painting.

Neither the sketch nor the design for this picture has survived, but there are preliminary studies of individual passages and figures. One is of the seated woman [95a],

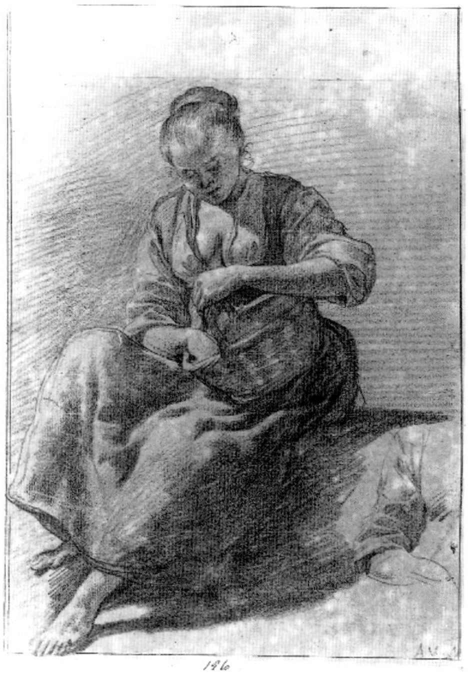

95a Adriaen van de Velde, *Seated woman*; red chalk, 28.3 x 20 cm. Netherlands, private collection

95b Adriaen van de Velde, *Seated woman with a basket and livestock*; red chalk, 19.3 x 29.8 cm. Amsterdam, Amsterdams Historisch Museum

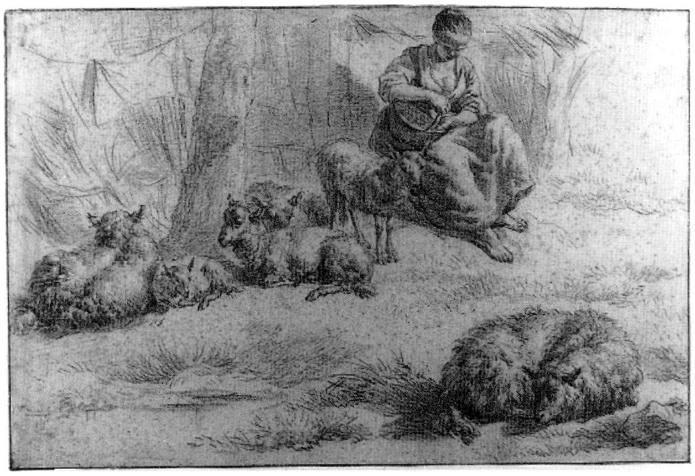

95c Adriaen van de Velde, *A cow and three sheep*; red chalk, 19.5 x 31 cm. Amsterdam, Amsterdams Historisch Museum

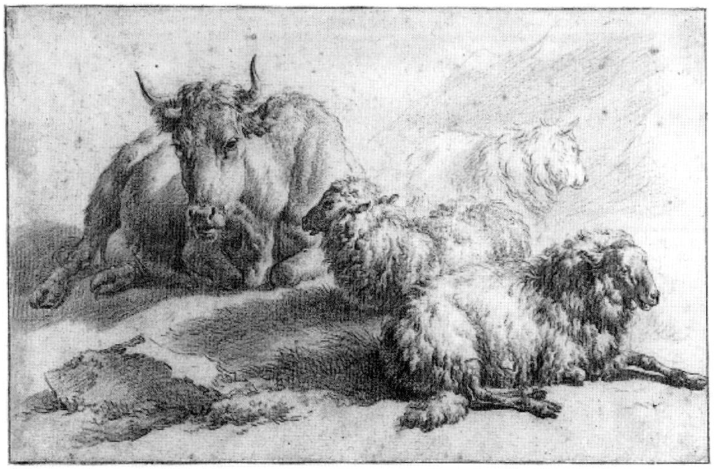

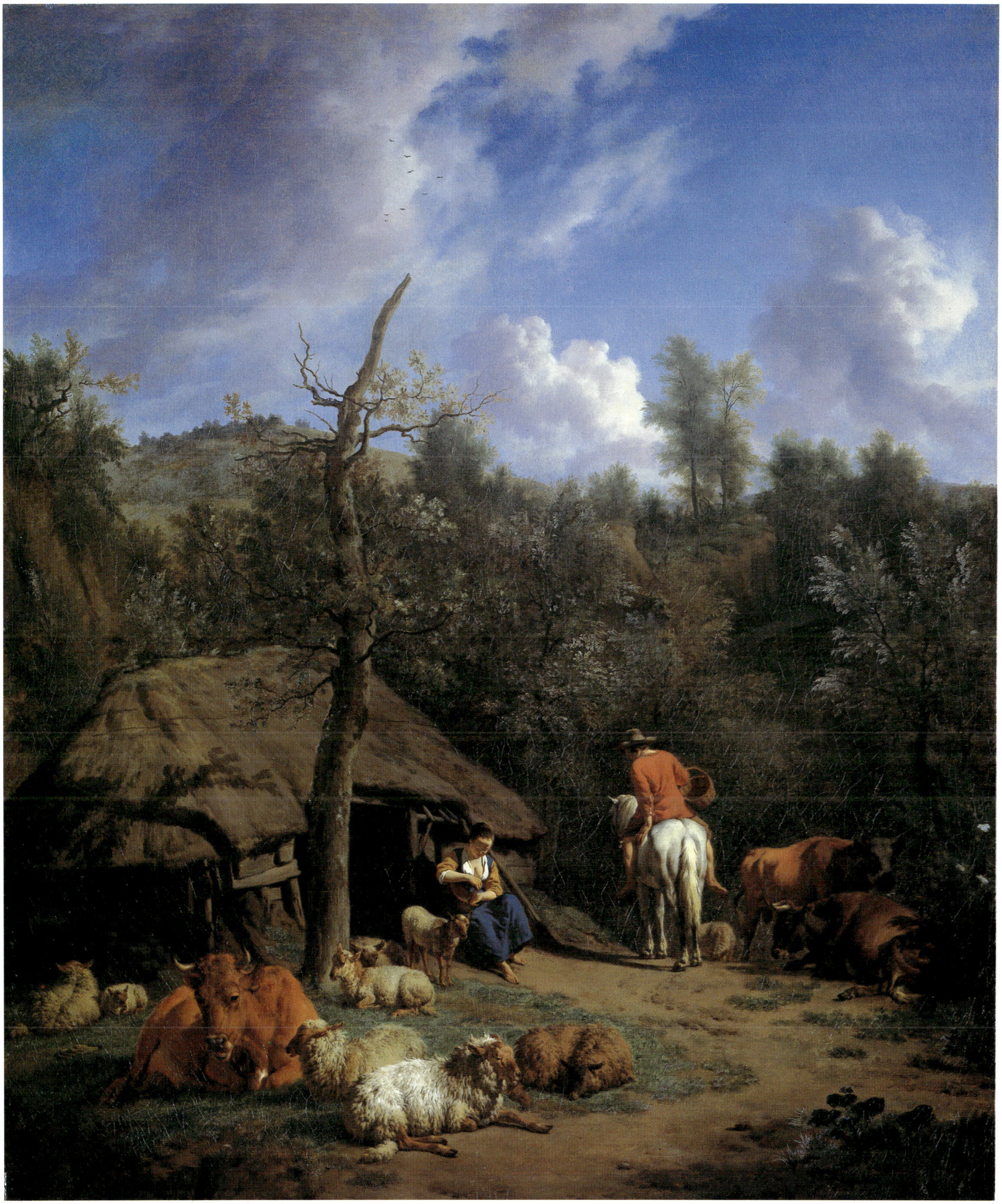

of which there is also an offset (Dresden, Kupferstichkabinett) showing her as she is in the painting. She reappears in the company of several sheep in a preliminary study for part of the full composition [95b], and there is yet another study of the cow and sheep in the foreground [95c]. A study of the hut from which the painting takes its name was once in the Hans van Leeuwen Collection. There is no known drawing of the horseman seen from the back, although there probably is (or was) one of him as well.

Given the lack of both the rough sketch and the detailed design, it is conceivable that Adriaen van de Velde put together a new composition from material he already had in stock, although one would like to believe that the painting would provide evidence backing Houbraken's assertion that the master made studies from nature 'until his death'. This highly talented member of the family of painters died in 1672 at the age of 36, one year after this picture was completed.

LITERATURE

Schatborn 1975; exhib. cat. Amsterdam/Washington 1981-82, pp. 116-117; exhib. cat. Dordrecht/Leeuwarden 1988-89, no. 32

Adriaen van de Velde (Amsterdam 1636-Amsterdam 1672)

96 *Reclining herdsman, c. 1670*

Red chalk over a sketch in black chalk, 19.9 x 29.1 cm
At lower left: *A. v.d. Velde. f:*
From the collection of Jacob de Vos Jbzn; acquired from the Vereniging Rembrandt, 1885
Inv. no. RP-T-1885-499

There are few 17th-century Dutch artists whose path from initial idea to finished painting can be followed as closely as Adriaen van de Velde's. When preparing for a painting he first made a small composition sketch. He then drew separate detailed studies from life of the figures that were to populate his landscapes, and from time to time he also used landscape drawings as guides for specific passages [95].

He often portrayed a figure twice on a single sheet in different poses or dress. This drawing of a young herdsman is a very fine example of such a variation on a theme, one sketch showing him with raised head in a pose midway between sitting and lying down, the other as he sleeps with his head on his right arm. The second drawing shows the man only as far as the waist,

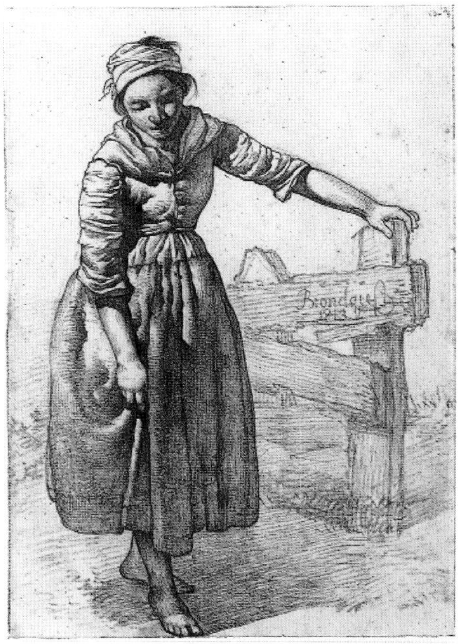

96b Albertus Brondgeest, *Girl standing by a fence*, 1813; red chalk, 24.8 x 17.9 cm. Amsterdam, Rijksmuseum, Rijksprentenkabinet

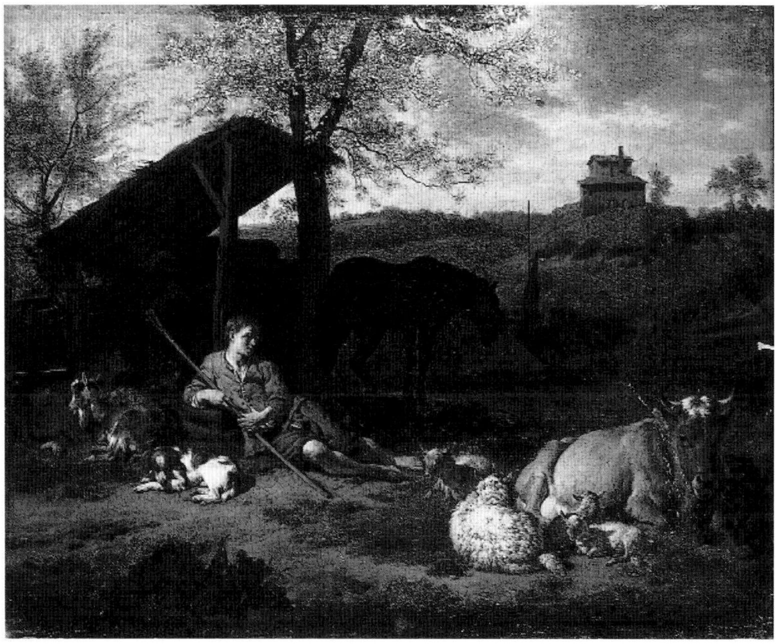

96a Adriaen van de Velde, *Landscape with reclining herdsman and livestock*; oil on canvas on panel, 31.5 x 40.8 cm. Karlsruhe, Staatliche Kunsthalle

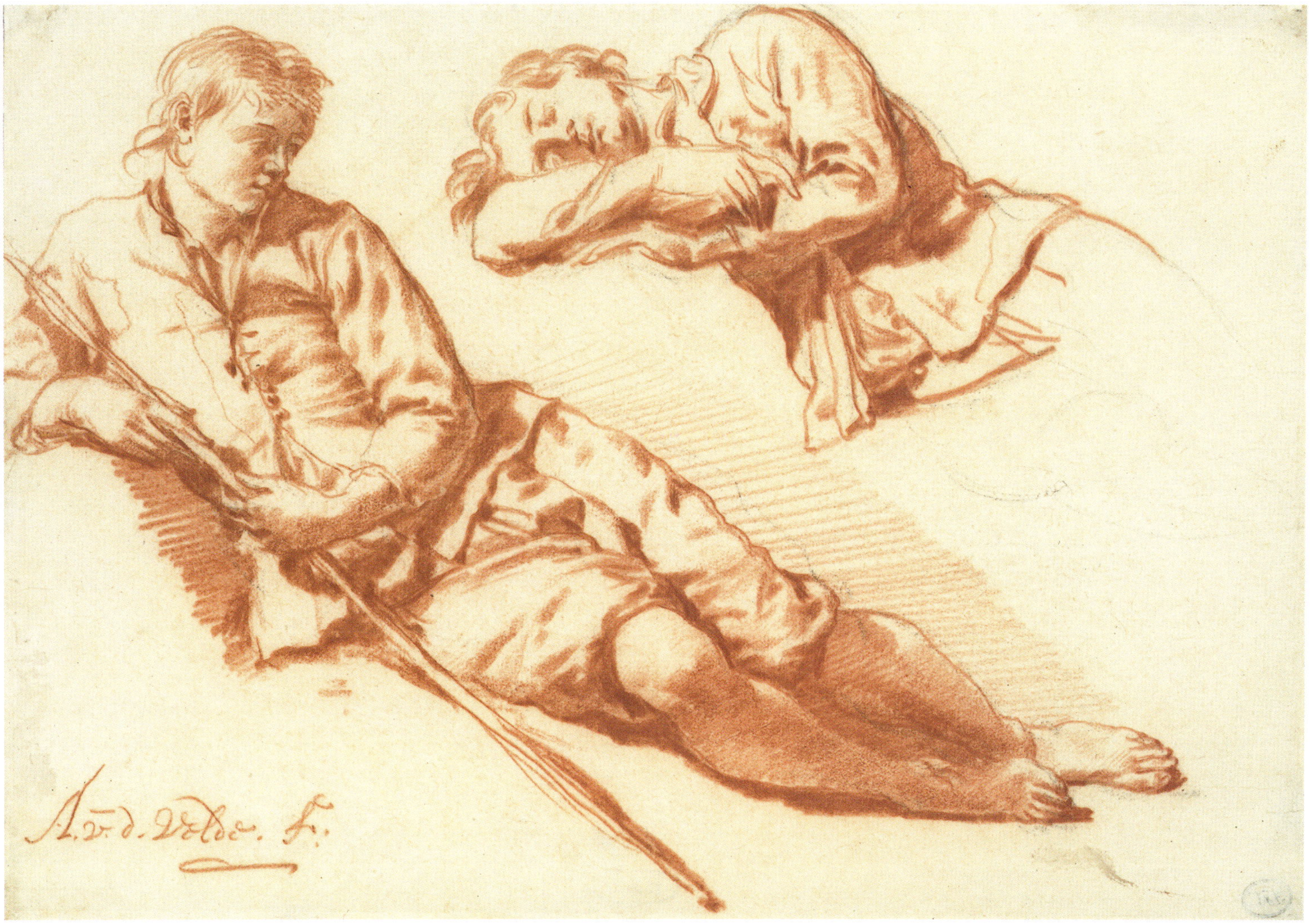

for since nothing had to be changed to the position of the legs why bother repeating something that had already been done? Moreover, Van de Velde often made offsets of his studies so that he could include a particular figure in a painting in mirror image if that suited him better. Rarely does one come across an artist who was so economical with his materials.

The Amsterdam herdsman in his reclining pose is found in a painting in the Staatliche Kunsthalle in Karlsruhe *[96a]*. The date is rather difficult to read, but is perhaps 1671. It will be clear from the above that the drawing may well have been made some years earlier.

Van de Velde's figure studies are among the finest of 17th-century Dutch drawings. They display a delicate precision that never descends into the finicky, and an intense concern for the rendering of light and shade. The remarkable qualities of his draughtsmanship were recognised at an early date, and various artists tried to imitate his style in the late 18th and early 19th century. A study of a young woman *[96b]* by Albertus Brondgeest, himself a collector and art dealer, would have been inconceivable without the example of Adriaen van de Velde.

LITERATURE

Exhib. cat. Amsterdam/Washington 1981-82, pp. 118-119, no. 94

Gerrit Berckheyde (Haarlem 1638-Haarlem 1698)

97 *The bend in the Herengracht near the Nieuwe Spiegelstraat in Amsterdam, 1672*

Oil on panel, 40.5 x 63 cm
At right, on a slab on the canalside: *G. BerckHyde 1672*
Purchased in 1980 from the collection of the heirs of J. Goudstikker, Amsterdam, with the aid of the Rijksmuseum-Stichting and the Ministry of Culture, Recreation and Social Affairs
Inv. no. SK-A-4750

Berckheyde's view of the 'golden bend' in the Herengracht is a marvel of precision. The houses, all brand-new and each with a character of its own, recede in an orderly rhythm, separated with clear-cut verticals amidst a web of diagonals beneath a sky layered with horizontals. There a few gaps in the dark frontage (the sun is in the south-west) where houses are yet to be built, and in the bend itself there are even glimpses through to the Nieuwe Spiegelstraat beyond. The brightly lit side walls lead the eye into the picture and temper the relentless march of the perspective. The northern frontage across the canal is in full sunlight, but due to its greater perspectival distance it does little more than give an indication of the width of the canal and the relative proportions of the houses, canalside and water.

The question of how Gerrit Berckheyde painted this marvellously accurate view is answered to some extent by a meticulous study on paper [*97a*]. That drawing explains a lot, but not everything. The artist probably had more preparatory material. The second house front from the right, for example, is more specific in the painting. The drawing would not have told him that one of the statues at the top was of Neptune (judging by the trident). There is also a coat of arms on the balustrade, and he would have missed that as well if he had been relying solely on the drawing. Added to that, the house was not completed until 1673, which makes it even more likely that Berckheyde had the design for the front elevation in his Haarlem studio, or a copy of it. Another interesting difference between the drawing and the painting is in the rendering of the water and the sky. The taut pattern of the water in the drawing has been transferred to the sky in the painting, while the reflections of the house fronts in the water enhance the subtlety of the painting. A second point is the detail of the two canalsides, with the drawing showing trees on the left and new plantings and one or more lampposts on the right. Their presence rules out the possibility of the drawing being a record of the painting. The marvellous regularity of windows and steps in this part of the picture, at precisely the point where they are hidden by the trees in the drawing, suggests that Berckheyde relied on his own power of imagination in this passage.

A second drawing [*97b*] gives the opposite view. The painting shows the canal from the bridge near the Leidsestraat, from the west in other words, but the other drawing shows it from the east. The style, which corresponds completely, as can be seen from the walls of the canalside, shows that the two drawings were made on the same occasion. Gerrit Berckheyde was

97a Gerrit Berckheyde, *The bend in the Herengracht*; pen, washed, 17.9 x 37.5 cm. Amsterdam, City Archives

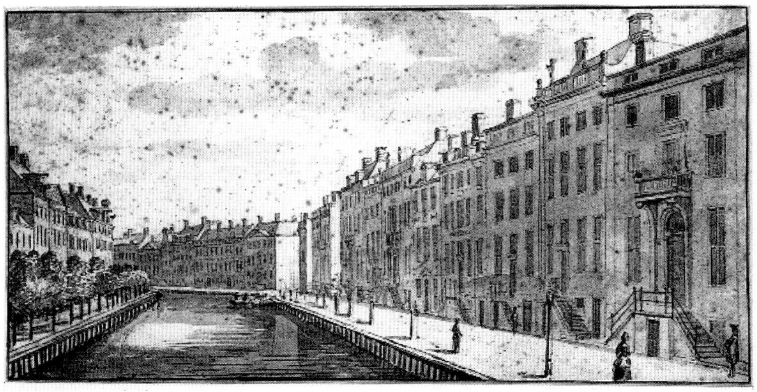

97b Gerrit Berckheyde, *The bend in the Herengracht*; pen, washed, 20.8 x 39.5 cm. Amsterdam, City Archives

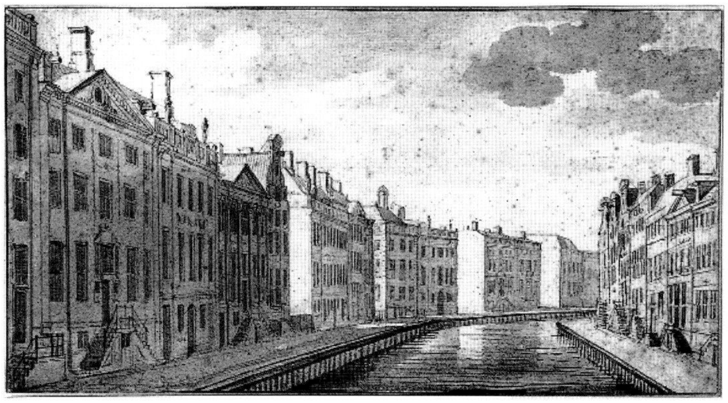

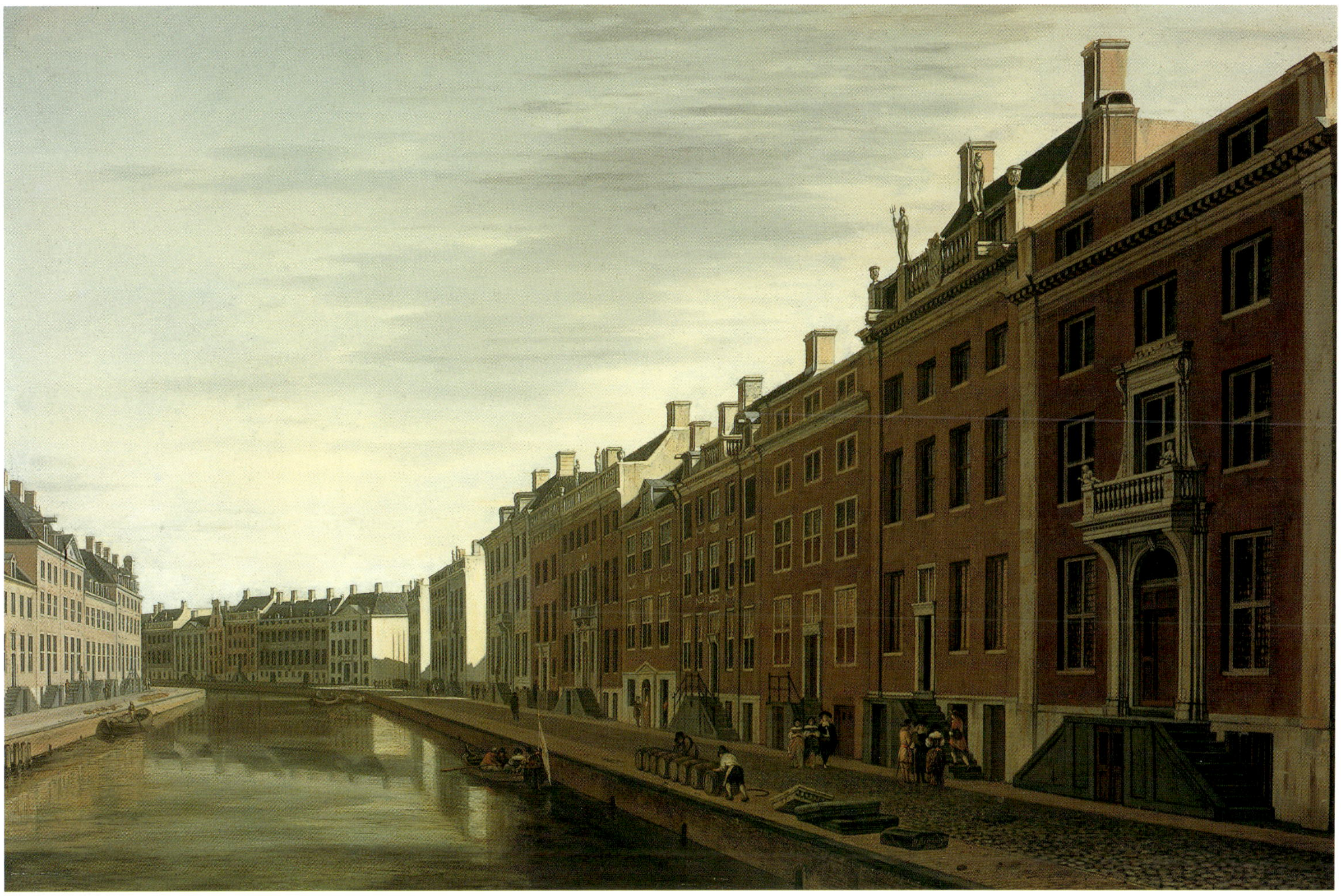

evidently planning to make two pendant paintings, and it is in that light that ideas about the possible patron should be examined. The owners of several of the houses have been cast in that role, but it is less likely that he or she owned more than one house than the possibility that a single patron had children living in different houses. It is very possible, of course, that the artist planned to make two paintings in the hope of finding a buyer among the wealthy homeowners in this exclusive part of town.

The year of execution, the 'year of disaster' 1672, is extremely important for the earliest history of the painting. The poet Joost van den Vondel associated the political and economic crisis unleashed by the invasion of parts of the Republic by neighbouring nations with a painting of the Herengracht by Gerrit Berckheyde, perhaps this very one.

On the New Herengracht by Berckheyde

Berckheyde paints the Herengracht
From life, and fine it is to behold.
Buy paintings, shun building.
Why? It is now French midnight,
So wait for a bright dawn.
House-building brings trouble and woe.

LITERATURE

Meischke 1973; Kloek 1989b; Lawrence 1991, pp. 63-64

Delft, Het Jonge Moriaenshooft faience factory under Rochus Jacobsz Hoppesteyn

98 *Two dishes with Chinese figures, c. 1685-1690*

Faience, multicoloured in the glaze, decorated in overglaze red and gold
h. 26 cm, w. 32.5 cm, and h. 26.5 cm, w. 33.5 cm
Purchased in 1962
Inv. no. BK-1962-62-a/b

These two dishes are from an ensemble of four which flanked two smaller and two larger trapeziform dishes so that their sides fitted, with an elongated octagonal dish placed in the middle. Sets of this kind are anachronistically referred to in the literature as 'rice-table garniture', a name prompted by the modern use of such side dishes. Indonesian cuisine was unknown in western Europe in the 17th century, and the set would actually have been used as a table centrepiece holding numerous pickled or possibly sweet titbits accompanying a main course or dessert. The large service which Wenzel Ferdinand, Prince Lobkowicz, ordered around 1685 from Lambertus Kleffius, owner of De Metalen Pot faience factory, originally contained six sets of this kind, all consisting of slightly smaller dishes, as well as numerous loose ones which were placed beside or near the diner's plate.

The two factories Het Jonge Moriaenshooft and Het Oude Moriaenshooft adjoined each other on the south side of Gasthuislaan in Delft. From the mid-1660s they were both run by the Hoppesteyn family. Jacob Wemmersz became the owner in 1664, and on his death in 1671 they passed to his widow Jannitge. When her second husband died in 1679 she continued the business jointly with her son Rochus. The factories flourished, producing goods of the highest quality, both technically and artistically. Jannitge Claesdr van Straeten, who was born in 1626 to a family of Delft faience potters, certainly played a supporting role at first, but as a widow she probably took over the management entirely, handling the commercial side of the business and possibly supervising the staff as well, leaving Rochus free to develop his artistic talents. The factories prospered as never before.

All the faience produced in Delft was decorated in blue alone until around 1670. That had long been the fashion, but it was one dictated by the market, which especially wanted objects resembling the blue and white porcelain that was imported from China until 1650 or thereabouts. Literal copies of that porcelain, and endless series of variations known as chinoiseries, were made for the European market for the next 25 years. Variations on that theme were introduced around 1670 by painting the chinoiseries purple and blue. Consumer demand for a few more colourful pieces was probably satisfied by the import of multicoloured Japanese porcelain known as Kakiemon ware.

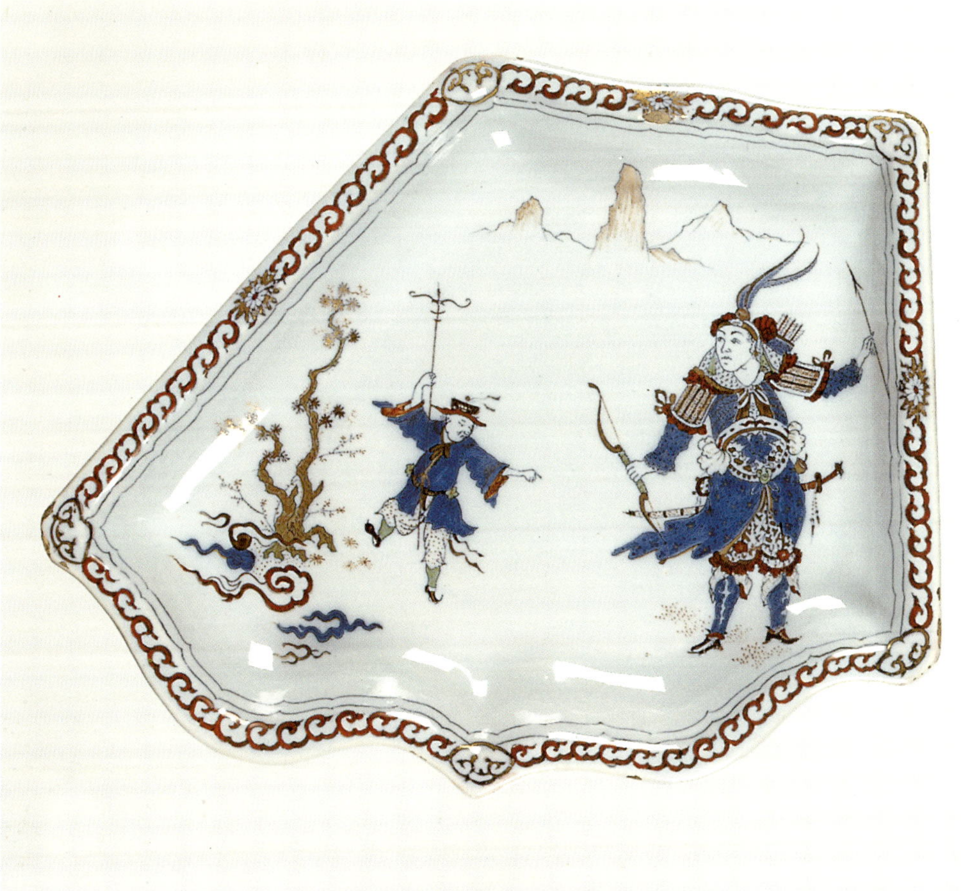

Shortly after 1680, Het Moriaenshooft started experimenting with colour. Blue, purple, yellow, green and orange could be painted on the powdered glaze into which it sank and fused during the high-temperature firing at 1,000° Celsius. Those colours were already known before 1650, but others, like red and gold, did not react well to such high temperatures. Until 1680-1690, all the colours on Japanese Kakiemon ware were painted overglaze, to which they were fused during a third firing at around 600° Celsius. Het Moriaenshooft developed this further with a mixed technique of high-temperature firing for blue, purple, green and so on, followed by a low-temperature firing in the muffle-kiln for red and gold. After the pre-1680 experiments with the combination of blue and purple, a more varied palette was just a matter of time, and soon more factories were producing objects painted in the new colours. The Hoppesteyns, mother and son, were among the first to do so, and at the time they were the only faience producers in Delft who experimented with the low-temperature firing technique.

Most of their pieces in this mixed technique are marked JW. It used to be thought that they dated from 1661-1671, when Jacob Wemmersz owned the factory, but it now seems that they were made in the brief period 1682-1686, when Jacob's widow Jannitge was running the business with her son Rochus. Jannitge died in 1686 at the age of 60, leaving everything to Rochus. After her death, it is assumed that the mark RHS stands for Rochus Hoppesteyn. He must have had a good sense of what the European elite wanted in the way of finery: large decorative pieces covered with a brilliant white glaze delicately decorated with a keen eye for detail.

LITERATURE

Lunsingh Scheurleer 1984, pp. 54-55

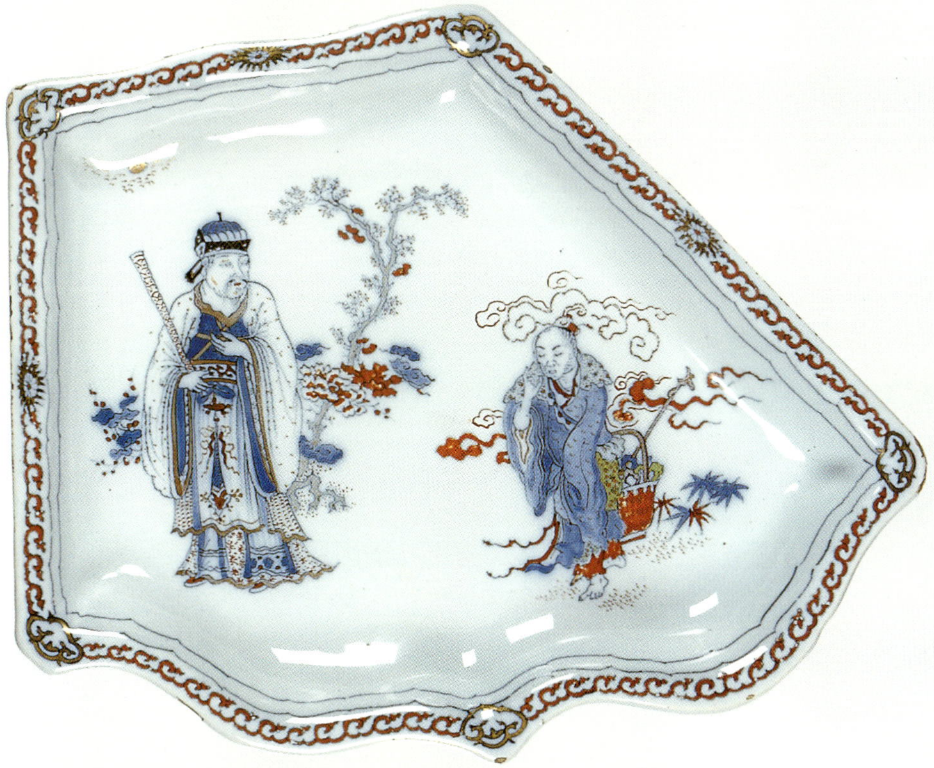

Gerard de Lairesse (Liège 1641-Amsterdam 1711)

99 *Cleopatra's banquet, c. 1675*

Oil on canvas, 74 x 95.5 cm
At lower right: *G. Lairesse inv.*
From the Van Loon-Van Winter Collection, Amsterdam (1878);
Insinger-Van Loon Bequest, 1903
Inv. no. SK-A-2115

Not so long ago Gerard de Lairesse was still being regarded as a representative of the late 17th-century 'decline' in the painting of the Golden Age. His international Classicist style was dismissed as 'un-Dutch' and hence uninteresting. He initially worked in Liège, moving to Amsterdam around 1666, and he did indeed look far more to the French for inspiration than to the Dutch—his great model being Nicolas Poussin. Nowadays he will be less readily taken to task for the 'un-Dutch' nature of his work. An unprejudiced look at *Cleopatra's banquet* makes one realise just how harmonious his compositions could be and how good he was at imitating textures and using colour. His Classicism can once again count on the appreciation it enjoyed in the 18th and early 19th centuries.

Painted around 1675, *Cleopatra's banquet* deals with the story of the wager between the Egyptian queen and her lover Mark Antony, who was in charge of the eastern half of the Roman empire. She had bet him that she could give a banquet costing 10,000 talents. It seemed impossible that the simple meal that was then served up could be worth that much, that is until Cleopatra dissolved one of her pearl earrings in wine and drank it down. When she was about to do the same with its companion, Lucius Plancus, who was adjudicating the wager, stepped in to prevent it, for she was obviously going to win the bet. It is that moment which is depicted so theatrically here, with the scene looking as if it was conceived according to contemporary Classicist ideas about stagecraft. The stagy effect is reinforced by the curtains at the top, and above all by the man standing in the foreground, who acts as a kind of intermediary between the public and the actors. The background architecture is also reminiscent of stage decor.

The caryatids at the back were copied from those in the Tribunal of the Town Hall built by the architect Jacob van Campen. De Lairesse probably chose this quotation because of Van Campen's Classicism, although it might have some meaning in the context of the story. The caryatid supposedly originated as an architectonic motif from the depiction of the Peleponnesian women who were compelled to carry an eternal burden on their shoulders as punishment for conspiring with the Persians against the Greeks. As such, De Lairesse's motif might allude to the fate awaiting the wily Cleopatra, for she was the woman who used all her charms to seduce Mark Antony and thus increase her influence in the Roman empire. The inscription on the etching which De Lairesse made after his painting [*99a*] also refers to the political power of Cleopatra's seductiveness: 'Quem Mars nunquam vicit Venus' (He whom Mars never conquered

99a Gerard de Lairesse, *Cleopatra's banquet*, c. 1675-1680; etching, 35.8 x 48.3 cm. Amsterdam, Rijksmuseum, Rijksprentenkabinet

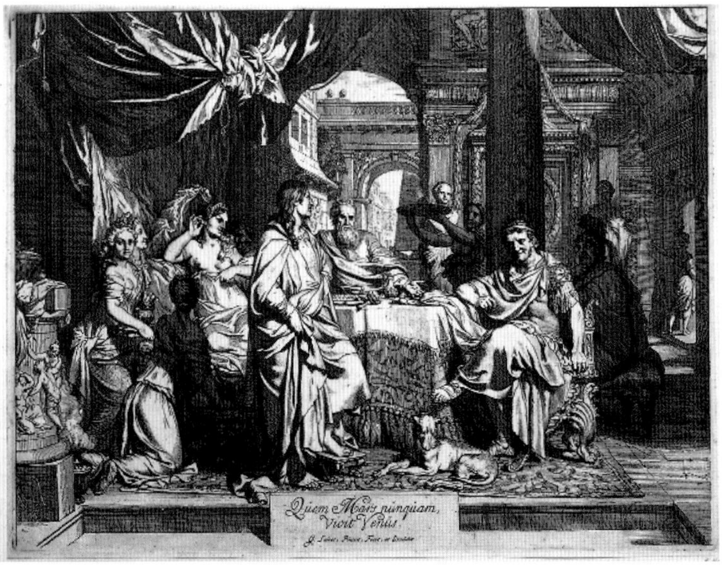

99b Gerard de Lairesse, *The death of Cleopatra*, 1686; oil on canvas, 74 x 95.5 cm. Toronto, Art Gallery of Ontario

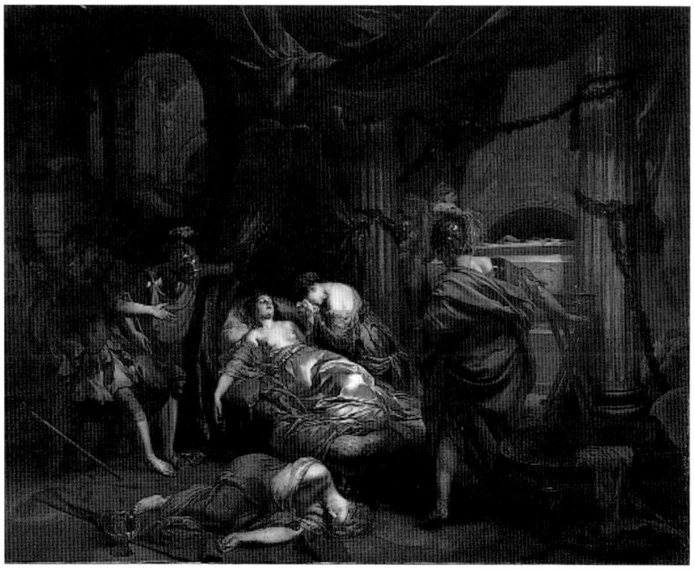

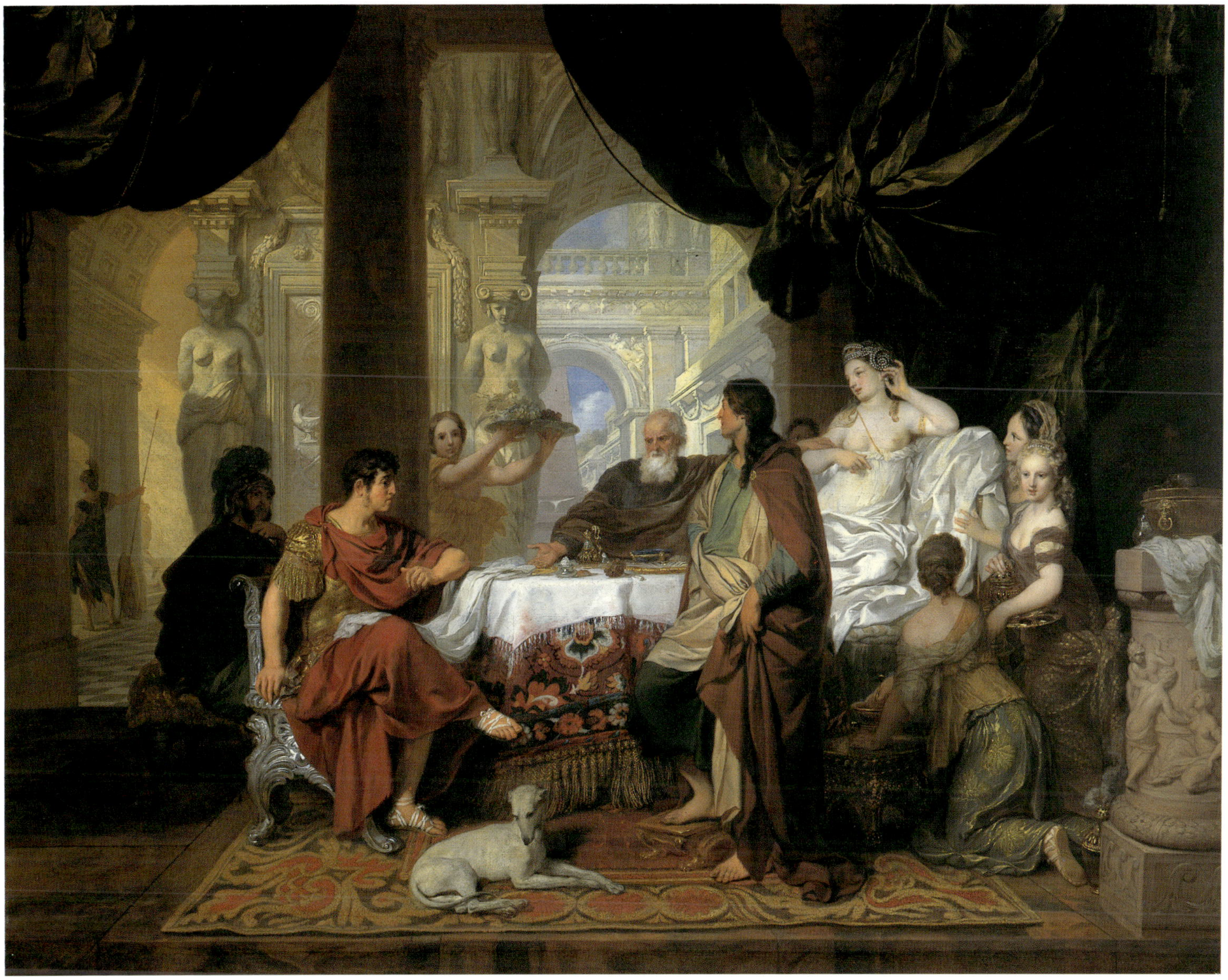

succumbed to Venus). Nevertheless, the caryatids do not necessarily refer to the punishment that a lust for power can bring. In his theoretical treatise *Groot schilderboek*, published in 1707, De Lairesse remarked in connection with Rubens's painting *Samson and Delilah* (London, National Gallery) that the statuette of Venus in it should not automatically be construed as a reference to Delilah's sensuality. In other words, the artist himself urged caution when interpreting such details. Another point is that De Lairesse omitted the caryatids in the etching, which suggests that the scene is not so much about the consequences of a lust for power as about the repercussions of lust in general (the vice of Luxuria), which inevitably leads to downfall. It is therefore likely that De Lairesse's *Death of Cleopatra* in Toronto [*99b*], which is identical in size, was made as a pendant to the painting in the Rijksmuseum.

LITERATURE

Roy 1992, no. P. 96; exhib. cat. Amsterdam 1993

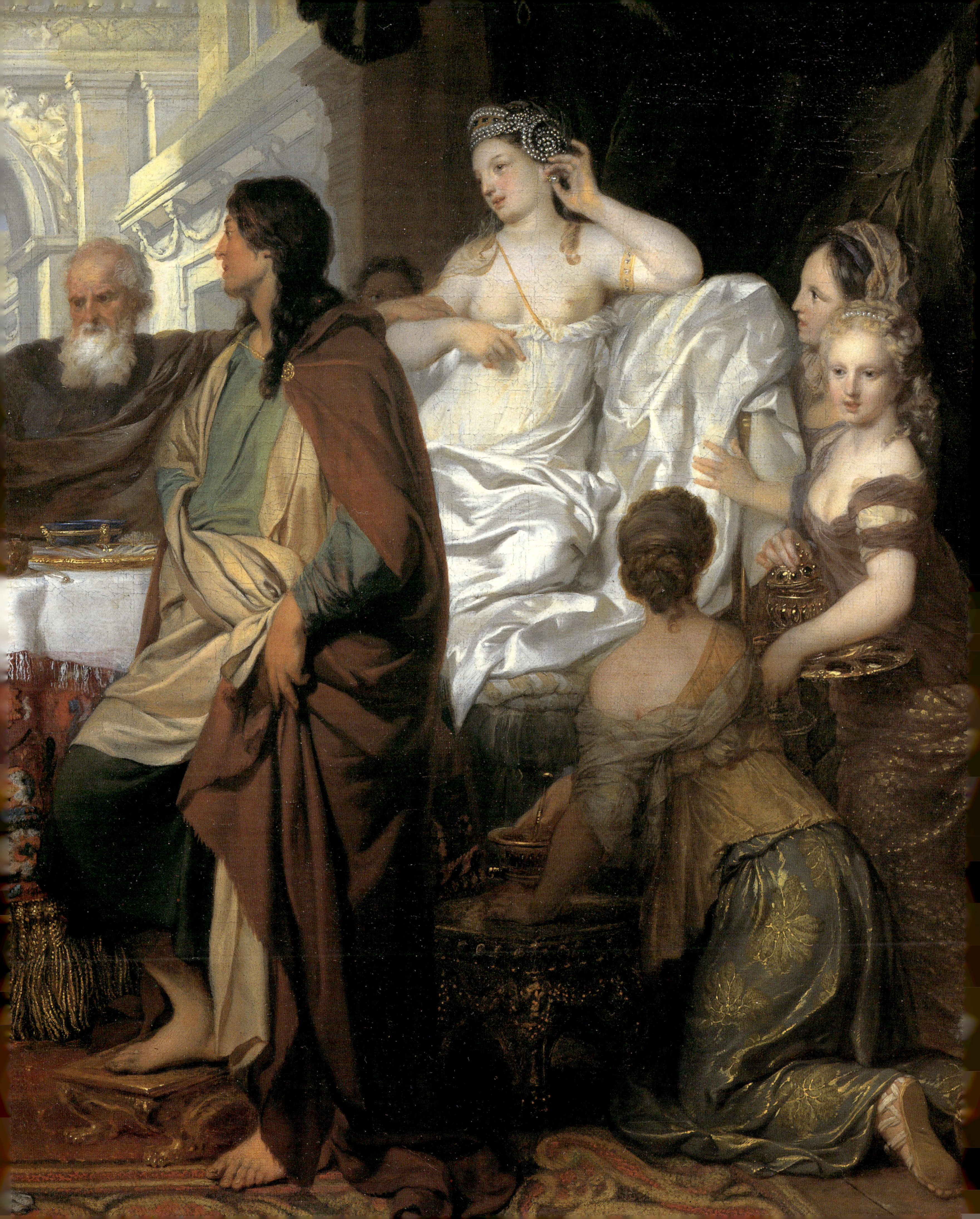

Melchior d'Hondecoeter (Utrecht 1636-Amsterdam 1695)

100 *The floating feather, c. 1680*

Oil on canvas, 159 × 144 cm
In the centre, on the rim of the pool wall: M.D. *Hondecoeter*
Probably made for Het Loo Palace; transferred to the vestibule of Soestdijk Palace in the 18th century; moved to Huis Ten Bosch in 1799 along with three other paintings by Hondecoeter, where it formed part of the National Konst-Gallerij when it opened in 1800
Inv. no. SK-A-175

Melchior d'Hondecoeter was born in Utrecht in 1636 to a family which had already produced several generations of artists. He was trained by his father, the landscapist and animal painter Gijsbert d'Hondecoeter, and after the latter's death by his uncle, the Italianate landscape painter Jan Baptist Weenix. Hondecoeter was active in The Hague from 1659 to 1663, where he was made dean of the painters' society. He married in Amsterdam in 1663 and lived there until his death in 1695.

Gijsbert d'Hondecoeter made paintings of the humbler kinds of poultry, a genre in which his son Melchior became a true specialist, but in keeping with the circumstances of his rich clientele he moved his scenes from the barnyard to the peacock courtyards and aviaries of stately country mansions. Hondecoeter often painted life-size, exotic birds against a background of garden statues, vases or fountains in the pleasure garden of a country retreat. Here he would certainly have been influenced by his apprenticeship to Jan Baptist Weenix, who was very gifted both technically and in his use of colour, and who had made an important contribution to the development of a style of painting that was both monumental and decorative.

The main customers for Hondecoeter's sumptuous paintings of birds in parks were Amsterdam's wealthy merchants and regents, who from the late 1660s loved to surround themselves with his works in their newly built, luxurious interiors. The scenes of expensive decorative birds in gardens clearly matched the aristocratic aspirations of the upper burgher class, who in addition to town houses had country seats built for them in their newly acquired manorial domains, some of which brought privileges that approached those of the nobility.

In the 1670s the stadholder, Prince Willem III, also fell under the spell of Hondecoeter's art, and rewarded him royally for it. His paintings hung in the stadholder's three palaces of Het Loo, Soestdijk and Honselaarsdijk. The earliest provenance of *The floating feather* is the hunting lodge at Soestdijk, but it probably did not arrive there until the 18th century, when Het Loo was vacated. The large canvas shows several ducks swimming in a pool in the foreground, on the surface of which floats the feather that gave the painting its popular name. On the left stands a white pelican, and among the birds in the background are a peacock and a flamingo. The monumental work is rounded off with a view through to a luxuriant garden.

LITERATURE
Stumpel 1995; Vlieger 1995

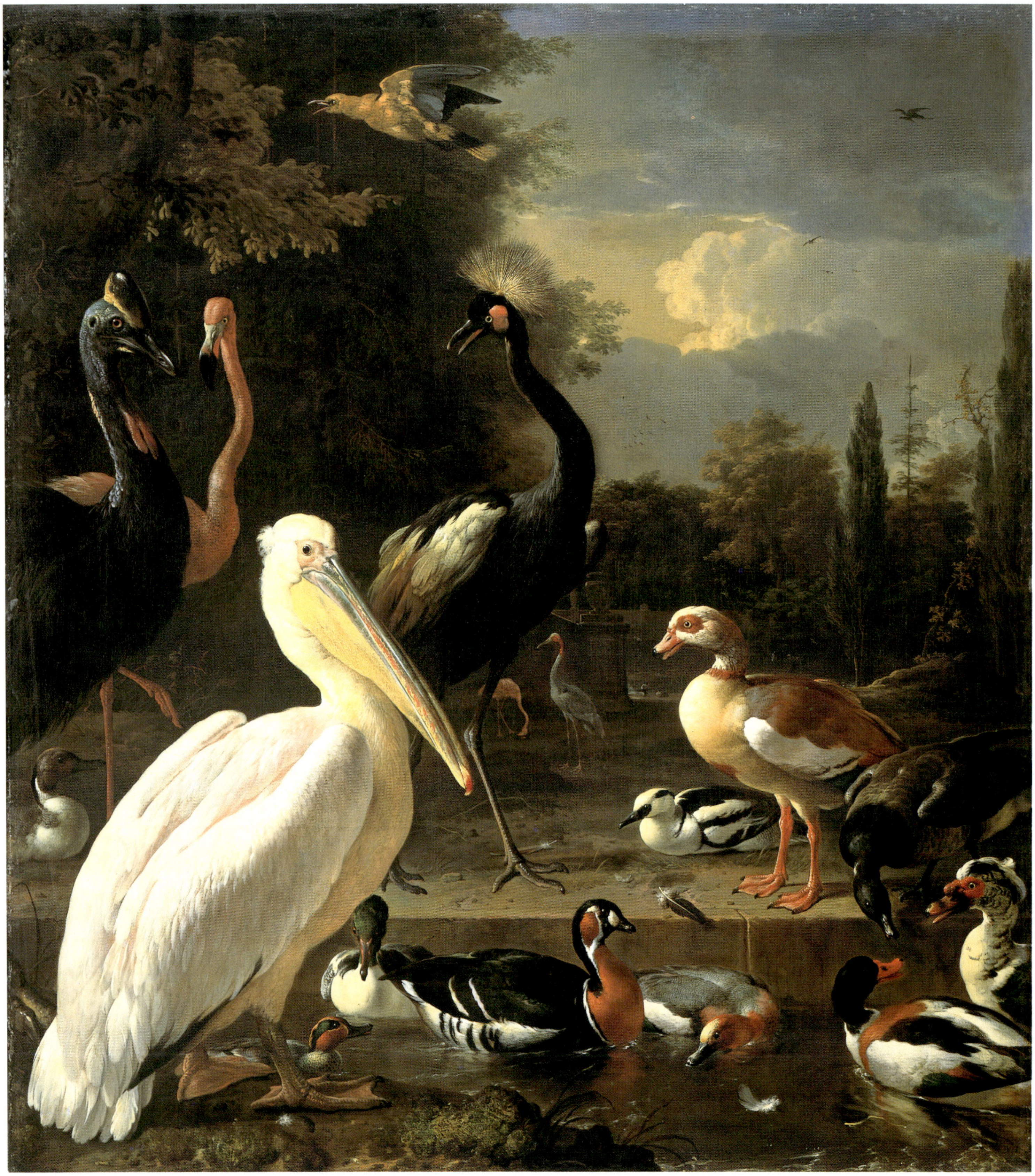

Amsterdam

101 *Petronella Oortman's doll's house, c. 1686-1705*

Cabinet: oak veneered with tortoiseshell and pewter; interior: various materials, h. 255 cm, w. 190 cm, d. 78 cm
Assembled for Petronella Oortman, Amsterdam; purchased in 1821
Inv. no. BK-NM-1010

The doll's houses made in Amsterdam in the second half of the 17th century have been admired since their creation, and are regarded as an inexhaustible source of information about the furnishing of grand merchants' houses in the heyday of the Dutch Republic. Doll's houses are found in other countries, of course, but nowhere else were they executed in such costly materials or was so much care lavished on the faithful reproduction of all sorts of domestic chattels, down to the very humblest. Because the houses have always been famous quite a lot is known about the women from the moneyed burgher class who put them together, but their reasons for doing so are still rather obscure. This one was made by Petronella Oortman (1656-1718), who as a wealthy widow married the silk merchant Johannes Brandt in 1686 and went to live with him in Amsterdam's Warmoesstraat.

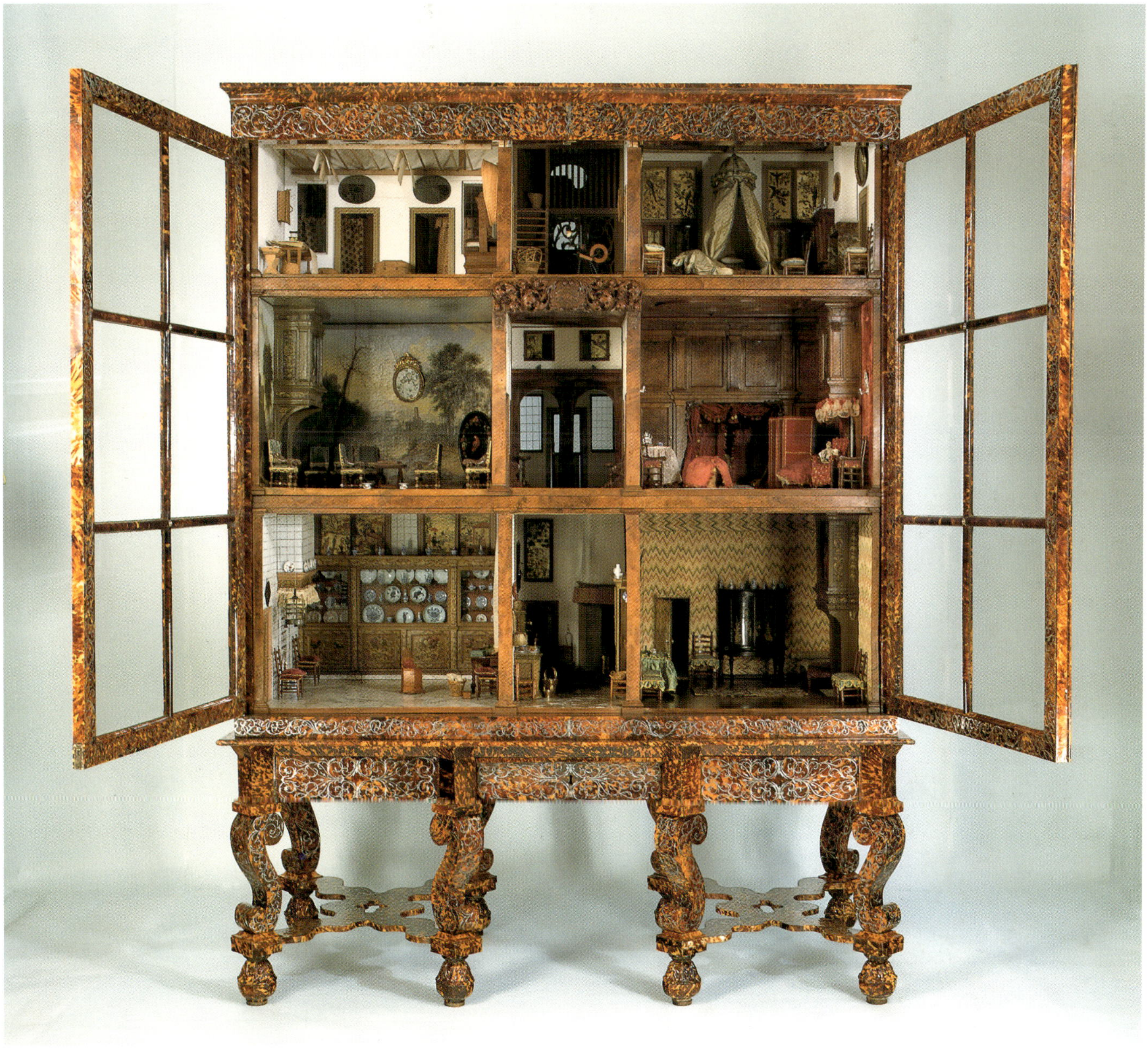

She started assembling her doll's house shortly after their marriage. The first thing that had to be made was the magnificent cabinet, which is one of the most ornate pieces of Dutch furniture to have come down to us from the closing years of the 17th century. The marquetry of pewter tendrils on a tortoiseshell base recalls the finest French work of the period. When the German traveller Zacharias von Uffenbach inspected the house in 1718 he was told that the cupboard was by a French cabinet-maker who had previously worked for the court at Versailles. It is striking that the Amsterdam doll's houses are in cupboards which do not differ essentially from other furniture used for storage. Petronella Oortman's is an early example of a display cabinet. In other countries, by contrast, the exteriors were often in the form of a house. The Dutch ones are in the tradition of collectors' cabinets or art cabinets—items of furniture designed to hold collections of costly or rare objects. They are the female variant, for all the known doll's houses were put together for and by women.

Their contents illustrate a woman's life in the home, with a lying-in room, kitchens and all the other rooms to be found in a well-run household. Women had for long played a leading role in the design of interiors, and this was to gain even greater weight in the 18th century. The vogue of the Dutch doll's house, which was restricted to a close circle, almost exclusively in Amsterdam, is a fascinating chapter in the history of this development, and one that is not easy to explain.

Reading from left to right and from top to bottom, Petronella Oortman's doll's house contains an attic drying room, an room for peat and provisions, a nursery, a drawing room, a hall with a garden beyond, a lying-in room, a display kitchen, a working kitchen with a cellar below, and a tapestry room [*101a*]. This particular doll's house has always been famous for the remarkable authenticity of all its parts. More than in any other doll's house, each object was executed wherever possible in the material used for the full-sized version. In addition, the proportions are very precise. Unfortunately all the dolls have disappeared, with the exception of a baby which was probably hidden in a cradle. The painter Jacob Appel made a 'portrait' of the doll's house around 1710 [*101b*], which shows that is was originally concealed from view by a yellow curtain. Crowned with 'cups' covered in fabric and with a valance along the top, it must have looked like a four-poster bedstead when the curtains were closed.

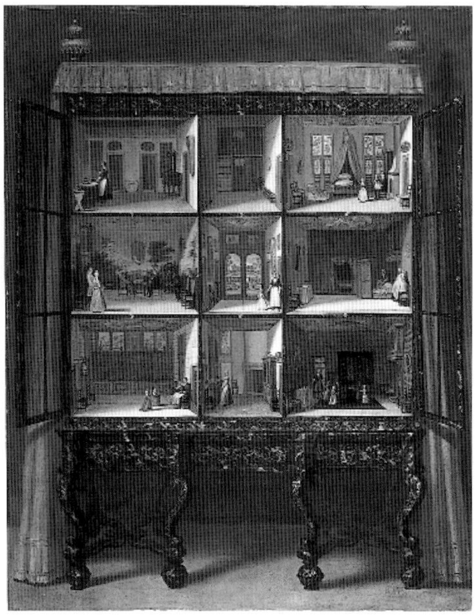

101b Jacob Appel, *Petronella Oortman's doll's house*; oil on vellum on canvas, 87 x 69 cm. Amsterdam, Rijksmuseum

LITERATURE

Pijzel-Dommisse 2000

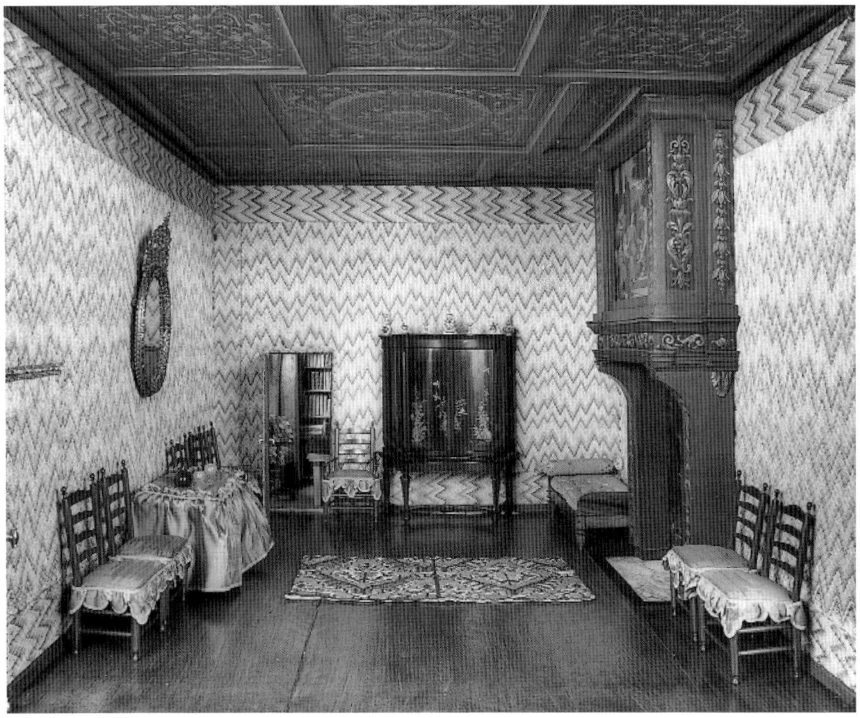

101a The doll's house with the doors open; the tapestry room with a lacquered collector's cabinet

Frans van Mieris (Leiden 1635-Leiden 1681)

102 *Woman writing a letter, 1680*

Oil on panel, 25 × 20 cm
At upper left: *F van Mieris fecit Anno 1680*
From the collections of D. Grenier, Middelburg (1712), Reygersbergen van Cauwerven, Middelburg (1765), G. Braamcamp, Amsterdam (1771), Randon de Boisset, Paris (1777), Beaujon, Paris (1787), Destouches, Paris (1794), H. van Wel, Brussels (1795); purchased in 1808 at the Van der Pot van Groeneveld sale in Rotterdam
Inv. no. SK-A-261

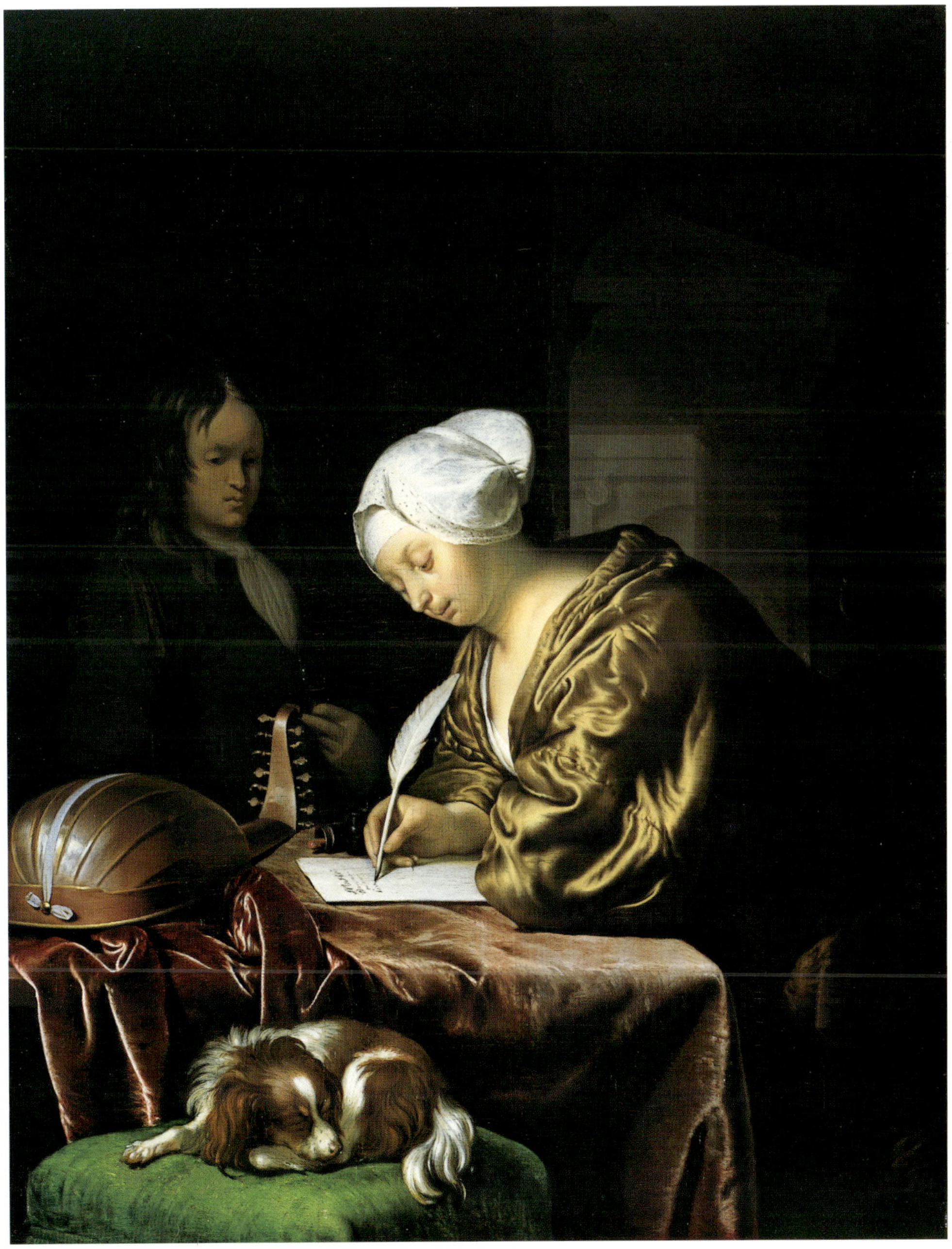

This perfectly preserved late work by Frans van Mieris the Elder, the patriarch of a famous Leiden family of painters, shows that the master, who was fêted during his lifetime and celebrated for his delicate touch until the mid-1800s, retained his fabulous technical refinement to the end of his life. It is also a typical example of Van Mieris's late style, which is characterised by the somewhat mannered faces, especially that of the woman writing the letter, and the slightly unnatural fall of the draperies, most of which are in exuberant, harsh colours. Nevertheless, this costly cabinet piece is superbly painted, and was undoubtedly meant to be held in the hand in order to admire the details.

The subject of a woman writing a letter is known primarily from the oeuvre of Gerard ter Borch, who is regarded as the founder of this branch of genre painting. There is a very fine example in the Mauritshuis in The Hague [*102a*], and it is fair to assume that Van Mieris knew that work or a similar one by the artist. There are two earlier variations on the theme by Van Mieris himself, both of them nocturnes like this one, which had been popularised by Van Mieris's teacher, Gerard Dou [*73*].

If one compares Van Mieris's small panel with Ter Borch's one is immediately struck by the fact that Van Mieris was mainly, if not exclusively, interested in showing his virtuoso ability to imitate textures, whereas Ter Borch, who was also no slouch in that respect, always tried to give his genre scenes a slightly ambivalent psychological charge, which is what makes them so intriguing [*72*]. In that respect Van Mieris is his inferior, so we only have the attributes on the table to tell us whether he intended communicating anything more than his virtuosity with this letter-writer. It has been suggested that the scene has an amorous dimension, with the epistle being a love-letter. In that reading, the lute, which was indeed cited as a symbol of the harmonious cohabitation of a husband and wife in the

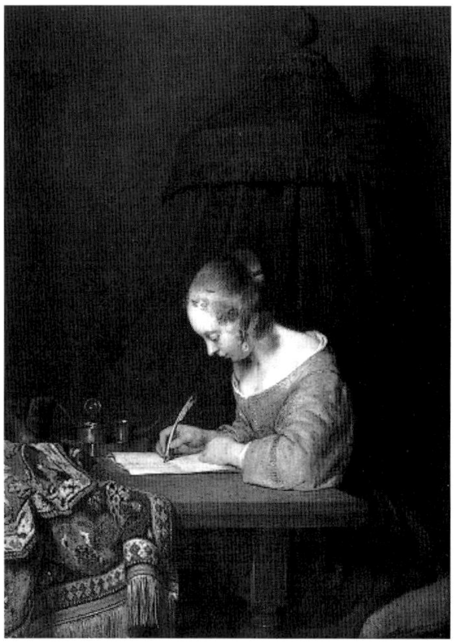

102a Gerard ter Borch, *Woman writing a letter*, c. 1655; oil on panel, 39 x 29.5 cm. The Hague, Mauritshuis

17th century, is there ready to be taken up by the woman's lover so that they can sing love songs together. However, it is a little odd to write a letter to a lover who is expected at any moment, and on top of that it is known that making music by oneself was not uncommon in well-to-do circles. The English diarist Samuel Pepys (1633-1703) repeatedly tells how he played music to divert himself. The lute could therefore be regarded simply as an utterly plausible attribute in a genteel interior. So we can only guess as to the nature of the letter this woman is writing, and perhaps that was (and is) what makes scenes of this kind so enjoyable.

LITERATURE

Naumann 1981, vol. 1, p. 111, vol. 2, p. 123, no. 118; exhib. cat. Leiden 1988, no. 27

Francis van Bossuit (Brussels 1635-Amsterdam 1692)

103 *Mars, c. 1680-1692*

Ivory, h. 44 cm
From the collections of Petronella Oortmans-de la Court, Leiden (1707) and Jeronimus Tonneman, Amsterdam; purchased in 1998 with the aid of the Vereniging Rembrandt
Inv. no. BK-1998-74

The sculptor Francis van Bossuit garnered great fame in Amsterdam because he transformed 'the hard ivory into a delicate softness with his chisel strokes, which sent the chips flying hither and thither'. The best illustration of that 'delicate softness' is provided by this monumental, free-standing *Mars*, which was rediscovered only a few years ago. It occupies a very special position within the known oeuvre of Francis van Bossuit, being the largest and only surviving free-standing ivory from his hand. Its discovery made it clearer than ever why he has been so famous since the 17th century, for our knowledge of his oeuvre has so far been restricted to small ivory reliefs carved and composed with great virtuosity, such as his *Venus and Adonis* [103a]. *Mars* is almost half a metre high, and was carved from a tusk with a diameter of at least 14 centimetres, the shape of which is reflected in the compact and slightly curved composition of the statue.

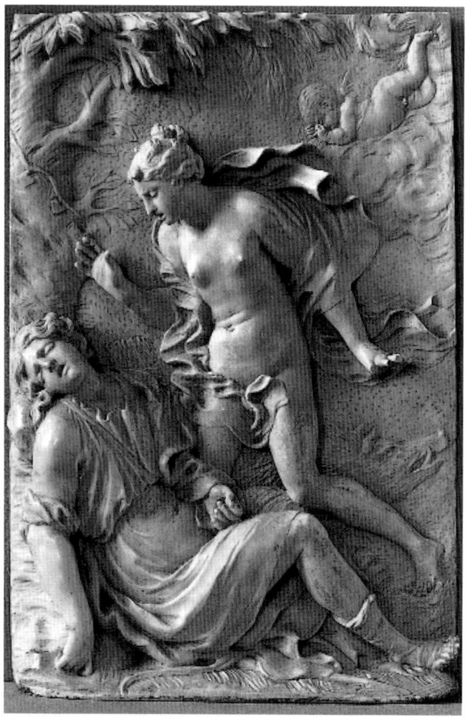

103a Francis van Bossuit, *Venus and Adonis*, c. 1682-1692; ivory, 18.1 x 12.5 cm. Amsterdam, Rijksmuseum

Francis van Bossuit carved *Mars* after his arrival in Amsterdam. Born in Brussels in 1635 and trained in Antwerp, he went to Rome in the 1650s and spent most of his career there. He settled in Amsterdam in 1680, where he lived until his death in 1692, rapidly gaining a high reputation. Van Bossuit's experiences in Italy formed the basis for an internationally inflected Baroque style, which in Amsterdam was to mix with the local influences of Artus Quellinus and Rombout Verhulst.

Mars was published as a work by Van Bossuit as early as 1727 in Mattys Pool's *Beeld-snyders Kunst-kabinet* [103b-c]. This remarkable work, an early example of an art book in several languages, is devoted entirely to the work of the ivory carver. It contains more than 100 engravings reproducing a considerable part of Van Bossuit's oeuvre. The prints, which are after drawings by Barent Graat, show the master's ivory, wooden and terracotta statues from different angles [103c]

When Graat drew the ivory *Mars* it was in the famous art collection of Petronella Oortmans-de la Court (1624-1707) along with nine other works by Van Bossuit. Her estate inventory of 1707 states that the 'ivory Mars by Francis' formed a pair with a *Venus*, and that both stood on ebony plinths. Today, however, the *Venus* is known

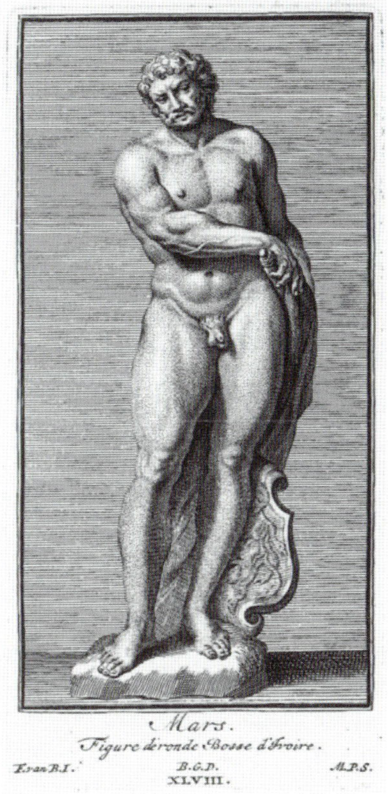

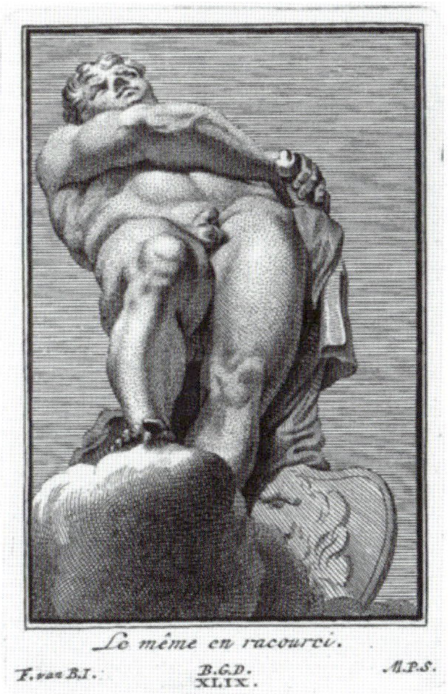

103b-c Mattys Pool after Barent Graat, *Mars by Van Bossuit, seen from the front and from below*; engravings from Mattys Pool, *Beeld-snyders Kunst-kabinet*, Amsterdam 1727, pls. XLVIII and XLIX

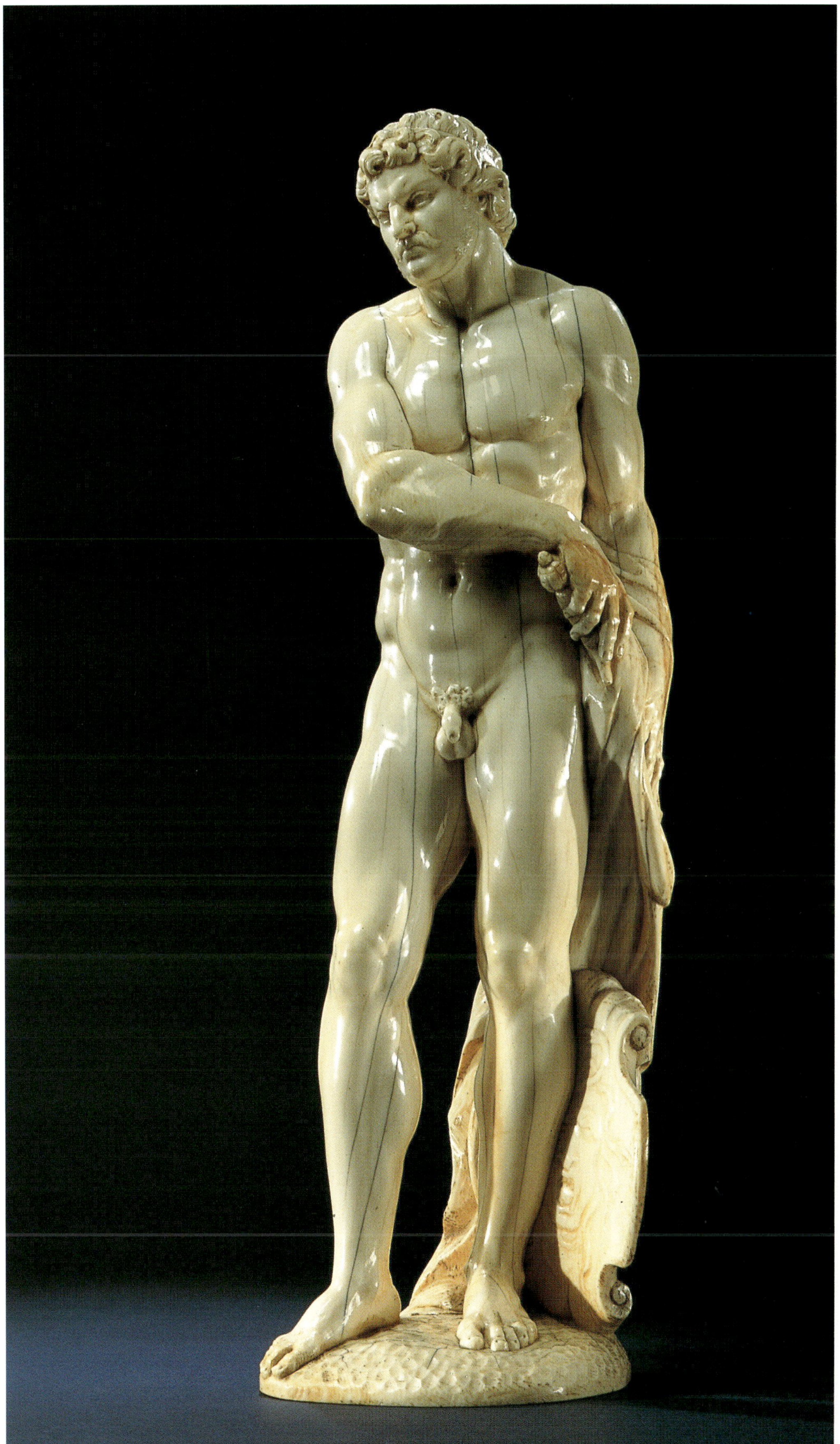

only from a drawing by the Leiden artist Willem van Mieris. It was a relatively rare scene of her with the love god Anteros, who is breaking the bow belonging to his little brother Cupid—a subject that can be traced back to an emblem by Alciati. Van Mieris drew several of Van Bossuit's ivories and incorporated them in his paintings. *Mars*, for instance, reappears in the guise of Odysseus in a painting of the Greek hero with Circe the sorceress. Such painterly reworkings of ivory compositions could be seen in the light of the traditional rivalry between painting and sculpture, but perhaps it was also encouraged by Van Mieris's rich patrons. In any event, they confirm the great esteem in which Francis van Bossuit's work was held.

LITERATURE

Theuerkauff 1975; Scholten 1999

Adriaen van der Werff (Kralingen 1659-Rotterdam 1722)

104 *Amorous couple in a park spied upon by children, 1694*

Oil on panel, 37 x 30 cm
At lower right: *Adrn. v. werff. fec./ Ao 1694*
From the Adriaan van der Hoop Collection; bequeathed to the City of Amsterdam in 1854; on loan to the Rijksmuseum since 1885
Inv. no. SK-C-265

Looking back on his successful career, Adriaen van der Werff disowned the works he had painted before 1697, judging by the paintings he catalogued the year he died. Not one 'notable worthy piece' left his studio prior to that date. He was dismissing the genre scenes and portraits he had painted before entering the service of the Elector Palatine—an extremely successful career move which was to earn him a fortune and a knighthood to go with it. His opinion, of course, does not do justice to the high standard of his work in those early years, of which this *Amorous couple in a park* is a masterly example.

A scantily clad shepherd, identified by the staff and recorder on the ground in front of him, embraces a half-naked young woman whose disarranged clothing conceals only the most delicate part of her anatomy. They are seated before a garden wall with a circular hole in it giving a view of a marble statue of Silenus. On the right, amidst the greenery, is a sculpture of a satyr dancing on a pedestal. Two boys on the right are spying on the lovers, the one in front holding a mask.

This erotic pastoral must have been regarded as very near the knuckle when it was made. Startlingly, the shepherdess's features bear more than a passing resemblance to those of the artist's wife, Margareta Rees, whose portrait he painted a few years later. Van der Werff's eclecticism is demonstrated by the fact that the statue of the dancing satyr was taken from an illustration in a book of 1668 by Jan de Bisschop, and the lusty shepherd in his impossible pose from an engraving after a design by Carlo Bonone, where the man embodies *The genius of the arts*. Van der Werff's later, strictly Classicist paintings are far more peaceful, harmonious compositions, but the mastery of the early works, with their melting brushwork, refinement of detail and delicate infusion of colour and tone, makes his later rejection of paintings like this one difficult to understand, to put it mildly.

LITERATURE

Exhib. cat. Amsterdam 1989-90, no. 57

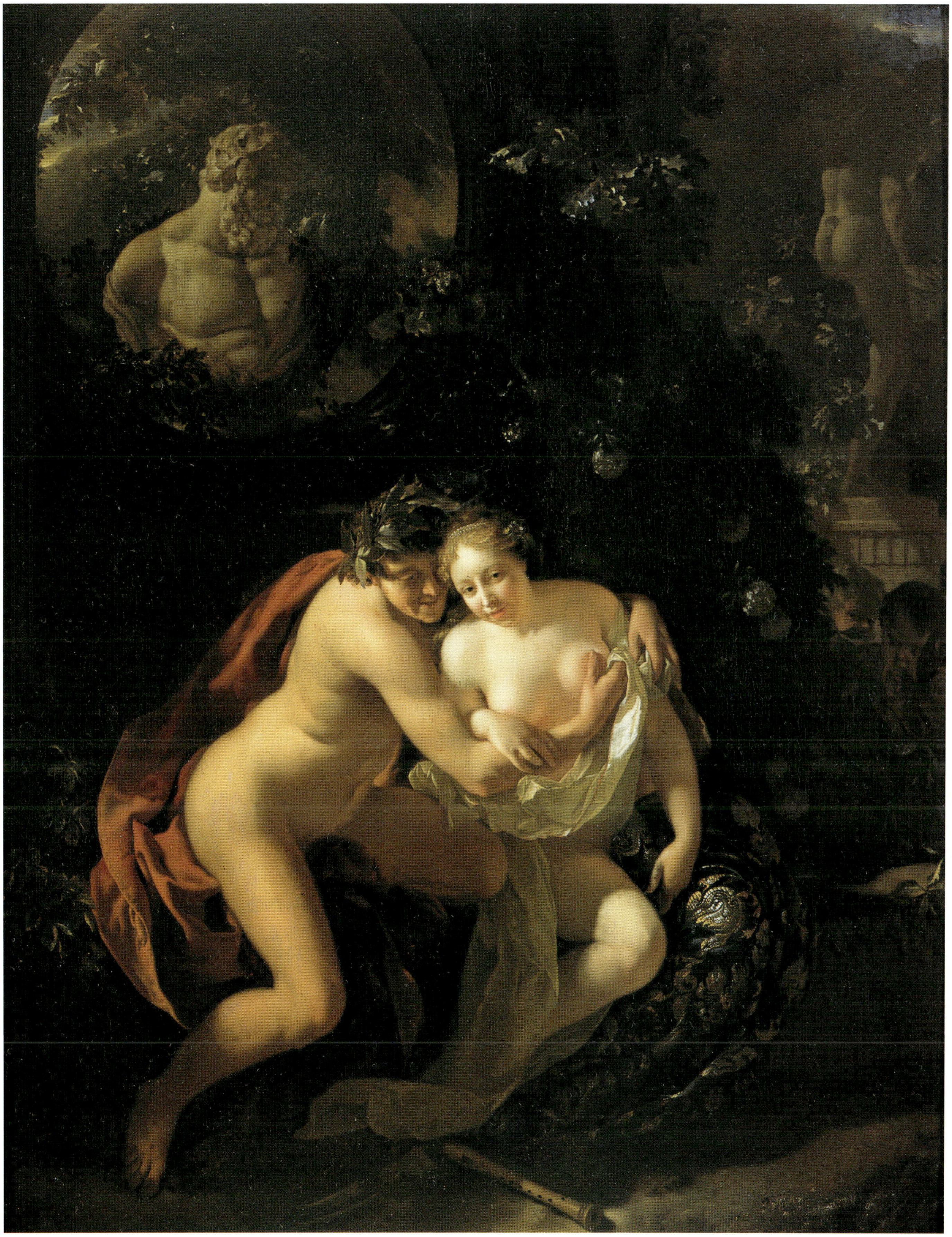

Adriaen Coorte (Middelburg ?-Middelburg ?)

105 *Still life with asparagus, 1697*

Oil on paper, on panel, 25 x 20.5 cm
At lower right, on the edge of the table: *A Coorte 1697*
A.A. des Tombes Bequest, The Hague 1903
Inv. no. SK-A-2099

Adriaen Coorte was the odd man out among the still life painters of his day. Towards the end of the 17th century there was a dramatic fall in the number of painters. In the sheer struggle for existence, fewer and fewer masters supplied an increasingly pampered public with work that became more and more elegant. That is particularly true of still life painting, where large sums were paid for extremely professional but sometimes rather decorative, empty pictures. The artists who profited most from this trend were Rachel Ruysch, Jan Weenix, Melchior d'Hondecoeter and Jan van Huysum. Outside this small coterie there seems to have been no room for more modest still-life paintings. Coorte's however, are an exception. His pictures stand out for their extreme simplicity, loving concentration, and the isolated look of a few shells or a handful of strawberries on a plinth bathed in a harsh, unrealistic, almost spectral light. He occasionally tried to produce rather more complicated compositions, but they were rarely a success. His fame in Middelburg in Zeeland, was for a long time no more than local chauvinism. It was only in the middle of the 20th century that an international public discovered the charm of his work, which was undoubtedly due to a love of the intimate detail and a rejection of the overwrought, those hollow demonstrations of painterly skill beloved of his successful contemporaries. What is so striking about the recent reappraisal of all five artists is that Coorte's star has not waned, probably because the contrast between him and the others, between simplicity and excess, has been found enriching.

The small painting in the Rijksmuseum is of a bundle of asparagus. It probably consists of more than 20 pieces, but Coorte shows just 7. The bunch rests on a single asparagus, tilting it back on the tabletop. The artist captured the appearance of the vegetables brilliantly: their creamy white colour tending towards purple, the scaly crowns and the stems cut aslant. The reddish brown, tufted piece of string casts a few subtle shadows on the whitish vegetables. The artist even included the mouldy, bad spots. By placing the asparagus in a bright light cast from the right and falling on a cracked stone tabletop he removed every association with the farmer, the marketplace and the kitchen. The painting is of asparagus, pure and simple, of the artistic potential of a bunch of vegetables.

Coorte usually painted in oils on paper which was then pasted onto panel, as he did here. It is not surprising, then, that a parallel is drawn with the many nature studies made in the 17th century, which were collected together in albums. Although Coorte sometimes produced small series of his simple still lifes, in pairs or fours, there is no question of the systematic approach inherent in the nature studies. His distinctive technique merely highlights his isolated position among the still-life painters of his day.

LITERATURE

Bol 1977; exhib. cat. Amsterdam 1999, no. 14

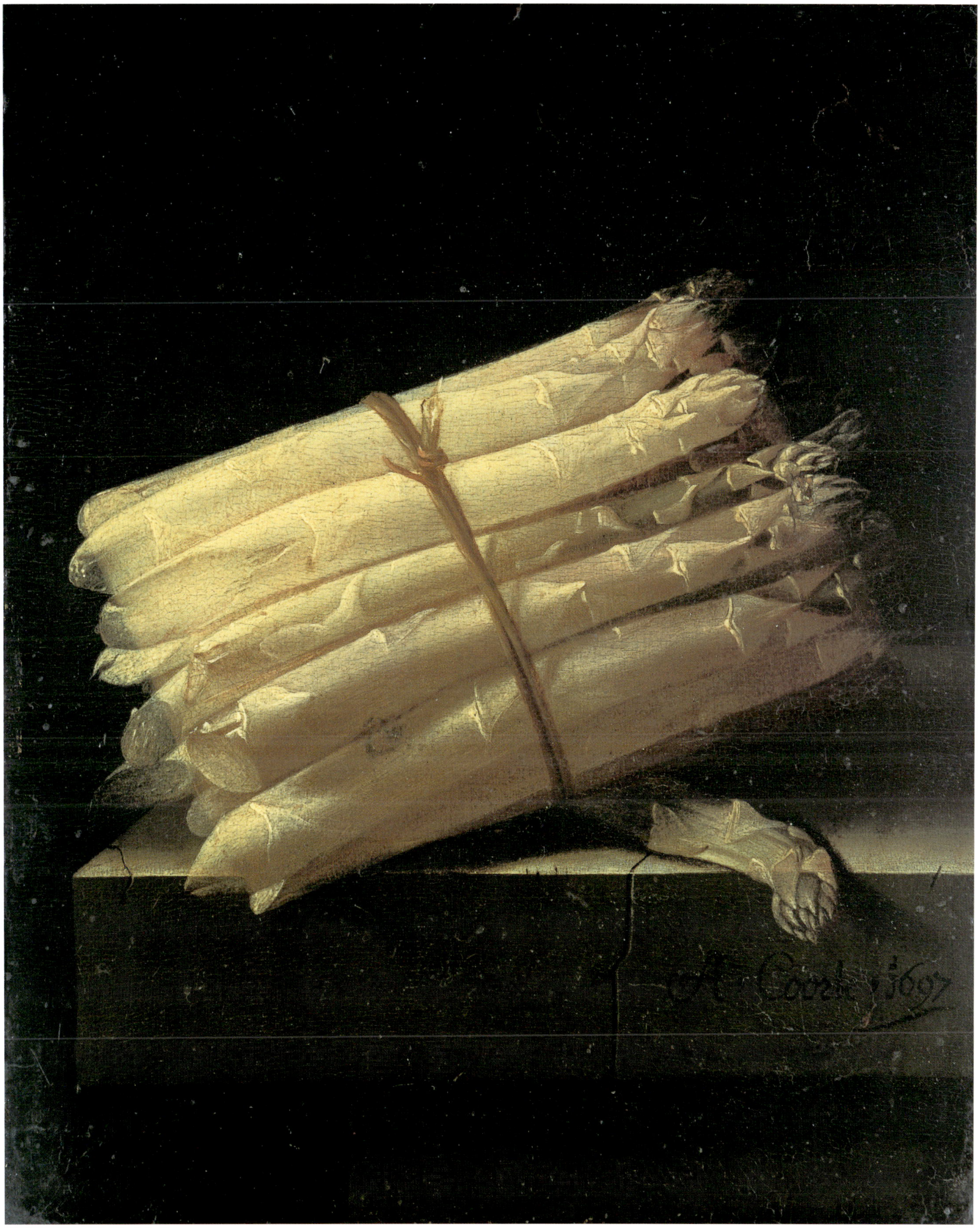

Adam Loofs (The Hague ? c. 1645-The Hague 1710)

106 *Silver candlestick with a female figure as the stem, 1687*

Silver, h. 28.6 cm, ø 13.4 cm
Marked on the underside of the foot-rim: The Hague assay mark, the Dutch lion, the year letter N (1687) and the master's mark AL in ligature beneath a crowned tree (Adam Loofs)
Purchased in 1966
Inv. no. BK-1966-10

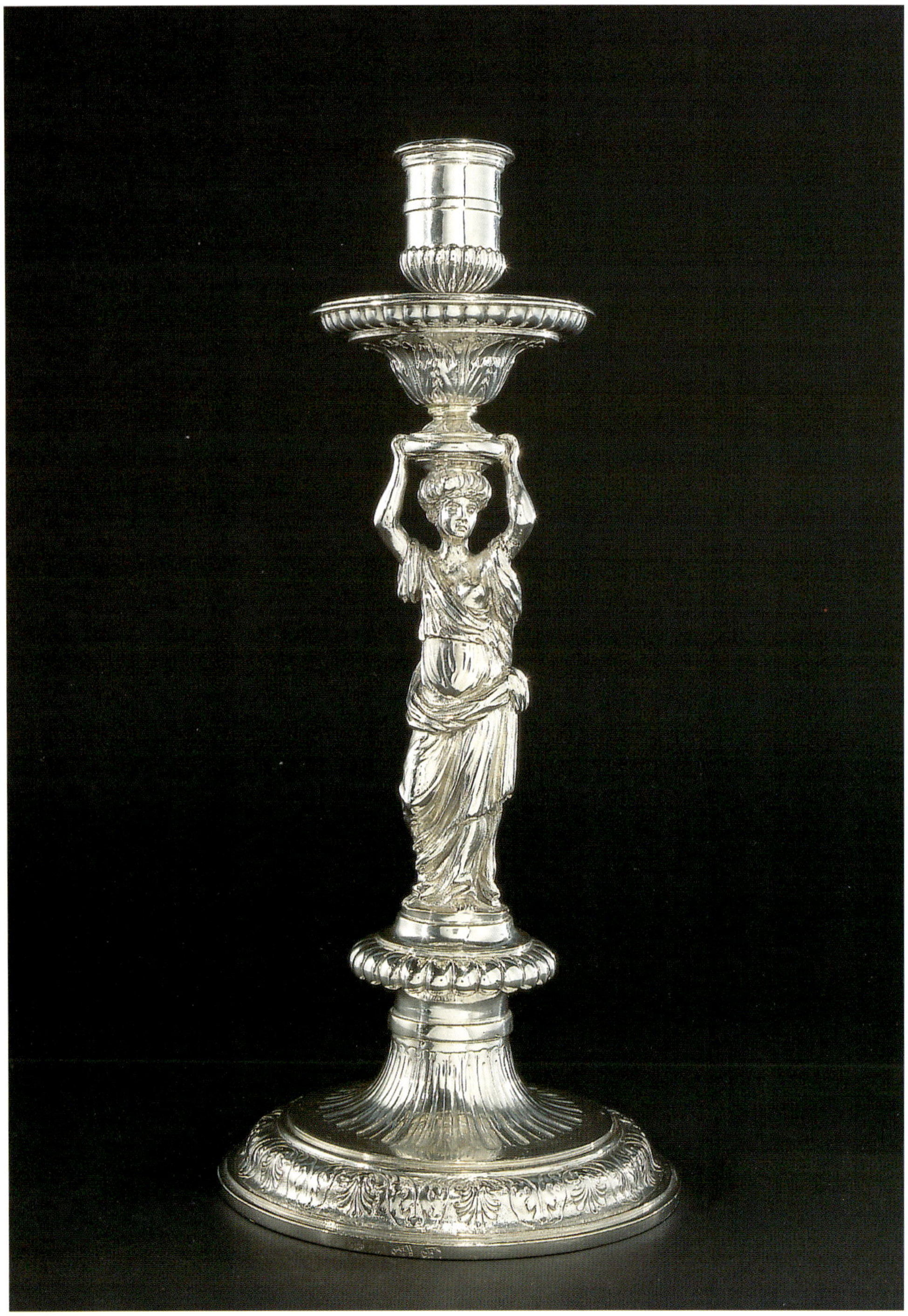

This is an early example in Dutch silver of the influence of the French style popular at the court of Louis XIV. It is not just the form that is distinctive, but above all the decoration with palmettes, acanthus leaves and 'fish-bladder' motifs. The Dutch silversmith Adam Loofs became familiar with the Louis XIV style while working in Paris in the 1670s.

On 1 May 1680, soon after his return to the Netherlands, the talented Loofs was appointed 'Gold and silversmith-in-ordinary and steward of the silver' to Stadholder Willem III. As steward of the silver he was responsible for the custody and condition of the gold and silver objects in the palaces in The Hague and of those in the country houses of the stadholder and his wife, Princess Mary. Loofs's principal position, though, was court silversmith. A 1697 inventory of 'His Majesty's gold and silver vessels [...] being in the custody and stewardship of Adam Loofs' shows that he had delivered hundreds of decorative and utilitarian objects to the court, including plates, dishes, beakers, bottles, chamber-pots, wine coolers and even furniture. Candlesticks are also listed, and it is very likely that this one also belonged to Willem III, for carved on the underside of the foot is the letter W.

It is odd that the stadholder should prefer Loofs, who had worked in Paris, to any of the long-standing Hague masters. He was probably attracted to the exceptional quality of Loofs's work, which reflected the style in vogue at the Sun King's court.

Loofs's oeuvre is closely related to that of French silversmiths of the late 17th century. The objects are generally monumental in structure, symmetrical in form, and decorated with motifs borrowed from classical antiquity.

The standing female figure, a caryatid, supporting the candle-holder may have been taken from an etching by Jean le Pautre (1618-1682) of c. 1675, which contains a design for a similar candlestick.

Le Pautre's prints with designs for gold and silver objects, pieces of furniture and fabrics were imitated by countless craftsmen in northern Europe, and candlesticks with stems in the form of female figures were also being made in England in the same period.

LITERATURE
Exhib. cat. Amsterdam/Toledo/Boston 1979-80, no. 87; Ter Molen 1987-88; exhib. cat. New York/Pittsburgh 1988-89, no. 67; exhib. cat. Amsterdam 2000b, no. 194

Delft, The Grieksche A pottery under Adriaen Kocks

107 *Two large tiles from a column, c. 1690*

Blue-painted faience, 62 x 61.5 cm
On loan from the Koninklijk Oudheidkundig Genootschap since 1955
Inv. nos. BK-KOG-2567 (above), BK-KOG-1681 (below)

The plans of King-Stadholder Willem III and his wife Mary Stuart to tile the walls of one or more rooms in their palace at Hampton Court outside London was part of the old Dutch tradition of sealing damp walls with glazed tiles. Dutch tile-makers were accustomed to executing large designs in the form of tableaux using ordinary tiles, the standard size of which in the 17th century was 5 inches square, roughly 13 x 13 centimetres. In the course of the century the innovative Dutch potteries managed to reduce the thickness of a tile to 7 millimetres and still make a completely flat product.

Few tile-makers in the province of Holland would have had any problem with the plan to tile the walls of the Water Gallery, a Tudor building in the palace grounds. Their products were so standardised and flat that the joins were almost invisible, resulting in magnificent tableaux. But the court's proposal to have the Water Gallery tableaux executed not on standard tiles but on panels measuring 2 feet by 2 feet (62 x 62 cm) must have made the project nearly unfeasible and caused all the Dutch potteries to despair. It was almost impossible to make such large sheets. They had to be thick enough but not too thick, but were too big for the largest sagger, so they had to be fired standing upright, packed between incombustible material, remain flat, and without the decoration running during firing.

Willem and Mary had followed in the footsteps of his grandmother Amalia van Solms by amassing a large collection of Chinese porcelain and delftware, which could be used to decorate walls and, in the case of the larger pieces, to lend further touches of splendour to a room. Delftware was painted in the Chinese manner, so could easily be displayed alongside real porcelain. With their plans for furnishing Hampton Court, Willem and Mary went a step further, ordering large vases and covered pots from Delft in a special new design and with decoration they specified themselves. When Willem was still just stadholder, before he ventured across the Channel to claim the throne of England, he had been advised on several building projects by the French Huguenot Daniel Marot (1661-1752), and although Marot's name does not appear in the financial accounts for building work at Hampton Court it can be assumed that he had a hand in some of the decoration and furnishing of the Water Gallery. The designs for the tiling, at any rate, appeared in print under his name around 1700.

The Delft pottery, De Grieksche A, which was run at this time by Adriaen Kocks, was capable of carrying out the commission to the specifications of such demanding clients. While it was still under the management of Kocks's brother-in-law, Samuel van Eenhoorn, it had made pieces for Het Loo Palace, Willem and Mary's country seat at Apeldoorn. Its leading position in Delft, and the homogeneity of the decoration of the tile panels and the large vases which are still at Hampton Court, make it likely that this was the pottery which supplied the tiling.

Building work at Hampton Court came to a halt after Mary's death in 1694. The Water Gallery was torn down before 1700, despite its recent rebuilding. The tile panels were probably ripped out, with

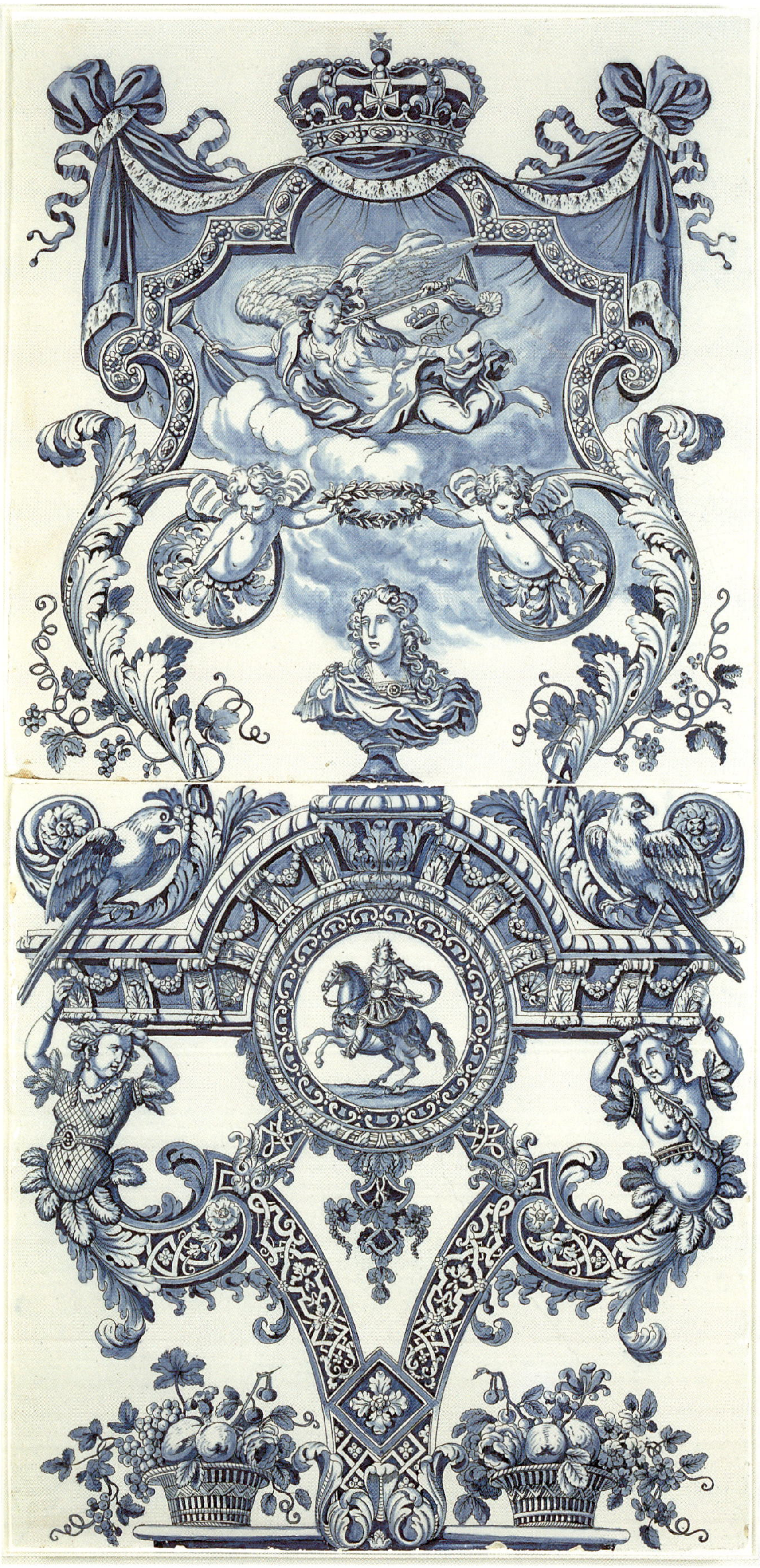

a courtier carrying off such fragments as were worth rescuing. Ten tiles from at least four ensembles appeared on the English art market in 1923. Five of them are now in the Rijksmuseum, while museums in New York, Sèvres, Copenhagen, London and Delft have one each.

LITERATURE

Lane 1959; exhib. cat. London 1964, no. 228; exhib. cat. New York/Pittsburgh 1988-89, no. 165

Northern Netherlands (The Hague ?)

108 *Table, c. 1700*

Limewood and oak (tabletop), gilt, h. 87.5 cm, w. 108.5 cm, d. 73.5 cm
From the H. Klugtkist Hesse Collection, Kollum; donated by the Commissie voor Fotoverkoop, 1937
Inv. no. BK-14980

After Willem III was made stadholder of the Seven United Provinces in 1672 the Netherlands regained a court culture, albeit on a modest scale, but it expanded after 1689, when he and his wife, Mary Stuart, became king and queen of England. They now needed objects which had no place in the homes of ordinary citizens—pieces fit for royalty, both for themselves and for members of their entourage. Although Willem's whole life was dominated by the struggle with King Louis XIV, the French court style was still the one to emulate. The main person who brought it to his court was Daniel Marot (1661-1752), a French Huguenot who had worked for Louis XIV at Versailles and elsewhere but who fled to the Dutch Republic after the Revocation of the Edict of Nantes. He was in an ideal position to advise the king-stadholder and his retinue about the customs and latest fashions at the French court, and he made designs in the French style for almost every part of palaces and their gardens.

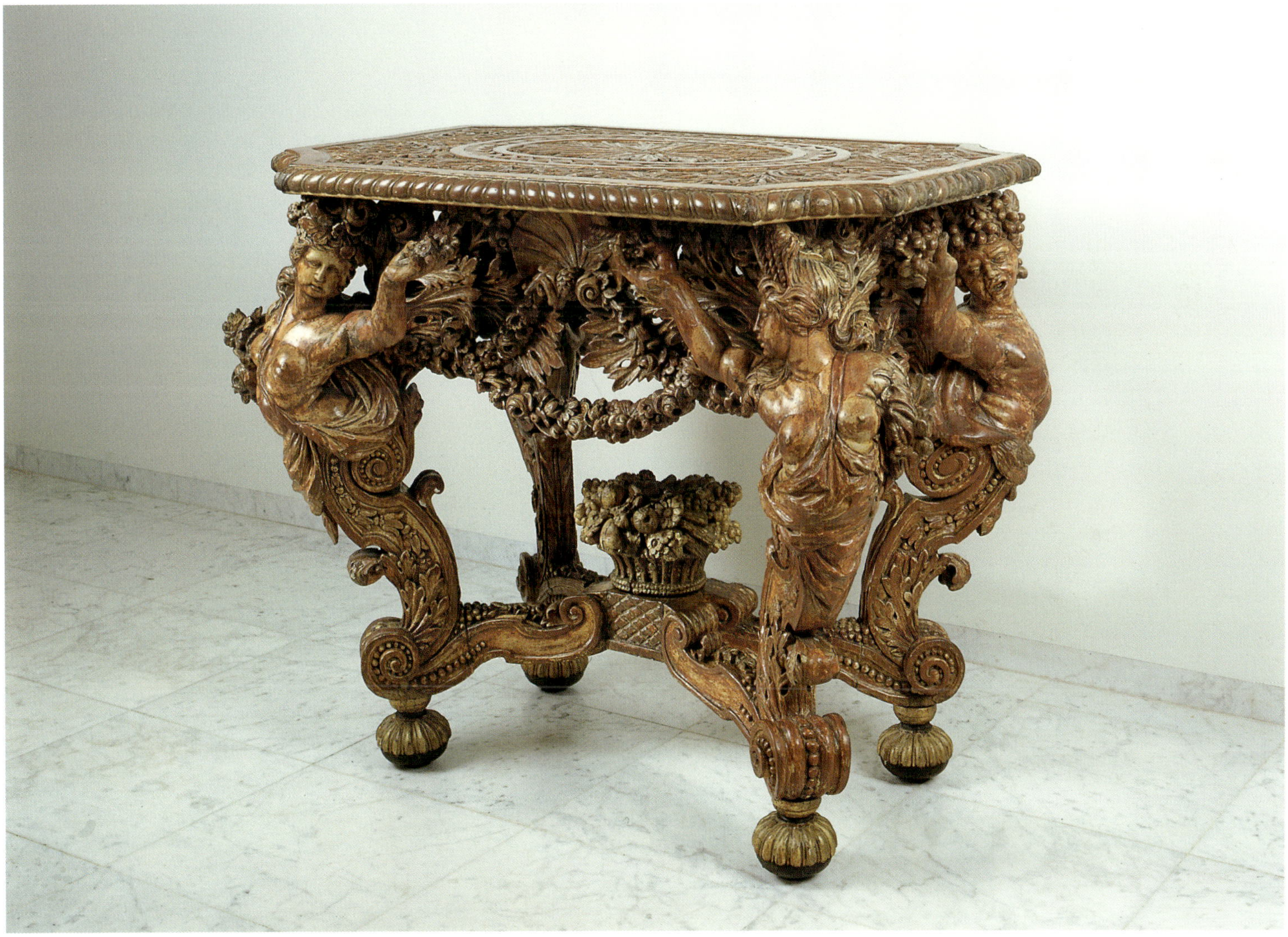

This carved table with its legs in the form of herms representing the four seasons is a piece of court furniture *par excellence*. The use of human figures gives it a grandeur which would probably have been considered unseemly in less elevated surroundings. Ornamental furniture of this kind at Louis's court was originally made mainly of silver, but the king was soon forced to have the pieces melted down to finance his wars, and he had them replaced with others executed in wood which was then gilt or silvered. Willem III also had fine pieces of silver furniture, and in his case too their prestige was certainly reflected in the wood imitations. This table with its squat, heavy forms was closer to French designs of the 1670s, like those of Jean le Pautre (1618-1682), than to Marot's engravings of some decades later. Many Huguenots sought refuge in the Netherlands, among them cabinetmakers, embroiderers and sculptors. This table is probably the work of one of those craftsmen, who brought about a synthesis between the old-fashioned forms he knew from his native country and the fashionable elements propagated by Marot, such as the distinctive angular curves of the stretchers. The makers of such distinctive court furniture were mainly active in The Hague.

The print by Le Pautre shows that a pier-table of this kind was often conceived in conjunction with two stands on either side and with a mirror above. These furniture ensembles, which were often placed between the windows, made for a powerful architectonic accent in the succession of rooms which was so typical of palace architecture in the late 17th century. That this specimen is indeed a pier-table is clear from the fact that the figures are turned towards the front and that the rear edge of the tabletop is undecorated.

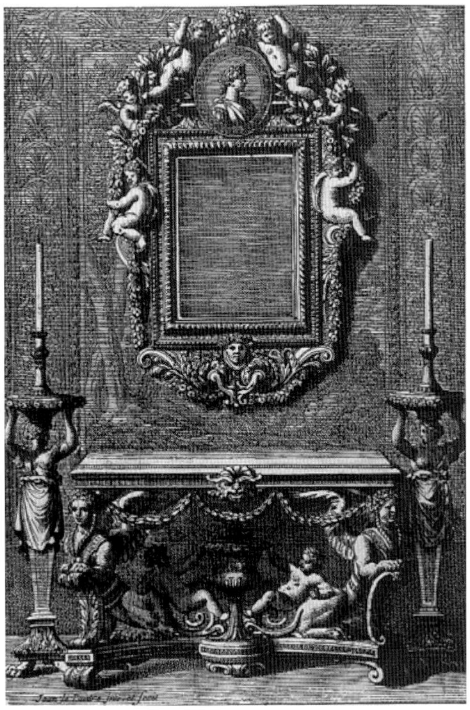

108a Jean le Pautre, Ornament print from *Livres de Miroirs, Tables et Guéridons*, Paris 1670

LITERATURE

Cat. Amsterdam 1952a, no. 315; cat. Amsterdam 1993b, no. 31

Detail of fig. 64 ▸

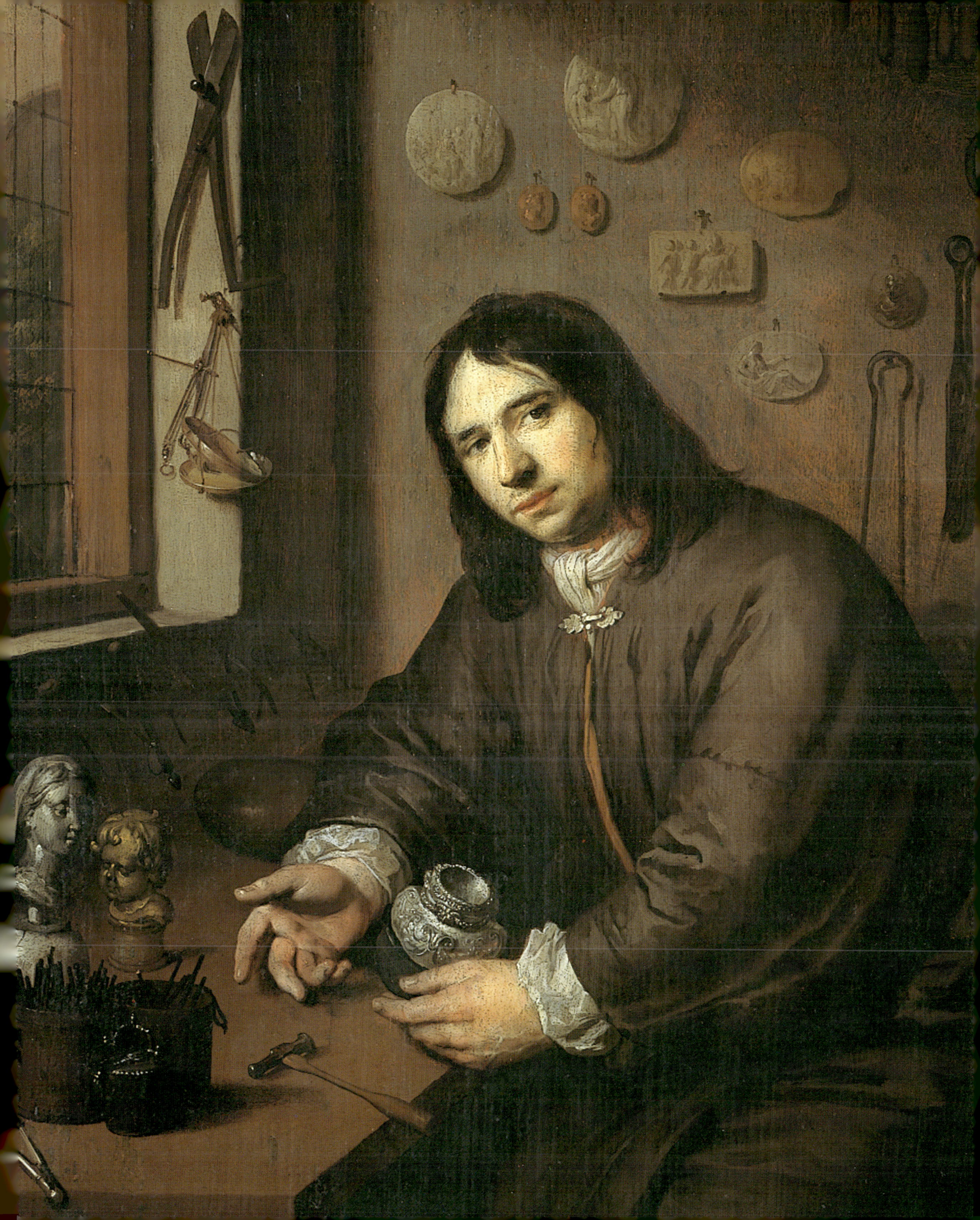

The materials and methods of the 17th-century masters

A trend that made a cautious appearance at the end of 16th century came to full fruition in the second half of the 17th. Art diversified into numerous specialities and specialists, there was scaling-up, rationalisation, mechanisation, a more efficient use of materials, an extensive division of labour, and even forms of mass production.

These developments are well illustrated by the production of delftware. Demand for it was stimulated at the beginning of the 17th century when oriental porcelain appeared on the European market after the Dutch captured two Portuguese ships laden with Chinese ceramics. There was enormous interest when the booty was auctioned in 1602 and 1604, and the Dutch East India Company itself began importing huge quantities of this 'carrack porcelain'.[1] Imitations were not long in coming. In 1667, Dirk van Bleyswijck, writing about Delft, said that 'Nowhere in the country is porcelain made more exquisitely and finely than in this city, where they appear to be emulating the Chinese most excellently'.[2] Production was on a large scale from the outset, and hundreds of millions of items were made. That this was done in Delft was not that unusual, for it had a long tradition of manufacturing ceramics in potteries and majolica workshops. That, though, was fairly cheap and crude earthenware covered with a transparent lead glaze. The output of earthenware in Dutch cities increased with the arrival of majolica potters after the fall of Antwerp in 1585, many of whom originally came from Italy. They covered the back of their wares with the cheap, transparent lead glaze, but the front with a white tin glaze which provided a fine finish. This white *bianchi de Faenza* was of a higher quality than the traditional, local product, and became the basis for delftware.

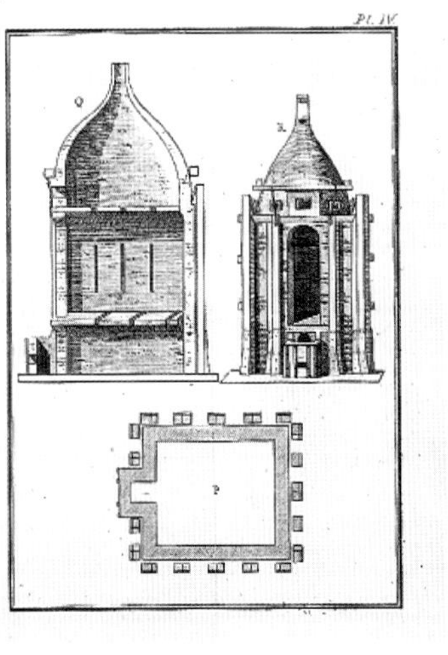

fig. 55 A potter's kiln, plate IV in *De plateelbakker of Delftsch aardewerk-maker: met plaaten*, Dordrecht 1794

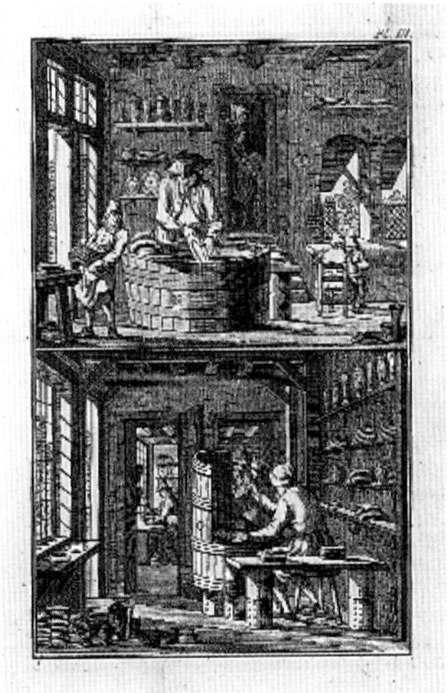

fig. 56 Applying the tin glaze, plate III in *De plateelbakker of Delftsch aardewerk-maker: met plaaten*, Dordrecht 1794

Kaolin, which is needed to fire true porcelain, was readily available to the Chinese, enabling them to produce clear white vitrified pottery with a thin, translucent body. The Delft potters had no kaolin at their disposal, so made do with alluvial clay, most of which came from the surrounding region and had to be mixed to obtain a workable material: 'Clay from Tournai or Brabant, German clay from Mülheim, a small town on the Ruhr in the Duchy of Berg, are brought here, black clay and Delft clay'.[3] These types of clay usually contain a lot of impurities, so require rinsing and sieving, which was usually done on the banks of the River Schie. 'The mixture, having been shovelled into a brass sieve or vat, then settles into the tray below, leaving behind the gross impurities or unsteeped parts in the sieve, with the remainder in the tray.'[4] When the tray was full the mixture was allowed to settle, with the water rising to the top and being poured off. The clay mixture, consisting of quartz, clay and feldspar, was then set out to dry until it had reached a kneadable consistency, when it was cut into square blocks and sent to the potteries.

The potter used a foot-powered wheel to throw vessels, and moulds into which the moist clay was pressed. Small parts like handles, spouts and decorations, were modelled by hand. When the object had been given its basic shape it was touched up with spatulas and then set aside to dry, allowing the water between the clay particles to evaporate. The object became harder and harder and eventually lost its plasticity. Once completely dry it was ready for firing in the large kiln in the potter's workshop (*fig. 55*).

An object fired in this way has a matt surface and is also quite porous, which is obviously totally unpractical for vessels designed to hold liquids. In addition, in Delft it had a reddish brown or yellowish colour. In order to correct this, the object was given a glaze — a thin layer of glass that melts into and onto the pores and seals them (*fig. 56*). This filled in any irregularities and gave the surface the look of porcelain. The addition of a little tin oxide to the glaze turned it an opaque white colour (*fig. 57*). The finishing touch was the addition of decoration that had a Chinese appearance, which could be done by grinding coloured glass with the glaze powder, or even more effectively by adding various metal oxides.[5]

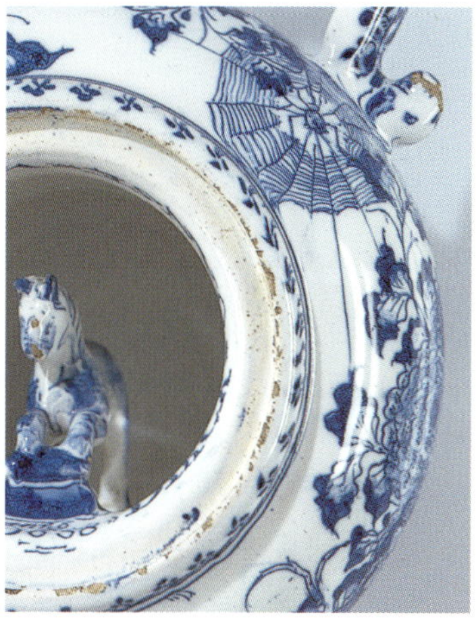

fig. 57 Faience jug, 1658, with damage revealing the original colour of the brownish clay beneath the bright white tin glaze. Amsterdam, Rijksmuseum

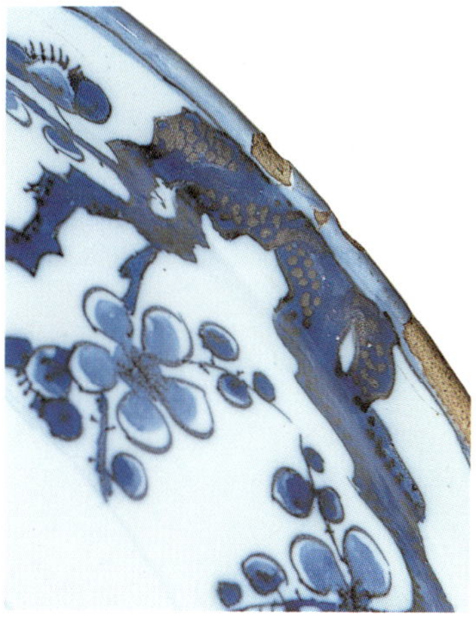

fig. 58 Delft, c. 1670-1685, *Large faience dish*, attributed to Lambertus Kleffius's factory, De Metalen Pot. The deep blue decoration was obtained by melting cobalt oxides (zaffer) in the glaze. Amsterdam, Rijksmuseum

Blue, the main colour used on Delft faience, was obtained from cobalt oxides, as it was for true Chinese porcelain. It was supplied to potters as 'zaffer', a name derived from the Latin *saphirus*. Zaffer is obtained by calcining cobalt ore with quartz sand and a flux, usually potash. The precise shade of blue was governed by elements like nickel, iron, manganese, silver and arsenic in associated minerals which are always present in the ore. They yielded colours ranging from a brownish black to a purplish violet. The main sources of zaffer were Schneeberg and Annaberg in Saxony.[6]

There were already eight Delft potteries using zaffer at the beginning of the 17th century, and in 1627 the faience potter Jacob van den Heuvel had 876 pounds of it in stock.[7] It was melted in the glaze, forming superb, deep blue patterns (*fig. 58*). Blue cobalt glass was used not only for ceramics, but when coarsely ground was also available as a painter's pigment called *smalt*.

SCULPTURE

Clay was also an important material for the sculptor. He used it to produce sketches, as well as for the initial form of a sculpture that was to be cast in bronze. Clay for sculpture has to be readily kneadable and flexible so that it can be shaped by the pressure of fingers and spatulas. It also has to have a certain degree of porosity and, when the object is intended to be permanent, must be easy to fire.

The modelling clay used in the 17th century was generally a mixture of clay itself, hydrated aluminium silicate and sand. Depending on the quality, the sand could be as fine as the clay particles, but also so coarse that the mixture felt rather gritty. Sculptors naturally preferred clay with a rather finer grain for smaller and more detailed works. If there was too much sand in the mixture, or it was too coarse, it first had to be leached out, because a surfeit of sand made it impossible to shape the clay properly.[8]

Once the sculpture had been shaped it was left to dry. The drying time depended on the thickness of the clay and the composition of the mixture. A porous clay, one containing a fair amount of sand, often dries with few if any cracks. Ball-clay, on the other hand, is very easy to work but shrinks so badly that it almost always cracks and loses its shape during drying and firing. The addition of some feldspar makes it a little more porous.

A sculpture modelled in clay was almost invariably hollow, particularly when it was to be fired. Sometimes it was first modelled as a massive object and then hollowed out at the back by scraping out the soft clay with a spatula, and sometimes it was built up as a hollow form from the start. A hollow sculpture of moist clay is less prone to collapse under its own weight. The sculpture also dries quicker if the core is removed. However, hollowing out the object was not just done to reduce weight or make it dry quicker; a hollow piece does not crack as easily as a solid one. The sculpture shrinks as it dries, but the clay on the outside shrinks more than that on the inside. This sets up tensions which can lead to shrinkage cracks (*figs. 59a-b*). If the object is hollow it will dry free of tension on both the outside and the inside. That is why Hendrick de Keyser deliberately tried to build up a terracotta bust with walls of equal thickness (*figs. 60a-b*).

fig. 59a Rombout Verhulst, *Portrait of Jacob van Reygersberg*, 1671 [77]. Despite the hollow structure, there are shrinkage cracks on the inside. Amsterdam, Rijksmuseum

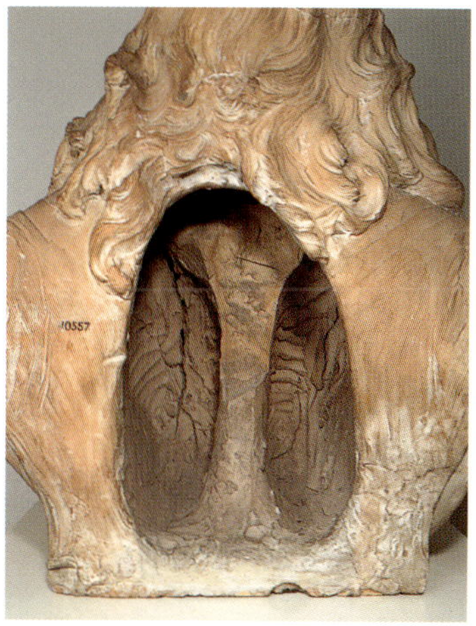

fig. 59b Exterior of *fig. 59a*

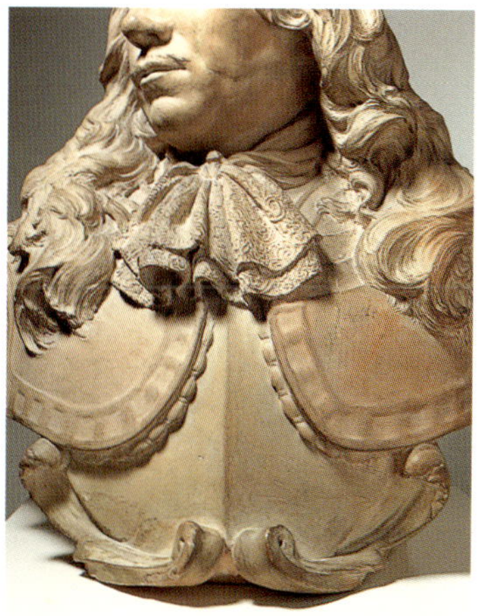

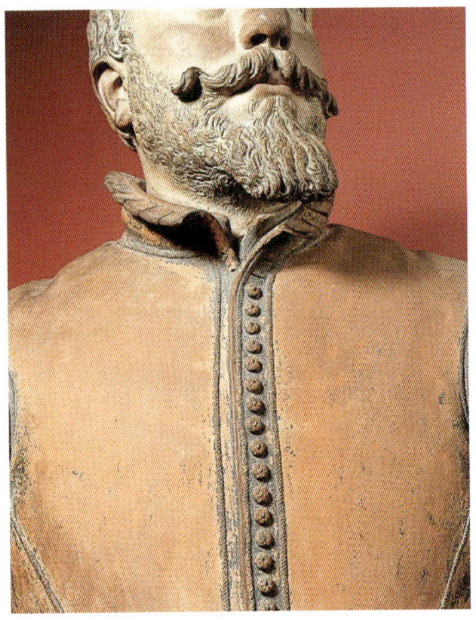

fig. 60a Hendrick de Keyser, *Portrait bust*, 1606, polychromed terracotta, h. 72.5 cm. Amsterdam, Rijksmuseum

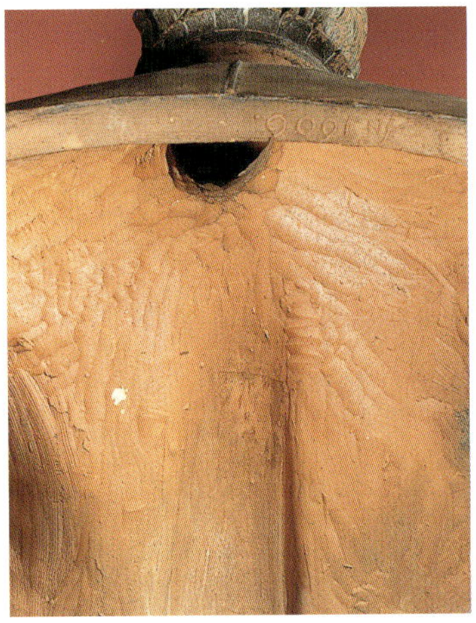

fig. 60b Back of *fig. 60a*

BRONZE

Clay was also involved in the production of bronze sculptures. Bronze is an alloy of copper and tin, generally in the ratio of 9:1, the precise proportions determining the properties of the bronze. A higher copper fraction often produces a slightly softer bronze, which is easier to work but is more susceptible to damage. Too much copper raises the melting-point of the alloy so high that it is difficult to cast. More tin lowers the melting-point and strengthens the bronze. The alloy usually contains smaller amounts of other metals like lead, arsenic, zinc, iron, silver or antimony. The composition of bronze is rarely constant. Old bronze cannons and church bells were sometimes melted down and the metal reused for statues, but unfortunately the reverse also happened.

The alloy is heated until it becomes extremely fluid and is then cast in the mould. The commonest way of casting was the lost wax method, the basic principle of which is extremely simple. The sculptor made a small wax figure which he then covered with plaster, The block was then left to harden and thoroughly dry out. Heating it to 70° Celsius melted the wax, which flowed out of the plaster mould. The hollow it left behind was then filled with the molten bronze alloy, and when that had cooled the plaster was broken off leaving a solid bronze figure. A good example of a sculpture produced in this way is Hendrick de Keyser's *Mercury* of 1611 (*fig. 61*). However, the method did have its limitations, for it restricted the size of a sculpture. Anything much larger than the *Mercury* became too heavy, and the amount of metal prohibitively expensive. Statues of any respectable size had to be cast hollow.

The basic form was then made of clay, which could be of inferior quality since it only needed to be a rough approximation of the planned sculpture. It often contained additives like sand, plaster, brick dust, straw, hair, horse manure and even old rags. The rough model made from this material was a little smaller and less detailed than the finished sculpture. For larger pieces, in particular, the basic form was held together on the inside by an armature of iron rods and wire. The clay was then applied around the armature. Once it had dried it was covered with a layer of wax. The desired form could then be modelled in the wax down to the finest details. The thickness of the wax layer naturally depended on the size of the sculpture, but it was important to apply it so that the walls of the finished bronze were the same thickness throughout. The wax was then covered with plaster, melted out and replaced with bronze to produce a sculpture consisting of a wall of bronze with a clay core.[9] The plaster on the outside and the core were then removed, leaving a hollow bronze sculpture. Everything modelled in the wax was faithfully reproduced on the surface of the bronze.[10]

The quality of a cast depends primarily on the speed with which the molten metal spreads through the mould cavity. When it flows through the narrow space between the core and the investment, as the outer plaster mould is called, air and gas bubbles can easily form and become trapped in the metal, weakening its structure. To prevent this happening, numerous small wax rods were attached to the wax model. They were melted out along with the wax of the model, leaving a channelling system of sprues and vents which accelerated the flow of metal through the cavity and allowed air and gas to escape. Once the bronze had cooled sufficiently and the outer mould had been broken off, the sculpture emerged with bronze

fig. 61 Hendrick de Keyser, *Mercury*, 1611; a massive bronze cast with the lost wax method. Amsterdam, Rijksmuseum

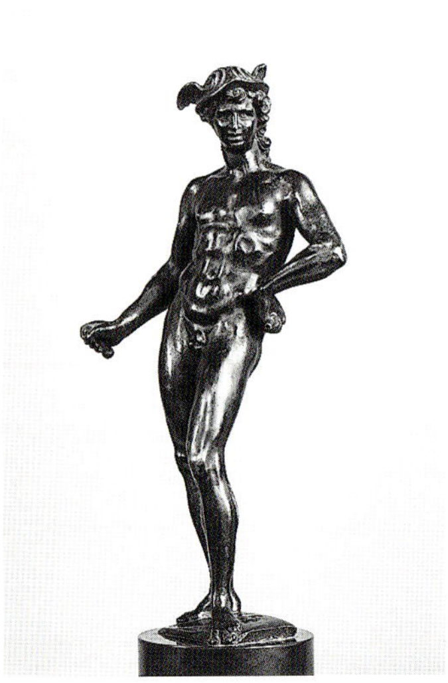

fig. 62 Martin Desjardins's unfinished equestrian statue in the Statens Museum for Kunst in Copenhagen

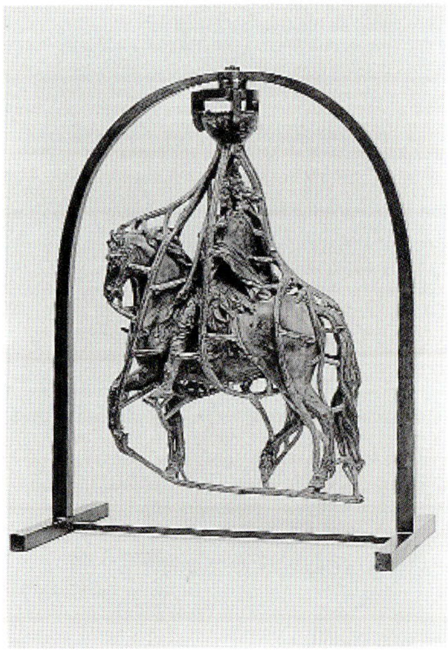

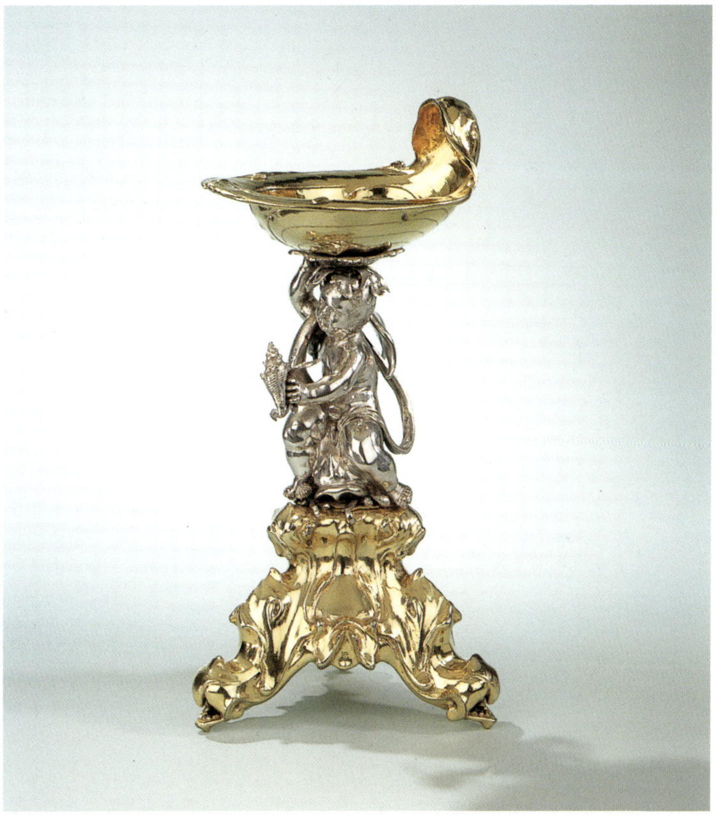

fig. 63 Johannes Lutma, *Salt*, 1639; cast and embossed silver, parcel-gilt [33]. The putto on the triangular base was cast with the lost wax technique in several versions as part of a larger series. Amsterdam, Rijksmuseum

rods sticking out of it. These were sawn off and all trace of them carefully removed. The unfinished equestrian statue by Martin Desjardins in Copenhagen's Statens Museum for Kunst gives an excellent idea of this aspect of casting bronze (*fig. 62*).[11]

GOLD AND SILVER

The famous silversmith Johannes Lutma used two different techniques for a series of salt-cellars (*fig. 63*). The salt-well at the top was beaten from a single sheet of silver, and is unique. The figures below, the stem in the shape of a small boy, and the foot done in the auricular style, were cast. By assembling stems and feet in different combinations he was able to produce a whole range of objects. For instance, the foot and the stem of this salt-cellar reappear as parts of a glass-holder in a painting by Willem Kalf [67].

Little has changed in the craft of silversmithing down the ages. The procedures followed by Lutma in the 17th century for his silver salt-well were almost identical to those described in the 12th-century treatise *Schedula diversarum artium*.[12] The raw material was sheet metal. The silver extracted from the ore had already been poured onto a smooth surface at the silver mine. It was then beaten into thin sheets on an anvil. The silversmith cut a piece out of the sheet in the approximate shape of the object he wanted to make. In this case it would have been a little smaller than the salt-well, because hammering increased its surface area. The flat sheet was then beaten roughly into shape on a steel anvil or stake. The hammer had two heads, a round one for imparting curves and a flat one for the level parts (*fig. 64*).[13] If the plate is hammered carefully it thins evenly all over. Hammering also distorts the metal and packs the crystals closer together (*fig. 65*).[14] This makes it stiffer and more difficult to work, so from time to time it has to be annealed. The metal was thus given its approximate shape with the hammer alone.[15] When it was thin enough and in almost the right shape the silver could be depressed or raised, and for this the silversmith used not the ordinary flat anvil but a 'stake'—a small anvil with an iron or wooden spike. The metal was shaped around the stake, which is how the salt-well was hammered further into shape. It

fig. 64 Dutch school, *Portrait of a silversmith in his workshop*, c. 1680; oil on panel, 45 x 38 cm. Hanging by the window is a pair of shears for cutting the silver to size. On the table is an embossing hammer. Amsterdam, Rijksmuseum

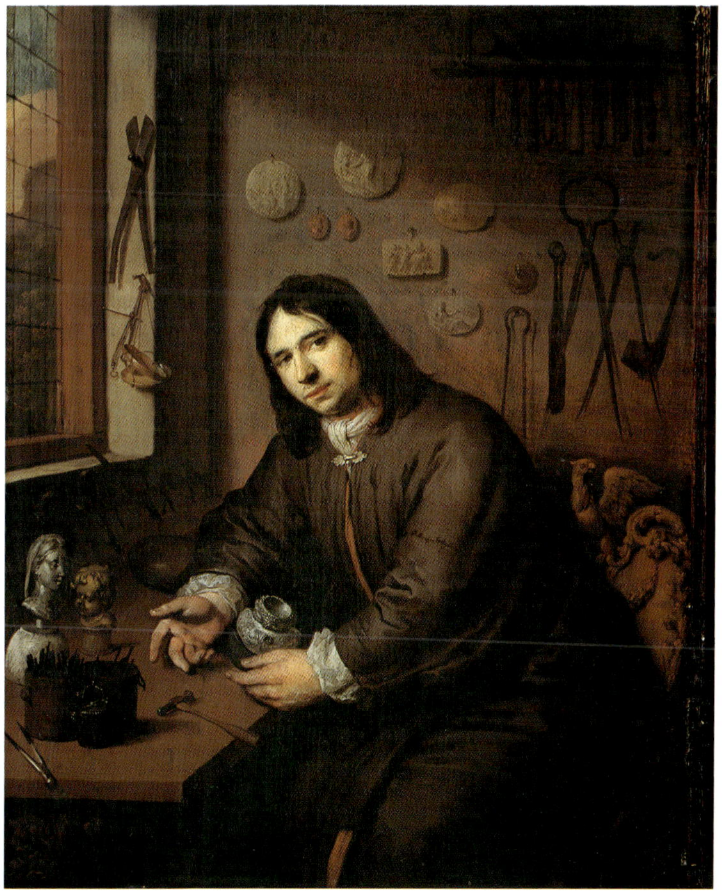

then had to be given its final form and detailing by embossing figures into the metal. Details were applied using small hammers or, more often, small punches—blunt iron chisels approximately 10-12 centimetres long. A silversmith usually had a large number of punches of different shapes.[16] The dish was chased from the front and embossed from the back (*fig. 66*). Hammers and punches removed any irregularities on the surface, and chasing added detail to the figures.

PRINTS

It is generally assumed that printmaking evolved from the goldsmith's practice of inking his engraved work and printing it on a piece of paper so as to have a visual record of it. The lines engraved in the metal were filled with ink, a piece of damp paper was placed on the plate, and the plate and paper were pulled through a press, which transferred the inked lines to the paper. Such impressions could be shown to prospective customers to give them an idea of the goldsmith's skill.

This intaglio technique soon developed into an artistic medium in its own right. At the beginning of the 17th century the complicated engraving technique was largely superseded by etching, in which the copperplate was covered with an acid-resistant layer called the ground. Lines could be incised in the ground with a sharp needle, exposing the underlying metal, which was 'bitten' with an acid. The plate was then cleaned, the etched grooves filled with ink, and the plate put into the press covered with a piece of dampened paper.

fig. 65 Microstructure of embossed metal displays deformed and compressed crystals. Etched, magnification 200x

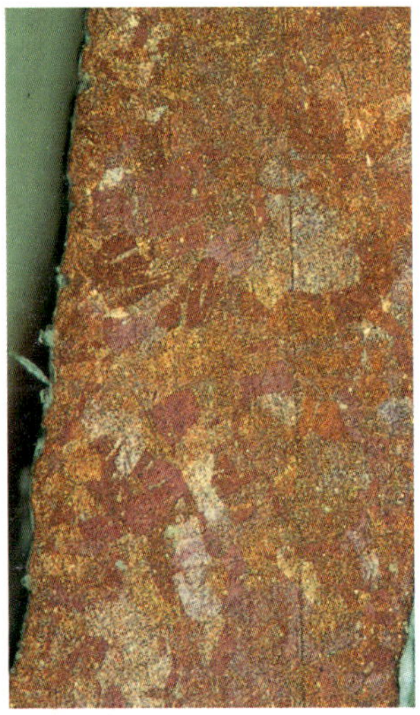

fig. 66 Johannes Lutma's salt (*fig. 63*) with traces of the embossing on the salt-well visible as tiny dents

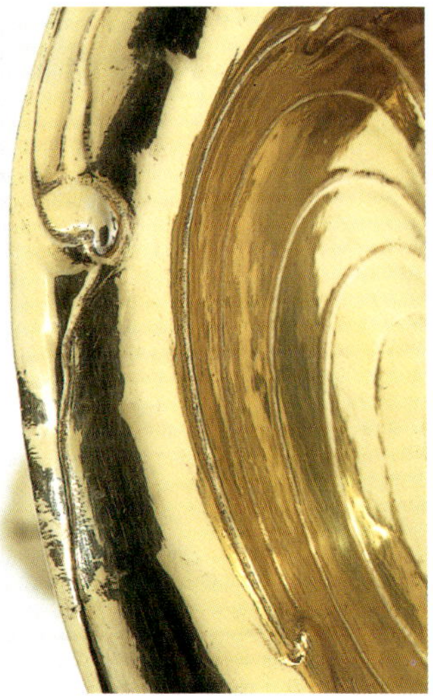

Woodcuts, engravings and etchings were eagerly collected in the 17th century, with prints being bought from bookstalls, print shops, at auctions and from publishers.[17] Collectors derived great aesthetic pleasure from prints, and artists often had a professional interest in them (*fig. 67*). The portrait painter David Beck (c. 1610-1656), for instance, used a print by Anthony van Dyck when he painted his portrait of Queen Christina of Sweden.[18] Prints, like sketchbooks, were thus also tools of the artist's trade.

The etcher worked on a copperplate which he ordered from a coppersmith. The plates were cut to size and hammered to a specific thickness and hardness. The hammering left the plate full of dents and scratches, which were removed by rubbing with various kinds of stone. The scratches left by the stone were eliminated by smoothing the plate with a very fine sort of stone or with a polishing iron, and the etching ground was then applied. One popular, hard ground consisted of a mixture of linseed oil boiled with resin and asphalt. After being applied to the plate it was left to dry before very delicate lines were drawn on it with a sharp needle. Rubens mentions a much softer ground in a letter to Pieter van Veen, in which he describes the technique used by Adam Elsheimer (1578-1610). The latter covered his copperplates with a soft white paste, and when he drew on this with his needle the exposed copper gave the effect of a red chalk drawing on white paper. Rubens went on to say: 'I do not remember the ingredients of this paste, although he very kindly told me'.[19]

Quite a few recipes for hard and softer etching grounds have survived. Almost all of them were made from beeswax, pitch, pine-resin, asphalt and vegetable oil in varying combinations and proportions, with the melting-point being kept low enough for the mixture to flow smoothly over a warm copperplate and be smeared out into a thin film with a feather.[20] The thinner the ground the easier it was to draw on.

This was usually done with a needle which was sharp enough to penetrate the ground but not the plate. Etchers generally used needles of differing thickness, with the thinnest and most pointed being reserved for the finest lines. A little more force was used with the thicker needles, which actually scratched the copper. Those incised lines, which were quite broad to start with, were widened even further by the acid. The etcher thus had a great variety of lines at his disposal.[21]

First, though, they had to be bitten into the plate by a corrosive substance. Seventeenth-century writings generally mention agents like copper or iron vitriol and various acids. The commonest mordant was a mixture of copper acetate, mercury chloride, vitriol and alum. A more powerful one was copper acetate mixed with alum, ammonium chloride (sal-ammoniac), tartrate, vitriol and ordinary kitchen salt dissolved in strong vinegar.[22] An artist could mix this kind of mordant for himself, but if he needed anything

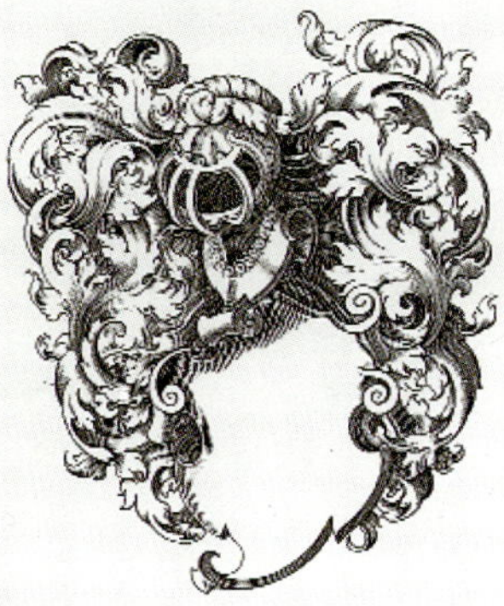

fig. 67 Coat of arms in the sample book by Michel le Blon, *Recueil d'ornaments...*, Amsterdam c. 1630

more powerful he had to go to a specialist like an apothecary. Saltpetre acid was made by distillers or refiners. Acids obtained by distillation were often so corrosive that they had to be diluted before use.[23] The copper exposed by the etching needle was easily etched simply by pouring the acid over it. A handier method was to line the edges of the plate with a 'dam' of beeswax, turning the plate into a tray which was then filled with the mordant.

The process was brought to a halt by rinsing the acid off with water once the lines were deep enough and the image sufficiently etched (*fig. 68*), at which point the plate was ready for printing. The artist did not always do this himself but left it to a professional printer, because a press was a sizable investment which most craftsmen could not afford.

The printer smeared ink onto the plate, ensuring that it penetrated deep into the etched lines. The plate was then cleaned so that the only ink was in the grooves. The final film of ink was removed by wiping the plate rapidly and lightly with the palm of the hand (*fig. 69*). The plate was then pulled through the press with a damp piece of paper, which picked up an impression of the inked lines in the plate.[24]

PAINTINGS

Almost all the wood used for paintings in the 17th century was oak from the lands around the Baltic. It was only later in the century that artists began working on tropical wood like mahogany and cedar. They bought their panels ready-made from members of the joiners' and cabinetmakers' guild. The panel-maker first let the imported wood dry out thoroughly—a process which could take four or five years. The timber was thin split and sawn to size, which was increasingly done in sawmills as the 17th century progressed. Small panels usually consist of a single plank, preferably sawn or split radially. Larger panels were made by cold-gluing two or three planks together. The gluing was sometimes reinforced with dowels, tenon and mortise joints, and even dovetail joints. Sapwood was generally glued to sapwood and heartwood to heartwood to prevent the panel warping due to uneven stresses. The panel could then be planed smooth and the back edges bevelled slightly to make it fit into the rabbets of the frame (*fig. 70*). The joiners sold panels in various sizes, most of which were based on local units of measure. The dimensions of a panel from Leiden were derived from the Rhineland foot of 31.394 cm (consisting of 12 inches of 2.616 cm), those from Amsterdam from the Amsterdam foot of 28.31 cm (11 inches of 2.57 cm).[25]

Painters occasionally worked on copper, usually for very small paintings meticulously executed with a smooth, egg-shell finish. Many artists who made these exquisite works on copper were from Antwerp, where there was an abundance of copperplates due to the city's role as a centre of the copper trade. Large amounts of the metal were traded and processed there, particularly after the Fugger family set up local offices of its Austrian, German and Hungarian copper mines. Working the copper consisted chiefly of beating the purified and molten copper into sheets. The artists who used those sheets naturally had no say in this process, which was the preserve of the specialist coppersmith. There are indications that the plates came in standard sizes. One inventory of 1632 lists 49 painted plates in 'Greek format', and 45 in a 'Passion format'. They were also identified by their cost: guilder plates, pound plates and so on.[26]

The size of a canvas could also be associated with local units of measure. Its width was governed by the width of the loom. Most of the looms in Twenthe and Brabant, the main sources of ship's canvas and bedtick (which was also used for paintings), were two

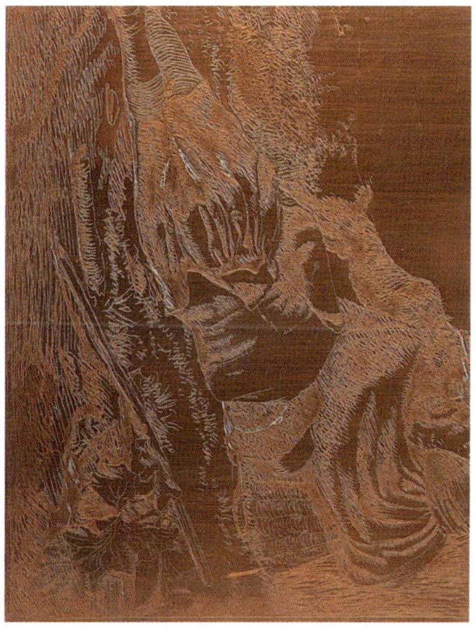

fig. 68 Detail of etched lines in a 17th-century etching plate

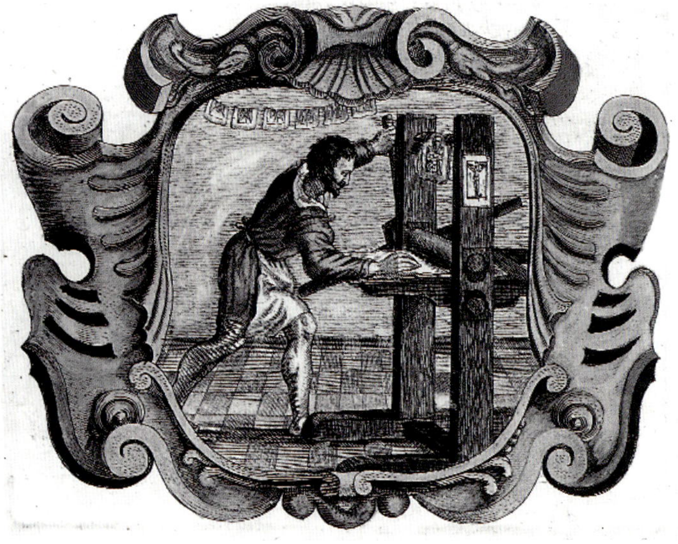

fig. 69 Plate-printer's press, emblem in Adriaen Poirters, *Afbeeldinghe van d'eerste eeuw der Societyt Iesu*, Antwerp 1640

fig. 70 The bevelled edges of a 17th-century panel

ells wide, which is around 138 cm. Strips were sewn together for larger works.

The canvas was stretched on a temporary frame, to which it was attached by pegs or nails, or was tied to a much larger frame with cords, with the edges of the canvas being doubled over to prevent tearing. Strainers of this kind were generally only used while the painting was being executed. Once completed, the picture was put on a permanent stretcher. Occasionally, though, one finds a painting which is still on its original strainer (*fig. 71*).

The panel or canvas has to be given a ground layer before it can be painted. Panel ground differed from those for canvas, their main purpose being to fill in any irregularities in the grain of the wood and provide a smooth surface to which the paint would adhere properly. A very suitable one was chalk ground up in a gelatine glue. This mixture was spread onto the panel in thin layers. The proportions of the ingredients was of crucial importance. If there was too much glue the ground would become hard and crack, and if there was too little it would absorb the binding medium of the paint layers, weakening the adhesion of the paint, which caused distortions between the different layers and blistering. Applying the ground was therefore another specialist task which was carried out by a primer. Once the ground had been laid it only had to be scraped smooth. In the course of the 17th century the chalk-glue ground was replaced by one made by grinding lead white in thin linseed oil, and that too was rarely done by the artist.

The ground layer on canvas had to fill the interstices of the canvas weave to provide a smooth painting surface. This generally required two ground layers. The first was applied directly onto the canvas and usually consisted of cheap materials like ochre, brown and red earth pigments and chalk. This brownish-grey layer often contained a little umber, the manganese in which accelerated the drying of the oil. Lead white was sometimes added to the mixture for the same purpose. The second layer was usually a little lighter in tone, and consisted of a smoothly applied mixture of lead white with some ochre and carbon black (*fig. 72*).

This gave the painter a smooth, warm grey surface on which to work. Occasionally the ground tone was not completely covered by the subsequent paint layers, allowing it to play a part in the overall visual effect of the painting.

The outlines of the scene were first drawn on the ground. This underdrawing could range from a few cursory lines to very precise contours which simply had to be coloured in. Just as a panel required a different type of ground from a canvas, so the underdrawing varied. That on the white ground of a panel was generally done in black chalk or black ink (*fig. 73*). The underdrawing on the usually light grey ground of a canvas was better applied with a light medium—a thin, almost ink-like lead-white paint (*fig. 74*).

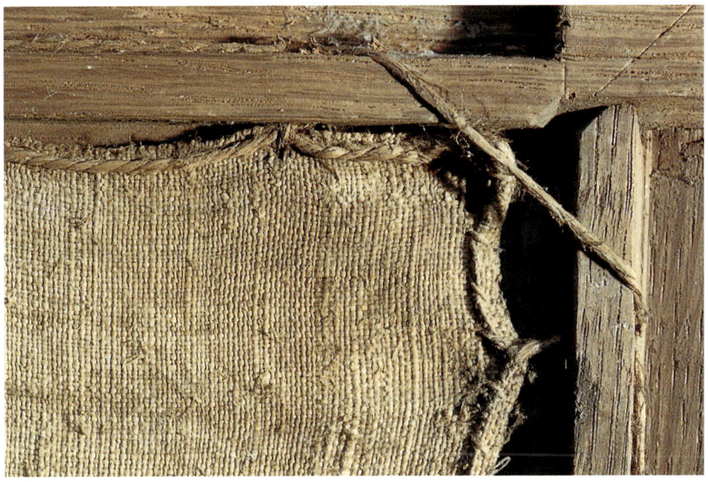

fig. 71 A 17th-century painting on its original stretcher

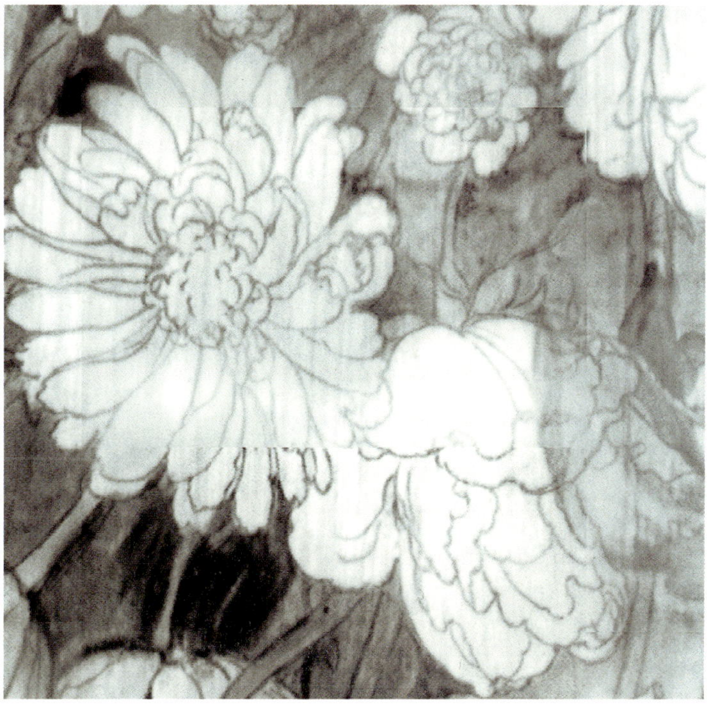

fig. 73 Infrared reflectogram of Balthasar van der Ast, *Still life with flowers*; oil on panel, 59 x 43 cm. It can be seen that the underdrawing was done with black chalk. Amsterdam, Rijksmuseum

If oil paint is applied directly onto the chalk ground of a panel, the binding medium is immediately absorbed, preventing the subsequent paint layers from adhering properly. The chalk-glue ground was therefore usually covered with a thin insulating layer of lead white. A little pigment was often mixed in, giving the panel some tone. Such a coloured underlayer could serve as a middle tone. This *imprimatura* provided the basic tone for the painting, with the lights being painted with pale pigments like lead white, lead-tin yellow or vermilion,[27] and the shaded passages with very dark pigments. The scene could be laid down with its main contrasts of light and shade very quickly, even with a very cursory under-drawing. It was a working method eminently suited to painters like Rembrandt and his pupils, who were noted for their rapid, painterly touch.

The basic tone consisted of a mixture of different pigments, and it sometimes seems that all the pigments on the artist's palette are found in the *imprimatura*. That is indeed the case. The remains of paint scraped off the palette at the end of the working day were often used for the purpose, as was the sediment at the bottom of the pot in which brushes were cleaned.

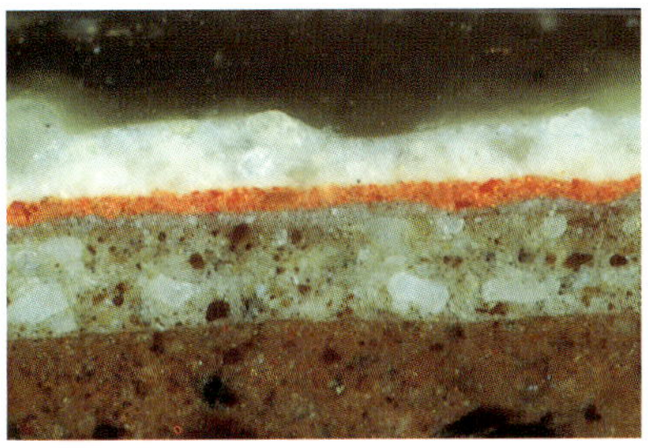

fig. 72 Paint cross-section from Abraham Mignon, *Still life with flowers and watch*; oil on canvas, 75 x 60 cm. The double ground of a painting on canvas is clearly visible. Magnification 320x. Amsterdam, Rijksmuseum

The pigments used in the 17th century differed little from those found in the two preceding centuries. One new colour was the attractive but unstable *schietgeel* ('fugitive yellow'). It was a bright

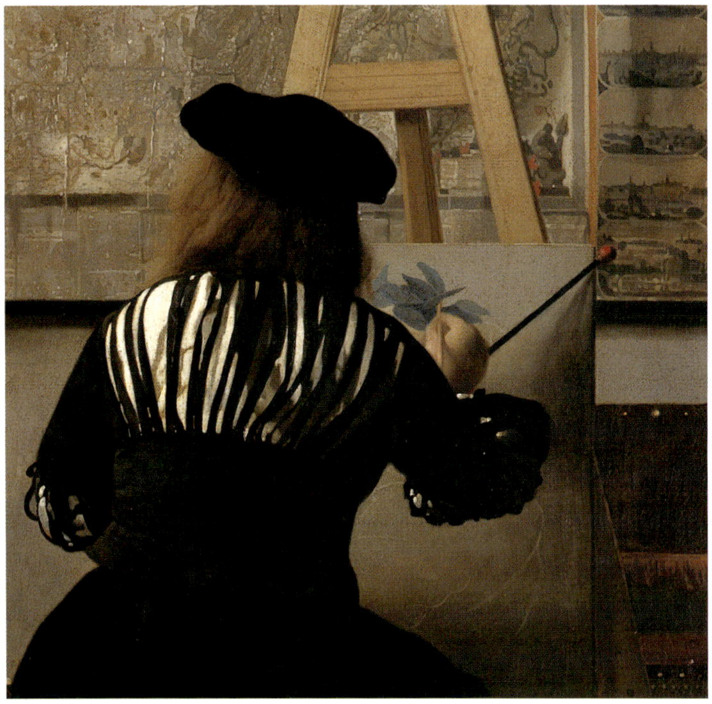

fig. 74 Detail of Johannes Vermeer, *Allegory of painting*; oil on canvas, 120 x 100 cm. The preliminary drawing on the grey ground was done with white paint. Vienna, Kunsthistorisches Museum

yellow, almost fluorescent lake made from plant extracts, notably unripe buckthorn berries (*Rhamnus catartica* L.), the leaves of dyer's broom (*Genista tinctoria* L.) and wild mignonette (*Reseda luteola* L.). This transparent lake enabled the artist to paint deep golden tones. The pigment was originally used in textile dyeing, before specialist pigment makers began supplying it to painters in the 17th century. The Amsterdam manufacturer Pekstok produced these yellow lakes and other colours on an industrial scale (*fig. 75*) by chemically attaching the colorants in the plants to a precipitate of chalk or aluminium hydroxide.[28] Because aluminium hydroxide is completely transparent, it was possible to make bright yellow lakes with a very deep lustre. The yellow lake was also combined with blue pigments to produce green, but in some cases the yellow in the mixture has faded completely, leaving just the blue. As a result, the greens in some 17th-century paintings now have a bluish, rather metallic colour. An example of this can be seen in Gabriel Metsu's *Woman eating* (*fig. 76*), where the green stalks and leaves of the bouquet in the vase have discoloured to a bright blue.

Another pigment produced by Pekstok was the so-called plain indigo, which originally was also used exclusively in textile dyeing. Unlike the yellow lakes, it did not have to be precipitated onto an inorganic substrate. When mixed with lead white it gave a light blue base tone. The painter could then put a darker tone over it with pure indigo as a glaze. Although indigo always retains a rather ashen hue, it could yield a very convincing blue provided the layers were carefully built up. It was also fairly cheap, certainly compared to other blue pigments, which could be a very important consideration if an artist had to paint extensive blue passages, as in civic guard portraits. Indigo was also used in smaller works,

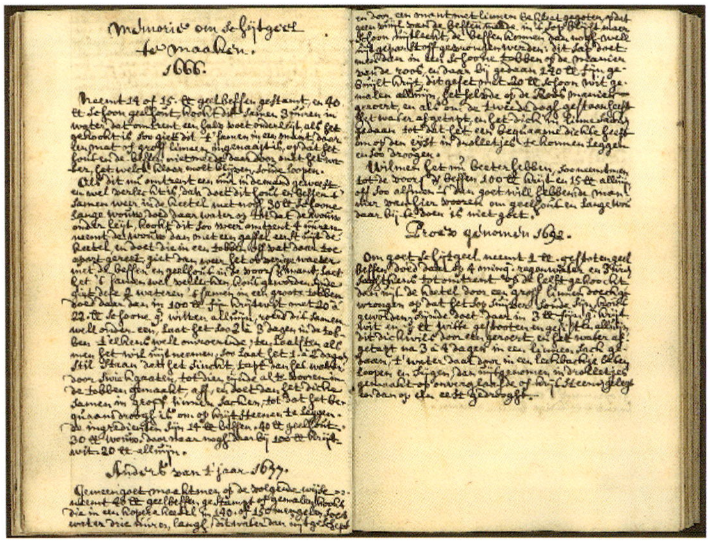

fig. 75 The manufacture of organic coloured lakes described in the Pekstok manuscript. Amsterdam, City Archives

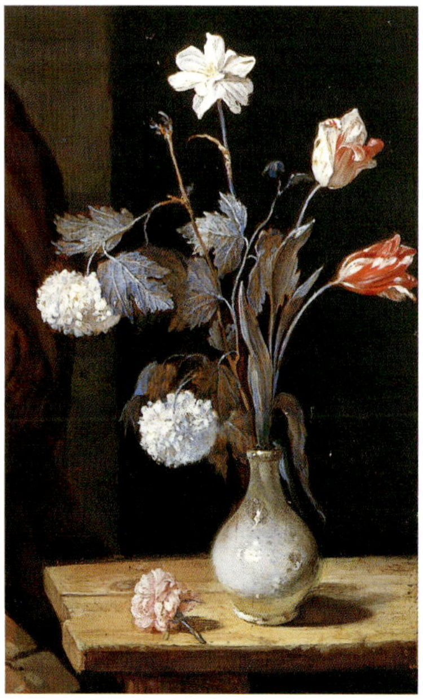

fig. 76 Detail of Gabriel Metsu, *Woman eating*; oil on panel, 33.5 x 27 cm. The fugitive yellow in a mixed green has faded, leaving only the blue. Amsterdam, Rijksmuseum

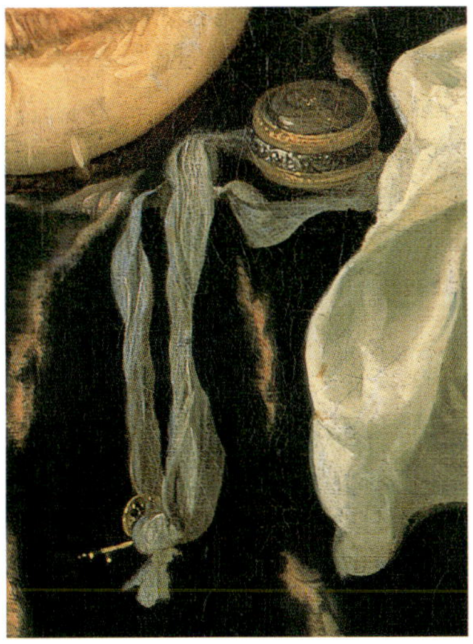

fig. 77 Detail of Abraham van Beijeren, *Still life*; oil on canvas, 126 x 106 cm. The blue ribbon was painted with a mixture of lead white and smalt. Amsterdam, Rijksmuseum

a fine example being one of the Rijksmuseum's showpieces, the *Portrait of a girl dressed in blue* by Johannes Verspronck [49].

Another new and inexpensive pigment was smalt. When extremely hot, molten blue glass is poured into water, it shatters into tiny splinters which can be ground into a powder. Smalt was fairly simple to produce for a glass-maker. Smalt in oil is rather transparent, and the only way to make it opaque is to mix it with lead white (*fig. 77*).

Cheaper pigments of this kind were often used for dead colouring, the first painted lay-in of the scene. The shapes of the individual objects were painted over the ground in monochrome areas of colour in order to establish the basic tonality in a neutral middle tone using a relatively inexpensive material. One passage, for instance, could be laid in with smalt, which was cheap, setting the basic blue tone, and could then be worked up with a transparent red lake. It was then finished off with a very thin layer of expensive ultramarine.[29] The costly blue tablecloth in a painting by Pieter de Ring was dead-coloured with a cheap mixture of lead white and indigo (*fig. 78*) before being worked up with ultramarine. The film of ultramarine is very thin, but was sufficient to give the painting the sumptuous look that the painter was after. Red draperies were also very amenable to laying in with dead colouring.[30]

Dead colouring was not just done for economic reasons but was part of the systematisation of an artist's output. The process resembles the three-stage system of laying in, deepening and heightening familiar from the watercolour technique. The greyish and blue draperies in the dress of Catharina de Witte painted by Caspar Netscher show how effective this approach could be. The shadows were painted in darker tones over the plain middle tone of each basic colour, and the heightening with white tones (*fig. 79*). This fits in with the advice of Gerard de Lairesse, who suggested that the artist should start a work by painting in a layer of dead colour for each individual area of the composition. That implied that each part was to be painted in evenly on the basis of a precise underdrawing, with the dead colour already approaching the desired colour of the finished picture.[31]

A flower still life, which required a very painstaking touch, demanded a systematic approach with *imprimatura*, dead colouring and finishing. Portraits and history paintings with many different coloured draperies also lent themselves to this method. The drawback is that the artist had to wait until one layer had dried before applying the next. Some subjects were also suited to a simpler and more direct method, with the sketch in a brownish paint and the

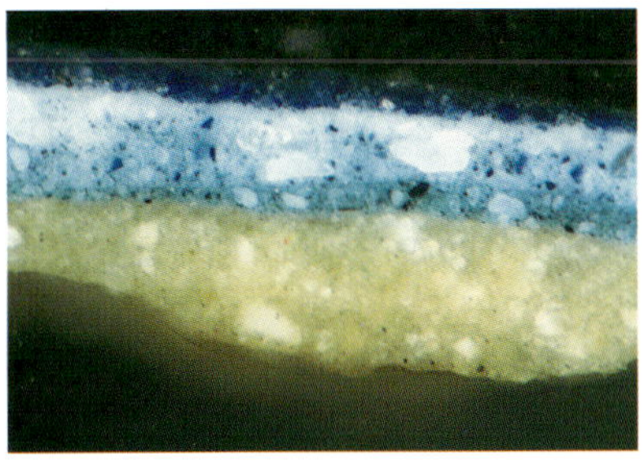

fig. 78 Paint cross-section from Pieter de Ring, *Still life with a golden goblet*; oil on canvas, 100 x 80 cm. From bottom to top: dead colouring of indigo and lead white; mixture of lead white and some ultramarine; dark blue glaze of pure ultramarine. Amsterdam, Rijksmuseum

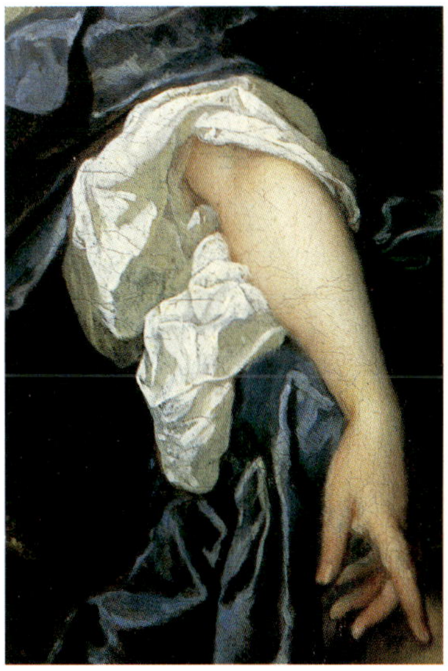

fig. 79 Detail of Caspar Netscher, *Helena Catharina de Witte, wife of Iman Mogge, Lord of Haamstede*; oil on canvas, 49 x 40 cm. The systematic build-up of the paint layers is clearly visible. Amsterdam, Rijksmuseum

dead colouring being highly worked up, leaving only sporadic finishing to be done.

That system was sometimes very suitable for landscapes. These cost very little, so landscapists were among the worst-paid artists, and could only keep their heads above water if their output was large. This high productivity also had consequences for the way in which the scenes were produced. There were endless variations on a single theme, with the same motifs constantly reappearing in different combinations. The 'tonal landscape', with its sober palette of a few harmonised colours, which became increasingly popular from the 1620s on, was ideal for rapid production. A number of those 'tonal' painters once entered into a wager. They each had to paint a landscape in one day which outdid the work of the others in quality ('in excellence and worth', as the chronicler put it). The first painter, François van Knibbergen, relied on his manual dexterity. Each brushstroke was perfectly placed first time. Everything that he set down 'fell from his brush like the letters from a writer's pen'. In the short time he needed he quickly added his signature in the wet paint using the handle of the brush (*fig.* 80). The second painter in the company, the marine artist Jan Porcellis, screwed up the tension by sitting down, looking, and doing absolutely nothing. He just sat there, drinking in the landscape. It was only as the day was drawing to a close, when he had imprinted the scene on his mind (by which time the spectators were beginning to get decidedly nervous), that he stirred, taking up his brushes and palette. He painted the scene that he saw in his mind's eye without needing to refer to the landscape again. He reproduced an internalised image, as it were. And then it was the turn of Jan van Goyen, who set to work with a vengeance, 'covering his entire panel in great swathes, here light, there dark, somewhat like a multicoloured agate or marbled paper. There were all sorts of pleasant drolleries to be seen in it which he made visible with little effort and many small touches of the brush, so that yonder there emerged a pleasing vista adorned with peasant cottages, and here an old town rampart, with gateway and dam, with reflections in the rippling water, with ships and boats laden with freight or passengers lowering or raising their sails. In short, his eye, as if directed to perceiving forms lain hidden in a chaos of colours, skilfully guided his hand and mind so that one saw a perfect painting before one could rightly make out his intention.'[32]

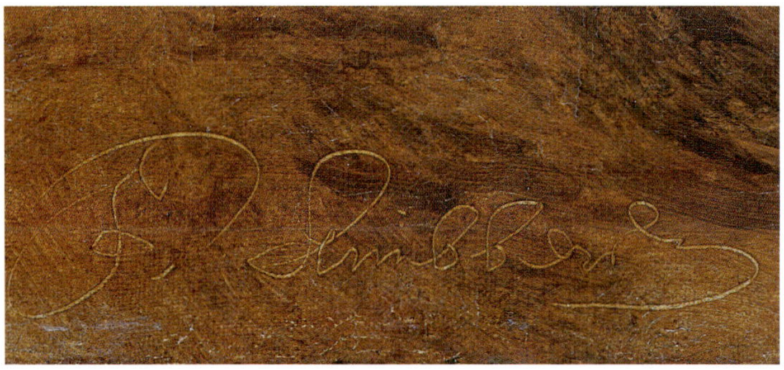

fig. 80 Detail of François van Knibbergen, *Panorama in the countryside around Cleves*; oil on canvas, 97 x 140 cm. The signature was scratched into the wet paint. Amsterdam, Rijksmuseum

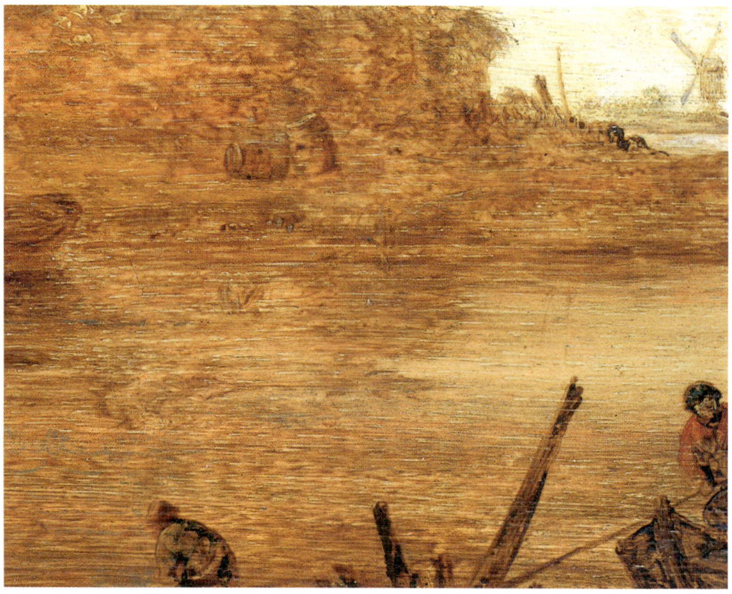

fig. 81 Detail of Jan van Goyen, *River view with sentry post*; oil on panel, 46 x 66.5 cm. Amsterdam, Rijksmuseum

Van Goyen's panels had the usual chalk and glue ground on which a preliminary drawing could be made before the dead colouring was laid in. Judging by the above account, he dispensed with that preliminary work on this occasion, dashing off a welter of dabs and strokes instead, and wildly smearing paint in every direction. The daubs could be interpreted any way one pleased. In other words, he had no need of sketches of the landscape in order to reproduce it in paint.[33] All that was required was a bit of paint and some imagination.

Van Goyen and other tonal landscape painters employed a limited palette for their work: a few ochres, burnt earth colours and umbers, all applied on a thin ground. That layer was not always present in Van Goyen's works, or was very thin indeed, and often there is some chalk in the *imprimatura*. Such a mixture was not only cheaper than an *imprimatura* of pure lead white but had the advantage of making the paint layer slightly transparent, revealing the pattern of the grain of the panel,[34] which could be incorporated in the painting (*fig.* 81).

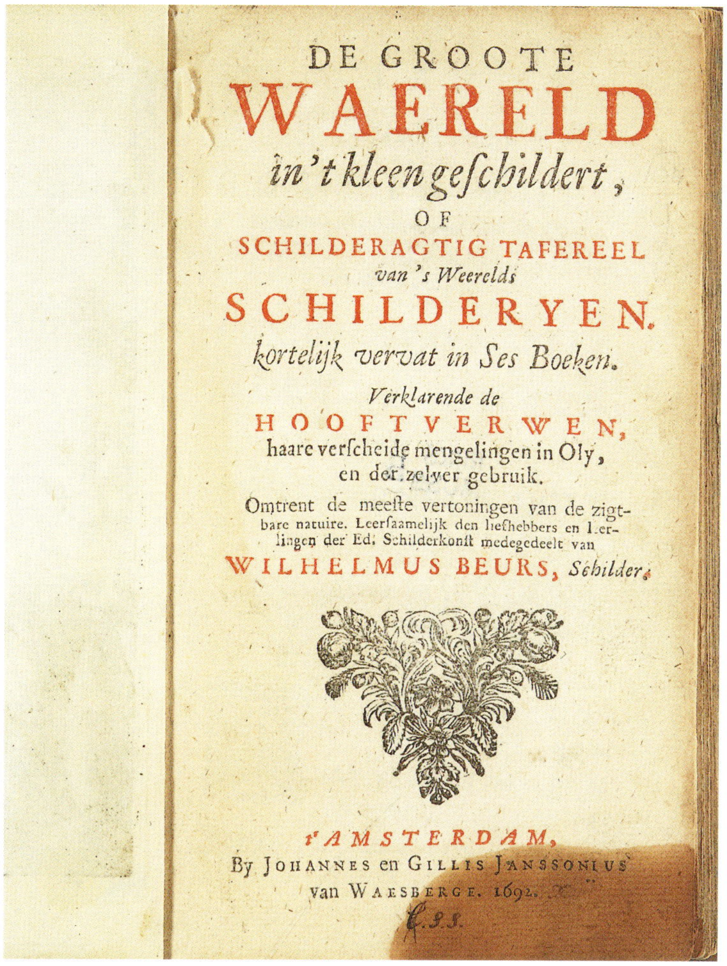
DE GROOTE
WAERELD
in 't kleen geschildert,
OF
SCHILDERAGTIG TAFEREEL
van 's Weerelds
SCHILDERYEN.
kortelijk vervat in Ses Boeken.
Verklarende de
HOOFTVERWEN,
haare verscheide mengelingen in Oly,
en der zelver gebruik.
Omtrent de meeste vertoningen van de zigtbare natuire. Leersaamelijk den liefhebbers en Leerlingen der Ed. Schilderkonst medegedeelt van
WILHELMUS BEURS, Schilder.
t'AMSTERDAM,
By JOHANNES en GILLIS JANSSONIUS van WAESBERGE, 1692.

fig. 82 Title page of Willem Beurs, *De groote waereld in 't kleen geschildert*, Amsterdam 1692, a painter's manual

DIVISION OF LABOUR

Painting output can also be increased by dividing up the various steps among the members of the workshop. Apprentices who had just started their training were set to work grinding pigments, preparing the colours and setting them out on the palette. Slightly more advanced pupils brought a painting to the dead colouring stage, leaving the master to finish it. Some workshops even had stocks of dead-coloured paintings which could be taken off the shelves and quickly completed. When the inventory of Pieter Lastman's estate was made there were still six dead-coloured panels in the studio. Nor was it uncommon for one artist to finish a painting which had been dead-coloured by another.

The allocation of tasks could also leave the dead colouring and finishing of crucial parts of a painting solely to the master, with the less important passages being handled by assistants. Portrait painters, especially, could gear up their output considerably in this way. Famous portraitists like Nicolaes Maes and Constantijn and Caspar Netscher were in the habit of working with templates for the bodies and dress of their sitters. They had already been painted in, so all the master had to do was add the head.[35] Conversely, he could paint the head first and an assistant then use the templates to insert the body.

This method was not only practical in that it made the fullest possible use of assistants, but also because it economised on costly materials. The painter only put the colours on his palette that he needed for a specific passage. If he was to paint a face he only required the colours for flesh tones: yellow and brown ochres, lead white, vermilion, red lake and a touch of black.

Apprentices gradually learned the tricks of the trade as they carried out the different tasks. The main problems concerned the use of colour to create the illusion of light, shade and three-dimensional forms. Very little was written about what a pupil learned during his apprenticeship, not because it involved studio secrets but mainly because it was so difficult to find the right words for a lucid description of the methods. It was far easier to give a practical demonstration. The commonest didactic model was learning by example and imitation. Broadly speaking, then, painters had little time for textbooks. The few technical sources to have come down to us from the 17th century are mostly either collections of recipes by people who were not, or no longer, painters themselves, such as those by the doctor Theodore de Mayerne or the historian Simon Eikelenberg, or writings by people of a more theoretical turn of mind like Gerard de Lairesse or Roger de Piles. Only the small book by Willem Beurs was written with truly didactic intentions (*fig. 82*). All of them, though, have one thing in common. They demonstrate how difficult it is to give written instructions for depicting a three-dimensional object on a two-dimensional plane. Often the authors do no more than make fairly general observations. Sometimes, though, there are slightly more specific instructions for suggesting volumes in space, the emphasis being on the observation of light and shadow on curved surfaces.

1 Carrack porcelain is so called from the name of the commonest Portuguese merchantman, the *carraca*. Most of it was from the period of Emperor Wanli (1573-1619) and his successors up to the fall of the Ming dynasty in 1644.

2 Dirk van Bleyswijck, *Beschryvinge der stadt Delft*, Delft 1667, p. 736: '[...] nergens werd het hierlands porceleijn subtijlder noch fijnder gewrocht als in dese stadt, daer in sij de Chinesen allerbest schijnen na te bootsen'.

3 *Hedendaagsche historie, of tegenwoordige staat van alle volkeren*, vol. 14, Amsterdam 1742, pp. 474-477. See also Gerrit Paape, *De plateelbakker of Delftsch aardewerkmaker: met plaaten*, Dordrecht 1794, p. 5: 'Doorniksche of Brabantsche aarde, Duische aarde welke van Muhlheim, een steedje aan de Roer, in 't hertogdom Berg, herwaards gebragt wordt, zwarte aarde en Delftse aarde'.

4 Paape, op. cit. (note 3), p. 7: 'Het Mengzel, in de koperen zeef of ketel geschept zijnde, zijgt vervolgens in den daaronder geplaatsten bak, blijvende de groove vuiligheid, of ongeweekte deelen in de zeef en de overigen in den bak achter'.

5 A little copper oxide, azurite or malachite—pigments also used by painters—imparted a deep green tint to the glaze. Manganese dioxide gave a purple colour. Yellow was obtained by adding arsenic oxides, antimony oxide or mixtures of tin oxide and lead oxide. Those lead-tin compounds could also be finely ground and used as a pigment in the painter's studio. See Cipriano Piccolpasso, *Li tre libri dell'arte del vasaio*, Florence 1976.

6 The presence of those elements made the preparation of zaffer a hazardous occupation: '[...] der staub vnd rauch von Cobalt sterbet vil Bergleut und Ertzscheider' ('[...] the dust and smoke of cobalt has killed many a miner and ore refiner'). Back in the 14th century the Italians were already making blue glass and a ceramic glaze with 'dell'azurro della magna, di quello che tinge el vetro'. See G. Milanesi, *Dell'Arte del vetro per musaico; tre trattatelli dei secoli XIV e XV*, Bologna 1864, pp. 80, 95.

7 See A. Hoynck van Papendrecht, *De Rotterdamsche plateel- en tegelbakkers en hun product, 1590-1851*, Rotterdam 1920, p. 21, 8 March 1627: '876 pond gebrande gesifte saffer, tot 38 gulden 't hondert, maeckt 322 guldens 10 stuijvers' ('876 pounds of roasted and sifted zaffer at 38 guilders per 100 pounds comes to 322 guilders and 10 stuivers').

8 B. Velde, *Introduction to clay minerals: chemistry, origins, uses and environmental significance*, London 1992.

9 L. Jans, H. Scheerder & F. Villanueva, *A cire perdue*, Amersfoort 1993

10 J. Ayres, *The artist's craft: a history of tools, techniques and materials*, Oxford 1985, pp. 162-168.

11 F.G. Bewer, 'Kunststuck von gegossenem Metall': Adriaen de Vries's bronze technique, in *Adriaen de Vries 1556-1626, imperial sculptor*, exhib. cat. Amsterdam (Rijksmuseum), Stockholm (Nationalmuseum), Los Angeles (The J. Paul Getty Museum)/Zwolle 1998, pp. 78-83.

12 W.L. Braekman, 'Secreten van een goudleermaker en van een edelsmid uit Mechelen', *Handelingen van de Koninklijke Kring voor Oudheidkunde, Letteren en Kunst van Mechelen*, 102/1 (1998), pp. 95-154.

13 Theophilus, *On divers arts: the foremost medieval treatise on painting, glassmaking and metalwork*, ed. J.G. Hawthorne & C.S. Smith, New York 1979, p. 150.

14 D.A. Scott, *Metallography and microstructure of ancient and historic metals*, Los Angeles 1991.

15 Theophilus, op. cit. (note 13), p. 150: 'Anneal it on live coals. When it has cooled by itself, work over the whole figure with hammers, always carefully depressing on each side and repeatedly annealing it'. See D.A. Scott, 'Technological, analytical, and microstructural studies of a Renaissance silver basin', *Archeomaterials* 5 (1991), pp. 21-45.

16 J. van Bennekom, 'Analysis of a silver plaquette made by the Flemish silversmith Mathias Melin', *Art Matters* 1 (2002), in preparation.

17 J. van der Waals, *De prentschat van Michiel Hinloopen: een reconstructie van de eerste openbare papierkunstverzameling in Nederland*, exhib. cat. Amsterdam 1988, pp. 16-28.

18 Ger Luijten & Saskia Sombogaart, '"...with the hand": the collecting of Van Dyck prints', in Carl Depauw & Ger Luijten, exhib. cat. *Anthony van Dyck as a printmaker*, Antwerp (Museum Plantin-Moretus/Stedelijk Prentenkabinet)/Amsterdam (Rijksprentenkabinet) 1999, pp. 9-18, esp. p. 11.

19 M. Roosens & C. Ruelens, *Correspondence de Rubens et documents epistolaires*, Antwerp 1898, p. 17. The English translation is from R. Saunders Magurn (ed. and trans.), *The letters of Peter Paul Rubens*, Cambridge (Mass.) 1955, p. 88.

20 J.G. van Gelder, 'Hollandsche etsrecepten voor 1645', *Oud Holland* 56 (1939), pp. 113-124.

21 A. Stijnman, 'Over veren, kaarsen en natte lappen: de etstechniek van Van Dyck en zijn tijdgenoten', in Depauw & Luijten, op. cit. (note 18), pp. 26-39.

22 Carel Batin, *Secreet-Boeck, waer in vele diversche Secreten ende heerlicke Consten in veelderleye verscheyden materien uit seker Latijnsche, Fransoysche, Hoochduytsche, ende Nederlandsche Authoren te samen ende bij een ghebracht zijn, door Dr. Carel Batin*, Dordrecht 1609.

23 Van Gelder, op. cit. (note 20).

24 A. Stijnman, 'De ontwikkeling van de houten etspers, 1460-1850', *Kroniek van het Rembrandthuis* 1-2 (1996), pp. 2-40.

25 J.M. Verhoeff, *De oude Nederlandse maten en gewichten*, Amsterdam 1983.

26 J. Bruyn, 'Een onderzoek naar 17de-eeuwse schilderijformaten, voornamelijk in Noord-Nederland', *Oud Holland* 93 (1979), pp. 96-115, esp. p. 97.

27 A. Wallert, 'Makers, materials and manufacture', in H. van Os *et al.*, *Netherlandish art in the Rijksmuseum 1400-1600*, Amsterdam/Zwolle 2000, pp. 254-255.

28 E. Hermens & A. Wallert, 'The Pekstok Papers; lake pigments, prisons and paint-mills', in *Looking through paintings*, (*Leids Kunsthistorisch Jaarboek* 11), Baarn/London 1998, pp. 269-294. The precipitate of aluminium hydroxide has no colouring properties of its own, but does have the ability to bind organic colorants to itself very firmly, such as the yellow flavonoids in plants, greatly increasing their colouring power and stabilising them.

29 See J.A. van de Graaf, *Het De Mayerne Manuscript als bron voor de schilderkunst van de barok, British Museum Sloane 2052* (diss.), Utrecht 1958, p. 149: 'Beau labeur en bleu. Faittes avec esmail & blanc de plomb (duquel tant plus y a, tant plus la couleur s'estend facilement) couchés le tout avec ces couleurs. Enfoncés avec Laque. Glacés par dessus avec Ultramarin'.

30 Van de Graaf, op. cit. (note 29), p. 151.

31 Gerard de Lairesse, *Groot schilderboeck, waar in de schilderconst in al haar deelen grondig werd onderweezen, ook door redeneeringen en prentverbeeldingen verklaard*, Haarlem 1740, vol. 1, p. 331.

32 Samuel van Hoogstraeten, *Inleyding tot de hooge schoole der schilderkonst: anders de zichtbaere werelt*, Rotterdam 1678, pp. 237-238: 'want hy zijn geheel paneel in 't gros overzwadderende, hier licht, daer donker, min nochmeer als een veelverwige Agaet, ofgemarbert papier, bestont allerley aerdige koddigheeden daer in te zoeken, die hy met weynig moeiten en veel kleyne toetsjes kenlijk maekte, zoo dat ginder een aerdig verschiet, versiert met boere gehugten, zich opdee; hier zagmen een oude steevest met poort en waterhooft voor den dag komen, en in 't aenkabbelende water wederglanssen, scheepen en schuiten, met vragt of reyzigers beladen, af en aen'haelen, en in 't kort zijn oog, als op het uitzien van gedaentens, die in een Chaos van verwen verborgen laegen, afgerecht, stierde zijn hand en verstandt op een vaerdige wijs, zoo dat men een volmaekte Schildery zag, eermen recht merken kon, wat hy voor hadt'.

33 When he was on his travels, though, Van Goyen made masses of sketches, many of which he incorporated in his paintings.

34 E.M. Gifford, 'Jan van Goyen en de techniek van het naturalistische landschap', in exhib. cat. *Jan van Goyen*, Leiden (Stedelijk Museum De Lakenhal) 1996-97, pp. 70-79, esp. pp. 76-77.

35 A. Blankert, 'Invulportretten door Caspar and Constantijn Netscher', *Oud Holland* 81 (1966), pp. 263-269. P. Huys Janssen & W. Sumowski, *Rembrandt's Academy*, Hoogsteder & Hoogsteder/Zwolle 1992, no. 31, Nicolaes Maes, pp. 240-243.

Detail of fig. 88 ▸

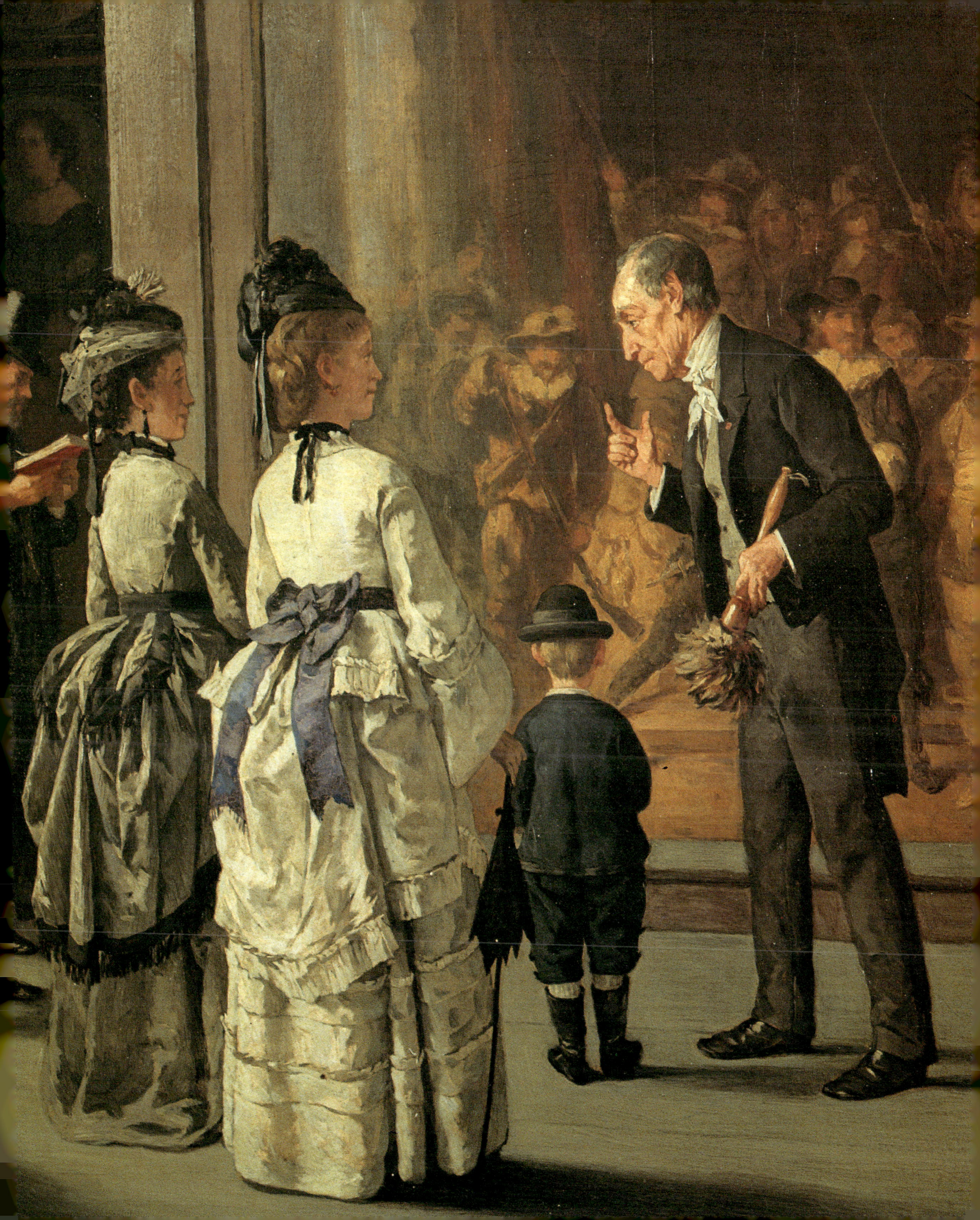

The changing picture of the art of the Golden Age in the Rijksmuseum

Seventeenth-century Dutch painting has played a key role in the Rijksmuseum's presentation throughout the 200 years of its existence. When the Nationale Konst-Gallerij (National Art Gallery) was founded at the end of the 18th century there was already an awareness that the 17th century was the most fertile period in the nation's past, both economically and artistically. The gallery, which was housed in five rooms in Huis ten Bosch palace between 1800 and 1805, had more than 200 exhibits illustrating Dutch history and painting, with a marked emphasis on the Golden Age. Today, at the beginning of the 21st century, the Rijksmuseum's collections have grown out of all recognition in both scale and diversity. As a result, the picture it provides of the art of the Golden Age has been radically expanded and altered.

For example, the Nationale Konst-Gallerij had no works by the most important 17th-century painters: Frans Hals, Rembrandt, Jan Steen, Johannes Vermeer and Jacob van Ruisdael. Only when it fused with other collections in the new Rijksmuseum building, which opened in 1885, was the basis established for the present, wide-ranging collections.

The dates of acquisition and provenances of the artworks discussed in this book (pp. 51-252) show how the collections were built up over a period of 200 years and augmented with loans, gifts and purchases. Happenstance, changing political circumstances and views played an important part in the process. Evolving art-historical ideas largely determined the museum's acquisition policy, particularly as it applied to the Golden Age.

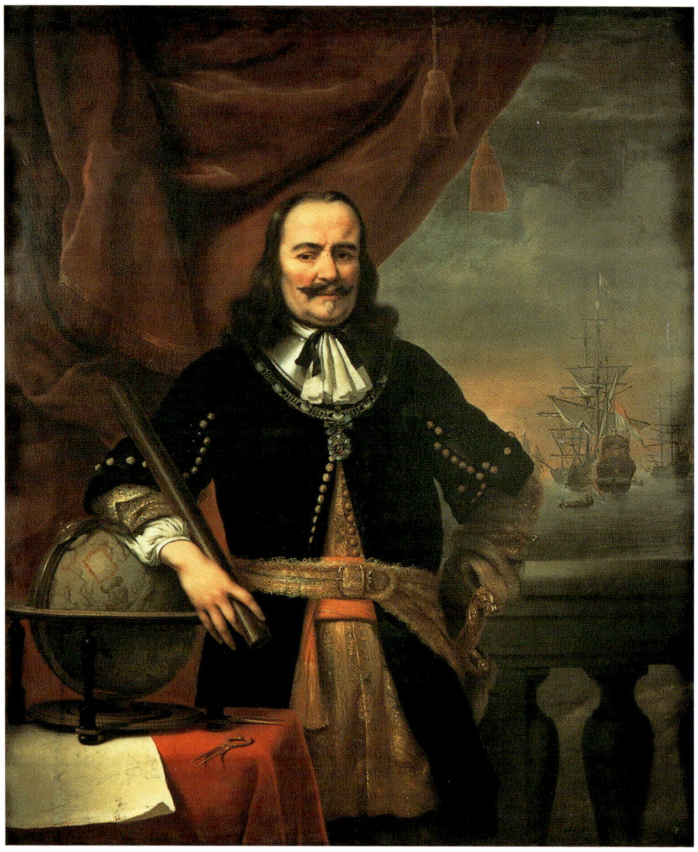

fig. 83 Ferdinand Bol, *Portrait of Michiel Adriaansz de Ruyter*, 1667; oil on canvas, 157 x 238 cm. Amsterdam, Rijksmuseum (on loan to the Nederlands Scheepvaartmuseum, Amsterdam)

THE NATIONAL ART GALLERY

The creation of a national museum was part of a wider effort on the part of the new regime to interest the Dutch in their history. Although the collections of the stadholder, Prince Willem V, had been carried off to Paris by the French, there were still plenty of paintings and objets d'art in the country's palaces and public buildings. They, together with a number of historical artefacts, comprised the collection of the new museum that opened its doors in Huis ten Bosch on 31 May 1800.

The first galleries were devoted to Dutch history, which was illustrated mainly with portraits of such naval heroes as Maarten Tromp and Michiel de Ruyter (*fig.* 83). There were also a number of 'national relics', such as De Ruyter's sabre, Tromp's commander's baton, the Sea Beggars' goblet and a 'gold cannon' (*fig.* 84). The painting *Fishing for souls* (*fig.* 85) which was attributed to Jan Brueghel

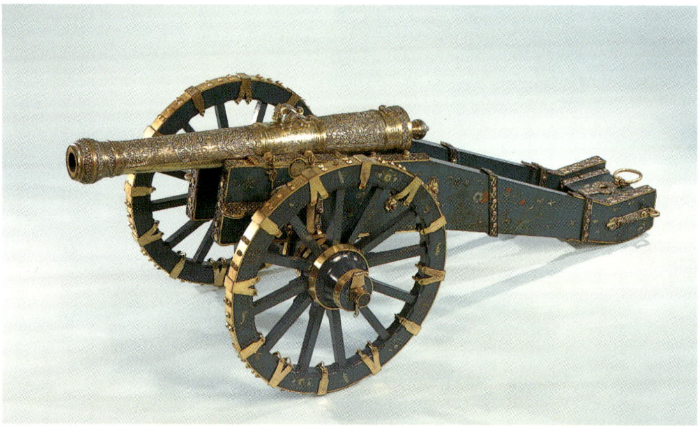

fig. 84 Sinhalese cannon, captured by the Dutch East India Company in 1765 and presented to Stadholder Willem III; bronze, silver, gold and rubies, 177 x 71 x 59 cm. Amsterdam, Rijksmuseum

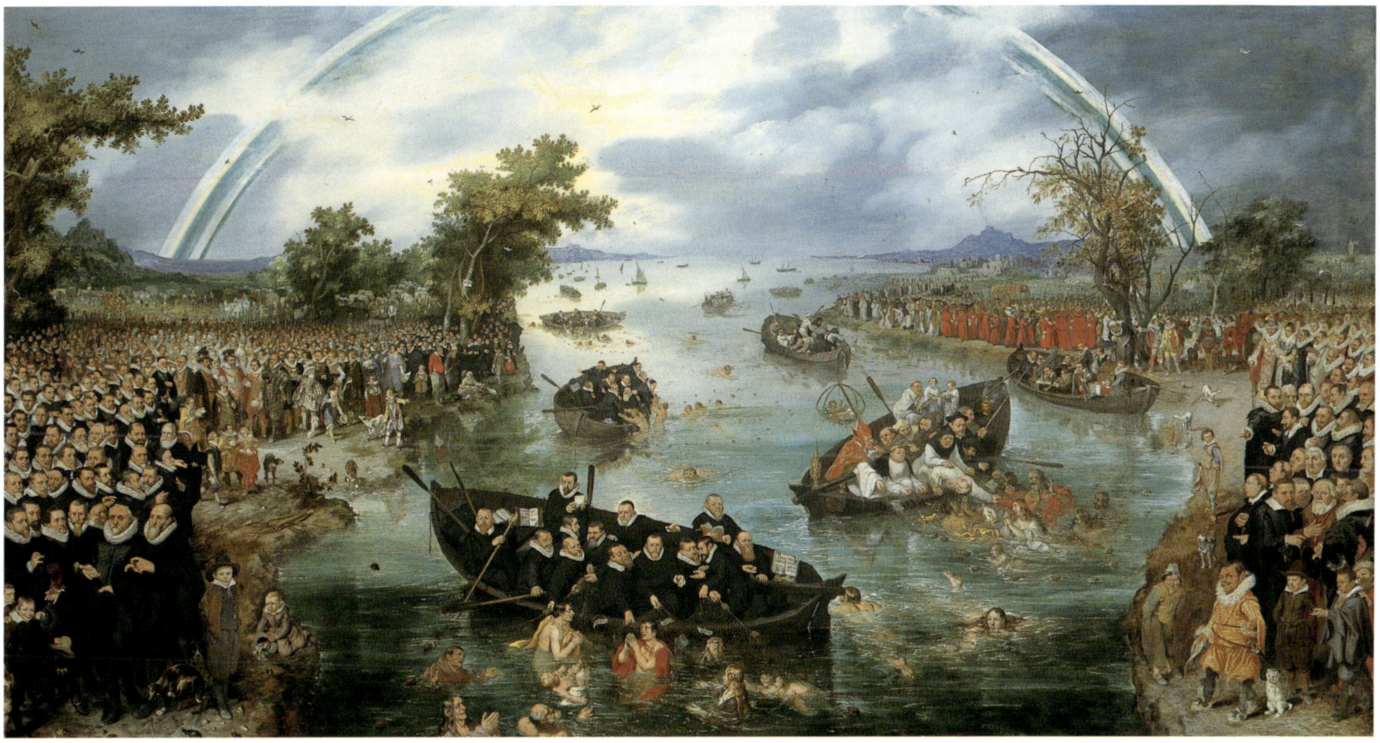

fig. 85 Adriaen Pietersz van der Venne, *Fishing for souls*, 1614; oil on panel, 98 x 189 cm. Amsterdam, Rijksmuseum

at the time, was regarded as a parody of religious sectarianism in the Republic. The next three galleries were hung with paintings by Italian, French and Dutch masters. Most of the Dutch paintings, which were overwhelmingly from the 17th century, came from the palaces at Het Loo and Soestdijk, with the result that the display was dominated by decorative works by artists active at the end of the century like Gerard de Lairesse (*figs.* 14, 86) and Melchior d'Hondecoeter [100].

The exhibition ended in the Oranjezaal, which was decorated with allegories glorifying Prince Frederik Hendrik. This great hall, which still exists, with its paintings executed between 1648 and 1652 by Jacob Jordaens, Caesar van Everdingen, Jan de Braij and others, is a unique, monumental ensemble of 17th-century Dutch and Flemish history painting (*fig.* 32).

All in all, the Nationale Konst-Gallerij gave a very one-sided view of painting from the Golden Age. It lacked not only works by most of the great Dutch masters but also cabinet pieces by painters like Gerard Dou, Frans van Mieris, Jan Steen and others which were the cornerstones of most 18th-century Dutch picture collections. The curators of the gallery must have been aware of these gaps, for their purchases in the early years went beyond works that were merely of historical interest, to encompass paintings by artists like Jacob van Ruisdael, Jan van de Cappelle [41], Albert Cuyp, Jan Steen, Rembrandt and Rubens. The sums involved were rarely large.

fig. 86 Gerard de Lairesse, *Diana and Endymion*, c. 1680; oil on canvas, 177 x 18.5 cm. Amsterdam, Rijksmuseum

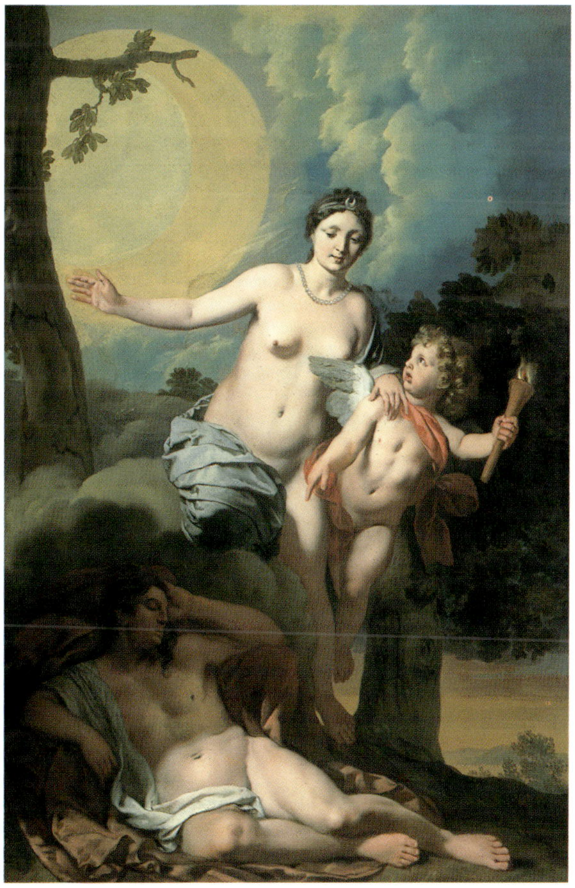

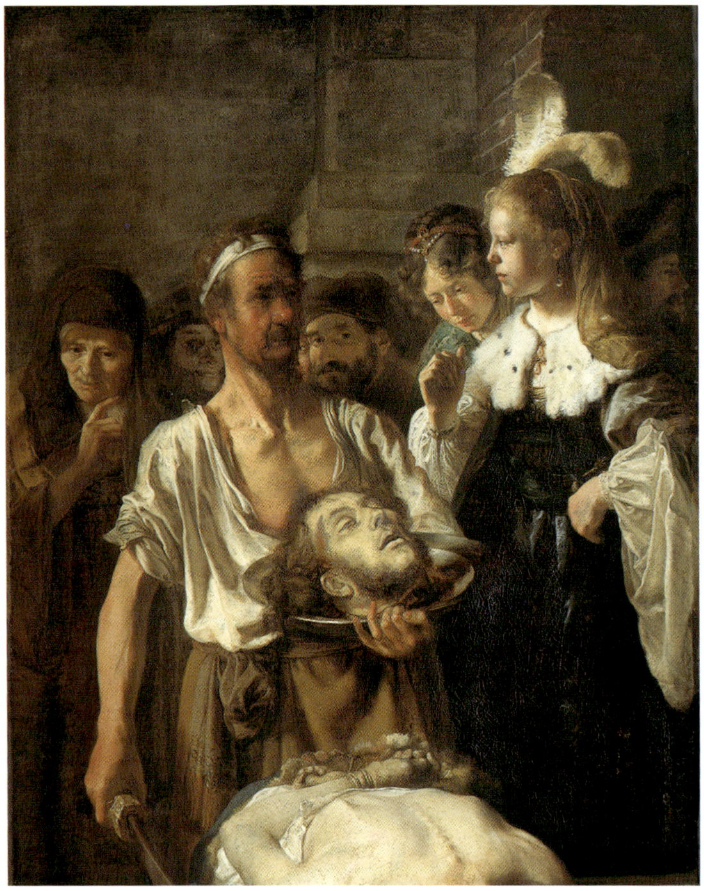

fig. 87 Carel Fabritius (attributed to), *The beheading of John the Baptist*, c. 1640; oil on canvas, 149 x 121 cm. Amsterdam, Rijksmuseum

Great and Small chambers of the Council of War, which were hung with paintings that had belonged to the city from the days when the building was still the Town Hall. On King Louis's insistence, seven of them were incorporated in the Royal Museum, including Bartholomeus van der Helst's *Celebration of the Peace of Münster* [48], the *IJ at Amsterdam with the Gouden Leeuw* by Willem van de Velde the Younger (*fig. 16*), and Rembrandt's *Night watch* [44] and *Syndics* [81]. Although short-lived, Louis Napoleon's rule (1806-1810) was a period when the museum came into its own.

Loans from the City of Amsterdam and the purchase of more than 200 paintings from two 18th-century Dutch collections changed the face of the museum by shifting the emphasis to the 17th-century Dutch school. Sixty-five paintings were bought at the auction of the Van der Pot cabinet in 1808, which was slanted heavily towards the great masters of the Golden Age [*32, 56, 73, 91, 102*]. The most expensive was Dou's *Night school* [73], followed by Paulus Potter's *Herdsmen with their cattle*. In June 1809 the museum acquired the 137 paintings in the Van Heteren Gevers Collection, which also consisted almost exclusively of 17th-century Flemish and, above all, Dutch cabinet pieces, the public favourites being Gerard ter Borch's *Paternal admonition* [72] and Jan Steen's *Feast of St Nicholas* [74].

THE RIJKS MUSEUM IN THE TRIPPENHUIS

In 1815, after the restoration of the House of Orange, it was decided to move the museum to the Trippenhuis, along with the Royal Academy. After the removal of the 'historical relics' and 'antiquities' to The Hague and Leiden in 1825, the Rijks Museum (National

The first purchase, made two weeks after the Konst-Gallerij opened, was of Jan Asselijn's *Threatened swan* [53], which was wrongly believed at the time to be an allegory of the defence of the Republic by Pensionary Johan de Witt against the twin threats of the House of Orange and England. In 1801 the gallery bought *The beheading of John the Baptist* (*fig. 87*) thinking it was a Rembrandt. Today it is attributed to Carel Fabritius.

The Nationale Konst-Gallerij in Huis ten Bosch had only a brief existence. Grand Pensionary Rutger Schimmelpenninck moved into the palace in 1805, forcing the gallery to relocate to the Buitenhof in The Hague. King Louis Napoleon, the brother of the French emperor Napoleon Bonaparte who was made king of Holland in 1806, renamed it the Koninklijk Museum (Royal Museum) and transferred it to Amsterdam.

THE ROYAL MUSEUM

The Royal Museum opened in Amsterdam on 15 September 1808 in the former Town Hall on Dam Square, which Louis Napoleon had commandeered as the Royal Palace. Part of it was housed in the

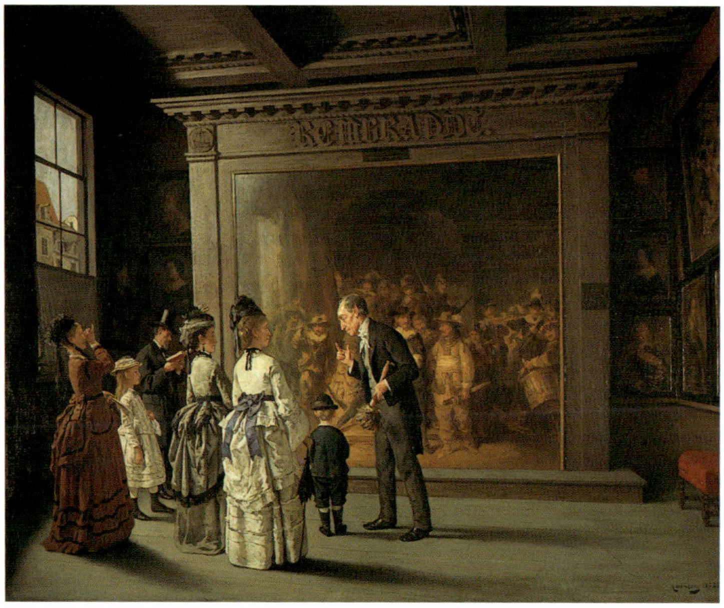

fig. 88 Augustus Jensberg, *Rembrandt's Night watch in the Trippenhuis*, 1880; oil on canvas. Malmö, Museum

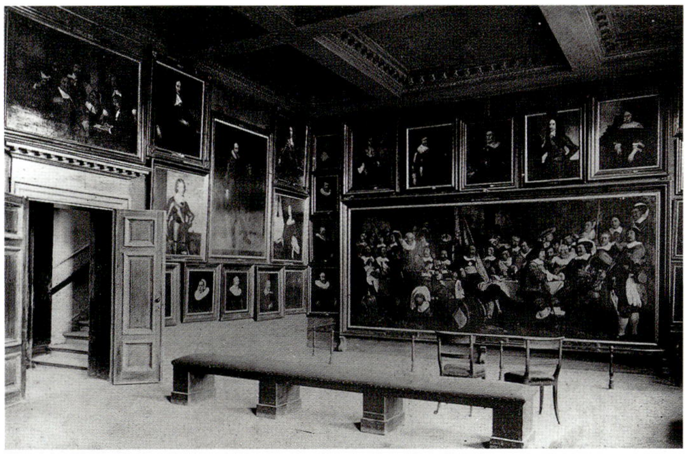

fig. 89 Gallery with Van der Helst's *Celebration of the Peace of Münster* and Rembrandt's *Night watch* (opposite wall) in the Trippenhuis, c. 1880

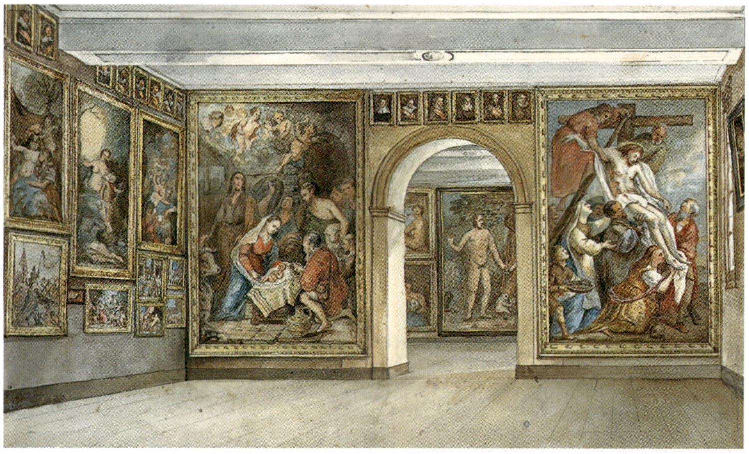

fig. 90 Gerrit Lamberts, *Interior of the Rijks Museum in the Trippenhuis, the large gallery at the front of the second floor*, c. 1838; watercolour, 23.5 x 41 cm. Amsterdam, City Archives

Museum) became a museum of paintings with a printroom attached. The building was not really large enough for the 500-odd paintings in the collection, which were exhibited on the first and second floors. The largest room, the anteroom on the first floor, housed 'the distinguished paintings relating to the nation's history and the portraits of our country's most famous men'. Rembrandt's *Night watch* and Van der Helst's *Celebration of the Peace of Münster* hung facing each other on the side walls (*figs. 88-89*). They were among the most famous works in the museum, and interestingly, public appreciation of them shifted in the course of the 19th century from the Van der Helst to the Rembrandt. The anteroom on the second floor was given over to the earlier paintings and other large history pieces (*fig. 90*), with pictures by artists like De Lairesse (*fig. 86*) and Caspar de Crayer. The still lifes, landscapes and genre scenes were consigned to smaller rooms at the back. The structure of the collection remained virtually unchanged until it moved to the new Rijksmuseum building in 1885, as did the way it was displayed.

The composition of the collection was fairly one-sided. Small works by masters like Nicolaes Berchem, Jan Steen, Jan van der Heyden and Philips Wouwerman were well represented, but in 1815 there was still nothing by Frans Hals, Meindert Hobbema, Gabriel Metsu, Aert van der Neer, Pieter de Hooch or Johannes Vermeer.

By now the Netherlands had a second museum of paintings in the shape of the Mauritshuis in The Hague, which housed the stadholder's collection after its repatriation from Paris. There, too, the accent was on painting of the Golden Age. The directors of both museums made it their policy to have at least one representative work by every Netherlandish master, Dutch and Flemish. That accounted for the sale of paintings in 1828 by artists who were already amply represented in both museums, the exchange of

fig. 91 Rembrandt, *The anatomy lesson of Dr Nicolaes Tulp*, 1632; oil on canvas, 169.5 x 216.5 cm. The Hague, Mauritshuis

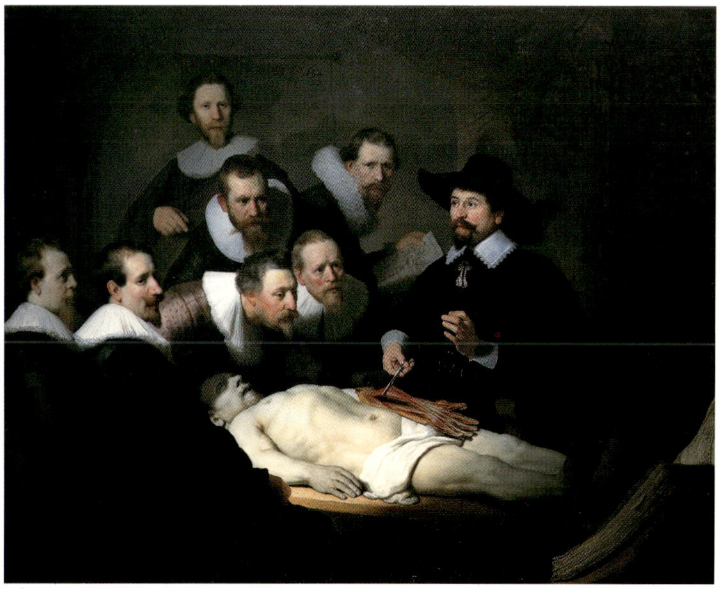

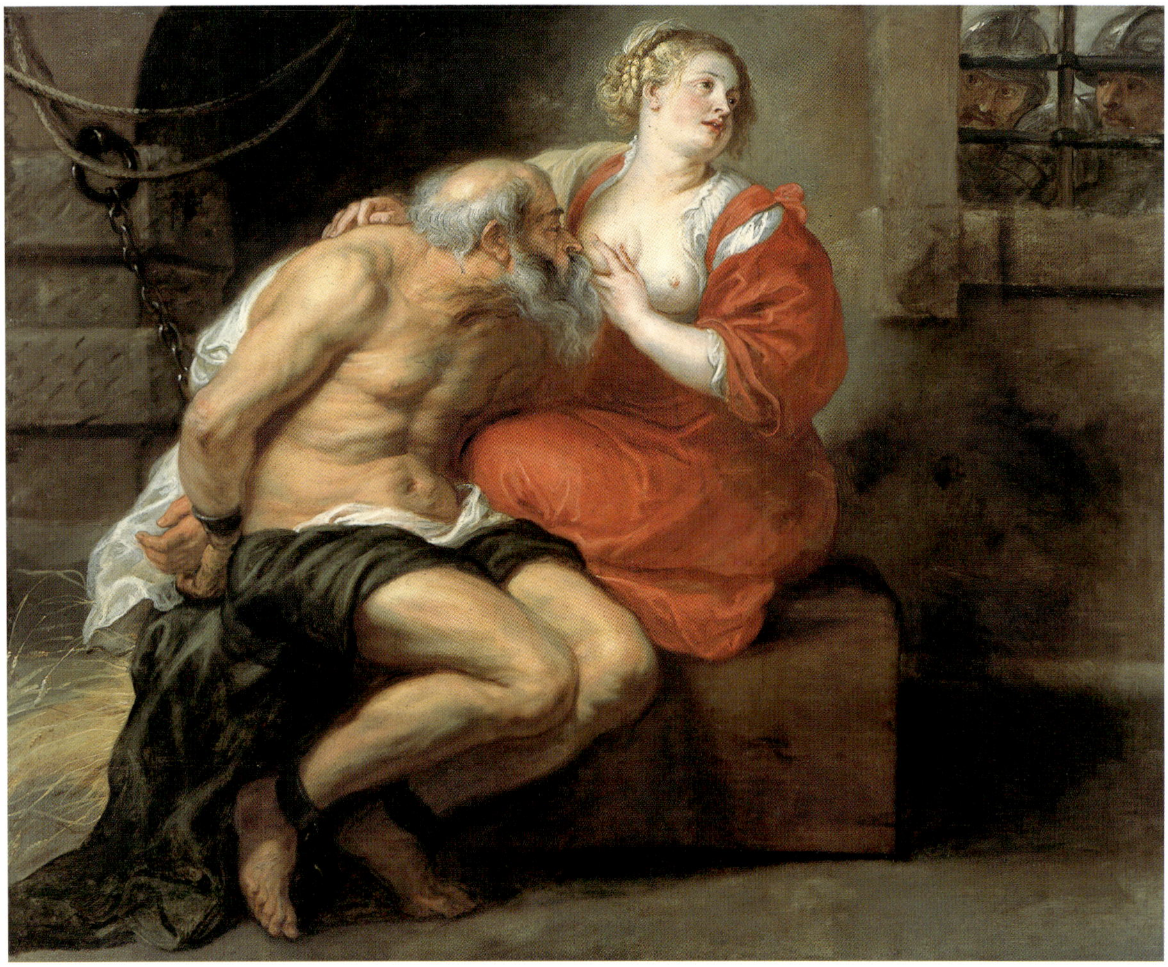

fig. 92 Peter Paul Rubens, *Cimon and Pero*, c. 1630; oil on canvas, 155 x 190 cm. Amsterdam, Rijksmuseum

works between them, and the suggestions for purchases submitted to King Willem I, on whom both institutions depended for financial support. The king had a marked preference for the Mauritshuis, which resulted in Vermeer's *View of Delft* going there after its purchase in 1822, against the advice of both directors. On the other hand, Adriaen van de Velde's celebrated *Hut* [95], which was bought the same year for a far higher price at the Brentano sale, went to Amsterdam. The king then proceeded to transfer Rembrandt's *Anatomy lesson of Dr Nicolaes Tulp* (*fig. 91*) from Amsterdam's Surgeons' Guild to the Mauritshuis in 1828, despite the fact that Cornelis Apostool, the director of the Rijksmuseum from 1808 to 1844, had made great efforts to acquire it and that most of the purchase money had come from the sale of paintings from the Rijks Museum.

The museum was more fortunate with its acquisition of two masterpieces by the then underrated Frans Hals: the *Merry drinker* [29] in 1816 and the *Marriage portrait of Isaac Abrahamsz Massa and Beatrix van der Laen* [28] in 1852. Other purchases, like Gerard van Honthorst's *Merry fiddler* [14] in 1824 and Paulus Moreelse's *Beautiful shepherdess* in 1817, added an unexpected realistic touch to the collection. However, it was to be a long time before the museum made room for the early 17th-century landscape and still life painters of Haarlem such as Esaias van de Velde and Avercamp, Pieter Claesz and Heda, let alone for history pieces by Dutch followers of Caravaggio like Hendrick ter Brugghen and Dirck van Baburen.

What it did try and do was acquire work by 17th-century Flemish artists. An exchange with the Mauritshuis in 1825 gave it Rubens's *Cimon and Pero* (*fig. 92*) and Anthony van Dyck's *Portrait of Nicolaes van der Borght* (*fig. 93*).

The acquisitions made by both museums, modest as they were to start with, came to an almost complete halt between 1830 and 1875, when the supply of funds slowed to a trickle. King Willem II, who succeeded to the throne on Willem I's abdication in 1840, was only interested in his private gallery, and the government was content to do nothing but administer the art that was already in the museums. Until 1875, then, the Rijks Museum simply marked time.

Sadly, almost nothing of the superb private collection which Willem II put together in the early decades of the 19th century remained in the Netherlands. It was a classic royal gallery, with

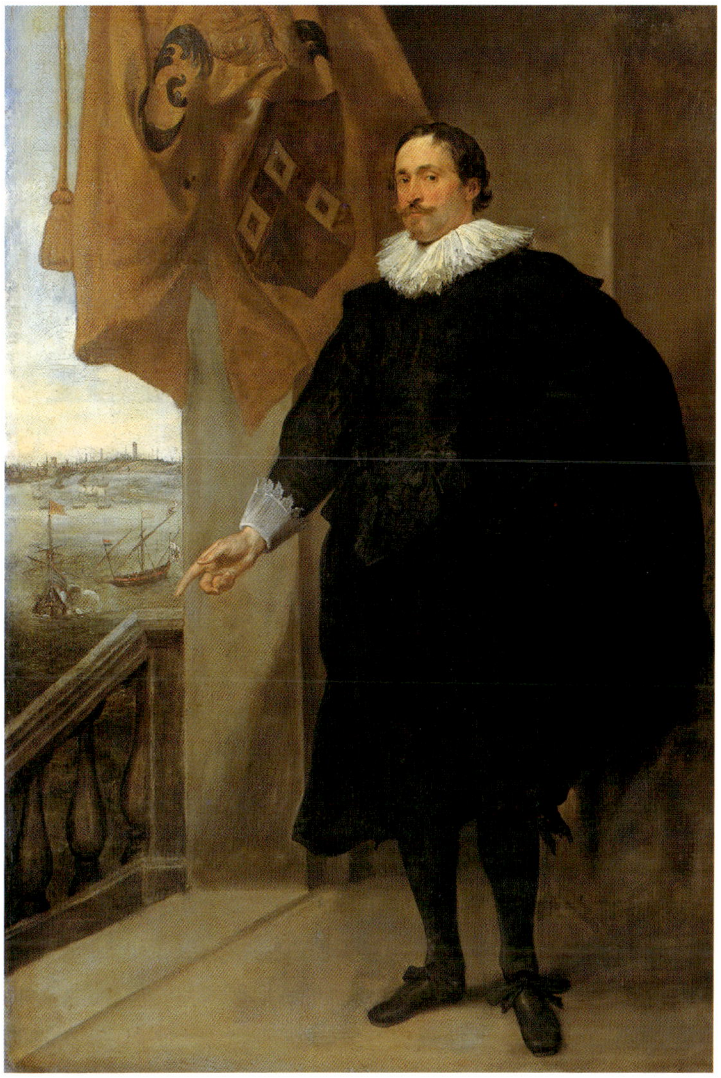

fig. 93 Anthony van Dyck, *Portrait of Nicolaes van der Borght*, c. 1620-1630; oil on canvas, 201 x 141 cm. Amsterdam, Rijksmuseum

important works by great names like Jan van Eyck, Raphael, Titian, Rubens, Van Dyck, Lorrain, Murillo and Rembrandt, and it would have given a Dutch museum an international character which is still lacking today. The paintings by Rembrandt, Ruisdael, Hobbema and Van der Helst were of a quality and stature that far exceeded anything in public museums. After Willem II's death in 1849 the collection was auctioned off in The Hague and disappeared abroad almost in its entirety. The Rijks Museum asked the minister to buy two magnificent works by Teniers and Hobbema, but he refused. In 1885 the Teniers did eventually come to the museum as part of the Van der Hoop Collection (*fig. 94*). The Minister of Home Affairs at the time was the Liberal leader Johan Thorbecke, who believed that the arts and sciences had no need of government subsidies.

Paintings by many Dutch masters had been snapped up by foreign buyers even back in the 17th century. Wilhelm van Bode, the German art historian, remarked in 1871 that 'anything in the many Dutch private collections that is not part of the fixtures and fittings has, with few exceptions, been peddled off abroad.' But then the tide began to turn. In 1870 the Rijks Museum received a substantial bequest from L. Dupper Wzn, a Dordrecht collector, comprising more than 60 17th-century Dutch paintings, most of them cabinet pieces [*39, 64b*]. This was the first in a series of gifts and bequests which strengthened the emphasis on the classic Dutch school. In addition, there was now talk of building a new museum.

The cluttered and cramped arrangement of the Rijks Museum in the Trippenhuis was attracting considerable criticism. Théophile Thoré, the famous connoisseur of Dutch painting who had rediscovered painters like Hals, Fabritius and Vermeer, delivered a scathing judgement in his *Musées de la Hollande* of 1858, published under the pseudonym William Bürger. In his view, a new building, a new hang and a new catalogue were essential if justice was to be done to the glorious 17th century. Thoré's book laid the foundations for a completely new view of the painting of the Golden Age, with the emphasis on everyday reality and with Frans Hals, Rembrandt, Jan Steen and Johannes Vermeer as the leading lights. To his mind there was little good to be said about later 17th-century painters like Van Mieris, Dou, De Lairesse and Wouwerman. *The night watch* [*44*], which Thoré considered to be the most beautiful painting in the world, finally won out over Van der Helst's *Celebration of the Peace of Münster* [*48*], which he felt was too smooth and detailed.

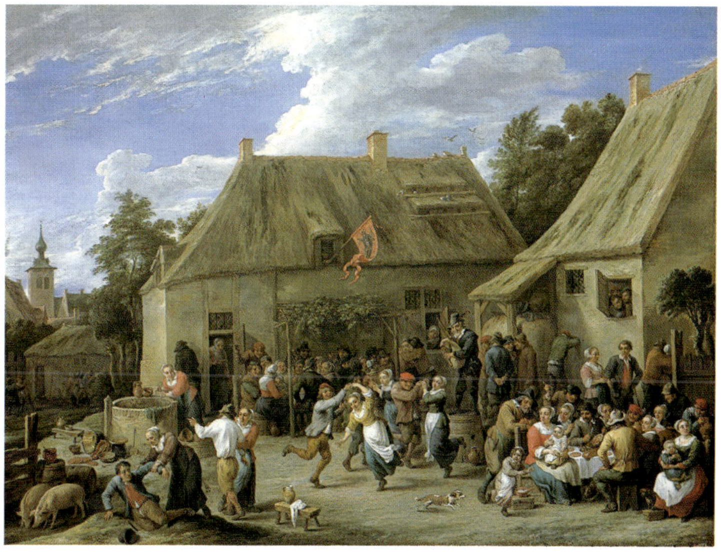

fig. 94 David Teniers II, *Country kermis*, c. 1650; oil on canvas, 78 x 106 cm. Amsterdam, Rijksmuseum (A. van der Hoop Bequest)

It was to be a long time before Thoré's vision gained acceptance in the Netherlands. Interest in the art of the glorious past was primarily historical and antiquarian, and was geared to preserving the country's historical heritage. In his celebrated article of 1873, 'Holland op zijn smalst' (Holland at its meanest), Victor de Stuers argued that the government should become more involved in preserving that legacy. In 1875 he became head of the Department of Museums and Monuments at the Ministry of Home Affairs, and he set to work with a vengeance. He took a decidedly broad view of the term 'cultural heritage'. After the lower house of parliament voted to build a new Rijksmuseum in 1872, De Stuers's efforts led to an active acquisition policy for the various collections that would be given a home in the new museum.

THE NEW RIJKSMUSEUM BUILDING

The reliefs, tile pictures and inscriptions decorating the exterior of the Rijksmuseum illustrate the origins and flowering of the culture of the northern Netherlands, which reached its apogee in the glorious Golden Age, although considerable space is also devoted to the middle ages and the Renaissance.

Rembrandt takes pride of place in 17th-century painting, and is depicted several times on the outside of the building. He is the central figure in a tile picture on the south front, which is now concealed by the *Night watch* annex (*fig. 95*). He represents the Golden Age in the stained glass windows in the main hall, with Lucas van Leyden as his counterpart for the earlier period of northern Netherlandish art. Frans Hals makes his first appearance in the medallions in the windows, alongside Memlinc and Raphael.

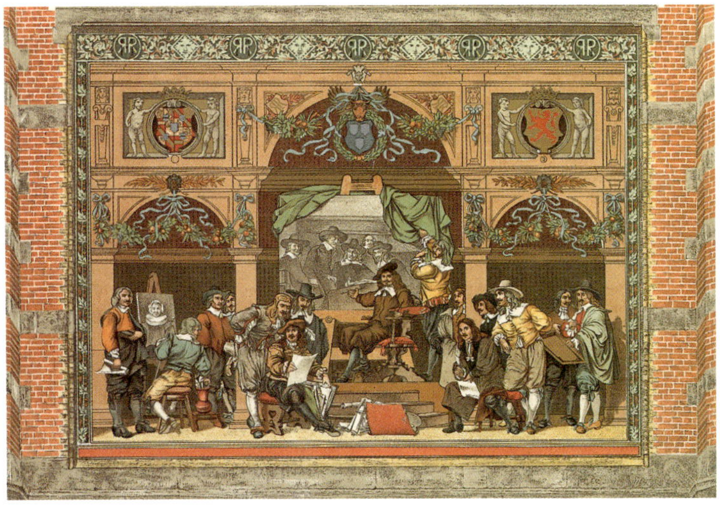

fig. 95 François Gillet, *Design for the depiction in enamel on lava above the gate at the back of the building: Rembrandt amidst his colleagues, with the Syndics*; lithograph in Victor de Stuers, *Musée National d'Amsterdam*, Amsterdam-Paris 1897

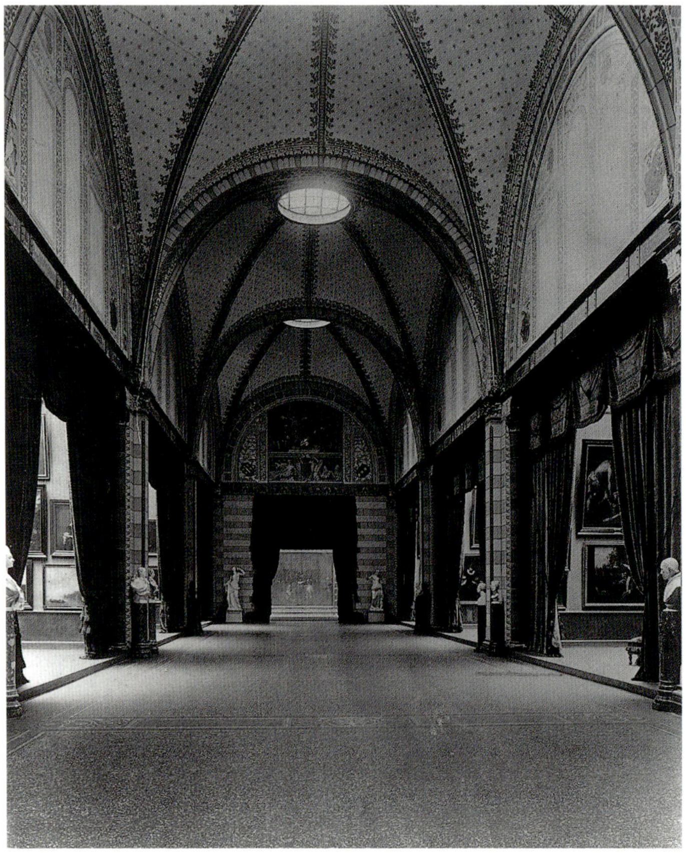

fig. 96 *The night watch seen from the Gallery of Honour*, 1898

Seventeenth-century art also dominated the museum galleries. The entire first floor was hung with paintings from the 15th to the 19th centuries, but most of the rooms were devoted to the 17th century. Rembrandt's *Night watch* was given a central position in a room at the end of the Gallery of Honour (*fig. 96*). The ground floor was occupied by the Nederlandsch Museum voor Geschiedenis en Kunst (Netherlands Museum of History and Art), which illustrated the various aspects of the history of Dutch art and culture.

THE NETHERLANDS MUSEUM OF HISTORY AND ART

Museums for the decorative arts opened in London, Vienna, Berlin and Hamburg in the second half of the 19th century with the aim of improving the taste of craftsmen and the general public. They also served as collections of examples to be studied by artisans and artists. In addition to this exemplary function, the interest in the applied arts as manifested in the Rijksmuseum after 1885 had a decidedly antiquarian nature.

The creation of a Dutch museum of decorative arts was the ultimate goal of the Koninklijk Oudheidkundig Genootschap, or KOG (Royal Antiquarian Society), which was founded in Amsterdam in 1858. The society's collection, which grew rapidly in the early decades of its existence through purchases, gifts and bequests, was exhibited at various venues in Amsterdam prior to 1885. Several galleries in the new Rijksmuseum were then filled with objets d'art belonging to the society: the Regents' Gallery, the Gilt-Leather Room and the Old Dutch interior. Most of the other objects went on display in the Netherlands Museum.

The Netherlands Museum of History and Art was founded by Victor de Stuers in 1875, and was housed in The Hague until the new Rijksmuseum was completed. The core collection consisted of objects of Dutch origin from the Koninklijk Kabinet van Zeldzaamheden (Royal Cabinet of Rarities) in the Mauritshuis. The non-western artefacts (mostly Japanese and Chinese) were exhibited in the Ethnographic Museum in Leiden. From 1875 onwards, Victor de Stuers sent many 'ancient relics' of very variable importance and quality to the Netherlands Museum, and with the other purchases and gifts the collection expanded rapidly. The museum's director was David van der Kellen Jr, one of the founders of the KOG, which set the stage for integrating both collections in the new Rijksmuseum.

The galleries with ecclesiastical architecture in the Netherlands Museum concentrated chiefly on the middle ages, but those with civic architecture focused mainly on the 17th century. They consisted of a series of old Dutch period rooms (*fig. 97*) complete with original panelling, ceilings and fireplaces and furnished with 17th-century objects and works of art—furniture, carpets, glass and silver. The arrangement followed the model Kellen had developed for presenting the KOG collections when they were spread over various locations in Amsterdam. There were also separate rooms for textiles, ceramics and porcelain, as well as an Admirals' Gallery with paintings of sea battles and portraits of naval heroes. The east courtyard was devoted to Dutch history, and the west courtyard to a survey of Dutch architectural sculpture using plaster casts from the national collection.

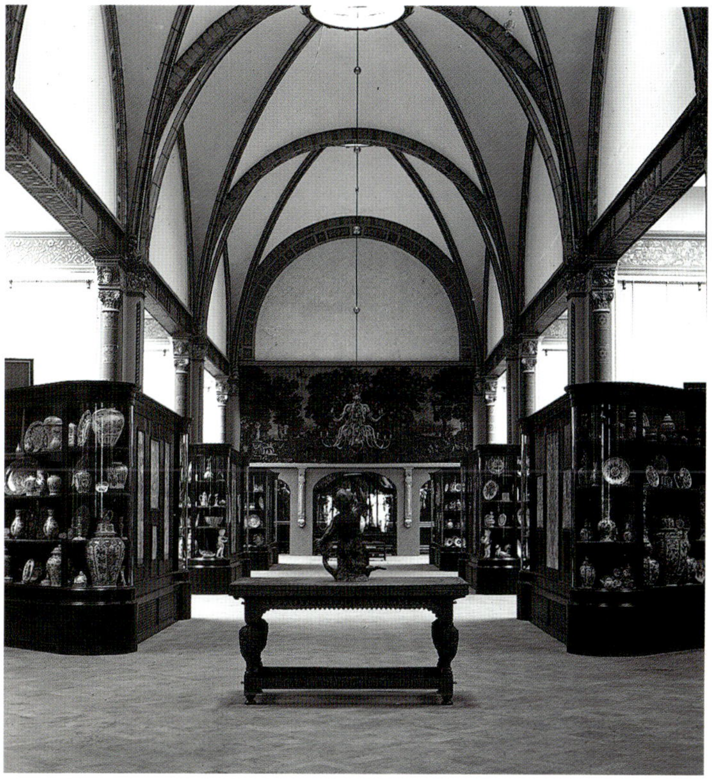

fig. 98 The Gallery of Honour with the display cases containing delftware from the Loudon Collection, c. 1930

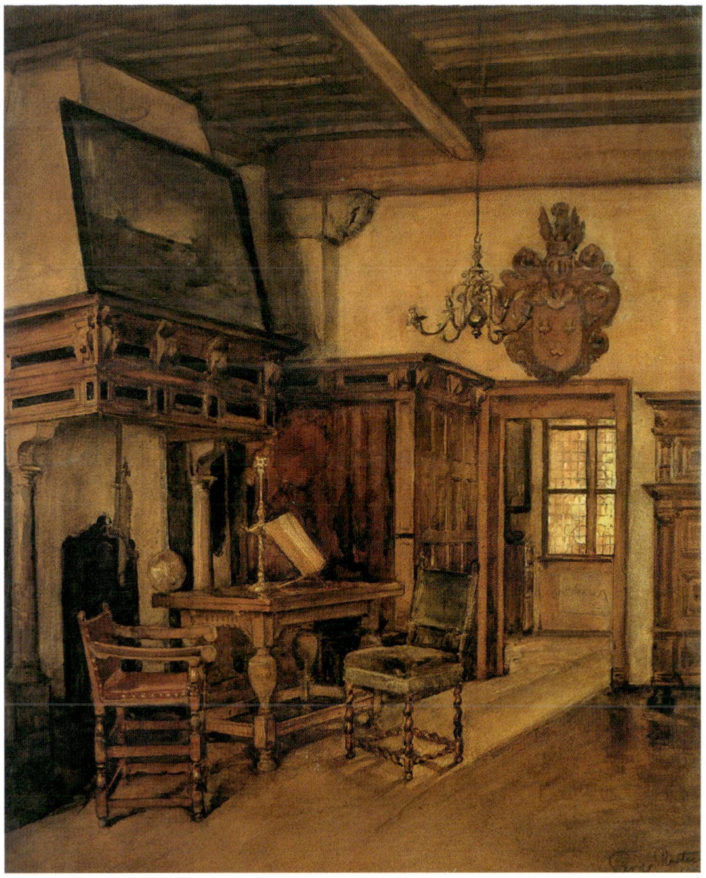

fig. 97 Georg Rueter, *Old Dutch bedchamber in the Nederlandsch Museum*, April 1894; watercolour and gouache, 58.5 x 48.5 cm. Amsterdam, Rijksmuseum

Neither the galleries with ecclesiastical architecture nor the period rooms were granted a long life. Changes in the arrangement of the displays in the early decades of the 20th century shifted the emphasis to stylistic developments within the various branches of the applied arts.

Bequests and gifts prior to 1900 greatly enriched the collection of 17th-century glass, particularly with engraved specimens [15, *69*], and furniture, silver and gold objects from the Golden Age were also well represented. There were particularly rich holdings of Amsterdam silver and gold, thanks to a loan from the City of Amsterdam, gifts and purchases. When the heirs of John F. Loudon presented the museum with an exceptionally fine collection of Delft faience in 1916, this branch of the applied arts could suddenly be displayed to excellent effect. Delftware had been rediscovered a few decades earlier and rapidly became the archetypical Dutch contribution to the European decorative arts, which is why it was exhibited in the Gallery of Honour until the Second World War (*fig. 98*).

A picture of 17th-century Dutch sculpture began to emerge when the collections of the City of Amsterdam, the KOG and those in The Hague were brought together in the Rijksmuseum [87]. It was then that Artus Quellinus's superb bust of Andries de Graeff returned to the Rijksmuseum [51]. Apostool had bought it for the museum in 1817, but it was later transferred to the Academy of Fine Arts in Amsterdam's Oudemanhuispoort. That was also the source of the unique collection of terracotta sketches and models that Quellinus had made for Amsterdam Town Hall [52], which belonged to the city. Purchases expanded the holdings of 17th-century sculpture with work by Hendrick de Keyser [4] and Rombout Verhulst [77].

At the beginning of the 20th century the purchases took on a more international air, consisting chiefly of Italian and French furniture, and eastern and Italian ceramics. However, acquisitions of Dutch objects continued to centre on the 17th century, with the French-inspired court art favoured by Stadholder Willem III being totally ignored.

THE RIJKSMUSEUM PRINTROOM

In 1816, the print collection of Baron Van Leyden, which Louis Napoleon had bought for the Royal Library in The Hague in 1808, was transferred to the Trippenhuis. Put together in the 18th century, it now forms the nucleus of the Rijksmuseum Printroom, its 70,000 prints providing a superb overview of European printmaking from the late middle ages to the end of the 18th century. The group of Rembrandt etchings, amounting to some 500 impressions, was remarkably fine and complete, and his contemporaries Hercules Segers and Adriaen van Ostade were also well represented [10, 71].

The collection could be examined by specialists, connoisseurs and artists in the lower gallery of the Trippenhuis. The collection was enlarged in the early decades of the 19th century, mainly with etchings by Rembrandt and reproductive prints, but then the printroom, too, was struck by the budgetary constraints which prevented any further purchases from 1840 on. It had almost no drawings, apart from the few bought under Louis Napoleon.

The appointment of J.P. van der Kellen as director of the printroom in 1876 marked the start of an active acquisition policy. He initially built up the collection of Dutch prints, and by adding several thousand sheets a year put together a very wide-ranging collection of 17th-century Dutch graphic art. Baron van Leyden had collected Dutch prints selectively and within an international context, but Van der Kellen's approach was all-inclusive. It is thanks to him and his successors that the Amsterdam printroom now contains an unrivalled reference collection of Dutch printmaking.

Van der Kellen also set himself the task of assembling a representative survey of Dutch drawings, which had been almost entirely lacking up until then. Once again there were budgetary restrictions. When the famous collection of drawings belonging to Jacob de Vos Jbzn came up for auction in Amsterdam in May 1883, a group of private individuals had to come to the printroom's aid. They founded the Vereniging Rembrandt (Rembrandt Society), raised a considerable capital sum, and gave the nation a large, interest-free loan. That money was used to buy almost 500 drawings, mostly from the 17th century [37, 50, 96]—one-third of De Vos's collection. That purchase laid the foundations for an overview of 17th-century Dutch drawing that grew apace in the next few decades. More than 5,000 drawings were bought in that period, while the print collection expanded from 70,000 to 125,000 sheets. In addition to purchases, the printroom received from the City of Amsterdam the 17th-century print collection of Michiel Hinloopen, which contained almost 50 works by Hercules Segers.

The period of vigorous growth which the printroom had enjoyed under Van der Kellen came to an end at the beginning of the 20th century. The collection continued to expand steadily, largely through gifts, but the very limited budget made spectacular purchases few and far between. One highlight came in 1931 with the Cornelis Hofstede de Groot Bequest of a large number of Rembrandt drawings. In the same period, Mr and Mrs De Bruijn-van der Leeuw were building up a collection of more than 500 etchings by Rembrandt [80], which in 1961 was added to the etchings from Baron van Leyden to make the printroom's Rembrandt collection the finest in the world.

THE RIJKSMUSEUM OF PAINTINGS

The collection of paintings grew steadily from 1875 through gifts, bequests, purchases and a major loan from the City of Amsterdam, trebling its size from 700 to 2,000, and this in turn transformed the nature of the painting galleries in the new building.

The loan from Amsterdam brought a large group of Amsterdam civic guard and regents' portraits into the Rijksmuseum, giving it a particularly rich showing of 17th-century group portraits executed in Amsterdam. As a result of this and the arrival of several large collections of family portraits, Dutch portraiture took a prominent place in the displays. The presentation of classic Dutch painting was also strengthened, especially when the Van der Hoop Collection came to the museum on loan from the City of Amsterdam.

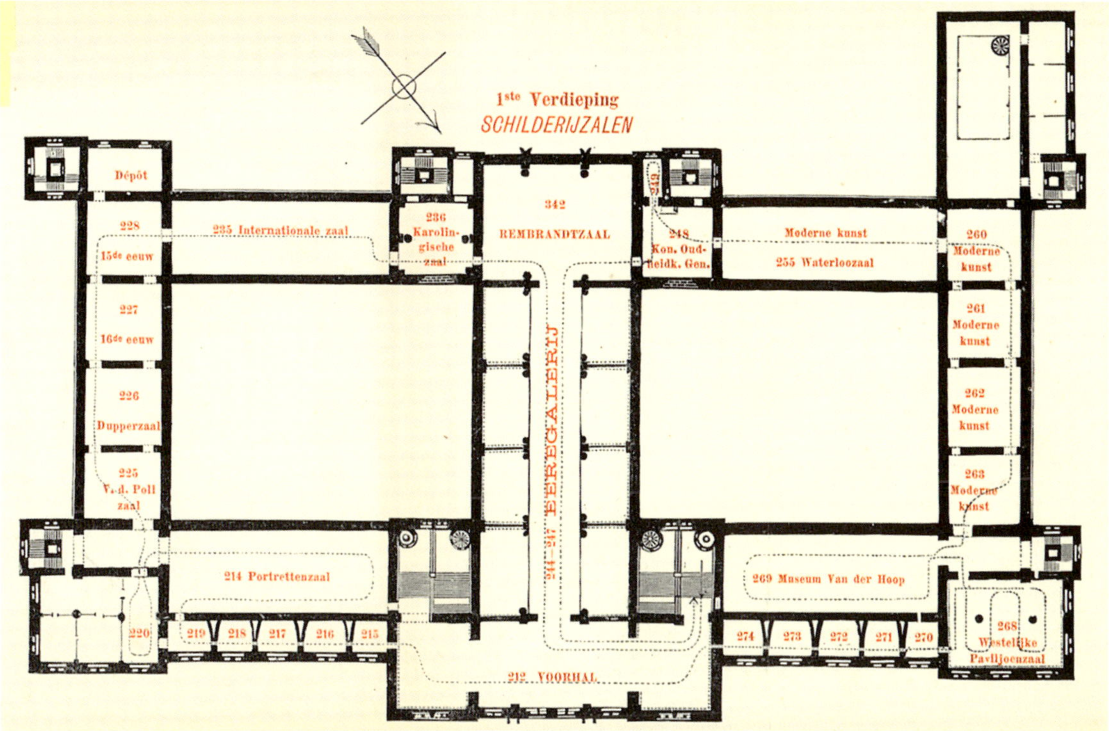

fig. 99 Ground plan of the first floor in the Rijksmuseum, in de *Wegwijzer door 's Rijks Museum*, 1898

The Amsterdam banker Adriaan van der Hoop left his collection to the city in 1854, and until 1885 it was exhibited in the Van der Hoop Museum in Oude Manhuispoort. The praise that Thoré showered on it in his *Musées de la Hollande* of 1858 gives an idea of its importance. In the very period when the Rijks Museum had almost no money to spend, Van der Hoop had the means to put together an exceptionally fine collection of 17th-century paintings, many of which are still among the Rijksmuseum's showpieces, such as Johannes Vermeer's *Woman reading a letter* (*fig. 101*), Rembrandt's *Jewish bride* [82], Ruisdael's *Windmill at Wijk bij Duurstede* [62] and many others [42, 55, 63, 64a, 104].

The accruing riches of the paintings collection were exhibited in the galleries on the first floor of the museum, where they filled no fewer than 67 rooms and cabinets (*fig. 99*). Visitors started the tour on the left side of the *Night watch* gallery, and as in the Trippenhuis the walls were completely filled with paintings (*fig. 100*). After a large room containing the foreign schools came two rooms covering the 15th and 16th centuries, followed by many more devoted to the 17th, with the Dupper and Van de Poll bequests and the Van der Hoop Museum being given a room apiece. The tour ended with several rooms of modern, mostly 19th-century paintings. Despite the wealth of the offerings, the hang of the rooms by subject (there was one large one for portraits, for example, and a smaller one for self-portraits) and by collection meant that there was no coherent overview of the development of 17th-century painting or of the work of the major artists, which in most cases was scattered over several rooms.

The museum's purchasing policy was designed to present 17th-century Dutch painting as comprehensively as possible, and the works it acquired reflected the art-historical views of the late 19th century. Archival research had unearthed a mass of new information about Dutch painters of the Golden Age, with the result that art history had become distinctly documentary in its approach. The

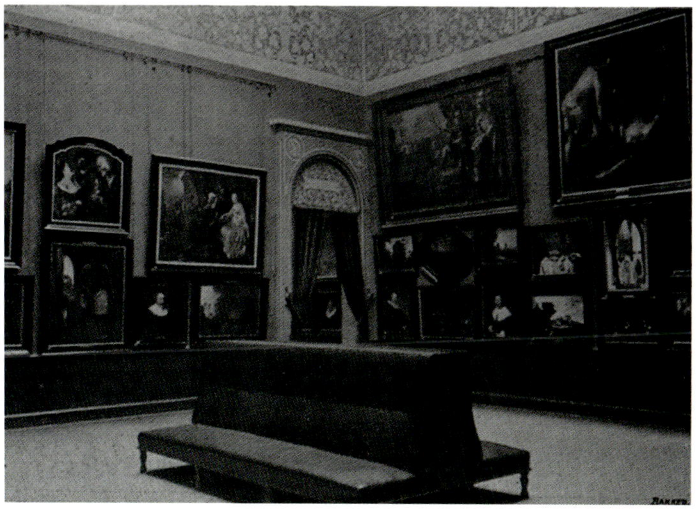

fig. 100 A gallery of paintings (room with 'Old Dutch art'), illustration in *In en om het Rijksmuseum*, 1909

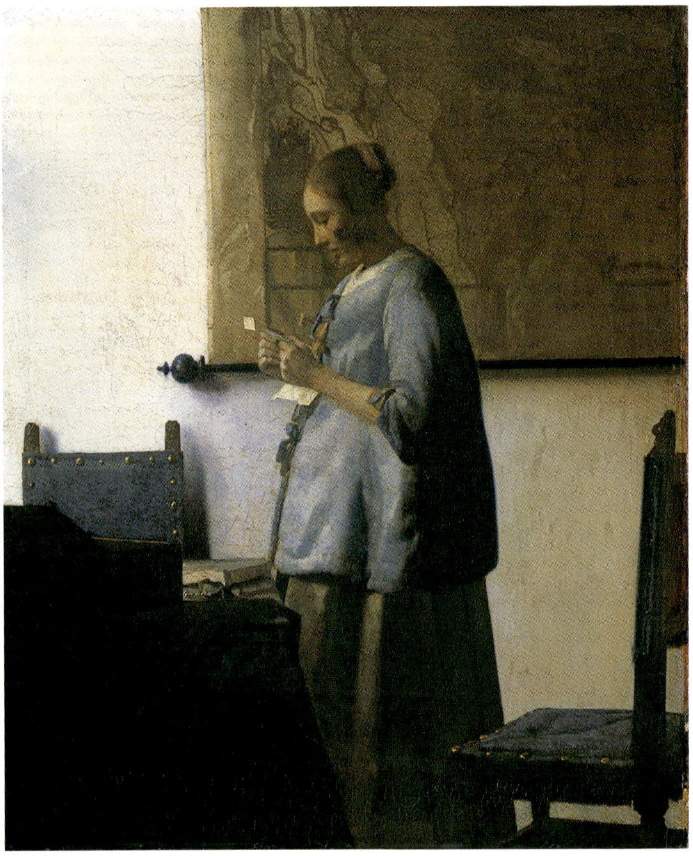

fig. 101 Johannes Vermeer, *Woman reading a letter*, c. 1663; oil on canvas, 46.6 x 39.1 cm. Amsterdam, Rijksmuseum (A. van der Hoop Bequest)

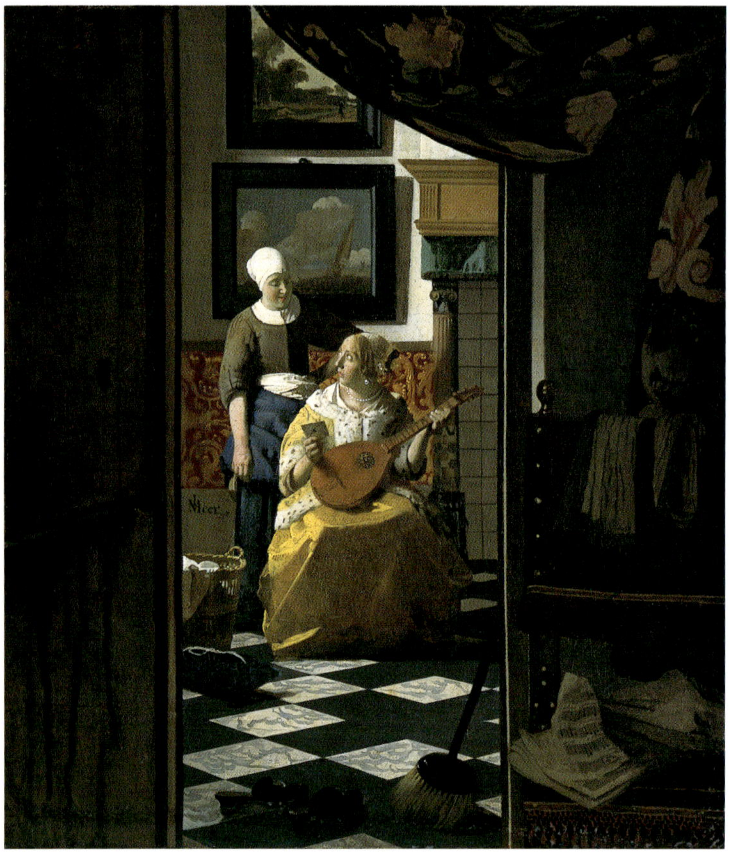

fig. 102 Johannes Vermeer, *The love letter*, c. 1669; oil on canvas, 44 x 38 cm. Amsterdam, Rijksmuseum

preference was for dated and signed works by artists who until then had often been unknown, which then formed the basis for reconstructing their oeuvres. Many of the purchases were of documentary importance. One remarkably fortunate one was Esaias van de Velde's *Ferryboat*, which was added in 1885 [8]. There was rarely enough money to spend a large sum on a painting, and it was only with the aid of the Vereniging Rembrandt that the museum was able to acquire Vermeer's *Love letter* in 1893 (*fig.* 102), a classic cabinet piece like Wouwerman's *Grey* in 1894 [94], and Avercamp's *Winter landscape* in 1897 [6]. The society came to the rescue again in 1900 to help the museum buy Rembrandt's *Stone bridge* [38] at a sale in London. It was the Rijksmuseum's first purchase of a painting by the master, for all his other works had entered the collection as loans, most notably the one from the City of Amsterdam. The Vereniging Rembrandt and the state joined forces in 1908 to buy 39 paintings from the Six Collection, among them Vermeer's *Kitchen maid* [84]. A fourth Vermeer entered the museum in 1921 when the oil magnate H.W.A. Deterding donated *The little street* [83] after buying it from the Six family. The acquisition of many hundreds of paintings in this period, with the Vermeers as the high point, made the Amsterdam collection the most comprehensive overview of 17th-century Dutch painting in the world. However, since most of the pictures were hung rather haphazardly, it could not have been easy to see the wood for the trees. The arrangement in the galleries was rarely chronological, and the various bequests were displayed in rooms of their own, with the result that the work of one and the same artist was often spread over several rooms.

THE RIJKSMUSEUM UNDER SCHMIDT-DEGENER

Under the directorship of Frederik Schmidt-Degener from 1922 to 1941 the emphasis shifted from historical and art-historical inclusiveness to quality. The museum was totally rearranged in the two decades preceding the Second World War, with the works of art being displayed in a more spacious and evocative way, and with a clear demarcation between art and history.

The collection of paintings was exhibited for the first time in more or less chronological order in the first-floor galleries, from the late middle ages to the late 17th century (*fig.* 103). Most of the rooms were devoted to the art of the Golden Age, preceded by early Netherlandish painting and supplemented with a few rooms of Italian, Spanish and Flemish works. Now, at last, the visitor was presented with a coherent chronological view of 17th-century art.

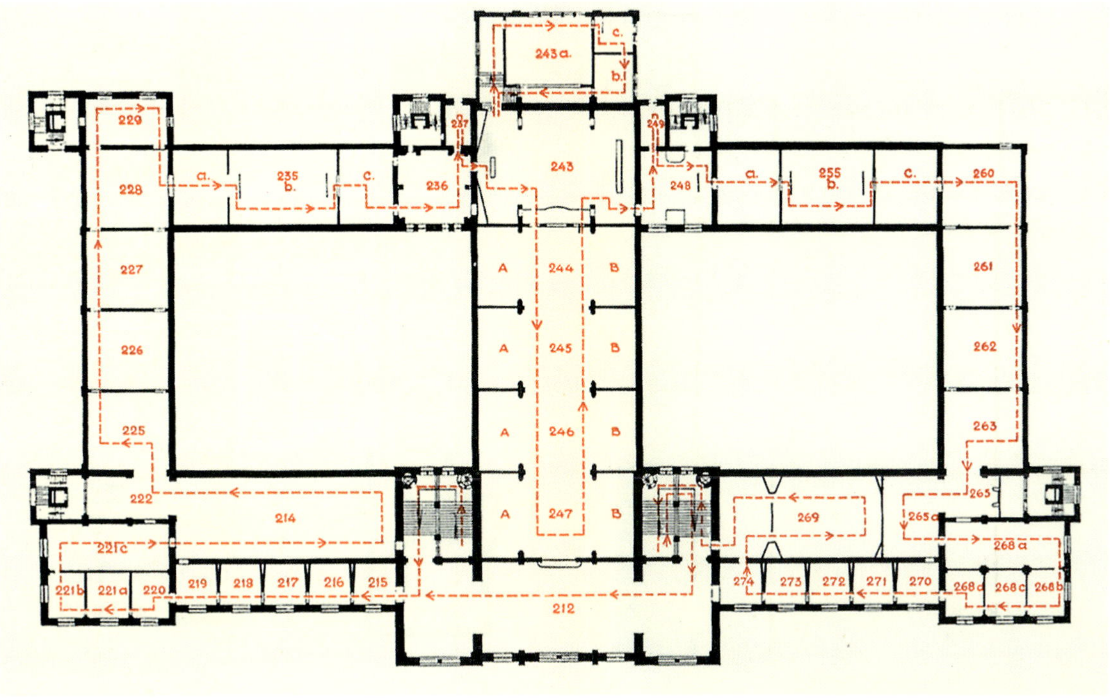

fig. 103 Ground plan of the first floor of the Rijksmuseum, in *Gids met afbeeldingen*, 1928

Rooms with paintings alternated with others containing 17th-century sculpture (De Keyser, Verhulst and Quellinus) and the applied arts (silver by Van Vianen and Lutma, and engraved glass). Delft faience adorned the Gallery of Honour, the cabinets of which combined the larger 'decorative' paintings with 17th-century furniture. The remaining collections of applied art and history retained their place on the ground floor and in the South Wing, which also housed the 18th and 19th-century paintings.

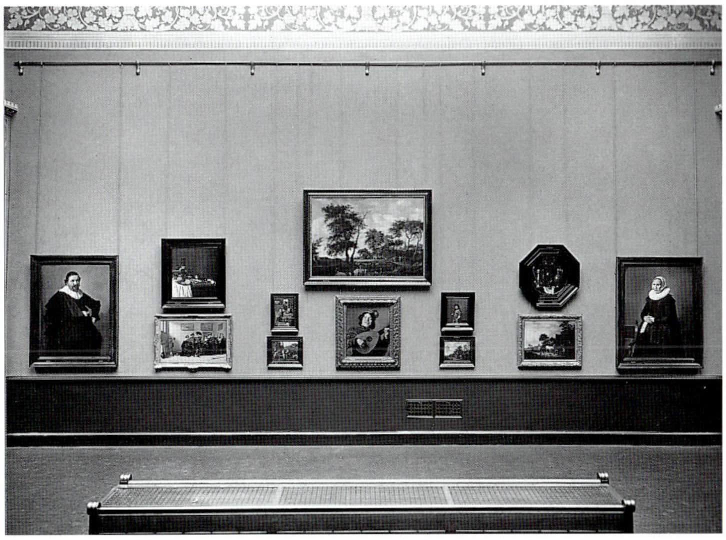

fig. 104 The 'Gallery of early Haarlem paintings' (room 227), c. 1930

In Schmidt-Degener's view, the aesthetic experience of a work of art was of prime importance. He wanted to display the 'lasting image of Dutch art' in which the leading roles were reserved for the great masters—Hals, Steen, Rembrandt, Saenredam, Vermeer and Ruisdael. 'Natural' realism was in and foreign influences out. As long as painters 'remained aloof from the European movements their creations were always new and fresh,' he believed. There was no room for Mannerists, Caravaggisti, Italianates, *Feinmaler* or Classicists. However, they were not banished from the museum altogether, for a few smaller rooms were reserved for the Italianates and the painters of the *beau fini*. Most of the history paintings were hung with the decorative works and 17th-century furniture in the cabinets of the Gallery of Honour.

It is not surprising that Schmidt-Degener was so much choosier than his predecessors. His slender budget, which was cut to a minimum during the years of the Depression, restricted his room for manoeuvre, and purchases of sculpture, decorative arts, prints and drawings were brought to an almost complete halt.

When it came to paintings, the Vereniging Rembrandt and a number of collectors were prepared to rally round when important works were up for sale. That was what happened with Verspronck's *Blue girl* [49] and Metsu's *Sick child* [75], both of which entered the museum in 1928 to bolster the 'lasting image'. The acquisition of Willem Buytewech's *Dignified couples courting* [24] in 1926 was a little outside the traditional idea of the Golden Age, but reflected

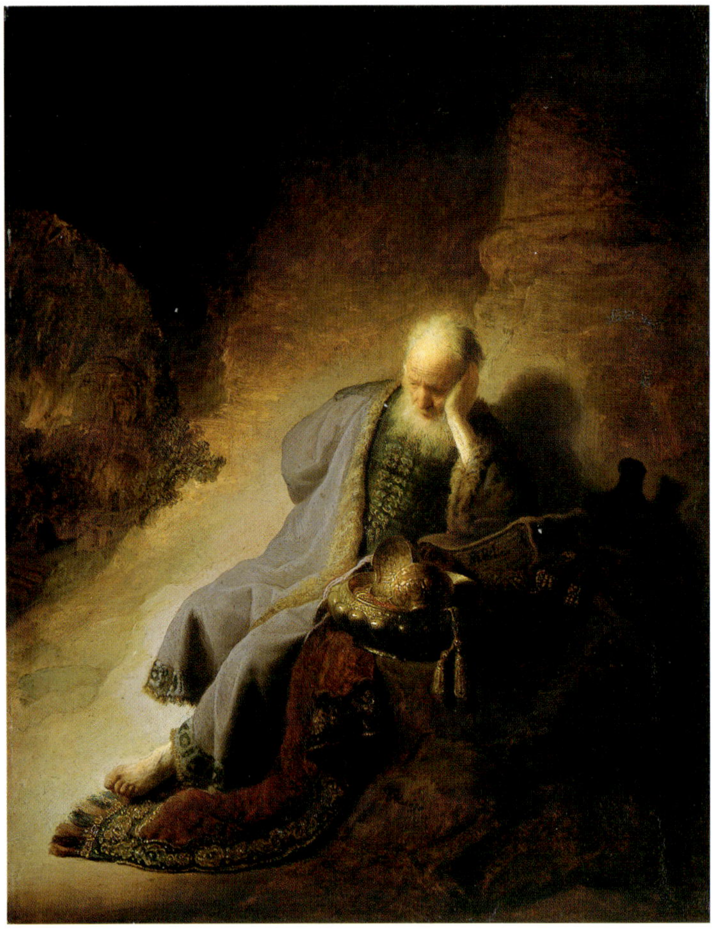

fig. 105 Rembrandt, *Jeremiah lamenting the destruction of Jerusalem*, 1630; oil on panel, 58 x 46 cm. Amsterdam, Rijksmuseum

a reawakened interest in the early 17th-century realism of the Haarlem school (*fig. 104*).

Schmidt-Degener was a great admirer of Rembrandt. He organised two exhibitions of his work (in 1932 and 1935) at a time when specialist shows were rarely staged in the museum, and acquired no fewer than seven of his works. Two of them, *St Peter's denial* and the *Portrait of Titus in a monk's habit*, both dated 1660, came from Russian collections. The final purchase in the series was Rembrandt's early masterpiece, *Jeremiah lamenting the destruction of Jerusalem* of 1630 (*fig. 105*), which was made with the assistance of various individuals and organisations, among them the Vereniging Rembrandt.

Rembrandt's work was also a key part of the collection which Mr and Mrs De Bruijn-van der Leeuw put together in the interbellum years in close consultation with Schmidt-Degener. Aside from the large collection of Rembrandt etchings mentioned above, they formed a select group of 17th-century paintings (among them his *Self-portrait as the apostle Paul*) and drawings, which was left to the Rijksmuseum in 1961 (*figs. 2-4, 10 and 11*).

THE RIJKSMUSEUM AFTER THE SECOND WORLD WAR

The aesthetic approach was retained when the Rijksmuseum was rearranged after 1945. The mixed presentation which Schmidt-Degener had introduced on a modest scale was abandoned, and there was a strict separation in the permanent collection between the departments of painting, Dutch history, and sculpture and the applied arts. If paintings were hung in other departments it was because of their documentary value in the case of history, and decorative qualities in the case of the applied arts.

The Department of Sculpture and Decorative Arts profited from the increase in exhibition space created by building on the inner courtyards. In more than 60 rooms spread over three floors in the western half of the museum it was able to display a multifaceted and dazzling overview of European sculpture and applied arts extending from the late middle ages to the early 20th century. This was made possible by the transfer shortly after the war of Dr F. Mannheimer's outstanding collection of decorative arts and sculpture.

In the past few decades the museum has actively pursued an acquisition policy designed to raise the quality of the collections over a considerably wider time-span than was customary before the war. The Dutch collection, for instance, was extended to cover the period 1680-1830, providing a place for the works made for the court of King-Stadholder Willem III. The existing collection of 17th-century Dutch decorative arts was also enriched with new purchases. Important silver objects by Paulus and Adam van Vianen [*1, 5*], Johannes Lutma [*33*] and other silversmiths [*19, 68*] were acquired after 1945, as were a layette cupboard [*59*], a cupboard attributed to Herman Doomer [*46*] and most of the tapestries by François Spiering [*3*].

Because drawings and prints can never go on permanent display, the importance and growth of the collections of the Rijksmuseum Printroom is mainly evident in the extremely varied series of temporary exhibitions and publications. The collection of 17th-century Dutch prints and drawings is unarguably the largest and most complete in the world, and plays a prominent role in the study of the period. The catalogues of the Hollstein series provide a crucial frame of reference in the realm of printmaking, and this is mirrored by the catalogues of the 17th-century Dutch drawings.

The Department of Paintings continued using the eastern galleries and Gallery of Honour on the first floor for the permanent collection, and until recently the 18th and 19th centuries were on display in the South Wing. The extensive holdings of 17th-century Dutch painting followed the 15th and 16th-century works in the eastern cabinets, in the Frans Hals Gallery and ended in the *Night watch* gallery, and that remained the situation until 1983. The Gallery of Honour housed Italian and Spanish paintings, 17th-century Flemish works and, until the 1970s, the Haarlem Mannerists

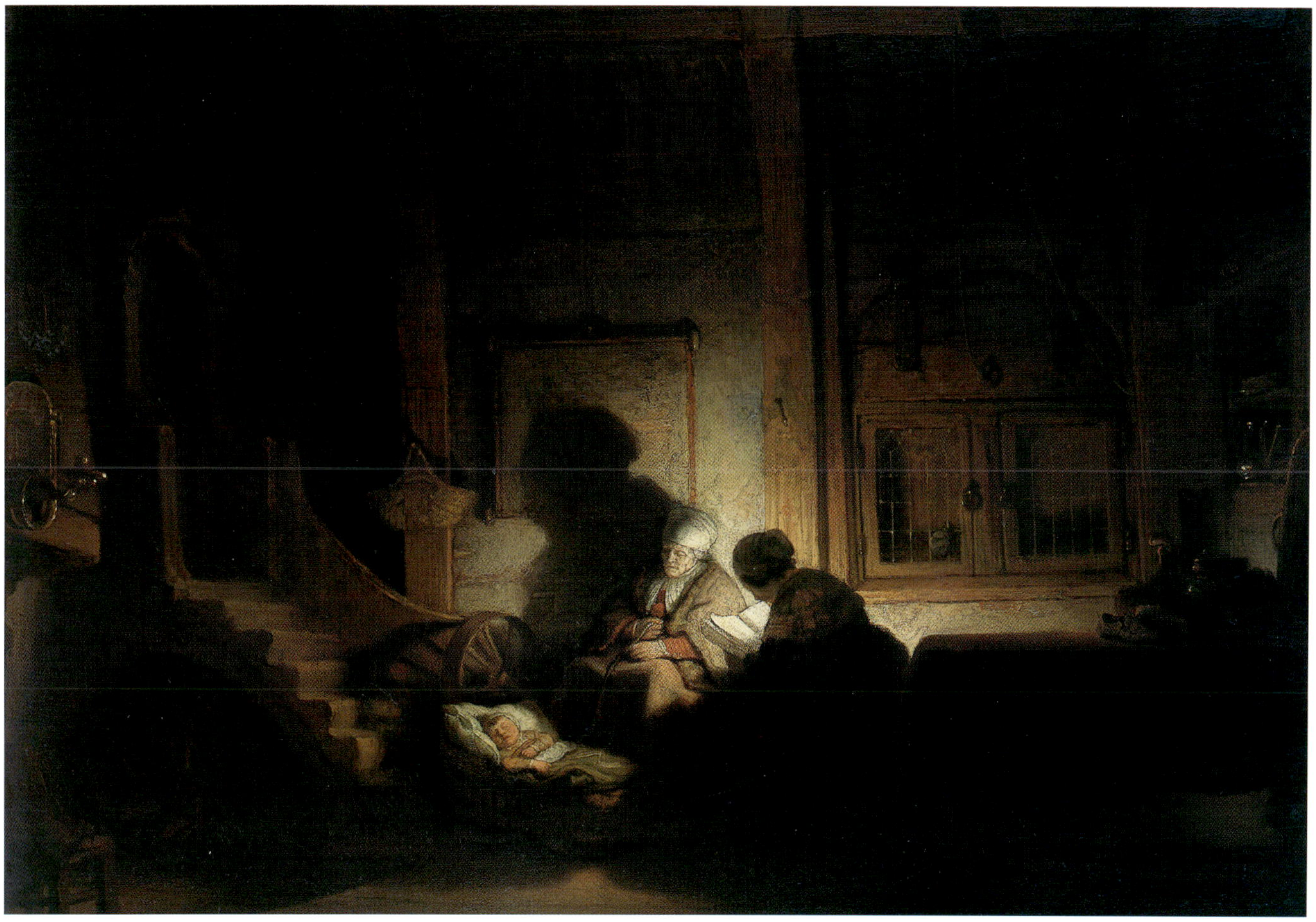

fig. 106 Rembrandt workshop, *The Holy Family at night*, c. 1645; oil on panel, 66.5 x 78 cm. Amsterdam, Rijksmuseum

and Utrecht Caravaggisti. When it and the *Night watch* gallery were renovated in 1983-1984, Rembrandt's painting was restored to its central position in the middle of the room, and the Gallery of Honour was given over to 17th-century Dutch paintings, notably the larger works (*fig. 107*).

The very active exhibition policy followed after the war focused specifically on undervalued aspects of the art of the Golden Age, such as Mannerism and the rise of realism (*Dawn of the Golden Age*, 1993-1994), genre (*Tot lering en vermaak*, 1976), history painting (*Gods, saints and heroes*, 1980-1981), the *Feinmaler* (*De Hollandse fijnschilders*, 1989-1990) and picture frames (*Prijs de lijst*, 1984). Many of these exhibitions resulted in purchases that enhanced the multifaceted picture of 17th-century art. Among them were paintings by Goltzius [12], Hendrick ter Brugghen [13], Pieter Codde [25] and Caesar van Everdingen [76].

The museum also acquired a considerable number of classic 17th-century Dutch masterpieces, including the large still lifes by Floris van Dijck, Pieter Claesz and Willem Heda [18, 34, 35], as well as monumental landscapes by Aelbert Cuyp and Philips Koninck [57, 61]. The latter two were bought in England, to which most large classic works of this kind were exported in the 18th century.

Rembrandt, the most versatile and best-loved master of the Golden Age, continued to have an important place in the Rijksmuseum's exhibition and purchasing policies. Exhibitions were devoted to him in 1956, 1969 and 1991/92. The first of these contained several works with doubtful attributions, but the later shows reflected the influence of the Rembrandt Research Project, which has pruned the number of works attributed to the artist considerably.

One of the victims of that research was *The Holy Family at night* (*fig. 106*), which was bought in 1965. It had been one of the most popular of Rembrandt's works since the beginning of the 18th century, when it was in the famous collection of the Duc d'Orléans in Paris. It has now been demonstrated beyond doubt that it was executed around 1640 in Rembrandt's workshop but that it is certainly not autograph. The Rembrandt Research Project has also given us a much better idea of the master's early work, and this led

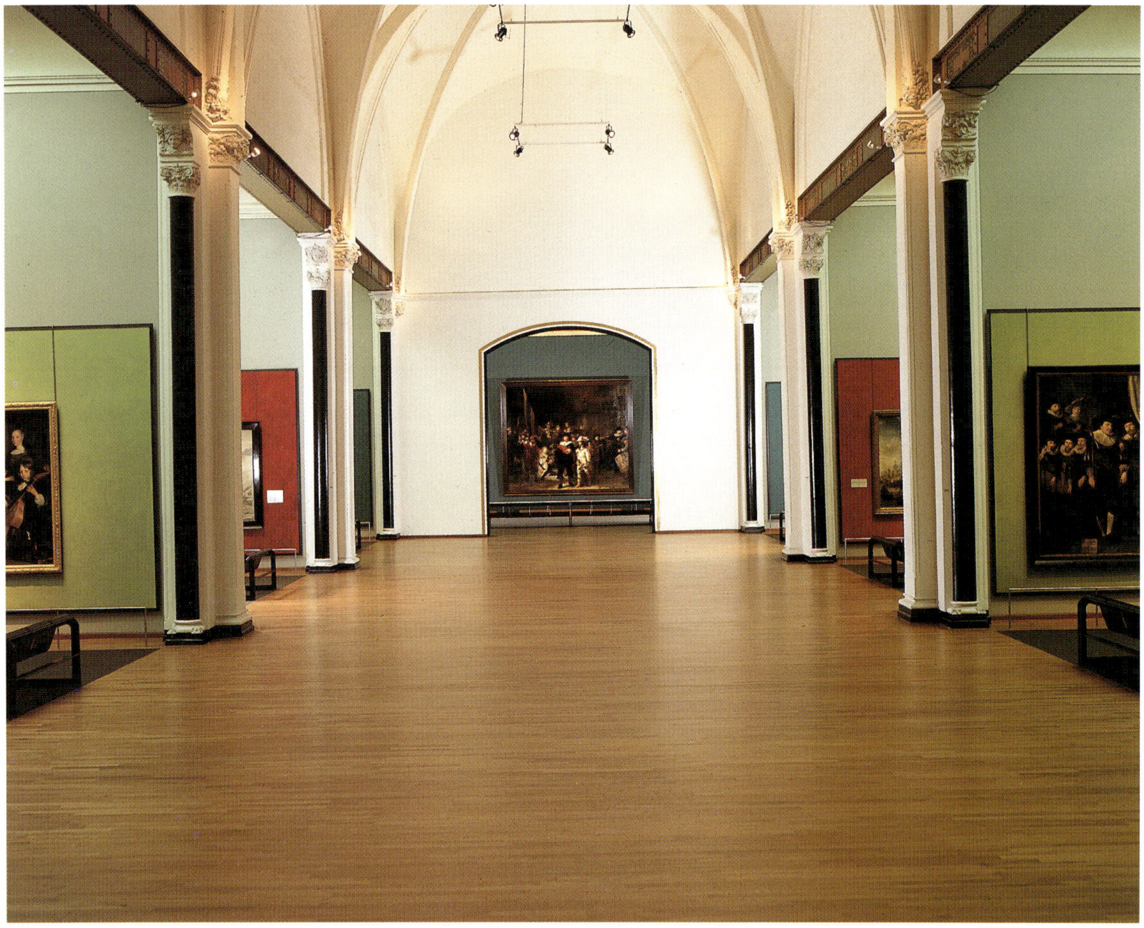

fig. 107 The Rijksmuseum's Gallery of Honour, 2001

to several acquisitions, among them the early *Self-portrait* [30] and *Tobias accusing Anna of stealing the kid* of 1628 (*fig. 12*). The imposing *Portrait of Johannes Wtenbogaert* of 1633 [31] was the most recent in the long line of purchases of paintings by Rembrandt in the post-war period. The Rijksmuseum now has 20 uncontested Rembrandts, all of which, apart from the four loans, were acquired in the 20th century.

The 'permanent image of Dutch art' has been substantially enriched and diversified in the past 50 years. It has been extended to embrace the Mannerists and Caravaggisti, as well as the Leiden *Feinmaler* and the Classicists. The survey of 17th-century art no longer peters out in the decade 1670-1680, as it does in most books on the subject, but now includes the court art made under the aegis of Stadholder Willem II. The lavish display of Dutch sculpture and decorative arts has proved to be a worthy counterpart to the paintings.

It is beyond question that the Rijksmuseum's collections illuminating the Dutch Golden Age are now the richest in the world in their scale, breadth and diversity. The prints and drawings form the largest component, and can be examined on request in the study room of the printroom, and are displayed to the museum visitors in temporary exhibitions. At present the collections of paintings, sculpture, decorative art and history are segregated in different gallery complexes, but from 2006/07, after the Rijksmuseum has undergone major refurbishment, it is planned to integrate them on the first floor. That new arrangement will enable more aspects of the diverse production of art in the period 1600-1700 to be illustrated than has been possible in this book, in which the accent is necessarily on painting.

FURTHER READING

On the 200 years of the Rijksmuseum's history: Van der Ham 2000; on its purchasing policy between 1800 and 1896: Bergvelt 1998; on the Koninklijk Museum: exhib. cat. Amsterdam 2000a; on the history of the Department of Paintings: cat. Amsterdam 1976, pp. 10-47, and cat. Amsterdam 1992, pp. 20-21; on the furniture collection: cat. Amsterdam 1952a, silver: cat. Amsterdam 1952b and cat. Amsterdam 1999, glass: cat. Amsterdam 1993a and cat. Amsterdam 1995b; prints and drawings: exhib. cat. Amsterdam 1987, cat. Amsterdam 1998, and exhib. cat. Amsterdam 2000c

Bibliography

Angel 1642
Philips Angel, *Lof der schilder-konst*, Leiden 1642; see also Hoyle & Miedema 1996

Arnold 1973
J. Arnold, 'Three examples of late sixteenth and early seventeenth century neckwear', *Waffen- und Kostümkunde* 2, no. 2 (1973), pp. 109-24

Baarsen 1989a
R.J. Baarsen, 'Adam van Vianen, kan met deksel van verguld zilver', *Bulletin van het Rijksmuseum* 37 (1989), pp. 201-03

Baarsen 1989b
R.J. Baarsen, 'Een Amsterdams zilveren zoutvat uit 1618', *Bulletin van het Rijksmuseum* 37 (1989), pp. 51-72

Baarsen 1989c
R.J. Baarsen, 'Luiermandskastje van eike- en notehout, Nederland, 3de kwart 17de eeuw', *Bulletin van het Rijksmuseum* 37 (1989), pp. 230-32

Baarsen 1996
R.J. Baarsen, 'Herman Doomer, ebony worker in Amsterdam', *The Burlington Magazine* 138 (1996), pp. 739-49

Bachmann 1982
F. Bachmann, *Aert van der Neer 1603/4-1677*, Bremen 1982

Beck 1972-87
H.U. Beck, *Jan van Goyen 1596-1656: ein Oeuvreverzeichnis*, 3 vols., Amsterdam/Doornspijk 1972-87 (vol. 4: *Künstler um Jan van Goyen: Maler und Zeichner*, Doornspijk 1991)

Beck 1993
S.E. Veldhuyzen (ed.), *David Beck, Spiegel van mijn leven: een dagboek uit 1624*, Hilversum 1993

De Beer 1993
G. de Beer, *Seesturm und Schiffbruch im Werk des Ludolf Backhuysen*, Kiel 1993

Bergvelt 1998
E. Bergvelt, *Pantheon der gouden eeuw: van Nationale Konst-Gallerij tot Rijksmuseum van Schilderijen (1798-1896)*, Zwolle 1998

De Bie 1661
Cornelis de Bie, *Gulden cabinet vande edele vry schilderconst*, Antwerp 1661

Bijl *et al.* 1994
M. Bijl *et al.*, 'Rembrandts Portret van Johannes Wtenbogaert, verwerving en restauratie', *Bulletin van het Rijksmuseum* 42 (1994), pp. 327-33

Blankert 1975
A. Blankert (with contributions by R. Ruurs & W.L. de Watering), *Vermeer of Delft: complete edition of the paintings*, Oxford 1978

Blankert 1982
A. Blankert, *Ferdinand Bol (1616-1680): Rembrandt's pupil*, Doornspijk 1982

Blankert 1991
A. Blankert, 'Vrouw "Winter" door Caesar van Everdingen', *Bulletin van het Rijksmuseum* 39 (1991), pp. 505-23

Boer 1994
E.M.A. Boer, 'Voor elc wat wils', *Antiek* 28 (1994), no. 4, pp. 17-23

Bok 1991
M.J. Bok, 'Ambrosius van Swol, vermaard beeldhouwer', *Kunstschrift* 35 (1991), no. 3, pp. 7-8

Bok 1992
M.J. Bok, 'De schilder in zijn wereld: de sociaal-economische benadering van de Nederlandse zeventiendeeeuwse kunst', in F. Grijzenhout & H. van Veen (eds.), *De Gouden Eeuw in perspectief*, Heerlen 1992, pp. 330-59

Bok 1994
M.J. Bok, *Vraag en aanbod op de Nederlandse kunstmarkt, 1580-1700*, Utrecht 1994 (diss. Utrecht University 1994)

Bok 1996
M.J. Bok, 'De Utrechtse verwanten van de beeldsnijder Albert Janszn Vinckenbrinck', *Amstelodamum* 83 (1996), no. 6, pp. 167-72

Bol 1962
L.J. Bol, 'Helena van der Schalcke als kind', *Openbaar Kunstbezit* 6 (1962), no. 32

Bol 1977
L.J. Bol, *Adriaen Coorte: a unique late seventeenth century Dutch still-life painter*, Assen 1977

Bol 1989
L.J. Bol, *Adriaen Pietersz. van de Venne: painter and draughtsman*, Doornspijk 1989

Boxer 1974
C.R. Boxer, *The Anglo-Dutch wars of the 17th century, 1652-1674*, London 1974

Brenninkmeyer-de Rooij 1982
B. Brenninkmeyer-de Rooij, 'Notities betreffende de decoratie van de Oranjezaal in Huis Ten Bosch', *Oud Holland* 96 (1982), pp. 133-90

Briels 1987
J. Briels, *Vlaamse schilders in de Noordelijke Nederlanden in het begin van de Gouden Eeuw, 1585-1630*, Antwerp/Haarlem 1987

Broulhiet 1938
G. Broulhiet, *Meindert Hobbema (1638-1709)*, Paris 1938

Brown 1981
C. Brown, *Carel Fabritius*, Oxford 1981

Brown 1997
C. Brown, 'The strange case of Jan Torrentius: art, sex, and heresy in seventeenth-century Haarlem', in R.E. Fleischer & S.C. Scott (eds.), *Rembrandt, Rubens, and the art of their time: recent perspectives* (Papers in Art History from The Pennsylvania State University, vol. XI), University Park 1997, pp. 224-33

Brulez 1986
W. Brulez, *Cultuur en getal: aspecten van de relatie economie-maatschappij-cultuur in Europa tussen 1400-1800*, Amsterdam 1986

Brusati 1995
C. Brusati, *Artifice and illusion: the art and writing of Samuel van Hoogstraten*, Chicago/London 1995

De Bruyn 1698
C. de Bruyn, *Reizen door de vermaardste deelen van Klein-Azië*, Delft 1698

Bruyn *et al.* 1982-89
J. Bruyn *et al.*, *A corpus of Rembrandt paintings*, 3 vols., Dordrecht/Boston/Lancaster 1982-89

De Bruyn Kops 1965
C.J. de Bruyn Kops, 'Kanttekeningen bij het nieuw verworven landschap van Aelbert Cuyp', *Bulletin van het Rijksmuseum* 13 (1965), pp. 162-76

Burgers 1999
C.A. Burgers, 'Notes on early Haarlem workshops of Passchier Lammertijn, Quirijn Jansz Damast and others: some facts and attributions', in R. Schorta (ed.), *Leinendamaste: Produktionszentren und Sammlungen*, Riggisberg 1999, pp. 239-49

Burke 1976
J.D. Burke, *Jan Both (ca. 1618-1652): paintings, drawings and prints*, New York/London 1976 (diss. Harvard University 1972)

Cat. Amsterdam 1880
[J.W. Kaiser], *Beschrijving der schilderijen van het Rijksmuseum te Amsterdam*, Amsterdam 1880

Cat. Amsterdam 1952a
Th.H. Lunsingh Scheurleer *et al.*, *Catalogus van meubelen en betimmeringen*, Amsterdam (Rijksmuseum) 1952

Cat. Amsterdam 1952b
A. Pit (ed.), *Catalogus van goud en zilverwerken*, Amsterdam (Rijksmuseum) 1952

Cat. Amsterdam 1973
J. Leeuwenberg & W. Halsema-Kubes, *Beeldhouwkunst in het Rijksmuseum*, Amsterdam 1973

Cat. Amsterdam 1975-79
A. Blankert, *Amsterdams Historisch Museum: schilderijen daterend van voor 1800*, Amsterdam 1975-79

Cat. Amsterdam 1976
P.J.J. van Thiel *et al.*, *All the paintings of the Rijksmuseum in Amsterdam: a completely illustrated catalogue*, Amsterdam/Maarssen 1976

Cat. Amsterdam 1985
P. Schatborn, *Drawings by Rembrandt, his anonymous pupils and followers*, Amsterdam (Rijksmuseum)/The Hague 1985

Cat. Amsterdam 1992
P.J.J. van Thiel *et al.*, *All the paintings of the Rijksmuseum in Amsterdam, a completely illustrated catalogue: first supplement 1976-91*, Amsterdam/The Hague 1992

Cat. Amsterdam 1993a
P.C. Ritsema van Eck & H.M. Zijlstra-Zweens, *Glass in the Rijksmuseum*, vol. 1, Amsterdam/Zwolle 1993

Cat. Amsterdam 1993b
R.J. Baarsen, *Nederlandse meubelen 1600-1800/Dutch furniture 1600-1800*, Amsterdam (Rijksmuseum)/Zwolle 1993

Cat. Amsterdam 1995a
F. Scholten, *Gebeeldhouwde portretten/Portrait sculptures*, Amsterdam (Rijksmuseum)/Zwolle 1995

Cat. Amsterdam 1995b
P.C. Ritsema van Eck, *Glass in the Rijksmuseum*, vol. 2, Amsterdam/Zwolle 1995

Cat. Amsterdam 1995c
R. Kistemaker *et al.* (eds.), *In beeld gebracht: beeldhouwkunst uit de collectie van het Amsterdams Historisch Museum*, Amsterdam/Zwolle 1995

Cat. Amsterdam 1998
M. Schapelhouman & P. Schatborn, cat. *Dutch drawings of the seventeenth century in the Rijksmuseum, Amsterdam: artists born between 1580 and 1600*, 2 vols., Amsterdam/London 1998

Cat. Amsterdam 1999
J.R. de Lorm, cat. *Amsterdams goud en zilver*, Amsterdam (Rijksmuseum)/Zwolle 1999

Chapman 1990
H. Perry Chapman, *Rembrandt's self-portraits: a study in seventeenth-century identity*, Princeton 1990

Chong 1987-88
A. Chong, 'The market for landscape painting in seventeenth-century Holland', in *Masters of 17th-century Dutch landscape painting*, exhib. cat. Amsterdam (Rijksmuseum) 1987-88

Van Dam 1989
J.D. van Dam, 'Vroege faience uit Delft (1625-1655) en de invloed op Japans porselein (1660-1670)', *Mededelingenblad Nederlandse Vereniging van Vrienden van de Ceramiek* 135 (1989), no. 3, pp. 4-18

Van Deursen 1991
A.Th. van Deursen, *Mensen van klein vermogen*, Amsterdam 1991

Duparc 1993
F.J. Duparc, 'Philips Wouwerman, 1619-1668', *Oud Holland* 107 (1993), pp. 257-86

Van Eeghen 1957
I.H. van Eeghen, 'De Staalmeesters', *Jaarboek van het Genootschap Amstelodamum* 49 (1957), pp. 65-80

Ekkart 1979
R.E.O. Ekkart, *Johannes Cornelisz. Verspronck: leven en werken van een Haarlems portretschilder uit de 17de eeuw*, Haarlem 1979

Ekkart 1999
R.E.O. Ekkart, 'Een man met ring en toetssteen door Werner van den Valckert', *Bulletin van het Rijksmuseum* 47 (1999), pp. 20-25

Evelyn 1935
J. Evelyn, *The diary of John Evelyn*, ed. E.S. de Beer, Oxford 1935

Exhib. cat. Amsterdam 1952
J. Bruyn *et al.*, exhib. cat. *Drie eeuwen portret in Nederland*, Amsterdam (Rijksmuseum) 1952

Exhib. cat. Amsterdam 1969
P.J.J. van Thiel (ed.), exhib. cat. *Rembrandt 1669/1969*, Amsterdam (Rijksmuseum) 1969

Exhib. cat. Amsterdam 1971-72
V. Woldbye & C.A. Burgers, exhib. cat. *Geweven boeket*, Amsterdam (Rijksmuseum) 1971-72

Exhib. cat. Amsterdam 1976
E. de Jongh *et al.* (eds.), exhib. cat. *Tot lering en vermaak: betekenissen van Hollandse genrevoorstellingen uit de zeventiende eeuw*, Amsterdam (Rijksmuseum) 1976

Exhib. cat. Amsterdam 1984
P.J.J. van Thiel & C.J. de Bruyn Kops, exhib. cat. *Prijs de lijst: de Hollandse schilderijlijst in de zeventiende eeuw*, Amsterdam (Rijksmuseum) 1984 (later translated into English as *Framing in the Golden Age: picture and frame in 17th-century Holland*, Amsterdam/Zwolle 1995)

Exhib. cat. Amsterdam 1984-85
K.A. Citroen *et al.*, exhib. cat. *Meesterwerken in zilver: Amsterdams zilver 1520-1820*, Amsterdam (Museum Willet-Holthuysen) 1984-85

Exhib. cat. Amsterdam 1987
M. Schapelhouman & P. Schatborn, exhib. cat. *Land & water: Hollandse tekeningen uit de 17de eeuw in het Rijksprentenkabinet*, Amsterdam (Rijksprentenkabinet) 1987

Exhib. cat. Amsterdam 1988
J. van der Waals, exhib. cat. *De prentschat van Michiel Hinloopen*, Amsterdam (Rijksprentenkabinet) 1988

Exhib. cat. Amsterdam 1989
J.F. Heijbroek (ed.), exhib. cat. *De verzameling van mr. Carel Vosmaer (1826-1888)*, Amsterdam (Rijksprentenkabinet) 1989

Exhib. cat. Amsterdam 1989-90
P. Hecht, exhib. cat. *De Hollandse fijnschilders: van Gerard Dou tot Adriaen van der Werff*, Amsterdam (Rijksmuseum) 1989-90

Exhib. cat. Amsterdam 1991a
A. Tümpel & P. Schatborn, exhib. cat. *Pieter Lastman: leermeester van Rembrandt/Pieter Lastman: the man who taught Rembrandt*, Amsterdam (Museum Het Rembrandthuis) 1991

Exhib. cat. Amsterdam 1991b
C. Tümpel *et al.*, exhib. cat. *Het Oude Testament in de schilderkunst van de Gouden Eeuw*, Amsterdam (Joods Historisch Museum) 1991

Exhib. cat. Amsterdam 1992
E. Bergvelt & R. Kistemaker (ed.), exhib. cat. *De wereld binnen handbereik: Nederlandse kunst- en rariteitenverzamelingen, 1585-1735*, Amsterdam (Amsterdams Historisch Museum) 1992

Exhib. cat. Amsterdam 1993
Jan Peeters *et al.*, *Het Paleis in de schilderkunst van de Gouden Eeuw*, Amsterdam (Koninklijk Paleis) 1993

Exhib. cat. Amsterdam 1993-94
G. Luijten *et al.* (ed.), exhib. cat. *Dawn of the Golden Age: northern Netherlandish art 1580-1620*, Amsterdam (Rijksmuseum) 1993-94

Exhib. cat. Amsterdam 1997
E. de Jongh & G. Luijten, exhib. cat. *Mirror of everyday life: genre prints in the Netherlands 1550-1700*, Amsterdam (Rijksprentenkabinet) 1997

Exhib. cat. Amsterdam 1998
P. van Coelen (ed.), exhib. cat. *Everyday life in Holland's Golden Age: the complete etchings of Adriaen van Ostade*, Amsterdam (Museum Het Rembrandthuis), 1998

Exhib. cat. Amsterdam 1999
A. Wallert (ed.), exhib. cat. *Still lifes: techniques and style*, Amsterdam (Rijksmuseum) 1999

Exhib. cat. Amsterdam 2000a
F. Grijzenhout, exhib. cat. *Een Koninklijk Museum: Lodewijk Napoleon en het Rijksmuseum 1806-1810*, Amsterdam (Rijksmuseum) 2000

Exhib. cat. Amsterdam 2000b
J. Kiers & F. Tissink, exhib. cat. *The glory of the Golden Age, Dutch art of the 17th-century: paintings, sculpture and decorative art*, Amsterdam (Rijksmuseum) 2000

Exhib. cat. Amsterdam 2000c
E. Runia, exhib. cat. *The glory of the Golden Age, Dutch art of the 17th-century: drawings and prints*, Amsterdam (Rijksprentenkabinet) 2000

Exhib. cat. Amsterdam/Boston/Philadelphia 1987-88
P.C. Sutton *et al.* (eds.), exhib. cat. *Masters of 17th-century Dutch landscape painting*, Amsterdam (Rijksmuseum)/Boston (Museum of Fine Arts)/Philadelphia (Philadelphia Museum of Art) 1987-88

Exhib. cat. Amsterdam/Cleveland 1999-2000
A. Chong & W. Kloek, exhib. cat. *Still-life paintings from the Netherlands 1550-1720*, Amsterdam (Rijksmuseum)/Cleveland (The Cleveland Museum of Art) 1999-2000

Exhib. cat. Amsterdam/Emden 1985
B. Broos *et al.*, exhib. cat. *Ludolf Bakhuizen 1631-1708: schryfmeester-teyckenaer-schilder*, Amsterdam (Nederlands Scheepvaartmuseum)/Emden 1985

Exhib. cat. Amsterdam/London 2000-01
E. Hinterding, G. Luijten & Martin Royalton-Kisch, exhib. cat. *Rembrandt the printmaker*, Amsterdam (Rijksmuseum)/London (British Museum) 2000-01

Exhib. cat. Amsterdam/Stockholm/Los Angeles 1998-99
F. Scholten *et al.*, exhib. cat. *Adriaen de Vries (1556-1626): imperial sculptor*, Amsterdam (Rijksmuseum)/Stockholm (Nationalmuseum)/Los Angeles (The J. Paul Getty Museum) 1998-99

Exhib. cat. Amsterdam/Toledo/Boston 1979-80
A.L. den Blaauwen (ed.), exhib. cat. *Nederlands zilver 1580-1830/Dutch silver 1580-1830*, Amsterdam (Rijksmuseum)/Toledo (The Toledo Museum of Art)/Boston (Museum of Fine Arts) 1979-80

Exhib. cat. Amsterdam/Vlissingen 1957
R. van Luttervelt, exhib. cat. *Michiel de Ruyter 1607-1957*, Amsterdam (Rijksmuseum)/Vlissingen (Nieuw Tehuis voor Bejaarden) 1957

Exhib. cat. Amsterdam/Washington 1981-82
P. Schatborn, exhib. cat. *Dutch figure drawings from the seventeenth century*, Amsterdam (Rijksprentenkabinet)/Washington (National Gallery of Art) 1981-82

Exhib. cat. Berlin/Amsterdam/London 1991-92
C. Brown *et al.*, exhib. cat. *Rembrandt, the master and his workshop: paintings*, Berlin (Gemäldegalerie Staatliche Museen Preussischer Kulturbesitz, Altes Museum)/Amsterdam (Rijksmuseum)/London (The National Gallery) 1991-92

Exhib. cat. Boston/St. Louis 1980-81
C.S. Ackley, *Printmaking in the age of Rembrandt*, Boston (Museum of Fine Arts)/St. Louis (St. Louis Art Museum) 1980-81

Exhib. cat. Delft 1996
M.C.C. Kersten *et al.*, exhib. cat. *Delftse Meesters, tijdgenoten van Vermeer: een andere kijk op perspectief, licht en ruimte*, Delft (Stedelijk Museum Het Prinsenhof) 1996

Exhib. cat. Delft/Cambridge/Fort Worth 1988-89
S. Segal (ed.), exhib. cat. *A prosperous past: the sumptuous still life in the Netherlands 1600-1700*, Delft (Stedelijk Museum Het Prinsenhof)/Cambridge, Mass. (Fogg Art Museum)/Fort Worth (Kimbell Art Museum) 1988-89

Exhib. cat. Dordrecht 1977-78
J.M. de Groot *et al.*, exhib. cat. *Aelbert Cuyp en zijn familie, schilders te Dordrecht*, Dordrecht (Dordrechts Museum) 1977-78

Exhib. cat. Dordrecht 1992-93
P. Marijnissen *et al.* (eds.), exhib. cat. *De zichtbaere werelt: schilderkunst uit de Gouden Eeuw in Hollands oudste stad*, Dordrecht (Dordrechts Museum) 1992-93

Exhib. cat. Dordrecht/Leeuwarden 1988-89
F. Grijzenhout *et al.* (eds.), exhib. cat. *Meesterlijk vee: Nederlandse veeschilders 1600-1900*, Dordrecht (Dordrechts Museum)/Leeuwarden (Fries Museum) 1988-89

Exhib. cat. Georgia 1994
S.W. Pelletier, L.J. Slatkes & L. Stone-Ferrier, *Adriaen van Ostade: etchings of peasant life in Holland's Golden Age*, Georgia (Georgia Museum of Art) 1994

Exhib. cat. Haarlem 1986
E. de Jongh, exhib. cat. *Portretten van echt en trouw: huwelijk en gezin in de Nederlandse kunst van de zeventiende eeuw*, Haarlem (Frans Halsmuseum) 1986

Exhib. cat. Haarlem 1988
M. Carasso-Kok & J. Levy-van Halm (eds.), exhib. cat. *Schutters in Holland: kracht en zenuwen van de stad*, Haarlem (Frans Halsmuseum) 1988

Exhib. cat. Haarlem/Antwerp 2000-01
J.B. Bedaux & R. Ekkart (eds.), *Kinderen op hun mooist. Het kinderportret in de Nederlanden 1500-1700*, Haarlem (Frans Halsmuseum)/Antwerp (Koninklijk Museum voor Schone Kunsten) 2000-01

Exhib. cat. The Hague 1967
B. Jansen *et al.*, exhib. cat. *Haags zilver uit vijf eeuwen*, The Hague (Haags Gemeentemuseum) 1967

Exhib. cat. The Hague 1992
B. Brenninkmeyer-de Rooij *et al.* (eds.), exhib. cat. *Mauritshuis in bloei: boeketten uit de Gouden Eeuw/Mauritshuis in bloom: bouquets from the Golden Age*, The Hague (Mauritshuis) 1992

Exhib. cat. The Hague 1994-95
A. Walsh *et al.*, exhib. cat. *Paulus Potter: paintings, drawings and etchings*, The Hague (Mauritshuis) 1994-95

Exhib. cat. The Hague/Cambridge 1981-82
S. Slive & H.R. Hoetink, exhib. cat. *Jacob van Ruisdael*, The Hague (Mauritshuis)/Cambridge, Mass. (Fogg Art Museum) 1981-82

Exhib. cat. The Hague/Münster 1974
J.P. Guépin *et al.*, exhib. cat. *Gerard Ter Borch, Zwolle 1617-Deventer 1681*, The Hague (Mauritshuis)/Münster (Westfälisches Landesmuseum) 1974

Exhib. cat. Leiden 1988
E.J. Sluijter *et al.* (eds.), exhib. cat. *Leidse fijnschilders*, Leiden (De Lakenhal) 1988

Exhib. cat. Leiden 1996-97
C. Vogelaar *et al.*, exhib. cat. *Jan van Goyen*, Leiden (De Lakenhal) 1996-97

Exhib. cat. London 1964
A.G.H. Bachrach (ed.), exhib. cat. *The Orange and the Rose: Holland and Britain in the age of observation 1600-1750*, London (Victoria & Albert Museum) 1964

Exhib. cat. London/The Hague 1999-2000
C. White & Q. Buvelot (eds.), exhib. cat. *Rembrandt by himself*, London (National Gallery)/The Hague (Mauritshuis) 1999-2000

Exhib. cat. London/Hartford 1998-99
P.C. Sutton, exhib. cat. *Pieter de Hooch, 1629-1684*, London (Dulwich Picture Gallery)/Hartford (Wadsworth Atheneum) 1998-99

Exhib. cat. Madrid 1999
S. Segal, exhib. cat. *Willem Kalf: original y copia*, Madrid (Museo Thyssen-Bornemisza) 1998

Exhib. cat. Melbourne/Canberra 1997-98
A. Blankert *et al.*, exhib. cat. *Rembrandt: a genius and his impact*, Melbourne (National Gallery of Victoria)/Canberra (National Gallery of Australia) 1997-98

Exhib. cat. New York 1979-80
C. Ryskamp, exhib. cat. *William & Mary and their house*, New York (The Pierpont Morgan Library) 1979-80

Exhib. cat. New York/Pittsburgh 1988-89
R.J. Baarsen *et al.*, exhib. cat. *Courts and colonies: the William and Mary style in Holland, England and America*, New York (Cooper-Hewitt Museum)/Pittsburgh (The Carnegie Museum of Art) 1988-89

Exhib. cat. Perth/Adelaide/Brisbane 1997-98
N. Middelkoop, exhib. cat. *The golden age of Dutch art: seventeenth century paintings from the Rijksmuseum and Australian collections*, Perth (Art Gallery of Western Australia)/Adelaide (Art Gallery of South Australia)/Brisbane (Queensland Art Gallery) 1997-98

Exhib. cat. Philadelphia/Berlin/London 1984
P.C. Sutton (ed.), exhib. cat. *Masters of seventeenth-century Dutch genre painting*, Philadelphia (Philadelphia Museum of Art)/Berlin (Gemäldegalerie, Staatliche Museen Preussischer Kulturbesitz)/London (Royal Academy of Arts) 1984

Exhib. cat. Rotterdam 1991
J. Giltaij & G. Jansen, exhib. cat. *Perspectiven: Saenredam en de architectuurschilders van de 17e eeuw*, Rotterdam (Museum Boijmans Van Beuningen) 1991

Exhib. cat. Rotterdam 1994-95
N. Schadee (ed.), exhib. cat. *Rotterdamse meesters uit de Gouden Eeuw*, Rotterdam (Historisch Museum Het Schielandhuis) 1994-95

Exhib. cat. Rotterdam/Berlin 1996-97
J. Giltaij & J. Kelch, exhib. cat. *Lof der zeevaart: de Hollandse zeeschilders van de 17e eeuw*, Rotterdam (Museum Boijmans Van Beuningen)/Berlin (Gemäldegalerie Staatliche Museen) 1996-97

Exhib. cat. Rotterdam/Frankfurt 1999-2000
A. Blankert *et al.*, exhib. cat. *Dutch Classicism in seventeenth-century painting*, Rotterdam (Museum Boijmans Van Beuningen)/Frankfurt (Städelsches Kunstinstitut) 1999-2000

Exhib. cat. San Francisco/Baltimore/London 1997-98
J. Spicer (ed.), exhib. cat. *Masters of light: Dutch painters in Utrecht during the Golden Age*, San Francisco (Fine Arts Museums of San Francisco)/Baltimore (The Walters Art Gallery)/London (The National Gallery) 1997-98

Exhib. cat. Utrecht 1965
A. Blankert, exhib. cat. *Nederlandse 17e-eeuwse Italianiserende landschapschilders*, Utrecht (Centraal Museum) 1965

Exhib. cat. Utrecht 1984-85
M.I.E. van Zijl & J.R. ter Molen, exhib. cat. *Zeldzaam zilver uit de Gouden Eeuw: de Utrechtse edelsmeden Van Vianen*, Utrecht (Centraal Museum) 1984-85

Exhib. cat. Utrecht/Braunschweig 1986-87
A. Blankert *et al.* (eds.), exhib. cat. *Nieuw licht op de Gouden Eeuw: Hendrick ter Bruggen en tijdgenoten*, Utrecht (Centraal Museum)/Braunschweig (Herzog Anton Ulrich-Museum) 1986-87

Exhib. cat. Utrecht/Braunschweig 1991
S. Segal, exhib. cat. *Jan Davidsz de Heem en zijn kring*, Utrecht (Centraal Museum)/Braunschweig (Herzog Anton Ulrich-Museum) 1991

Exhib. cat. Utrecht/Frankfurt/Luxembourg 1993-94
P. van den Brink *et al.* (eds.), exhib. cat. *Het gedroomde land. Pastorale schilderkunst in de Gouden Eeuw*, Utrecht (Centraal Museum)/Frankfurt (Schirn Kunsthalle)/ Luxembourg (Musée National d'Histoire et d'Art) 1993-94

Exhib. cat. Washington/Amsterdam 1996-97
H.P. Chapman *et al.*, exhib. cat. *Jan Steen: painter and storyteller*, Washington (National Gallery of Art)/ Amsterdam (Rijksmuseum) 1996-97

Exhib. cat. Washington/The Hague 1995-96
A.K. Wheelock Jr (ed.), exhib. cat. *Johannes Vermeer*, Washington (National Gallery of Art)/The Hague (Mauritshuis) 1995-96

Exhib. cat. Washington/London/Haarlem 1989-90
S. Slive (ed.), exhib. cat. *Frans Hals*, Washington (National Gallery of Art)/London (Royal Academy of Arts)/Haarlem (Frans Halsmuseum) 1989-90

Exhib. cat. Washington/London/The Hague 2000-01
R. Baer *et al.*, exhib. cat. *Gerrit Dou 1613-1675*, Washington (National Gallery of Art)/London (National Gallery)/The Hague (Mauritshuis) 2000-01

Floerke 1905
H. Floerke, *Studien zur niederländischen Kunst- und Kulturgeschichte: die Formen des Kunsthandels, das Atelier und die Sammler in den Niederlanden vom 15.-18. Jahrhundert*, Munich/Leipzig 1905

Franits 1993
W. Franits, *Paragons of virtue: women and domesticity in seventeenth-century Dutch art*, Cambridge 1993

Fremantle 1959
K. Fremantle, *The baroque town hall of Amsterdam*, Utrecht 1959

Frijhoff & Spies 1999
W. Frijhoff & M. Spies, *1650, Bevochten eendracht*, The Hague 1999

Gaastra 1991
F.S. Gaastra, *Geschiedenis van de VOC*, Zutphen 1991

Gaehtgens 1987
B. Gaehtgens, *Adriaen van der Werff 1659-1722*, Munich 1987

De Gelder 1921
J.J. de Gelder, *Bartolomeus van der Helst: een studie van zijn werk, zijn levensgeschiedenis, een beschrijvende catalogus van zijn oeuvre, een register en 41 afbeeldingen naar schilderijen*, Rotterdam 1921

Gerson 1936
H. Gerson, *Philips Koninck: ein Beitrag zur Erforschung der holländischen Malerei des XVII. Jahrhunderts*, Berlin 1936 (reprinted Berlin 1980)

Gerson 1942
H. Gerson, *Ausbreitung und Nachwirkung der Holländische Malerei des 17. Jahrhunderts*, Haarlem 1942

Van der Giesen 1997
I. van der Giesen, *Pieter Xavery: genre in zeventiende-eeuwse beeldhouwkunst*, Amsterdam 1997 (graduate thesis, Vrije Universiteit)

Giltay 1980
J. Giltay, 'De tekeningen van Jacob van Ruisdael', *Oud Holland* 94 (1980), pp. 168-74

Goedde 1989
L.O. Goedde, *Tempest and shipwreck in Dutch and Flemish art: convention, rhetoric and interpretation*, University Park/London 1989

Goeree 1670
W. Goeree, *Inleydingh tot de praktijck der al-gemeene schilder-const*, Middelburg 1670

Grijzenhout 1984
F. Grijzenhout, 'Tempel voor Nederland: de Nationale Konst-Gallerij in 's-Gravenhage', *Nederlands Kunsthistorisch Jaarboek* 35 (1984), pp. 1-75

Grisebach 1974
L. Grisebach, *Willem Kalf 1619-1693*, Berlin 1974

Gudlaugsson 1959-60
S.J. Gudlaugsson, *Gerard Ter Borch*, 2 vols., The Hague 1959-60

Haak 1968
B. Haak, *Rembrandt: zijn leven, zijn werk, zijn tijd*, Amsterdam 1968

Haak 1984
B. Haak, *The Golden Age: Dutch painters of the seventeenth century*, New York 1984

Van Hall 1958
H. van Hall, 'Portret van een Blaeu of van Abraham Casteleyn?', *Oud Holland* 73 (1958), pp. 51-54

Halsema-Kubes 1991
W. Halsema-Kubes, 'De Noordnederlandse beeldhouwkunst in de 17de eeuw', *Kunstschrift* 35 (1991), no. 2, pp. 16-25

Van der Ham 2000
G. van der Ham, *Tweehonderd jaar Rijksmuseum: geschiedenis van een nationaal symbool*, Amsterdam 2000

Harwood 1988
L.B. Harwood, *Adam Pynacker (c. 1620-1763)*, Doornspijk 1988

Haverkamp Begemann 1959
E. Haverkamp Begemann, *Willem Buytewech*, Amsterdam 1959

Haverkamp Begemann 1973
E. Haverkamp Begemann, *Hercules Segers: the complete etchings*, Amsterdam/The Hague 1973

Haverkamp Begemann 1982
E. Haverkamp Begemann, *Rembrandt: the Nightwatch*, Princeton 1982

Hesselink 1997
L. Hesselink, *Het goud- en zilversmedengilde te Amsterdam in de 17de en 18de eeuw*, Utrecht 1997 (graduate thesis, Utrecht University)

Hoekstra 1996
F. Hoekstra, 'Het "ideale paar" van Rembrandt', *Antiek* 31 (1996), no. 2, pp. 59-65

Hollstein
Hollstein's Dutch and Flemish etchings, engravings and woodcuts, ca. 1450-1700, Amsterdam 1949-78, Roosendaal 1988-93, Rotterdam 1997-

Hoogewerff 1919
G.J. Hoogewerff, *De twee reizen van Cosimo de' Medici Prins van Toscane door de Nederlanden (1667-1669)*, Amsterdam 1919

Hoogewerff 1947
G.J. Hoogewerff, *De geschiedenis van de St. Lucasgilden in Nederland*, Amsterdam 1947

Hoogewerff 1952
G.J. Hoogewerff, *De Bentvueghels*, The Hague 1952

Van Hoogstraeten 1678
Samuel van Hoogstraeten, *Inleyding tot de hooge schoole der schilderkonst: anders de zichtbaere werelt*, Rotterdam 1678

Houbraken 1718-21
Arnold Houbraken, *De groote schouburgh der nederlantsche konstschilders en schilderessen*, 3 vols., Amsterdam 1718-21

Hoyle & Miedema 1996
M. Hoyle & H. Miedema, 'Philips Angel, Praise of painting', *Simiolus* 24 (1996), pp. 239-48

Huygens 1987
C. Huygens, *Mijn jeugd* (trans. and annotated by C.L. Heesakkers), Amsterdam 1987

Israel 1995
J.I. Israel, *The Dutch Republic: its rise, greatness, and fall 1477-1806*, Oxford 1995

De Jager 1990
R. de Jager, 'Meester, leerjongen, leertijd: een analyse van zeventiende-eeuwse Noord-Nederlandse leerling contracten van kunstschilders, goud- en zilversmeden', *Oud Holland* 54 (1990), pp. 69-111

Jansen 1997
G.M.C. Jansen, 'Paulus geneest de kreupele man te Lystra uit 1663 door Karel du Jardin (1626-1678)', *Bulletin van het Rijksmuseum* 45 (1997), pp. 179-89

De Jongh 1967
E. de Jongh, 'Zinne- en minnebeelden in de schilderkunst van de zeventiende eeuw', *Openbaar Kunstbezit* 11 (1967), no. 29

De Jongh 1981-82
E. de Jongh, 'Bol vincit amorem', *Simiolus* 12 (1981-82), pp. 147-61

De Jongh 2000
E. de Jongh, *Questions of meaning: theme and motif in Dutch seventeenth-century painting*, Leiden 2000, pp. 105-27

De Jongh & Vinken 1961
E. de Jongh & P.J. Vinken, 'Frans Hals als voortzetter van een emblematische traditie: bij het huwelijksportret van Isaac Massa en Beatrix van der Laen', *Oud Holland* 76 (1961), pp. 117-52

Judson 1959
J.R. Judson, *Gerrit van Honthorst: a discussion of his position in Dutch art*, The Hague 1959

Judson & Ekkart 1999
J. R. Judson & R.E.O. Ekkart, *Gerrit van Honthorst (1592-1656)*, Doornspijk 1999

Kauffmann 1977
H. Kauffmann, 'Jacob van Ruisdael: "Die Mühle von Wijk bei Duurstede"', in L. Grisebach & K. Renger (eds.), *Festschrift für Otto von Simson zum 65. Geburtstag*, Frankfurt 1977, pp. 379-97

Keyes 1984
G.S. Keyes, *Esaias van den Velde 1587-1630*, Doornspijk 1984

Kilian 1994
J.M. Kilian, *The paintings of Karel du Jardin (1626-1678)*, Ann Arbor 1994

De Klerk 1986-87
E.A. de Klerk, 'Academy-beelden and teeken-schoolen in Dutch seventeenth-century treatises on art', *Leids Kunsthistorisch Jaarboek* 5/6 (1986-87), pp. 283-88

Kloek 1989a
W.Th. Kloek, 'Willem Claesz Heda, stilleven met vergulde bokaal, 1635', *Bulletin van het Rijksmuseum* 37 (1989), pp. 224-27

Kloek 1989b
W.Th. Kloek, 'Gerrit Adriaensz Berckheyde, De bocht van de Herengracht bij de Nieuwe Spiegelstraat te Amsterdam, 1672', *Bulletin van het Rijksmuseum* 37 (1989), pp. 238-39

Kloek 1992
W.Th. Kloek, 'Over Rembrandts Portret van Uyttenbogaert, nu in het Rijksmuseum', *Bulletin van het Rijksmuseum* 40 (1992), pp. 346-52

Kloek 1998
W.Th. Kloek, *Een huishouden van Jan Steen*, Hilversum 1998

Kluiver 1995
J.H. Kluiver, 'Adriaan van de Venne's "Gezicht op de haven van Middelburg", geïdentificeerd als het vertrek van Robert Sidney in 1616', *Oud Holland* 109 (1995), pp. 121-42

Kruimel 1971
H.L. Kruimel, 'Rondom de Van der Schalcke-portretten van Gerard Ter Borch', *Jaarboek van het Centraal Bureau voor Genealogie* 25 (1971), pp. 224-29

Kuznetzow 1974
J.I. Kuznetzow, 'Nikolaus Knupfer (1603?-1655)', *Oud Holland* 88 (1974), pp. 169-219

De Lairesse 1740
Gerard de Lairesse, *Groot schilderboek*, 2 vols., Haarlem 1740 (revised edition, ed. princ. Amsterdam 1707)

Lane 1959
A. Lane, 'Delftse tegels uit Hampton Court en Daniel Marot's werkzaamheid aldaar', *Bulletin van het Rijksmuseum* 7 (1959), pp. 12-21

Lawrence 1991
C. Lawrence, *Gerrit Adriaensz. Berckheyde (1638-1698): Haarlem cityscape painter*, Doornspijk 1991

Lemmens 1964
G.Th.M. Lemmens, 'De schilder in zijn atelier', in exhib. cat. *Het schildersatelier in de Nederlanden*, Nijmegen (De Waag) 1964, pp. 5-26

Liedtke 1982
W.A. Liedtke, *Architectural painting in Delft*, Doornspijk 1982

Lourens & Lucassen 1994
P. Lourens & J. Lucassen, 'Ambachtsgilden in Nederland: een eerste inventarisatie, *NEHA Jaarboek* 57 (1994), pp. 34-61

Luijten 2000
G. Luijten, *Rembrandt's etchings*, Amsterdam (Rijksmuseum)/Zwolle 2000

Lunsingh Scheurleer 1942
Th.H. Lunsingh Scheerleer, 'Het Amsterdamsche St. Josefgilde, in het bijzonder met betrekking tot de meubelmakers', *Historia* 8 (1942), pp. 33-44

Lunsingh Scheurleer 1984
D.F. Lunsingh Scheurleer, *Niederländische Fayence*, Munich 1984

Van Mander 1604
Karel van Mander, *Het schilder-boeck*, Haarlem 1604

Manke 1963
I. Manke, *Emanuel de Witte 1617-1692*, Amsterdam 1963

De Marchi & Van Miegroet 1995
N. de Marchi & H.J. van Miegroet, 'Art, value and market practice in the Netherlands in the seventeenth century', *Art Bulletin* 76 (1994), pp. 451-64

Martin 1906-07
W. Martin, 'The life of a Dutch artist in the seventeenth century', *BM* 7 (1905), pp. 125-28, 416-27; 8 (1905-06), pp. 13-24; 10 (1906-07), pp. 144-54, 363-70; 11 (1907), pp. 357-69

Martin 1913
W. Martin, *Gerard Dou: des Meisters Gemälde*, Stuttgart/Berlin 1913

Meischke 1973
R. Meischke, 'Gerrit Adriaensz. Berckheyde: Bocht in de Herengracht te Amsterdam', *Openbaar Kunstbezit* 17 (1973), pp. 25-27

Meischke 1978
R. Meischke, 'Buitenverblijven van Amsterdammers voor 1625', *Jaarboek Amstelodamum* 70 (1978), pp. 82-106

Merrifield 1967
M.P. Merrifield, *Original treatises on the arts of painting*, 2 vols., New York 1967, vol. 2, p. 769

Meyer 1958
E.R. Meyer, 'Gabriël Metsu (1629-1667): Het zieke kind', *Openbaar Kunstbezit* 2 (1958), no. 29

Miedema 1986-87
H. Miedema, 'Over vakonderwijs aan kunstschilders in de Nederlanden tot de zeventiende eeuw', *Leids Kunsthistorisch Jaarboek* 5/6 (1986-87), pp. 268-83

Miedema 1987
H. Miedema, 'Kunstschilders, gilde en academie: over het probleem van de emancipatie van de kunstschilders in de Noordelijke Nederlanden van de 16de en 17de eeuw', *Oud Holland* 101 (1987), pp. 1-34

Miedema 1980
H. Miedema, *De archiefbescheiden van het St. Lukasgilde te Haarlem 1497-1798*, 2 vols., Alphen aan den Rijn 1980

Ter Molen 1983
J.R. ter Molen 'De betekenis van loterijen voor de studie van de Nederlandse edelsmeedkunst', *Antiek* 18 (1983), pp. 65-75

Ter Molen 1984
J.R. ter Molen, *Van Vianen: een Utrechtse familie van zilversmeden met een internationale faam*, 2 vols., Rotterdam 1984

Ter Molen 1987-88
J.R. ter Molen, 'Adam Loofs, zilversmid van de Koning-Stadhouder: enkele nieuwe aspecten van zijn leven en werk', *Antiek* 22 (1987-88), pp. 518-26

Ter Molen 1992
J.R. ter Molen, 'De loterijprent van Durgerdam: een overzicht van het Nederlandse zilver uit de late zeventiende eeuw in woord en beeld', *Antiek* 27 (1992), pp. 112-32

Von Moltke 1965
J.W. von Moltke, *Govaert Flinck 1615-1660*, Amsterdam 1965

Von Moltke 1994
J.W. von Moltke, *Arent de Gelder: Dordrecht 1645-1727*, Doornspijk 1994

Montias 1982
M. Montias, *Artists and artisans in Delft: a socio-economic study of the seventeenth century*, Princeton 1982

Montias 1987
M. Montias, 'Cost and value in seventeenth-century Dutch art', *Art History* 10 (1987), pp. 455-66
Du Mortier 1984
B.M. du Mortier, 'De handschoen in de huwelijkssymboliek van de zeventiende eeuw', *Bulletin van het Rijksmuseum* 32 (1984), pp. 189-201
Du Mortier 1989
B.M. du Mortier, 'Een paar geborduurde handschoenen, Nederland, ca. 1622', *Bulletin van het Rijksmuseum* 37 (1989), pp. 204-05
Muller 1880
S. Muller Fz, *Schilders-vereenigingen te Utrecht: bescheiden uit het Gemeente-archief*, Utrecht 1880
Mundy 1925
P. Mundy, *The travels of Peter Mundy in Europe and Asia, 1608-1667*, IV (Travels of Europe), ed. R Carnac Temple, London 1925
Naumann 1981
O. Naumann, *Frans van Mieris (1635-1681) the Elder*, 2 vols., Doornspijk 1981
Neurdenburg 1930
E. Neurdenburg, *Hendrick de Keyser, beeldhouwer en bouwmeester van Amsterdam*, Amsterdam 1930
Neurdenburg 1948
E. Neurdenburg, *De zeventiende eeuwsche beeldhouwkunst in de noordelijke Nederlanden*, Amsterdam 1948
Nicolson 1958
B. Nicolson, *Hendrick Terbruggen*, The Hague 1958
Van Os 1992
H.W. van Os, 'Hoe Rembrandts Uyttenbogaert in Nederland terugkwam', *Bulletin van het Rijksmuseum* 40 (1992), pp. 343-45
Paludan 1999
C. Paludan, 'Nogle europaeiske damaskmanufakturer i 16.-19. årh.', in C. Paludan & B. Wieth-Knudsen (eds.), *Damask og Drejl: Dækketøjets Historie i Danmark*, Copenhagen 1989
Panhuysen 1996
B. Panhuysen, 'The early modern free-rider: the history of insiders and outsiders of the Amsterdam and Haarlem Tailors' Guilds', in *Guilds and guildsmen in European Towns - 16th to 19th Century*, ESTER seminar Amsterdam, 14 November 1996, p. 6
Pfister 1972
M. Pfister, 'Trasimenischer See oder Zürichsee?', *Bulletin van het Rijksmuseum* 20 (1972), pp. 177-81
Pijzel-Dommisse 2000
J. Pijzel-Dommisse, *Het Hollandse pronkpoppenhuis: interieur en huishouden in de 17de en 18de eeuw*, Amsterdam (Rijksmuseum) 2000
Raupp 1984
H.J. Raupp, *Untersuchungen zu Künstlerbildnis und Künstlerdarstellung in den Niederlanden im 17. Jahrhundert*, Hildesheim 1984
Reiss 1975
S. Reiss, *Aelbert Cuyp*, London 1975
Ritsema van Eck 1980
P.C. Ritsema van Eck, 'Drie glazen uit het museum van het Koninklijk Huisarchief', *Nederlands Kunsthistorisch Jaarboek* 31 (1980), pp. 161-68
Robinson 1974
F.W. Robinson, *Gabriel Metsu (1629-1667): a study of his place in Dutch genre painting of the Golden Age*, New York 1974
Robinson 1990
M.S. Robinson, *Van de Velde: a catalogue of the paintings of the Elder and the Younger Willem van de Velde*, 2 vols., London 1990
Rosenberg 1928
J. Rosenberg, *Jacob van Ruisdael*, Berlin 1928
Rowlands 1979
J. Rowlands, *Hercules Segers*, Amsterdam 1979
Roy 1992
A. Roy, *Gérard de Lairesse (1640-1711)*, Paris 1992
Russell 1975
M. Russell, *Jan van de Cappelle 1624/6-1679*, Leigh-on-Sea 1975
Schapelhouman 1986
M. Schapelhouman, '"in yver ten konsthemel uitbonzen": over twee tekeningen van Mattheus Terwesten', *Bulletin van het Rijksmuseum* 34 (1986), pp. 177-82
Schatborn 1975
P. Schatborn, 'De Hut van Adriaen van de Velde', *Bulletin van het Rijksmuseum* 23 (1975), pp. 159-65
Van Schendel 1956
A. van Schendel, 'De schimmen van de Staalmeesters', *Oud Holland* 71 (1956), pp. 1-22
Schneider 1990
C.P. Schneider, *Rembrandt's landscapes*, New Haven/London 1990
Schneider & Ekkart 1973
H. Schneider & R.E.O. Ekkart, *Jan Lievens: sein Leben und seine Werke*, Amsterdam 1973
Scholten 1991
F. Scholten, '"Mea sorte contentus": Rombout Verhulst's Portrait of Jacob van Reygersbergh', *The J. Paul Getty Museum Journal* 19 (1991), pp. 65-74
Scholten 1993
F. Scholten, 'De Nederlandse handel in Italiaans marmer in de 17de eeuw', *Nederlands Kunsthistorisch Jaarboek* 44 (1993), pp. 197-214
Scholten 1999
F. Scholten, 'Een ijvore Mars van Francis: de beeldsnijder Van Bossuit en de familie De la Court', *Bulletin van het Rijksmuseum* 47 (1999), pp. 26-43
Schwartz & Bok 1989
G. Schwartz & M.J. Bok, *Pieter Saenredam: the painter and his time*, Maarssen/The Hague 1990
Slive 1970-74
S. Slive, *Frans Hals*, 3 vols., London/New York 1970-74
Slive 1995
S. Slive, *Dutch painting 1600-1800*, New Haven/London 1995
Sluijter 1999
E.J. Sluijter, 'Over Brabantse vodden, economische concurrentie, artistieke wedijver en de groei van de markt voor schilderijen in de eerste decennia van de zeventiende eeuw', *Nederlands Kunsthistorisch Jaarboek* 50 (1999), pp. 113-43
Smit 1990
F.G.A.M. Smit, *Anna Roemers & Maria Tesselschade and their engravings on glass*, Peterborough 1990
Sousa-Leao 1973
Joaquim Sousa-Leao, *Frans Post*, Amsterdam 1973
Staring 1927
A. Staring, 'De beeldhouwer Pieter Xavery', *Oud Holland* 44 (1927), pp. 1-15
Steland-Stief 1971
A.C. Steland-Stief, *Jan Asselijn nach 1610 bis 1652*, Amsterdam 1971
Stumpel 1995
J. Stumpel, 'Van veren en verven: over het mirakel van geschilderd gevogelte', *Kunstschrift* 39 (1995), no. 4, pp. 36-41
Sumowski 1983-94
W. Sumowski, *Gemälde der Rembrandt-Schüler*, 6 vols., Landau/Pfalz 1983-94
Sutton 1980
P.C. Sutton, *Pieter de Hooch*, Oxford/New York 1980
Taylor 1995
P. Taylor, *Dutch flower painting 1600-1720*, New Haven/London 1995
Temple 1972
Sir William Temple, *Observations upon the United Provinces of the Netherlands*, Oxford 1972, p. 78
Theuerkauff 1975
C. Theuerkauff, 'Zu Francis Van Bossuit (1635-1692), "beeldsnyder in yvoor"', *Wallraf-Richartz-Jahrbuch* 37 (1975), p. 178
Van Thiel 1967
P.J.J. van Thiel, 'Philips Konincks Vergezicht met hutten aan de weg', *Bulletin van het Rijksmuseum* 15 (1967), pp. 109-15
Van Thiel 1975
P.J.J. van Thiel, 'Een stilleven door Pieter Claesz', *Bulletin van het Rijksmuseum* 23 (1975), pp. 119-21
Van Thiel 1983a
P.J.J. van Thiel, 'Werner Jacobsz van den Valckert', *Oud Holland* 97 (1983), pp. 128-95
Van Thiel 1983b
P.J.J. van Thiel, '1928 Johannes Verspronck: Portret van een meisje in het blauw', *Bulletin van het Rijksmuseum* 31 (1983), pp. 210-11

Van Thiel 1989a
P.J.J. van Thiel, 'Hendrick Goltzius, Lot en zijn dochters, 1616', *Bulletin van het Rijksmuseum* 37 (1989), pp. 124-40

Van Thiel 1989b
P.J.J. van Thiel, 'Pieter Codde, de terugkeer der jagers, 1633', *Bulletin van het Rijksmuseum* 37 (1989), pp. 219-21

Van Thienen 1957
F.W.S. van Thienen, 'Jan Steen (1626-1679): het Sint Nicolaasfeest', *Openbaar Kunstbezit* (1957), no. 32

Thornton 1998
P. Thornton, *Form & decoration: innovation in the decorative arts 1470-1870*, London 1998

Tümpel 1993
C. Tümpel, *Rembrandt*, Antwerp 1993

Vecht 1968
A. Vecht, *Frederik van Frytom 1632-1702: life and work of a Delft pottery-decorator*, Amsterdam 1968

Vlieger 1995
E. Vlieger, 'Melchior d'Hondecoeter (1636-1695), "der beste mahler umb vögeln zu mahlen"', *Kunstschrift* 39 (1995), no. 4, pp. 16-23

De Vries 1977
L. de Vries, *Jan Steen 'de kluchtschilder'*, Groningen 1977 (diss. Rijksuniversiteit Groningen)

De Vries 1991
J. de Vries, 'Art History', in: D. Freedberg & J. de Vries (eds.), *Art in history, history in art: studies in seventeenth-century Dutch culture*, Santa Monica 1991, pp. 249-82

De Vries & Van der Woude 1995
J. de Vries & A. van der Woude, *Nederland 1500-1815*, Amsterdam 1995

Vroom 1980
N.R.A. Vroom, *A modest message as intimated by the painters of the 'monochrome banketje'*, 2 vols., Schiedam 1980

Van de Waal 1956
H. van de Waal, 'De Staalmeesters en hun legende', *Oud Holland* 71 (1956), pp. 61-107 (reprinted in translation in H. van de Waal, *Steps towards Rembrandt: collected articles 1937-1972*, Amsterdam/London 1974, pp. 247-92)

Wagner 1971
H. Wagner, *Jan van der Heyden 1637-1712*, Amsterdam/Haarlem 1971

Walford 1991
E.J. Walford, *Jacob van Ruisdael and the perception of landscape*, New Haven/London 1991

Walsh 1989
A.L. Walsh, *Paulus Potter: his works and their meaning*, Ann Arbor 1989

Welcker 1979
C. Welcker, *Hendrick Averkamp (1585-1634), bijgenaamd 'de stomme van Campen' en Barent Avercamp (1612-1679), 'schilders tot Campen'*, revised edition by D.J. Henbroek-van der Poel, Doornspijk 1979 (ed. princ. Zwolle 1933)

Westermann 1997
M. Westermann, *The amusements of Jan Steen*, Zwolle 1997

Van de Wetering 1997
E. van de Wetering, *Rembrandt: the painter at work*, Amsterdam 1997

Van de Wetering 1999-2000
E. van de Wetering, 'De meervoudige functie van Rembrandts zelfportretten', in: exhib. cat. London/The Hague 1999-2000

Wheelock 1975-76
A.K. Wheelock Jr, 'Gerard Houckgeest and Emanuel de Witte: architectural painting in Delft around 1650', *Simiolus* 8 (1975-76), pp. 167-85

White 1999
C. White, *Rembrandt as an etcher: a study of the artist at work*, New Haven/London 1999 (2nd edition)

Van der Woude 1991
A.M. van der Woude, 'The volume and value of paintings in Holland at the time of the Dutch Republic', in D. Freedberg & J. de Vries (eds.), *Art in history, history in art: studies in seventeenth-century Dutch culture*, Santa Monica 1991, pp. 285-329

Van der Woude 1997
A. van der Woude, 'De schilderijenproductie in Holland tijdens de Republiek: een poging tot kwantificatie', in A. Schuurman *et al.* (eds.), *Aards geluk: de Nederlanders en hun spullen van 1550 tot 1850*, Amsterdam 1997, pp. 223-58

Zeldenrust 1983
M. Zeldenrust, 'Aert van der Neers Rivierlandschap bij maanlicht opgehelderd', *Bulletin van het Rijksmuseum* 31 (1982), pp. 99-104

Index

PHOTOGRAPHIC ACKNOWLEDGMENTS

Every effort has been made to inform all the relevant institutions and individuals about the publication of the photographs in this book. Should an inadvertent omission have been made, please contact the Exhibition Office, Rijksmuseum, Amsterdam.

The photographs were supplied by the photographic departments of museums and private individuals mentioned in the captions, to which the following should be added.

Fig. 1	Museum Purchase 1913.69
Fig. 25	Photo: Speltdoorn & zoon
Fig. 26	Photo: H. Lilienthal
Fig. 30	Photo courtesy of Kunsthandel Premsela & Hamburger, Amsterdam
Fig. 32	Koninklijke Verzamelingen, Huis ten Bosch (photo: Tom Haartsen, Ouderkerk a/d Amstel)
Fig. 34	Photo: Studio Beekmans, 's-Hertogenbosch
Fig. 38	Sammlung der Zeichnungen und Druckgraphik, Staatliche Museen zu Berlin, Preussischer Kulturbesitz, KdZ/SZ 5239. Photo: Jörg P. Anders
Fig. 62	Photo: Hans Petersen
[6a]	Copyright IRPA-KIK, Brussels
[7a]	Photo: Jörg P. Anders
[14a]	Photo: Elke Walford, Hamburg
[17a]	Photo courtesy of the Universiteitsbibliotheek, Nijmegen
[32a]	Photo: Tom Haartsen, Ouderkerk a/d Amstel
[65a]	Photo: Louis Lemaire (commissioned by the Stichting Manifestatie Historisch Interieur 2001)
[65b]	Photo courtesy of the RKD, The Hague
[71a]	Art Resource, NY
[78a]	Photo: De Jongh, Lausanne